News Clippings from Nephi, Levan, Mona, Utah

1851 - 1889

Compiled from the Deseret News, Deseret Evening News, Deseret Weekly, Salt Lake Herald, Salt Lake Tribune, Eastern Utah Advocate, & contributions from other regional papers.

Often while working on family history (genealogy) I wonder about more than is listed on the pedigree sheets and am so grateful for their sacrifices and love for the generations to follow.

Some of the names include: Aagaard, Abbott, Adam, Allison, Andrews, Asher, Bagley, Bailey, Bamford, Barber, Barnett, Barton, Baxter, Bell, Belliston, Benson, Betts, Bigler, Bailey, Blackburn, Blackett, Booth, Borrowman, Bowles, Brafford, Broadbent, Broadhead, Brown, Bryan, Bulger, Butterfield, Campbell, Cannon, Carter, Cazier, Chapman, Chappell, Chase, Christenson, Claridge, Coleman, Cook, Crabb, Crandall, Crawley, Crockwell, Cummings, Curtis, Darton, Downs, Dye, Ellertson, Ellison, Elmer, Evans, Ewing, Fellows, Foot, Foote, Fouks, Frederick, Funk, Gadd, Gamet, Gardner, Gardiner, Garrett, Gerrard, Gibbs, Gifford, Gilson, Goldsborough, Goss, Grace, Greenbaigh, Goble, Goldsborough, Goodwin, Grever, Grover, Gusten, Harley, Hartley, Hague, Hanchett, Harley, Harris, Hawkins, Hayward, Hague, Haws, Haynes, Healy, Heath, Henriod, Heywood, Higbee, Higgins, Holden, Hollinshead, House, Hoyle, Hoyt, Hubbard, Hudson, Huggins, Irons, Jackson, Jaques, Jenkins, Jones, Joseph, Kay, Kendall, Kiene, Kinkie, Knight, Knowles, Lang, Larson, Lewis, Littley, Lordon, Love, Mangum, Marcer, May, McConkie, McCune, Meeks, Mendenhall, Merrifield, Midgley, Miller, Morgan, Mullineux, Nuttall, Oakey, Olinton, Olsen, Ord, Orme, Ostler, Pace, Parkington, Partington, Pass, Patterson, Paxman, Paxton, Pepper, Perkins, Petersen, Peterson, Pickston, Pierce, Pitchforth, Platt, Price, Pyper, Randall, Rasmussen, Reid, Richard, Riches, Ritchee, Rockwell, Rollins, Rowley, Schofield, Schrouder, Scott, Sells, Shaw, Shell, Shepherd, Sidwell, Siler, Sinclair, Smith, Snow, Sorenson, Sowby, Sparks, Spencer, Sperry, Stanley, Stephenson, Starr, Storrar, Stubbs, Sutton, Svenson, Swensen, Taylor, Teasdale, Thay, Thorp, Thygessen, Tidwell, Tingey, Tolley, Tranter, Tunbridge, Turner, Tybert, Udall, Valaride, Vickers, Wallace, Wandell, Warner, Warwood, Webb, Wenn, Williams, Wignal, Wilson, Winn, Witbeck, Wolf, Worwood, Wright, Young, and many, many, more.

Some of the articles are easier to read than others, please consider that some are over 100 years old.

ISBN-13:978-1546587224

ISBN-10:1546587225

Deseret News
December 13, 1851

For the Deseret News.

Mr. Editor—Sir:—I left the city of Nephi, located on Salt Creek, Juab valley, on the 25th ult.

About 12 houses have been erected; viz: 3 built of adobies, 2 of willows plastered inside and out, 1 two story house built of 4 inch plank, and the balance of logs obtained from a distance of ten miles.

Our roofs and flooring are principally of lumber cut at Hamilton & Potter's mills, San-Pete valley distant about 30 miles from Nephi.

A large quantity of hay was cut by the first settlers, probably more than will be needed for their stock, unless the winter should be uncommonly severe. The altitude of Nephi City, according to observations made by professors Pratt and Carrington, is 4425 feet, and one hundred and twenty-five feet higher than Temple Block, G. S. L. City.

Wood, feed, and mowing land are convenient, and the clay and soil make an uncommonly heavy adobie.

On my way up, I met bros. Foote and Gifford with their families, moving to the settlement. Bro. Z. H. Backster is making preparations for building a grist mill, next season.

Up to the time of my leaving, not more than 2 inches of snow had fallen in the valley, at any one time.

Very respectfully,

J. L. HEYWOOD.

Deseret News
May 1, 1852

The Comissioners appointed by the Legislature to locate the capitol at Fillmore, left this city Oct. 21, accompanied by brothers Young, Kimball, and others, who visited Fillmore, Manti, Nephi, Provo. and other places, and returned Nov. 7. The Legislature accepted the report of the commissioners. confirmed the location of the site for the public buildings at Fillmore. 38 deg. 58m. 40s. N. L.; 4789 feet altitude; and men are engaged for their erection. The Legislature will continue to meet at this city, till the new capitol is prepared for their reception, having purchased the Council House for that purpose.

Missionary Report.

Bro. Richards:

On the 2nd inst., I left this City, in company with bro. S. M. Blair, on a mission to Fillmore City and the intervening valleys and settlements of the Saints, to preach the Gospel and speak to the Saints the peaceable things of the kingdom; and after an absence of 16 days, we have been permitted to return to the City, and found all well, and believing that you, in connection with your readers generally, would like to know how we found things, and of the prosperity of the Southern settlements; I thought to furnish you the following items, taken from our journal.

We passed directly to Fillmore City, and then commenced to preach, (with one exception, we preached at Provo City, on our way to Fillmore.) We found the settlement at Fillmore in a thriving condition, its beautiful location is unsurpassed in the valleys of the mountains, the scenery picturesque, the crystal streams that it is situated on, lovely to behold; while the surrounding hills, vales and mountains lie beneath the green carpeting of the well known mountain grass, as green at this season of the year as the sage grass is in May; combined with the facilities of firewood, building material, &c., and last, not least, the very best of soil for agricultural purposes, lying adjacent to the city plat, a good share of which has been put into cultivation by its citizens, the past season, and to their credit be it said, that they have the finest arrangements for irrigating their lands in their large and commodious sects, as well as the best cultivated fields and fence lands we have examined in the valleys; and they now have stacked in their stack yard some 8000 bushels unthrashed wheat, besides Oats, Corn, &c., which is laid out on the plan of the face of a compass, each man having a front running to a point in the center, upon which a circle is struck sufficiently large for to set a machine to thrash their grain, and thus is every thing arranged and all that we have to regret, was that we found but 18 families who had acted on the counsel given them and stopped or gone to that place.

We preached there on Sunday the 8th twice, and felt a good spirit prevailing, and the people rejoicing in the new and everlasting covenant, but very desirous to have an increase of their numbers, for they feel themselves rather in the minority, when compared with their red-faced brethren around them; and they need more help to carry out their improvements, that they have on hand in Saw and Grist Mills, building, &c., and they sent their request by us through a vote, with uplifted hands to the Presidency, for more settlers, if it should meet their minds, with which we concurred and felt to bless the people in the name of the Lord and pray for their prosperity.

On the 9th we left for San Pete Valley, Manti, and at night reached the Sevier River, where we passed bro. T. B. Foot, building a bridge across the river and which to our great joy and satisfaction, on our return we found complete, and had the satisfaction of being the first to cross it after it was finished, and we pronounced it a good substantial bridge, and felt much credit was due bro. Foot.

On the 10th, we reached Manti City, and truly our hearts felt to rejoice, and felt to praise the Lord when we beheld what improvements our brethren had made; and how our Father had blessed the labor of their hands, for truly, we exclaimed, the city of "Stacks" for all seemed to be the owner of stack yards, and we found the people in a prosperous condition.

We spent one day with the good people, and preached both evenings to a crowded house of Saints; and truly we were reminded of the day of Pentecost, for the Lord was surely with us and all felt to praise the Lord. We found the people had not only an abundance of grain, but also all kinds of vegetables, Pumpkins, Squash, &c., and for a sample I brought 2 fine heads of Cabbage home which were presented me by elder Billingsly; the citizens have erected a good Stone Fort in the city, 10 rods square, 8 or 10 feet high. A general spirit of improvements appears to be the order of the day. On the 11 inst., the first stone residence was finished belonging to President B. Young. We found only eight families of this Fall's emigration in this lovely valley. What has become of the emigration of Utah?

On the 12th, we set out for Nephi, Juah Valley, and reached it about five o'clock p. m.; preached in the evening to the Saints and had a season of rejoicing, found 26 families of the Fall emigration at this point, and Nephi begins to extend her borders and assume quite a village appearance, and is truly situated in the heart of a valley capable of sustaining thousands. They are erecting a Grist mill, and a Saw mill is much needed.

Nov. 13th, left Nephi and dined at Clover Creek at bro. Love's, member elect for Juab. Clover Creek, the evening reached at Payson, Peteetneet Creek, and preached to a crowded house, and much to our joy and their satisfaction. Payson is a beautiful settlement, as much so as any in Utah Valley. We found 22 families of the Fall emigration at that point.

Saturday reached the lovely site of Springville, were the busy buz and clattering wheels of wagons and constant stir of men and boys. bespeak that enterprising industry for which its citizens and presiding officers are characteristic. At 11 o'clock a. m., we preached at the house of President Aaron Johnson, a new building just erected. The Hall in which we preached is some 20 by 15 feet, were we found him and his worthy Councilors and his bro. Lorenzo Johnson, with a crowded house of Saints. We felt free and spoke as we felt, and all seemed to be in and to enjoy the Spirit of the New and Everlasting Covenant, and for which we felt truly to rejoice. At the earnest solicitation of our worthy brothers M. Miller and Johnson we stopped for the day, and in the evening we had the privilege of enjoying one of the most social parties, that it has been our lot to share in the valleys of the mountains, and about 8 o'clock p. m., a new impetus was given to our party by the arrival of bros. Erastus Snow, and F. D. Richards, bound for Iron County, and truly we left Springville and with it our blessings we left Springville and with it our blessings, and praying that Our Father might continue his blessings with the Saints at that place, as he has done in the days that are past.

15th, we reached Provo City agreable to previous appointment, and preached at 11 o'clock a. m., and 2 p. m., and a more attentive congregation we have not met with on our mission, the house was crowded, and it was said some 500 could not be seated in the house. Truly our hearts felt to rejoice and praise the Lord for the good measure of his Holy Spirit we enjoyed while addressing the Saints, for the Spirit seemed to run from heart to heart and all felt to rejoice and say thy will, and not mine be done. Of the City of Provo we can truly say a more industrious and enterprising people cannot be found, and Union and Peace seems to be their motto; for we enjoyed that Spirit in their midst while bros. Carter, Bird, and others shared with us, their kind and hospitable roofs; may the Lord bless them and prepare them for his coming and glory is our prayer.

16th, we left for Dry Creek, Utah Valley, and preached to a large congregation of Saints, we found them in a prosperous condition and enjoying a good degree of the good Spirit, as was manifested on their attendance and many more we learn would have been out but we learned that some of the enterprising brethren had sought out a Valley which they call Cedar Valley west of the Jordan River south of Tooele Valley, that abounds in fine land, timber, and grass, distance from G. S. L. City about 35 miles, and was absent making their improvements preparatory to moving their families; and we felt they are engaged in a good enterprise and with success.

17th, arrived at home and we thought to thus report ourselves and our mission to you and the Saints. Bro. Richards we omitted to say that bro. Tomkinson at Fillmore has in successful operation a Pottery and says he can make ware as good as Liverpool ware, from the material found there. Of the emigration, we think that one half of it has stopped in Utah Valley.

Yours truly in the bonds of the New and Everlasting Covenant.

E. T. BENSON.

G. S. L. City, Nov. 18th, 1852.

We feel that it would be wiser for the brethren to exert themselves in strengthening Fillmore, and other weak settlements, than in opening new Valleys; for when the brethren extend their settlements beyond their own inherent power to maintain themselves against Indian invasions, their lives, property and all are endangered: and if by extending beyond that point, they should need protection, they must be dependent on others who already have enough to do to protect themselves, and thereby the whole community are liable to suffer.

Deseret News
December 11, 1852

NEPHI CITY, JUAB COUNTY,
Sept. 30, 1852.

Editor Deseret News:

Perhaps it may be useful to some of your readers to learn something of this new settlement, and other settlements in Juab county.

Our first survey commenced on the 25th Sept, 1851, and our settlement consisted during the following winter, of twenty families. On the first Monday of May last, our city election took place, when the following officers were elected agreeable to the provisions of our city charter, viz:

Mayor—Josiah Miller.

Aldermen—Timothy B. Foote, Charles H. Bryan, John Carter, Isaac Grace.

Councilors—Amos Gusten, John Cazier, David Webb, James Crabb, Cleon Elmer, Levi Gifford, Ichabod Gifford, Thomas Tranter, Miles Miller.

Recorder, Assessor and Collector—Z. H. Baxter.

Treasurer—Wm, Cazier.

Marshal—Israel Hoyt.

Supervisor of Streets—Charles Sperry.

During the spring and summer, our settlement has been augmented by a few families. In Dec. last, three families commenced a settlement upon Clover creek in this county, about eight miles north of Nephi, and where there is an extensive range for stock, which is also one of the prominent advantages throughout Juab valley. Fire wood is abundant, and convenient of access; some very good timber from the mountains, and it is believed that with a few hundred dollars expense in road work, large quantities of timber can be obtained.

The crops in this county both of wheat, corn, oats and potatoes, are considered equal to any first crops that have been raised in this Territory.

On the 25th of September, being the anniversary of the survey of Nephi, our community partook of a sumptuous feast prepared by the Mayor and Aldermen of our infant city, which, to say the least, was good enough. Prest. Isaac Morley and the Hon. B. F. Johnson were among our invited guests. After listening to appropriate remarks from various individuals, the revelation as contained in the "Deseret News extra" was read upon the occasion, whereupon Prest. Morley made some highly appropriate remarks, calculated to promote "peace on earth, and good will towards all men."

Respectfully,
J. L. HEYWOOD.

NEPHI, Nov. 13, 1852.

ED. NEWS:—An inquest was held this day by our city authorities upon two dead bodies found in the forks of Salt creek, within the corporation of Nephi. One of the bodies was discovered on the 12th inst., where it had apparently been dragged into some brushwood near the creek. He was a middling sized man, five feet nine inches nigh, dark brown hair, apparently about twenty-three years old; a bullet appeared to have entered the forehead, near the centre. The skin on the right arm was considerably fractured. An U. S. Military overcoat with "U. S." on the buttons, with the initials of "T. B." on the lining of the same, was found lying across the body, which had the appearance of having been dead five or six weeks. The remains of a camp fire was near the body; also a small camp kettle, and a pair of shoes.

On the 13th while the jury were preparing to hold

the above inquest, another body was found about nine
rods from the former. He appeared to be a man
about twenty-one years of age; five feet ten inches in
height, sandy hair, light complexion, with a bullet
mark through the neck, apparently dragged to the spot
where found among some bushes.

On the 2nd of Oct. last, four men, with one pack
horse, were seen to go to the place where these bodies
were found. Some Indians recollect hearing on the
same night, the report of four guns.

Yours, &c.,

J. L. HEYWOOD.

P. S. The last described body had, apparently, an
officer's coat, of fine quality of cloth, and both bodies
had military pants.   J. L. H.

[Nov. 2nd reached us, at which date it does not appear that the inquest had given their decision, we
therefore leave it as we find it, with this suggestion,
if editors east and west, will copy, light may be thrown
on the case, by the marks specified, for in all probability, the dead, and others once with them, were travelers
from the States to California, and of their names, and
where from, and where after, so far as particulars are
concerned, the citizens of Utah are ignorant. If any
thing appears to the contrary, we will publish it. Mr.
Heywood is Marshal of the Territory, and what he
has stated, we rely on as correct.

Since writing the above we understand that a
stranger of suspicious appearance, having more guns,
pistols, &c., than is common for travelers, passed
through Iron County, on his way to California; but
at that time it was not known that crimes had been
committed.

Deseret News
January 8, 1853

we would suggest to the Post Masters of
Provo, Salt Creek, and Ogden, to write to the first
Assistant Post Master General, Washington, to
change the names of their several Post Offices, from
Utah Lake to Provo City; Salt Ceeek to Nephi
City; and Brownsville to Ogden City; let each hav
its right name. We understand that the Post Maste
at Fillmore has attended to this.

Deseret News
February 5, 1853

LOCAL CORRESPONDENCE.

SAN PETE.

Manti City, Dec. 31, 1852.

Editor News:—

We have no communication with any other settlement owing to the great depth of the snow on the divide below this and Nephi, which is from 4 to 6 feet deep, so it is reported by Messrs. Dodge, Frink, Averett and Lewis who arrived here on the 29th inst. having been out six days from Nephi. The snow here is only about 12 inches deep, and is now going off very rapidly, so rapidly that I think there will be an express sent out to Nephi next week, we are doing well in Manti, all is peace and plenty, no sickness and death has not visited our camp since June. We have plenty of fire wood to burn, and plenty to eat; the products of San Pete Valley. We have not had a mail in a month or more but we hope for better things in the Spring.

We are troubled but little with the Red men.

Yours,
A. L. SILER.

From the same source, under date of Jan. 2nd we have a long report of a sleigh ride party, dance, feast, speeches, songs and music by the Seventies in San Pete, which came off on New Years, attended with every demonstration of pleasure usual to saints on such occasions; but we have not room for the report entire.

Deseret News
February 19, 1853

LOCAL CORRESPONDENCE

San Pete.

Manti, Jan. 25th, 1853,

Mr. Editor,

On Sunday last 23rd inst., the mail arrived in this city, for the first time this year, brought by Artemas Millet, resident of this city, his route was from Nephi to the Severe, thence up to Manti, and travelled comfortably with an ox team. Why can we not have a mail once a month, at least on this route in the winter? [We could if government would make appropriations, Ed.]

The mail brought to us your over welcome "News," to tell us what is going on in the various departments of the Bee-hive, the world, and that the work of the Lord is rolling throughout the nations, after we have been locked up in the icy embraces of a Deseret winter for two months, it is truly cheering to the saints in Manti to read the News.

When President Young was here last spring, he directed the millers to give the Indians what wheat they needed, and grind it for them, which has amounted to 50 bushels or more, at $2 per bushel, what wheat is worth here, and this is the way the President fights the Indians, and saves powder and lead, the Indians were in need at the time and took most of it in about 2 weeks and went on their winters hunt.

Large quantities of saleratus earth have been boiled down for the purpose of making soap, a portion of which did not succeed for that, and was converted into saleratus. The saleratus springs, 4 miles south yield a heavy per centage of saleratus, easier procuring it than to bring it from Independence Rock.

We have had an open winter in Manti, though the snow may have been from 2 to 4 feet deep, we have not felt its effects as we should have done had it been 1 foot all the time. Many cattle have wintered themselves and are doing well.

A. L. SILER.

P. S. Two deaths in Manti since April last, one from drowning, one from a fall which broke his skull, and not a case of sickness except sister Ritchee, reported, we are so high the miasma never reaches us, some comfort for being in a high altitude.

☞ Bro. Samuel Pitchforth writes from Nephi, March 1st, 1853, to Joseph Cain:

We have enjoyed ourselves first rate this winter; we have had first rate meetings and the spirit of God is with us. I have never lived in a place where the Saints were more united than they are in Nephi. We have had a dancing school in operation for some time; also a cyphering school. We have a broom maker in our city who intends planting 10 acres this season, and will supply a great many with brooms. There is a grist mill building, and a saw mill will be built this season. The brethren intend putting in a great deal of grain this season, so that there will be some to spare next season for our brethren and the Indians. The Walkers work first rate; you may see them all over Nephi carrying water, chopping wood, assisting to haul wood, and I understand they where very useful last harvest. When we have grain to spare, we can employ them to good advantage for us, and themselves; we never give them anything but what they must work for it; by doing this way, they don't get so impudent!

Bro. Heywood has been lecturing on the history and geography of the countries that our elders have been sent to, and his lecturing has awakened the brethren on the subject so much that he intends organizing a literary association, on next Saturday evening. He also proposes to the members to subscribe towards a library; so you can see that our president don't intend Nephi to be far in the rear. There has been several meetings with the Indians, all tending towards our peace, and their improvement. I like the place, also the Saints who dwell here.

BROOMS.

I wish to inform the inhabitants of Utah Territory, that I intend to engage in the manufacture of Brooms. I have prepared machinery and intend to raise fifteen acres of Broom Corn this season, and having had experience in the business, for I have made forty thousand for New York City market. I will make a good article of Brushes and Brooms and will sell them from twenty to twenty five cents each which I think will be cheaper to the inhabitants of the Territory than for them to raise Broom Corn and make Brooms without machinery. I intend to send them to the different settlements in the Territory. In the Tithing Office G. S. L. City, will be supplied of my make after the first of October next.

WM. H. CARPENTER.

Nephi City, March 1st, 1853.
march19-9-3in

DIED.

At Nephi, Juab County, February 22nd, 1853, SAMUEL, son of Samuel and Sarah Ann Pitchforth, aged 3 days.

Indian Difficulties.

It is well known to the residents of this Territory that the Indian Chief, Walker, has been surly in his feelings and expressions at divers times and places within our borders, for more than one year past, and that he has repeatedly endeavored to raise an excitement and open war out of small pretexts, that in former times he would have smiled at. It is equally well known that, in the midst of all Walker's follys, Gov. Young has pursued an invariable, and uniformly mild course towards him and his tribe, and has counseled our citizens so to do, and that counsel has been followed in all the settlements without any deviation worthy of notice, but it at last appears that all this does not prevent a still greater exhibiton of perfect folly and wickedness on the part of Walker.— His cunning and treachery, his thieving and murderous propensities have outweighed the constantly open and extended hand of utmost kindness, and on a mere pretext, which he could have satisfactorily arranged in a moment, had he possessed a spark of good feeling, he has declared open war. On the 17th inst., hostilities commenced by a menace on Springville, in Utah county, but the inhabitants receiving timely notice, and being numerous and watchful, no damage was done. On the 18th, Walker and his two brothers Arrapin and Ammon with many of the tribe were camped on the Peteetneet, just above Payson, in Utah county, and as Arrapin was riding from the town to his camp he passed close by Alexander Keele, who was on guard, and though another Indian was near by, as near as the spectators could judge it was Arrapin shot Keele dead on the spot, and this too, after having partaken of a hospitable meal in the fort with all apparent friendliness. The Indians then moved up Peteetneet Kanyon, the rear firing heavily as they passed, upon some half dozen families in the Kanyon, but injuring nothing but their clothing, and leaving quite a quantity of balls in the buildings. On the 19th, Col. Peter W. Conover started from Provo city with 150 men, to assist the weak settlements on the route, reconnoitre, and rendezvous and await further orders at Manti, in San Pete valley, which place he reached on the evening of the 20th. Still the Indians were not idle on the night of the 19th, nor dismayed by the force sent out, but undertook to surprise the post at Pleasant creek in San Pete county, and were fired upon by the guard, and it is supposed that one Indian was killed, the whites sustaining no injury; and on the same night they stole several head of cattle from Manti, several miles south in the same county, stole three horses from Nephi City, in Juab county, and wounded William Jolly in the arm, while on guard at Springville; thus demonstrating that they were in some force, very hostile, and acting in good concert. On the night of the 2th an attempt was made to steal horses from the Allred settlement, which is between Pleasant creek and Manti, and the guard was fired upon at Nephi city. On the 24th, Clark Roberts was shot in the shoulder, and John Berry in the wrist, by Indians secreted in the vacated houses at Summit creek. Roberts and Berry were bringing in express, and within twenty minutes after they reached Provo city, twenty mounted men were out in pursuit of the aggressors, with what success is not yet known. This is a brief detail of the events of the outbreak so far as information has reached us up to the 26th inst., at 4 o'clock p. m. We also print in this number the orders, and instructions issued by the Governor and Ex-officio Superintendent of Indian Affairs, and Lieut. Gen. D. H. Wells, up to same date.

July 27th, 2 o'clock P. M. We stop the press to announce further news from the seat of Indian hostilities, which arrived per express, at half past 7 o'clock this morning, from Col. Peter W. Conover. Col. Conover states that a scouting party, sent out by him from Manti, under command of Lieut. Col. Jabez Nowlin, fell in with a company of twenty or thirty Indians, on the 22d inst., about 10 miles east of the Pleasant Creek Settlement, who were addressed by the Interpreter of the party, and replied they were our enemies and commenced firing; Col. Nowlin immediately charged upon them and killed six, the rest scattering and escaping; returned on the 24th with his company all safe. This completes the detail of acts and losses on either side up to date.

DIED.

In the South Cottonwood Ward of Scarlet Fever, after an illness of 4 weeks and 4 days, EMILY ANN, daughter of A. O. and Emily Smoot, aged 18 months and 21 days.

Sweet babe, thou art gone
To the mansions of bliss,
To join with thy kindred
Thou hadst before this;
And have left us behind
That loved thee so dear,
But soon we shall meet thee
In that brighter sphere.

June 28th, killed instantly by falling off a wagon in this city, JOHN ALMA, son of Thomas and Ann Cottam, aged 10 years 11 months and 19 days. St. Louis Republican please copy.

May 23th, at Nephi City, Juab County, of Erysipelas, JAMES HOYTE, aged 67

Deseret News
October 15, 1853

Indian Difficulties.

The Indian chasing, alluded to in our last, occur-red on the 26th of last month, under the command of Major Stephen Markham. The Indians were found encamped near the mouth of Salt Creek, after some firing by both parties, in which C. B. Hancock was slightly wounded, and four or five Indians supposed to be killed, Major Markham withdrew and returned home.

On the 30th of September, Wm. Nelson, William Luke, Wm. Reed and Thos. Clark, started with two ox teams, loaded with wheat, to come from Manti to his city. They camped about daybreak, of Oct. 1st, at the Uinta Springs, just East of Salt Creek kanyon, where some Indians killed them all, and horribly mutilated their bodies, which were brought into Nephi, and buried.

On the 2nd inst., in a skirmish at Nephi, eight Indians were killed, and one squaw and two boys taken prisoners.

On the 4th inst., John E. Warner and William Mills, were killed by Indians, 3 or 400 yards above the grist mill, near Manti.

Deseret News
December 15, 1853

DEATHS.

In Payson, Nov. 24, 1853 at the house of B. F. Johnson, ORSON H. MURRY, aged 15 years.

———In Nephi, June 30'h Charles H., son of Charles H., and Miranda Bryan; aged 22 months.

———Dec. 4th; John H., son of Charles H. and Jane Bryan; aged 19 years.—Sangamon Journal Ill. please copy the two last names.

PROPOSALS for Carrying the MAILS.

PROPOSALS for carrying the Mails of the United States, from the 1st day of July 1854, to the 1st day of July, 1858, in the Territory of Utah, will be received at the Contract Office of the Post Office Department, in the city of Washington, until 9 A. M. of the 3rd of April, 1854, (to be decided by the 23rd of April, 1854.) on the routes and in the times herein specified, viz:

12523 From Sacramento City, by Carson Valley, in Utah, and Box Elder, to Salt Lake, 900 miles and back, once a month.

Leave Sacramento at 6 a m on the first of each month:

Arrive at Salt Lake in four weeks;

Leave Salt Lake at 6 a m on the first of each month;

Arrive at Sacramento City in four weeks.

Bids to carry once a fortnight will be considered.

12707 From Dalles, by Fort Boise, and Fort Hall to Salt Lake, in Utah, 800 miles and back once in two months.

Leave Dalles at 9 a m on the first day of every other month:

Arrive at Salt Lake in four weeks.

Leave Salt Lake City at 9 a m on the first day of every other month;

Arrive at Dalles in four weeks.

Bids for monthly trips are invited.

12801 From Salt Lake City, by American Fork, Provo City, Springfield, Payson, Summit Creek, Nephi City, Fillmore City, Red Creek, Parowan, Johnson's Springs, Coal Creek, Santa Clara, and San Bernardino, Cal., to San Diego, 1000 miles and back, once a month.

Leave Salt Lake City on the 20 of each month;

Arrive at San Diego by the 18th of the next month;

Leave San Diego on the 20th of each month;

Arrive at Salt Lake City by the 18th of the next month.

12802 From Salt Lake City, by Draperville [Willow Creek,] Lehi City, American Fork, Pleasant Grove, Provo City, Springville, Palmyra, Payson, Salt Creek, to Manti, 133 miles and back, once a week.

Leave Salt Lake City every Monday at 6 a m;

Arrive at Manti by 8 p m Tuesday;

Leave Manti every Thursday at 6 a m;

Arrive at Salt Lake City by 8 p m Friday.

12803 From Salt Lake City, by Fort Laramie to Council Bluffs, in Iowa, 1000 miles and back, once a month.

Leave Salt Lake City on the 10th of each month,

Arrive at Council Bluffs by the 8th of the next month;

Leave Council Bluffs on the 10th of each month;

Arrive at Salt Lake City by the 8th of the next month.

Separate proposals for the part beyond Fort Laramie are invited. Also, bids to run the whole route twice a month each way.

12804 From Salt Lake City, by Miller's Creek to Brownsville, 40 miles and back, twice a week.

Leave Salt Lake City Mondays and Thursdays at 5 a m;

Arrive at Brownsville by 8 p m same days;

Leave Brownsville Tuesdays and Fridays at 5 a m;

Arrive at Salt Lake City by 8 p m same days.

12805 From Salt Lake City to Tooele City, 35 miles and back, once a week.

Leave Salt Lake City every Monday at 6 a m;

Arrive at Tooele City by 8 p m;

Leave Tooele City every Tuesday at 6 a m;

Arrive at Salt Lake City by 8 p m.

FORM FOR A BID.

Where no change from advertisement is contemplated by the bidder.

"I (or we, as the case may be) [here write the name or names in full] of [here state the residence or residences] hereby propose to carry the mail on route No.——from——to,——as often as the Postmaster General's advertisement for proposals for the same, dated October 13, 1853, requires, in the time stated in the schedules contained in said advertisement, and by the following mode of conveyance, to wit: [Here state how it is to be conveyed.] for the annual sum of [here write out the sum in words at full length.]

Dated   [Signed.]

Form of a Guaranty.

The undersigned undertake that if the foregoing bid for carrying the mail on route No.——be accepted by the Postmaster General, the bidder shall, prior to the 1st day of July next, enter into the required obligation to perform the service proposed, with good and sufficient sureties.

Dated   [Signed by two guarantors.]

Form of Certificate.

The undersigned (postmaster, Judge, or a Clerk of a court of record, as the case may be) certifies that he is well acquainted with the above guarantors and their property, and that they are men of property and able to make good their guaranty.

Dated   [Signed]

JAMES CAMPBELL,
Postmaster General.

POST OFFICE DEPARTMENT, OCT. 13, 1853.
dec10-25tf

ACTS AND RESOLUTIONS
Of the 3rd Session of the Legislature of the Territory of Utah.

PUBLISHED BY AUTHORITY.

AN ACT

Relating to the United States Courts for the Territory of Utah.

SEC. 1. Be it enacted by the Governor and Legislative Assembly of the Territory of Utah, That the First Judicial District shall embrace and be composed of Great Salt Lake, Davis, Weber, Tooele, and Utah counties, and all regions of country lying east, north and west of said counties; and the Second of Juab, San Pete, and Millard counties, and all regions of country lying south of the south latitude of Utah county, and north of the south latitude of Millard county; and the Third of Iron county, and all regions of country lying south of the south latitude of Millard county.

SEC. 2. The Hon. Leonidas Shaver, Associate Justice, is assigned to the First Judicial District, and shall hold courts annually as follows, viz: On the first Monday in December in Great Salt Lake City; on the first Monday in March in Ogden City; on the third Monday in March in Provo City; and on the second Monday in August in Fort Supply.

SEC. 3. The Hon. Lazarus H. Reed, Chief Justice, is assigned to the Second Judicial District, and shall hold courts annually as follows, viz: On the third Monday in October in Nephi City; on the last Monday of October in Manti City; and on the second Monday of November in Fillmore City.

SEC. 4. The Hon. Zerubbabel Snow, Associate Justice, is assigned to the Third Judicial District, and shall hold court annually as follows, viz: On the third Monday in November in Parowan City.

SEC. 5. A Supreme Court shall be held annually on the first Monday in January in Great Salt Lake City.

SEC. 6. Each session of said Courts shall be kept open at least one day; and no session shall be legal except an adjournment in the regular term.

SEC. 7. Upon the petition of not less than one hundred legal voters and tax-payers residing in any Judicial District, the Judge of said District shall hold a special session of court at the time and place specified in the petition, unless a remonstrance to said petition is seasonably presented to the Judge, and signed by a larger number of like qualified signers than said petition has, in which case a special session shall not be held; and a like course by the required number of like qualified residents of this Territory shall obtain or prevent a special session of Supreme Court.

SEC. 8. All other laws and doings of the Legislative Assembly on the subject of this Act, are hereby repealed.

Approved Jan. 13th, 1854.

The foregoing is a true copy of the original Act on file in my office.   A. W. BABBITT,
Sec'y. of U. T.

RESOLUTION

To Encourage the Raising of Flax and Hemp.

1. Be it resolved by the Governor and Legislative Assembly of the Territory of Utah, That the sum of four hundred dollars be and the same is hereby appropriated out of any moneys in the Treasury not otherwise appropriated, to be paid in awarding premiums as follows:

2. The person that shall raise the greatest number of bushels of flax seed and greatest amount of lint from two acres of ground, shall be entitled to a premium of one hundred dollars; the person raising the greatest number of bushels from one acre, shall be entitled to sixty dollars; and the person raising the greatest number of bushels from one half acre, shall be entitled to forty dollars.

3. The person who shall raise the greatest number of pounds of hemp lint from two acres, shall be entitled to one hundred dollars; the person raising the greatest number of pounds from one acre,

shall be entitled to sixty dollars; and the person raising the greatest number of bushels from one half acre, shall be entitled to forty dollars.

3. The person who shall raise the greatest number of pounds of hemp lint from two acres, shall be entitled to one hundred dollars; the person raising the greatest number of pounds from one acre, shall be entitled to sixty dollars; and the person raising the greatest number of pounds from one half acre shall be entitled to forty dollars: Provided, that no more than one of the above premiums on flax seed, or hemp lint, shall be awarded to the same person.

4. All claims for the above premiums must be accompanied with sufficient evidence of the amount of ground sown; the number of bushels sown, and how the ground was prepared; and that it was raised in the year 1854 by the person claiming the premium; and be accompanied by a written statement of the amount of seed sown, number of acres, kind of soil, and how prepared, when sown, when harvested, and quantity of lint. Said evidence and statement must be filed with the Auditor of Public Accounts on or before the 1st of December next.

5. As soon after the 1st of December as practicable, the Auditor shall give each successful claimant an order on the Treasurer for the amount of premium due.

Approved Jan. 13th, 1854.

The foregoing is a true copy of the original Resolution on file in my office.

A. W. BABBITT,
Sec'y. of U. T.

AN ACT

Defining the Boundaries, and for the organization of Green River and Summit Counties, and defining the Eastern boundary of Davis County.

SEC. 1. Be it enacted by the Governor and Legislative Assembly of the Territory of Utah, That all that section of country, bounded north by Oregon, east by the Territorial line, south by the parallel of the thirty ninth degree and thirty minutes north latitude, and west by a north and south line that intersects Sulphur creek where the present emigration road crosses it, is and the same shall hereafter be called Green River county.

SEC. 2. That the Probate Judge for said county, when elected, shall be authorized and empowered to organize the same, when in his opinion it shall become expedient and necessary; also, to locate and establish the county seat in said county.

SEC. 3. That all that section of country, bounded north by Oregon, east by the west line of

A RESOLUTION

Exempting the Members of the Legislative Assembly of the Territory of Utah, from Arrest and Summons, during the sitting of the Legislature, and while going to and from the same.

Be it resolved by the Governor and Legislative Assembly of the Territory of Utah, That the members of the Council and House of Representatives, shall be privileged from arrest and summons, during the session of the Legislative Assembly, or during the time of their going to, and returning from said session, except for treason or murder; and no suit at law against any member, shall be prosecuted during said session.

Approved, Jan. 14th, 1854.

The above is a true copy of the original Resolution on file in my office.

A. W. BABBITT,
Secretary of U. T.

Green River county, south by a parallel line forming the southern boundary of Great Salt Lake county, and west by a parallel line forming the eastern boundary of Weber county, is, and the same shall hereafter be called Summit county, and is attached to Great Salt Lake county for election, revenue, and judicial purposes.

SEC. 4. Davis county shall be bounded on the east by Summit county.

SEC. 5. All laws and parts of laws conflicting with this Act, are hereby repealed.

Approved Jan. 13th 1851.

The above is a true copy of the original act on file in my office. A. W. BABBITT,
Sec'y. of U. T.

RESOLUTION

Offering a Reward for the Discovery of Coal Bed near Great Salt Lake City.

Be it resolved by the Governor and Legislative Assembly of the Territory of Utah, That the sum of one thousand dollars be and the same hereby appropriated, out of any money in the public Treasury not otherwise appropriated, as a reward to any resident of this Territory who will open a good coal-mine not less than eighteen inches thick, within forty miles of Great Salt Lake City, in any accessible position, and that can be profitably worked; and when the Governor shall become satisfied of the fact, he may draw on the Treasury of the Territory for the amount in favor of the person entitled to it; and the Governor shall control said coal mine until further provided for by law.

Approved Jan. 14th, 1854.

The above is a true copy of the original Resolution on file in my office.

A. W. BABBITT,
Sec'y. of U. T.

AN ACT

Containing Provisions applicable to the Laws of the Territory of Utah.

SEC. 1. Be it enacted by the Governor and Legislative Assembly of the Territory of Utah, That all questions of law, the meaning of writings other than laws, and the admissibility of testimony, shall be decided by the Court; and no law, nor parts of laws shall be read, argued, cited or adopted in any Court, during any trial, except those enacted by the Governor and Legislative Assembly of this Territory, and those passed by the Congress of the United States when applicable; and no report, decision, or doings of any Court shall be read, argued, cited, or adopted as precedent in any other trial.

SEC. 2. The repeal of a law does not revive one previously repealed by it, nor affect any rights, duties, or penalties which have arisen under it.

SEC. 3. Laws, and parts thereof, and words and phrases, shall be construed in accordance with the customary usage of the language.

SEC. 4. Words used in one tense may include either; and words used in one gender may include either; the singular may be read plural, and the plural singular; "person" may include a partnership, and a body corporate and politic; "writing" may include printing; "oath" may include affirmation or declaration; "signature" or "subscription" may include a mark, with the person's name written near it, and witnessed by one who can write. "Property" includes everything usually bought and sold, unless restricted. Joint authority given to three or more persons is given to the majority, unless restricted.

Approved Jan. 14th, 1854.

The above is a true copy of the original Act on file in my office. A. W. BABBITT,
Sec'y. of U. T.

Deseret News
March 30, 1854

Report of the 37th Quorum.

The following is a list of the presidency and members of the 37th quorum of seventies, and their present residences; organized, in Great Salt Lake City, January 12, 1854:—

Presidents:

Cyrus H. Wheelock, John Lyon, Jesse W. Crosby, Jonathan Midgley, David J. Ross, George Halliday, Claudius V. Spencer, Great Salt Lake City.

Members:

John M. Jones, John P. Smith, William Derr, William Smith, John Lowe, John G. Chambers, Andrew J Allen, Henry Maiben, John Miller, William Chatwin, Thomas Higham, Edward Allen, Eli Harrison, Hamilton G. Park, John Hawkins, John Griffiths, James Ririe, Jasper Thornton, Josh. T. Arrowsmith, Jacob S Ferrin, Thomas A. Dowell, James Lethan, Henry Ballad, Lemuel A. Davis, William Plunkett, Francis D. Clift, James V. Young, Elisha H. Rodgers, James M. Brown, James Spillett, Joseph Morris, John S. Wright, Samuel F. Neslin, Isaac C. Morris, Alfred Lamb, George Openshaw, John Harris, John Spriggs, Edwin L. Parry, James Belliston, William Parry, Joseph Hodgetts, Abraham Greenhalgh, James Newton, John S. Barnes, Richard Rostron, Henry Walsh, Henry George, William N. Fife, James Durney, Joshua Midgley, Arthur Stayner, Edmund Pugh, James Blackham, George T. Marsh, Andrew J. Tayson, John T. Morris, George Light, James Edwards, Eugene Henroid, Great Salt Lake City.

Charles Barnes, Lehi City.
James Quayle, Grantsville.
George Kendall, Nephi City.

The members of said quorum are requested to communicate at the first opportunity with the clerk, if they should detect any errors in the above list, or in case of removal to any other part of the Territory. It is also the desire of the presidency that each member, when absent on mission or otherwise, should write a communication (post paid) to the president or clerk at least once a-year, that their standing may be known. The meetings of the quorum are held every Friday evening at the 14th Ward school house, and the spirit manifested at those meetings is of the most exhilarating character, and truly refreshing to all who attend. It is the duty of every member resident in this city to attend these meetings. Members of other quorums are not prohibited from attending, but are at liberty to mingle their testimony with ours.

JOHN G. CHAMBERS, Clerk.

Deseret News
April 14, 1854

For the News.

Report of the Seventies of Nephi.

Dear President Richards:—

We, the seventies of Nephi, wish to inform our brethren, through the columns of the News, that we hold regular meetings on Wednesday and Sunday evenings, and are alive in the gospel of Christ. Our desires are to assist in rolling on the great work of this last dispensation; we find it very profitable meeting often together. The presidents of this place request us to preach to the saints, which we do cheerfully, in turns. We herewith send our names, &c and to what quorum we belong.

Acting President at Nephi: John A. Woolf, 18th quorum.

Members.—Andrew Love, 8th.; Wm Meeks, 6th.; Samuel Pitchforth, Thomas Wright, Edwin Harley, 24th.; Israel Hoyt, 22nd., Barnabas Merrifield, 2nd.; Miles Miller, 10th.; John Pyper (president), Alexander Gardner, William Holden, 27th.; John Borrowman, Z. H. Baxter, 9th.; Edward Ockey, Benjamin Riches, George Barber, 17th.; Samuel Barnett, sen. 23rd; Timothy S. Hoyt, 32nd.; Ichabod Gifford, 11th.; Abel Butterfield, 5th., George Kendall, 37th.; James Rollins, 25th quorum.

The following are attached to no quorum:— Amos Gustin, William H. Carpenter, George Cummings, Charles Sperry, William Lang, Absolom Woolf, John Cazier.

SAMUEL PITCHFORTH,
Clerk of the Seventies at Nephi.

Nephi Fort, March 15th., 1854.

Nephi,

August 12th, 1854.

EDITOR OF THE NEWS:—

Sir:—We enjoy a reasonable portion of health, and a good degree of union and peace; are at peace with the natives, &c. The grasshoppers and bugs have been doing their work. The beet crop is entirely, and the potatoe crop mostly destroyed, and much injury is done to wheat, and oats, and water very scarce for what is left; Salt creek not being so high as usual, nor retaining its height so long. So all is right; the destroyer cut off what the water would have failed to irrigate; so we see the hand of the Lord in it.

The people are satisfied with the place, and show a disposition to build it up. The city wall is progressing, and large quantities of the finest quality of hay are being rolled into our place every day from our rich, luxuriant meadows. Our wheat and oat harvest has just commenced. Our corn will be late. Our crops will be about an average. Considerable smut in wheat.

We still herd our cattle, stand guard, and carry our small arms with us into the fields. Our herding costs us about 10$ per day, 3,650$ per year. Our guarding will cost 50 cents per watch of two hours, four watches, two men on at a time, 4$ per night, 1,460$ per year; added to the above, makes a sum of 5,110$.

We expect to close our city wall by Conference, and have a time of rejoicing; and may we all pull together, and make a long pull, and a strong pull.

PHILOMEN.

United States District Court

FOR THE SECOND JUDICIAL DISTRICT, in session at Nephi City, Oct. 18, Chief Justice Kinney presiding; on motion of Joseph Holman, Eq., U. S Attorney for the Territory of Utah,—

SYLVESTER MOWRY, of Rhode Island,

BENJAMIN ALLSTON, of South Carolina, and

ROBERT O. TYLER, of Connecticut,

were admitted to practise as Attorneys and Counselors at Law, and Solicitors in Chancery before the United States Courts in and for the Territory of Utah

Indians.

We learn from br. Dimick B. Huntington, Interpreter for Col. Steptoe in the late trip to Fillmore, that he talked to the Natives around Nephi, Manti, and Fillmore, instructing them plainly and fully in the best course for them to pursue in order to secure to themselves the most real benefit. He told them to throw off their idle habits, cease their begging, and go to work; that the whites had to work for what they had, and were tired, and out of patience with supporting them in idleness, impudence, and thievery; and they need not expect many more presents unless they assisted in obtaining their own subsistence. They made no reply, but were very friendly, and as winter is at hand, we shall probably hear of no Indian disturbance until Spring; and if we are strictly wise, prudent, and prepared, we may escape further annoyance, except from now and then a reckless individual whose case can be easily disposed of, as his tribe will hunt him out, and deliver him up.

Nov. 15, br. Edward Dalton, just arrived from Parowan, informs us that Walker and several of his band passed thro' Parowan the day he left.— They were on their way south, and appeared very friendly. A large number of Utahs were met in Beaver valley. They felt well, did not beg, but wished to trade.

Nephi,
Nov. 20th, 1854.

Mr. Editor—Dear Sir: We are prospering in our labors upon our City Wall; the most of it is twelve feet high, and the remainder about nine. The gates are hung, and were locked on the night of the 18th inst., and guard dismissed, thus affording us a time of rejoicing. We now feel to claim the promise of the protecting hand that should be over us, on the completion of this work, to preserve our lives, and to enable us to wield a greater influence over the natives, that we may stay their hands from bloodshed, and also their wrath, to the end that we may live in peace, and safety, together with our wives and little ones. We still maintain our amicable relations with the natives. There are very few in our midst, or round about our borders.

Nov 30 is appointed for feasting, and merry making, to celebrate the great event of closing up our city.

Most of our citizens have been re-baptized according to express command, washing away their sins and walking in newness of life, thus manifesting their faith by their works.

Yours in the faith,   BULLOMEN.

Celebration at Nephi.

Nephi, December 4th, 1854.

Editor of the Deseret News:—

Sir, We are happy to inform you that peace prevails in our midst. Our City wall and gates being nearly completed, and our grain, &c., being well secured, we concluded to meet en masse, and rejoice in feasting, dancing, and praising the Lord, for the great blessings we have enjoyed during the past season.

The following Committee being appointed viz:

J. G. Bigler,	T. B. Foote,
C. H. Bryan,	Josiah Miller,

George Kendall.

They announced a feast for Thursday, November 30th, and the two following days. At noon the people assembled and partook of a bountiful feast, consisting of every variety the season afforded. At 2 p. m. the meeting was called to order by President Bigler. Chanting by the Choir. Prayer by Elder George Kendall. An original poem composed by Elder Kendall, was sung. Speeches by Timothy B. Foote, Mayor of the City, and President Bigler. Toasts by Samuel Pitchforth, Peter Munzer, George Kendall, Andrew Love, and George Spencer. Song, "Merry Mormons," by William Evans, Music by the Cotillon Band; Song, "You can't come in," (original) by George Barber, speech by George Kendall. At 5 p. m. the inhabitants were organized into companies of ten families, with a captain to each ten, three companies to occupy the Hall each evening. Benediction by William Cazier. Patriarch. Friday, 2 p. m. the citizens assembled in high spirits. Singing and Prayer. Speech by President Bigler, followed by appro-priate remarks from the brethren, and a large number of toasts, and sentiments by David Webb, Abel Butterfield, John Mangum, William Cazier, and others. Comic Song by William Throp. At 5 p. m. the meeting adjourned to 10 a. m. of the following day. Saturday 10 a. m. the people were called together by the sound of horn, and firing of cannon. Meeting opened by singing and prayer. Speeches by Bishop Bigler, Kendall, and others. Many toasts and sentiments were given. A Song, composed by Mary Pitchforth, was sung by the choir. Toast, may the spirit which pervades this feast fill Nephi's Missionaries Sly and Gustin, with joy and consolation, S. Pitchforth.

Mayor T. B. Foote, proposed that this feast be annually celebrated on the first day of December. Carried unanimously. Appropriate remarks were made by the Bishops, and the meeting adjourned to 4 p. m. for dancing, which was spiritedly participated in, until twelve o'clock. Thus joyously terminated the feast of Nephi.

Yours truly,

JACOB G. BIGLER,
President.

R. BENTLY,
Clerk.

UNITED STATES MAIL.
UTAH.

POST OFFICE DEPARTMENT,
December 5, 1854.

PROPOSALS for carrying the mails of the United States from the 1st day of September, 1855, to the the 30th day of June, 1858, (inclusive) in UTAH TERRITORY, will be received at the Contract Office of the Post Office Department, in the city of Washington, until 9 a.m. of the 15th day of June, 1855, to be decided by the next day, on the routes, and in the time herein specified, viz:

12806 From Salt Lake City, by Neff's Mill, Mill Creek, Holladay's Settlement, Little Cottonwood, and Draperville, to Mountainville, 20 miles and back, once a week.

Leave Salt Lake City every Thursday at 7 a. m.;
Arrive at Mountainville same day by 7 p. m.;
Leave Mountainville every Friday at 7 a. m.;
Arrive at Salt Lake City same day by 7 p. m.

12807 From Salt Lake City, by Taylorsville, West Jordan, Gardner's Mills, Bingham, and Kanyon, to Cedar Valley, 45 miles and back, once a week.

Leave Salt Lake City every Thursday at 7 a m.;
Arrive at Cedar Valley next day by 12 m.;
Leave Cedar Valley every Friday at 1 p.m.;
Arrive at Salt Lake City next day by 6 a. m.

12808 From Tooele City to Grantsville, 12 miles and back, once a week.

Leave Tooele City every Tuesday at 8 a. m.;
Arrive at Grantsville by 12 m.;
Leave Grantsville every Tuesday at 1 p.m.,
Arrive at Tooele City by 5 p. m.

12809 From Nephi City, by Fillmore City, Corn Creek, Parragona, and Parowan, to Cedar City, 180 miles and back, once a week.

Leave Nephi City every Monday at 6 a.m.,
Arrive at Cedar City next Friday by 6 p. m.

Leave Cedar City every Monday at 6 a.m.;
Arrive at Nephi City every Friday by 6 p.m.

NOTES.

No pay will be made for trips not performed, and for each of such omissions not satisfactorily explained three times the pay of the trip may be deducted. For arrivals so far behind time as to break connexion with depending mails, and not sufficiently excused, one-fourth of the compensation for the trip is subject to forfeiture. Fines will be imposed, unless the delinquency be promptly and satisfactorily explained by certificates of postmasters, or the affidavits of other creditable persons, for neglecting to take the mail from or into a post office, for suffering it to be injured, destroyed, robbed, or lost; and for refusing, after demand, to convey the mail as frequently as the contractor runs, or is concerned in running, vehicles on the route.

The Postmaster-General may annul the contract for repeated failures to run agreeably to contract; for disobeying the Post Office laws or instructions of the department, or for assigning the contract without the assent of the Postmaster General.

The Postmaster General may alter the schedule. He may also order an increase of service on a route by allowing therefor a pro rata increase on the contract pay. He may also curtail or discontinue the service, at pro rata decrease of pay, if he allow one month's extra compensation on the amount dispensed with. No extra pay will be allowed for excess of actual over-advertised distance if the points to be supplied are herein correctly stated. The bids should be addressed to the Second Assistant Postmaster General, superscribed "Mail proposals in the Territory of Utah."

The contracts are to be executed and returned to the department by or before the 1st day of September, 1855. For further particulars as to conditions to be incorporated in the contracts see advertisement for California, Oregon, Utah, &c., dated 13th October, 1853.

JAMES CAMPBELL,
Postmaster General.

Trip to Manti.

EDITOR OF THE NEWS:—

Sir:—I left this city on the 8th inst., in company with Dr. Garland Hurt, Indian agent for Utah, to visit the Indians in the southern settlements, there being great excitement among them in consequence of Walker's death.

The Indians at Lehi were friendly, and disposed to work; those at Springville were cross, and excited, ready to accuse the Mormons, while they themselves live by begging, and have burned up two miles of fence.

Those at Payson were friendly, and anxious to farm in the Spring. Wah-woo-ner, the one who killed Keel, was at Nephi, making heavy demands upon the inhabitants for cattle and flour, but to no effect.

At Fort Ephraim there were a number of the Po-eooteh-i-ches and Shib-e-re-ches from the Uinta country; they appeared friendly.

On arriving at Manti we found Arapeen very friendly, and quite humble. He was anxious to be chief in Walker's place. He has had a remarkable vision, about Walker's death, which he told us. It appears that Walker, while gambling with some Pah-van-tes, broke a blood-vessel, which caused his death. Ar-a-peen thinks the Pah-van-tes made bad medicine for him. Walker had his senses until the last, and requested his brothers to kill a Pi-ede woman (who was in a delicate condition), to strangle, with lassoes, two Pi-ede girls, and bury alive a Pi-ede boy ten years old; to kill sixty horses, and six sheep. Twenty of the horses ran off, while the others were being killed.

On our return to Palmyra we visited Pe-tetenect's band, and found them very friendly, and lazy. Dr. Hurt took much pains to instruct and encourage the natives in doing right; and manifested a lively interest in improving their condition. At the next new moon, all the neighboring tribes are to meet at Nephi to elect a chief.

Yours respectfully,

D. B. HUNTINGTON,
Interpreter.

G. S. L. City, Feb. 16, 1855.

Deseret News
March 8, 1855

AGENTS.

The following persons are requested to act as Agents of the Deseret News Vol. 5:

GREAT SALT LAKE COUNTY.

Kanyon Creek Ward	A. O. Smoot.
Gardner's Mill, Mill Creek	Robt. Gardner.
Mill Creek	Alex. Hill.
Big Cottonwood	Lyman Stevens.
South Cottonwood Ward	And'w. Calhoun.
Union	S. Richards.
Drapersville	Wm. Draper.
West Jordan Ward	Joseph Harker.

TOOELE COUNTY.

Richville	J. Rowberry.
Tooele City	Eli B. Kelsey.
Grantsville	Thos. H. Clark.

DAVIS COUNTY.

Stoker	John Stoker.
Centerville	A. B. Cherry.
Farmington	Jas. Leathead.
Kaysville	Saml. Henderson.

WEBER COUNTY.

Ogden City	J. G. Browning.
Bingham's Ward	E. Bingham.
South Weber	Thomas Kington
East Weber	A. Wordsworth.
North Ogden Ward	Thomas Dunn.
North Willow Creek	C. W. Hubbard.
Youngsville	Eli H. Pierce.

UTAH COUNTY.

Provo City	D. Carter.
Springville	Aaron Johnson.
Lehi City	David Evans.
Mountainville	Isaac Houston.
Cedar Valley	Allen Weeks.
American Fork	L. E. Harrington.
Pleasant Grove	Wm. G. Sterrett.
Palmyra	John W. Berry.
Payson	Chas. B. Hancock.
Juab County	T. B. Foot.
San Pete County	George Peacock.
Millard County	S. P. Hoyt.

IRON COUNTY.

Parowan	J. C. L. Smith.
Cedar City	Isaac C. Haight.
Washington County	John D. Lee.
San Bernardino, Cal.	D. M. Thomas.

Report of the 15th Quorum.

About three fourths of its members have reported and forwarded their genealogies to the Quorum, and are of good report. The Quorum meet at Alfred Randall's, the first Sunday of every month at 6 o'clock p.m.

All the members belonging to this Quorum who have not reported themselves are requested to do so forthwith by letter to the clerk, post paid.

Any member of the Church that can give information of the whereabouts, death, or apostacy, if any, of the following named members, will confer a great favor to the Council.

William Smith, Hugh Walker, Silas S. Davis, Elijah Haws, Ephraim Cheney, Henry More, Joseph Hutchinson, Silas Nowel, Jeremiah Root, John Pickels, Nathan Butler, James M. Johnson, Rufus B. Linnel, George W. Spiluger, George W. Fowler.

SIMEON A. DUNN, Weber Co.

H. W. MIKESELL, G. S. L. City.

A. RANDALL,   "

E. K. FULLER, on mission to States.

W. W. WILLIS, Cedar City.

WILLIAM MEEKS, Nephi.

CHAPMAN DUNCAN, G. S. L. City,

L. R. CHAFFIN, Clerk.   Presidents.

AN ACT

In relation to the compilation and revision of the Laws and Resolutions in force in Utah Territory; their publication and distribution.

SEC. 1. Be it enacted by the Governor and Legislative Assembly of the Territory of Utah: That the following compilation of the laws shall be published with the amendments and alterations therein specified, and the new amendments therein made are valid in law; all laws and resolutions not included in said list, the laws and resolutions of the present session excepted, are deemed repealed, obsolete or not necessary to reprint.

SEC. 2. The following is the compilation above referred to:

Book.	Page.	Approved.	
1	3	Sept. 17, 1787.	Constitution of United States and amendments.
2	83	March 18, 1849.	Constitution of the State of Deseret.
			Ordinances of the State of Deseret.
2	90	Jan. 15, 1850.	Providing for State and County Road Commissioners.
			Sec. 1. insert "2 years" instead of "4 years."
2	92	Feb. 28, 1850.	Incorporating the University of the State of Deseret.
			Sec. 11 leave out, numbering the other sections accordingly.
			Sec. 14 changed to read, "The Secretary and Treasury shall each present a full and explicit report in writing of the situation, funds, and doings of the University in their several departments, by the 15th of October in each year, to the Auditor of Public Accounts."
2	94	March 2, 1850.	In relation to County Recorders: leave out sec. 6.
2	95	" "	Creating a Surveyor General's office.
			Sec. 1, insert "2 years," instead of "4 years."
2	96	" 29, 1850.	Prohibiting the sale of arms, ammunition, or spirituous liquors to the Indians.
2	96	Dec. 9, 1850.	To control the waters of the Twin Springs, and Rock Spring, in Tooele valley, and county, for mills and irrigating purposes.
2	96	" "	Concerning City Creek and kanyon.
2	97	Jan. 9, 1851.	Granting the waters of North Mill Creek kanyon, and the waters of the next kanyon north, to Heber C. Kimball.
2	97	Jan. 19, 1851.	To incorporate Great Salt Lake City.
			Sec. 5, insert "April" instead of "March."
			Sec. 38 and 44, insert "Probate Court," instead of "County Court."
			Sec. 47, and 48 not reprint.
2	105	Jan. 9, 1851.	In relation to the timber in the mountains, west of Jordan.
2	106	" "	In relation to the timber in the kanyons and mountains leading into Tooele valley, and the kanyons between Salt Lake Valley and Tooele.
2	107	Jan. 18, 1851.	Pertaining to North Cottonwood kanyon,
			Sec. 2, leave out.
2	107	Feb. 6, 1851.	To incorporate Ogden City.
			Sec. 5, insert "April" instead of "March."
			Secs. 38 and 44, "Probate Court" instead of "County Court."
			Sec. 47, not reprint.
2	114	" "	To incorporate the City of Manti.
			Sec. 5, "April" instead of "March."
			Secs. 38 and 44, "Probate Court" instead of "County Court."
			Sec. 47, not reprint.
2	122	" "	To incorporate Provo City.
			Sec. 5, "April" instead of "March."
			Secs. 38 and 44, "Probate Court," instead of "County Court."
			Sec. 47, not reprint.
2	129	" "	To incorporate Parowan City.
			Sec. 5, "April" instead of "March."
			Secs. 38 and 44, "Probate Court" instead of "County Court."
			Sec. 47 not reprint.
2	136	Feb. 8, 1851.	Incorporating the Church of Jesus Christ of Latter Day Saints.

1	115	Feb. 3, 1852.	Section 1, "2 years" instead of "4 years."
1	117	March 6, 1852.	To create the office of County Treasurer in each county of the Territory of Utah, and to define the duties thereof.
1	143	March 3, 1852.	In relation to crimes and punishments.
1	143	Feb. 5, 1852.	Providing for the bridging of ditches or seets leading across the highways.
1	160	Feb. 5, 1852.	To provide for the further organization of the Militia of the Territory of Utah.
1	161	Feb. 18, 1852.	Section 26, Paragraph 4, leave out and number accordingly.
1	161	Oct. 4, 1851.	In relation to the inspection of spirituous liquors.
1	162	March 3, 1852.	Locating the county seat of Davis county.
1	169	Feb. 3, 1852.	To provide for the organization of Millard county, and to name the seat of government.
			Defining the boundaries of counties.
1	170	Feb. 5, 1852.	Granting the control of waters from Mill creek, in Great Salt Lake county, unto Willard Richards.
1	170	Feb. 16, 1852.	Granting waters of Mill creek unto President Brigham Young.
1	171	Feb. 18, 1852.	For the improvement of Big Kanyon Creek road.
1	173	Jan. 16, 1852.	In relation to the waters of American creek in Utah county.
1	176	Feb. 10, 1852.	Creating the office of Code Commissioners and prescribing their duties.
			To incorporate Cedar City, in Iron county, Utah Territory.
			Section 5, insert "April" instead of "March."
1	184	Feb. 5, 1852.	Section 47 leave out.
			To incorporate the City of Lehi.
			Section 5 insert "April" instead of "March."
1	192	Feb. 13, 1852.	Sections 47 and 48 leave out.
1			To incorporate Fillmore City in Millard county.
1			Section 5, insert "April" instead of "March."
1	200	March 6, 1852.	Section 47, leave out.
2	5	Dec. 23, 1852.	To incorporate Nephi City.
			In relation to the Militia.
2	6	Dec. 30, 1852.	Section 5, omit.
			Regulating the mode of procedure in civil cases in the Courts of the Territory of Utah. Section 14 revised, "When complaint is made and substantiated against a non resident, or absentdent debtor, and the plaintiff has given the requisite security, the court shall issue an order to the proper officer to take his property, or sufficient thereof to liquidate the debt and costs; and appoint three competent persons who shall proceed forthwith under oath to appraise the property; whereupon the Court shall advertise its order in one newspaper printed in this Territory, and send a copy thereof to the defendant, if his residence is known or presumed, and shall offer the property to the plaintiff for his acceptance, and if refused shall proceed to sell the same at public or private sale for money, at not less than three fourths its appraised value, and pay the demands, and deposit any surplus into the County Treasury, to the credit of the defendant; and such defendant may be heard in the matter at any period within seven years."
2	10	Jan. 3, 1853.	Regulating elections.
2	13	Jan. 13, 1853.	To prevent the needless destruction of Fish.
2	14	Jan. 17, 1853.	To incorporate the Deseret Iron Company.
2	17	" "	Granting unto Daniel H. Wells, the right to erect ferries across Green River, and to control the same.
2	18	" "	To incorporate the Provo Canal and Irrigation Company.
2	20	Jan. 21, 1853.	To incorporate the Provo Manufacturing Company.
			Section 7, leave out.
2	23	Jan. 21, 1853.	To incorporate the City of Springville.
2	30	" "	Regulating the mode of procedure in criminal cases. Section 27, insert after the word "court," the words "and shall search for and take persons, papers, or property concealed, and is empowered to break any and every description of fastenings, or enclosures, and to take any steps necessary to enable him to execute an order or judgment.
2	33	Jan. 21, 1853.	Granting unto Charles Hopkins and others the right to build a bridge across the river Jordan.
2	34	" "	Authorizing the erection of a ferry or ferries on Ham's Fork River.
2	37	" "	Concerning a ferry or ferries across Bear River, and a bridge across the Malad.
			Section 6, leave out and number accordingly.

MEMORIALS TO CONGRESS.

SEC. 3. The Hon. Evan M. Greene, is hereby appointed and authorized to attend to the publishing of said list together with the Laws, Resolutions and Memorials of the present session, and may call to his assistance such clerks as shall be necessary to aid him therein.

SEC. 4. There shall be published five thousand copies thereof, with full and complete marginal notes, index and contents—including the Declaration of Independence and Articles of Confederation, the Constitution of the United States and Amendments thereto, the Constitution of the Provisional State of Deseret, the Organic Act, with the list of Memorials attached, and their indexes.

SEC. 5. There shall also be published three thousand copies of the Journals of the present session of the Legislative Assembly, including the Governor's Message and Proclamations, in book form.

SEC. 6. The Secretary of the Territory is hereby required to furnish the Governor of each State and Territory with one copy each of the Laws and Journals, and the Governor of Utah Territory with twenty five copies of each, the Laws and Journals, two copies of the Laws and one of the Journals to each of the members of the present Legislative Assembly, and one copy of each to each officer of the two houses, two copies of each to each of the Judges of the Supreme and Probate Courts in the Territory, and one copy of each to each of the clerks of the Supreme, District, and Probate Courts, one copy of each to the United States Marshal and each of his deputies, and the United States District Attorney for the Territory of Utah, and one copy of each to each civil officer in the Territory of Utah, including the Mayor, Aldermen, Recorder, and Marshal of each incorporated city; one copy of the Laws to the commandant of the Nauvoo Legion, the commandant of each Military District, and the Commandants of each Brigade, Regiment and Battalion, and their staff officers respectively, and captains of companies; to the Utah Library, and the Library of the University of the State of Deseret each five copies of the Laws and Journals, and two copies each, to each other public Library in the Territory.

Approved January 19th, 1855.

Deseret News
June 27, 1855

GRASSHOPPERS, &c.—Hon. Calvin G. Pendleton, arrived in this city from Iron co., on the 24th.; general health among the people; the grasshoppers have destroyed all the grain at Paragoonah, nine-tenths at Parowan; all the wheat at Fort Johnson, and about one-tenth of the grain at Cedar city; the grain at Harmony is uninjured.

The bursting of a cloud on the mountains about the first of June, washed away the house of Elder Benjamin R. Hulse in Cedar city, and injured several others. The fields look like a desert and every separate bench appears to be hatching out fresh crops of grasshoppers. Several companies have started to the 'Pangwitch' lake, on fishing excursions. The water is lower than has ever been known before, and but a small portion of the land resown can possibly be watered. A small party has also started to the Santa Clara mission to plant corn. The people of Iron co. are in first rate Spirits. The Public Square at Parowan city (10 acres) has been planted with potatos in the hopes that the united efforts of men, women, and children, chickens, ducks, turkies, &c., &c., may save a sufficiency to have occasionally a little potato soup next winter.

Nine tenths of the wheat crops are destroyed at Fillmore. Chalk Creek very low, fresh recruits of grasshoppers hatching on the benches. The fields at Nephi city look like the seat of desolation.

Excursion to Fillmore,

By Hon. John M. Bernhisel, accompanied by Lieut. Gen. D. H. Wells.—Our delegate, and Gen. Wells left this city, Tuesday, 21st inst., and drove to Springville. On the 22nd they reached Nephi, and on the 23rd arrived at Fillmore, 152 miles south of this city.

They visited the south wing of the State House, whose walls are of red sandstone, where they found the workmen busily engaged in placing the flagging in the basement story, laying the floors in the first and second stories, and arching the ceiling of the large hall in the upper story, preparatory to lathing and plastering.

The sash were all in, and outside doors all hung, and a temporary entrance stairway finished.

The work on the building will soon be ready for the plasterers and painters, who it is expected will be immediately sent from this city; and all efforts are being made to complete the rooms so far as to comfortably accommodate the Library, and the next Legislative Assembly, which adjourned to meet on the second Monday of December at that place.

Corn and potatoes at Fillmore, and at other places between here and there, look promising for a fair crop; but grain and hay are an entire failure, except at Springville and Provo, where they will probably have wheat sufficient for their own consumption; there is considerable hay cut at Pleasant Grove and American creek.

Kanoshe and all the Indians met with on the route were very friendly, tho' as usual, very burdensome upon our young settlements, in their affectionate method of constant begging, and supplying themselves liberally with corn and potatoes from the fields.

After tarrying over night at Fillmore, and finishing the transaction of such business that devolved upon them, they started on their return on the 24th, and reached this city about half past 11 a. m. of the 26th, in excellent health and spirits.

Report of the 21st Quorum.

The following is a list of the Presidency and Members of the 21st Quorum of Seventies, and their present residences so far as known:—

PRESIDENTS.

Nathan B. Baldwin, Fillmore; Alonzo Lebarron, Payson; James Beck, Stephen Hales, David Wilkin, Ephraim K. Hanks, Geo. W. Taggart, G. S. L. City.

MEMBERS.

Orrin D. Farline, Robert Crookston, Orlando F. Mead, Samuel L. Jones, Simon Noel, James Tanner, James Shanks, Wm. Robinson, Hans Hanson, Luther S. Hemmingway, H. L. Southworth, John Squires, Nells Hanson, Andrew Overlade, Wm. Anderson, Samuel Cornaby, Wm. Jackson, Andrew Beardalson, Wm. Barnes, Gammer Heyward, Richard V. Morris, Wm. R. Jones, John T. Evans, Canute Hanson Brown, James Hanson, Alvah Fester, Gorgen Daniels, Genhard Jensen, Alonzo H. Russel, Jens Thomsen Balle, Daniel Gamble, James Woods, Wm. Price, G. S. L. City.

Thos. Charlesworth,* Orson Tyler,* Isaiah Huntsman, Fillmore.

Beverly C. Boren,* Allen D. Boren,* Coleman Boren, Elijah Allen, Provo.

John Galaher,* John W. Dutson, St. Louis.

Thos. Adair,* John Mangum,* Geo. Spencer,* Thos. Carter, Nephi.

Thos. Steed, North Cottonwood.

Wesley H. Seabury, Little Cottonwood.

Edmund Pace, Session's settlement.

Abram Durphy, Coal Creek*.

Nathan Lewis, Battle Creek.

Walter F. Smith, Orrice C. Murdock, Lehi city.

Sidney A. Hanks on mission to Society Islands.

Enoch B. Tripp, mission to the States.

Hugh Conway Morris, Little Salt Lake.

Geo. A. Day, Tooele city.

Wm. R. McClean, Kay's Ward.

John Wakely, on mission.

S. Hadlock, unknown; Merril Wheeler, San Bernardino.

Those whose names have a star attached to them are requested to send in their genealogies immediately.

The members scattered abroad are requested to report themselves, as we wish to know the standing of every member of the Quorum.

The Quorum meets regularly every first and third Sunday evening in each month at the house of David Wilkin in the 17th Ward at 6 o'clock, all members living in the city are expected to attend, and all others as often as circumstances will permit. We want none but active, lively members in the Quorum, such as are determined to magnify their priesthood, pay their tithing, and assist all in their power to roll on the Kingdom of God.

By order of the Council.

ORLANDO F. MEAD, Clerk

IMMIGRATION LIST.

The following is the list, so far as we have received it, of the names of the heads of families, single individuals, number of horses, oxen, cows, wagons, &c., of this year's immigration:—

The * indicates returning missionaries.

FIRST COMPANY—John Hindley, Captain.

Peter Burgess	William Knowles
David P Barnes	William Knox
Miles Rostan	Daniel Lunn
Charles L Walker	Willard G McMullen*
George H Barnes	Henry McMullen
James Ashton	Edward A Miles
John Buckwalter	J W Myers
Henry S Buckwalter	Henry Misanger
B Bunnell	John H Picknell
James Fywater	Edwin Pearse
James Barker	Josiah Pearse
Zechariah Astell	Priam Pearse
Cyrus Averey	Henry Perry
William Avery	W A Perry
William Beasley	Allen T Riley
J Brown	Robert Redford
Josiah Brown	George Sant
Peter A Boyl	B N Stanford
John W Coward*	Enos Stokey
John Clegg	John Singleton
D S Caspar	David Stromple
John Coomish	Thomas Swindlehurst
William Coomish	Ephraim Turner
Jacob B Carr	John Thornley
James Crancher	Robert Thornley
David Duncan	George S Williams
Henry Dinwoody	Thomas Williams
Samuel Glascon*	E Williams
James Gibbons	George Water
William Gough	Jefferson Wright
George Greenwood	Arthur Wright
John Hindley	Asa Wright
Abraham Lawer	John Worley
Darius Longee	Weber Worley
David Louden	Henry L Worley
John Knowles	

67 women and 66 children. 46 wagons, 226 oxen 54 cows, 14 horses and 4 mules.

SECOND COMPANY----Noah T. Guyman, Captain.

Jacob F Secrist* (dead)
Osmon M Duel
Minnie Wagner
John Ethrington 4
John Pugh 4
Ann Haslep 3
Mary Ann Thorne
John Mewey 4
John Lang 2
James Jordan 6
Thomas C Stayner 3
Henry Randall
Edmund Ellis
Peter Horrocks 4
John Prescott
John Chisnall
Henry H Morgan
William Kershaw
James Domville 2

Samuel Ackerley 2
James Prescott 6
U M Dougal 3
Joseph Lyon
Daniel Horrock (died) 5
William Thomas
Charles Smith*
Noah T Guyman*
Ralph Blanch 3
Robert Telford 2
Edward Kendall 3
William Kendall 3
James Mather 6
William Grundy 2
George Ogleby 8
Peter Furlong 3
Edward Falconer (4 died) 8
James Welch (1 died) 6
Thomas Morgan (1 died) 7

DANES.

Erick G M Hougan*
Johan Tralsen 3
C Christiansen
S Halvorsen 3
J Sandersen 2
G Ericksen
N A Mauritzen 2
H Ericksen 4
H Christiansen 5
M Larsen
M Poulsen 3
E Otesen
N Widergren 4
J Christensen
Simon A Rase 3
Christine Jensen
H J Johansen 7
Alexander Dahl 2
Anders Monsen
Rasmus Brun 4
E Johnsen 4
Peter Nielsen 4
Lars Tofte 3
Peter Andersen 5
Peter Staffensen 4
S Biarnesen 2

Jens Jensen 5
A E Ericksen 2
J L Lund 2
Jens Skrader 4
H P Larsen
A M Nielsen
Hans Jensen
Karen Andersen 8
J C Sorensen 8
A C Brawand
A C Larsen
Hans Ottesen 5
R Nielsen 4
A C Andersen 5
J Christensen 3
O P Larsen
Christian Andersen 7
J Eilertsen 6
P Jespersen 3
L P Lund 6
N H Beck 3
Ola Andersen 7
Niels Capsen 2
H Petersen 9
L C Kier 5
J Nielsen 2

E G Hansen	4	Niels Jensen	2
Niles Petersen		Niels Johnsen	2
Nicolai Dorius	2	J C Petersen	2
Ingri Jonsen	2	J J Svane	5
Martin Brun	5	Hans Hansen	5
M Nielsen	2	Jens Petersen	6
C Petersen		E C Ottesen	
Jorgen Hansen	2	R N Beck	4
Jorgen Rasmusen		N Clemensen	2
Jens Poulsen		M Christensen	3
Anton Christensen	7	P O Hansen*	
O K Beck	2	H O Lundblad	5
Lars Olsen	3	Peter Hansen	4
Lars Franzen	2	A Fullgren	3
M F Hageman	2	Jens Jensen	3

58 wagons, 231 oxen and 190 cows.

FOURTH COMPANY----Richard Ballantyne, Captain.

Wm Glover*		Amelia Longford	2
John Bushby		Charles Livingston	8
Thomas Barrat	3	Samuel Mulliner	3
Elizabeth Boory		Charles Monkcom	2
George Bill	3	Mary Morris	
Anna Bander		Berthia Mullinax	2
Timothy Adams		Hector McQuarry	
Sarah A Bane		William McFarlane	9
James Bush	8	James Moore	2
Robert Baxter	6	Angus McDonald	2
Esther Birch		Sarah Matthews	3
Barry Beeby		George Mayer	
William Beard	7	John Mottssee	
George Butcher		Samuel Martin	6
Ami Bird	5	Mary Mors	

Casper Bruner		James McCracken	
William Bishop	3	Elizabeth Nish	3
George Bourne		Samuel Ostler	2
Joseph Birch	5	Thomas Orr	4
Charles Cranford	3	Andrew Odnatt	
Anna Crouther		Robert Nish	2
Daniel Caveen	5	Caroline Opterholda	
John Clark		George Neasham	
Henry Clegg	2	Thomas Palmer	3
George Cushing	3	Mary Pearce	
Francis H Congriffe	2	Susanna Preston	
John Chance		George Pickering	
Mary Clemens		Mary Porter	

Ann Cole		William Pitt*	
Jane Clayton	4	Josiah Fent	2
Elizabeth Daviess		Mary Prosser	
Emma Dewey		Skaderick Peters	2
James Davis	2	Elizabeth Pinder	2
Elizabeth Dimant		Jane Pilkington	
Griffith Davis		John Pickett	2
Emma Davis		Frederick Rushton	6
Ann Finch		Mary Reid	
Sarah Franks	2	Charles Ramsden	4
Trena Fisher		James Robson	5
Charles Ford		Joseph Race	2
Thomas Floyd		William Race	5
Mark Fletcher	3	Jane Saunders	2
James Gardener	2	Thomas Sutherland	
Arnold Goodliffe		Ellen Stevens	
John Grimatt	8	Thomas Stanger	4
Mary Greene		John Story	3
William Hapley	5	Thomas Stevenson	3
Mary Harper	4	John E Sheldon	3
William Horrinkson	3	Daniel Skelding	4
Anna Hurst		James Stevenson	2
Elias Hunt	2	William H Sterrock	6
David Hilton	3	Michael Saunders	
Charles Hogg	3	George Simonds	5
James Hadley	2	Elizabeth Saunders	2
Emma Hodges		Mary A Spencer	3
Charles Hartley	5	John Thomson	
Harriet Hindford	2	William Thomson	6
Phillip Hewitt	2	Robert Thomson	2
William Hunt	4	Benford Thimbeby	
David Hutchinson	6	Otho Teasdale	
James Hardman	5	George Thomson	
Jacob Handermann		Thomas Taysem	4
Jacob Hook	8	Sarah Williamson	
Ann Jenkins		Thomas Wilson	
William Julian	3	Harriet Wendford	
Thomas Joice	4	John Warwood	5
Phillip Jones		Jane Walker	
James Inshaw		William West	7
Margaret Johnson	3	Samuel Ware	6

Jane Johnson		Thomas B Wadman	
Isaac Knowles	5	Elizabeth White	
Thomas Knowlden	2	James Warlton	8
Josiah Knowlden		Sarah A Wickle	2
Charles Kidgel	2	James Wall	2
William Kent		James Westwood	6
Mary A. Loveless		John Vest	6
Mary Lockhead		Catharine Vealey	
Samuel Langfield		Marion Young	3

402 persons; 45 wagons; 220 oxen; 48 cows; 3 horses.

FIFTH COMPANY---Moses Thurston, Captain.

William Brown 2
Clark Baker
John Arnold
Thomas Brooks Bell
Annie Allsworth
William Burnett
Eliza Ann Bunting 2
Sarah Bradbridge
James Aiken
Charles Butterfield
John Brownlow
Charles Bohnford
Richard E Davies 3
John Evans
Hudraw Ferguson 7
Philip Gems 10
Duncan Ferguson
Elizabeth Galgalland
John Giles 4
Aaron Garlick 3
Abraham Helm 13
Annie Hampton
William Horsley
Samuel Howard
Francis Hawkes 2
John W Jenkins 2
Joseph Inchin 2
George Knowlden

Thomas Lee 2
Annie Liversidge
Richard Morgan 4
John B Maiben 2
Thomas Margetts*
John Moore 5
Thomas Norn 7
Thomas Peake
James Pailing 3
John Robinson 4
James Robson
John Rigby
Charlotte Riley
Eliza Richards
John Sheffield 2
Joseph Seale 2
John Stout 3
Joseph Shaw 1
Charles Tuckett 7
John Todd
Robert Wright 8
Ruth Wickens
John Wood 8
George Williams 3
Isaac White 2
Francis White 7
William Wilkstonholme
Jesse Youngblood

33 wagons, 234 oxen, 28 cows and 12 horses.

SIXTH COMPANY---P. E. F. Co.--- C. A. Harper, Captain.

John Allen 2
A S Burton
Dominie Bodrer
Jeanette Bland
Alfred J Atkinson 7
George Burton
Thomas Burton 3
Ann Bradley
Emma Burdsley
Rachel Bowen
Samuel Burt 2
Jane Couthanche
Daniel Cadorett
Domnico Bordrane
Alexander Couderwood
Samuel Crawford 4
Hamel Chapman
Agustus Dunin
Joseph Dunkley 2
————Dufresne
William Davies 4
Rees Davies 7
John Edwards 3
Abraham Enouf
James Endriel
William Ferne 4
Susan Dolbel 2

Henry J Jones
William Jones 3
William T Kilburn 4
Samuel Langlois 7
Henry Lucas 5
Mary Ann Lapworth
John D Malan 9
D Meiklejohn
John Memnott 5
John N Morriss 3
Sinah Pugh
Francis Romreal
Mary Robertson
Emma Roe 4
Andrew Robertson
Ann Reese
John Reese 3
William Richards 5
Ephraim Rollins 4
Francis D L George 4
John La Sener 7
James Shanks 5
Robert Sneder
James Squires 2
Mary Ann Williams
Rhoda White 4
Edwin Watts 2

John Lee Gresley
Daniel Graves 9
Henry Goddard 2
William Gorringe 4
Cornelius Green 2
George George 3
William Harden 3
Elizabeth Howard
Sarah Howlet
Louisa Hulse
Ann Hughes 6
Mary Hiles
Samuel Handron
Elizabeth Jean
Henry Jones 4
Rosser Jenkins 2

Ann Taylor 3
Mary Parker
Joseph Perkins 3
Jane Price 2
Jeremiah Price 7
Thomas Painter 5
W Thomas 4
Henry Powell
Jenkin Williams
Salina Williams
Thomas Williams
William Vest 3
Josiah Young 8
Robert Toring 4
Catharine White 2

INDEPENDENTS (so called)

Charles A Harper*
Lucy L Brown
Jane Brown
Ann Brewerton
Kitty Bumpton
G W Bramwell 3
Martha Barton
Margaret Griffiths
William Hanson 2
Morgan Jones
Marr Harris
Jane Jackson
William James 4
Thomas Jeremy* 3
Elizabeth Jones
Henry Liversidge 4
Jane C Martin

Dwight Martin 2
John Marral 2
John Parkin 5
Caroline Pill 2
Joseph Perry
William Rust*
William Rowan 3
Joseph D Reynolds
David Reese 2
William Reese 6
Edward Sutherland
Daniel Thomas
Harriet Taylor
Thomas Turner
David Williams
Sarah Williams
Thomas Williams 8

39 wagons, 220 oxen, 30 cows, 1 horse and 1 mule.

SEVENTH COMPANY------Isaac Allred, Captain.

Henry Ashcroft 2
U Anderson
E C Brand 2
J Bond
G Brown
Thomas Brian
Fred Branson
R Drummond
J M Coombs
Thomas Colborn
G Gurstang
J Galland
Mary A Griffin
Samuel Hardy
James Harper
Nephi Hampton 4
L Hambley 3
Samuel Hambley
Edley F Hampton
Caleb Hartley
S Low
Amos Lower

Elizabeth Hardy
Thomas Morgan 2
N Morris
F Mainwaring
W V Morris
James Munroe 4
J Nelson 2
Isaac Richards
James Pace
G Robinson
J Redfurn
T Stolworthy 2
William Stewart
James C Sly*
J Timmins
Enoch Trenter
Enoch Richew
William Warner 2
L Woolman 2
J Walker
Ann Webb
James Wright

42 men, 13 women, 7 children, 38 wagons, 234 oxen, 1 horse and 1 mule.

APPOINTMENTS.

At a quarterly conference held in Tooele city, Dec. 8 and 9, the following resolutions were adopted:—

Resolved, that a quarterly conference be held in Grantsville, to commence on Saturday, Dec. 8.

Resolved, that a quarterly conference be held in the Tabernacle in Great Salt Lake City, to commence on Saturday, Dec. 22.

Resolved, that a quarterly conference be held in Union Fort, to commence on Saturday, Jan. 6, 1856.

Resolved, that a quarterly conference again be held in Tooele city, to commence on Saturday, Feb. 2.

Resolved, that Joseph Young, Zera Pulsipher, Henry Herriman, Horace S. Eldredge, Lorenzo D. Young, Thomas Grover, John Lyon, Levi Richards and George Woodward fill up the intervals of time between the quarterly conferences, by individual preaching in the various settlements in the Sixth Missionary District.

W. WOODRUFF.

Report of the 16th Quorum of Seventies.

PRESIDENTS:

George D. Grant, on mission to England.

Albert Merrell, G. S. L. City.

Benjamin T. Mitchell, do.

Burr Frost, on mission to Australia.

James G. Willis, on mission to England.

James Ferguson, " Ireland.

William M. Thompson, G. S. L. City.

MEMBERS:

George Rhoads, Mill Creek.

Harry S. Dalton, Robert McMichael, Daniel M. Bell, Sugar House Ward.

Charles Williams, William P. Smith, Nathan Smith, Joseph Griffiths, Union.

Charles Green, South Cottonwood.

John Barrow, William H. Carpenter, John McIntyre, William Kelly, John Jackson, Thomas Johnson, William Robinson, Thomas S. Williams, William J. Larkins, G. S. L. City.

William Box, George Grover, John Gibbs, Box Elder.

John W. Clark, Grantsville.

Benjamin Clegg, William Pope, Tooele City.

Arnold Potter, William A. Gwither, San Bernadino.

John Marriott, John Bright, Ogden.

William B. Simmons, Amos P. Stone, Bountiful.

Edwin Walker, Farmington.

Samuel Payne, Kay's Ward.

David Crockett, Payson.

Lorin Simmons, Springville.

Alfred D. Young, Cable C. Baldwin, Provo.

Jeremiah Bingham, Petetenete.

Edward Robinson, Lake City.

William Daily, Fort Johnson.

Madson D. Hambelton, Nephi City.

Thomas Mackey, John Mackey, West Jordan.

James McGaw, on mission to United States.

John Ostler, William Martindale, on mission to Texas.

Thomas E. Ricks,   „   Los Vegas.

Eleazur King, Manti.

Henry H. Overly, Pitsburgh, Carll county, Indiana.

Joseph Armstrong, Kanesville, Iowa.

Harry Call, Jordan P. Henderson, John Harden, Henry Fairbanks, John Cunningham, Henry Sprague, Henry H. Overly, James C. Williams, Chancey Pack, Leonard Hill, John B. Hill, Charles F. Hill, Dominicus Elmore, report yourselves and give your genealogies to the clerk by letter or otherwise, or your places will be filled up with active members.

N.B. The quorum meets in the house of President Benjamin T. Mitchell, in the 15th ward, the first and third Saturday in the month, at 6 o'clock p.m.

WILLIAM M. THOMPSON, Clerk.

CORRESPONDENCE.

G. S. L. CITY, December 15, 1855.

TO THE EDITOR OF THE NEWS

Sir:—Thinking, perhaps, that a short sketch of a tour I have just had, in company with Major Garland Hurt, Indian agent, to Utah, Juab, Millard and Sanpete counties, would not be altogether uninteresting to you, the following is at your disposal:—

The agent went for the purpose of visiting the different bands of Utahs in that section of the Territory, and to select suitable places to establish and locate Indian reservations, with a view to persuade the poor unfortunate Indians to forsake their nomadic for a civilized life.

We left this city, Tuesday, Nov. 27, numbering seven in company. We found no Indians, however, until we got to Springville; we had some conversation with them, gave them some clothes, and then they said they felt very well. Here our party was joined by Levi G. Metcalf, Indian interpreter.

We arrived at Nephi Saturday, December 1st. Here we found some more of nature's children; they all felt first-rate at our telling them that we wanted them to go to work and raise grain like the white man, that they and their families might not suffer when it became cold and their country destitute of wild game.

We tarried at Nephi over the Sabbath, owing to the agent's health, he having taken a cold after he had left the city, which caused an abscess to come upon his upper lip, which was very annoying and made him quite sick. The next day, being able to proceed on our journey, we went and examined the facilities for farming on Chicken creek; we found some very good land, but water rather scarce. Here we camped for the night.

The next morning we were en route for Fillmore city by the dawn of day, distance near 60 miles; having a mule team, we were under the necessity of improving our time to make the desired point, which, however, was obtained through the united energies of our drivers, and no small quantity of buckskin, about 9 o'clock in the evening.

Here we found all well, and preparing to receive the legislative members. We had a visit early next morning from Konosh, chief of the Pah-vantes. He was much pleased at seeing his father, (as he called the agent) and said he knew that he had good advice for himself and his people. We told him that we wanted him and his men to accompany us on the morrow to Corn creek, where the Indians have been trying to farm this season.

Accordingly, next day, we examined the prospects of making an Indian reservation. We found, as we thought, good land and a plenty of water for a large farm for the Indians. We then returned to Fillmore city; tarried next day, made many presents to the Indians, and were well pleased at the arrival of His Excellency the Governor and suit all well and in good spirits.

We then set out next day to visit a location in San Pete county. Here we found a very good place for a farm, and saw Arrapine and his band at Manti; had a conversation with him and found him feeling well disposed towards the whites, and ready to punish the offender of justice, on his part. We also made his band, and a band of the Sanpitches many presents, such as blankets, coats, pants, caps, shirts, &c.

On our return home, we were informed at Springville, that some of the Indians had been stealing horses some time since, and the whites were trying to take the offenders, which made Squashhead and some others of the band quite angry. We saw Squashhead, and he said that he did not want anything but that which was right. He being very deceitful, there was no use to place any dependence on what he said. I have not since learned what disposition they made of the prisoners.

We arrived in this city on the 14th inst., and found all well at home. You will please excuse haste, and believe me, yours, &c., with respect,

LYMAN S. WOOD, U. S. Indian Interpreter.

G. S. L. CITY, Dec. 18, 1855.

MR. EDITOR:—As several of the persons who escaped from the massacre at Elk mountains have asked me to present their claims for property lost in that unfortunate affair, I take occasion to suggest that they all make out their claims in due form, and forward them to me at my office, in G. S. L. City, as soon as practicable.

G. HURT, Indian Agent.

Deseret News
January 2, 1856

NEPHI, Dec. 24, 1855.

EDITOR OF THE NEWS:

Dear Sir:—As the mountains are again capped with snow and the mail routes almost impassable, I thought a word from Nephi might be interesting.

We enjoyed ourselves in our annual feast, which came off on the last of November and first of the present month, our house not being large enough to accommodate all at once.

We have had the pleasure of hearing from several of the missionaries sent to visit the saints, and rejoiced in their instructions, for the spirit of their calling truly attended their labors.

Through the blessings of our Heavenly Father enough has been raised to sustain us till next harvest. Our city is improving; several good houses have been built this season.

Br. Samuel L. Adams has a machine to make cut nails nearly finished. Our meetings are well attended, and a lively spirit prevails. Dancing is not neglected.—Yours in the covenant of peace, SAMUEL PITCHFORTH.

Deseret News
January 23, 1856

CORRESPONDENCE.

HOME MISSIONARY OPERATIONS.

NATIONAL TEMPERANCE HALL, Grand Terrace, Broadway, Fillmore, Jan. 12, 1856.

HON. ELIAS SMITH:

Dear Sir:—Lest I should be found an unfaithful steward, by neglecting to report minutes of our missionary proceedings, I will hereby present you a very short account of our meetings, while on the journey as well as in this city, and leave the legislative proceedings for the Hon. Albert Carrington to report.

On Monday, Dec. 31, I left Great Salt Lake City for Fillmore, in company with Hon. L. Snow, J. C. Wright and L. Farr. We proceeded to Lehi, and held a meeting with the people.

Governor Young, and Presidents Kimball and Grant had proceeded on to Pleasant Grove. Our honorable chaplain, P. P. Pratt, met with an accident just before we entered into the city of Lehi. His coach was drawn by four spirited mules; and while approaching the city, he took a seat in front beside the driver to view the scenery, or for some other cause, and in an unguarded moment he happened to touch one of the wheel mules with a whip, switch, or something, and he kicked up and hit him upon the leg, and came near breaking it: he was lame for many days. At the same moment, the mules struck into a speed, which if it had been upon some roads might have endangered the lives of the passengers; but being upon a smooth, level road, they passed through the gate into the city, where they were fully reigned up and stopped without any damage. The chaplain was not able to attend meeting.

The assembly was addressed during the evening by O. Pratt, E. T. Benson, W. Woodruff, and Erastus Snow. A variety of subjects were spoken upon, but mostly including the practical duties of life: all appeared edified.

Jan. 5, we rode to Nephi. We here met with the Presidency and most of the northern members of the Legislature. We held a meeting during the evening with the citizens of the place; they were addressed by E. Snow, O. Pratt, E. T. Benson, and W. Woodruff; and we had a good meeting.

On the 6th, we crossed the Sevier, and drove to the Round prairie, and camped for the night in company with the Governor and the majority of the members of the Legislature. We had evening prayers, and the encampment was entertained with several appropriate songs from Elders Erastus Snow and Jacob Gates.

On the 7th, we drove to Fillmore, and took up our residence in various parts of this city, during a legislative session of forty days.

On the 8th, we had an evening meeting in the School-house: the people were addressed by E. T. Benson and W. Woodruff.

On Sunday, the 9th, the citizens and many members of the Legislature attended meeting at the School-house, and were addressed by the chaplain, Elder P. P. Pratt. He gave an interesting rehearsal of his first travels through this country in the dead of winter, as far as Iron county, before there was any settlement south of Provo, and the difficulties which he and his company had to pass through. He then took up the coming forth of the Book of Mormon; pointed out those prophecies which had been fulfilled since it came forth, and referred to many which are yet to be fulfilled. He pointed out the various times when blood had been shed in this church, for maintaining the gospel of Christ, which was still unavenged. Many excellent remarks were made by the Speaker.

On the 10th, the people again assembled this evening at the School-house, and were addressed by James Brown, W. Woodruff, and Elder Ray. Among the subjects dwelt upon was the progress of the kingdom of God, the necessity of prayer, the wickedness of the world, and the approaching judgments of God.

On the 12th, attended meeting at the School-house in the evening. The people were addressed by Elder Orson Pratt for one hour upon the gifts and graces of the church, and the importance of our calling upon God in mighty prayer and faith, in order that we might rend the veil, and obtain those great blessings which the ancients enjoyed.

He was followed by Lorin Farr, who gave an exhortation to the people upon what brother Pratt had said, and urged the people to listen to the servants of God.

He was followed by W. Woodruff, who spoke of the great duties and responsibilities which rests upon us as saints and elders in Israel in the proclamation of the gospel to this generation, the building up of Zion, and in the relationship which we sustain to the house of Israel, and especially the Lamanites.

On the 14th, the people were addressed in the evening by Phineas Young, who spoke of his visiting the Lamanites in former days; said he had distributed the Book of Mormon to their chiefs, from the Cherokees to Florida. He gave Mr. Rop one, the present chief of the Cherokees. He was followed by Elders Lorenzo Snow and Samuel W. Richards, who spoke much to the edification of the people.

On Sunday, the 16th, the people assembled at the School-house, and were addressed in the forenoon by the chaplain of the Council, Elder P. P. Pratt, upon the practical duties of every day life.

President Brigham Young preached to the people in the afternoon upon the subject of building up Zion; took for his text, "Arise and shine, O Zion, for thy light is come, and the glory of the Lord is risen upon thee;" and was followed by President Heber C. Kimball; I reported both sermons.

U. S. Mail to Manti.

THE SUBSCRIBER begs leave to inform the citizens of Utah, that the United States Mail Coach for Manti will leave Great Salt Lake City, every Thursday, at 6 a.m., and arrive at Manti every Saturday at 6 p.m.; returning, will leave Manti every Monday at 6 a.m., and arrive at G. S. L. City every Wednesday at 6 p.m.

Passengers or parcels for Union, Draperville, Lehi, American Fork, Pleasant Grove, Provo, Springville, Palmyra, Payson, Nephi, Fort Ephraim, and Manti, will be carried on reasonable terms.   JOHN DAILY.

Apply to Col. Hosea Stout, Agent.
Great Salt Lake City, July 25, 1855.   20tf

Missionaries.

Names and Residences of those now appointed to go on missions, and their destination, as read from the stand in the Tabernacle in G. S. L. City, Sunday, Feb. 24, 1856.

TO GREEN RIVER.

From Springville—Myron Crandall, James Oakley.

From Palmyra—Alexander Robertson, Stephen Markham, William Berry.

From Provo—William M. Daniels, Aaron M. Daniels, George Porter, James A. Ivie, Lucius N. Scovil, Edson Whipple, John H. Van Wagoner, Clinton Williams, John Sessions, Alva Downey, George B. Teeples, Peter W. Conover.

From Tooele—Eli B. Kelsey, Eli Lee.

From Great Salt Lake City—Jerome B. Kempton, Addison Everett, William Snow, Curtis E. Bolton, James Baldwin, William Bird, Thomas Jenkins, Isaac Duffin, E. P. Duzette, Daniel Greenig, Jonathan Harrison, Edward T. Mumford, David Mustard, Henry Cooksley, Spencer Wiltbank, George Shell, William W. Sterrett, Joseph A. Thompson, William K. Parker, Robert Carter, William M. Thompson, Thomas Frazier, James Young, John A. Wakeham.

From Payson—Jeremiah Bingham.

From Nephi—William Meeks.

From Lake City—Arza Adams.

TO THE NORTH.

From Ogden—William S. Lish, William Shaw, Thomas Bingham, John Campbell 2nd, Clifton Browning, Buthrea C. Hadlock, Crandall Dunn, Bailey Lake.

From Centerville, Davis County—George Dolton, Henry A. Cleveland, Solomon Connolly, Henry R. Cleveland, Thomas Brandon, Woodruff Brandon, Henry Russell, David Russell.

From Farmington—Jacob Miller.

From Stoker's Ward—Charles Parks, Thomas Abbott.

From Great Salt Lake City—William J. Perkins, Thomas Carloss, Lott Huntington, Thomas Day, James Gammell, Alexander Hill, sen., Richard Margetts, Wallace McIntyre, Charles Thomas, James Walker, John Walker, Henry Walker, John Preese, James Watson, William Price, William Empy.

From Nephi—George Barber.

From Battle Creek—John Holman.

From Lehi—Sylvanus Collett, John R. Murdock.

From Western Jordan—Joseph Harker.

From Provo—Simon Kelting.

TO LOS VEGAS.

From Great Salt Lake County—Williams Camp, John S. Fullmer, Lewis Robins, Lorenzo Brown, Andrew Cahoon, Almon L. Fullmer, Thomas Hall, Hyrum Kimball, George Mayer, Samuel Thompson, Aaron Farr, Alexander A. Lemon, Justin Merrill, Samuel Turnbow, Ute Perkins, Daniel Shearer, Allen Stout, John Snider, William Moss, Francis Boggs, Jacob L. Workman, Elijah K. Fuller.

From Provo—Edson Barney, Philander Colton.

From Parowan—Miles Anderson, John Lowder.

From Beaver County—Beeson Lewis.

From Palmyra—William W. Riley, John H. Redd.

TO EUROPE.

From Fillmore—Peter Robinson, Thomas R. King, John A. Ray, Edwin Holden.

From Davis County—Jesse Hobson

From Utah—Lorenzo Hatch, Isaac Higbee, William Pace, William Miller.

From Great Salt Lake City—Orson Pratt, Ezra T. Benson, Orson Pratt, jun., Phineas H. Young, Miles Romney, James Beck, James Ure, Truman O. Angel.

From Lehi—James Taylor.

TO AUSTRALIA.

From Provo—Andrew Jackson Stewart (the surveyor), Thaddeus Fleming, Joseph A. Kelting.

From Great Salt Lake City—Louis R. Chaffin, Zerubbabel Snow, James Phelps.

From Battle Creek—George Clark.

TO THE EAST INDIES.

From Great Salt Lake City—Thomas S. Johnson.

From Provo—William M. Wall, Alexander P. Chesley, George Parish.

From Springville—Martin Crandall, Joseph Kelly, William Bird, John Whitbeck.

The brethren who cannot go without leaving their families upon the hands of the Bishops, had better stay and provide for their families before they leave. By order of the First Presidency.

Deseret News
March 5, 1856

The CALIFORNIA MAIL arrived late on the 1st. inst., and was not very burdensome in transportation, as it contained but few letters, one or two dozen exchange papers, no Harper's, no Graham's, 10 Godey's and a few papers in the Sullivan package.

Had it not been for several bundles of 'The Mormon,' from 40 to 43 inclusive, the mail would have been light indeed.

The carriers encountered a violent snow storm on Pine creek; it lasted 38 hours, covered Baker's Pass to the depth of 2 feet, and compelled the feeding flour to sustain the animals. Deep mud in Pauvan valley, and another storm, which set in at the Sevier and lasted until they reached Nephi, caused further detention, and the storms were very cold and severe upon both the men and animals, but br. Conger successfully struggled through all difficulties, as he always has.

It is shameful that a mail which is so regularly and promptly carried, and almost without exception makes such good time, should be of so little actual benefit. There is miserable mismanagement somewhere; who is to blame?

Deseret News
April 2, 1856

DIED:

In Ogden city, March 11, DUNBAR WILSON, aged 50 years.

He was born in Chittenden county, Vermont, was baptized in Ohio, Richland county, May 23, 1836; endured with his brethren the persecutions of Missouri in 1837, 8, 9; was ordained a High Priest in Nauvoo; arrived in Great Salt Lake City in 1853; settled in Ogden City. His last hours were calm and peaceful, and he died as he lived, full of faith in the work of the latter day, and of a glorious resurection.

At Springville, on the 28th of Feb., of croup, ELEANOR RYALLS, daughter of Walter S. and Martha Savage, aged 1 year and 6 months.

In this city on March 28th 1856, HENRY STEPHEN son of George and Sarah Ann Hales, aged 1 year, 2 months and 25 days.

In Nephi, Juab co., on the 19th inst, SEREPTA M., daughter of J. L. & M. S. Heywood, aged 2 years and 7 months.

In this city on the 21st inst, MARY ALICE, daughter of James and Mary Standing, aged 3 years, 4 months and 15 days.

DIED:

At Nephi City, on the 27th of last month, of canker, JOHN SAMUEL, the infant son of John and Sarah Kienke, aged 1 year and 17 days.

In Weber county, on the 9th of April, AMELIA, wife of Thomas Chapman, aged 39 years. Millenial Star please copy.

Small Pox.

Members of the Assembly report that, while on their way to Fillmore, on their arrival at Nephi they were requested to be a little cautious as to where they put up for the night, as the small pox was in that place. It is just such unwise conduct and back-end-forward notifications that keep this loathsome disease in fuel and opportunity. Why not all, and especially all Bishops and Probate Judges, recollect and give heed to the counsels of the First Presidency on this subject, as printed in not-far-back numbers of the News?

Those counsels are just as applicable in localities where the small pox has found entrance, as they were at first; to persons having it, or exposed to it, as they were to Matthews' company; and will continue to be so, until that disease is entirely banished. But how long, think you, will it take to accomplish that object, if the infected and exposed are allowed to remain or go at random, and the traveling public and neighbors merely notified to watch out where they stop or pass, after unwarnedly driving into danger?

Such a course stifles out the disease, with the same effect that accompanied a stupid act in a northern settlement. A person had been exposed and was very wisely put in quarantine, but after tarrying a few days was released upon his plea of no 'danger from him,' and forthwith he broke out with the small pox in the midst of a thickly settled neighborhood. It thus escaped from one to many, and we have not learned whether it has yet been expelled from that region.'

Deseret News
June 3, 1857

Deseret News
July 1, 1857

Trip to Iron County.

GREAT SALT LAKE CITY,
June 19, 1857.

TO THE EDITOR OF THE DESERET NEWS:

Dear Sir: For the last two months I have been on a visit to the extreme southern settlements; and have thought it advisable to furnish a few items for insertion in the 'News.'

Having been kindly invited by President C. C. Pendleton to accompany him as far as Parowan, Iron county, I accepted the invitation, and arrived in that elevated region of country after ten days easy travel, in company with Elder Isaac Laney and lady.

A home missionary being a rare visitor there, you may judge my reception was of the most welcome and pleasing kind.

As President Dame was absent with the Governor (North) and the brethren had not been catechised, preparatory to the renewal of their covenants, it was thought advisable, by Bishop Tarleton Lewis, (who was one of the wounded at the

Hauns' Mill massacre) and the authorities that I should catechise and baptize them, which duty I attended to.

I visited, in company with brs. Pendleton and Dalton, jr., the noble pinery in the first left hand kanyon. which presents the appearance of splendid parks, reaching to the summits of the highest mountains; some of the pines are 5 feet across the butt; very lofty and free from knots.

In the mountain heights around Parowan there seems to be enough firewood within five hours reach of wagons and oxteams to supply the inhabitants of this Territory for years to come. On account of the elevated position of Parowan—1381 feet above this city—the air is much cooler; and the winds blow with much force and frequency.

I visited Fort Harmony and explored the mountains around Ash creek and the Rio Virgin on foot in company with brs. Peter Shirts, Ingram and an Indian. We discovered a large mound of crystalized gypsum in broad sheets and other forms.

From information received from one of the brethren who had been visiting at the new cotton farm, he stated that the company were well satisfied with the location; that the indigo seed which I brought from the Upper Provinces of India, sent by Governor Young in advance of the company, had been put in—was up and flourishing; that a dam had been made about a mile above the intended settlement and that good pasture and firewood had been found within 10 miles distance.

They have commenced building on the site of the new city, brother Wm. Wesley Willes and others having taken the lead. Bishop Smith has commenced a large Tithing Office and Store House and the Saints are all on the alert for moving to the new location, a short distance from the one now occupied. I also visited Johnson's Fort, and Shirt's creek, small settlements for farming and grazing.

The new settlement on Beaver creek, 210 miles south of this city, where there are already quite a number of families, presided over by Bishop Philo Farnsworth, bids fair to soon realize the predictions of Pres. H. C. Kimball respecting its capabilities and prosperity; though only a year old it presents most of the pleasing features of much older settlements. For water, land, timber and grazing privileges it stands second to none in the valleys. Br. Thompson and others are erecting a saw mill.

I also paid passing visits to Buttermilk Fort, Nephi City, Summit creek, Battle creek and Spanish Fork; where all the pleasing signs of improvement are visible.

At Spanish Fork, Bishop Butler and the brethren had united in building a timber bridge across the principal stream, which was accomplished in a week and at a cost of twelve hundred do'lars.

I visited the Sabbath and daily schools in the different settlements, which are conducted in a very orderly and creditable manner, considering the many disadvantages they have to contend with in respect to the supply of school requisites.

In conclusion it may be remarked that as a general thing a most excellent spirit prevails among the Saints in the different settlements, of which the Indians partake; and many of them are industriously assisting the brethren in farming operations and kanyon work. Ammon is farming extensively at Beaver; has built him a log cabin, keeps his sheep and chickens; calls his squaws 'women,' talks English as much as possible and strives to be one with the brethren.

A short time ago, he dreamed that he met the Great Spirit, with whom he walked on a very handsome, slippery pavement, that the Great Spirit shook hands with him, and told him if he would quit stealing, when he died, he should be in the same place with him, but if not he should never enjoy that privilege. At Harmony on the death of a squaw, the friends applied to Bishop Davis for a coffin and the privilege of burying her among the 'Mormons.'

From the observations I have made I am of opinion that there is a much better chance for the working man in the south than in and near the city; unless it be among those who are imperatively required to assist in the public works.— The only complaint I heard is, 'we are so far from head quarters;' but then say they, 'the re-reports of the discourses of the authorities which we read in the 'Deseret News,' in some measure make up the deficiency. I remain yours faithfully, in the Kingdom of God.   WM. WILLES.

Report of the 39th Quorum.

The 39th Quorum of Seventies are hereby notified that their next regular meeting will be held at Jackson's Hall, 14th ward, on Saturday, 11th July, 1857, at 7 o'clock p. m., and fortnightly from that date at the same place, until further notice. A punctual attendance of the members residing in the city is requested. Country members are required to report quarterly by letter, and all who have not handed in their genealogies to forward them immediately to the clerk.

A list of the Quorum is subjoined.

PRESIDENTS.

Daniel McIntosh, on mission to U. States.

Lorenzo Brown, G. S. L. City.

J. W. Young, on mission to England.

C. H. Bassett, G. S. L. City.

H. C. Jackson,　　do

J. Hatch, Nephi.

J. T. Caine, G. S. L. City.

MEMBERS.

R. H. Attwood, J. V. Adams, M. Anderson, B. F. Blake, N. L. Christenson, W. Dye, R. L. Kemeson, W. I. Kilpack, P. H. Lutz, J. Mather, M. Meeks, N. Olsen, R. Patterson, A. Taylor, C. F. Thomas, G. Wilding, W. Jones, W. Moors, G. S. L. City.

T. H. Latey, on mission to England.

J. R. Young, on mission to Sandwich Islands.

J. Read, A. Cooksley, Fort Supply.

R. B. Margetts, on mission to Salmon River.

Samuel Allen, R. Johnson, Manti.

J. Boswell, D. H. Bowen, R. Easton, J. White, N. Morris, Iron county.

J. G. Brown, J. Bishop, South Willow Creek.

A. N. Monteith, A. Medcalf, W. Knudsen, G. Reader, F. F. Hansom, Box Elder.

D. Cook, Davis county.

Edward Clift, Pleasant Grove.

T. Doxey, H. J. Hartley, J. Rowland, Ogden.

G. Clayton, J. Shipley, H. Layton, W. F. Littlewood, Lehi.

D. Grundy, Farmington.

C. Lapwood, Payson.

E. W. Pell, California.

T. Parkinson, Tooele.

E. Sleeman, North Willow Creek.

H. Tingey, Sessions' Settlement.

John Wilkie, Nephi.

R. Smith, G. J. Taylor, Kaysville.

W. Rylance, Jared Campbell, John Mower, Samuel Campbell, John Dunn, North Ogden.

John Robinson, David M. Perkins, East Weber.

R. H. ATTWOOD, Clerk.

Deseret News
August 5, 1857

NEPHI—4TH AND 24TH.

At Nephi we are rejoicing in the abundant blessings of our Heavenly Father. Our crops are the best this season that we have even seen. The sides of Mt. Nebo have yielded an abundant supply of water. Harvest has commenced. Much has been done on the county road in Salt Creek Kanyon. Adobies are being made and a cellar dug for a meeting house 60 feet by 40, and many good buildings are going up. A general time of health and peace prevails.

The celebration of the 4th was conducted with the usual mountain feelings of loyalty which characterizes the inhabitants of Utah. Military review, orations, songs and dancing were the order of the day. The Declaration of Independence was read by Elder Saml. Pitchforth. and fired up the spirit of '76. Both native and adopted citizens expressed themselves ready to stand in its defence.

Synopsis of the celebration of the 24th.

At day break a salute of musketry by Capt. J. G. Bigler's Company. Capt. Sperry's Band serenaded the city.

At sunrise the stars and stripes were unfurled.

At 9 a.m., the escort was formed by Lt. John Kienkee, Marshal of the day, marched through the principal streets, called at Prest. Bigler's residence and escorted the President and his Council to the newly erected Bowery.

Deseret News
March 17, 1858

Report of the Seventh Quorum of Seventies.

PRESIDENTS:

Randolph Alexander, G. S. L. County.

Luman A. Shirliff, Ogden City.

James L. Thompson, Spanish Fork City.

James W. Cummings, G. S. L. City.

Wm. M. Allred, Grantsville, Tooele Co.

Simpson D. Huffaker, South Cottonwood Ward.

James M. Barlow, G. S. L. City.

MEMBERS:

Thomas McTaggart, Wilson Lund, A. D. Boynton, Jas. Bird, Geo. W. Price, James Hale, Marcena Cannon, Nelson W. Whipple, Charles Colebrook, Isaac Hunter, James Pullen, Peter Beckston, O. F. Atwood, David McKenzie, Brigham Y. Lamb, Ralph Smith, Joseph Shaw, Thomas Mercer, George E. Bowrne, Thomas Copley, John G. Lynch, Great Salt Lake City.

H. P. Olsen, George Tiffany, John W. Browning, Owen Cole, John Martin, Wm. Burch, Chas. Woods, Thos. W. Jones, Geo. Hutchings, Wm. A. Allred, Silas H. Tracy, John Brimhall, John M. Foy, David H. Stephens, Nathaniel Leavitt, Ogden City.

William K. Rice, Joseph France, Farmington, Davis County.

Israel J. Clark, Haskil V. Shirtliff, Salmon River mission.

Jesse Hobson, mission to England.

Hugh Syme, John Harvey, James B. Porter, Stephen Nixon, Nathan W. Packer, Provo City.

William J. Jolly, Payson.

Thomas M. Alexander, G. S. L. County.

William Myers, Centerville, Davis County.

Isaac Bowman, American Fork, Utah County.

Charles A. Davis, Spanish Fork City.

George W. Bradley, Nephi City, Juab Co.

Peter O. Hanson, Hans C. Hanson, Manti City, Sanpete County.

Andrew L. Siler, Brigham City, Box Elder Co.

Joseph A. Allred, Kaysville, Davis Co.

JOHN G. LYNCH, Clerk.

G. S. L. City, March 10, 1858.

Deseret News
January 5, 1859

Died:

In Nephi city, Juab county, December 25, ORSON ALBERT, son of Charles and Elsa Price; aged 1 year, 10 months and 8 days.

Southern Utah.

From our own Correspondent.

PAROWAN, Feb. 16, 1859.

There is nothing of much interest going on in this part of the Territory. Winter still reigns, but the southern slopes of the mountains are becoming more bare, affording good range for our stock, but there is still considerable snow on the bottoms. Peteetneet's band of Utahs have gone over to the Sevier. The horses they were supposed to have taken have all been found; but they have several in their possession which are supposed to have been taken from Nephi city.

A new saw mill is being erected by Messrs. G. A. Smith, James Lewis and N. S. Hollingshead, which is expected to be in operation in about two months, and which will add materially in supplying the increasing demand for lumber.

The Parowan Dramatic Association is about closing its season, having performed a variety of plays in a manner that has given general satisfaction, considering the many disadvantages under which its members have labored.   Yours &c.,

SOUTHERNER.

FATAL ACCIDENT.—Samuel Henriod, of Nephi city, about seventeen years of age, had the misfortune some two weeks since, to have a harrow fall on him, the teeth of which were very sharp; one of the teeth entered his body near the heart, inflicting a mortal wound of which he died in a few days.

Terms for holding U. S. Courts.

UTAH TERRITORY, ss.:

At a meeting of the Justices of the Supreme Court of said Territory at Great Salt Lake City, in the county of Great Salt Lake, on Saturday, the eighteenth day of June, in the year of our Lord one thousand eight hundred and fifty nine, the said Justices order and appoint the holding of the terms of the District Courts of the said Territory, until otherwise appointed, to be held annually at the times and places following, viz.:

That the District Court of the first Judicial District shall be holden at Nephi, in Juab County, on the fourth Monday in August of each year.

That the District Court of the Second Judicial District shall be holden on the first Monday in September, at Genoa, in Carson County, in each year.

That the District Court of the Third Judicial District shall be holden at Great Salt Lake City, in Great Salt Lake County, on the fourth Monday in July, in each year. And each of said District Courts may sit until the first Monday in November, if the business thereof shall require it.

D. R. ECKELS,
Chief Jus. of Sup. Court,
CHAS. E. SINCLAIR,
Asso. Jus. Sup. Court,
JNO. CRADLEBAUGH,
Asso. Jus. Sup. Court.

THE FORGERY CASE. — McKenzie accused of forgery and taken to Camp Floyd on the 10th inst., has since undergone an examination before Chief Justice Eckles, at the head quarters of the 5th Infantry, two of his accomplices, Wallace and Brewer, turning States' evidence. Their testimony as reported was that McKenzie engraved the plate and struck off the blanks for the drafts in this city, and that they took them to Camp Floyd and filled them up there and Brewer passed one, upon which Wallace immediately informed the Quarter-Master and had Brewer arrested. McKenzie was required to give bail in the sum of $3,000 for his appearance at the District Court at Nephi on the 4th Monday in August next, and Wallace to give bond in the sum of $10,000 and Brewer $9,000 for their appearance there as witnesses in the case.

Wallace is highly lauded by some for the service he has rendered the Government and the merchants and traders in exposing the counterfeiting scheme of this trio, and they have intimated that he should be pecuniarily rewarded for so doing.

In our opinion the whole story has not been told yet, and that there were more than three interested in the concern, and further, that Government may not be under so much obligation to those who have availed themselves of the protection offered or sought by becoming witnesses, as some have supposed.

Matters in San Pete County.

G. S. L. City, July 8, 1859.

EDITOR DESERET NEWS—DEAR SIR:—

Having recently made a tour through the Southern settlements as far as Manti, in company with J. D. T. McAllister, I thought perhaps a brief account of our journey would not be uninteresting to the readers of the News

We left this city on the 17th of June ultimo, and arrived at Manti on the 24th about 12 o'clock m. We held meetings in every settlement (except Mountainville and Pondtown) between Salt Lake and San Pete counties on our outward trip. When we arrived in San Pete we proceeded direct to Manti, the most southern settlement in the county, and on our return, visited and held meetings in the several settlements in that county.

We found the Saints generally prospering and enjoying the Spirit of God, although there are some who profess to be Saints that are a disgrace to their profession and to humanity. Such, however, did not lack for *spirit* for they were thoroughly inspired by the spirit of alcohol.

There is in most of the settlements we visited a tolerable fair prospect for a good harvest of grain, although in some, the crickets and grasshoppers have materially injured the crop. Mountainville, Santa Quin and Nephi have suffered the most from those Intruders. The wheat in San Pete county (about six thousand acres) although late looks well, and promised a good crop.

Two new settlements have been formed in San Pete county this season. One about twenty five miles east of north from Manti on Pleasant creek, called I believe Mt. Pleasant. They have about one thousand acres of wheat growing. There is in that vicinity an abundance of wood, water, stone and timber, in fact every facility for an extensive settlement. The people were living in wagons and brush shanties, but had commenced a stone wall four feet thick at the bottom, which when completed is designed to be twelve feet high and two feet thick at the top, and to enclose six acres of ground, to be finished by the 24th inst. Within that enclosure they purpose building their houses, and when that is done I think their families will be secure from Indian depredations.

The other new settlement lies about ten miles south of west from Mt. Pleasant, near the Sanpitch river, on the direct route from Salt Creek to Manti, and is called Moroni. They have sown about three hundred acres of wheat. They have also laid off a city and are building on their city lots instead of forting in. The facilities there are abundant for a large settlement.

After visiting those settlements and transacting our business with the Bishops we started for home, where we arrived on the 2d inst.

I would say in conclusion that although the prospect bids fair for a good harvest, the people have need to preserve their grain and not dispose of it for a mere nominal sum, as some have heretofore done, and those who will obey this counsel will see the day when they will thank God for having done so. Famine and the sword will desolate the earth, and that event is nearer at hand than many are aware of. Oh! that the Saints would be wise.

In haste, I am your servant and friend,

J. W. CUMMINGS.

Deseret News
July 27, 1859

INFORMATION WANTED.—Thomas Ord, of Nephi, who had been laboring for Woolley, Davis & Co., in Little Cottonwood kanyon, came to the city a few weeks since in ill health and, by invitation, went to Mr. Gilbert Clements' to stay till his health should improve so that he could go to work again, or return home. He had not been at Mr. Clements' long before it became apparent that his mind was impaired, at times, to some extent. The best of care was taken of him, but his lunacy continued to increase till Monday the 18th inst., when it became necessary to watch him closely to prevent any unpleasant occurrence. Mr. Clements reported the fact to the proper authorities, and steps were immediately taken to have him properly taken care of, and to return him as soon as circumstances would permit to his family at Nephi. That evening during the temporary absence of the man who was taking care of him, he escaped from the room through a window, and all efforts to find him that night and since, were and have been unavailing.

From the report of a person from the south, the next day after his escape, it was thought that he had started for home, but if so, he did not reach Nephi, or had not the last that was heard from there. His wife is now in the city, and much distressed by the unhappy occurrence, and if any person, far or near, has seen him or knows where he can be found, they are requested to report immediately, either at our office or to Mr. Clements, in this city, or to some officer whose duty it is to see after persons in his situation.

Since writing the foregoing we have been informed that the suffering man was seen in East Temple street on Wednesday morning following his escape, and in the course of that day in the 1st Ward, by persons who knew him, but had not been informed of what had transpired. It is feared that he has gone into the mountains and perished there.

He is about 5 feet 2 inches high, large prominent forehead, blue eyes, light brown hair. Had on when he left a black hat, checked shirt and blue drilling pants.

Deseret News
August 3, 1859

RETURNED HOME.—Mr. Ord, whose escape in a state of mental aberration was noticed in our last issue, has been heard from, having returned to his family at Nephi. It seems that after leaving this city he made his way by some circuitous route to Camp Floyd, where,

like others who have been similarly afflicted, he claimed protection, imagining from the promptings of the evil spirit that afflicted him that he had done something for which he might be killed, if not protected. From Camp Floyd he went home by the west side of Utah Lake, thus eluding the search that was made for him. From report he is no better.

Deseret News
August 31, 1859

CHIEF JUSTICE ECKLES' COURT.— We publish in this number the proceedings of the court in the First District at Nephi, during the first four days of the session, and shall continue to keep our readers apprised of its doings from week to week during the continuance of the present term. We have no comments to make at present, further than that Judge Eckles manifests a desire to be more expeditious in the transaction of business than has been common of late in this Territory.

Deseret News
September 7, 1859

The Court at Nephi.

It will be seen by the minutes of the court in the First District, that the judge has discharged both the grand and traverse juries and metamorphosed himself into a "committing magistrate," for which transformation, the Federal judges in this Territory unquestionably have a patent. If they have not, they had better file a *caveat* in the Patent Office without delay to prevent others from availing themselves of the benefits that may accrue from their invention.

Report says that the judge intends to summon another grand jury, but we put but little reliance in rumor in these days. If another jury is to be arranged, it will in all probability be comprised of citizens of the Territory, the sutlers, gamblers and camp followers as in and and about Camp Floyd, from which were taken fifteen of the twenty four grand jurors and ten of the petit jurors, who tried McKenzie, discharged by the court, have not, it seems, the ready cash to pay for their board just now, and the citizens of that little town, do not seem disposed to trust that class of men to any great extent, under existing circumstances; thinking, perhaps, that if they should the pay would never be forthcoming; which would be a very natural conclusion.

If the men who composed those juries could have got one hand into the Treasury of the United States, and the other into that of this Territory, they no doubt would have been willing to have attended the court *ad infinitum*, without making "presentment" in relation to the state of *finances*.

The history of the judicial proceedings in Utah during the years 1858–9 will no doubt, be read with interest in days to come. So much wisdom and purity has been displayed, and the laws have been so strenuously enforced (?), especially in relation to *gambling* and other vices that disgrace humanity, the period in question will undoubtedly be spoken of as one of the most remarkable in the history of Utah and of jurisprudence.

Who would, if disposed, find any fault with the proceedings of the courts, and the general administration of justice in this Territory? Our friends of the *Mountaineer* do not fully concur in all the movements that have been and are being made, nor in all the doctrines that have been promulged. They may think differently hereafter; but we shall not quarrel with them if they do not.

thereof into fruitful fields, and they would not have done it if there had been any other place on the earth, where they could have dwelt in peace.

THE COURT AT NEPHI.—Judge Eckles adjourned his court on the 4th from Nephi to Camp Floyd, after having done an incredible amount of business, for this country, as there was one man tried and sent to the penitentiary and some half-dozen civil cases disposed of mostly by default, in the short space of two weeks. The judge must have a remarkable taste for camp life or he would not so soon have adjourned his court to the head-quarters of the army stationed in Utah, when there was so much to be done in bringing offenders to justice, as he alleges, in his district, for the ostensible purpose of issuing naturalization papers to some of the soldiers who may wish to become citizens of the United States, most of the 'rank and file' having been born on the other side of the Atlantic, as native-born citizens do not like to serve their country in that capacity under existing circumstances.— In the opinion of most men,it would have been better for the judge to have attended to the more important matters first, and not gone back to camp till he had made at least one effort to punish some of the host of murderers that are said to dwell in his district. Why not do something besides talking about crime when justice to the guilty as well as to the innocent demands it?

From Juab County.

NEPHI CITY, Sep. 23, 1859.

EDITOR OF DESERET NEWS—DEAR SIR:

Knowing that you feel interested in hearing from the various locations in the mountains, I venture to write, informing you how the Nephites are prospering. Generally speaking, we are rejoicing in the blessings of health and peace; although many children have been, and some are sick of bloody flux. A few deaths have occurred of late.

Our wheat crop was very light, compared with former seasons; but what has been raised is generally free from smut. Our corn crop is very good, exceeding that of previous years. Potatoes will I think yield middling well.

In regard to improvements, not much has been done during the past season. The most extensive are the machinery and buildings erected by Messrs. Adam, Grace & Baxter, nail manufacturers. Their rollers, shears and cutting machines are fitted up in good style. I understand that when they get their new machinery into operation, which will be shortly, they will be prepared to roll out hoop iron, nail rods, &c.; also to turn out nails of all kinds more abundantly than at the present.

Messrs Gardner & Andrews are putting their saw mill in good order.

Br. C. Price has just returned from the Sevier bridge. He has been repairing it and it is now in good condition.

Our day and Sunday schools have been and are still prospering under the able management of br. J. Midgely. On Saturday last, 17th inst., our annual Sunday school festival came off, and we had a first-rate time. The recitations did credit to both scholars and teachers. Some good instructions were given by Pres. J. G. Bigler.

Capt. Sperry's Band was in attendance, and assisted much to enliven the occasion.

Teachers, scholars and parents have manifested a lively interest in supporting this school, and I hope that the teachings given from Sabbath to Sabbath will not soon be forgotten by those who have and will attend the Nephi Sunday school.

The Indians in this vicinity are friendly disposed, and all things seem to move on about as usual. Yours, respectfully, S. P.

[For the Deseret News.

Southern Tour of Messrs. Lyman and Rich.

On the 8th of November, at 11 o'clock, we left on our visit to Southern Utah. Our conveyance was furnished by our generous friend, br. Lott Smith. As we left there were some indications of stormy weather; but we had no storm to trouble us.

On the evening of the 10th, we arrived at Nephi and, on the day following, crossed the mountians by the Bloody Pass into San Pete, passing through the young, but thriving settlement of Moroni. At night, we arrived at Ephraim and attended meeting.

On the following morning, after holding public meeting, we then traveled to Manti, where we remained until the afternoon of Sunday, the 14th, when we left in company with Major Snow and ten men, who traveled and camped with us at the warm springs, near the Sevier river and twenty miles from the bridge.

On Monday morning, we parted with our friends and reached Fillmore at night. Continuing our journey south as far as Fort Clara, we found the Saints generally pleased with our visit and disposed to listen with apparent interest to our instructions.

We organized Lower Beaver Ward and ordained br. Jas. H. Rollins, bishop and president.

The people of the South report their grain and cotton crops as better than formerly.— Their yield of molasses from the cane was also good, although inferior in quantity, from the imperfect quality of their mills, which were of wood.

The sale of molasses and also cotton for grain and other produce is more or less difficult, on account of the very great disparity between the respective amounts realized from the cultivation of the land; as, for instance, the man who raises wheat will realize from thirty to sixty dollars for the products of one acre of land, estimating his wheat at two dollars per bushel; when, from the same quantity of land, from one to two hundred gallons of molasses are produced; which, being held at $3 per gallon, giving the producer from $300 to $600 for the cultivation of his land—a very considerable amount for every acre so cultivated, above what can be realized by the producer of wheat.

The above is approximately correct. Such relative change in the price of cotton and molasses as would tend to give greater equality to the proceeds of a given quantity of land, could not fail to benefit the country and the people generally.

We had good weather and good roads until our return to Salt Creek settlement.

We were out thirty days, traveled some eight hundred miles and held twenty-nine meetings.

AMASA LYMAN,
CHAS. C. RICH.

We may have something to say on the subject of prices hereafter.

[For the Deseret News.

From Juab County.

NEPHI CITY, Dec. 8, 1859.

EDITOR OF THE NEWS—DEAR SIR:

With pleasure I sit down to communicate a few items from Juab.

Since my last, the health of our city has improved. Peace, as usual, prevails. The appearance of old Mount Nebo forcibly reminds us that winter has duly arrived, bringing very severe frosts. A person who has lately come from Camp Floyd informed me that he saw a man at Mr. C. W. Webb's (near Goshen), who had his limbs very severely frozen, having lost his way in going from Lehi to Camp Floyd and wandered two days and nights without food and, no doubt, would have perished if a person driving a team had not accidentally came across him. I was also very sorry to hear that brs. James & Joseph Allred had their feet and hands severely frozen in going from this place to Uinta Springs, being necessitated to camp out on the divide between this and San Pete valley, on Monday night last.

Wagons are daily passing on their way to California after goods. Quite a train passed to-day, belonging to Mr. C. Crisman.

Our meetings and schools are well attended. On Sunday morning last we were favored with a discourse from Elder Amasa Lyman. He reasoned on the necessity of our living so that at all times we might enjoy the Spirit of peace, creating a heaven at home. In the evening we were also much edified in hearing from Elders Rich and Lyman, when they advanced glorious principles, plainly marking out the line of our every day duty. They were severe on the horse and mule thieves who infest this southern part of the Territory.

The *Deseret News* arrives here on every Friday evening and is to us all a welcome visitor, being well stored with news and useful information. It seems to please every class, for all can find something therein to suit their fancy. The page "For Farmers and Gardeners" is highly interesting and will, I believe, be an effectual means of inspiring many to improvement in those respects; of which we in this part of the Territory, as well as elsewhere, have great need. Our desires are earnest for its success and the consummation of all the improvements it advocates.

Yours respectfully,

MONA.

From the Late Capital.

FILLMORE, January 4th, 1860.

EDITOR DESERET NEWS:—

Thinking perhaps that you would like to hear from this part of the Territory I take my pen to write you a few lines relative to what has been transpiring in this city since the commencement of the holidays and other matters that may be of interest to your readers.

The weather has been unusually cold since the commencement of December and there has been snow enough to make very good sleighing most of the time, which our citizens have improved so extensively that the snow is nearly used up. Since the commencement of the new year the weather has been more mild and pleasant.

Sleigh riding and other amusements have been the order of the day for the last two weeks, and dinner, pic-nic and dancing parties have been well attended and on such occasions the *pungoes*, as the natives call them, have had to move lively.

On Sunday morning, last — New Year's Day—a sleigh with four drove up and, on going to the door, I was very agreeably surprised to find that it contained Elders Orson Hyde and E. T. Benson, who were accompanied by two brethren from Nephi. After the usual New Year's salutations, they came in and warmed themselves and, as it was nearly meeting time, they soon repaired to the school house, which was well filled on the occasion, and taught the people the principles of life and salvation during the day and evening and also on Monday and Monday evening and on Tuesday till after 2 p.m., much to the edification and satisfaction of those who were in attendance. It was truly a rich treat to the Saints in Fillmore.

About 4 p.m. on Tuesday they started on their return home, leaving their blessings with the Saints and all that desire to do right.— Bishop Brunson and a few of our citizens accompanied them as far as Cedar Springs, where they remained over night and this morning at 7 o'clock they proceeded on their journey and the Fillmore brethren returned home.

We are all well.

Yours in the covenant of peace,

S. P. HOYT.

Fourth of July Celebrations.

The patriotic people of Ogden city celebrated the eighty-fourth anniversary of our national independence, very appropriately, according to the report with which we have been favored, much after the old fashioned custom, in which all heartily participated without that burdensome pomp and parade that often attend such occasions.

The appropriate salutes were fired by Maj. McGaw's Light Artillery, there was a small but respectable military parade under the direction of Col. Gamble, and a public assemblage of the citizens at which speeches were made by Gen. West, Maj. McGaw and others.

The day passed off without disorder or accident, with the "Star Spangled Banner" floating over the city as proudly as it ever waved since the Declaration of American Independence.

At American Fork, the day was celebrated by the burning of large quantities of gunpowder, not by discharging cannon, as they have none of that kind of arms in that place, the raising of the national flags, a procession, an oration, speeches, toasts, &c.

No very lengthy report of the proceedings has been furnished, the reporter merely announcing the fact that the day was observed by the people of that small town in the foregoing manner, in commemoration of the signing of the Declaration of Independence, and to manifest their appreciation of the principles of liberty therein set forth.

At Nephi, the county seat of Juab county, a very imposing scene was displayed on the return of the national anniversary, but the booming of cannon was not heard among the notes of joy that were uttered or sent forth on that occasion, the men of war in that city having failed thus far to provide themselves with such weapons of defense. In musketry, however, they are not deficient, and they were used on that day in lieu of arms of larger caliber. The people were awakened at early dawn by the discharge of fire-arms and by music by Capt. Hawkin's Brass Band. The Stars and Stripes were unfurled and floated in the breeze during the day. There was a grand procession in the forenoon, also a large assemblage at the Bowery, where after the reading of the Declaration of Independence, Judge Love, the orator of the day, delivered a short oration and the Hon. J. G. Bigler, Mayor of the city, made a patriotic speech.

A sumptuous dinner was provided, of which all the citizens, without distinction, partook in old fashioned style; after which, speeches were made; toasts and sentiments offered and songs were sung, the whole interspersed with the enlivening music of the Band.

The committee of arrangements consisted of Messrs. G. Kendall, H. Brown, M. Miller, W. Broadhead and E. Harley.

It may be considered unnecessary to add that not only at Nephi, but at Ogden and American Fork, after the usual ceremonies of the celebration were performed, the balance of the day and evening was devoted to various kinds of amusement, and that dancing in particular was indulged in quite extensively.

TWENTY-FOURTH AT MORONI.

At sunrise the Stars and Stripes were run up to the top of the liberty-pole and three volleys, followed by a "feu-de-joie" were fired by the riflemen; immediately after which the Nephi Brass band struck up "Hail Columbia," followed by the Moroni Martial band, with some soul stirring airs.

The Presidency of the Branch, Committee of Arrangements, some of the principal citizens of San Pete and Juab counties and the Brass and Martial bands in carriages, proceeded through the principal streets of the city — the bands sending forth their stirring strains to welcome the joyful day.

At nine the inhabitants, with numerous visitors from Manti, Fort Ephraim, Mount Pleasant, Fountain Green and Nephi, assembled under the spacious bowery, erected for the occasion in front of the meeting house, and were formed in procession by W. P. Jolly, Marshal of the day, in the following order:

1st—Advance guard of ten riflemen.
2nd—The Martial and Brass bands.
3rd—The choir of Moroni.
4th—The pioneers and Mormon Battalion.
5th—24 Fathers, with banner.
6th—24 Mothers, with banner.
7th—24 Young Men, with banner.
8th—24 Young Ladies, with banner.
9th—24 Little Boys, with banner.
10th—24 Little Girls, with banner.
11th—The citizens.
12th—Rear guard of twenty riflemen.

The procession then proceeded to the residence of Bishop G. W. Bradley, where he was received by an escort of riflemen and presented with a beautiful banner chastely designed, and executed by Mrs. Emily B. Spencer, accompanied with some appropriate remarks.— The escort now conducted the Bishop, accompanied by some distinguished citizens and the Committee of Arrangements, to the place assigned them in the procession, which then proceeded through some of the principal streets and returned to the bowery.

After all were seated, the services commenced by the Brass band playing "O'er the gloomy hills of darkness."

Prayer by the Chaplain, N. Higgins.

Music by the Martial band.

An oration was then delivered by Elder J. Hatch.

Soul-stirring addresses were also delivered by Bishop J. G. Bigler, of Nephi; Hon. Geo. Peacock, of Manti, and M. McCune of Moroni.

The choir then sung the following original song, composed for the occasion by Emily B. Spencer:

THE VALES OF DESERET.

Within the vales of Deseret
We've found a peaceful rest;
And here the love of liberty
Burns in each honest breast.

With toil the bees of Deseret,
Have beautified these vales;
For here the hum of industry
Hath rung o'er hills and dales.

And here from mobs and violence
We sought our liberty;
Among the red men's mountain homes
We sing that we are free.

Though clouds have hung o'er Deseret
And darkness shrouded all,
They have dispersed and fled away—
Sol's rays now on us fall.

And we in lovely Deseret,
Will sing that we are free,
And shout hosannah cheerily—
God gave us liberty.

The whole assembly then sat down to a sumptuous feast; after which dancing and other amusements were indulged in till supper time, interspersed with songs, toasts and sentiments.

Dancing was resumed after supper and kept up with great spirit until a late hour.

Not a jar occurred to interrupt the harmony and enjoyment of the day.

GEO. SPENCER, REPORTER.

From Juab County.

A correspondent at Nephi in narrating the progress of events in Juab county says, that the citizens there are generally enjoying the blessings of health and peace and that their crops are abundant.

The cold, dry, backward spring operated very unfavorably to the farming interests, and most of the fields sown or planted had to be watered before the seed came up, in consequence of which, the crops are late and the harvest season has not yet ended. The grasshoppers and crickets have done less damage there this season than formerly.

A small settlement has been formed at Clover creek, and another on Chicken creek, the former six or eight miles north, and the latter fifteen miles south of Nephi.

The money appropriated by the Legislature last winter for the improvement of the road in Salt Creek kanyon has been expended as provided, and the road made passable by that means and similar appropriations made by the County courts of Juab and San Pete.

Home manufacturing is a subject to which the Nephites have given much attention, and there are few families there who do not manufacture the greater part of the cloth from which their wearing apparel is made, and it is supposed that there are more sheep in that county than in any other in the Territory, according to the number of inhabitants.

The people of Nephi are evidently striving to keep up with the spirit of the times, and while engaged in producing the necessaries and comforts of life, extending settlements, building houses, repairing roads and improving their social condition in many ways, they have not been unmindful of mental improvement, and have provided good schools for the rising generation and are taking measures for the procurement of a library and the establishment of a reading room, that all who have a desire to increase their stock of knowledge by such means can have the privilege at a comparatively trifling expense.

President Young's Trip South.

We have been favored with the following brief account of the late excursion of President Young and others to Manti, by a scribe who was one of the party:

On Wednesday, October 24th ult., Presidents B. Young and D. H. Wells, accompanied by Elders Joseph Young, Jesse C. Li tle, Robert T. Burton, John T. Caine, Geo. D. Watt, A. M. Musser, Theodore McKean and Albert Dewey, left G. S. L. City and rode to Lehi, where a meeting was held in the evening, Prest. B. Young and Elder H. S. Eldredge preached.

On Thursday the company proceeded to Pleasant Grove, where two meetings were held; one at half-past 2 p.m., at which Presidents Wells and B. Young preached; and the other in the evening, which was opened with prayer by Prest. B. Young, after which the people were addressed by Elders J. T. Caine, A. M. Musser and Joseph Young; concluding remarks by Prest. B. Young.

On Friday, 26th, the company proceeded to Provo, and while there were joined by Elders Geo. A. Smith and R. L. Campbell.

Saturday, 27th.—The Saints at Provo met at 11 a.m. Elder Orson Hyde opened the meeting by prayer. Elders Dan. H. Wells and O. Hyde preached.

Afternoon, the congregation was addressed by Elders Joseph Young, George D. Watt and Prest. B. Young.

Evening, the Seventies had a meeting, and Prest. Joseph Young, Elders A. M. Musser, Dominicus Carter and James W. Cummings preached.

Sunday, 28th.—The meeting hall was crowded by 10 a.m. Several from Lehi, American Fork, Pleasant Grove and Springville, were present. Prest. Brigham Young preached.

Afternoon, Prest. D. H. Wells and Elders Robert L. Campbell, John T. Caine, A. M. Musser, Joseph Young, Geo. A. Smith and Prest. B. Young addressed the meeting.

Early the in evening the wind commenced blowing from the north. The brethren from the settlements north of Provo, in Utah county, as they were returning home were met by the storm on the Provo bench, where they were brought to a halt, their animals refusing to proceed, but after a protracted, and, at times, doubtful contest, the parties reached Pleasant Grove.

On Monday morning the mountains east of Provo appeared to have received a "light impression." About noon, the President and party started south, encountering a slight snow storm. Bishop Henson Walker and Louis Robison joined the company, which arrived at Payson about 5 p.m., where Presidents Joseph Young, D. H. Wells and Elder Geo. A. Smith preached. Here Prest. Heber C. Kimball joined the company, having rode from G. S. L. City in two days, and encountered a severe storm, while in feeble health, which was the cause of his not starting with the company; he was accompanied from American Fork by Bishop L. E. Harrington.

Tuesday, 30th.—Morning clear and cold, ice half an inch thick on the water courses. Brigham Young, jun. arrived at 8 a.m., having left G. S. L. City on Monday at 5 p.m.

The party, joined by David Fairbanks, left Payson about 10.30 a.m., and arrived at Nephi about 4 p.m., after a pleasant ride. In the evening Presidents Young, Kimball, Wells, and Elders Geo. A. Smith, G. D. Watt and Robert L. Campbell addressed as many of the Saints as could get within the walls of their small meeting-house.

Wednesday, 31st.— The Presidency and party left Nephi about 11 a.m., and arrived at Moroni at 4 p.m. Weather mild.

Evening, Presidents Young, Kimball, Wells and Elder Geo. A. Smith preached to a large assembly of Saints.

Thursday, Nov. 1st.—Hard frost during the night. The company proceeded to Manti; held meeting in the evening, when Elders Joseph Young and Geo. A. Smith preached, and Elder Orson Hyde related a dream.

Friday, 2d.— Pleasant day, cool. Presidency and company visited their old acquaintances, and tried to find what improvements had been made there.

In the evening, Elder A. M. Musser delivered a lecture on the manners and customs of the Orientals inhabiting Hindostan, and was followed by Prest. Brigham Young, who made some appropriate remarks. Prest. Kimball, through indisposition, did not attend the meeting.

Saturday, 3d.—At 10 a.m. the Manti meeting-house was crowded, and many were unable to gain admittance. Presidents Joseph and Brigham Young preached.

In the afternoon, Prest. Wells, Elders Robt. L. Campbell, Geo. A. Smith and Prest. Brigham Young preached. Prest. Kimball's health did not admit of his being present.

The Seventies met in the evening, having extended a general invitation to the Saints to attend. Elders Joseph Young, Lewis Robison, John T. Caine, Wm. Bench, D. H. Wells and Orson Hyde preached.

Sunday, 4th.—Prest. Kimball's health improved. The Presidency and party, accompanied by many from Manti, returned to Fort Ephraim, where a large stone meeting-house, 60 feet by 44 had been inclosed, and the floor laid.

This was the only meeting-house south of Provo, which comfortably convened those who were eager to hear and see the Presidency and party on the journey.

At 10 a.m. meeting was called to order by President Brigham Young who opened by prayer, dedicating and setting apart their spacious hall to the use of the Saints. Presidents B. Young and H. C. Kimball preached, much to the edification of all present.

Afternoon, the congregation was addressed by Elders D. H. Wells, Geo. A. Smith, Joseph Young and Prest. B. Young. The remarks of Prest. B. Young on this occasion were exceedingly interesting and instructive.

In the evening the Seventies held a meeting at which others were present, Prest. Joseph Young having extended a general invitation. He preached, and gave directions about the Quorum reports, etc. Elders Orson Hyde, Robert T. Burton, Geo. A. Smith and Prest. Wells addressed the meeting.

Monday, 5th.—The Presidency and company left Fort Ephraim at 8 a.m., halted an hour near Fountain Green, and arrived at Nephi at 5 p.m.

On Tuesday returned to Provo; and on Wednesday, about sunset, arrived at G. S. L. City, having been absent fifteen days.

The tour, as a whole, was very pleasant and agreeable. The Saints were highly pleased to see and hear the Presidency; to whom it was no doubt gratifying to realize, as Prest. Wells remarked, that "the spirit and blessing of God predominated throughout all the settlements in these valleys."

That this visit of the Presidency and party may prove a lasting blessing to those favored with their administrations, is the desire and humble prayer of your correspondent, in the name of Jesus Christ. Amen.

Deseret News
February 6, 1861

Supreme Court.

After a session of four weeks the Supreme court adjourned yesterday, until the 4th Monday in April.

On Monday, the case of Thorp vs. the People of Utah was reversed, and the plaintiff held to bail in the sum of $3,000, to answer at the next term of the District court, to be held in this District on the 2d Monday in March.

The case of David McKenzie, who was sentenced to the Penitentiary in Judge Eckles' court, held at Nephi, August, 1859, was argued and judgment reversed, and an order issued to the Warden of the Penitentiary for his immediate release.

The court appointed the times of holding the District courts, for United States business, as follows:

First District in Provo, on the 4th Monday of March; 2d District, in Carson city, on the 2d Monday of August; 3d District, on the 2d Monday of April, in this city, and annually thereafter. The term in this District to be three weeks, and in the first and second Districts, two weeks.

The following persons were appointed United States Commissioners:

1st District—Isaac Bullock, Charles W. Wandell, Frederick C. Robinson, Charles B. Stebbins, John A. Ray, T. B. Foote and Wm. Crosby.

2d District—John C. James.

3d District—Wm. Bell, Hosea Stout, David O. Calder, Wm. A. Carter, S. W. Richards, Aaron F. Farr, Jonathan C. Wright, Ezra T. Benson and Evan M. Greene.

Several important decisions have been made by the Court during the session on which we have not now time to comment but intend to refer to them hereafter.

Deseret News
March 13, 1861

Tour Through the Southern Counties.

Elders George A. Smith, and Joseph A. Young returned on Thursday evening last from a tour through the southern counties, having been absent about forty-six days, during which time they travelled eight hundred and forty miles. They left this city immediately after the adjournment of the Legislature, and had an exceedingly cold, uncomfortable, stormy time on their outward bound trip, till they reached the Rim of the Basin. Their progress was much impeded by the snow, which was very deep most of the way, and the roads unbroken, there not having been much traveling in that direction during the winter.

After passing through Utah and Juab counties, they visited nearly or quite every city, village, town and settlement south of Nephi, preaching to and teaching the people wherever they went, adjusting difficulties occasionally, and setting things in order in places where they found them disarranged, so far as was possible, and time would permit.

They report that many of the former citizens of Fillmore have moved to the new settlement on the Sevier, thirty miles west of that place, where a town has been surveyed, called Deseret City, which bids fair to be a place of some consideration, as the facilities for farming there are good, the soil being of excellent quality for this country, and water abundant. There are many others who are preparing to go there from Fillmore this spring.

The settlement at Minersville is represented as being in a prosperous condition. The citizens there have recently built a commodious school house, and those engaged in mining have erected a new smelting furnace; but it seems that they are not getting out much lead, either because they lack the means to carry on the business successfully, or from some other cause not reported. The lead is said to be very easy of access, and the ore exceedingly rich; and if those now engaged in the business do not or cannot make it profitable, others should take hold and smelt out a sufficiency of lead, to supply the market, at prices that will exclude importation, and so low that some enterprising person or company may be induced to commence the manufacture of paints, for which there is, and will be a great and increasing demand.

At Cedar City, a large Social Hall is being built and the work far advanced. Other improvements there are in progress or in contemplation.

The settlements in Washington county are progressing as fast as circumstances will permit. Substantial improvements are being made, and not only the production of cotton is engaging the attention of the people, but they are entering extensively into the grape growing and fruit raising operations. At Santa Clara nine acres of suitable land had been prepared for a vineyard, and the cuttings were in readiness for setting out as soon as the time for planting should arrive. Several others were preparing to plant smaller vineyards, and many grape cuttings were planted last season; some of them producing grapes. In these matters Mr. W. E. Dodge has taken the lead, and to his exertions and examples, the citizens of Southern Utah are much indebted for the spirit of improvement infused into their minds, from which, if they continue to progress as they have for the last two years, they will ere long reap a rich reward. Mr. Dodge has a large nursery of fruit trees of many varieties, and if there are any in that region who have not, as yet, commenced planting out trees for fruit, ornament and shade, they should lose no time in doing so. The satisfaction of having made the effort to raise fruit of such kinds as will grow there, will amply repay them for the time and money thus expended, even if their efforts are not crowned with complete success; but of that there seems to be no doubt.

Mr. J. D. Lee is erecting a fine flouring mill at Washington, the county seat, the walls of which are of stone. A new town called Tonoquint has been commenced about two miles from Heberville. Several new settlements have been made in that county recently, but such is the nature of the country that no very large towns may be expected to spring into existence there at present, the cultivable lands being somewhat limited in extent and confined principally, if not entirely to the margin of the streams, the intervals of which are generally very narrow, but the soil is exceedingly rich.

A new road has been made between Washington and Santa Clara, which can be traveled at all times, a convenience not attending the old road in times of high water. Suitable and commodious school houses have been built in all the principal settlements, some of which, as well as many of the dwelling houses, in the absence of glass, have mica, commonly known as isinglass windows, of which mineral there is an abundance in that region of country.

The people in every settlement in that county, with the exception of Toquerville, Pocketville and Grafton have been more or less afflicted with fever and ague during the past year, and at the time Elders Smith and Young were there, nearly one-third of the people were shaking occasionally, but no person had died from the effects of that chilling feverous disease.

A LITTLE TOO LATE.—Hon. Wm. H. Hooper, in a letter to President Young, announces that among the last official acts of Mr. Buchanan, he extended his pardoning power to David McKenzie who was illegally convicted and sentenced to the Penitentiary during the sitting of Judge Eckles' court at Nephi, in August 1859. What motive actuated him in granting a pardon at that late hour after having delayed so long, with a full knowledge of the facts before him, which were set forth in the petition asking for his release from illegal confinement, which petition was forwarded to him nearly one year ago, we are not advised. At all events he was so slow to hear, that his pardoning act was of no avail: the Supreme court having set Mr. McKenzie at liberty long ago, on hearing the case upon a writ of error. The proceedings in the matter were declared illegal and void.

Good News from the South Country.

On Saturday evening last, Elder John B. Maiben returned from a business tour through the southern part of the Territory, on which he started from this city on the 1st instant. He reports having met President Young and party at Cove creek, some thirty-eight miles below Fillmore, on the evening of Monday the 20th, where they camped that night, and would arrive at Beaver the next day. On Wednesday, the 22d, it was intended to visit Minersville, eighteen miles west of Beaver, and probably the party would not reach Parowan till Friday evening. They were all well and in fine spirits, and had traveled from Fillmore to Cove creek on the day they were met by Elder Maiben.

At Fillmore, which place they did not reach till Sunday the 19th, a meeting was held in the afternoon. A large congregation assembled, which was addressed by Presidents Young and Wells, Elder John Taylor and Bishop Hunter. President Joseph Young, who accompanied the party as far as Fillmore, held meetings there on Monday and Tuesday evenings.

Elder Maiben brings a good report of matters and things in the Southern settlements, and especially of the crops in Washington county, which he says looked remarkably well. The wheat was in the boot and barley was further advanced. He saw corn three feet high that had not been planted a month. The prospect for fruit below the Rim of the Basin is excellent. The grape vines are luxuriant, and apple, peach and other fruit trees remarkably thrifty and some very young trees heavily laden with fruit.

The express which left this city for the President's party late on Wednesday night, was met ten miles beyond Nephi, and would arrive at Beaver before the departure of the company from that place, for Parowan on Friday morning.

PRESIDENT YOUNG'S VISIT SOUTH.

From notes furnished us by Elder Woodruff we have selected the following items in relation to the late trip of President Young and party to and through the southern counties.

On Wednesday, May 15, President Young and company—consisting of Prest. D. H. Wells, Elders Wilford Woodruff, John Taylor, George A. Smith and Joseph Young; Bishop Hunter, Mayor A. O. Smoot, Gen. G. D. Grant, Professor Carrington, Surveyor-General Fox, Commissioner McKean, Sheriff Burton, and several other citizens of distinction left Great Salt Lake City, at 8.30 a.m., and drove to American Fork, where they arrived at 2 p.m. As notice had been circulated that the meeting-house at that place would be dedicated by President Young, many of the Saints from Alpine, Lehi, Battle Creek and Provo had assembled to the number of four times as many as could be convened inside of the building, which is about 35 feet by 50, and a substantial, well-finished house.

After Bishop Harrington had opened the doors and as many people as the building could hold had crowded in, with little apparent diminution of the concourse outside, President Young went out of doors and, standing in a wagon, preached to the large assembly, followed by Presidents D. H. Wells and Joseph Young.

At the close of the meeting, the President requested the Elders, Bishops and presiding officers present to convene inside, and in a few moments, the house was again filled to its utmost capacity. President Young then made a few remarks and offered a dedicatory prayer.

The company left American Fork on the morning of the 16th, and passing through Provo, reached Springville at 12.30 p.m , at which place President Young preached at considerable length.

In the afternoon the company proceeded to Payson, where the people convened in the evening, at about eight o'clock, and were addressed by Prest. Young and Elder John Taylor.

On Friday, 17th, the company proceeded to Nephi, and held a meeting at five p.m., which was addressed by Prests. D. H. Wells and Joseph and Brigham Young, and Elder Woodruff. George W. Bryan was ordained a Bishop.

The company, having been considerably increased in numbers in passing through Utah and Juab counties, when it left Nephi, consisted of 64 souls, including 48 men, 14 women, and two children, with 23 carriages, 21 horses and 42 mules.

The company drove to Round Valley, Millard county, on the 18th, and held a meeting there in the evening. Elder John Taylor preached. That is a new settlement, consisting of only nine families.

Leaving Round Valley, Sunday morning, the company proceeded to Fillmore, and in the afternoon held a meeting, at which Prests. B. Young and D. H. Wells preached, and were followed by Elder John Taylor and Bishops A. O. Smoot, E. D. Woolley and Edward Hunter. A portion of Prest. Young's address was on the resurrection of the dead.

At Fillmore on the morning of the 20th, President Joseph Young left to return home, the rest of the company proceeding to Cove creek, a distance of thirty-five miles, which they made by 3.20 p.m., and encamped. There is at that ranch a corral, two houses, one dug-out, and three families, including five men, who had sown nine acres of grain. An extensive range surrounds the ranch, and there is an abundance of sulphur in the vicinity.

The next morning the company proceeded to Pine creek, where Samuel White and several others were commencing a settlement, and from thence continued on to Beaver, where a meeting was held at 4 p.m. President B. Young preached, followed by Elder Grant, President Wells, and Elders G. D. Watt and John Taylor, and Bishop E. D. ley.

On Wednesday, the 22d, the company proceeded to Parowan, arriving at 3 p.m. A meeting was held in the Tabernacle at 6 o'clock in the evening. President B. Young preached, followed by Elders John Taylor and W. Woodruff, and Bishop E. Hunter.

Leaving Parowan on Thursday morning, they proceeded to Cedar city, where they arrived at noon. The Saints assembled at 4 p.m. in the Social Hall, and were addressed by President Young, followed by President Wells and Elders W. Woodruff and John Taylor.

In the evening Bishop Woolley, and Elders W. Woodruff and George Goddard preached in the same place.

From Cedar city, on Friday, the company went to Pinto ranch, twenty-eight miles south-west of that place, where there were six families, including ten men, with eight houses. The country at Pinto is well adapted to grazing, and some good dairies are kept there; also about eight hundred sheep and goats are pastured there. At 6 p.m. an express arrived with letters, papers, etc., from this city, and the DESERET NEWS EXTRA of the 22d ult. The Saints met at br. Robinson's where President Young preached.

On Saturday, 25th, the company traveled through the Mountain Meadows, and passing over the rim of the Basin, camped a short distance below Gun-Lock fort, traveling about thirty-five miles.

Passing down the Santa Clara, and winding up through "Jacob's Twist," the company arrived at Santa Clara fort at noon of the 26th, distant from G. S. L. City three hundred and thirty miles. Two meetings were held at that place, at which President B. Young, Elder G. A. Smith, President Wells, Elder John Taylor and Bishop E. Hunter preached.

At Santa Clara there are several fine young peach orchards. It is estimated that one thousand bushels of peaches will be produced there this season. Jacob Hamblin has one hundred bearing trees. Mr. W. E. Dodge has a fine young orchard and vineyard, consisting of apples, peaches, apricots, nectarines, plums, pears, quinces, almonds, figs, English walnuts, gooseberries, currants, and Catawba, Isabella, and California grapes, all in a thrifty and promising condition.

The cotton crop looked very well, but was not as forward as usual, and crops in general were backward.

On Monday, the 27th, the company went to Tonaquint, situated at the junction of the Santa Clara with the Rio Virgen, about eight miles south-easterly from Santa Clara fort, and the most southern settlement in the Territory. A meeting was held at 10 a.m. Elders Woodruff, Taylor, Stewart, Bishop Hunter, and Presidents Wells and Young preached. The company then proceeded to Washington and held a meeting at 4 p.m., which was addressed by President Young and Bishops Smoot, Woolley, and Sharp.

Washington is the county seat of Washington county, and is situated near the Rio Virgen, some ten miles east of Santa Clara.

The company proceeded to Toquerville the next day, eighteen miles, where the Saints were addressed by President Young, Bishop McCullough, Dr. S. L. Sprague, and Elders George Goddard and G. A. Smith.

At this place, as at some others in that vicinity, the citizens use isinglass for windows, said to be a very good substitute for glass.

On Wednesday, 29th, passing over a very rough country, through narrow defiles, they went to Pocketville, or Virgen city, eight miles, and held a short meeting, where President Young addressed the Saints.

They then proceeded to Grafton, six miles, crossing the Virgen, which is there a beautiful stream, four times. A meeting was held there which was addressed by President Wells, Elders Woodruff and Taylor, and President Young. They returned to Toquerville from Grafton that evening.

The company arrived at Fort Harmony on their way homeward on the 30th, and held meeting at 5 p.m. Presidents Young and Wells addressed the Saints.

The next day, 31st, the company returns"

to Cedar city, where the whole party partook of a sumptuous public dinner, prepared by the citizens, and a meeting was held at 5 p.m., at which Elder John Taylor, and President Wells preached.

Another express from G. S. L. City, arrived late in the evening.

The next day, Saturday, June 1st, they came to Parowan and, on Sunday the 2d, the Saints there were addressed in the forenoon by Prest. Young and Elder Taylor, and, in the afternoon, by Prest. Wells, Elder Woodruff and Prest. Young.

On Monday the 3d, Prest. Young and most of the company took the road to Minersville, thirty-five miles distant from Parowan, in a north-westerly direction. The road was found to be very rough. They arrived at Minersville at 3 p.m., and held a meeting in the evening. Presidents Wells and Young addressed the congregation.

On Tuesday, the party visited the lead mines, some four miles from Minersville and then went to Beaver, where the balance of the company were met and all sat down to a sumptuous dinner prepared for them by the citizens. After dinner, they came to Indian creek, six miles from Beaver, and encamped there for the night. On the 5th, they dined at Corn creek, and camped at Meadow creek, eight miles beyond Fillmore, that evening.

Arriving at Fillmore next morning, they took breakfast there and then came to Round valley, where they halted for about an hour. A short distance this side of Round valley, the express, which left this city the evening before, was met. At the Sevier, as they passed, some twenty lodges of Yampa Ute Indians were encamped near the bridge, having a large number of horses. Chicken creek was the camping place of the party that night, having traveled fifty miles that day.

They came to Payson next day and dined, then to Spanish Fork, where Elder John Taylor preached. The distance from Spanish Fork to Chicken creek is fifty miles.

On Saturday, 8th, the company breakfasted at Springville, at 6 a.m., dined at American Fork at noon, and arrived at home at 6 p.m., traveling some sixty miles, most of the way in the rain, which was considered an agreeable change, as there had been no falling weather in the southern counties for a long time, and they had traveled the entire distance out and back, as far as Spanish Fork, through the dust, greatly agitated by the wind, which had blown almost constantly all the time they were traveling.

The President and party enjoyed excellent health during their absence from the city, with some few exceptions, and aside from the dust, had a very pleasant trip.

Deseret News
June 19, 1861

Death of Ammon.

The well known Utah Indian Ammon, half brother to the late celebrated chief, Walker, died in his camp at the mouth of Bingham's kanyon, on the 12th instant, as reported by Mr. Huntington, Indian interpreter. He had been sick a long time, of disease contracted by coming in contact with christian civilization, as practised by a Federal prosecuting Attorney at Nephi, while a District court was in session there some years since, but whether the disease was engendered at that time or since the army came to Utah, our informant saith not.

His death is said to have been extremely agonizing, and one of his horses was killed before the vital spark had fled, and four afterwards in accordance with the religious rites and ceremonies of the Indians on such occasions.

Deseret News
December 25, 1861

Married:

In this city, on Dec. 12, 1861, by Elder John Tooned Major WM. PITT and Miss MARY JANE COLLINS DYER, formerly of Swansea, South Wales.
. Mill. Star please copy.

In this city, Nov. 5, by Bishop A. Hoagland, Mr. SMITH B. THURSTON, of this city, and Miss MARY ISOM, late of Birmingham, England.

In this city, Nov. 8, by Bishop A. Hoagland, Mr. DANIEL A. HUSSEY, of Mill Creek, and Miss SARAH LOUISA BRIDGES, late of Birmingham, England.

In this city, Oct. 27, by Elder John M. Chicester, Mr. WM. PULSIPHER and Miss ESTER CHIBESTER.

In this city, Oct. 27, by Bishop D. Pettegrew, Mr. RICHARD J. MILLS and Miss CHARLOTTE GILES, both from Walsall, Staffordshire, England.

In Nephi city, Oct. 19, by Elder Peter Stubbs, Mr. GEORGE SHELL and Miss SARAH HOYLE.

Deseret News
January 15, 1862

Died:

In this city, Dec. 19, 1861, of ulcerated sore throat, SARAH IDA, daughter of Joseph L. and Sarepta M. Heywood, aged 10 years, 5 months and 3 days.

At Nephi city, Juab county, Dec. 29, 1861, of consumption, JAMES RANDALL, aged 64 years, 6 months and 6 days.

In this city, Jan. 3, 1862, ROYAL WILLIAM, son of Royal and Elizabeth Barney, aged 17 days.

At South Cottonwood, Jan. 8, 1862, JANE, wife of Matthew Rowan, aged 34 years, 11 months and 8 days.

Deseret News
February 12, 1862

Died:

At Nephi City, Juab county, January 14, of inflammation, CHARLOTTE, wife of John Andrews, aged 42 years, 5 months and 8 days.

Deseret News
March 19, 1862

ELECTION AT NEPHI.

Nephi, March 4th, 1862.

EDITOR OF THE NEWS:

Last Monday the Election day, (being the first election held under the Constitution of the State of Deseret,) was an interesting time in this city, and throug out this county. At an early hour, Capt. J. Hawkins' Brass Band serenaded the streets. About ten a.m., a large number of citizens had assembled themselves at the meeting house, and the general feeling was that they would spend a portion of the day together—the house was soon in order, and Charles H. Bryan was chosen chairman, and Samuel Pitchforth, secretary of the meeting. The "Star Spangled Banner," was played by the Band. To be brief Mr. Editor, we enjoyed ourselves much, hearing speeches, songs, toasts and some first rate music from Hawkins' Band—a strong Union sentiment prevailed. We were favored with short speeches from the following well known gentlemen: Hon. Hosea Stout, Timothy B. Foot, Esq., Dr. Matthew McCune and John Borrowman, Esq., (Prosecuting Attorney for this county) all spoke in favor of sustaining the Constitution of the United States, and the Constitution of the State of Deseret, and considered that this people had proved themselves worthy of a State Government.

With due respect, I remain,

SAMUEL PITCHFORTH.

Deseret News
April 9, 1862

Died:

In Nephi City, March 26, in child-bearing, SARAH, wife of Thomas J. Schofield, and daughter of William and Eliza Foster, of Nottingham, England, aged 21 years 6 months and 17 days.

Deseret News
May 14, 1862

Died:

In this city, on the 11th inst., of bronchitis and lung disease, JOSEPH WILLIAM, son of Samuel W. and Mary Ann P. Richards, aged 6 years, 3 months and 16 days.

At Nephi City, April 7th, of inflammation of the lungs, JOSHUA HOLDEN, aged 62 years and 3 months.

At Nephi City, April 21st, of convulsions, SARAH ELLEN, infant daughter of David and Sarah Frances Canier.

Deseret News
June 18, 1862

Mail Lettings.

From the temporary derangement of the mail service to the east of this city, we have been unable to publish at an earlier date the lettings of the mail routes in the Territory. The contractors need not, however, fail to enter upon the discharge of their duties to the public on the 1st of July—they will see at a glance that they have to jump right into the business.

The route 14601, from Brigham city, by Providence, Millville, Hyrum, Wellsville and Mendon to Logan, 55 miles and back, once a week, has been awarded to O. P. Rockwell, at $350 per annum.

The route 14603, from Cedar city, by Summit, Hamilton Fort, Harmony, Toquerville, Washington and Tonaquint, to Santa Clara, 70 miles and back once a week, to O. P. Rockwell, $800.

The route 14604, from Cedar Valley to Gardiner's Mills, 40 miles and back, to O. P. Rockwell, $300; route to be extended to Salt Lake city, pro rata.

The route 14606, from Fillmore city, by Beaver, Parowan and Summit, to Cedar city, 110 miles and back once a week, to John White, $1,475.

The route 14607, from Nephi city, by Ephraim, Fountain Green and Moroni, to Manti, 41 miles and back, once a week, to O. P. Rockwell, $350.

The route 14605, from Ephraim, by Limhi, and Mount Pleasant, to North Bend and back once a week, likewise the route 14613, from Salt Lake city, by Tooele, to Grantsville, 55 miles and back, once in two weeks, have not been awarded to bidders, as the Department is waiting for offices on those routes. If the citizens on those routes take any interest in postal communication with "the rest of mankind," they should immediately take the proper measures, if not already attended to, to notify the Post Office Department, through the Hon. J. M. Bernhisel, of the places where Post Offices could be well established for the general convenience, giving name of place and county, with the name of reliable persons for Post Masters, and there is no doubt of the offices being established and the contracts awarded to the lowest bidders.

We are pleased to notice that in the awarding of the contracts, the Department has not changed the semi-weekly mails from this city to Fillmore, and from here to Brigham city, as it was intended and advertised in the call for 'proposals.' The change from semi-monthly to weekly mails, from Fillmore city to Cedar city, and from the latter place to the Santa Clara will, no doubt, be very serviceable to the southern portion of the Territory. For these very important changes, and for retaining the semi-weekly mails north and south, the Territory is indebted to the good offices of Mr. Chas. Watrous, the special agent of the Post Office Department on the Pacific, who, in his passage through this city, last February, took particular pains to ascertain the proper *demands* of the citizens for postal communication with the extending settlements. Though Mr. Watrous was very desirous of carrying out the retrenchment order of the day, a ready perception of the necessary wants of the citizens prompted his favorable recommendation to the *Department* for the adoption of those routes for the present, and we have no doubt that a proper representation of what is required in other settlements would find as favorable attention.

Deseret News
July 9, 1862

SEVIER RIVER FERRY.—The traveling public, especially those desiring to go southward, beyond Nephi, may be glad to learn, that a ferry boat has been built at the crossing of the Sevier of sufficient capacity to carry any wagon, not a "land schooner," and by swimming their stock travelers can now pass in that direction without hindrance.

Deseret News
August 6, 1862

Died:

At Mill Creek, Aug. 3°, CLARISSA, daughter of Geo. and Mary Gates, aged 9 years, 6 months and 25 days. [Millennial Star, please copy.

At Nephi City, on the 20th of July, 1862, of Inflammation of the bowels, THOMAS CORBETT, aged 52 years and 3 months.

At Springville, Utah county, July 28th, in childbed, AMY ELIZABETH, wife of George W. Brown, and daughter of Levi W., and Clarissa Hancock, aged 26 years, 2 months and 14 days.

At North Ogden, MARY JANE, daughter of Morgan and Margaret Vaughn, aged 2 years, 8 months and 9 days.

JUAB COUNTY FAIR.

Nephi, Juab County, }
Sept. 29th, 1862. }

Editor Deseret News.

Dear Sir:—Knowing that you are interested in anything that is conducive to the happiness of the people of the State, we send you the report of the Fair held by the Nephi branch of the D. A. and M. Society in this place on the 27th inst. This being the first Fair of the kind held in Juab county, considerable anxiety was manifested for its success, and we can truly say, that it has exceeded our most sanguine expectations.

An opinion has prevailed in this county that fruit could not be raised here, but the exhibition of peaches, plums, apples and grapes, showed that such an opinion was utterly fallacious. The people of this county are beginning to wake up in relation to such matters, and it is hoped that the time is not far distant when Juab county will be able to successfully compete with her sister counties in the production of those comforts, which it is the privilege of the bees of the hive of "Deseret" to enjoy. Not desiring to be tedious we close by subscribing ourselves, Yours truly,

T. B. Foot, President.

Thomas Oad, Secretary.

List of successful competitors at the "Fair" held in Nephi, Juab county, September 29th, 1862.

Class A.—Stock.

Best one year old bull, T B Foot
do cow and calf, Chas H Bryan
do stallion, T B Foot
do mare and colt, T B Foot
do sow, John Brough

Class B.—Field Crops.

Best 5 acres wheat, John Vickers
do 2 " do
do 5 acres oats, Saml Scriggins
do 2 " Saml Claridge
do sugar cane, Thos Tranter
do " corn, Saml Scriggins

Class C.—Vegetables.

Best dozen tomatoes, J Midgley
do peck potatoes, John Brough
do squashes, John Esplin
do pumkins, Geo Kendall
do cantaloupes, David Udall
do carrots, Thos Barton
do quart beans, do
do onions, Miles Miller
do green kohl rabbi, C H Bryan
do colored peppers, Ed Ockey

Class D.—Fruits and Flowers.

Best plums, Ed Harley
do colored flowers, Mrs A Bigler

Class H.—Clothes, Dry-goods, etc.

Best 5 yds colored flannel, John Andrews
do 5 yds white linsey, do
do " colored " C H Bryan
do " jeans do
do woolen shawl, John Andrews
do madder root Saml Pitchforth
do wool filling, Ed Ockey
do " stocking yarn "

Class L.—Women's Work.

Best patchwork quilt, Mrs Taylor Jackson
do needlework, Mrs Chas H Bryan
do childs' hood, Miss Lovette Bigler

Class M.—Produce.

Best butter, C H Bryan
do molasses do

CORRESPONDENCE

G. S. L. City, Oct. 2, 1862.

Friend Elias:

I wish to give you a short sketch of my observations from Sanpete county to this place.

On Saturday, the 27th ult., I had the pleasure of attending the county fair of Juab county at Nephi, which went off with considerable spirit. The exhibition of field crops and cane was creditable, but the home department excelled anything that I expected to witness—jeans, linseys, shawls and yarn equal to anything that I have ever seen in Utah. The yarn spun from wool and cotton, native production, could not be excelled. There was a beautiful specimen presented to me, on which was written, "Spun by Rachel, a native." Madder, and yarn colored with the same, was on their tables, showing that the growing of madder in that county was a success. The ladies' department was well represented in home-spun, hosiery, quilts, needle-work, etc. The show of fruit and flowers was very gratifying, especially in a land that has long been supposed, would produce nothing but wheat. It is but just to say that the notice given of the fair was very short; but, for all that, it was decidedly a success, and much credit is due the directors for their undefatigable labors in getting up the fair.

From Nephi I proceeded down Salt Creek to Goshen, over which route a road might be made that wou'd save travel enough in one year to the southern settlements to defray the expenses of making the same.

The harvesting at Goshen was mostly done, and the stacks were beginning to appear, which I fear will soon hide the houses (gardens I saw none); but if the threshing machines continue to run at the rate that they have been working, the stacks will rapidly disappear, the wheat get into the bins, and the straw on the sheds.

Arriving at Fort Crittenden, I found an old pile of ruins, interspersed with a few good buildings; but, for all that, every place is inhabited, that is tenantable or can be rendered so. Everybody was on the look out for Col. Conner and his boys; and if he should not arrive this fall, all will be disappointed—some pleasantly, others vice versa.

I met with Col. Cummings assessing taxes for revenue purposes at this place. One or two breweries, some stores and whisky shops, were all he had to operate on—not a very pleasant job for him, certainly.

Leaving the Fort, I crossed Jordan on an excellent flat boat at the upper ferry, and arrived in this place on the 1st instant.

I remain, yours,

A Traveler.

PREPAYMENT OF LETTER POSTAGE.

We are informed by the Postmaster of this city that a large number of unpaid letters are usually dropped into the post office box every Sunday, from which it is inferred that many of the newly-arrived immigrants are unacquainted with the American postal law, which requires the prepayment of all letters sent to any portion of the United States, and also to certain foreign countries, and that also in the new style of stamps. All such letters are "held for postage," and unless prepaid by stamps, are sent to the Dead Letter office.

The following are now in the office in this city:

Chas. P. Dubois, Woodland, Cal.;
Hannah Slayner, Leavenworth City; 2
Geo. Cane, Santa Fe;
Amos Cram, Meredith Village, N. H.;
W. J. Thomas, Euclid, Ohio;
C. H. Raven, Vallejo, Cal.;
Mrs. Mary E. Birnes, Throopsville, N. Y.;
E. B. Bond, Peoria, Ills.;
Thomas Gaxton, Fort Desmoines, Iowa;
John Walker, Lone City, Cal;
Mrs. Mary D. Wilson, New Philadelphia, Ohio;
Miss M. L. Deighan, Mansfield, Ohio;
Mrs. Susan Gamet, Nephi;
Raamus Neilson, Box Elder;
Caroline McIntyre, St. George;
Peter Makkeyram, Cedar City;
M. Yates, Lehi;
Mr. A. Hunter, Florence, Nebraska Territory;
G. J. Taylor, Kaysville;
Thos. Boulder, Ogden;
Jewdith Anderson, Box Elder;
J. B. Thompson, Trail Creek, Colorado Territory.
Farley B. Granger, Alvarado, Cal.

Deseret News
February 11, 1863

SALT, SALT, SALT!

FOR SALE, in any quantities, at my Salt Works, in Sal Creek Kanyon, which I warrant to be the finest article manufactured in the Territory.

For Sale also at Nephi.

53-4   T. BOOTH, Proprietor.

Deseret News
April 29, 1863

LATEST FROM THE PRESIDENT'S PARTY.—By persons from the south, we have been informed that in consequence of the prevailing snow-storm on Thursday last, President Young and company remained at Nephi, and did not proceed on to Sanpete county till Friday morning. As we were locking up last evening, we received a communication from our correspondent dated at Manti, on Sunday morning, the 26th, from which we learn that the President and company went from Nephi to North Bend on Friday, passing through Fountain Green and Moroni, and from thence via. Mount Pleasant, Springtown and Ephraim to Manti on Saturday. On Sunday the party would return to Ephraim where two meetings would be held, after which they would return to Manti that evening. On Monday they would proceed to Gunison, and from thence to Fillmore on Tuesday.

Deseret News
May 6, 1863

INCIDENTS OF TRAVEL.—PROGRESS OF PRESIDENT YOUNG AND COMPANY.

Nephi, April 23, 1863.

EDITOR NEWS:—The snow storm mentioned in the postscript of my communication of yesterday, continued until about noon to-day, which keeps us here until to-morrow. At 12 o'clock, m., another meeting was held, and instruction given of much practical utility, by Prest. Brigham Young, Elders G. D. Watt and J. W. Young, on the subjects of agriculture, horticulture, manufacture, home industry, domestic economy, education, etc., which was listened to with deep attention.

During the afternoon a few hours were spent in passing round through the town, to witness the improvements which have been recently made. We first visited the meeting-house which is in progress of erection. Its dimensions are 44 by 64 feet. Its height from the ground to the top of the steeple is to be 80 feet. It is well roofed, but the tower has not yet been erected. A wall which serves as a support for the weight of the tower, takes off 11 feet of the main room, which forms an outer court. The floor is laid; the stand which is in the east end is finished substantially with good design, and the singers' desks are being constructed in the west end of the room. A considerable amount of lumber has been prepared and put together for the seats, and all the work on the window castings is well executed. The whole super-structure rests upon a stone foundation, rising some four feet above the ground. The cornice is not completed; but the design is to carry out President Young's counsel and complete the entire building this season. One year ago last fall the rock foundation was laid, and one year ago this spring they commenced moulding the adobes and laying the walls.

We next examined the saw-mill, which carries an upright saw, but that is about to be removed, when a circular saw will supply its place. Adjacent to this mill is a tannery, where a good business is done in the tanning line.

Next we examined the foundation which has been laid for a grist-mill, which is intended to be completed this season, by James Hague.

We then went to the nail factory, owned by Adams & Jones, with which we were well pleased. Mr. Adams stated, that they could roll out and cut from eight hundred to one thousand pounds of nails per day. Success to their business. Attached to their establishment is also a good shingle machine, nearly completed. We then examined a set of rollers for grinding cane, which would certainly not be discreditable to mechanics of any country, in their execution. They were forged by Adams & Jones, and fitted up by Charles Kemp, at a cost of about $250. There is also a chair factory here, with turning lathes attached, which we did not examine.

The Social Hall of which I have before spoken, in which we partook yesterday of such a bountiful repast, has all been built, even to getting the timber from the kanyon, since last December. Its dimensions are 55 by 32 feet. It is to be arched over head; not yet plastered. It is a neat, commodious little hall, and will be used for meetings until the meeting house is completed.

The Bishop's new frame house is 18 by 40 feet, a story and a half high, two rooms above and below, with eight feet passage, and a cellar under the entire building. It is well lighted, and when painted will be a delightful residence. It cost perhaps fifteen hundred dollars—rather more than adobe; but it will be better.

Vickers & Salsbury are manufacturing salt, taken from the mountains six miles from here, in Salt Creek kanyon. It is blasted from the solid rock, mixed with red clay. It yields about seventy per cent. It is pulverized; placed in boilers containing water and boiled about two hours; then drawn off into vats and left to settle, when the brine is drawn from the vats into other boilers and boiled down to salt. Its quality, the manufacturer informs me, is superior to any manufactured in the Territory, and the demand for it much greater than can be supplied.

I have been thus particular in noting the different items of improvement here, hoping it may encourage the citizens of Nephi, still to persevere in all works of useful improvement; and I need not disguise the hope that at least two settlements through which we have past—much older and more numerously settled than this—will profit by their example, at least in the matter of meeting-houses and other public buildings. I need not name them here, as it is a proverbial fact, that two large, old settlements between this and Salt Lake City, cannot boast of a meeting-house or any public building now in the state of completion. I believe, however, there are private companies in each of these places, who have been enter-

prising enough to build halls, which are actually rented for meetings—it is so much better financeering for a wealthy community, abounding in cattle, horses and mules, farms, etc., to rent than to build. I refrain from saying more.

In the morning, the weather permitting, we go on to Sanpete, where I expect to write again.

GOSHEN ONCE MORE!!

Goshen, Utah Co. July 6, 1863,

EDITOR NEWS:

DEAR SIR:—It has long been a subject of consideration; also a very great desideratum to have a good substantial road constructed through Goshen kanyon, at the head of Goshen valley, leading into Juab valley, by which the traveling distance between the southern portions of the Territory and G. S. L. City would be shortened some 25 miles and the traveler furnished a better and more convenient road than that through the settlements by way of the old route. Whether the work of making the road had been considered so great an undertaking or not, I cannot say, but up to the time of President Young's visit at Goshen, on his homeward bound trip, from "the land of cotton," no measures were taken for its accomplishment. When here, the President instructed Bishop Price to advise with the bishops of Nephi and Santaquin, also with Mr. Levi Stewart, and get their co-operation in the matter, and so get the job put through in quick order.

On Monday the 1st ult., the road having been previously surveyed, and all things got in readiness; the Santaquin forces, under command of Bishop McBride and the Goshen forces, under Major Enoch Williams, made a simultaneous attack upon the no th end of the kanyon, where such picking and shoveling and smashing and crashing among the gravel and rocks, thereabouts had not been heard for a long time past. That portion of the work allotted to Santaquin was put through in double quick time, which, doubtless may justly be attributed to the peculiar tact and energy of Bishop McBride, who like a brave general, never forsook his men or deserted his post, until the victory had been achieved. Goshen did good execution and won a brilliant victory over the rocks and other obstructions before leaving the field of action.

It would be unjust here, not to mention that much praise is due Major Williams, who with true Irish grit, (good luck to his ould shore,) stuck to the pick and the shovel like a hungry man to a plum pudding, never dodging a particle during the whole engagement. When last heard from, Bishop Bryant, of Nephi, and Mr. Stewart had not commenced their division of the work, but judging from the known character and energy of the parties, when once commenced it will soon be driven to a completion.

This route furnishes an abundance of good feed for teams, also firewood and water in great plenty, has no mud holes or bad pitches, or hills, and is entirely free from gravel, except a little in the kanyon, and the road is slightly declining from the head of the kanyon to the point of the lake near Lehi bridge, a distance of thirty five miles, at which point the traveler can strike the old route again, or continue on the west side of the Jordan, as there is but little difference in the quality of the routes; but should the anticipated improvements be made at the point of the mountain, east of the river, that would decidedly be the better road.

The morning of the Fourth was ushered in here by a national salute, by Major William Price's battalion of Infantry, Nauvoo Legion and the raising of a splendid pole of rare proportions, taken from near the summit of one of the highest peaks of the Wasatch range, and but a short distance from the celebrated Mount Nebo, upon which a beautiful and newly-made flag (the voluntary donation of the ladies of this place) was soon unfurled to the then gently stiring winds, revealing the glorious Stars and Stripes, as it played fantastically in the breezes. The remainder of the day was spent in a manner highly illustrative of the energy and patriotic zeal of the people. Towards the close of the day we were unexpectedly favored with a visit from the Spanish Fork brass band, whose well-timed and sweet sounding notes gave new fervor to the spirit of the occasion.

The programme for the twenty-fourth promises a grand concern. First upon the list are processions of juveniles, under the supervision of their respective teachers, with banners; bearing appropriate mottoes and inscriptions, to be followed by brilliant and spirit stiring effusions, from orators selected for the occasion; after which, the mammoth table is to be set, upon which is to be served up, in

good order, a superior dinner, consisting of, as a ground work, a bountieous supply of good roast beef and mutton, with a suitable quantity boiled, of course; to which in resubstantial viands are to be added, and an almost indiscribable amount of every conceivable and come-atable dainty which the country afford s, to be part cipated in by all who may be present, and wish to partake of the teeming luxuries, to be followed by a good y number of appropriate toasts, etc., and to conclude with a grand pic-nic ball.

The people of Goshen are feeling well. They were much encouraged by the late visit and fatherly counsels and instructions of the President, and are determined to go ahead and make themselves more worthy of his kind approval and paternal attention.

GOSHENITE.

Deseret News
October 7, 1863

BRANCH FAIRS.

We have before us reports of the "Cedar Ward branch" and the "Nephi Auxiliary branch of the D. A. & M. Society fairs, held at the former place on the 5th and at the latter on the 26th ultimo. The show of stock at Cedar was much larger and superior to that of last year, and in "real substantial articles"—in clothing, in the products of the field, garden and dairy, there was marked improvement. At Nephi, the "substantiability of the articles exhibited" was the prominent feature. Colored flannel, strong jeans and Scotch plaid were very attractive and shared the attention with the home-grown

madder and other dye-stuffs. Fruit and garden produce were abundant and excellent in quality. In addition to the specifications, the reports exhibit that, with proper care and dilligent attention, the citizens are satisfied everything can be grown or manufactured in those places that will make any people "happy and comfortable." The reports before us are well written and would read well, but we are f reed to omit them from our columns. We are pleased to notice the growing progress of the people in the direction of "real substantial articles." They have our warmest sympathy and best wishes for a still better future.

HOUSE OF REPRESENTATIVES.

January 21st.

MORNING SESSION.

House met at 10 a. m. Speaker in the Chair. Roll called. Quorum present. Prayer by the Chaplain

Mr. Pitchforth presented the petition of C. H. Bran and 60 others, praying for a renewal of the Nephi City Charter. On motion of Mr. Richards, the petition was referred to the Committee on Corporations.

Mr. Pitchforth presented the petition of R. Wilson Glen and 26 others, praying for the organization of a new county in the southern part of Sanpete county. On motion of Mr. Patton, the petition was referred to the Committee on Counties.

Thomas Callister, to whom was referred "An Act changing the County Seat of Summit county" reported favorably to the same, which was read and on motion of Mr. Long, was laid on the table to come up in its order.

Mr. Thurber, to whom was referred (H. F. No 29,) "A bill for the encouragement and advisement of Agriculture, Manufacture, and for other purposes," begs leave to report unfavorable to the passage of said bill On motion of Mr. Woolley the report was accepted and the Committee discharged from further duties on the subject.

F. D. Richards, to whom was referred the Report of a special Committee on amount of appropriation by Congress, yet unexpended for the completion of Utah Penitentiary, report that inasmuch as there is now before the House, Memorials from the Council to the Secretary of the Treasury, and to Congress, asking that the amount already applied may be made available; and that an additional amount of $12,000 be appropriated for the completion of the Penitentiary, it appears superfluous to present further Memorials on the subject. Your Committee therefore, ask to be excused from further consideration of the subject. On motion of Mr. Long, the Report was accepted and the Committee discharged.

Mr. Long moved that the Committee on Claims and Appropriations be instructed to incorporate in the Territorial Appropriation Bill, the sum of $66 for services rendered by John H. Hardy, as Engrossing Clerk of the House during the present Session. Seconded and carried.

Mr. Rockwood, to whom was referred (H. , . No. 38,) "Territorial Appropriation Bill," begs leave to report the same back with amendments, which was read as amended. On motion of Mr. Thurber the bill passed to its third reading and so passed. The title was read and approved.

On motion of Mr. Long, the House adjourned for one hour.

AFTERNOON SESSION.

House met at 2 p. m. Speaker in the chair. Roll called. Quorum present.

Resolution in relation to "publishing and distributing the Laws of the Thirteenth Annual Session," which was read the second time. On motion of Mr. Preston, said resolution was read the third time and adopted. The title was read and approved.

Resolution authorizing J. F. Kinney to collect certain moneys due the Territory of Utah, which was read, and on motion of Mr. Preston, adopted.

"An Act changing the County Seat of Summit" Said county seat is hereby located at Coler ' in said county, which was taken up on its second reading. On motion of Mr. Lunt, the bill was read the third time by its title, and so passed. Title of said bill was read and approved.

A message from the Council was received and read, announcing their concurrence in (H. F. 37,) "An Act to amend An Act Incorporating the Deseret Agricultural and Manufacturing Society," approved Jan. 17, 1856. Also their passage of (C. F. 19,) "An Act to incorporate the St. George Library Association." Also adopted "Memorial to Congress for the admission of Utah as a State," which are respectfully forwarded for your action.

(C. F. No. 19,) An Act to Incorporate the City of St. George Library Association, was taken up and read the first time. On motion of Mr. Maughan, said bill was read the second time. On motion of Mr. Pratt, said bill was read the third time by its title and so passed. The Title was read and approved.

"Memorial to Congress for the admission of Utah as a State," was read, and on motion of Mr. Lunt, adopted.

On motion of Mr. Richards, the House took a recess of half an hour.

On re-assembling, (H. F. No. 33) "An Act concerning joint enclosures and division fences," was taken up on its second reading. On motion of Mr. Maughan, said bill was read the third time by its title. On motion of Mr. Long, said bill passed. The title was read and approved.

(H. F. No. 41,) Mr. Farr presented An Act to incorporate the "Ogden City Library Association." On motion of Mr. Long, the bill passed to its second reading by sections. On motion of Mr. Van Cott, the bill was read the third time by its title, and so passed. The title was read and approved.

The following was received and read.

Executive Department, Utah Ter.,
G. S. L. City,
Jan. 21st, 1864.

The Hon. John Taylor, Speaker of the House of Representatives.

Sir:—I have approved and signed the act entitled "An Act in relation to fires on the public domain," and have deposited the same in the office of the Secretary of the Territory. I have also approved and signed the memorial entitled "Memorial to the Hon. Post Master General," which as soon as recorded I shall forward to that office.

AMOS REED, Acting Governor.

The following was received and read.

Executive Department, Utah Ter.,
G. S. L. City,
Jan. 21st, 1864.

To the Hon. Council and House of Representatives of the Legislative Assembly of Utah Ter.

Gentlemen:—Before your final adjournment I deem it proper to inform you that I am constrained to withhold my signature and approval from the act entitled "An Act concerning mining claims," my reasons for this course are many, and I deem it necessary only to advert to some of them. In my annual Message your attention was called and favorable consideration asked to the new field of enterprise, which the working and discovery of mines of precious metals opens to the people of this Territory. I regarded these discoveries as in the highest degree important and matters of a sincere congratulation to you and your constituents, and indulged the hope that the Legislature would esteem it a duty and a privilege to enact such laws as would tend to promote, encourage, and foster mining.

AMOS REED, Acting Governor.

The following was received and read:

Council Chamber, Jan 21st, 1864.

To the Honorable Speaker and House of Representatives—Gents: The accompanying bill (C. F. 21,) "An Act pertaining to damage done by stock," has passed the Council and is now sent for your concurrence. (H. F. 40,) "An Act changing the County Seat of Summit County," not concurred in, and their concurrence in resolution giving authority to J. F. Kinney to collect a certain amount due the Territory.

DANIEL H. WELLS, President.

Said bill (C. F. 21,) "An Act pertaining to damage done by stock," was read the first time. Said bill was read the second time. On motion of Mr. Pitchforth, was read the third time by its title, and so passed. The title was read and approved.

On motion of Mr. Lunt, the House adjourned to Jan. 22d, at 10 a. m. Benediction by the Chaplain.

HOUSE OF REPRESENTATIVES.

January 22d.

House met at 10 a. m. Speaker in the Chair. Roll called. Quorum present. Prayer by the Chaplain.

The following message from the Council was received and read :

Hon. Speaker and House of Representatives—Gentlemen : Your "Territorial Appropriation Bill" has passed the Council with amendment, and is respectfully sent to your honorable body for concurrence in said amendments. Do you concur? The Council has also passed the accompanying bill (H. F. 22,) "An Act requiring owners of cattle to mark or brand them." which is respectfully submitted for your action thereon.

Very respectfully.

DANIEL H. WELLS. President.

The "Territorial Appropriation Bill" was taken up, read as amended, and the amendment concurred in, except that pertaining to Mr. East's claim, which was stricken out by the Council.

(C F. 22,) "An Act requiring owners of cattle to mark or brand them," was read; pending discussion on the bill the following message from the Governor was received and read :

Executive Department,)
U T, G S L City, }
Jan. 22d, 1864.)

The Hon. John Taylor, Speaker of the House of Representatives—Sir. I have approved and signed the following acts to-wit : " An Act to incorporate the Seventies' Library and Reading Room Association," "An Act to incorporate Provo City," "An Act to amend An Act incorporating the Deseret Agricultural and Manufacturing Society." Also the resolution entitled "Resolution giving authority to Hon. John T. Kinny to collect certain amounts due the Territory," and have deposited the same in the office of the Secretary of Territory.   AMOS REED,
Acting Governor.

"An Act concerning a ferry or ferries across Bear River. and a bridge across the Malad," was taken up and read a first time.

(This act authorizes Joseph Young, sen , to control a ferry or ferries on Bear River, between a point one mile below where the present ferry crosses the river, to a point up said river one half mile easterly from the place where the old ford usually called the California Ford, crosses Bear River in Box Elder county, and was adopted to meet the objections of the Governor who had vetoed a bill on the same subject a few days before.—Rep.)

On motion of Mr. Wright, the bill was read the second time. On motion of Mr. Pitchforth, it was read the third time and so passed. The title was read and approved.

(The bill finally passed both Houses, and was signed by the Governor on the last night of the session —Reporter.)

(C F No 22,) "An Act requiring owners of cattle to mark or brand them," (pending the consideration of which the Governor's Message was read,) was read the second time and amended. The bill was read the third time, and on motion of Mr Callister, passed. The title was read and approved. (This bill having passed both Houses, was vetoed by the Governor, or rather, was not approved by him.)

Mr Eldridge reported back petition of citizens of Nephi considering the time too limited at the present session to frame a bill of the measure ask ed for in said petition

On motion of Mr. Rockwood, the Committee were relieved from the further consideration of the subject.

Mr. Wandell presented a bill entitled "An Act concerning Mining Claims," which was read the first time, and on motion of Mr. Pratt, was read the second time, (after a short discussion between Messrs. Wandell and Pratt covering the same points which have heretofore been reported, the enacting clause of said bill, was, on motion of Mr. Pratt stricken out, and so endeth the last chapter of the Mining bill. Mr. Pratt seemed to be leader and spokesman of the policy of decided enmity to the development of mining, and was backed by a majority of the Legislature. If Mr. P thinks his policy will win, all right, but we think he will find himself thoroughly mistaken.)

Mr. Fair, to whom was referred petition of Z. Snow and others, requesting that the law regulating fees of certain officers be amended, reported that the Committee did not deem it expedient to undertake to amend the laws relating to the fees of officers, so late, in the Session. On motion of Mr. Fair, the Committee were relieved from further duties on the subject.

Mr. Pitchforth presented a bill entitled "An Act to incorporate the Nephi Library and Reading Room Association," which was read the first, second, and third time, and on motion of Mr. Preston, passed. The title was read and approved.

Mr. Callister, to whom was referred petition of the citizens of Richland, in Sevier valley, praying for the organization of a new county, to be called Sevier, reported adversely to granting the petition. On motion of Mr. Long, the House went into Joint Session in the Representatives Hall.

Upon dissolution of the Joint Session, the House resumed the consideration of (H. F. No. 45,) "An Act granting unto Lewis Robinson and Joshua Terry, the right to establish and control a ferry or ferries on Green river," which was read the second time, and on motion of Mr. Woolley, passed. The title was read and approved.

the Committee were relieved from the further consideration of the subject.

On motion of Mr. Maughan, the House took a recess for one hour.

AFTERNOON SESSION.

House assembled at half past 1, p. m., as per adjournment. Roll called. Quorum present.

A message was received from the Council as follows:

The Council has concurred in (H. F. No. 11.) "An Act to incorporate the Ogden City Library Association." The Council does not concur in retaining the account of Mr. East, in the Appropriation Bill, considering it County business. The Council concurs in (H. F. No. 9.) "An Act in relation to Territorial, County, City and School Taxes," with amendments; also in "Resolution changing the location of the road in Summit county," between Peeks creek and Chalk creek.

Respectfully,
DANIEL H. WELLS, President.

On motion of Mr. Richards, the House concurred with the Council in the striking out of the Territorial Appropriation Bill, the claim of E. W. East.

(H. F. No. 9,) "An Act in relation to Territorial, County, City and School Taxes," was read as amended, and on motion of Mr. Richards the House concurred with the Council in the amendments thereto.

"Resolution changing the location of the road in Summit county, between Peck's creek and Chalk creek," was read as amended. On motion of Mr. Wall, the amendments thereto were concurred in.

Mr. Preston presented "An Act granting to Lewis Robinson and Joshua Terry, the right to establish and control a ferry or ferries on Green river," which was read the first time. Pending the further consideration of this bill, the House went into Joint —

(This bill was less fortunate than the Green river franchise, as it failed to receive the sanction of the Governor. So Joshua Terry and Lewis Robinson, can't control all of Green river, or monopolize that stream crossed by the entire emigration from the East to the West.)

Mr. Wandell presented a bill entitled "An Act for the protection of growing crops," which was read the first time. On motion of

Mr. Wright, the bill was laid on the table.

(Mr. Wandell seems to be in bad luck; he didn't start a bill during the session that wasn't bounced, badgered, slaughtered, or like Desdemona, most foully smothered, in one way or another.)

On motion of Mr. Long, the House adjourned until 6 p. m.

EVENING SESSION.

House met pursuant to adjournment. Speaker in the Chair. Roll called. Quorum present.

"An Act granting unto President Brigham Young the right to make a toll road in Tooele County," was read the first and second time. On motion of Mr. Johnson, the bill was read the third time and so passed. The title was read and approved.

(This bill grants an important franchise to Brigham Young—not President Young. Although it was just introduced after 6 o'clock, p. m., it had three readings in the House, as many in the Senate, and was approved by the Governor before 10 o'clock; a species of rapid legislation, which, if it don't betoken haste, certainly does expedition—sharp's the word)

Executive Department,
G. S. L. City, Utah Ter.,
Jan. 22d, 1864.

The Honorable the Speaker and House of Representatives—Gentlemen : I have approved and signed the following acts, to wit: "The Territorial Appropriation Bill," "An Act in relation to Territorial, County, City and School taxes." AMOS REED,
Acting Governor.

Mr. Hunt, to whom was referred a manuscript on Military Tactics, etc., reported the same back, and recommended it be laid on the table as unfinished business, to come up

in set forth, we are determined not to suppose ourselves not mistaken. On motion of Mr. Fair, the above resolution was adopted.

Mr. Thurber presented the following Resolution, which was received and read.

Resolved, That we highly appreciate the candid, courteous and impartial manner in which the Hon Speaker, has discharged the duties of his office during the present Session, and that we unanimously tender to him our

next Session,—the time being too short to act on so important a matter. On motion of Mr. Lunt, the report was accepted, and the matter laid over as unfinished business.

On motion of Mr. Rockwood. a note was addressed, and forwarded to the Council, enquiring as to the fate of the "General Incorporation Act."

Mr Wandell presented the following resolution: Be it resolved by the Council and House of Representatives of the Territory of Utah, that the thanks of the Assembly be tendered to His Excellency the Acting Governor for his courteous and gentlemanly bearing towards the Legislature, and for the general interest manifested by him for the welfare and peace of this Territory. On motion of Mr. Johnson, the above resolution was adopted.

Mr. Wright presented the following resolution, which was received and read: Resolved, by the Speaker and House of Representatives of the Legislative Assembly, that the thanks of this Assembly be, and are hereby tendered to his Excellency, Hon. Amos Reed, acting Governor, for his very gentlemanly, obliging and respectful conduct to the members and officers of this House universally from the beginning to the last expiring moments of the Session. He has almost universally approved our acts, and in the few instances of non-concurrence in our enactments, his friendly communications explanatory of his reasons, have carried respect to every member's heart. He has, to be sure, weighed our acts with great deliberation, but the difference in judgment is of so venial a character as to not merit consideration(!) We met friends, we separate much more so, and in the opinion and expressions of our feelings unanimously here-

thanks, also our best wishes for his future welfare, prosperity and happiness. On motion of Mr. Hunt, the above resolution was adopted.

A message was received from the Council announcing their unanimous approval of the joint resolution complimentary to the acting Governor, and returning the same for engrossment. — DANIEL H. WELLS, President.

The Speaker acknowledged the tribute of

respect paid to him by the House, and testified to the reciprocal feelings existing in his bosom towards the members, and expressed his wishes for their future happiness and prosperity.

Having finished their business and while waiting the action of the Governor on several franchise acts, which engrossed so much of the attention of this Legislature, the House started in for a little fun, and numerous were the stories, of a highly moral cast we have no doubt, but we couldn't exactly see it, were humorously told by the several members. Mr. Pratt started the ball by presenting a bill entitled "An Act legalizing mules as animals," Be it enacted by the Governor and Legislative Assembly of Utah, that all mules are declared to be animals, but of what species is not yet fully determined.

On motion of Mr. Hunt, the bill was laid on the table, (on the ground, we presume, that it was unconstitutional for members' to introduce or vote on a measure in which they were personally interested.) On motion of Mr. Pratt, the Clerk, for the benefit of the House, read Josh Billings' celebrated essay on mules.

We could have wished that there had been a longer space of time between the reading of the essay (considering the subject) and the following Message from the Governor, which was received and read. The connection between the two documents was hardly apparent, notwithstanding the approval of the Bear river franchise:

Executive Department, }
Utah Ter., G. S. L. City, }
Jan. 22d. 1864. }

To the Hon. Speaker and Members of the House of Representatives—Gentlemen: I have approved and signed "An Act to incorporate the Ogden City Library Association." Also the resolution entitled "Resolution authorizing a change in the location of the road in Summit County, between Peck's Creek and Chalk Creek." Also an act entitled 'An Act to Incorporate the Nephi Library and Reading Room Association.' Also an act entitled 'An Act concerning a ferry or ferries across Bear River, and a bridge across the Malad.'

AMOS REED, Acting Governor.

A message was received from the Council with an accompanying resolution, complimentary of Gov. Reed in his double capacity as Acting Governor and Secretary of the Territory. (The resolution will be found at length in the proceedings of the Council.) The House unanimously concurred in the resolution, on motion of half a dozen members.

Mr. Richards presented Memorial to the Sec. of War, requesting him to remove the present location of Camp Douglas, said camp being within the corporate limits of G. S. L. City. The resolution broadly characterizes the Camp as a nuisance, and in terms, spirit and animus that can only be apologized for as being presented on the eve of final adjournment, when good jokes are current and at a par. Whether this memorial was intended as a set off to Mr. Pratt's mule bill, or the Clerk's mule story, or that of Mr. Wright about a harrassed young man in Arkansas, we don't know. The members didn't laugh, but we took it as the best joke of the evening.

Mr. Wandell moved that the Memorial be indefinitely postponed.— (Bully for Mr. Wandell—but it was no go.)

Mr. Wall lived out among the Indians, and the people in his neighborhood had a great deal of trouble turning out to defend their homesteads from Indians.(!) (Oh! fid, Mr. Wall, how can you—Do you recollect what Falstaff says about this world?) He wanted the soldiers scattered out where they could defend the country from Indians and not housed up in Salt Lake where there was no difficulty existing or apprehended.

Mr. Wandell was surprised at such a document. He had early learned that courtesy and kindly expressions accomplished more than insulting language. He believed in treating every man and every set of men with respect. He was sorry the Memorial was presented. Its only result was to outrage and insult the denizens of Camp Douglas. It was casting a stone in a direction whence we would not like stones to be thrown at us. He did not believe the author was in earnest

Mr. Wall considered himself insulted by the remarks of the last speaker. He intended none to Camp Douglas. The soldiers he regarded as his friends, sent here by his parent Government to protect him against Indians. He wanted them scattered about and did not like all of such a good thing to be bestowed on the Metropolitan citizens of Great Salt Lake City.

Mr. Richards disclaimed any intention to insult anybody. The Grand Jury had presented the Camp as a nuisance because it necessarily used and injured the water on which thousands of people depended for culinary purposes. He claimed his right of petition as an American citizen. It was a respectful petition to the proper authority to remove or abate what a Grand Jury had denounced as a nuisance. He proposed to ask in proper terms, as was his right, under the Constitution, for this relief. For anybody to take exception to this course made him suspect that all was not exactly right. It aroused his suspicions. Gen. Connor and the troops came from California, a land of sunshine and showers, where the bountiful earth yielded its harvests without the adventitious aid of artifical irrigation; while here, the water of ten streams was necessary for farming or gardening purposes. Hence Gen. Connor was not probably aware of the perhaps unintentional evil he was inflicting by depriving a third of the people of this city of pure and wholesome water.

He desired to present the facts in respectful terms to the proper authorities. If the soldiers at Camp had the good feelings which actuated himself and he believed the people at large in their intercourse with them, no offence could be taken at the Memorial.

Mr. Pratt moved the adoption of the Memorial. Carried. Mr. Wandell alone, voting NO, in the tones of a Stentor and amid the frowns of his colleagues.

A message was received from the Council announcing their adoption of Memorial to the Secretary of War.

On motion of Mr. Long, the House dissolved.

Benediction by the Chaplain.

[BY AUTHORITY.]

AN ACT

Concerning a ferry or ferries across Bear river and a bridge across the Malad

Sec. 1. Be it enacted by the Governor and Legislative Assembly of the Territory of Utah: That Joseph Young, sen. have the right to establish and control a ferry or ferries on Bear river, for the term of four years from and after the passage of this act; at such place or places as will best subserve the public interest between a point one mile below where the present ferry crosses the river and to a point up said river, one-half mile easterly from the place where the ford at present used crosses Bear river in Box Elder county.

Sec. 2. The said Joseph Young, sen., shall be allowed to take toll on said ferry or ferries at the following rates, viz:

For every vehicle not over two thousand pounds $2 00

For every vehicle over two thousand pounds and less than three thousand pounds $3 00

For every vehicle over three thousands pounds and less than four thousand pound $4 000

For every vehicle over four thousand pounds $5 00

For all pack animals, each 00 50

For horses, mules, jacks 00 25

Oxen or cows, each 00 25

For all colts, calves, sheep, goats or swine, each 00 10

For each footman 00 25

Sec. 3. The said Joseph Young, sen., shall keep a good bridge on the Malad on the main road leading to the northern part of this Territory at a convenient point to accommodate the travel crossing the aforesaid ferry or ferries going westerly towards California, and is authorized and empowered to collect toll thereon at the following rates, to wit:

For carriages, carts and empty wagons, each 00 75

For every loaded wagon $1 00

For all pack animals, each 00 20

All loose animals and footmen shall cross toll free.

Sec. 4. The said Joseph Young, sen., shall give bond and security to be approved by the Territorial Treasurer and filed in his office, in the penal sum of five thousand dollars ($5,000) payable to the people of the Territory of Utah, conditioned for the faithfully carrying out the provisions of this act, and to indemnify any person for damages they may sustain on account of neglect, or carelessness, on the part of the proprietor of said ferry, ferries or bridge, while receiving toll therefrom.

Sec. 5. If any person or persons shall establish a ferry within the aforesaid described limits on Bear river, or establish a ferry or bridge on the Malad, within one mile each way from said Joseph Young, sen's., ferry or bridge, and take toll thereon, without a grant from the Legislative Assembly, shall forfeit and pay to the people of the Territory of Utah, the sum of five hundred dollars ($500) for each and every such offence of taking toll on said ferry or bridge, to be collected as an action of debt.

Sec. 6. The said Joseph Young, sen., shall during the first week in November annually make a true report under oath to the Territorial Treasurer of the amount of moneys and property received for toll on said ferry and bridge, and pay ten per centum of the aforesaid moneys and property into the Territorial Treasury, to be held for the benefit of common schools, and to be expended as may be provided by law.

Sec. 7. All acts or parts of acts in anywise conflicting with this act are hereby repealed.

Approved January 22, 1864.

AN ACT

To incorporate the Nephi Library and Reading Room Association.

Sec. 1. Be it enacted by the Governor and Legislative Assembly of the Territory of Utah: That Thomas Ord, Jonathan Midgley, Thomas J. Schofield, Benjamin Riches, Andrew Love, Jacob G. Bigler and George Kendall, of Nephi City, and their successors in office, are hereby constituted a body corporate with perpetual succession, to be known and styled the "Nephi Library and Reading Room Association," and shall have power to purchase, receive and hold property; to sue and be sued, to plead and be impleaded; defend and be defended in all courts of law and equity and in all actions whatsoever, and to do and perform all things that may of right pertain to their duties in the regulation, control and suitably providing for the interests and in carrying into effect the objects of this organization; and the above named persons are hereby appointed a Board of Directors of said association, until an election shall take place.

Sec. 2. That a Board of Directors shall be elected by the members of said association, on the fourth Monday in February, 1864, and thereafter annually. The Directors shall have power to appoint a Secretary, Treasurer and Librarian, and such other officers as may be deemed necessary; also to fill any vacancy that may occur in the board; at the close of their term of office, they shall present to the association a report of the number of books, papers and other publications on hand; the amount of moneys received and disbursed during the year, the numbers of books donated, and by whom; also the amount incurred for services of Librarian and other incidental expenditures. A majority of the Directors shall constitute a quorum to do business and for the proper management of the Library and Reading Room. They shall have power to frame bye-laws, which upon receiving the sanction of two-thirds of the members present at any stated meeting, shall be in full force.

Sec. 3. That the Library and Reading Room shall be for the use and benefit of the public, subject to such regulations as may in the bye-laws be prescribed.

Sec. 4. Conditions of membership shall be as made and provided by law.

Approved January 22, 1864.

AN ACT

To incorporate the Saint George Library Association.

Sec. 1. Be it enacted by the Governor and Legislative assembly of the Territory of Utah: That Orson Pratt, senr., Erastus Snow, F. B. Woolley, A. M. Cannon, Jacob Gates, Orson Pratt, junr., James G. Blake, their associates and successors in office are hereby constituted a body corporate, to be known and styled Saint George Library Association, and shall have power to purchase, receive and hold property, real and personal, to sue and be sued, plead and be impleaded, defend and be defended in all courts of law and equity and to do and perform all things that may be necessary and proper to enable them to carry into effect the objects of the association in the diffusion of knowledge by establishing a library of books, maps, charts, and scientific instruments, connecting therewith a reading room *and scientific and other popular lectures.* And the above named are hereby appointed a Board of Directors of said Association until superceded as provided in the following section.

Sec. 2. A board of seven directors may be elected by the members of said Association on the second Monday of November annually who shall hold their office for one year, and, until their successors are duly elected, and they shall have power to appoint a President, Secretary, Treasurer and Librarian, and such other officers as may be deemed necessary, and define their duties and to enact such bye-laws as may be necessary for the proper management of all business of the Association. A majority may form a quorum to do business and they may fill any vacancy in the Board until the next regular election.

Sec. 3. This Association may raise means by shares, contributions, and donations for the purchase of books, maps, charts, etc., and for leasing and erecting suitable buildings for the library, reading room, and lectures, and new members may be added on such conditions as may be prescribed in the bye-laws of the Association, and the library and reading rooms shall be opened for the use of the public, or books loaned out under such regulations and at such times as the Board of Directors may determine.

Approved January 22, 1864.

Deseret News
March 30, 1864

Married:

In this city Feb. 20, ALEXANDER GARDNER, of Nephi city, and JANE OKAM, late from Deptford, England. [Mil. Star please copy.

Deseret News
May 4, 1864

LIBRARY AND READING ROOM.—The Secretary of the Nephi Library and Reading Room favors us with a communication in which we are pleased to learn of the general progress of that settlement, and of the contemplated building of a commodious Library and Reading Room there. *Our correspondent suggests a little poking at other settlements on the same score—they will take it kindly, we expect.* There are few men now at the head of settlements who do not fully appreciate the advantage of intellectual developement. It is fully a quarter of a century since sensible men came to the conclusion that mind governed matter, and in the struggle for supremacy, science was victor over the animal.

Deseret News
August 10, 1864

FROM JUAB COUNTY.

NEPHI, Juab county, July 28, 1864.

EDITOR OF THE NEWS:

DEAR SIR:—Feeling interested in reading the various communications, which appear in the NEWS from time to time, I am prompted to send a few items which I hope will prove interesting to your readers.

The ever to be remembered Fourth and Twenty-fourth days of July, were duly observed by the inhabitants of this city and county in a style characteristic of the people of Utah.

The orations, songs, toasts and music were all good, very good.

OUR CROPS.—We have a fair chance of securing our breadstuffs. Considerable wheat and oats will be raised, but the amount will fall far short of what many anticipated, in fact we shall have but little grain to spare— and all seem inclined to hold on to that little, until they can command a price that will pay them for the laborious work of raising grain in a climate like this, where the farmer has to spend so much time in irrigating his land.

Corn and cane are not so good as in former years. Hay and potatoes about an average.

OUR STOCK are doing well, and the wise policy of our Bishop in having the stock not needed, either for work or milk, removed to a good herd ground, has proved beneficial to our grain and hay, and also preserved the feed around home for our teams and milch cows. We have learned by experience, that it is not wisdom to have over one thousand head of cattle roaming around our fields and destroying the home range when good feed is abundant only a few miles away.

Much has been done in the way of fencing a new field containing over 600 acres, which has been enclosed, and also two large meadows. This has taken over eight miles of fencing, and taking into consideration that kanyons had to be opened to obtain poles, we feel that a good deal has been done in a short time. All have been busily employed, in fact, hands could not be hired at any price.

Mr. John Hague's new grist mill is doing good business, as also the Nephi tannery owned by Messrs. Andrews & Bosnell, and br. L H Bax er has a fine nursery started.

In conclusion, I feel happy to state that the people of this city are healthy and a united spirit prevails. Yours respectfully,

SAMUEL PITCHFORTH.

VISIT TO SANPETE COUNTY.

G. S. L. City, Aug. 15, 1864.

Editor Deseret News:

Sir:—There is nothing more worthy of observation to the traveling community than the condition of the roads, and having just returned from a visit to Sanpete, I will mention a few places that require immediate attention. First, the bridge over Little Cottonwood, near Kesler's mill, the small one just beyond it, and the one opposite Bishop Cahoon's: the planks on each of these are getting loose, and a few hours labor with two or three new planks would render them secure for months to come. The next place when an effectual improvement can be made at a small cost, is on the north side of Provo river, where a few hours labor in removing the large cobble stones would be particularly beneficial to the traveler, and equally so to his animals; then, on leaving Spanish Fork city, there are two streams of water crossing the road, and the banks on each are so abrupt, as to render them difficult to get over, further on and near Pangent Springs, 12 miles from Salt Creek, there is an elbow leading off the main road, where all the travel seems to go, on account of some bad place that needs attention. The last place worthy of remark, is on the county road, on leaving Nephi for the kanyon, just after crossing the bridge over Salt Creek, where there are several steep pitches that threaten the traveler with a broken axle-tree, or a summerset. With these few exceptions, the roads were never in a better condition than at present, for safe traveling, and as President Young, and others, expect shortly to visit the southern country, those whose calling authorizes them to act in the forenamed localities, will no doubt appreciate the motive in directing their attention to the same. A hint to the wise is sufficient.

Those who have a taste for the beautiful, in flowers, shrubs, choice fruits, etc., just call on friend Graves as you leave the city of Provo, and you will find him perfectly at home in that department; further south, at Spring Lake Villa, where only two or three years ago, all was barrenness, now an almost endless variety of fragrant flowers, drest in every conceivable attire of richest hues and trees laden with fruit of only two years growth. There lives Joseph E. Johnson, whose indefatigable labor and devotion to his garden studies, place him in the foremost rank of our Horticultural citizens. A few miles further, on Summit, lives Abel Butterfield, rather slow, but sure in his operations, he has some of the choicest flavored black currants in the Territory. He has also a large nursery, and fine growing orchard.

The next thing of note that greets the eye of the traveler is the lofty white steeple of the meeting house in Nephi, which can be distinctly seen for many miles before you reach the city. This building when completed will be equally an honor as well as an ornament to the place, and may those whose means were freely donated towards its erection, live many years to worship in it.

Leaving Nephi for Sanpete county, a few hours ride brought me to Uinta or Fountain Green, Moroni, Fort Ephraim and Manti, at each of these settlements, men and teams were equally busy in hauling hay, to be in readiness for the harvesting of grain which was nearly ready. Occasional showers of rain for a few weeks past, had proved a great blessing through the county. On Sunday, July 31st, a cloud burst near Fort Ephraim, and the storm came pelting down in such torrents on the city, as was never known before, the creek overflowed its banks, and for a time seemed to threaten everything with destruction, but being of short duration, and local in extent, it soon abated, and but little damage was done.

Having traveled over the entire Territory during the past two years, visiting over eighty settlements and some of them several times, it is very gratifying to observe the rapid improvements that a few months will develope, in such places where the leading spirits are men of taste, wisdom and enterprize, not only in the erection of meeting houses, good and substantial habitations, planting out orchards and shade trees, but in having good fences, and keeping every crossing place leading to and from the settlement in thorough repair. All these combined must certainly tend to render such cities far more inviting to those whose councils and countenances are both cheering and instructive, than where improvements, like angels visits, are few and far between, and where a crossing place three months ago, was very bad and dangerous, is a great deal worse to-day. Such things, however, I am happy to say, are among those that are past, and men appointed now to keep bridges and crossings in repair, are selected for their judgment and determination that the traveling community shall not any longer be jeopardized in life, property and limb by having to cross such dangerous places, as used to exist before they were appointed to office.

The shattered condition of one or more bridges near this city, on the State Road, will of course be immediately made good by our prompt and enterprizing supervisors. thanks of the whole portion of community will therefore be due to those whose duties require them to keep the roads in good repair, (and actually do so) and in their behalf I subscribe myself your friend and well-wisher,

GEORGE GODDARD.

PRESIDENT YOUNG'S TRIP SOUTH.

By letters received from Elder George D. Watt, we learn that President Young and company left Pleasant Grove about 9 a. m., of the 2d inst., passed through Provo and arrived at Springville in time for dinner. There was a general turn out to meeting. Elders D. O Calder, J. T. Caine, R. T. Burton, E. T. Benson and Geo. A. Smith addressed the congregation. The topics of discourse were "the proper training of children, the necessity of doing unto others as we would that they should do unto us, etc. etc."

The company arrived in Payson at 6 p. m. A meeting was held at 7, at which Elders L. Snow, and John Taylor preached. Leaving Payson at 9 o'clock the next morning the company proceeded to Nephi. Elder G. A. Smith stopping to preach to the residents of Willow Creek. The Nephi brass band and a military escort met the President 3 miles out from Nephi. The account of the reception is furnished by br. Watt as follows:

Bishop Bryan, desirous of giving President Young a hearty welcome to our City, appointed the following Brethren a committee to make the necessary arrangements for the reception: A. Love, S. Pitchforth, J. G. Bigler and G. Kendall.

On Friday the committee dispatched br. Mitchell to Payson to learn the time President Young would arrive and the probable number of his company, who returned at one on Saturday morning bringing the information that President Young would arrive at one p. m., and that his company numbered about 30 persons. A mounted guard under the direction of Cap. John Kienke met the President at Willow Creek and escorted him to Nephi. About 3 miles from Nephi, the Committee,

Bishop Bryan, the Nephi Brass Band were waiting by the road side, and the band struck up a lively air—they took their places next to the guard and escorted the company in.

On arriving at the City, the "Star Spangled Banner" was observed floating from several places.

As the company proceeded we were met by the following companies, who welcomed the President, etc., with a smile and bow. 1st. On the east side of main street were stationed the High Priests; on the west side were the schools of Nephi, under the direction of superintendent Ord. and teachers J. Midgley and sister A. Bigler. As the company turned to the east we were met by the 49th and Mass Quorum of Seventies; the Elders, Priests, Teachers, Deacons and members were out in quite a respectable number.

David Udall had charge of arranging the companies, who were stationed as above.

At 4 p. m. the President preached an excellent discourse which is to be furnished for publication when the company return. Elders F. D. Richards, D. McKenzie and E. T. Benson followed.

Meetings were held on Sunday, and discourses delivered by Elders John Taylor, W. Woodruff, L. Snow, G. A. Smith and President Young. The Nephi band accompany the President south.

At Round Valley a meeting was held in the evening of Monday, Elders W. Woodruff, E. T. Benson, G. A. Smith, President Young and G. D. Watt spoke, but the reporter says that it was too dark most of the time to take notes. Elder O. Hyde joined the company at Sevier bridge, and A. M. Lyman at Round Valley.

On Tuesday, the 6th, the company reached Fillmore, and held meeting at 2 p. m. Elders F. D. Richards, L. Snow, John Taylor and W. Woodruff preached.

Another meeting was held on the 7th. Bishop Callister, Elder O. Hyde and President Young addressed the meeting. The President's remarks are said to have been very instructive; but are reserved for publication in full.

SKETCH OF PRES. B. YOUNG'S TRIP SOUTH.

On the 1st ult. Pres. Brigham Young and company left Great Salt Lake City to visit our southern settlements. He was absent twenty nine days, and traveled between 700 and 800 miles.

Of the Twelve, George A. Smith, Wilford Woodruff, John Taylor, Ezra T. Benson, Lorenzo Snow, and Franklin D. Richards joined the company in Great Salt Lake City; Orson Hyde at Sevier river bridge, Amasa Lyman at Fillmore, and, on the return, Erastus Snow joined the company at Round Valley. There was no formal organization in traveling, for every person seemed to know his place and duty, and not a single murmur of discontent, unhappiness or fault finding occurred to ruffle the continued peace that prevailed during the journey.

Thirty seven settlements were visited and thirty nine meetings held, in which 124 discourses were delivered. The teachings were rich in counsel and good, sound instruction, which, if observed, will bring to the saints spiritual and temporal salvation, and were impressed upon every honest heart by an unusual unction of the Holy Spirit, greatly edifying the saints and strengthening them in their most holy faith.

The receptions given to the President and his company evidenced the universal confidence and good feelings of the people towards the constituted authorities of the Church. "The President's visit" was made a time of jubilee, feasting and rejoicing; the schools were out, headed by their teachers, and children gave their joyous bows of welcome as we passed; young men and maidens said: "Welcome President Brigham Young and company"; the stalwart farmer, mechanic and lumberman ceased for a time their labor to join in the general rejoicing and merry making, and the veterens bared their silvered heads in token of welcome. Companies of horsemen and bands of music, with colors flying, and in some instances platoons of beautiful girls dressed in white met the company to escort them into the cities and bid them welcome.

At Nephi, C. H. Bryan, Bishop, a wagon and team was fitted out for the Brass Band of that place, who courteously tendered their services to the President and company during the trip. It would be no easy task to say too much in praise of the brethren composing that Band; for they were ready on all occasions to awaken their beautiful strains, and both man and beast were comforted and inspirited by the sweet influences of their music. The Brass Band of Nephi formed an important item in the President's trip, and they will be held in grateful remembrance.

The land, where the water was naught and the soil barren, is now a land of flourishing cities; where frost, desolation and sterility characterized regions, now productive farms, thrifty orchards, and fragrant flower borders flourish. The company were regaled with melons, peaches, apples and other fruits of this lately barren section. Wheat and corn in abundance are produced on the Rim of the Great Basin. Wherever the saints have settled God has healed the waters, and blessed the land. It was said anciently "The wilderness and the solitary place shall be glad for them; and the desert shall rejoice, and blossom as the rose. It shall blossom abundantly, and rejoice, even with joy and singing: the "glory of Lebanon shall be given unto it, the excellency of Carmel and Sharon, they shall see the glory of the Lord, and the excellency of our God." This has been verified before our eyes.

When the company descended to the settlements south of the "Rim" they feasted upon the fruit of the vine, the cotton plant was exposing its fiber to the busy fingers of the gatherer, and every person seemed alive in the work of improvement and self preservation.

May the heavenly impressions received during the President's trip south in September, 1864, never be effaced from the minds of the participants.

G. D. WATT, Reporter.

Deseret News
November 9, 1864

In Mona, Juab county, Nov. 2, MARY ELLEN, daughter of John and Elizabeth Partington, of inflammation of the lungs, aged 2 years, 2 months and 3 days. [Mil. Star please copy.

Deseret News
December 14, 1864

HOME ITEMS.

NEPHI.—Bro. Samuel Pitchforth writes, Nov. 29, that Bro. Russell has finished plastering the Meeting House in Nephi, and that the gypsum hard finish, cornice and center pieces reflect much credit on the workmen.

The Social Hall in that city is being plastered.

Bishop Bryan is regaining his health.

Deseret News
January 25, 1865

At Nephi, Juab co., Jan. 13, of convulsions, JOHN TAYLOR, infant son of Samuel and Sarah Ann Pitchforth.

The babe was born and died during his father's absence from home, representing the interests of his county in the Legislative Assembly. [COM.

Deseret News
February 8, 1865

GOOD NEWS TO TRAVELERS.

PERSONS traveling to and from the southern part of the Territory, or to Southern California, will find good entertainment on reasonable terms at the Nephi House, Nephi City.

☞ Meals at all hours. Good stabling, and a good supply of Hay and Grain always on hand.

HENRY GOLDSBOROUGH,
Proprietor.

Deseret News
March 1, 1865

NEPHI, Feb. 16th, 1865.

EDITOR DESERET NEWS:

SIR—On their outward bound journey, Elder G. A. Smith and those accompanying him gave the saints in Nephi much valuable instruction, and we expect to hear from them again this evening on their return.

Bishop Bryan is doing all he can towards finishing our meeting house, and we expect to have it ready for dedication by the time President Brigham Young makes his annual southern trip.

The Juab Dramatic Association presented last evening, for the first time, Damon and Pythias, and the Green Mountain Boy. They were warmly applauded.

To-morrow evening they present Damon and Pythias, and Sketches in India. This will be the Benefit night for our Orchestral Band, which is ably conducted by Capt. C. Sperry.

The heaviest fall of snow this winter occurred on the night of the 14 inst.

S. PITCHFORTH.

Deseret News
April 12, 1865

Died:

In Nephi city, March 11, of inflammation of the lungs, EMALINE ELIZABETH, daughter of Martin and Annie Littlewood, aged 2 years and 2 months.

GONE TO NEPHI.—Prest. Young, accompanied by the brethren of the Twelve in this city and others, start this morning for Nephi to hold a two-day's meeting. They will hold meetings at Lake City, Spanish Fork and Santaquin by the way.

Correspondence.

PRESIDENT YOUNG'S TRIP TO UTAH COUNTY CONTINUED.

EDITOR DESERET NEWS:

DEAR BRO:—On Thursday, 8th, the President and party, including Elder Geo. Q. Cannon, whose name was inadvertently omited in the report of Wednesday, left Payson about half past nine in the morning for the Farm.

INDIAN ETIQUETTE.

As the company approached the Farm, a small party of Indians, stationed on a rising ground, notified the main body of the fact, and in a few minutes after the party arrived the Indians came gently sauntering down on horseback, seemingly endeavoring to keep up an appearance of dignity. All the chiefs were present except San-pitch, who had taken suddenly indisposed for the occasion,—indisposed to attend the meeting or be a participator in

SIGNING THE TREATY.

After a few brief and pertinent remarks by Col. Irish, the chiefs manifested their willingness to sign, and attached their marks to the document, old Sow-e-ett leading, as the oldest chief, Kon-osh, by his manner, seemed to think that simply putting his mark to the paper was rather small business. I afterwards learned that he prides himself somewhat on his ability to write his name,—a very laudable source of pride, for, as is well known, Indians generally are in much the same condition of ignorance with regard to caligraphy, that the mailed knights of christendom mostly were who bore the banner of the cross against the Saracens, to rescue Palestine from their infidel hands.

THE TALK AFTERWARDS.

Col. Irish pointed out to them that if they lived up to the conditions of the treaty, they might date the commencement of a career of prosperity from that day, encouraging them to do so.

President Young advised them to remember the good advice given them, to learn to read and write and increase in intelligence, stating, in connection, that Col. Irish had done all he possibly could for them, and that he was their friend; he then blessed them.

Kon-osh, Tabby and Sow-ok-soo-bet indulged in a short talk each, expressive of their good feelings; after which the President strongly advised them not to punish the innocent for the misdeeds of the guilty, and if any of their own or other bands should commit depredations, to catch the guilty ones and deliver them up to the authorities of the whites for trial.

MEETING AT SPANISH FORK.

Before the "big pile" of presents for the Indians were distributed, Prest. Young and company started for Spanish Fork, and held meeting there in the meeting-house, a very large congregation having assembled. The President said that though he had passed through Spanish Fork, in company with his brethren, several times without holding meeting, it was not because he was not in fellowship with the people there. His feelings were good towards them. He then encouraged them in building good houses and making improvements of every kind that would tend to make their homes places of beauty and increased comfort,—abodes of elegance, taste and happiness.

Elder John Taylor spoke on the benefits resulting from studying and living according to principles of truth, pointing, as an illustration, to the recent treaty made with the Indians and the confidence they had manifested in President Young, a confidence that had grown up in them because he had always spoken and acted truthfully with them.

The President then made some remarks on the book entitled "Joseph Smith and his Progenitors," requesting those who had copies to let him have them, and receive value for them if they desired it.

Elder Geo. Q. Cannon followed on the difficulties to be encountered by the servants of God in educating the people; and noticed some of the erroneous ideas that had been entertained by many with regard to the building up of Zion, showing that we must cultivate the faculties and abilities with which the Lord endows us, and the opportunities placed within our reach, to quali-

fy us for the duties which we are and will be required to perform.

After remaining over night in Spanish Fork, shortly after eight o'clock on Friday morning, the company started to hold

ANOTHER MEETING AT SPRINGVILLE,

which had been appointed for eleven o'clock.

Elder F. D. Richards treated on civil and ecclesiastical government, showing that when righteously administered the civil law is an auxiliary of the ecclesiastical. He deprecated opposition in elections, reasoning that it was a lack of understanding that led men to pursue such a course.

Elder W. Woodruff showed that opposition to the order of the kingdom of God is the road to apostacy. He exhorted the Saints to diligence and faithfulnes in the discharge of their duties. Elder D. J. Ross followed in a few remarks; after which Elder Geo. A. Smith strongly exhorted the Saints to faithfulness, recalling instances of individuals rising in opposition against the Prophet Joseph, pointing out that it led to their apostacy and their eventually participating in shedding his blood.

Elder Geo. Q. Cannon quoted from Lehi's vision in the Book of Mormon, of the iron rod and the tree of life, reasoning that if the people will cling fast to the Priesthood and the word of God, they will not wander into by and forbidden paths; although mists gather around them and darken their way, they have something to guide them, which, if they hold on to, will enable them to reach the goal and secure eternal life.

Prest. Young adverted to some of the privileges of the Saints. Speaking of elections, he said the electors should get together a few days prior to the election, and if there was any opposition to raise it and dispose of it then; fix upon a man and be united in favor of him, and that union would give him a power to magnify his office for good, which otherwise he could never have. He encouraged home manufactures and spoke of the purity and cleanliness that would be in the Centre Stake of Zion when it is built up, and the beauty of the city.

In the afternoon the company returned to Payson, preparatory to holding a two days meeting in the new Bowery there, appointed to commence on Saturday morning at ten o'clock. Next morning, according to appointment, the meeting commenced. The

AUDIENCE AT PAYSON

numbered, I judged, a little over 8,000 persons, assembled from the various settlements from Lake City to Manti. Happy faces, smiling countenances and pleasant looks abounded. Everybody seemed to have come for the purpose of enjoying themselves and to be instructed and strengthened in good works, which the teachings and exhortations from the stand were well calculated to do.

THE SINGING AND MUSIC

were beautifully executed by four good choirs from Springville, Spanish Fork, Payson and Nephi, and the excellent band from Nephi, which accompanied the President on his southern trip last summer, and afforded so much harmonious gratification to the company and the settlements through which they passed. The singing was very finely rendered; the music of the band delightful; the green foliage of the bowery afforded a cool and pleasant shade from the nearly vertical rays of the sun which streamed down with almost prostrating force.

After singing and prayer,

THE MORNING MEETING,

on Saturday, was addressed by Elder Geo. A. Smith, who made a few remarks on the object of holding the meeting, which was to get the brethren together to counsel and instruct them on various matters pertaining to their progress in the work of the Lord. He noticed some of the difficulties of labor and necessity which had to be met by the settlers in these mountains, and their tendency to keep the time so employed that it required some self-denial at times to leave them and gather together in meetings; advising them to leave their labors at home and concentrate their thoughts on the object for which they had come together.

Elder A. O. Smoot followed in some brief remarks; after which, Elder Geo. Q. Cannon spoke of the blessings we enjoy as a people, and the willingness of our Father and God to bestow blessings upon us if we will faithfully live for them; treated on the vague and erroneous ideas entertained by our fathers and ourselves of the Gospel previous to its revelation through the Prophet Joseph, and of the many causes we have for gratitude to God for the abundance of His mercies and the promises made to us. Bishop A. H. Raleigh then made a few remarks, and was followed by Bishop Hunter in some good and fatherly counsel.

President Young touched upon the difference between preaching the gospel to the world and gathering the people who received the testimony of the truth, and perfecting the Saints when gathered together. Boys and men of but little experience can preach the Gospel to the nations, but it requires men full of wisdom and of large experience to guide the gathered Saints in the road to perfection and exaltation. In the

AFTERNOON MEETING

President Young preached a short discourse on the comprehensiveness of the Gospel, taking for his text "life and death," and showing that we have embraced a system of life and salvation which preserves each and every individual, and which preserves all things in their order as they are brought forth; every thing which appertains to life, which tends to preserve and make it happy, is embraced in the Gospel, and the opposite is death, dissolution and destruction. Elders Seymour B. Young and John W. Young then made a few remarks each, when Elder Orson Hyde, who had come up from Sanpete, spoke of the recent Indian outrages, and pointed out the imperative necessity of the brethren being fully armed and equipped, expert in the use of their weapons, all provided with horses, saddles, and other articles necessary for a military outfit, and prepared at all times for any emergency that might arise; to be always prepared for danger is the most certain way of always avoiding it. Elder R. T. Burton made some excellent remarks upon the same subject, and was followed by Elder J. R. Winder in a similar strain.

Prest. Young took up the declarations that the Lord will fight the battles of his people, and that it is his business to provide for them, showing that if to obtain the latter blessing requires the exercise of our abilities and industry, we have no right to claim the former unless we act according to the counsel given to us and do that part of the work devolving upon us. He touched upon the great amount of stock the people have more than they can take care of, and advised them to keep the quantity they can feed and properly attend to, and dispose of the surplus for the purpose of procuring those things which they lack and which present and prospective exigencies require them to have. Your correspondent spoke for a few minutes, and was followed by Elder John Taylor in a short exhortation to the Saints to be faithful and diligent in righteousness, that they might be co-workers with the Lord for the accomplishment of his holy purposes; after which the meeting adjourned until the next morning.

THE SUNDAY MEETINGS

were very largely attended, and much valuable instruction and counsel were imparted. Elders W. Woodruff and F. D. Richards occupied most of the time in the morning, exhorting and teaching the Saints; after which the President gave some excellent counsel to the singers, while expressing his pleasure at their proficiency and sweet music, and spoke briefly on the subject of education.

In the afternoon Elders Geo. A. Smith, John Taylor and Orson Hyde spoke on various topics of interest; President Young following with some remarks explanatory of the treaty made with the Indians. He called attention to the administering the sacrament, noticing how few in blessing the bread and water followed the form laid down in the Book of Doctrine and Covenants. He then bestowed his blessing upon the congregation, and the meeting terminated with music by the Nephi Band.

THE RETURN TRIP

presented but little of interest to chronicle. Immediately after the close of the meeting, the company bade good by to the kind brethren of Payson, and started for Provo, which was reached in the evening. Remaining over night there, a start was made next morning a little before nine o'clock, and after halting at Lehi for dinner, the city was reached at half past six in the evening, all feeling well and having heartily enjoyed the trip. An escort under Col. Pace accompanied the President from Provo to Lehi, where they were relieved by a company of the Lehi cavalry.

Good feelings, good health and the ministrations of the Holy Spirit were enjoyed by the company going and returning, and were manifested in the various settlements where a halt was made.

Yours Respectfully,
E. L. SLOAN.

Deseret News
July 5, 1865

CONTINUATION OF PRESIDENT YOUNG'S TRIP TO NEPHI.

We arrived in Payson early in the evening of the 22d, where a treat awaited us in the sweet strains from the Salt Creek Brass Band. We spent the rest of the evening in the enjoyment of a social party, wherein, to good music, we went forth in the dance. An escort attended the company from Provo, under the command of Col. Pace, who is always ready.

Friday, 23d.

The brethren of the Twelve went on ahead of the President, to Summit or Santaquin settlement, to commence the meeting appointed. The President and those with him left Payson about 10 a.m., and arrived at Summit about noon, where we found the meeting progressing, Elder Wilford Woodruff having addressed the Saints on spiritual and temporal salvation.

Elder Franklin D. Richards urged the necessity of training our children in the faith of the Lord Jesus, and in every kind of useful education, with a view to their being useful in the kingdom of God in a time to come; and wished the parents of children to observe the counsel of President Young, and keep their children at school instead of turning them out on the prairie to herd stock and study mischief.

Elder Geo. A. Smith was glad to see the people here so comfortable and increasing in population. He expected by means of some "Mormon" magic to see a good meeting house springing up upon this beautiful site, with a spire much higher than any other in the Territory. Cap. Hooper was presented before the people as delegate to Congress. The vote in his favor was unanimous. Elder Hooper tendered his thanks to the congregation for their reception of him as prospective delegate. He spoke of the blessings of unity and the benefits of education. He urged the people to educate their children, that they may be able to carry on this great work when we are gone, and touched upon the importance of making our cities places of architectural, horticultural and floral beauty.

After singing Elder John Taylor discanted upon politics, defining them as they now exist, and showing how political men feel and conduct themselves towards each other. We are aiming to get at correct politics, correct morals and correct religion, and trying to find out the best possible manner in which to obtain the common necessaries, comforts and luxuries of life. Then we have to inform ourselves on the politics and laws of nations, to understand them for our own benefit. While we are loyal citizens of the United States, still it is part of our faith, that the time will come when all nations that will not acknowledge God and His rule will be broken to pieces and pass away, to give place for the kingdom of God and the rule of Him whose right it is to reign. Those who seek to stop the progress of the work of God may as well try to stop the sun in its course. We are in the hands of God, and it is for us to know His will and do it as fathers and mothers, and as Elders in Israel, that we may be prepared to receive the blessings of Jehovah upon the earth, and that our children and children's children may be owned and crowned the sons and daughters of God forever.

Pres. Young addressed the meeting half an hour. Dinner over, the President and company proceeded to Nephi, which was reached, after a very dusty drive from Santaquin, about 8 p.m., where a social party was attended, at which all enjoyed themselves in the dance with zest and spirit. Elders Orson Hyde and Amasa M. Lyman had reached Nephi during the day and were awaiting the arrival of the President and company.

Saturday, June 24th.

This morning at ten o'clock the new house of worship was filled with Saints; the meeting was called to order by President Brigham Young, when Elder Geo. A. Smith offered the following dedication prayer:

Our Father who art in heaven, we come before Thee in humility at this time for the purpose of dedicating unto Thee this house which has been erected by Thy servants,—a house for Thy worship. We pray Thee to cause Thy Holy Spirit to rest upon us, that we may be united in heart and soul and mind who are now engaged in this dedication, that Thy Spirit may dictate such words and sentences as shall be pleasing in Thy sight.

We present before Thee the lot or parcel of ground which has been set apart and appropriated for the erection of this building, and upon which it stands; and we dedicate the same unto Thee for a house of worship, that it may be holy unto the Lord; and pray that Thy watchful care and protecting hand may be over it, that it may never be polluted by wicked men, but ever remain holy for the worship of Thy name, and may it never be occupied for any other purpose.

We dedicate unto Thee the corner stones which have been laid as supports for the four corners of this house. May Thy blessings rest upon them, that they may remain firm in their beds to fulfil the duties reposed upon them in their places in the foundation. We also dedicate unto Thee all the stones composing the foundations of this house, and the sand and lime of which the cement is composed which binds them together; may Thy blessings be upon all the materials of the foundation which underlies this structure, may it remain in strength to the praise and honor of Thy name.

Hear our feeble prayers, O Lord, as we dedicate unto Thee the brick and morter, and lintels, and fastenings, and frames of which the body of this building is composed; may Thy blessing rest upon them, and may Thy watchful care and persevering arm be over them, and may Thy peace, our Father, be upon them.

May the several workmen who have labored in preparing the rock, and in procuring and putting the material of this house together be blessed in the labor which they have performed, and may they rejoice therein all their days.

Wilt Thou also cause Thy blessing to rest upon all the material of wood of which this building is composed; let Thy protecting hand be over it that it never may be consumed by the devouring elements, but that it may be preserved from decay and remain long to be a blessing for thy people. Let Thy blessings be upon all the materials of brass and iron, upon the bolts, the screws, the locks, the nails and the springs, and upon the glass, the paint, the varnish, the oil, the putty and the plaster, all of which we dedicate unto Thee as offerings, and testimonials of the labor and faithfulness and diligence of Thy Saints who reside in this city called Nephi.

Cause Thy choice blessing to rest upon every one of the brethren and sisters and friends who have contributed to the erection of this house; may the light of Thy Spirit rest upon them as they offer it unto Thee, to be holy for Thy worship, that Thy Saints may assemble here in peace, to worship Thee and partake of Thy holy sacrament, and to receive instruction, and counsel, and wisdom, that the light of Zion may shine upon them. And cause that no evil dominion shall ever be over it, that it may never fall into the hands of the wicked, but let it be preserved a holy house unto Thee as an evidence of the fidelity, faithfulness, patience and industry of Thy people, and as a blessing unto them, that therein they may receive instructions, and their children after them, in all things pertaining to salvation, to truth, to light and glory.

While we dedicate unto Thee this house, we pray for the bishop, (George W. Bryan) who presides over this department of Thy kingdom, with his counselors, elders and teachers and all those who are associated with him in the ministry of the gospel to this people. May the inspiration and power of the Holy Spirit rest upon them, and make them ministers of salvation to Thy people in this place, even to those over whom they preside. We pray also that Thy blessings may rest upon the singers and musicians who will make sweet melody within these walls; may Thy peace be upon them, and inspire them continually with the light of Thy Holy Spirit, that they may sing with the spirit and with the understanding also, and in a manner acceptable unto thee.

We dedicate unto Thee this pulpit which has been prepared, from which Thy servants shall speak forth Thy truth and dispense Thy word to Thy Saints, together with the tables attached to the pulpit, on which the bread may be broken and the wine poured out to represent the body and blood of Jesus Christ, whose body was mangled and whose blood was poured out for the redemption of those who believe. May this stand never be polluted by wicked and unrighteous men, nor, for evil purposes, but may it be preserved holy for Thy service. We also dedicate unto Thee the seats and enclosure devoted to the singers and musicians, also the seats and benches with which this house is furnished; may they be holy unto Thee; and when Thy people shall assemble in this house to worship Thy name, then let the peace of God, which passeth all understanding, fill it and abide upon them; and here may the repentant sinner find peace to his troubled spirit, the sick find health, those who mourn, comfort and consolation, and the wavering and unbelieving strength in the Lord.

May Thy blessing be upon Thy servant Brigham whom Thou hast called to preside over Thy Saints in the last days. Give unto him a healthy and strong body, and a powerful and active mind, and wisdom above all men, and enable him to foresee the evil which may threaten himself, and which may threaten Thy people, that he and they may hide themselves; and let every arm that is raised against him and against Thy people be paralyzed, and may the light of Zion shine through Thy servants unto Thy people who are scattered upon the face of all the earth, and may he live to lead Thy Saints back to Jackson County, to the land of the New Jerusalem and of the great temple which shall be erected in that place in these last days.

Remember, O Lord, Thy servant Heber, and may Thy Spirit rest upon him in power, and heal his body, and comfort his mind, and enable him to magnify his high and holy calling as first Counselor to thy servant Brigham; and may he live long upon the earth to aid in rolling forth Thy great work for the redemption of our race.

May thy peace rest upon Thy servant Daniel, and we pray thee to give unto him that understanding and ability and power to faithfully perform the duties of the calling placed upon him, that he may be enabled to magnify the same to the honor of Thy great name. Heal his body, and let good health rest upon him, and may all those of Thy servants who are associated with him in the European mission, have power to deliver thousands of the honest poor, who desire to serve Thee, and bring them to Zion, there to keep and observe Thy holy word.

We pray Thee to remember the Twelve Apostles of Thy Church, and quicken them with the gift and power of the Holy Ghost, and fill them with wisdom and knowledge to magnify their calling before Thee; and may Thy servant Orson Hyde, who presides over this Quorum of Thy Church, stand forth in the midst of his brethren and the people as a flaming herald of salvation. Let Thy blessing rest upon all the members of this Quorum of Thy Church, collectively and individually, and upon their families and all that thou has given unto them.

Bless thy servant John Smith, Patriarch of Thy Church, and enlighten and strengthen his mind, and may he be enabled to stand forth in the dignity and power of his holy calling, and with power preach salvation to the world. Loose his tongue that he may utter Thy word. May the earth tremble under his feet and great fear rest upon the ungodly, and may he be filled with blessings to Thy people.

May thy blessings be on the Quorums of the Seventies, High Priests, Bishops and Elders, and upon all the members of all the other Quorums of Thy Church in Zion and in all the world; and let Thy light shine forth through them from nation to nation, that the kingdom of heaven in the last days may be like a city that is set on a hill that cannot be hid.

Gather out from the midst of thy people, in the valleys of the mountains, all hypocrites and those that work iniquity and are not willing to keep Thy laws, but who come into our midst for the purpose of making mischief and of bringing oppression and misery on Thy people. May they be powerless in all their evil designs, and be made to depart from Zion; may disgrace cover them; and, inasmuch as they will not repent, may they be cut off from the face of the earth and that speedily.

Look down in Thy great mercy upon the Lamanites who dwell in the midst of this land, and who dwell with Thy people. Incline their hearts unto Thee, and cause that they may receive the teachings of Thy servant Brigham and his brethren, that they may come to a knowledge of their fathers, and cease their barbarous and savage customs, and learn the ways of righteousness; and may those who refuse to listen to the counsels of Thy servants, and to the voice of the Holy Spirit, and will continue to shed the blood of the innocent, and who will cling to the rules and regulations of the Gadianton robbers of old, may they wither away and be destroyed, may the hand of death fall heavily upon them, and may they from this time henceforth be unable to bring evil upon Thy saints, but may Thy saints be preserved, and all the honest in heart in the midst of the mountains. Bring the Lamanites to a knowledge of Thee and of their fathers, that they may assist Thy people, and unite with them in building up the New Jerusalem in the last days, which Thou hast promised to Thy people in the midst of this land.

We now pray Thee to remember our enemies, even the enemies of Thy work and kingdom, and look upon them in the midst of Thy wrath, and in Thine hot displeasure consume them who have shed the blood of the prophet, or consented thereto, and driven and afflicted Thy saints from place to place, and those who have laid plans and concocted schemes to bring mischief upon Thy people. Let them cease to bring evil and distress upon the righteous, and, in the language of Thine ancient prophets, let them be cursed and destroyed from under heaven. Let Thy blessing, O Lord, rest bountifully upon all high-minded, honorable men, who seek to preserve unto the children of men their constitutional rights and privileges, and who do good to Thy people; and let every man who shall raise his puny arm, and exert his influence for the distruction of Thy saints, suffer Thy vengeance, and become as the dream of a night; may they pass away and their place not be known among men, nor to history.

May Thy peace dwell upon the inhabitants of Zion, and Thy blessing upon all the efforts of Thy saints in building to Thy name a temple in Great Salt Lake City; and so control the hearts of all men, that nothing shall be interposed to hinder in the least the progress of Thy work in the last days. Pour out in abundance Thy Holy Spirit in the hearts of Thy servants and handmaidens, that they may remember their prayers before Thee, and educate their children in Thy ways, and set good examples before all mankind, and may the light of Zion burst forth, and the kings of the earth soon come to the brightness of her rising, and the kingdoms of this world become the kingdoms of our Lord and His Christ.

We dedicate and devote ourselves unto Thee and unto Thy service; and we dedicate this meeting unto Thee, that it may be holy, with all that pertains thereunto; and we ask Thee to accept of our offering, and hear, O Lord, O hear this our petition, in heaven Thy dwelling place, and seal upon us the blessings of light, life, glory and peace, with all that we can desire in righteousness and use profitably for the building up of Thy kingdom and advancement of Thy work on the earth; and thus we pray unto Thee in the name of Jesus Christ: Amen.

The Spanish Fork choir sang an anthem, after which Elder Orson Hyde addressed the Saints. He remarked, This house is now dedicated to the Lord, after the many hard labors and obstructions thrown in the way of its progress to completion have been overcome; and as sure as the brethren have triumphed in accomplishing this work, so will the time come when this kingdom will triumph over all its enemies, and the top stone will be laid with hozannahs to the Lord. We may love the earth as we love the mother that gave us birth, for God has pronounced all things very good and pure to those who are pure. It is for us to attend to the duties assigned us; and so sure as we are diligent in building up the kingdom of God, we shall obtain all the riches, wealth and grandeur that we can enjoy. The Lord will withhold no good thing from them that walk uprightly. This house has been dedicated; when the foundation of this kingdom was laid it was also dedicated by the best blood that ran in the veins of mortals; and we are the honored instruments appointed to build upon that foundation that was laid in the blood of our brethren, and to prosecute the work to its glorious consummation, and labor on until iniquity and sin are banished from the earth, and this kingdom bears universal rule.

Elder John Taylor spoke of the

Elder John Taylor spoke of the almost universal darkness and blindness that have existed from the begining, showing that even God's chosen people wandered in blindness and disobedience, while living under the sound of the prophets' voices. It has remained for us to live in that day which the prophets longed to see, when the Holy Priesthood should be revealed in its fulness, giving keys and powers to mankind for the redemption of the living and the dead. We are diverse from all those people who have lived previous to this day, except Enoch and his faithful band. We are living in the direct rays of revelation from God. We know that the hand writing of the Lord is written on the wall, relating to all nations,—"You are weighed in the balances and found wanting." The priesthood of God is laid upon us, notwithstanding all our weakness and follies; God has set His name upon us, and set us apart for His service, given us His priesthood which has the right to act in His name in all the earth. Then, what manner of men ought we to be? There is a connection between us and the heavens, and God is trying to infuse into our bosoms the great principles which dwell in His own.

Pres. Young spoke a few minutes, and the meeting adjourned.

Afternoon.

The Saints met under a spacious bowery situated on the north side of the meeting house.

Elder Wilford Woodruff addressed the meeting, and dwelt upon the subject of dedicating land and houses of worship to the service of God. We have been laboring in weakness from the beginning, and when we build a house like this, and dedicate it to God, it is so much gained, and thus, being sustained by His power, we shall little by little sanctify ourselves and the earth to the Lord, and ultimately establish that kingdom which shall never have an end.

Elder Stenhouse bore testimony to the preaching of the brethren on this trip, and expressed his satisfaction at the remarks of Elder Taylor, and others, in relation to politics and religion.

Elder Geo. A. Smith then presented Cap. Hooper as delegate for Congress, who received a unanimous vote and responded as in former places.

After a few remarks from Elder Geo. A. Smith on the Homestead Act, the meeting adjourned.

Sunday, 28th, 10 a.m.

Elder H. S. Eldredge had never regretted that he had embraced the gospel. There has constantly been a desire in his heart to be faithful to his holy religion. He was glad to see the improvements made among the Saints for the last fifteen years, and the readiness with which they have responded to every call made upon them, for he had seen, when on the frontiers gathering up the Saints, hundreds of wagons and teams that had come down from the mountains for that purpose. He encouraged the Saints to pursue home industry for self-sustenance and independence.

Elder Geo. Q. Cannon said, when we

have been scattered and peeled and afflicted by the violence of our enemies, our Heavenly Father has comforted us and turned aside the evil they sought to bring upon us. The ancient prophets could see the grand consummation of all things, but the steps by which this consummation should be reached has been hidden in a great measure. It is on this account that the faith of the Saints in all ages has been and is tried. It is necessary that we should walk by faith and not by sight. The increased experience of the Saints, since our leaving Nauvoo, has created an increase of faith among the people in those men whom God has placed to preside over them. We are being taught in the best of all schools to prepare us to bear off the kingdom of God upon the earth. We are gaining knowledge in the first of all arts, that is the art of living. Our people are becoming wise in erecting buildings and in creating other conveniences. Our growth is not too fast. I would rather see the people developing slowly and surely. When nations and kingdoms are developed too rapidly they are apt to come soon to an end. Soon ripe soon rotten. This kingdom will never come to an end. Spoke of the training of our children; was glad to see the respect manifested by the schools which welcomed the President and his company while passing through the settlements to this place. The standard of training in the world is not our standard, and while we remain in the minority we appear unfavorable to them; it requires those who have knowledge like us to understand us. But what is unpopular now will in a few years become popular; then will

the gentiles come to our light, which will arise in resplendant glory in the latter days. We can wait our time with joy, for there is no blessing adapted to our circumstances to-day that God does not bestow upon us. We can worship our God without fear, while we wait the development of His purposes; for everything is ours in the gospel.

Elder Franklin D. Richards. We are here in these mountains taking solid comfort and not in homeopathic doses either. Through the joys of the gospel we forget the embarassments and trials of life. Whenever we have been obedient the triumphs of the Saints have been easy and glorious. There is a safety in following out the counsels of the servants of God which is salvation to us. He complimented the people of Nephi on the fine meeting house they had erected; he exhorted them to continue improving in architecture, to plant out good orchards and shade trees, adorning and making pleasant their city, and to be careful and energetic in having their children well educated.

After singing and prayer, meeting adjourned for an hour.

Afternoon.

Elder Lorenzo Snow addressed the congregation on the blessings to be derived from obedience to the commandments of God and hearkening to the whisperings of the Holy Spirit. We are but children in the knowledge of the truth, and as the child developes and matures so we must grow in knowledge, understanding and power. Israel of old dreaded the Egyptians, but the Almighty preserved them, led them into the wilderness, fed them there, and would have permitted them as a body of people to pass into and enjoy the promised land had it not been for their unbelief and transgressions. So will He preserve us if we are faithful and obey His will. It is satisfactory to see the progress the Saints have already made; it is encouraging; yet all we have is but committed to our stewardship. Let us live so that the power of God may be with us, and all will be well.

President Young spoke about an hour, and the meeting was dismissed.

After meeting the President and company drove back to Payson and remained there over night.

Monday, 26th.

This morning at about 6 o'clock, we pulled out from Payson, traveled to Springville and took breakfast there.

At half past eleven we started for American Fork, where we arrived about 3 p.m., and at 4 attended a meeting of the Saints.

MEETING AT AMERICAN FORK.

Elder Franklin D. Richards addressed the meeting on the advantages of union of effort among the Saints to extend the cords of Zion beyond their own limits as settlements, and in aiding each other in making public improvements.

Elder H. S. Eldredge exhorted to confidence, and expressed his gratitude for the privilege of traveling with the brethren to visit the Saints.

Elder John Taylor said, the most effectual way of blessing ourselves is to bless others; if we would do good to ourselves let us do good to others. By obedience we obtain blessings, and they will be increased upon us as we become more obedient to the will of God. He pointed out the manifest mercies of the Lord to His people and to all the human family; should we not, therefore, love, honor and obey Him? The man who fears God and keeps His commandments,—his peace shall flow like a river and his righteousness as the waves of the sea. No power can hurt the Saints if they do not hurt themselves, by neglecting to keep the laws of God and abide in His revelations.

Elder W. Jennings bore testimony, in briefness, to the work of the Lord.

Elder Wilford Woodruff said, in reading over my journals, I am astonished at the fulfillment of the prophecies of the prophet Joseph, and others, which I have written years ago. There need not any of us wish for revelation; we live in it. Can a man preside over a people like this and not have revelation? President Young governs this church by counsel, and not by commandment. If we lived under the law of Moses, we should be obliged to make all our improvements by law; but we are counseled and persuaded to do right, and this is the freedom of the gospel which we enjoy. Let us lay the counsels of God to heart. When Pres. Young rebukes, individually or collectively, his rebukes are given by the spirit and power of God and should not be trifled with. This is our probation, and the old prophets and Saints are looking upon us; let us be faithful unto death that we may have a crown of life.

Pres. Young then addressed the Saints. His remarks at the various meetings on the trip were reported phonographically and will be published in a more extended form than the synopsis of this report.

About 9 o'clock, on the morning of the 27th, the President and company rolled out of American Fork and arrived in Great Salt Lake City at 2 p.m.

During the visit, as on similar occasions, the President was greeted and welcomed by escorts bearing the flag of our nation, schools attired in their best, carrying flags with mottos of welcome inscribed upon them, and by bands of music and choirs of singers. It seemed as though the people vied with each other in their eagerness to show their hearty welcome to the prophet of God, and to his traveling companions.

G. D. WATT, Reporter.

Deseret News
August 2, 1865

JUAB COUNTY.—Bro. Samuel Pitchforth, in writing from Nephi, reports that the recent copious rains have very much improved the crops in Juab county, and the people rejoice at the prospect of an abundant harvest.

Correspondence.

PRESIDENT YOUNG'S TRIP SOUTH.

Lehi, Sept. 4, 1865.

EDITOR DESERET NEWS:

This morning at half-past ten o'clock President Brigham Young of the First Presidency, Elder Geo. Q. Cannon, and a portion of the traveling company left Great Salt Lake City to visit the settlements in the southern parts of this Territory. Elders Lorenzo Snow and E. T. Benson, started at nine o'clock, in advance of the President, and were at this place when we arrived. Elders C. C. Rich and Franklin D. Richards came up to the company at the Hot Springs, where an escort from Lehi met us. We arrived in Lehi at half-past four, and there met with Elder Geo. A. Smith who had preceded us some few days. Elder Woodruff is still behind and expected in every minute. After partaking of a public dinner we repaired to the meeting house, where a crowd of people were assembled to hold meeting.

MEETING AT LEHI.

Pres. B. Young spoke a short time, and was followed by

Elder Ezra T. Benson, who spoke of the good resulting to the Saints in the various settlements through the visits of the President and those traveling with him. The blessings of the Lord have been very visibly poured out upon His people in these valleys during the past season. The President promised last spring, at Conference, that we should have abundant crops this season, and the heavens have poured down rain in a manner never witnessed here before, causing abundant plenty to smile around, where it was supposed the crops would be a failure. The words of President Young have been fulfilled, and the people have received the promised blessing, as they will always do so long as they keep the commandments of God.

Elder Geo. Q. Cannon:—We enjoy blessings that we cannot comprehend in their fullness. One thing we can understand and put into practice,—we can be obedient, and we can be humble. God has given unto us this power, and we know what the result will be of our hearkening unto the counsels of His servants. We have never been in any circumstance but what we could, if we lived for it, enjoy the Spirit of the Most High. You may surround such a people with the most adverse circumstances, and they cannot be crushed, for they know the power that will deliver them and give them the victory. There is every incentive for us to be diligent and faithful. We live in a dispensation in which we know the gospel will be triumphant and the Priesthood will rule throughout the whole earth. We have no cause to fear. The path we are traveling in is endless; and if we pursue it faithfully we shall be brought back into the presence of God.

Many of our elders have gone as missionaries to the nations and have left their families among us. These should

should dispense to them a portion of the blessings which God has so abundantly bestowed upon us; and I have no doubt but what the Saints will respond to any call that may be made upon them.

Elder Charles C. Rich said he remembered the time when he was called upon to come out to the Rocky Mountains to hunt out a home for the Saints. He had a large family and little for them to live upon. He believed it was the word of the Lord and he left his family in the hands of God, and they were provided for. There is a class of individuals who have followed the counsels of their own hearts to make wealth, but the advantage has always been on the side of those who have obeyed the counsels of the servants of God. How can the Lord use us build up His kingdom if He cannot dictate us. If we cannot be controled and dictated by His servants we cannot be controled and dictated by Him. Some imagine they must have a special call to build up the kingdom of God; but there is room enough for all to labor in this work, if they are disposed to do so. It is the duty of all to learn what is right and then do it. When there is no manner of iniquities practiced in our midst, then we will not be afflicted with evil, and the blessings of God will be upon all that we possess.

Elder Lorenzo Snow:—I would not be afraid to predict riches on the heads of the Saints, if they would keep the commandments of God and be at all times willing to properly dispose of that which the Lord gives to them. When we receive the glory which God has for us, we shall discover that the path of poverty is but a small portion of experience. Job loved God and loved to keep His commandments better than he did riches. The Lord will fulfil His promises to this people, and they will be rich in all things, but they should not wait until they are rich before they learn to exercise the principles of generosity. He enjoined upon the Saints the importance of being counseled by the Lord, through His servants, and in all things seeking to keep His com-

Pres. Young, in behalf of the company, returned thanks to the bishop and people of Lehi, for the kind hospitality which they had shown to him and his company in passing and repassing through this settlement. He then blessed the people and dismissed them.

Sept., 5th.

We partook of a public breakfast at half past nine this morning and rolled out of Lehi for Goshen, which we reached after a dusty drive at a quarter past three o'clock.

The west side of Utah Lake is the least adapted for agricultural purposes, but presents the finest view of the Lake, and the romantic scenery which surrounds it. Here we have a succession of promontaries, bays and inlets. We can see almost at a glance 200 square miles of water, with an average depth of twelve feet; and it is not difficult to see in a future day, when our contemplated canal is opened from the source of Jordan to Great Salt Lake City, a profitable traffic established, by means of this lake, between the northern and southern settlements of Utah.

GOSHEN

is situated on the south extremity of Utah Lake, upon a low clay soil of an indefinite depth, largely impregnated with alkali salts in the subsoil. The houses are built of logs, mud etc. We passed through this city two years ago, and we are able to see some progress in its growth; but a green tree is difficult to be found, for the people think that fruit cannot be raised here, and they will no doubt continue to believe so until they plant the trees and make the experiment.

After we got the dust so far cleansed out of our eyes, off our faces and clothes as to make us look like white folks, and had refreshed ourselves with the good things which the land of Goshen provides, we repaired to a comfortable, well put up and well seated bowery, situated on the south side of a good log schoolhouse to hold meeting. Bishop Woolley opened the meeting with prayer, and

Elder F. D. Richards, arose to address the meeting. This was the first time he had ever visited Goshen, and he was thankful to meet with a healthy and cheerful company of Latter-day Saints here. The Lord has brought us to these mountains to rest from the persecutions our former friends would heap upon us, and that we might gain strength in the service of the Lord. We are here to increase in strength, in power and in faith and holiness before the Lord, and to keep the law of God which we could not keep in the lands of our nativity. The Saints are increasing in faith and good works, and greatly in numbers; the little stone is becoming a strong nation. Here we have peace. In the morning we can kneel before the Lord in our families, and invoke His blessing; in the evening we can call upon His name, and offer thanks to Him; and we can grow up in Christ our living head. Here we can realize the hand of God made manifest for the salvation of His people; and our hope is made bright that in the future we shall still enjoy the favor of God, and our generations after us. Let us keep the covenants we have made with the Lord and with one another, and never submit to sin, that we may attain to all the gospel promises unto us.

President Young spoke for half an hour.

Elder E. T. Benson:—Your circumstances here this evening are very different from what they were some eight years ago. Then there were but a few people here; now there is quite a little settlement. The object of our coming to see you is to speak the truth, and if you are in the dark to bring you to the truth. If the people here do not practice upon the good instructions which they hear this evening, they will be worse off next year than they are at present. Get the Spirit of the Lord, and the spirit of the times which is to improve the land that the Lord our God has given unto us, planting trees and shrubs and vines to make genial shades, and to produce fruit which is good for man. When we have not a green thing to afford shade, the rays of the burning sun are distressingly uncomfortable. Plant out currant trees, and trees of every kind here, that will yield fruit for your children to eat, and to shade them and their mothers when they are out of doors. Obey the counsel of the President, and in so doing you will bless yourselves.

Elder Lorenzo Snow.—Had we come to this Territory and done nothing in the way of improvement, the Lord would not have been satisfied with us. It is a part of the gospel of salvation to attend to these improvements in the name of the Lord, doing what we do as a matter of duty that we owe to the Almighty. It is the business of the Saints in the last days to build cities in the name of the Lord. We should not go about this business as the world does. There is nothing discouraging to the people of Goshen if they do everything the Lord has given them ability to perform.

The speaker gave a brief history of his mission to Box Elder, and continued,—Anything accomplished in the way of improvement is not done without considerable exertion. In a few years we shall see beautiful orchards here, and shade trees, and good houses to live in, and good houses to worship our God in; and your young men and maidens will grow up in improvement and in the fear of the Lord; and this visit will be the moving cause of this beneficial change. We must use our means and our talents to accomplish all that is required of us. Follow the counsels given by the servants of God, and you will prosper and your hearts shall be glad and you shall see the salvation of God.

Elder C. C. Rich spoke on the principle of making home into heaven,—but it was too dark to report after him.

Meeting dismissed by Elder Geo. Q. Cannon.

September 6.

The company rolled out at a quarter past eight o'clock this morning, accompanied by a few of the brethren and sisters of Goshen to the southern line of their "Big Field," where we passed through an arch composed of fresh cedar bows intermingled with flowers and mock oranges, with a motto, "We shall," crowning the whole. This motto of two words was suggested by a remark made by the President last evening in the meeting. He proposed to exchange the name of Goshen for "Shall I?" as being more appropriate to the vacillating state of the minds of the people in that place, as to whether they shall commence and improve by planting trees and building good houses or not. We traveled over a new road through a kanyon, which saved many miles travel, and arrived at Nephi at one o'clock.

MEETING AT NEPHI.

At four o'clock we met the people in their new meeting house.

Prayer by Elder Geo. Q. Cannon.

Elder Ezra T. Benson.—This is the fourth trip south which the President has made this season, in company with his brethren, not because we have not business to attend to at home, but our object in visiting the Saints is to encourage them to be faithful, to magnify their Priesthood and build up the kingdom of God on the earth. I can bear my testimony that a great deal of good results to the Saints from these visits, not only in encouraging the Saints to work righteousness, and exercise increased diligence in spiritual matters, but the roads are made better, the bridges are mended and new ones made, new and better boweries and places of worship are built, and there is a general spirit of improvement made manifest. The people are also made to realize that there is a prophet in the land, through whom God speaks to His people; and the Saints are cheered and comforted and built up in their most holy faith. We have peace around us to-day, and we have the privilege of worshipping God without molestation. Since the Saints have been led to these valleys have we not prospered? We have; and the man who has been the most strict in obeying the voice of the servants of God has been prospered the most. We are apt to be lifted up in the pride of our hearts in the days of our prosperity, and we are not so humble before the Lord. We may love money and prosperity, but there is no enjoyment like that that is enjoyed through obedience to the gospel of the Son of God. There is no situation in life in which so much satisfaction can be enjoyed as in doing our duty towards God and one another; and this is the channel through which God will bless, happify and exalt mankind. Why should not our feet be fast in these mountains? We have the wisdom, the light, the Priesthood and the power of God with us; and if this fail us it is because we are not faithful. We are not led by the imaginations of men's hearts, nor by dreams and visions given to this person or that, but we are led by the prophet of God, and his word inspired

by the Almighty is our guiding star.

It is very easy for us to defile ourselves before the Lord, and cause Him to hide His face from us. This is not done all at once, but it comes about by our first refusing to perform some duty required of us, and then continuing in the downward path.

Elder Charles C. Rich said, it is our privilege to so learn and comprehend the principles that pertain to the kingdom of God that we can adopt them in our lives. It would be better for us if we did this more than we do. We have been taught by the traditions of our fathers that we must go away from this earth to find heaven. I want to stay on this earth and get wisdom and knowledge to make myself and everybody more happy. When our President speaks to the people he tells them how to make their heaven here. He teaches them to live righteously, to build good houses and plant trees for fruit and shade, and we see the result of this kind of teaching; we see heaven springing up in our homes by carrying out his instructions. If we are not willing to be governed by the principles of truth in this world, I do not think we shall be willing to do it in another world. Some people think that we shall learn the principles that govern in the heavens all at once, when we pass through the vail of death. I cannot see that we can attain to this knowledge there in any different way from we do here,—by learning one truth at one time, and progressing from one truth to another. Our whole object and aim should be to do right; and to do this we must be subject to the dictation of those who know what is right.

The Lord has said he will prove us in all things, and to be prepared to be thus proved we must be found ready and wide awake, and faithful in every duty, little or great, that we may be saved in this world and in the world to come.

Elder Wilford Woodruff.—I have been acquainted with President Young for over thirty years as an Elder in Israel, and I have never heard him give counsel that was not followed with blessings to those that obeyed it. The Lord has made us free agents, and if we wish to travel the path to heaven we must obey the laws that will guide us there. In my visits with the President among the Saints I discover an increasing spirit of obedience and union among the people. The Saints should be united in elections, as in building a temple, or in doing anything else that is required of them. Unless we carry out this principle in all our acts and labors we do not feel right and we cannot prosper. I want to see all the Latter-day Saints united upon the principles of life and salvation. The Lord has given us the Holy Priesthood to save ourselves, our wives, our children and our dead. Whenever the Saints are disunited upon anything, their progress in holiness stops right there. We are free agents and can go to heaven or to hell as we please; but upon the matter of the kingdom of God we must be willing to be united as one man if we desire to receive salvation,

for it is upon this principle that the heavens are governed. We are called to build up this kingdom, and no greater honor was ever conferred upon any beings in heaven or on the earth.

Elder F. D. Richards.—A few years ago this place was a wilderness in the possession of Indians; now, here are hundreds of Saints in good and happy circumstances, with an excellent house in which to worship God, and they are visited by the servants of the Most High who gives them words of life or words of death as they are obeyed or disobeyed by the people. A great deal depends, some times, upon little things, which lie at the foundation of our faith, the which if we neglect, will be ruinous to our progress. No man has a right to choose to do wrong, but all have a right to choose to do right; and if we choose to do wrong the consequences will fall upon our own heads. This is the state of feeling and society which the enemies of truth desire to bring about among this people. No people can be excused when they become divided where there are inspired men of God to guide and counsel them.

Elder Geo. A. Smith made a few remarks upon the late election; after which Bishop Bryant offered some explanations, and

Pres. Brigham Young followed for a short time on the same subject, when the meeting was dismissed.

We attended a party at eight o'clock; the dancing was continued with an unflagging spirit until a late hour. The President retired early.

Yours, etc.,
Geo. D. Watt.

Correspondence.

CONTINUATION OF PRESIDENT YOUNG'S TRIP SOUTH.

Sept. 7, 1865,

EDITOR DESERET NEWS:

Took our journey from Nephi at 8 a. m., drove against a head wind and through clouds of dust all day, arriving in Round Valley at 4 p. m. Elders F. D. Richards and A. M. Musser parted from the company at Chicken Creek settlement to visit Gunnison and the settlements on the Sevier, expecting to join the company again at St. George. They were accompanied by a sufficient escort of mounted men for safty. Bishop Callister arrived here this morning and several brethren with him from Fillmore, among whom were the Fillmore brass band. Improvements in this place have been limited since the President's last visit; considerable labor has been expended this year, however, in getting more water to the settlements. One saw mill has been put up; but their grinding is done at Fillmore, twenty-four miles from Round Valley. There are about forty families in the settlement.

Died:

In Nephi, Juab co., Oct. 25, FRANKLIN R. infant son of Edward and Esther Oekey, aged 14 months and 8 days.

Died.

In Nephi, Juab Co., Nov. 24th, ALVA S., son of Alva and Anna Foster, aged 2 years, 8 months and 2? days; also the next day their daughter JANE SOPHIA, aged 8 years, 6 months and 9 days.

Utah Produce Company

—:o:—

PROSPECTUS.

THE excessive fluctuations in the price of the products of this Territory, and of flour more particularly, that have hitherto occurred, have operated alike injuriously to both the producer and the consumer, until it has become a matter of necessity that some efficient action be taken to remedy this evil, and secure to the citizens of this and adjacent Territories, as nearly as the nature of circumstances will permit, a uniform price for a reliable brand of flour. And inasmuch as all previous efforts to accomplish this, have been at best partially successful, (consequent upon their being based on individual action, and the necessities of many having compelled them to sell flour at a sacrifice, that the condition of the market did not warrant;) we now propose that a Company be formed, of sufficient capital to obviate the necessity of selling, except at a fair price; and thus to insure to the producer, remunerative rates for his products, and at the same time to supply our neighbors constantly, with a first class article of flour, at a price so low as to supercede the necessity of its importation from California, Oregon, or the Missouri river. The necessity of this measure is so obvious, that we confidently expect the co-operation and favor, not only of the citizens of this Terrieory, but those of Idaho and Montana also, and are sanguine that all parties concerned will be benefitted to the extent that this and kindred associations become general. For the accomplishment of this end, we recommend the formation of similar Companies in the principal settlements of this Territory, which, to work harmoniously, it is deemed important should act in unison with and under the direction of this the parent association.

It is also proposed that this Company act as Storage and Commission Merchants, both in this city and in Montana, to receive flour and other produce from the companies to be formed in the various settlements, as well as from individuals, and, as soon as the finances of this Company will permit, to make advances on all consignments.

CONSTITUTION.

Sec. 1. The name of this Company shall be the Utah Produce Company, and its duration shall not be less than three years.

Sec. 2. The amount of its Capital Stock shall be One Hundred Thousand Dollars, to be increased when deemed necessary by the Stockholders representing two-thirds of the paid-up Stock, to be divided into shares of one hundred dollars each.

Sec. 3. The Company are fully authorized to do business, when two hundred shares are subscribed.

Sec. 4. The business of the Company shall be to deal in grain, flour, and such other commodities as the President and Directors may think proper, both by purchase and on commission and of transporting the same to market for sale.

Sec. 5. The powers of the Company shall be exercised by a President and Five Directors, who shall appoint a Treasurer and Secretary. The Treasurer shall give such bonds as the President and Secretary may require.

Sec. 6. The President and Directors shall be elected by the Stockholders, and hold office for one year, or until their successors are elected and enter upon the duties of their office.

Sec. 7. No person shall be eligible for office, who is not both a Stockholder and a resident of this Territory. All officers are eligible for re-election.

Sec. 8. Whenever deemed necessary by the President and Directors to call a meeting of the Stockholders, the Secretary shall give ten days' notice of the time and place thereof, by publication in some local newspaper.

Sec. 9. A number of persons representing more than one half of the paid-up Stock, are necessary to constitute a quorum to do business in all general meetings of the Stockholders. Each person shall be entitled to as many votes as he holds shares.

Sec. 10. The Secretary shall keep the books of the Company, which shall be subject to the inspection of the Stockholders, including a book containing the names of all the Stockholders and when they became such, together with the number of shares held by each respectively.

Sec. 11. The President and Directors shall have power to make such bye-laws as they may deem necessary for the business of the Company.

Sec. 12. A dividend of profits shall be declared and paid every six months.

Sec. 13. This Constitution may be altered or amended by a vote of the Stockholders, representing two-thirds of the paid-up stock.

TO THE MILLERS OF UTAH.

We beg to inform you that a Company has been formed in this city, called the "Utah Produce Company," with a capital of One Hundred Thousand Dollars, for the purpose of dealing in flour and other home products, the former being its speciality. The object of the company is to obtain for the farmer a remunerative price for his grain, by securing to the consumer, both in this Territory and elsewhere, a brand of superfine flour uniformly good; and for the furtherance of this object, we solicit your aid and co-operation, by doing all in your power to prevent any but fine flour, free from shorts, from leaving your mills; and suggest that you make only two qualities of flour—the first to be branded with the name of the mills and "SS", to be equal in quality to Tanner's and Allen's "SS", and another, branded SS extra, of a still finer grade. Special care should also be taken that each sack contains 98 pounds.

Thus we will immediately raise the reputation of our flour, and, as a consequence, its commercial value. That you may realize to what extent we have injured ourselves by sending indifferent flour to the mining districts, we would call your attention to the quotations made in the *Montana Post* of September last for the different kinds of flour, viz:—

St. Louis, for Sack of 98 lbs.,			$28.00
States,	"	"	24.00
Salt Lake,	"	"	18.00

Now if we cannot at present make as fine flour as that made in St. Louis (although some of our wheat is equal to any in the world), we certainly can make at least as good an article as that known as "States," and by doing so get six dollars per sack more for it in gold. The difference between the cost per sack consists simply in the difference in value of about 8 lbs of shorts and the same quantity of flour, which you are aware will not exceed fifty cents. Hence we find we have been losers of five dollars and-a-half per sack, sold in Montana, and as FORTY THOUSAND SACKS have been shipped from this Territory to that market during the past season, TWO HUNDRED AND TWENTY THOUSAND DOLLARS have been lost to the people of Utah in one year. Does not this imperatively demand that efficient steps be at once taken to remedy the evil and put a stop to this "penny wise and pound foolish" policy?

Much more on this subject could be said, but we believe enough has been mentioned to enlist your attention and induce you to unite your efforts with ours for the accomplishment of this public good.

E. HUNTER, President.
L. S. HILLS, Secretary.

A. O. SMOOT,
H. S. ELDREDGE,
JOHN SHARP,   } Directors.
H. W. LAWRENCE,
W. S. GODBE.

Great Salt Lake City,
March 19, 1869.

w-3t

[BY AUTHORITY.]

AN ACT.

Defining the boundaries of Counties and locating County seats.

SEC. 1. Be it enacted by the Governor and Legislative Assembly of the Territory of Utah: That all that portion of Utah Territory bounded north by a line running due east from a point four miles north of the north east corner of Fort Harmony, east by Colordo Territory, south by Arizona, and west by a line running due north from the southern boundary of Utah Territory, passing through the largest mineral spring at the mouth of the Rio Virgen kanyon, until it reaches the summit of the dividing ridge between the Leverkin and Ash creeks, thence north-easterly along the summit of dividing ridge to its intersection with the line first above mentioned, is hereby made and named Kane County, with County seat at Grafton.

SEC. 2. All that portion of the Territory bounded north by a line running due west from the northern boundary of Kane County, east by Kane County, south by Arizona, and west by Nevada is hereby made and named Washington County, with county seat at St. George.

SEC. 3. All that portion of the Territory bounded south by Washington and Kane Counties, west by Nevada, north by a due east and west line crossing the military road on the summit of the ridge dividing Little Salt Lake and upper Beaver Valleys, and east by Colorado Territory is hereby made and named Iron County, with county seat at Parowan.

SEC. 4 All that portion of the Territory bounded south by Iron County, west by Nevada, north by a line running due east and west through a point two miles due south from the south side of Fort Wilden on Cove Creek, and east by the range of mountains dividing Beaver and Panvan Valleys from the Valley of the Sevier is hereby made and named Beaver County, with county seat at Beaver.

SEC. 5. All that portion of the Territory bounded south by Iron County, west by Beaver County, north by an east and west line crossing the road on the summit of the dividing ridge between Mary's Vale and Alma, and east by Colorado is hereby made and named Piute County, with county seat at Circleville.

SEC. 6. All that portion of the Territory bounded south by Beaver County, west by Nevada, east by the summit of the mountains separating the Sevier from Panvan and Round Valleys, following said summit east of the lake in Round Valley and north of Round Valley to its intersection with the Sevier river, thence down the channel of said river to the mouth of its lower kanyon, thence due west to Nevada is hereby made and named Milliard County, with county seat at Fillmore.

SEC. 7. All that portion of the Territory bounded south by Piute County, west by Milliard County, north by an east and west line crossing the road at the ford of Willow Creek between Gunnison and Salina, and east by Colorado is hereby made and named Sevier County, with county seat at Richfield.

SEC. 8 All that portion of the Territory bounded south by Milliard County, west by a line drawn due north from the north line of Milliard County to the most western peak in the range of mountains between Tintic Valley and Meadow Creek, thence along the summit of said range to its intersection with the range between Tintic and Rush Valleys, north of the summit of the range between Tintic and Rush Valleys and the summit of the range between Tintic Valley and Cedar and Goshen Valleys and the summit of the range between Goshen and Juab Valleys and the summit of the high ground and range between Utah and Juab Valleys, and east by the summit of the Nebo range of mountains

to the highest southern peak of said range of mountains, thence on a straight line south-westerly to the north boundary of Milliard County, crossing the Sevier river at the upper Bluff Rock at the south end of Cedar ridge is hereby made and named Juab County, with county seat at Nephi.

SEC. 9. All that portion of the Territory bounded south by Sevier County, west by Juab County, north by the summit of the range of mountains between Sanpete Valley and Spanish Fork river and along the summit of said range until it intersects Green river, thence by a line drawn due east from said intersection to the thirty-second meridan west from Washington city, and east by said meridan is hereby made and named Sanpete County, with county seat at Manti. *Provided*, that the hay ground of Thistle Valley shall be included in Sanpete County.

SEC. 10. All that portion of the Territory bounded south by Juab and Sanpete Counties, west by the summit of the range between Cedar and Rush Valleys, north by the summit of the cross range between the Oquirh and Wasatch mountains, east by the summit of the range passing around the head of Dry, American Fork, Battle, Hobble and Spanish Fork creeks and a line drawn due north and south across Provo river, at a point one-fourth of a mile above the north fork of Deer creek of said river, to intersect at each extremity of said line the summit of the last named range, is hereby made and named Utah County, with County seat at Provo.

SEC. 11. All that portion of the Territory bounded south by Utah and Sanpete Counties, west by Utah and Great Salt Lake Counties, north by the summit of the range of mountains south of the head waters of East Kanyon and Silver creeks, following said summit to the points where the road leading to Great Salt Lake City and Rhodes' Valley crosses, thence south to Provo river at the high bluff below Goddard's ranch, thence along the channel of said river to its head waters, thence easterly to the summit of the range of mountains north of Uintah Valley, thence along the last named summit and south of Brown's Hole to the thirty-second meridan west from Washington City, and east by said meridan is hereby made and named Wasatch County, with county seat at Heber City.

SEC. 12. All that portion of the Territory bounded south by Utah County, west by the summit of the range of mountains between Great Salt Lake and Tooele Valleys, and a line running from the northern termination of said summit through Black Rock on the south shore of Great Salt Lake, north by the shore of said

Lake easterly to the mouth of Jordan river, thence by the centre of the channel of said river to a point due west from the Hot Springs north of Great Salt Lake City, thence by a line running due east to said Hot Springs, thence by the summit of the spur range terminating at said Hot Springs to its intersection with the summit of the Wasatch mountains, and east by the summit of said mountains is hereby made and named Great Salt Lake County, with county seat at Great Salt Lake City.

Sec. 13. All the islands in Great Salt Lake are hereby attached to Great Salt Lake County for election, revenue and judicial purposes; and judicial jurisdiction of all acts and transactions done or entered into on the waters of Great Salt Lake and on so much of its beach as is not included in any county is hereby given to Great Salt Lake County and the Judicial District to which said county at the time belongs.

Sec. 14. All that portion of the Territory bounded south by Great Salt Lake County, west by the eastern shore of Great Salt Lake, north by a line running due east from a point on said shore to a point in the centre of the channel of Weber river due north from the northwest corner of Kingston Fort, thence up the centre of said channel to a point opposite the summit of the Wasatch mountains, and east by the summit of said mountains is hereby made and named Davis County, with county seat at Farmington.

Sec. 15. All that portion of the Territory bounded south by Davis County and the dividing ridge between Ogden Hole and Weber Valley, west by the eastern shore of Great Salt Lake, north by a line drawn due east from a point on said shore to the Hot Springs by the Territorial road north of Ogden City, thence by the summit of the spur range terminating at said Hot Springs to its intersection with the summit of the Wasatch mountains, east by the summit of said mountains, passing around the head waters of Ogden river, is hereby made and named Weber County, with county seat at Ogden City.

Sec. 16. All that portion of the Territory bounded south by Weber County, thence by the shore of Great Salt Lake, following said shore around the head of Bear River Bay, Promontory Point, the north end of said Lake, and thence southeasterly to a point where it is intersected by latitude forty-one degrees north, thence by said latitude to the summit of Pilot Peak, thence due south thirty minutes of latitude, thence by latitude forty degrees and thirty minutes north, west by Nevada, north by latitude forty-two degrees, and east by the summit of the range of mountains east of Malad Valley, crossing Bear river at the centre of its lower kanyon, and thence southerly along the summit of the Wasatch mountains and passing around the head waters of Box Elder and Willow creeks is hereby made and named Box Elder County, with county seat at Brigham City.

Sec. 17. All that portion of the Territory bounded south by Juab and Milliard Counties, west by Nevada, north by Box Elder County, and east by the west and south shores of Great Salt Lake and Great Salt Lake and Tooele Counties is hereby made and named Tooele County, with county seat at Tooele City.

Sec. 18. All that portion of the Territory bounded south by Wasatch County, west by Great Salt Lake County, north by the summit of the range of mountains forming the upper kanyon of East Kanyon creek, thence northerly along the summit of the range of mountains between said creek and Weber river, thence across said river to, and along the summit of the high land between Pumbar or Lost and Echo Kanyon creeks, thence to, and along the summit next north of Yellow creek to Bear river, thence easterly across said river to the summit of the divide between Bear river and the tributaries of Green river, and east by the summit of said range is hereby made and named Summit County, with county seat at Wanship.

Sec. 19. All that portion of the Territory bounded south and east by Summit County, west by Great Salt Lake, Davis and Weber Counties, and north by Weber County and a line running from a point in the eastern boundary of Weber County nearest the most eastern head waters of Ogden river along the summit of the high lands or range passing around the head waters of Pumbar or Lost creek easterly to the point where the north boundary of Summit County crosses Bear river is hereby made and named Morgan County, with county seat at Littleton.

Sec. 20. All that portion of the Territory bounded south by Morgan, Weber and Box Elder Counties, west by Box Elder County, north by latitude forty-two degrees north, and east by the summit of the ridge of mountains between Cache and Bear Lake Valleys is hereby made and named Cache County, with county seat at Logan City.

Sec. 21. All that portion of the Territory bounded south by Summit and Morgan Counties, west by Cache County, north by latitude forty-two degrees north, and east by the summit of the divide between the waters of Bear river and the tributaries of Green river is hereby made and named Richland County, with county seat at St. Charles.

Sec. 22. All that portion of the Territory bounded south by Wasatch County, west by Summit and Richland Counties, north by latitude forty-two degrees north, and east by Colorado and Dacotah Territories is hereby made and named Green River County, with county seat at Fort Bridger.

Sec. 23. When any uncertainty or dispute arises as to what county an act or transaction has transpired in, either of the counties in which it is fairly presumable such act or transaction has occurred is hereby authorized to have jurisdiction in the case.

Sec. 24. All laws in relation to the boundaries of counties and locating county seats, conflicting with this Act, are hereby repealed

Approved January 16th, 1866.

Deseret News
July 12, 1866

LATEST FROM JUAB.—Through the courtesy of Elder R. L. Campbell, we learn, by letter to him from Elder S. Pitchforth, that the people of Juab Co. in general and of Nephi in particular, are prospering and on the alert to protect themselves and property against any attack from marauding savages. A careful distribution of men was being made, at date of writing, 2nd inst., to watch for some Indians, supposed to be in the mountains contiguous from certain signs that seemed to indicate their presence.

Deseret News
August 16, 1866

Correspondence.

NEPHI, Juab Co., August 4th, 1866.
EDITOR DESERET NEWS,

DEAR BROTHER:—There was every prospect of raising this season the largest amount of grain ever raised in this county until yesterday, when we were visited by one of the severest storms ever before known in this region.

About 1 p.m. of yesterday the wind began to blow briskly from the south, and in a short time immense clouds of dust came rolling along, causing for a short time almost total darkness, and the rain began to fall in torrents.

The great amount of damage done to our crops can not at present be fully realized or estimated. Wheat and Oats are beaten to the ground, which will cause much more labor in order to secure the crops. There is every reason to believe that late wheat (of which there is considerable) will be much injured by the rust which has already made its appearance. The storm has also done much damage to the crops at Chicken Creek and Clover Creek settlements.

Since my last I am sorry to have to report that a little boy, of about ten years of age, the son of one of the "Battalion Boys" our late worthy brother James C. Sly, had his arm much injured by falling from a mule. The injury done was so great that amputation became necessary, which was performed by Dr. Lane, of Springville. The little fellow is doing well, but mourns over the loss of his arm.

The settlement at Clover Creek is being built up under the management of Elder Edward Kay, and I am pleased to report that the inhabitants of that place have built a large and substantial School House, which is so far finished as to be of use.

Very respectfully,
SAMUEL PITCHFORTH.

Deseret News
September 6, 1866

Died:

In Nephi City, Juab Co., August 25, AXIE MELISSA, infant daughter of Henry and Susannah Goldsbrough, aged 1 year, 4 months and 15 days.

UNITED STATES MAIL, UTAH TERRITORY.

POST OFFICE DEPART-MENT, WASHINGTON, October 31, 1866.

PROPOSALS will be received at the Contract Office of this Department until 3 P. M. of February 15, 1867, for conveying the mails of the United States in the Territory of Utah, from July 1, 1867, to June 30, 1870, on the routes and by the schedules of departures and arrivals herein specified. (Being routes established by Acts of Congress approved March 14, and July 18 and 26, 1866—and others)

Decisions announced by February 23, 1867.

16,627 From Nephi, by Severe Valley and Fort Gunnison, to Saint George, 245 miles and back, once a week. Leave Nephi Monday at 7 A. M.; arrive at Saint George Friday by 7 P. M., leave Saint-George Monday at 7 A. M., arrive at Nephi Friday by 7 P. M.

16,628 From Logan to Oxford, 25 miles and back, once a week. Leave Logan Monday at 7 A. M.; arrive at Oxford by 5 P. M.; leave Oxford Tuesday at 7 A M.; arrive at Logan by 5 P. M.

16,629 From Huntsville to Bennington, 20 miles and back, once a week. Leave Huntsville Monday at 6 A. M., arrive at Bennington by 12 M.; leave Bennington Monday at 1 P. M., arrive at Huntsville by 7 P. M.

16,630 From Logan to Dexton, 25 miles and back, once a week. Leave Logan Monday at 7 A. M.; arrive at Dexton by 5 P. M.; leave Dexton Tuesday at 7 A. M., arrive at Logan by 5 P. M.

16,631 From Lehi, by Cedar Valley, to Fairfield, 15 miles and back, once a week. Leave Lehi Tuesday at 7 A. M.; arrive at Fairfield by 12 M.; leave Fairfield Tuesday at 1 P. M.; arrive at Lehi by 6 P. M.

For Form of Proposals, Guaranty and Certificate, and for instructions, requirements, &c., bidders are referred to the general advertisement of Utah routes, dated July 31, 1865, at the principal Post offices.

ALEX. W. RANDALL,
Postmaster General.

de8-4w}

A Southern Railroad.

ormer issues we called attention to the importance of a railroad hence through rn Utah to Pahranagat valley in South- evada, and connecting with the head- of the Colorado river at or above Call-

Indeed, it be not already demonstrated, nt facts have been developed to give onable assurance that the Colorado river tined soon to become an important in the conveyance of freight to the in- of the continent, and the channel for portation of the rich ores of Arizona and plus products of Southern Utah. It o said to be navigable for a certain of steamers for a distance of at least undred miles from its mouth. The t so-called head of navigation is but three hundred and fifty miles from the f Great Salt Lake, and presents the t and most feasible means of bringing marts the goods and necessaries now ed to long overland travel.

ing to California, the distance over plains and rugged snow clad moun- to the head-waters of the Sacramento, ards of six hundred miles; eastwardly, distant from the Missouri river more welve hundred miles. Over the one or her of these two routes come all our

s, not only for home consumption, but stribution to the Northern and Southern ents of Utah, and Montana Territory. Eastern route is absolutely closed to trains, from November to April by of want of feed for cattle and mules, the Western can scarcely be said to be

Yet it is a fact that goods can be ited from San Francisco to the mouth of Colorado by sailing vessels at little greater o than from the same point to Sacra- , and can be laid down at Callville from York or Boston at less actual cost than hison or Omaha, or the Missouri river. the Amazon is to South America, and ather of Waters to the Mississippi Valley, lorado is to the rich fields of Arizona opulous parts of Southern Utah.

to make it practicably available to us, ed a railroad from this city to some point t river. In a former article we suggested uch a road would probably connect at ur Pahranagat with a road already pro- from San Francisco via Los Angeles an Bernardino to the head-waters of the ado, and eventually become an import- uxiliary, if not the main trunk of the Atlantic and Pacific Railway. We see by California press is taking the same f the subject and pressing it upon the ion of capitalists. The *Alta* some time spoke encouragingly of the project, and ockton *Independent*, referring to a former in this paper, says:

VIDETTE tells us that the road can be
ly built, as there are no high mountains
come, and for the same reason can be
d the year round. There is no snow
be crossed This railway is of quite as
importance to San Francisco as to Salt
and the Chamber of Commerce ought
less a communication to the Senators
representatives from the Pacific States,
them to use all honorable means to
built as soon as possible—securing all
vernment aid they can toward the enter-

San Francisco capital ought, more-
to invest largely in its stock. But it
l not terminate at the head of Colorado
ation. The proper and western terminus
an Francisco; striking across the Colo-
t the Rapids, thence over the table lands
vidence Mountain, into San Bernardino,
rough that county and Los Angeles into
ad of the Tulare Valley by one of the
or four passes near Kern Lake; from
a point of intersection with the West-
acific Railroad, at or near the city of
ton.

argue that San Francisco, having a
r interest in it than any other part of
ald, ought, by her influence and capital,
d this road. It would place her forever
d the reach of rivalry on the Pacific;
without counting anything upon her
gh trade with the East, by the way trade,
avel alone, would more than double her
rce. It would form the trunk of a
great railway system, tapping Los An-
Owen's Valley, the country of central
na, (useless without railways,) but es-
lly the great valley of San Joaquin, which
largest body of good agricultural land
of the Missouri river, mostly of little
ut now, because shut out from a market.
behooves Utah to bestir herself in this

r. On no part of the continent –not
up the level valley of the Platte– could
road be constructed at less cost per mile
from here to Callville. Very little grad-
excavating would be necessary, no large
ns to be spanned with costly bridges, and
ly a hillock to be leveled. For three
red miles the road would pass through a
settled and fertile region abounding in
ng cities, towns, and settlements. Ameri-
olk, Provo, Springville, Nephi, Fillmore,
an, Cedar, St. George and others, being
ost prominent.

rould not be amiss for the Legislature,
will meet to-day, to appoint a commit-
gather, or rather compile the statistics
nd, relative to the population, resources,
cts, etc., of Southern Utah, and embody
in an authentic report. Capital East
West is seeking objects of remunerative
tment, and we know of none which prom-
Larger results than a railroad over the
suggested. To Utah and her every inter-
would be invaluable.

...e first Victims of the Crusade.

...he "council" of the Church leaders, which ...recently been the subject of the interest ...correspondence between the Gentile mer- ...nts of this city and Brigham Young, is ...ing its effect. It may, and probably will ...gratifying to those leaders to know that ...ever little effect, the Church order may ...on the proscribed Gentiles here, in ...outer counties and more remote settle- ...ts the interdiction of trade with Gentiles ...eing implicitly obeyed. In Nephi, about ...hundred miles south of this city, the Gen- ...firm of Firman & Munson has been com- ...ed to close its doors. One of the firm was ...berly a Lieutenant in the Nevada Volunteers ...the other a Lieutenant in the Michi- ...Cavalry. Not long since, with a degree ...nterprise which seemed so sadly wanting ...he Mormons themselves, these gentlemen ...hased a stock of goods and opened a ...ral store at the place named. They were ...g a thriving trade, and the people of the ...hborhood were not compelled as formerly ...nd to Salt-Lake City whenever they want- ...pound of sugar, or a new calico dress. ...ct the establishment was a great conven- ...e to the people. No word of complaint ...ever been urged against either of the firm ...eing bad citizens or obnoxious to the Mor- ...s—except that they are Gentiles. The ...r day they were waited on, informed of ...Church counsel forbidding trade with Gen-

and their business was broken up. They look elsewhere for custom, no matter important or convenient their enterprise be to the people, for the fiat has gone ... In this city, it is true that Mormons ...ell as Gentiles do a little thinking for ...selves, and despite the Church thunders ...ormer exercise a little independence in ...matter of trade. But in the settlements ...is no influence to break or expose the ...ch tyranny, and the Bishops are masters ...e situation. When Simon says "wiggle- ...le," all hands forthwith wiggle-waggle, ...hen Simon says "down," all thumbs go

...other instance has come to our knowl- ...of the admirable working of the "freezing ...process. Mr. J. H. McGrath, an enter- ...g Gentile merchant of this city, had es- ...hed a small branch of his house at ...ican Fork, in Utah county, and left an ...in charge. He, too, was doing a thriv- ...ade, much to the convenience of the ...settlement. Yesterday his agent ar- ...n this city with the pleasant intelli- ...that Church counsel had done the busi- ...and it was no use staying longer. The ...ing out" system was working admirably. ...hen it is added that with a very few ...ions in the hundred towns and settle- ...there is hardly a store to be found— ...that in most cases the bishops have a ...stock of groceries and dry goods— ...may be more method in this supposed al madness than would appear at first

We do not know that it is a fact that
ntile merchants of the settlements—
w there are—sell better goods and at
r prices than the Church stores have
the habit of doing, but, if, as we sus-
the case, this is true, the people must
veriest dolts not to know and appreciate
in all its bearings.

whether this is so or not, the action of
rch leaders in interdicting trade with
, avowed as it is by Brigham Young,
the press and pulpit, exposes the
which actuates the Mormon leaders,
early than would columns of mere
pposition or denunciation. It is the
intolerance lying at the foundation of
le system, which under the guise of a
organization, undertakes to meddle
gulate and despotically control tem-
atters. It is all moonshine to quote
titude that the Mormons like other
ave the right to deal with whom they
nd then, as Brigham does, ask, with
croiss and sublime self-complacency,
ebody to point out the clause in the
ation which restricts the right! We
Brigham's enunciation of that right,
because he seeks by organized and
Church influence and dictation to
that right among his followers, that
can complain. It is the merest sub-
to say that neither intimidation nor
is used, but that the people are only

n up in business, and their custom-

ed" not to trade with the ungodly

In no civilized country in the
es a direct order from the Govern-
nctioned by heavy penalties, meet
o implicit obedience from the people
s the so-called "counsel" of the bish-
ôh. And whether it be by intimida-
ercion, or a wide-spread belief that
ent will follow the least infringement,
the world to judge.

it is, that whatever may be the
ae people in the settlements do not
heir own choice or free will in these
but obey "counsel" as they receive
he bishops. In his response to the
ae merchants, Brigham Young inti-
at his "influence" was to be used,
t Gentiles generally, but only against
this city, whom he characterized
ain class doing business here," and
grievously offended personally. How
iance is to be placed on that state-
y be judged by the two instances
e in the proscription of Messrs.
Munson, and Mr. McGrath in the
ements. They certainly do not fall
e list, which Brigham would make
be opposes. They are proscribed

ers forbidden, by Church odict, from dealing
with them, because they are Gentiles, and for
no other reason. Thus does Brigham Young
prick the bubble he himself has blown, and
would fain have the world believe there's sub-
stance in it.

Brigham's "Reply," Again.

At the Tabernacle last Sunday, Brigham Young re-enunciated from the stand his determination that the Mormons should not only keep aloof from unsaintly associations, but must withdraw their patronage from the Gentiles. This doctrine—the new, or rather the renewed crusade—is taught through the press and enforced from the pulpit. Nor, as we have shown, is it confined to this city—where Gentiles most do congregate—but from one end of the Territory to the other has the fiat gone forth, and bishops, elders, deacons and teachers, from the greatest to the least, are engaged in the work of proscription. The card of Brigham Young in reply to the proposition of the merchants of this city, sought to make it appear that the proscription, though general in its terms, was intended only for a few persons who had made themselves personally obnoxious, by some real or fancied transgression against the notions or interests of the Mormons. But the shallowness of this pretence hardly needs the exposure it has met. It was evidently not intended for home consumption, but for a foreign market. That the bane and the antidote might go together, we gave yesterday a brief account of the working of the thing in Nephi and Spanish Fork. Notwithstanding, we are assured that in both instances we gave the version most favorable to the Church leaders, we are fully prepared to have our account and comments set down

as "slander, misrepresentation and persecution." This seems to be the standing poor defence of a certain class of would-be defenders not of the Mormon religion, but of the teachings of the Mormon leaders. We are content that it should be so, and to rest satisfied that out of their own mouths and by their own acts shall they be judged.

But the disingenuousness of the defence of Brigham Young, in his card, is shown by some of the broad statements with which he seeks to justify his crusade on the merchants.

Passing by as utterly unworthy of dignified response, the mere wordy abuse of those who seem to have excited the especial ire of the signer of the card, we find one specific cause of complaint to be, that "they" (which ever of these merchants may be comprehended in that pronoun) "have kept liquor and surreptitiously sold it in violation of law." Now, we submit that even if any or all these merchants were to plead guilty to the charge, it is not so very heinous an offence as to call down on their heads the severe anathemas levelled against them. That the selling of liquor is not in itself so grave a crime, may be fairly affirmed, when it is stated that for a long time the Church Liquor Store sought to maintain a monopoly of the traffic, and afterwards the City Government (but another name for the Church authorities) prohibited by highly penal ordinances anybody but itself from dealing in spirits. Nay, while authorizing itself to deal out ad libitum "liquid damnation," it proclaimed every other dealer in it a "nuisance," to be abated, either by law or by police raids.

But coming back to the specification in the charge, we ask, which one of the merchants "surreptitiously sold liquor in violation of law." If Brigham Young, or any of his satellites, ever had any evidence of such violation of law, it was his duty to cause the arrest and conviction of the offender, which would hardly have been difficult, seeing they have the courts, police, juries and appliances under their sole control. And if he has not such evidence, how can he deliberately undertake to pen the charge? Does not the head of the Church thus convict himself of either neglect of duty as a citizen and conservator of the morals and laws of the community, or of making an unjustifiable, unjust and unfounded charge against the character of some of our best citizens? We leave him to answer, either through his newspaper or to his own conscience, and perhaps the answers as they may be recorded in the one or the other, will be found widely variant. The further suggestion that "they" have endeavored to bias the minds of the Judiciary to give decisions favorable to "their" own practices, is too vague to require a response. The inuendo would seem to be that some attempt at corruption had been made by somebody, but it is too shadowy and meaningless to merit more than the sneer it will unquestionably receive, both from the Judiciary and the merchants.

The next and final specification, propounded like the rest behind an interrogation point, is, that "they have entered into secret combinations to resist the laws and thwart their healthy operation, and refused to pay their taxes and to give the support to schools required by law." This charge "has this extent no more," that a large number of the merchants refused to pay a most onerous tax, levied under the guise of a school law, and united openly and publicly in testing its validity before the Courts. Without reviewing the law in question, it is sufficient to say that it allowed taxation without limit, was wholly without restriction or guards, and susceptible of the most outrageous oppression from beginning to end. The case was carried to the Supreme Court, and after elaborate argument and consideration was pronounced by that high tribunal just what we have said it was. In fact so transparent were its manifold defects that the last Legislature, without waiting for the action of the Courts, repealed it, and substituted another in its place.

The merchants desired to know if they were entirely at the mercy of such laws as a Utah Legislature might choose to pass, whether constitutional or not. They appealed to the Courts, and the deliberate action of the latter has fully vindicated their course, and should have been sufficient to have protected them from the aspersions which we are now noticing. So much then for the sweeping charges of Brigham's "Reply." In the language of Sir Charles Coldstream, when he looked into the crater of a defunct volcano, "there's nothing in it."

[Communicated.]

To Brigham Young.

In accordance with our promise we again address you and beg leave to respectfully assure you of our most distinguished consideration. Trade, with the Gentile merchants, still continues good, notwithstanding the horrible condition of the public approaches to the city, and will gradually grow brisker and brighter as the roads become harder, and the intelligent husbandmen of the surrounding country can conveniently and safely drive into the metropolis of Utah, to purchase such articles of merchandise as the necessities of themselves and their families demand. Towards Spring we turn our eyes, and visions of mercantile success fill the brain. High hopes of colossal fortunes to be reaped in the future, in this Territory, by the exercise of mercantile energy, enterprise, and integrity, buoys us up at the close of this year, and incites us to fresh action.

It is now one week since you were addressed on a subject of no ordinary importance to lovers of truth, fair play, and justice. You stepped a little to one side after declining the proposition of twenty-three mercantile firms made in good taste and in a business like manner to the "Leaders of the Mormon Church," and you made twelve direct and serious charges against the "class" "doing business in the Territory" who are not members of the Mormon Church; not one of which you attempted to substantiate by facts, although called upon to do so.

1. You charge us with being the "avowed enemies" of this community. We demand your proofs or the retraction of the charge.

2. You charge us with seeking the disruption and overthrow of the community. Proofs are also needed in support of this allegation.

3. You charge us with circulating the foulest slanders about the old citizens. Pray, when?, and whose?........ ....You charge .... vile have been used to produce nefarious ends. In what way? Do explain!

5. You charge us with using the patronage of the people to destroy them. Really, Bro. Brigham, were you jesting? If you were not, you can scarcely contemplate that your naked assertion, unsupported by one scintilla of evidence, and in the face of a denial and a *demand* for proofs, will be entitled to much respect with the world.

6. You charge that we would coin the hearts blood of the people here to bring our machinations to a successful issue. What machinations? You are quite vague in this specification, and you are expected to be more definite in all your future charges, proof or no proof.

7. You charge us with having done all in our power to encourage violations of law. What law? and when was its violation encouraged? and by whom?

8. You charge us with retarding the administration of justice. How? and when?

9. You charge us with fostering vice and vicious institutions. This is a very grave charge, preferred by a minister of religion, against peaceable and law-abiding citizens, who would not exchange their precepts of morality with him without feeling they had the worst of the bargain. Come out with the proof of your charge.

10. You charge us with opposing the will of the people unanimously expressed. This, too, is a wondrously vague accusation, and unless you particularize people will fail to see the enormity.

11. You charge us with increasing disorder in this city. Can you, sir, sustain this soft impeachment? If you can, do so.

12. You charge us with having done all in our power to change the peace and quietude of the city into lawlessness and anarchy. Is it true we have done so? State when the effort was made; by whom made; and whether success crowned the effort.

Your "corrupt and venal press," if the use of one of your chaste and christianlike expressions is permissable, has published, and republished, your calumnious reply, and advertises that the demand is so great for the famed literary effusion of your life, that it is to undergo still another edition. An offer was made to your publisher of the original letter of "one of the signers of the card" to yourself, to accompany your "reply," but was declined. The reason that prompted that offer was the announcement that the entire correspondence was to be republished, and fearing that an excuse might be made that it would not be copied from the "corrupt and venal press," the original was tendered. But no, it was not to see the light of publicity by the means in your power, and the flimsy pretext that it was not signed by all the merchants who signed the card, advanced for its exclusion. That argument goes farther than you intended. The card was addressed "to the leaders of the Mormon Church." You individually reply. "One of the signers of the card" takes you to task for your reckless and calumnious assertions.

It would be well for the bane and antidote to go together. It is no evidence of moral courage to wantonly assail the characters and impugn the motives of your fellow men through the columns of a partizan press, and refuse them an opportunity to be heard in refutation. Error, even, can be safely tolerated in any community when truth and reason are left free to combat it. No harm could possibly arise to the readers of your paper by a perusal of both sides of the question. If you are correct in your wholesale charges against American merchants in Utah, controversy, sir, can only confirm your correctness.

But, sir, it has been hinted that something akin to sordid avarice, and entirely foreign to the charity preached by the Nazarene and his humble apostles, better than eighteen centuries ago, and which have been handed down from sire to son to the present day, prompted the serious allegations in your famed reply. After the exaction of the decimal portion of the produce and profits of each year are poured into your coffers, ostensibly

for religion, must the remaining nine-tenths be diverted into channels where you are accused of having extensive monetary interests, where the least possible amount of mercantile commodities may be exchanged for the greatest possible amount of money or produce? Is it to become a rule of your faith that you, and others, blessed with large fortunes and immense credit, at home and abroad, may purchase with impunity goods in large or small quantities from Gentile and Jew, and that the same privilege is to be denied to the mass of the people? Is not the saving of a dollar or two on a pair of boots, or the price of a pair of pantaloons, as much of, an object to the honest, hard-working laborer or farmer, who may have a family dependent on his toils and frugality, as a thousand or tens of thousands of dollars may be to you and the merchant princes you are fostering and favoring?

Perhaps you may be surprised that there is any one who has the hardihood to doubt the soundness of your views on commercial matters, or call their correctness in question. I beg you to believe I have great faith in the cherished principles of free speech and a free press—the groundwork of American liberty—and consider them always potent for good, where the condition of society is not reduced to organized ignorance and stupidity. The sincerity of your religious belief, or the correctness of the tenets of your faith, are in no wise questioned. That is a matter exclusively between man and his Maker, and any officious intermeddling or interference that would rob the creature of one motive of devotion towards the Creator is little short of sacrilege. Besides it would be against the spirit of our laws and contrary to the genius of our institutions. But when you, or any one else, arrogates to dictate how all the temporal affairs of life are to be conducted, to arouse jealousies and prejudices among men, instead of allaying them, and use your immense influence to injure others in their goods and property—aye, in their good name—be not surprised in finding us publicly protesting. It would be strange if the representatives of three million dollars worth of property in Utah, and possessing a credit of double or triple that amount outside in the Atlantic and Pacific States, were tamely to submit to

Pacific States, were tamely to submit to your efforts, involving their financial ruin, and that, too, on the soil of a Republic which fosters and protects its citizens in their commercial pursuits and enterprises against oppression and outrage to the uttermost bounds of the earth. Do you call it fair and equitable to impose licenses upon merchants—collect them under pains and penalties—and then poison the minds of the people against trading with them? Is that the reciprocity that should exist? When your people, as you familiarly call them, took the produce of their farms in other days to California, Nevada, Colorado, Idaho and Montana, and received the highest market price in glittering gold in return, you were not so strenuous in having them trade exclusively with each other. You did not then use coercion or intimidation; nor did you "counsel" them, as you facetiously term working on their eternal hopes and fears, by assuring them if they do not follow your counsel they will be cut off from the Church and go to hell. If it is a sin, a violation of any of the commands written by the finger of Omnipotence on the fractured tablet of the Decalogue, or of the laws of love and charity bequeathed by his Divine Son to weak erring humanity to trade with Jew or Gentile, is not the discovery quite recent for one supposed to be in communication with God, and acquainted with his laws, which are the same to-day, and yesterday, and forever? Is it right, honorable or legal when words nor grass will will do, to use intimidation and coercion to compel merchants to close their stores, as was recently done at Nephi? Is it not a weak confession that your people will buy where they can buy cheapest, notwithstanding your "counsel" to the contrary? Aye, sir, the time may come when your abusive discourses and speeches for your views statesship temporal money be out of taste with your people, and you, big with speech, like Fanfaroni, inquire,

What is't that boils within me?
Is't the throes of nascent genius?
Is't the strife of high immortal thoughts to find a vent?
Or is it wind?

Regretting that you have neglected to say more on this subject, as you led us to believe you would, allow me to say that, as heretofore, we shall demean ourselves as good citizens. Wishing you the enjoyment of health and happiness, we "will have more to say on this subject," bye and bye.

ONE OF THE SIGNERS OF THE "CARD."

Deseret News
January 30, 1867

Died.

At Nephi City, Juab Co., Nov 29, 1866. JANE, wife of Theophilus Everett, aged 54 years.

Sister Everett, was born at Amherst, State of New Hampshire; was baptized by Elder E Snow, in Salem, Mass., 1842; came to Utah, in Captain Willes company, in the summer of 1866; was beloved by all who had the pleasure of her acquaintance; and bore a faithful testimony to the truth of the Latter-day work. Her end was peace indeed.—[COM.

NEPHI, JUAB CO., March 1.

EDITOR DESERET NEWS:

Roads good or bad, mud or no mud, the southern mail Company brings our mails in schedule time, and the NEWS, ever welcome, comes regularly to hand; every item, sermons, editorials, communications, clippings from other journals, friendly or otherwise, are all read with interest, for in times like these, when outsiders talk of swallowing our Utah—our "Mountain Home"—to receive the NEWS and *Telegraph* regularly is a treat.

Here, in Juab, we are all getting along in about the usual way—enjoying ourselves the best we can, leaving our destiny in the hands of God; from former experience, we have proved that He is our Friend and that we are His people, and that, if we obey His laws and the instructions given by His servants, all will be well.

During the past winter influenza, affections of the lungs and bad colds have prevailed to some extent; delicate and aged people have suffered much, and some few deaths have occurred. Last week we were called to part with our beloved and much respected sister Thurza, wife of Edwin Harley; over four hundred persons attended her funeral. Sister Caxler, wife of our respected Patriarch, and several other aged sisters are very sick, and little hopes are entertained of their recovery.

Elders Hyde, Lyman and E. Snow, on their way home from the Legislative Assembly, held meetings here, giving the Saints much valuable and timely instruction.

Elder Snow, on the 11th of Feb., accompanied by Bishop C. H. Bryan, Judge Jacob G. Bigler, Presidents of Seventies, S. Pitchforth, J. Pyper and T. S. Hoyt and other Elders visited the Saints at Chicken Creek; two good meetings were held, and a Branch of the Church organized there; Elder Abraham Palmer was appointed Presiding Teacher, and Elders J. Wilson and W. Morgan his assistants. Elder Snow gave the Saints of this Branch much choice and fatherly teaching which, if observed, will enable them to have good meetings, and peace and union in their families and settlement. He instructed the Bishop and President of Seventies at Nephi to visit them and send elders often to hold meetings with the Saints at Chicken Creek, also with those who reside at Mona (Willow Creek).

The 49th and 71st Quorums of Seventies meet together once a week, and have good meetings.

Our Social Hall has been often occupied during the winter with balls, social parties, dramatic representations, and concerts. The Juab Dramatic Association have had two excellent social parties, performing the "Golden Farmer" and "Deaf as a Post," which, with dancing made a fine evening's entertainment. During the coming week Bernard Snow will appear in the characters of Rolla and the Stranger. Professor Tullidge's concert went off well, and was a treat to all who love good singing. More anon.

Respectfully,
SAMUEL PITCHFORTH.

Correspondence.

PRESIDENT B. YOUNG'S TRIP SOUTH.

Nephi, Juab Co., April 25, 1867.

EDITOR NEWS:—

The President and party arrived at Dry Creek, in G. S. L. Co., at 1 p.m. of Monday, 22nd, when we were met by two platoons of cavalry, who escorted the company to Willow Creek, where the people, including the school children with a multitude of banners, greeted the arrival of the President. After a short time for refreshments, we repaired to the meeting house, which was filled to overflowing, when Presidents Young and Wells, and Elders John Taylor and W. Woodruff, respectively addressed the meeting, each occupying about 20 minutes; they were pleased to meet the people so comfortably situated with regard to a meeting house, and to see the care and pains bestowed upon the education of the young, as evinced by the display of maps, charts, globes, diagrams, drawings, &c., &c., suspended on the walls of the meeting room, which is also used for school purposes; and felt to bless the people and bid them God-speed.

On Tuesday morning, at half past 8, the company rolled out for American Fork. We were met at Dry Creek, Utah Co., by the American Fork band, in a large wagon drawn by four grays, and some citizens on horseback, who accompanied us to the town. The people being assembled in the bowery in front of the meeting-house, which was too small for the occasion, many of the citizens of Lehi and Battle Creek being present, Elders Geo. Q. Cannon, W. Woodruff, J. F. Smith and John Taylor, and Presidents D. H. Wells and B. Young respectively addressed the Saints, on the subjects of the Word of Wisdom, unity, improvement, economy, &c. Pres. Young advised them to take their present meeting-room for a school-house, and build another suitable to meet in.

Meeting being over due respect was paid to a comfortable dinner prepared at bro. Hindley's after which the company moved on to Provo, where a meeting was held in the evening in the basement of the new meeting-house, which is now soon to be completed. Here Elders C. V. Spencer, A. H. Raleigh and President B. Young alternately spoke on various interesting and important and subjects.

On Wednesday, at 11 a.m., meeting was held at Springville, a crowded congregation being assembled. Elders W. Woodruff, J. Taylor, J. F. Smith, A. M. Musser and President B. Young spoke. Before the meeting closed, Elders W. Woodruff, Geo. A. Smith, (who joined us Provo,) Geo. Q. Cannon and others, left for Spanish Fork to fill an appointment at 2 p.m. Soon after the meeting opened, however, the President arrived. Elder Geo. Q. Cannon, Pres. D. H. Wells and Elder Taylor addressed the meeting.

After stopping a few minutes for dinner we drove on to Payson, being met by a large company of cavalry, some distance from the town, and by a youthful band of musicians as we approached. The streets were filled with school children, and people, old and young, with banners &c., expressing welcome to the servants of the Lord. It is quite evident that the good people of Payson are greatly blessed with a numerous posterity, all healthy, well clad, bright and happy, as only Utah's children are.

In the evening meeting was held in the theatre, which was filled to overflowing. Pres. Young expressed his kind and fatherly feelings for the Saints at this place, and elsewhere; gave some good counsel, kindly admonition and exhortation; and Pres. Wells followed with good instructions to the people in relation to their treatment of and conduct towards the Indians, urging the manifestation of kindly, conciliating, friendly and patient feelings on the part of the Saints, instead of harboring contemptible and degrading feelings of revenge and malice,—thus acting nobly instead of descending to the level of the savages. Elder Geo. A. Smith followed and spoke about ten minutes, relating the fable of the farmer, who discovered a snake almost frozen to death, and, moved with sympathy, put it in his bosom, where it soon recovered, and in reward for his kindness, buried its fangs in his bosom, from which he died; aptly and forcibly comparing it to the Latter-day Saints feeding and sustaining their avowed enemies.

S.

Correspondence.

Great Salt Lake City, April, 29.

EDITOR DESERET NEWS:

President Young and company left this city on Monday morning, April 22nd, at ten o'clock, on a tour to "Dixie." They arrived at South Willow Creek at 2 p.m., held meeting in the afternoon and stopped over night. On Tuesday morning at 10 o'clock, started for Provo, arriving there at 5.30 p.m. Held meeting in the evening.

On Wednesday morning, at 9 o'clock, started for Springville, where they held meeting at 10 a.m. Then proceeded to Spanish Fork, where they took dinner, and held meeting at 2 p.m. Then proceeded to Payson, reached there at 5.30 p.m., and held meeting in the evening.

On Thursday morning, at nine o'clock, started to Santaquin and held meeting. Then proceeded to Nephi, arriving there at 3.30 p.m., held meeting at 5 p.m.

Friday morning, at 9 o'clock, started for Scipio, (Round Valley,) arriving there at 4.30 p.m.; held meeting in the evening.

Saturday morning, at 8.45, started for Fillmore; arrived there at 1 p.m., and stopped over night.

On Sunday held meetings mornin and afternoon, took supper and then started at 4.20 p.m., for Corn Creek, and stopped over night. This morning left Corn Creek, and will arrive at Beaver this evening.

The health of the company is good, and they are enjoying themselves very much.

R. M. WILKINSON,
Operator.

Died.

In Nephi, Juab County, March 29, MARGARET, wife of William Cazier, aged 62 years and 18 days. She joined the Church in Moultrie County, Illinois, in the spring of 1845, and emigrated to the mountains in the fall of 1851.—[Com.

Correspondence.

NEPHI CITY, Juab Co.,
July 13, 1867.

EDITOR OF THE DESERET NEWS:

DEAR BR.—Through the blessings of our Heavenly Father, we have thus far escaped trouble from the Indians, our stock is doing well, being herded in Pigeon and Chicken Creeks.

CROPS.

The season opening unusual late, our field crops are much behind time, and in many instances not very promising. Sugar cane is almost an entire failure, but we have plenty of water and it is hot enough to force our crops along at a rapid rate.

FRUIT.

Our gardens and orchards are doing well, and it is quite cheering to see the prospect that many have of having considerable fruit. A few years ago our climate gave Indian corn a hard push to mature, and many would not believe that fruit could ever be successfully raised in as high a location as on Salt Creek. Our soil was always considered to be of a cold and backward nature; but thanks be to Israel's God we can now behold apple, plum, peach and apricot trees in full bearing, and if it had not been for a very unusual frost in June, some would have had considerable grapes.

EDUCATION.

We have three schools in full operation; Elder Love is teaching in the Social Hall; Elder J. Midgley opened on Monday last, a school, in the new school house in the 1st school district; and Elder J. Chapman, is teaching quite a number at his private residence.

Our Sunday school is well attended, and much interest is manifested, both by the superintendent, Elder Samuel Claridge, and the brethren who assist in teaching the children. Simple and instructive lectures have been delivered before the school, on the principles of our holy religion. Elder W. Warwood is teaching phonography.

IMPROVEMENTS.

Nephi is extending her boundaries on the north, six blocks, and buildings are going up on the new survey, which is well adapted for gardens and orchards, the cañon wind keeping off the frost some time longer than on the south side of the city.

An addition of several hundred acres of land has been laid out and fenced in on the north of the new field, the soil of which is well adapted for corn and sugar cane.

Br. John Andrews has been doing good business with a first class carding machine, which he purchased from Pres. B. Young.

Br. Henriod has been experimenting on burning brick, and we hope to be able, before long, to report some good brick buildings going up.

HIGH WATER.

Salt Creek has been very high, doing much damage to the road in the cañon. The bridge at the Forks is washed away and the channel of the creek is washed much deeper and wider than it was before.

Considerable labor had to be performed in order to secure the Sevier bridge, and keep open the road.

We have not as yet discovered any gold mines, but if rumors are true, we expect to obtain some of the precious metal for our products: may our motto ever be *stay* at *home* and mind our own *business.*

Our mails come prompt to time, and the NEWS, *Telegraph* and *Juvenile Instructor* are ever welcome.

Respectfully,
SAMUEL PITCHFORTH.

Deseret News
August 7, 1867

Nephi, July 25th, 1867.

Editor "News"—The twentieth anniversary of the arrival of the Pioneers into these, then sterile, valleys was celebrated at this place in a joyous manner. At sunrise the "Old Flag" was unfurled, and saluted by a volley from Capt. J. Kienke's company of infantry. The "Star Spangled Banner" was played by Capt. Hawkins' band, after which till half past nine o'clock they promenaded the town serenading many of the old permanent citizens. At that hour the people assembled in the meeting house, and, after being called to order by the Chairman of Committee of Arrangements, the choir under the presidency of elder William Evans sang "Lo! the Gentile chain is broken;" prayer by Chaplain, Patriarch Wm. Cazier. A speech, showing the importance of the occasion was then delivered by elder Andrew Love, and the song "Don't find fault with thy brother" was sung by Messrs. Thomas P. and George P. Carter brothers. Songs, recitations, and toasts, interspersed with music from the brass and orchestral bands, were the order of the morning. Miss Elizabeth Parks sang that heart-thrilling song, "Write a letter to my Mother," and "I hardly think I will," both calling forth hearty applause. The Philharmonic Society, under the leadership of br. Thomas P. Carter, performed well some most excellent pieces. The Nephi Sunday scholars, guided by br. John Millar, song "Sound the loud timbrel." Br. Samuel Claridge sang an original song composed by himself, "Marching home to Zion," tune: "Sherman's march.

After some appropriate remarks from the Chairman of Committe, and prayer by the Chaplain, the meeting dispersed at twelve o'clock, all seeming satisfied with the forenoon's entertainment.

At half past two, the juvenile portion of the community were freely given the use of the Social Hall for a dance, which was merrily indulged in by them till five. At eight o'clock the adult population enjoyed a dance with singing and recitations, which was kept up till 2 o'clock a.m. of the 25th.

The crops are looking well, some fall wheat has already been cut.

The gold fever has not yet reached Nephi, the inhabitants apparently, thinking more of the golden wheat fields than of hunting for gold.

Committee of arrangements:—George Kendall, John Pyper, Jonathan Midgley. Thomas Ord, Reporter.

Deseret News
August 21, 1867

Since the Indian raid near Parowan, (an account of which we published at the time), strong guards have had to be kept up at all the settlements between that place and Nephi, which is very onerous, especially during the period of haying and harvesting.

Deseret News
September 18, 1867

FROM NEPHI,—By letter from Elder S. Pitchforth, dated Nephi, Sept. 10th, we learn that the "grasshoppers" are there in vast hosts, they have done considerable damage, and were not satisfied at date of writing.

There had been considerable sickness among children, several of whom have died.

Thrashing had commenced.

Deseret News
January 15, 1868

Died:

At Nephi City, Juab Co., Dec. 9th, Wm. Furner, aged 33 years, 6 months and 22 days.

Bro. Furner was a native of Bread, Sussex, England. He was baptized by Elder Eastwood, August 6th, 1851, and emigrated in the Hand Cart Company, 1856, and settled at Nephi. He was ordained a member of the 49th Quorum of Seventies under the hands of Pres. Samuel Pitchforth, Sept. 6th, 1867. Ever since his residence in the valleys, he was engaged in herding stock for the citizens of Nephi, and was much respected for his honest and upright principles. He lived and died a Saint of God, leaving a wife and son to mourn his loss. [COM.

Mil. Star please copy.

Deseret News
February 12, 1868

Died:

At Nephi, Jan. 27th, 1868, of convulsions, Paul, infant son of Thomas and Jane Stephenson, aged 6 months and 4 days.

Deseret News
March 18, 1868

NEPHI, March 6th, 1868.

Editor Deseret News:—Dear Bro.,—Having a few leisure moments, I improve them by writing you a few lines.

On Monday, the 2d inst., I left home in company with Elder Erastus Snow, for a tour to "Dixie." Drove to Milo Andrus', where we were kindly entertained for the night.

On Tuesday, 3d inst., drove to Provo, where we arrived quite late, the roads being very bad. At American Fork and Battle Creek we noticed that the people were working some in their gardens, and saw one or two plows running, and were reminded in several ways that seed time is at hand.

Wednesday, 4th inst., we called on President Young, and were (as usual) a little late, the President was in his carriage about starting down to Bro. Madsen's fishery, at the mouth of Provo river. We found Bro. M. a whole-souled, big-hearted patriarch, though not very old. His family are all workers, and everything around the place indicated thrift. He told us that during the past winter, himself and family had manufactured seines, nets, lines, and other implements which would have cost, had he purchased them, not less than five hundred dollars. He had raised the flax, dressed it himself, and others of his family had carded and spun the twine, and he had knit his seines during winter evenings. He also told us that he had three years' breadstuff on hand. After drinking a glass of Danish beer (very mild drink) we took our leave of this truly enterprising man, and returned to Provo city.

After dinner, we drove to Spanish Fork, where we stayed all night. In the evening we attended a lecture in the school house. Bro. W. D. Jones was the lecturer. Subject—"The manufacture of iron and its uses." The lecturer handled his subject very well, for a new beginner. After the lecture, Bro. Snow was requested by Bishop Thurber to make some remarks, which he did to the joy of all present. His subject was the union of the Saints, and the necessity of sustaining ourselves. He urged upon the Saints the importance of sowing the usual (or even greater) amount of grain, and not to be frightened at the prospect of grasshoppers; for if we do not sow, we cannot expect to reap.

Thursday 5th, we started from Spanish Fork, about 10 o'clock, and drove over to Spring Lake Villa, where we took dinner with our enterprising friend Benj. F. Johnson. In the afternoon, drove to Mona, (What's in a name?) where we stopped over night, being kindly entertained by Bro. Ed. Kay.

In the evening meeting was held, Bro. Snow and myself speaking. This place, (Mona,) is capable of being made into a a very pretty little town. The new town being laid out on a high, gravely ridge, with plenty of water, and near the base of the mountain, will make it a good fruit growing spot. And as the settlement has plenty of hay land, and a good range for stock, we may reasonably expect to see a flourishing place in a few years.

This morning snow covered the earth to the depth of three or four inches. We drove over to Nephi, where we will remain till to-morrow. The people in this place are somewhat nervous in regard to the grasshoppers, but the Bishop says they will sow most of their land notwithstanding.

This is an enterprising place, and though only two years since I was last here, yet I see many and marked improvements. Four good schools are kept here, and what is best, all are taught by our own teachers. There is a manifest improvement in the great work of Education.

Your Brother in the Gospel,
Jos. W. Young.

Deseret News
May 6, 1868

NEPHI, Juab County,
April 27th, 1868.

Editor Deseret News.—Dear Sir:—The citizens of this county are doing their best to plant and sow enough for themselves and the grasshoppers who are hatching out in some places in countless numbers.

There has been considerable sickness during the Winter and Spring, influenza and whooping cough prevailing. At the present time the health of the people is improving.

During the Winter lectures have been delivered before the Seventies, by Elders W. Riches, J. Miller, D. M. McCune, T. Crawley, W. Worwood and S. Pitchforth, on various interesting subjects.

The Nephi Sunday School has prospered under the management of Elder Samuel Claridge, and is well attended.

The desire to plant out orchards and make improvements is on the increase; and we hope before many years to raise all the fruit we shall need.

A new town site has been surveyed between Chicken and Pigeon creeks, on the east side of the valley, some three and a half miles north-east of the old Chicken creek settlement. A field has also been surveyed and improvements have commenced. The new location is called Levan. Some few families have moved their houses from the old settlement, and the prospect is that the place will soon be built up. It is well situated and bids fair to become a choice location for a small settlement.

Respectfully,
SAMUEL PITCHFORTH.

Editor Evening News:—When Payson was first settled it was found impossible to water sufficiently 200 acres of land with Peteetneet Creek. The water has however increased, and a number of springs have broken out, and farm has been added to farm and field to field up till the present time; and a reservoir has been made on the south side of the town to contain the water, to be used in times of scarcity, after the spring floods are passed.

In 1850 a petition was made to bring the waters of Summit Creek to that place. This not being granted, B. F. Johnson, Esq. made a settlement at Summit Creek, in 1851, supposing there would be water enough for a farm. In 1853 it had grown to a considerable village, when it was vacated on account of Indian difficulties. Ferney Tindall was killed by the Indians at this place; and O. C. Roberts and J. W. Berry were wounded while carrying an express. Abel Butterfield saved his life, and that of several others by running toward the Indians calling for others to follow, although no others were near, having arms.

Late in the Fall, the Indians burned the village, and next day came into Payson and sued for peace.

In 1854 the settlement was renewed, but for several years the crops were destroyed by crickets and grasshoppers, until the people got discouraged with farming and many left the place. The beauty of its situation attracted others, and the waters have increased until it has become a thriving agricultural district, producing many choice fruits.

A city site has been surveyed on Clover Creek, which bears the name of *Mona*. Several log and adobe houses have been erected within the last year; gardens have been fenced and fruit trees planted, some of which are in blossom. As an evidence of thrift, Br. John Kay has built a good frame barn which is well finished; and in this country where lumber and other building materials are so scarce it is quite an uncommon thing in so new a town.

Bros. Andrew Love and John A. Wolf settled on this stream in 1852, put land under cultivation, and built houses, but vacated the place in 1853 on account of Indian hostilities. A band of Indians attacked their corral, at night, which contained a herd of cattle in the charge of Br. Burns, and kept firing for several hours; the corral was defended by Lieut. Burns and eleven herdsmen. The Indians afterwards reported that five of their number died of their wounds, and one had both arms broken, who recovered. Isaac Duffin was wounded in the knee and several cattle were wounded and a few killed.

"Hoppers" are reported numerous, and are doing some damage at Nephi. Crops are looking exceedingly well, a large part being Fall grain.

GEO. A. SMITH.

MOUNT PLEASANT, Sanpete,
May 10th, 1868.

Editor Deseret News:—Our meeting on Friday evening at the Nephi Meeting House, was well attended, the audience giving strict attention, and the singing excellent. Four addresses were delivered. Elders Pace and Thurber spoke on the measures necessary for the prevention of a recurrence of Indian hostilities; Elder Joseph F. Smith and myself on the benefits resulting from a proper classification of labor, and kindred subjects recommended at the last Conference.

Saturday morning we turned to the eastward, our way leading through the far-famed Salt Creek Cañon. The thickets of brush and the immense number of secret lurking places, along the road, render it one of the most dangerous passes, in times of Indian hostilities, in the mountains. A traveler has but little opportunity to escape an ambuscade in any part of it, and the eastern portion may not inappropriately be called "Bloody Pass." In 1853, four of the brethren were killed by the Utah Indians near the Uinta Springs, their bodies being horribly mutilated and left till an armed party came in search of them, who saw the Indians near by on the hill, taunting them, and daring them to approach, the Indians having taken a position for defence.

In 1858 another tragedy resulted in the destruction of a family by the San Pitches, who fired upon the unarmed and unsuspecting travelers from concealment in the bushes; and an ox harnessed up and hitched to the shaves of a cart, ran away in fright to Nephi, where his appearance lead to the discovery of the bodies. It is a historical fact, that every Indian engaged in this affair died of a loathsome disease resembling consumption.

In 1867, one man was killed, another wounded, and a herd of cattle driven off by the Utah Indians, in the same locality. The horrible scenes that have occurred along this route, must stir up the soul to earnest prayer that the descendants of Lehi may "cease their savage customs" "and live with God at home," at least, that this picturesque cañon may never again be stained with human gore.

Crossing the divide we encountered a severe rain storm. We held meetings at Fountain Green and Moroni yesterday, and to-day at North Bend and Mount Pleasant, each one of the party occupying a portion of time addressing, invariably, full and attentive audiences.

The "hoppers" are not so numerous in this as in Utah Valley; they have not as yet done any harm. Crops look excellent.

GEO. A. SMITH.

THE
DESERET TELEGRAPH COMPANY

HAS ESTABLISHED

TELEGRAPH OFFICES

At the following places, viz.:—

Cache County,
LOGAN, *County Seat.*
Wellsville.

Box Elder County,
BRIGHAM CITY, *County Seat.*
Willard City, or North Willow Creek.

Weber County,
OGDEN CITY, *County Seat.*

Davis County,
Kaysville.

Salt Lake County,
SALT LAKE CITY.

Utah County,
PROVO, *County Seat.*
American Fork.
Springville.
Spanish Fork.
Payson.
Santaquin.

Juab County,
NEPHI CITY, *County Seat.*
Mona, or Willow Creek.)
Chicken Creek.

Sanpete County,
MANTI, *County Seat.*
Fountain Green.
Moroni.
Fairview, or North Bend.
Mount Pleasant.
Springtown.
Fort Ephraim.
Fort Gunnison.

Millard County,
FILLMORE CITY, *County Seat.*
Scipio, or Round Valley.
Cove Creek.

Beaver County,
BEAVER CITY, *County Seat.*

Iron County,
PAROWAN, *County Seat.*
Cedar City.

Washington County,
ST. GEORGE, *County Seat.*
Kanarra.
Washington.
Toker.

Salt Lake City, May 18, 1868.

d152:1w-s30:2w-w16:4w

NEPHI, May 28th, 1868.

Editor Deseret News.—I came to Far West in 1837, and bought of the United States a quarter section of land, on Long Creek, four miles south-east of Far West, the title to which I hold to this day. Of this I fenced and broke forty acres. On the evening after the Saints were compelled to deliver up their arms to Gen. Lucas, I was with Bro. James Hendricks, who was wounded in the Crooked River battle, with whom I watched all night, and in the morning as soon as it was light I started to the camp to see the prisoners. I soon met a sentinel, but passed on without speaking or being questioned. I met about thirty horsemen who ordered me to surrender, and I told them that I had surrendered and given up my arms the day before; which command by the horseman and reply by me was repeated three times. Two of them then rode up to me, one on each side, and took me by the coat collar and started off at full speed dragging me into camp where they let me down. This heroic deed (!)was greeted by the crowd and horsemen with terrific yells of applause. They repeatedly threatened to shoot me and cursed each other for not doing so. This conduct astonished me, as I had been a prisoner of war in the hands of the British in 1813, and was treated with civility.

I passed on and came to where a guard was placed around the prisoners,—Joseph Smith, S. Rigdon, L. Wight, C. Baldwin and Geo. W. Robinson, and I think another, but I am not certain, who were seated in a wagon, from all of whom I received a bow of recognition except from S. Rigdon, who sat with his head down and his face buried in his hands.

I walked around the entire guard, composed of about 200 men, who stood shoulder to shoulder around the prisoners, and was frequently saluted with terrible oaths and told to look for the last time on my Prophet, for his die was cast, &c. After passing around the guard, I passed on and met Wm. E. McLellan, formerly one of the Twelve Apostles. He was armed. I asked him to explain why he was there. He said "The Bible and all religion are matters of speculation and priestcraft, from beginning to end, and 'Joe' is the biggest speculator of them all." I told him that I had heard him bear testimony that Joseph was a Prophet and that the Book of Mormon was true, and now he said to the contrary; and I asked him if he would tell me which time he lied! A crowd having gathered, McLellan slunk away, and I never saw him again.

Soon after this I met Rufus Allen who had been a prisoner in the camp all night. Among some beef cattle in a yard I saw a yoke of oxen which belonged to his father, and asked him why he did not turn them out, but he thought it unsafe to do so. I watched an opportunity, let down the bars, and turned the oxen towards home.

I then went to the court martial. Gen. Lucas was presiding. After some discussion, Lucas announced that Joseph Smith was found guilty of treason against the Government, and was sentenced to be shot on the public square of Far West at 8 o'clock the next morning.

General Dohlphan, who was a witness of the trial, said, "Gentlemen, your proceedings are as illegal as hell, and if the decision of this court is executed it will be d——d cold-blooded murder; and neither I nor my brigade will stay here to witness it. Joseph Smith is a civilian, and not subject to court martial in any way; and if he was who is your court composed of? One half of them are a set of G——d d——d priests and are not military men under any circumstances whatever, and have no right to sit on a court martial."

After this I returned to Far West, and then to my home.

T. B. FOOT.

Deseret News
June 24, 1868

FATAL ACCIDENT.—As Bro. James G. Pyper and his wife and infant daughter, were on their way from Fairview, Sanpete Co., to Nephi City, with a part of a load of flour, on the 14th inst., when about one mile above the forks of the creek, in the kanyon, the horses, through some unaccountable management, ran off a dug-way and precipitated Bro. Pyper, his wife and their little child, into a ravine near the bridge, which was 12 feet deep. The wagon and the load turning over so encumbered them that they could not extricate themselves, until assisted by Bro. George Thatcher, of Provo, who came by half an hour after the occurence. The little child was found dead, having been found drowned in the water at the bottom of the ravine. The mother was badly injured. Brother Pyper escaped with but little injury. Every person who knows the fearful and dangerous place where the accident happened, can not but know that they were saved only by a miraculous power.

Deseret News
July 1, 1868

Yesterday, at 4 p.m., a meeting was held in the Meeting House, at which the Nephi Female Relief Society was organized, the following were appointed officers of the same, Presidentess, Amelia Goldsborough; Counselors, Elizabeth Kendall and Jane Picton; Secretary, Amey L. Bigler; Treasurer, Francis Andrews. Interesting remarks on the duties of the above society, were made by Bishop Bryan, Patriarch W. Cazier, and Elders J. Pyper, J. Midgley and S. Pitchforth.

I am very sorry to report that the locusts have done immense damage to our crops, but they are leaving very fast.
Respectfully,
SAMUEL PITCHFORTH.

Deseret News
July 8, 1868

RECEIVED.—We are obliged to Bro. Jonathan Midgley for a report of the proceedings at the meeting in Nephi, on Wednesday last, 24th. Our correspondent, in accepting our thanks, will see that a full report has been already pub-

lished in the NEWS, from the pen of Bro. Samuel Pitchforth, which obviates the necessity of publishing that now forwarded by him.

NEPHI, Juab Co., July 5th, 1868.

Editor Deseret News.—At daybreak yesterday the citizens were aroused by the firing of small arms. At sunrise the National Flag was unfurled, and saluted by a volley from the infantry commanded by Adjutant Charles Price; also by the Nephi Brass Band under Capt. Gustave Henriod. At 8 o'clock the Sunday Scholars met at their respective school houses, and were marched by their several Superintendents to Bishop Charles H. Bryan's residence, when a procession was formed in the following order by Dr. M. McCune, Marshal of the day: Advance guard; Nephi Brass Band; Bishop Bryan, and William Cazier, Patriarch; County Judge, Hon. Jacob G. Bigler and Selectmen Hon. G. Kendall, Isaac Grace and David Udall; Major Timothy B. Foot and Major P. Sutton, commanding District, with Adjutant C. Foote; Committee of Arrangements; Sunday School scholars, in care of Superintendent Samuel Claridge; Sunday School scholars, in care of Superintendent William Knight; citizens; rear guard.

After parading several streets, the procession halted where it was formed, when the children, led by Elder John Millar, collectively sang, "In our lovely Deseret;" the Brass Band played "Hail Columbia," after which the procession was dismissed.

At half-past ten the children and citizens assembled in the Meeting House and were called to order by Hon. Jonathan Midgley, County Sunday School Superintendent. Music by the Brass Band and singing by the Nephi Choir, in charge of Prest. William Evans; prayer by the Chaplain, William Cazier; and an Oration by Judge Bigler, on the Declaration of Independence.

The exercises were conducted by Elder Midgley without programme, and all went off spiritedly.

At 2 o'clock the scholars met at their school houses and enjoyed merry dancing till half-past five, under the guidance of their Superintendents.

In the evening there was an adult dance in the Social Hall. All was peace and good order, nothing having occurred to mar the enjoyment of the day.

J. Midgley, George Kendall, Thomas Ord, Samuel Claridge, Samuel Pitchforth, Matthew McCune, William Knight, Committee of Arrangements.

THOMAS ORD, Reporter.

NEPHI, August 7, 1868.

Editor Deseret News:—Dear Brother: On the evening of the 24th of July last, I mailed you a full report of the celebration of that day in Nephi, which has not reached you—this makes the second letter that I have mailed within a few months, which has failed to reach its destination. There must be some great neglect in some of the post offices in regard to handling mail matter.

The 24th was celebrated in this place with much spirit: we had a grand procession, a speech from your humble servant on the travels of the Pioneers, and the causes which induced them to leave the land of civilization and launch out into the American desert and hunt a home amid the wilds of the Rocky Mountains. Songs, toasts, music from Capt. G. Henriod's band, and dancing for both juveniles and adults closed the day. The committee of arrangements were W. E. Neslin, C. Foot and S. Lintore. Marshal of the day, T. Cazier; chaplain, Wm. Cazier.

Harvesting and hay cutting are right on hand—and we are thankful for what the hoppers have spared—enough with care, to last until another harvest; corn and potatoes are growing fast. Reapers and mowing machines are doing good business.   Respectfully,

SAMUEL PITCHFORTH.

Deseret News
September 23, 1868

PRESIDENT'S MOVEMENTS.—President Young and company left Payson at 9.15 this morning, and held meeting at Santaquin at 10 a.m. He goes to Nephi to-night and stays there till Monday.

Deseret News
September 30, 1868

PRESIDENT YOUNG'S TRIP SOUTH.

NEPHI, Sept. 20, 1868.

Our last letter terminated rather abruptly. Before we had finished we accidentally snuffed the candle out, and as everybody was in bed and we could find no matches we were under the necessity of breaking off. Payson possesses a rare postmaster in the person of Bro. John T. Hardy; he is a model officer, and discharges the duties of his position with fidelity and ability. We had heard his good qualities spoken of and we had an opportunity of testing them, we were under the necessity of awakening him to write the last line or two of our letter, and to direct and post it. The alacrity and pleasure which he evinced in waiting upon us relieved us from the embarrassment we otherwise would have felt in disturbing his slumbers.

In the description of our reception at Spanish Fork we omitted to describe a banner which had inscribed upon it "Spanish Fork Silk." The letters were formed of cocoons, and the border of raw silk. The silk worm eggs were brought from England by Bishop A. K. Thurber, when he returned last year from his mission to that country. Attention is being paid here, we understand, to this culture. It will be found to be a remunerative business here as well as in other settlements in the Territory. From Spanish Fork we drove to Payson, where we met with the people at 7 p.m. The hall was very crowded, and, as a consequence, oppressively hot. Elders Joseph F. Smith, George Dunford, Thos. Taylor and A. M. Musser and President B. Young addressed the people. At 8 a.m. the next day a school of the prophets was organized, after which the company drove over to Santa Quin. We were greeted with the usual reception here, as at Payson, of children, with banners, and the adult population. Presidents Joseph Young and D. H. Wells and Elder Geo. Q. Cannon spoke to the people. After dinner we started for Nephi, eighteen miles, or, according to some, twenty miles, distant, and reached there after a drive two hours and a half. The reception the company met with here was a remarkable one. The Brass Band, which is in the first class of musicians, under the leadership of Captain Gustave Henriod, was at the edge of the town waiting for us, and marched into the town at the head of the company discoursing sweet music as they went. Opposite the meeting house the street was spanned by an arch of evergreens, which with the wings, occupied the entire street. Over the centre of the arch were the words "ZION'S CHIEFTAIN EVER WELCOME." After passing through the arch the people extended the whole length of the street up to the Bishop's. The number of children was something astonishing for a place no larger than Nephi. Accustomed as we are to seeing children in great abundance their numbers here surprised us. Probably the explanation is found in the inscription which we noticed on one of the banners which the children carried, "Monogamy at a Discount." A monogamist in the company remarked that the only fault he could find with the sight was, "he had no hand in producing it."

THE MEETINGS.

A meeting was held this evening, which we were kept by business from attending. President Joseph Young, Elders Joseph F. Smith, Joseph W. Young, A. M. Musser, Thos. Taylor and Geo. Dunford attended the meeting and all, we believe, spoke. From the character of the speakers you may be sure the matter was good.

This morning at sunrise the band serenaded the houses at which the President and the other members of the company put up. At 10 a.m. the meeting house was crowded to its utmost by the people. We noticed faces of residents of Payson, Santaquin, and Sanpete valley, and some also from Provo. Last night President Orson Hyde, accompanied by Bishop A. J. Moffitt, Col. R. N. Allred and a company of men under the command of Major Abner Lowry, arrived here from Sanpete valley. He was at meeting this morning, and in good health. In the afternoon he was indisposed and was unable to attend. The speakers in the morning were President D. H. Wells and Elder Woodruff. In the afternoon Elders George Q. Cannon and J. W. Young addressed the congregation, which for greater convenience and space met in the bowery at the side of the meeting house. The afternoon meeting, upon motion of President Young, was resolved into a special conference. Nephi was organized into a Stake of Zion, and Jacob G. Bigler was appointed President; and the following elders were selected as members of the High Council: Edward Ockey, Samuel Claridge, Matthew McCune, Israel Hoyt, Timothy S. Hoyt, Andrew Love, George Kendall, Timothy B. Foot, Jacob G. Bigler, Jr., David Cazier, Samuel Cazier, Wm. H. Warner. A school of the prophets was also organized after the dismissal of the afternoon meeting. At 7 p.m. the people assembled in the meeting house and were addressed by President Joseph Young and Elder Musser.

We shall leave Nephi and its hospitable citizens in the morning, carrying with us pleasant remembrances of the kindness we have received, especially from Bishop C. W. Bryan and family. We meet at Fountain Green at noon tomorrow, and then drive to Moroni where we stop the night.

Deseret News
October 21, 1868

Died:

At Nephi City, October 3, 1868, Agnes Ostler daughter of David and Anne Ostler, aged two years and two weeks.

Mill Star please copy.

NEPHI, Oct. 14, 1868.

Editor of the Deseret News: — Dear Sir—I am sorry to have to report that we have considerable sickness among our children. Dysentery and scarlatina, accompanied with ulcerated sore throat, are the prevailing diseases. Our much esteemed brother and sister Orme, of this place, have lost four out of a family of five, and their only remaining one is still much afflicted. We sympathize much with the bereaved parents, as will many of the English Saints, to whom Elder Orme was favorably known while he labored in the ministry. The following are the names and ages of their children, also the times of their deaths. Charles Frederick, died September 15, aged 3 years, 4 months and 10 days; Richard, September 23, aged 5 months and 5 days; Mary Elizabeth, September 28, aged 4 years, 7 months and 15 days; Isaac Joseph, October 10, aged 7 years, 6 months and 11 days.

On last Sunday afternoon, your humble servant and Elder McConnall, of Cedar City, had the pleasure of laying before the Saints of Nephi some of the good teachings of Conference, which caused them to rejoice, and all, by their cheerful faces, showed that they were on hand to sustain the Kingdom of God.

We are thankful to President Young for the organization of a Stake of Zion at Nephi, also for a branch of the School of the Prophets, which will have a tendency to cause the Saints to be more united.

Our crops of potatoes and corn turn out better than was expected.

William Jennings & Co. have moved their branch store into a commodious building erected by bro. J. Hague, where they are doing considerable business.

Very respectfully,

SAMUEL PITCHFORTH.

WEATHER ITEM.—By Deseret Telegraph we are informed that the weather at Logan is a little cloudy and cold; Brigham City, rather cloudy, with indications of a storm; American Fork, warm and cloudy; Springville, cloudy, and looks like storming soon; Payson, cloudy, and looks like storming; Nephi, cloudy, with the appearance of a storm, but pleasant; Moroni, very cold and cloudy, with indications of a storm; Fairview, cloudy and warm, snowed on the mountains last night; Mount Pleasant, cloudy and mild; Fillmore, pleasant; Cove, clear and pleasant, but hard frost last night; Beaver, clear and pleasant, scarcely a cloud visible; Cedar, very clear and pleasant, hard frost last night and rather cool this morning; Toker, clear and pleasant, heavy frost last night; St George, clear and pleasant, with thermometer at 55°

LEVAN.—Br. James Wilson, writing from Levan, near Chicken Creek, on the 23rd, says: "This place was first settled last March, by a number of the old settlers from Chicken Creek, under the direction and counsel of Br. Erastus Snow. We have a beautiful location for a city. Good fruit raisers tell us we can raise all kinds of fruit here. Nearly all the settlers have put out fruit trees and they grow finely. There is an abundance of range for stock, timber is near by, and we have every facility for making a large and prosperous settlement. Br. Samuel Pitchforth, of Nephi, is our President. He is doing all he can to build up the place and invite good Latter-day Saints here. We have about twenty-five families here at present. The town is laid off in blocks 26 rods square, principal streets eight rods wide, cross streets six rods wide. Our farming land is below the town. We have a day school here, under the direction of one of our sisters; an evening school under the direction of Br. Isaac Pierce; and a Sunday school under the superintendence of Br. James Wilson and Br. Isaac Pierce. All is peace, and good feelings prevail in this settlement.

We feel the want of a Post Office very much. We cannot get our papers regularly; sometimes we get them when they are a week old and sometimes not at all."

LEGISLATIVE.

Feb. 11th, 1869.

Mr. E. Snow presented a petition of J. G. Bigler, and eighty-seven others, citizens of Nephi and Levan, praying for an appropriation for road purposes, which was read and referred.

Died:

In New Harmony, Washington Co., January 25, 1869 of consumption, Omer H. Heywood, (Lamanite) supposed to be about 21 years old. He was purchased from captivity in 1853, by Br. Z. H. Baxter, of Nephi City, by whom he was given to the undersigned; in whose family he remained until his death. He came upon the Southern Utah mission in 186?; did military duty assisting in carrying out the orders of Brig. General Erastus Snow to build forts upon the frontier in 1866; and was much respected by all who knew him.

JOSEPH HEYWOOD.

Deseret News
March 17, 1869

Died:

At Nephi, Nov. 16th, 1868, Brother James Shaw. He was born Nov. 19th, 1801. He was in Nauvoo with the Saints and came to these valleys in 1850, and ever remained true to the cause of truth.

Also at the same place on the 3d inst., Mary Bamford, born August 9th, 1790. She left England with her family in the ship *Berlin*, in 1848, and came up to the Bluffs, where she buried her husband. In 1852 she came to Utah, where by her faithful, kindly spirit she won the love and esteem of all who were acquainted with her. —COM.

Deseret News
March 31, 1869

Died:

At Nephi, Juab Co., on the 3d inst., of scarlet fever, Emily, daughter of David and Elizabeth Udall, aged 9 years, 1 month and 27 days.

Also at the same place, of the same disease, on 9th inst., Nancy Maria, daughter of Andrew and Sarah M. Love; also of the same disease, on the 14th inst., Joseph, infant son of the above A. and S. M. Love.

Also on the 20th inst., of the same disease, Sarah Lucretia, daughter of Thomas and Sarah Tranter, aged 9 years, 1 month and 26 days.

The above little sisters were regular attendants at the Sunday School, and were admired for their kind and gentle dispositions, and being prompt and attentive to their studies.—COM.

Nephi, March 22, 1869.

Ed. Deseret News:—Dear Bro.—The heavy rains which have fallen during the last two weeks have delayed the spring planting, but they have been good for the fall grain, of which a large amount was sown last fall. From the appearance of the mountains there is every prospect of there being an abundance of water the coming season, and the people are preparing to put in crops on an abundant scale. We have been blessed with a mild and pleasant winter and our fruit trees appear promising, many are intending to plant out fruit trees, grape vines and mulberry cuttings, on quite a large scale, silk culture, co-operation, wine making, &c., seem to be looming up and the spirit of improvement is abroad among the Saints.

The Juab Co-operative and Commercial Association is flourishing, and the establishment is doing a good cash business. It has purchased the extensive stock of the Nephi Branch of the Eagle Emporium. The Institution is offering goods at reasonable rates. The following gentlemen are the officers of the Association: President, Jacob G. Bigler; Directors, John Vickers, David Udall, Mathew McCune, and John Hague; Treasurer, Timothy B. Foot; Secretary, Samuel Pitchforth.

The Ladies' Relief Society, under the management of Sister A. Goldsbrough, is doing much good.

Our Sunday schools are in a prosperous condition, the south district school, on the 7th inst., had an interesting exhibition which was a decided success, and reflected much credit on the teachers of the school. A number of prizes were given to the children.

We have four day schools, which are well attended. The two principal ones are taught by bros. A. Love and W. Rellay.

I am sorry to have to report that there is a great deal of sickness among our children. The scarlet fever, of a very malignant type, has been raging for some time in this place. Bros. Udall, Love, Webb, and Tranter, have lost children of great promise, and many children are still afflicted with this disease.

Peace and union prevail throughout the country and our officers of the law have to farm for a living, there being no cases on the docket. Industry and sobriety characterise the people, who are prospering under the direction of President Bigler.

The DESERET NEWS is ever welcome, but when the Weekly does not arrive until Saturday we are much disappointed.

Respectfully,
SAMUEL PITCHFORTH.

Deseret News
June 2, 1869

Died:

At Nephi, Juab county, May 15th, Ruth Eliza, infant daughter of William and Emma Hayward, aged 9 months and 27 days.

THE FOURTH IN THE SETTLEMENTS.

At Nephi the national flag was hoisted at sunrise, with the accompaniments of music and musketry. At ten o'clock there was a meeting of the citizens, who were regaled with music, songs, and an oration.

NEPHI, June 30, 1869.

Editor Deseret News:—Dear Sir—The crops in this county are very promising, and the farmers are looking forward to an abundant harvest, and the people will rejoice in "the harvest home." Our orchards and gardens are full of choice fruit—apple, pear, plum, apricot, cherry trees are doing well and many will be blest with being rewarded for the care and labor they have expended in planting out orchards. Grape vines and small fruits are also bearing abundantly and the crops of vegetables of all kinds were never better.

The Nephi Co-operative Mercantile and Manufacturing Institution is doing a good business; the people, without exception, supporting it.

On Saturday last, by invitation, I attended the annual meeting of the Nephi Female Relief Society. The room was tastefully decorated; there was a fine display of articles manufactured by members of the Society, which numbers one hundred and forty-six. Quilts, pieced and wove, rugs, table and stand covers, shirts, hats, stockings, socks, mittens, gloves, slippers, crotchet work, etc., were exhibited and were a credit to the Society, and the cheerful and smiling faces of the sisters, indicated that they were united in the good work.

Sister Amelia Goldsbrough gave an interesting account of the organization and progress of the Society, and felt proud of the support she had received from the officers and members of the same. Sister A. L. Bigler read the statistical report of the Society, which showed the finances of the same to be in as favorable a position as could be expected, considering that the locusts destroyed the crops of last season. Much credit is due to the Presidentess and the officers of the institution for the manner in which the business has been conducted. Valuable instruction was given by President Jacob G. Bigler, Bishop C. H. Bryan, Elders E. Ockey, S. Pitchforth, G. Kendall, B. Riches and J. Miller, on the duties and callings of the officers and members of the Society, and all felt pleased to meet with them and see the progress the sisters were making.

The Society had rendered timely assistance in many cases of sickness and want, for which it will receive the blessings of the grateful.

I am pleased to say that of late there has been no deaths from the epidemic which prevailed here during last winter.

Yours, very respectfully,

SAMUEL PITCHFORTH.

SUICIDE AT NEPHI.—We learn by Deseret Telegraph Line that shortly after sunset last evening Mr. William Stanly, of Nephi, committed suicide by blowing off the upper part of his head with his gun, causing immediate death. The deceased was very much respected for his honesty, faithfulness and industry.

LEVAN.

The celebration commenced at daybreak, with a salute of artillery. The flag was raised at sunrise, and was saluted by the firing of 22 guns. The teachers and Sunday School scholars assembled in the bowery at eight o'clock a.m., with banners bearing appropriate mottoes, and there formed a procession and marched through the principal streets, thence repaired to the residence of Bro. Elmer Taylor, where they were joined by President Pitchforth and party, when they returned to the bowery precisely at 11 o'clock a. m.; when the following programme was presented:

House called to order by the Marshal. Singing by the choir, prayer by the Chaplain, Singing by the choir. Oration by Bro. Geo. Gardner, Orator of the day; singing; Reminiscence of the pioneers, and history of the church by President Samuel Pitchforth; singing; Benediction by the Chaplain.

At 2 o'clock p.m., the tables were set, and all partook of a sumptuous dinner provided by the sisters.

At 3 o'clock p.m., the juveniles enjoyed themselves dancing, the evening was devoted to the same amusement by the adults. All appeared to enjoy themselves; and everything went off agreeably.

Yours truly,
HEBER HARTLEY.

Deseret News
August 18, 1869

NEPHI.—An esteemed correspondent writing from Nephi, says "a very large amount of grain will be raised this season in Nephi; the harvest is pressing and hands are few. I understood that the telegraph operator at this place reported the shocking case of suicide which took place here on last Wednesday evening, when Bro. Wm. Stanley shot himself, blowing off one third of his head. An inquest was held and the jury gave a verdict that the deceased was laboring under a temporary fit of insanity. No one can give any reason why Bro. S. killed himself; he was a good, peaceful citizen, about twenty-six years of age, and leaves a wife and four children to mourn his loss.

"On the election ticket, voted at the last election, Pres. Jacob G. Bigler was the nomination for Councilor for Millard and Juab counties, and Samuel Pitchforth Representative for Juab county."

Deseret News
September 1, 1869

LEVAN.—We learn through a letter from Elder Samuel Pitchforth to Robert L. Campbell, Esq., that they are hauling rock and otherwise preparing to build a meeting-house at Levan. The building is to be 36 by 20 feet. That settlement, the letter states, is in a prosperous condition, the crops are good and the location is well adapted for fruit. Speaking of his home in Nephi, Elder Pitchforth says: "We should be pleased to show you our fruit, flowers, etc., twenty-five varieties of grapes, three of which are bearing, also some choice kinds of cherries, plums, pears, apricots, gooseberries, strawberries, currants, etc.; of flowers we have dahlias, roses, gladiolus, tuberroses, stocks, petunias, bleeding hearts, etc. We have now twelve kinds of dahlias in bloom, and have had more than that number of roses blooming.

Deseret News
October 6, 1869

THE STORM.—The first snow of the season fell in this valley during the night, and to-day it is far too dreary, chilly and squally to be comfortable. It is a most disagreeable day. By Deseret Telegraph Line we learn that at Springville the weather is cold, the wind blowing and the rain falling fast; at Payson, Mona and Nephi it is cold, rained considerably during the night, and at the latter place a little snow fell; at Mount Pleasant and Scipio it is cloudy and cold; at Fillmore it snowed a little last night; at Tokerville the weather is clear, the wind blowing slightly, there has been no frost there as yet this fall; at Ogden the weather is very stormy.

Deseret News
October 13, 1869

ESTRAYS.

I HAVE in my possession the following described animals—

One Brown HORSE, 12 or 13 years old, branded No. 8 on left shoulder and thigh, Y on left shoulder and thigh, and O on left thigh.

W

One Red Spotted Grey 2-year old STUD, no marks or brands.

The above named animals, if not claimed within 30 days from the date of advertising, will be sold at Nephi City Stray Pound.

ISAAC GRACE,
Nephi City Poundkeeper.

873 2 x 33 1

Deseret News
November 17, 1869

SHOOTING AFFRAY.—A telegram from Nephi, Juab County, received this afternoon per Deseret Telegraph Line, says:

A shooting affray took place near here last night, between the Postmaster of Treasure city, White Pine, and a man who had been engaged by him to take charge of a ranch owned by him near Treasure city. On Sunday last the man in charge of the ranch left it, taking with a number of stock teams and wagons, which he has since sold. The Postmaster, hearing of his departure, started in pursuit and overtook him at about midnight last night, while camped three miles north of this place, and there shot him. The Postmaster says he did not intend to kill him, but being excited, the pistol went off easier than he could have supposed.

The Postmaster came in and gave himself up for trial.   OPERATOR.

Deseret News
December 1, 1869

STATE OF THE WEATHER.—Received per Deseret Telegraph line, yesterday:

Logan, cold and cloudy, looks like snow; Kaysville, dismal and chilly, appearance of snow soon; Brigham, cold and cloudy, like rain; Springville, been snowing all day, now about four inches deep; Nephi, snow about five inches deep, thawing, clearing off; Scipio, very cloudy have very muddy roads, some snow; Provo, snowing.

Deseret News
December 15, 1869

DIED suddenly on the 20th of Nov., at the residence of Elder A. F. McDonald, Provo, Mary, relict of the late John Sutton, of Nephi, aged 71 years.

Deseret News
January 19, 1870

JUAB COUNTY.—Elder Samuel Pitchforth of Nephi City, has paid us a short visit, and borne his testimony in relation to matters in general in Juab County. At Nephi the people are prosperous and comfortable. Co-operation is thriving, and the dividend lately declared amounted to four per cent. per month, and would have been larger but for a quantity of old stock, bought at high rates, still remaining unsold. This dividend was exclusive of a large quantity of grain on hand and a building owned by the share-holders.

The members of the Female Relief Society gave parties on the evenings of the 5th and 7th instant, in behalf of their institution, in the Social Hall, which was elegantly decorated with mottoes, paintings and fine specimens of their own work, such as quilts, etc. The ladies did the honors on the occasion, and conducted the affair with great *eclat*. No gentlemen were entitled to numbers, the ladies having entire control. Sperry's band was engaged for the occasion and discoursed most eloquently. President Bigler and the authorities of the city were present, and there was a first rate time, the characteristics of the affair being peace and good order.

Schools are receiving a good share of support in Nephi: three are constantly running. Bro. W. R. May is very successfully conducting a fine select school. His school room is well provided with maps and globes and the best educational works, from which instruction is imparted on the most approved methods.

Levan and Mona are also doing well: the new meeting-house at the former was dedicated on Christmas day, since which time several parties have been held within it walls. The citizens of Levan are prospering, and are pleased with the location of their settlement!

Mona is being fast built up, and is increasing in size and importance. The health of the county, generally, is good.

Deseret News
January 26, 1870

MASS MEETING AT NEPHI.—The ladies of Nephi held a mass meeting on the 14th, to express their indignation at the bills before Congress presented by Cragin and Cullom. The attendance was large, the meeting-house being well filled. Mrs. Amelia Goldsbrough was called to the chair, and Mrs. Amy S. Bigler was chosen Secretary. A number of speeches were made by the ladies and the meeting was highly interesting and spirited. The speakers characterized the bills as malicious and infamous and designed to subvert the rights of civil and religious liberty. The originators and authors of the measures were characterized as too contemptible for notice from high-minded ladies; but the speakers expressed themselves confident that Congress would not countenance their efforts by so illiberal and unjust a proceeding as the passage of either of the bills, which would be an indelible blot on the national escutcheon.

ADDITION TO THE MUSEUM.—Bro. John W. Shepherd, of Levan, Juab Co., presented to to the S. L. City Museum to-day, thro' Hon. S. Pitchforth, and by his suggestion, a seed from the East Indies, called the Buffalo Seed, from its close resemblance to the head of a buffalo; also a Japanese silver coin, rectangular in form, about an inch long, the thickness of a half dollar and covered with Japanese characters.

Bro. Shepherd was formerly a steward on an Oriental steamer that plied between London and the East Indies, and during a term of service of eighteen years' duration, he had opportunities to collect many things rare and curious from Oriental climes; and it is not improbable that other specimens from this gentleman will help to enrich the Museum. Others in the Territory may go and do likewise with the greatest propriety.

Deseret News
February 23, 1870

PURE SALT.—Hon. S. Pitchforth, of Nephi, Juab County, presented us to-day, on behalf of the manufacturers, Messrs. Salisbury, Warner & Co., of Nephi, a very fine specimen of table salt, made from a spring, oozing from a rock near Nephi. This salt is declared to be free from any mineral mixture, and to be perfectly pure. The manufacturers can furnish it in Salt Lake City, at prices to suit the times.

Deseret News
March 9, 1870

Died:

At Levan, Juab County, March 1st, of measles and inflammation of the chest, Seth Franklin, son of James and Elizabeth Wilson, aged 1 year, 1 month and 14 days.

THE LADIES' MASS MEETINGS—THEIR TRUE SIGNIFICANCE.

On the 13th of January the first indignation meeting, to protest against the bill in Congress designed to suppress the patriarchal marriage system in Utah, was held by the ladies of this city. Since then similar meetings have been held in the principal cities and settlements of the Territory, and we have received the reports of the same from:—Pleasant Grove, Salem, Millville, Richmond, Wellsville, Springville, Nephi, Grantsville, Milton, Fairfield, Kanosh, Hyrum, Fillmore, Willard, Scipio, Rockville, American Fork, Farmington, Mount Pleasant, Springtown, Fountain Green, Toquerville, Alpine City, Porterville, Franklin, Mona, Spanish Fork, Manti, Lehi, Cedar City, Payson, West Jordan, Beaver, South Jordan, Clarkston, Logan, Brigham City, Clifton, Paris, Parowan, Hebron, Pinto, Pine Valley, Centreville, Weber City, South Cottonwood, Minersville, Newton, Virgin City, Kaysville, Smithfield, Washington, Adamsville and Greenville.

Several of these reports we have published in a condensed form, in the columns of the NEWS; we should be glad to publish all, but lack of space and a fear that a repetition of sentiments exactly similar, would prove tedious to the majority of our readers compel us to refrain. We intended to publish the names of the officers and speakers at the various meetings, believing that they deserve to be held in remembrance, but instead of that, we shall hand them all, with the reports of the speeches they have furnished us, to President Geo. A. Smith, Church Historian, that they may be preserved in the archives of the church. The number of ladies who have attended these meetings amount in the aggregate to not less, we feel confident in saying, than twenty-five thousand, and twentyfi-ve thousand women voluntarily assembling for such a purpose,—to endorse patriarchal marriage and to protest against legislation designed to suppress it, is without a parallel in the world's history, and furnishes an incontestible proof that the women of Utah, when brought to the test of principle, can be as firm and decided in their integrity as the sterner sex.

An impartial person, on perusing these speeches printed in the NEWS, will at once discard the idea that the ladies of Utah are the degraded, spiritless and ignorant creatures that their traducers have represented them. Their utterances, on the contrary, have evinced as much intelligence and culture as the same number of ladies chosen promiscuously from any community in the world would have done on this or any other subject. While to suppose for a moment that such a number of women can be degraded, or that they are so completely devoid of the refined instincts peculiar to woman, as to vote for the spread of female degradation is simply preposterous. The comments of the press on these meetings have, in many instances, been very flattering, and have proved that the protests of the ladies of Utah have commanded a large share both of attention and respect.

Unprecedented as are these meetings in character and object, we regard them as possessing far more significance and importance than the mere gathering together and the passage of the resolutions at first sight evince. The ladies of Utah in carrying out this programme have well earned and deserve the respect and thanks of their sex throughout the whole world, for they have inaugurated the *first efficacious* movement for the social redemption and elevation of the female sex.

Prostitution, or the "social evil," as it is called, which is corrupting the vitals and undermining the foundation of every nation in Christendom is exciting much fear, and scientific and philanthropic men in every nation are more than ever in earnest seeking a remedy. But they all admit that they have little hope. The ladies, too, in this country and in various parts of Europe, painfully aware of the increasing degradation of their sex, are striving in their way to elevate it to a higher plane; but their labors have effected little good. Judging by the pertinacity with which they are laboring to secure female suffrage one might be led to suppose that they regard that at least as the chief ingredient of a panacea for the ills that the sex labors under. But with the suffrage in their hands we fear that they would fail in effecting the reformation they desire.

The key to the solution of the social problem, and the extinction of the "social evil" has just been given by the ladies of Utah, in their protest in favor of, and their expressed determination to support and spread plural or patriarchal marriage. The world, after taxing the resources of their wisest and best, is still crying aloud for this great boon; but in Utah the problem has been solved, for in a community numbering not less than from a hundred to a hundred and fifty thousand members, possessing all the passions and frailties of their fellow creatures elsewhere, the "social evil" and what are termed "sexual diseases" have been trodden down and out of existence and a system instituted under which their development is rendered impossible. We know that thousands, when talking about polygamy in Utah, will manifest their ignorance and prejudices so far as to talk about "legalized prostitution." But this is sheer nonsense. Let them turn their attention to those countries where prostitution is legalized and they will find the same results there as in the United States where it is not sanctioned by law. In those countries as well as in this there are thousands of walking pest houses spreading diseases which are destroying

the stamina and corrupting the life blood of the whole race, and this is the result of prostitution, whether sanctioned or proscribed by legislative enactments. But no such results follow patriarchal marriage, and those who declaim against it, as instituted in Utah, and compare it with legalized prostitution, might, with as much propriety, compare the odor of the full blown rose with the abominable stench of the skunk.

God, through the Prophet Joseph Smith, revealed the plural marriage system, and the great design of its revelation was to relieve the earth from that terrible curse that now threatens it with destruction. The world with all their philosophy and science will fail to find any remedy for their "social evil." This is a remedy of which God is the Author; all others will fail. Its efficacy has been demonstrated here, and, sooner or later, all mankind will gladly acknowledge it in their faith and practice in order to escape destruction.

Viewed in this light, and this is the true light in which to view them, these demonstrations of the ladies of Utah possess deep significance; and in making them they have done more to provide a remedy for the curse of the age than all the social science congresses that ever assembled, or than all the combined efforts of the "strong-minded" have yet accomplished; in fact they have laid the sure foundation for the social and physical redemption not only of their sex but of the whole race, and in time to come they will receive the thanks and honor to which such a step entitles them.

THE PRESIDENT AND PARTY.—By Deseret Telegraph line we learn that the President and party held a meeting at Payson last night. The speakers were Bishop L. D. Young, Elders B. Young, jr., and C. R. Savage, and President Geo. A. Smith. The party started this morning at 9-40 for Nephi, holding meeting at Santaquin. They will stay at Nephi over night. All are well.

The returning party addressed a crowded meeting at American Fork last evening. Elders John Taylor, Wilford Woodruff, Geo. Q. Cannon, Joseph F. Smith and Heber P. Kimball spoke; the meeting was an excellent one. The same Elders met in the School of the Prophets with the members belonging to that place, Lehi, Pleasant Grove and Mountainville.

RECOVERING.—We learn from Ogden that the Honorable F. D. Richards, who has been suffering from a severe attack of inflammatory rheumatism, is recovering. This will be gratifying intelligence to his numerous friends.

Deseret News
March 16, 1870

FILLMORE CITY, March 3, '70.

Editor Deseret News—Dear Sir—

I had the pleasure of joining the President and party, yesterday afternoon, just south of the Sevier bridge. I had supposed that some of the members of the company had been sending you items respecting the progress, etc., of the party; but I learned this evening that no letter had as yet been written.

The following is a list of persons constituting the company, viz: Presidents Brigham Young and Geo. A. Smith, with their ladies; Bishop L. D. Young, Elders Brigham Young jr., J. W. Young, Chas. R. Savage, Levi Stewart, John S. Hollman, John Squires, O. P. Arnold, John H. Smith, Nathaniel V. Jones, E. W. VanEtten, A. M. Musser and lady, and Masters Brigham and Albert C. Young, with eight vehicles and some twenty-eight animals. The brethren have been very busy since quitting the city, having held meetings at American Fork, Provo, Payson, Santaquin, Nephi, Scipio, Holden, and at this place.

You are well aware that traveling every day and attending meetings every evening, and sometimes at midday, is very laborious work. The two inches of snow that fell last night have made the roads very sloppy up to date. No accident of moment has occurred to mar the pleasure of the company. As usual, the Saints everywhere give evidence of the pleasure they have in seeing and hearing the Presidency and Elders; meeting houses are all too small to hold the people. Bros. Young and Smith do their share of the preaching, and the former is driving his own team.

In meetings and in private talks almost every conceivable duty devolving on the Saints is made plain, and the people are strongly urged to observe and faithfully perform them.

I almost forgot to mention that Bishop A. J. Moffit and lady joined us last night at Scipio.

At Manti, the people seem to be taking hold in good earnest to build a commodious meeting house to be 80 by 55 feet, of white sard-stone, a considerable portion of which is already quarried and on the ground.

Some of the Bishops have been placing cedar posts, 7 feet long, in the ground by the side of each telegraph pole, so as to maintain its perpendicularity after the pole has rotted off. It is expected that every pole on the line, now some six hundred miles long, will soon be stayed in like manner. This will, in the long run, prove economical, although costing considerable now. The cedar posts, if cut when the sap is down, and of the right sort, will last for years in the ground.

We expect to reach Cove Creek Fort, to-morrow p. m., and no doubt will spend Sabbath at Beaver.

More anon.

Yours respectfully,

A. MILTON MUSSER.

Deseret News
June 20, 1870

LEVAN. — By a communication from Elder Isaac W. Pierce, dated, "Levan, Juab county, June 15th," we learn that matters are moving along comfortably at that place, under the presidency of Elder Samuel Pitchforth. The grasshoppers have done great damage to the small grain crops, but the people are busy re-planting, and the pests were on the wing, northward. The damage to the gardens is but trifling. The settlers have enlarged their field this Spring, and have now 1,050 acres of good farming land enclosed. The co-operative store and Female Relief Society are in a flourishing condition; also the Sunday and day school. General good health prevails, and the people are alive to the work of God.

Deseret News
July 13, 1870

NEPHI.

At sunrise the "old flag" was unfurled to the breeze and saluted by infantry in command of Adjutant Charles Price.

At nine a.m., the people assembled at the meeting-house, when they were called to order by the Marshal of the day, Samuel Cazier. Singing by the Nephi choir. Prayer by the Chaplain, Patriarch William Cazier.

The Declaration of Independence was read by Thomas Ord. Oration by Andrew Love, after which, singing, recitations, etc., interspersed with music, was in order, and the hours passed happily till twelve o'clock, when the meeting was dismissed by the Chaplin.

At two p.m. the juveniles assembled under the bowery and enjoyed themselves lively till six.

In the evening there was an adult dance in the Social Hall. The day was fine, and everybody seemed to enjoy themselves finely notwithstanding the threatenings of "Bill Cullom."

Charles Sperry, John Kienke, David Cazier, Committee of Arrangements. Thomas Ord, Reporter.

Salt Lake Herald
July 14, 1870

NOTICE.—On and after Friday, July 15th, an express and letter mail will be forwarded from the office of Wells, Fargo & Co., via southern stage line, to Pioche (Meadow Valley mines), Provo, Nephi, Fillmore, Beaver, Cedar, St. George and intermediate points in southern Utah.

Leaving Salt Lake City every Friday at 8 a. m.; arriving at Pioche on Monday at 4 p. m.

Returning, leave Pioche every Wednesday at 8 a. m., arriving at Salt Lake City on Saturday at 4 p. m.

THEO. F. TRACY, AGT.

Deseret News
August 3, 1870

THE ELECTION.—The following special dispatch to the NEWS, of the returns of the votes cast in the settlements, up to 2 o'clock this afternoon, has been received by Deseret Telegraph line:

Logan	345
Kaysville	214
Payson	400
Springville	386
Mt. Pleasant	271
Nephi	174
Fillmore	162
Fairview	99
Moroni	44
Ogden	362
Manti	182
Scipio	117
Provo	531

The vote polled in this city, up to half past 2 o'clock was as follows: 1st Precinct 420; 2nd Precinct 700; 3rd Precinct 412; 4th Precinct 1118.

Deseret News
August 10, 1870

A NEW TELEGRAPH OFFICE.—We are informed that superintendent Musser, o the Deseret Telegraph Co., opened a new office at Levan, Juab Co., yesterday afternoon. Miss Elizabeth Clarrige assumes the duties of operator at this new office.

Deseret News
August 24, 1870

Died.
In Levan city, Juab county, on the 15th inst., of inflammation of the bowels, Isaac Daily, son of George H. and Sarah Pierce, aged 5 months and 3 days.

Salt Lake Herald
August 27, 1870

GONE SOUTH.—Presidents Young, Smith and Wells, Elder B. Young, jr., General Burton, Col. Winder, Major Huntingdon, and some other gentlemen, start on a trip south this morning and will be gone probably about three weeks, except President Geo. A. Smith, who will only go as far as Nephi with the company and then return to the city. We wish them a pleasant journey and safe return.

UTAH NEWS.

Movements of President Young's Party.

[By Deseret Telegraph to the HERALD.]

Springville, August 29.—The following is the list of the President's company going south. Presidents B. Young and D. H. Wells, Elders B. Young, jr., R. T. Burton, Jno. R. Winder, J. W. Fox, A. E. Hinkley, Briant Stringam, D. B. Huntington, O. P. Arnold, Willard Young and A. M. Musser, President G. A. Smith and Elders A. K. Thurber and Jno. H. Smith go with them to Nephi.

Yesterday they had two good meetings at Provo. Presidents Joseph and Brigham Young spoke in the morning, Presidents B. Young and G. A. Smith in the afternoon. General and wholesome instructions were given to large and attentive audiences.

Chauncey Turner, an old member of the church, was buried yesterday at Provo.

At the meeting here last evening there was a full house. Presidents Young, Smith and Wells and Bishop Smoot spoke, giving excellent teachings.

The company take dinner at Santaquin to-day, and stay at Nephi to-night.

NEPHI, Aug. 29th, 1870.

Editor News:—I telegraphed you a list of the President's company from Springville yesterday p.m. The party, quitting your city at different times of the day on Saturday last, reached American Fork, Pleasant Grove and Provo in a scattered, but not at all demoralized, condition. All feel well and start out on this visit as missionaries, to do the Saints good.

President Joseph Young's remarks, on Sunday morning, at Provo, related mostly to his experience on his late mission to Europe. He manifests much solicitude for the poor of the old country, and had he the means at command every Saint would be most kindly remembered by this philanthropist.

President Brigham Young followed in remarks directed pungently to those who had promised succor to their poor friends, to those who had borrowed money to help themselves to Utah and have neglected to refund, to the many who have been assisted to immigrate by the P. E. F. Co., but do not pay up, and to all in anywise under obligations to the ungathered Saints.

At the afternoon meeting, at Provo, President Brigham Young again addressed the large congregation. He said that the Saints could leave their homes, property, etc., at the bidding of the devil, as at Kirtland, in Missouri, Illinois and other places, while many object to give a few of the many dollars they possess in peace, to assist in gathering the poor, etc., and object to do many things the Lord asks them.

President George A. Smith followed, much in the same strain, urging the people, with much force, to remember the poor abroad that they may be gathered to enjoy the blessings of God in these peaceful valleys.

I almost forgot to refer to the very excellent singing by Bro. Daniels' choir.

The Provo Woolen Factory is progressing finely. It will be, when completed, a fine and much needed structure.

The Dusenberry Bros. are alive in school matters. The President paid them a handsome compliment in respect to their school. He also referred, with pleasure, to the success attending your labors in the manufacture of type, paper, etc.

At six p.m. the good people of Springville met to hear the President and his counsellors, who addressed the large and eager audience in a very encouraging and comforting manner.

The roads are very dusty; fruit in most settlements abundant, as also grain in Utah and in this county.

Major Powell, illustrious for navigating the great Colorado, is, with his company and outfit, on his way south. We pass and re-pass each other daily.

At meeting here this evening President Smith and Elder Hyde addressed the Saints.

President Hyde and a number of the Bishops from Sanpete came over to see the President.

In haste.

A. MILTON MUSSER.

Deseret News
September 28, 1870

Died.

At Levan, Juab County, of cholera infantum, on the 20th of September, 1870, James Hartley, son of James and Elizabeth Wilson, aged 2 months and 20 days.

Deseret News
October 12, 1870

Died.

At Nephi, Juab county, September 9th, at 11 o'clock p.m., Thomas Midgley, Senr., after 23 days of severe affliction.

Salt Lake Herald
October 29, 1870

ARRIVAL OF THE STAGE ROBBERS. —There was considerable excitement on East Temple street and at the City Hall yesterday evening, on the arrival of the men engaged in the late stage robbery, in charge of U. S. Deputy Marshal Duncan and Hugh White, Esq., proprietor of the Southern Stage line. When they got into the City Hall, McKay had a reckless devil-me-care look, with a good deal of snap about him that was indicative of mischief with a fair opportunity. The other two presented an ordinary appearance. From Mr. White we gained the following facts. He, (Mr. White) was at American Fork when he received word of the robbery, and started south immediately, On the way he received a telegram that the men had been caught. When he arrived at Nephi the robbers bore themselves rather defiantly, as if those who had arrested them had made a mistake and had taken the wrong men. But the evidence against them was too strong, and finally St. Ledger agreed to show

where the plunder was concealed. Mr. White took him in his buggy to Levan, and there he discovered the fruits of the robbery in a sort of cellar, near the house where the three men had been stopping, and close by a hay stack where they had camped. Five hundred and forty dollars in gold and twelve dollars and seventy-five cents in silver, with a hundred and sixty-five dollars in currency which had been taken from the registered package sack were recovered, being all that was stolen.

The driver had identified the men as soon as he saw them, McKay as the one who had robbed the coach, St. Ledger as the one who had covered the driver with a shot-gun, and Heath as the one who stood by the coach with a pistol, while McKay "went through" it.

Sheriff Cazier of Juab Co., who arrested them with his posse, received a dispatch to bring them up to Provo and deliver them to the United States Marshal. He brought them up on Thursday and turned them over yesterday morning. They were ironed and left Provo at 10 a.m. yesterday, arriving in this city at 5 p.m. in the evening. They are in confinement in the city prison. Mr. White speaks in the highest terms of the energy manifested by the Sheriff of Juab County and the citizens of Nephi.

McKay and St. Ledger are well known in this city, the former having been proprietor of and the latter connected with, the Revere House for a length of time. Heath is a discharged soldier, formerly belonging to the 9th regiment of U. S. infantry.

Deseret News
November 2, 1870

ROBBERS CAUGHT.—We learn, per Deseret Telegraph line, that there is every reason to believe that the parties who committed the stage robbery near Nephi, on Monday night, have been captured and are now in custody. Yesterday Sheriff Cazier and *posse* found two men lurking about a mile from the spot where the robbery was committed. On being interrogated they gave conflicting and unsatisfactory answers. When asked if any one else was with them, they stated that a companion was then about a mile eastward, and that he had lost a dog for which they were hunting. The man alluded to was found one mile westward, and, when questioned, said he had not lost a dog. It is suppposed that these men had secreted the treasure in that vicinity, and were watching an opportunity to convey it away. On examination, it was found that the shoes of the prisoners corresponded exactly with the tracks at the scene of the robbery. One of the prisoners had a nail in the centre of the sole of his shoe, the imprint of which was plainly visible in some of the tracks. They were identified by the stage driver. Up to last night the treasure had not been found, but a party of men were searching for it.

The names of the three prisoners are McKay, St Ledger and Heath. They were transient residents of Levan, Juab Co. They will shortly be handed over to the custody of the U. S. Marshal.

THE MAIL ROBBERS.—We have received the following per Deseret Telegraph line:

NEPHI, October 27, 7 p.m.—Four hundred and forty dollars in coin, taken from the coach by the robbers, are recovered. The registered papers, etc., are cut up so that they cannot be identified, with the exception of one package.

St. Ledger gave information where the money was, but it is thought that he knows where there is more. He says that McKay, Heath and himself started out for the purpose of robbing the mail. They were going north to rob the Montana coaches, but a friend of McKay's told him that the treasure box only went occasionally on the Montana coach, and when it went it had an armed force with it; and they concluded they would come down this way. They had three shot guns and three revolvers, which they got just for the business, and had kept concealed while staying at Levan.

St. Ledger says there was nothing in the treasure box, and only sixty-three dollars in currency in the register sack. He says McKay has that in his pocket. He also says he don't know where the guns and pistols are; McKay hid them—stuck them in the mud, muzzle down, in Levan field somewhere.

It is thought that McKay got more money than he let St. Ledger and Heath know of.

EXAMINED. — Yesterday the men charged with robbing the mail coach south of Nephi, were brought up before Judge Strickland and held over for trial at Provo. Mr. Hugh White, proprietor of the stage line; Sheriff Cazier, of Juab county; Mr. S. Memmott, the stage driver; Mr. Charles Price, one of the passengers, and Judge S. P. McCurdy, another of the passengers were examined. Bail was refused for the prisoners, whose trial, we understand, will commence on January 2nd, 1871.

SANPETE MAILS.—The following communication was received on Friday from a gentleman of Mount Pleasant, Sanpete Co.:

Mount Pleasant, Sanpete,
Nov. 9, 1870.

Editors Herald:—You will please ventilate the question why we of Sanpete are subject to the annoyance of seeing our local mail, which intersects at Nephi, come and no papers; this happening repeatedly. Now, do you firstly put the papers in due form, time and season in the Salt Lake office? If so, as the Sanpete mail is not opened, only at Nephi to put in all letters gathered for Sanpete between Salt Lake City and Nephi; it follows, of course, presuming that Mr. White delivers the mail in due schedule time to T. B. Foot, P. M., of Nephi, that the fault is at Nephi, or the schedule time of the Sanpete mail is too early for the locomotiveness of the aforesaid great Southern mail route; in which case, please ask Col. Wickizer to alter the time, so as to promote proper intersection and the arrivals of the city sheets so desirable just now. DATA.

The difficulty complained of was caused thus: Sanpete has lately received a tri-weekly mail from Nephi, but Mr. Moore, Postmaster in this city, who had been sending the sack twice a week as before, was not apprised of the change until Tuesday last. Upon receiving the information he made up a sack and dispatched it on Wednesday morning; and the mail for Sanpete now goes every Monday, Wednesday and Friday, so that our friends in that county will get their papers by due course of mail.

We trust Col. Wickizer, when he returns, will be as prompt in dealing with the Ophir, Cache Co. and Rich Co. matter, as Mr. Moore has been in this; and would also request his attention to the necessity of increased mail facilities for West Jordan and Bingham.

Deseret News
November 23, 1870

LEVAN.—Brother James Wilson, of Levan, Juab county, writes on the 14th inst., that the settlement is progressing, good houses are being built and other improvements made by the citizens. A good Sunday school is in operation; and in two weeks time a day and evening school will be started in the New Meeting House, which will then be finished. Co-operation is flourishing: On the 1st instant stock was taken and a dividend of thirty per cent in six months was declared.

Salt Lake Herald
December 6, 1870

[By Deseret Telegraph Line.]

ESCAPING PRISONERS SHOT AND KILLED IN JUAB COUNTY.

Nephi, Dec. 5.—On the 30th of November information, under oath, was filed before G. Gardiner, J. P., of Levan precinct, that Richard Soper and Antone Varlardie were guilty of the crime of committing rape on their step-daughters, children of ten, eleven, twelve and thirteen years of age, both men being married and having children. Writs were issued and the prisoners examined. On the 1st of December, at 2 p.m., the evidence being plain and positive, the prisoners of their own choice and free will made a public confession of their guilt. They were committed for trial, and a constable was ordered to deliver them, for safe keeping, into the hands of the Sheriff of this county. On the 2nd inst., as they were being conveyed under guard of five men to Nephi, at a place called Cedar Point, the prisoners gave a yell, at the same time springing out of the wagon. The horses became frightened, and by the time the guard was out of the wagon the prisoners were about seventy-five steps away. The constable ordered them to stop or they would be fired on. They paid no attention, making their way up the hills into the cedars, the guard running and firing when opportunity presented. After a chase of from half to three-quarters of a mile the prisoners were brought down by being shot, and died a short time after. The constable came to Nephi and gave information of the facts in the case, whereupon the Coroner issued a writ to the Sheriff, who proceeded with the constable to the above-mentioned place and brought in the bodies. An inquest was held upon the bodies before the Coroner and a jury of respectable citizens, and the witnesses were duly examined.

GENTLEMEN'S LIST.

Alamande F	Anderson D P
Almy T J	Alexon M
Barnes F	Britell C K
Barratt C C	Burras F
Beckwith T S	Byrn J T
Birdsall D H 5	Burk J M
Bingham E	Burke J
Blake W	Burt A
Bolser B S	Brown D B
Bredeson O	
Carey M'D	Cole G
Carney W J	Cottle H
Coein L	Cooper & Bros 2
Caldwell C	Cowley W J 2
Clayton J	Cooper H S
Claye J R	Cowan J
Church H C	Couer L
Chrestensen C	Coombs H S
Davis R	DeColbert J
Davis J D	Derby J E
Dahl A	Dodd, Brown & Co
Dalman A	
Edginton W W	Eriezon C L
Edwards F	Evans D
Elliott R W	Evans J
Eddy B E	
Fisher W	Fuller M A
Fisher D M	Furgeson P G
Foulke H	Forgensen O
Gilliam C H	Gottfredsen J
Gillispie P	Goddard J S
Gordon J	Gray M P
Hall J K	Hinkley A E
Harkness M K	Howard S
Hawkins T	Holman E
Hershey A E	Hoffar N S 2
Haywood G	Hoffman G F
Harris M	Hoffman F A 4
Harrier W H	Hoge E D
Haskell J M	Hudson J
Harris T W	Hutchinson G
Hardy M	Humpry G F
Hensser J	Hunter A
Heart L	
Ingalls L	

LIST OF LETTERS

Remaining in the office at Salt Lake City, on the 5th day of December, 1870, which, if not called for within one month, will be sent to the Dead Letter Office.

LADIES' LIST.

Ball P	Brewer A
Blodsoe E M	Bullock E
Boyes E	
Chapman A M	Cook I J
Cheshire Mrs	Collett M
Harman S	Hoss A
Hanchett A	Hoagland S
Hayes M J	Holden E
Hassel A M	
Jenson G	Jones I J T
Jones J	
Leaver M S	Lithle F
Littlefield L	Lyon A
Littlewood A	
McMurrin J 2	Miller M A
Martin A	
Nowell E	Norman E
Fetterson C	Philster F
Richards A	Romans E
Smith M	South K
Smith F	Snyder S
Stewart F	Soranson L
Sessions P	Stone M P
Sesem M	
Taylor L	Thayn E
Taylor M E	Tolly S
Walsh S	Whitmore M
Wickli M	

Jairson A A	Jonason S
Jackson N	
Kelsey J B	Kidden J H
Kennsen R	Kingsberg J
Lang J	Linquest N C
Latimer T	Lincoln S H
Larson J	Livingston J
Liter W H	Loughner J
Leinhart G	Loey T T
McGhie J 2	Middleton F
McGrath M	Mills J
McCoy J	Miller R
McMasters J	Morrison S
McGrath M W	Mott G
Manning S S	Morris J J
Marston A R	Murdock W C
M J S Messrs	
Neal "Bro"	Neimoyir J
Neilson H	Nimoyer C
Needham J	Nichols D C
Napper J	Nystrom P T
Oldfield W	
Patterson A S	Patterson A
Patrick R	Pugmire J
Perkins W T	Potest Mr
Pike J W	
Ranc S	Ries G K
Reynolds G	Richards J W
Reece G	Richards J
Ralph B W	Riche W 2
Redfield W	Rockwell O P
Richards E	Roper A
Riter S W	Rose H
Richton E	Rolfe B
Smith E	Stephenson P C
Smith J T	Sloane E
Smith T G M	Simpson T
Smith J	Sims G
Smith Bros	Sisson J
Smith J F	Sowderi J
Smith J	Sproule A
Smith J F	Sparks F
Smith W	Spence
Savage J N	Swein R
Schuartz W	Sweetman C H
Stuart W M	Swinde G
Stewart W T	Sinclair B
Tyler J P	Trulson A
Thomas T	Twede C F
Thorp J	Thruelson J A
Toby M	Tuddenham J

Vandement J	Vance J
Waller J	White J M
Weggeland D	Wixcey J J
Williams J M	Wilding G
Williams M	Wildpret G A
Williams W B	White J
Williams J G	Worth L W
Williams R	Wright R

Persons inquiring for the above letters are requested to state when advertised.

J. M. MOORE, Postmaster.

HELD FOR POSTAGE.

Andrews J, North Ogden
Allmon Miss E, Provo, U T
Baily A, Ithica, Riche Co, U T
Bawson F, Rock Springs
Brown & Deal, Nevada City, Cal
Butterworth Mr, Flat Rush, N Y
Calvert E, Provo, U T
Chadwick Miss M, Oswego, N Y
Messrs Flies, Allen & Moody, 77 Broad
  street, Utah
Rees E M, Helena, M T
Tolley W, Nephi City, U T
Weyman M, Huntsville, U T

J. M. MOORE, Postmaster.

Deseret News
December 7. 1870

Nephi, Dec. 5.—On the 30th of November, information, under oath, was filed before O. Gardner, Justice of the Peace of Levan Precinct, that Richard Soper and Antone Variardie were guilty of the crime of committing rape on their step-daughters—children of 10, 11, 12 and 13, both men having married women having children. Writs were issued and the prisoners examined on the 1st of Dec., at 2 p. m., the evidence being very plain and positive, the prisoners of their own choice and free will, made public confession of their guilt. They were committed for trial and a constable was ordered to deliver them, for safe keeping, into the hands of the sheriff of this county. On the 2nd inst., as they were being conveyed, under a guard of five men, to Nephi, at a place called Cedar point, the prisoners gave a yell, at the same time springing out of the wagon. The horses became frightened and by the time the guard was out of the wagon the prisoners were about seventy-five steps away. The constable ordered them to stop or they would be fired on. They paid no attention but kept making their way up the hills into the cedars, the guard running and firing when an opportunity presented. After a chase of from half to three quarters of a mile the prisoners were brought down by being shot, and died a short time after. The constable came to Nephi and gave information of the facts in the case, whereupon the coroner issued a writ to the Sheriff who proceeded with the constable to the above mentioned place and brought in the bodies. An inquest was held upon the bodies, before the coroner and a jury of respectable citizens, and witnesses were examined.

Salt Lake Herald
December 24, 1870

THE MEAT MARKET.—If any evidence was wanting of the excellence of our ranges for raising choice meats, the present Christmas display in the Meat Market would furnish it. From the east, west and north is the flesh of animals fat enough to feast the eyes of an epicure. Levi Garrett has mutton from Rhoad's valley and beef from Skull valley, that show how succulently rich is the feed on those ranges. George Chandler has large and fat beef and mutton from Bear Lake valley, which may be called a kind of paradise for stockowners; he has also, among other meats, an immense hog grown in Tooele. Jennings & Paul have a splendid show of meats, principally from Rhoad's Valley, with three enormous hogs, one grown by John Hague, of Nephi, and the other two by Wm. Jennings, of this city. Charles Popper shows what kind of fat stock can be made on the range north of Bear river; and so on through the market, on both sides. The beef, mutton, pork, venison, fowl and bear meat make a display that any stock-raising country might be proud of. It is to be hoped that Utah will not again import beef, as has been done within the past few weeks; but that our stock-raisers will exert their energies to supply the entire home demand and open a large export trade. Such meats as are in the market to-day would find ready sale anywhere.

Deseret News
January 11, 1871

NEPHI, Juab Co., Jan. 6.
On the 4th ult., coal was discovered three miles south of this city and three miles east of the State road. Three veins were found, one seven inches, one two and a half feet and one ten feet thick.

Deseret News
January 18, 1871

TELEGRAPHIC.

Reduction of Tariff on the Deseret Telegraph Line.

ON and after January 16th, 1871, messages of ten words or less will be sent from Salt Lake to and from Franklin and intermediate points, and to Gunnison, Levan and intermediate points, for 25 cts; additional five words or fraction, 10 cts.

From Salt Lake to and from St. George and intermediate points south of Levan, 50 cts; additional five words or fraction, 20 cts.

From St. George to and from Nephi, Gunnison and intermediate points, 25 cts; additional five words, 10 cts.

Between all points north and south of Salt Lake, 50 cts; additional five words or fraction, 20 cts.

A. MILTON MUSSER, Supt.
s100 & w51-2w

MORE MINERAL DISCOVERIES.—
We learn that argentiferous galena
has been discovered within a reasonable distance of Nephi, in the neighborhood of Mount Nebo, and that the
prospects are favorable. This, with a
late discovery of coal near Nephi will
draw increased business to the capital
of Juab county. With the completion
of the extension railroad to Payson,
Nephi will become a place of considerable importance, as the centre not only
of a fine agricultural and pastoral region, but of mineral development as
well.

COAL AT NEPHI.—The following
telegram was received yesterday, by
Deseret Telegraph line:

Nephi, Utah. 24.—John Hague, of
this city, and H. Carlson of Fairview,
have commenced opening coal mines
discovered by them on the 4th of January. The prospects are favorable.
Experienced judges declare it, beyond
all doubt, to be a valuable coal bed.

Died.

At Levan, Juab County, Utah, on the 18th ult., of old age, Christian Christiansen, sen., aged 80 years, 9 months and 11 days.

Father Christiansen was a native of Denmark, and was born April 7th, 1790, at Dolby, in the parrish of Wiborg. He was an able school teacher for thirty-five years, and Deacon of the Lutheran Church in his native Parish for fifteen years, during which time, he was much respected, being noted for his great piety.

On the 10th of June, 1852, he was baptized a member of the Church of Jesus Christ of Latter-Day Saints by Elder Christian Christiansen, jun., his youngest son, who was the first Elder ordained in Denmark, under the hands of Elder E. Snow.

Father Christiansen was ordained a High Priest by Elder John Fosgreen, and emigrated from Denmark, in company with his son, in the Fall of 1852, arriving in Salt Lake Valley, Sept., 1853. He resided in Salt Lake City until the move, when he settled at Nephi, in the Fall of 1859. He moved to Fort Ephraim, Sanpete County, where he remained until the Fall of 1869, when he removed to Levan. On the 30th of April 1870, he was ordained by Elder E. Snow a Patriarch. His first wife, mother of his children, died in Salt Lake City in the spring of 1859. He now leaves behind him, a wife, three sons and one daughter. His eldest son resides in Denmark, the other of his children are in Utah, and attended his funeral, which took place at Levan on Saturday Jan. 21st, and was one of the largest ever attended in this county, many of his friends coming from Sanpete County, and also from Nephi

Father Christianson, enjoyed the use of all his faculties until the last moment, giving full instructions about his funeral, blest his children and friends, requesting them not to mourn at his death for he was going to join his wife and friends and was anxious to be released from his body that he might preach to his friends behind the veil. His end was peace, for he lived and died a man of God and a patriarch in Israel.—COMMUNICATED BY S. P.

NOTICE!

TO WHOM IT MAY CONCERN. Cash entries of the following Town Sites were made at the Land Office in Salt Lake City, U. T., as follows, to wit:—

On the 5th of June, 1869, for Nephi, viz:—Section Four, North-west quarter of Section Nine, East half of the North-east quarter of Section Eight, East half of the South-east quarter, South-east quarter of the North-east quarter, and Lot One of Section Five, Township No. 13, South of Range one East, and South half of the Southwest quarter of Section No. 33, Township 12, South of Range One East. In all containing one thousand one hundred and twenty one acres and fifty-two parts of a hundreth.

On the 5th of June, 1869, for Mona, the North-west quarter of the South-west quarter, and the South-west quarter of the North-west quarter of Section 32, and South-east quarter of North-east quarter, and Northeast quarter of South-east quarter of Section 31, Township No. Eleven South of Range No. One East, containing in all one hundred and sixty acres.

On June 7th, 1869, for Levan, the North-east quarter of Section No. 31, and South half of South-east quarter of Section No. 30, in Township No. 14, South of Range No. One East, containing in all two hundred and forty acres.

The above entries have been suspended for further proof, and this is to hereby notify all claimants that on the 13th day of next March, at 0 a.m., I will appear at the United States Land Office in Salt Lake City, Utah Territory, to make the necessary proof, and show that I am entitled to have the entries of the said land confirmed under the town site act of March 2d, 1867, for the use and benefit of the inhabitants of the aforesaid towns, at which time and place above mentioned any person or persons, so disposed can appear and contest.

JACOB G. BIGLER,
Probate Judge, Juab Co., Utah.
Nephi, Juab Co., Utah.

Deseret News
February 22, 1871

DIED

At Levan, Feb. 11th, 1871, of lung fever, Almon Martin Valarida, son of Annia Valarida; aged 5 months and 15 days.

At Nephi, Juab County, Utah Territory, on the 6th inst., of inflammation of the lungs, Elder George McCune, aged 24 years, 1 month and 10 days.

The deceased was born at Fort William, near Calcutta, Bengal, India, on the 27th December, 1846, where his father and mother at that time resided, his father, Dr. Mathew McCune, being an officer in the East India Company's service. The deceased was baptized when eight years of age, a member of the Church of Jesus Christ of Latter-day Saints. On the 10th of December 1856, in company with his parents, he left India for Utah, arriving in Salt Lake City on the 29th day of September, 1857, the family making Farmington, Davis County, their place of residence. In 1858 they moved to Nephi, where they have continued to reside.

On the 11th of January, 1868, deceased was married to Elizabeth, eldest daughter of Thomas and Sarah Wright, of Nephi, and on the 10th of the following March he was ordained a member of the 49th Quorum of Seventies. He leaves behind a wife and two little sons, father, mother, brothers and sisters to mourn his loss, who have the sympathies of a great many true friends, whose prayers ascend daily for their comfort and consolation.

The funeral of the deceased took place at 2 p.m., on Tuesday, the 7th, being attended by over 300 persons. The Nephi choir and brass band (of which he was a member) took part in the services. Suitable remarks were made by Elders S. Pitchforth and George Kendall. Brother McCune was noted for his industrious habits, and he died in full faith of the gospel.
Communicated by S. P.

We extend our sympathy and condolence to the wife and parents of Brother McCune, in their bereavement and sorrow. The dispensations of Providence seem to fall with peculiar severity, when the young and promising are suddenly snatched away by death; and, under such circumstances, words of sympathy and condolence are all but powerless to assuage sorrow. Faith in the promises of the gospel of Jesus Christ, is the only thing on earth at all effectual at such times; and we pray that faith and the comforting influences of the Holy Spirit may impart to the members of the deceased's family all the comfort possible under their bereavment.

Deseret News
March 15, 1871

DIED.

At Nephi, on the 24th of February, 1871, of inflammation of the stomach, GEORGE W., son of Edward and Hannah Jones.

NEPHI MINING DISTRICT.—A dispatch yesterday to the HERALD, from Nephi, reports the formation there of a mining district, with the reported discovery of several rich ledges. The existence of paying ores there has been known for years to prospectors, who have passed over and examined the mountains in that region, and it would not surprise us if the Southern Utah R. R. would not get down to Payson one hour too soon, if soon enough, to meet the requirements of mines being developed in the mountains south of that point.

LEVAN, Juab Co.,
March 21st, 1871.

Editor Deseret News:—Reading with interest the many communications which appear in the NEWS from various parts of our "Mountain Home," has induced me to give you a few items of the welfare of our settlement. The citizens of Levan have enjoyed themselves much the past winter. Our meetings have been well attended, and parties and dances have not been neglected.

The Female Relief Society of Levan gave their annual social parties on the evenings of the 17th and 18th inst. Much credit is due the committee of arrangements, Sisters H. Christianson, S. Wilbeck and Sister Edwards, for the energetic manner in which the parties were conducted. The meeting house was beautifully decorated with a choice selection of pictures, banners, mottoes and evergreens. Elder George Rowley, our blind organist from American Fork, gave some accompanyments on the organ, which enlivened the entertainment. By request, our President, Hon. S. Pitchforth, made a few remarks, speaking of the pleasure we have as a people in mingling together in social parties.

Our farmers are busy preparing for the work of the season. The Farmers' and Gardners' Club is in successful operation, having had many interesting meetings during the winter, at which the subjects of farming, stock raising, and the culture of fruit, silk, &c., were discussed.

Bro. George Rowley gave a concert on Monday the 20th inst., assisted by E. Lambert, I. W. Shepherd and a few of the choir; he had a full house, and all went home well paid.

Very respectfully,
JOHN W. SHEPHERD

Deseret News
April 12, 1871

CONFERENCE AT NEPHI.—Hon. Samuel Pitchforth, of Juab Co., informs us that a conference of that Stake of Zion was held at Nephi on Sunday last, Prest. J. G. Bigler presiding. Representatives were present from Levan and Mona. Prest. Orson Hyde was also present and addressed the conference. The general church authorities were sustained. Branch conferences had been held at Mona and Levan the previous Sunday.

A new Court-House is in progress at Nephi, 57 by 47, the basement to be built of rock, with cells.

Prospecting for mineral continues vigorous; but the settlers, as usual, give their attention to their farms.

The Co-operative stores are prosperous.

Deseret News
May 17, 1871

GONE SOUTH.—Professor W. E. Wallace has gone on a professional tour through the settlements south, as far as Nephi, Juab Co.. He gave an exhibition of his system of horse training at Draper to-day. All who witnessed his exhibitions here were unanimous in the opinion that his is a very superior system; and we trust he will succeed in imparting a knowledge of it to a great many of the people throughout the Territory. After his return to this city the Professor purposes giving an exhibition in this city, the proceeds of which will be handed over to the P. E. fund.

Salt Lake Herald
May 18, 1871

NEW MINING DISTRICT.—A new mining district, named Pope's District, after the discoverer, Mr. Pope, has been organized west of Nephi, Juab County, commencing at the North Meadow Bridge, thence west to the east end of Tintic district, south to the Sevier river, east to Chicken Creek, and north to the place of beginning. Some seven ledges have been already located. One ledge, the Star of the West, is being worked by the "Western Union Mining Company," and a shaft nine by seven feet is being sunk. Our correspondent will post us as to progress.

Deseret News
May 31, 1871

NEPHI, 25.

We have to announce the death of one of our much respected citizens, Isaac Grace, after an illness of nine weeks. He got wet in a rain storm and took cold, which brought on chronic diarrhea, which terminated his life this morning at eight o'clock. Brother Grace was born in Liverpool, England, April 27th, 1820. He settled in Nephi in the fall of 1851. He was a thorough young man and filled many responsible positions here. He was a great support to our Nephi choir, from its organization. He leaves a wife and seven children and many friends to mourn his loss.

Deseret News
June 7, 1871

NEPHI, 31.

An Eastern company is about building extensive reducing works at the head of Lower Salt Creek Canyon, where rich discoveries of ore have been recently made.

DIED.

At Levan, Juab Co., on the 25th ult., CACILIUS, son of F. A. and Lillie Petersen, aged 4 months and 8 days.

Skandinavien Stjerne, please copy.

Salt Lake Herald
July 2, 1871

ACCIDENT. — Yesterday a young man from Nephi, named John Cazier, while watching the balloon ascension met with a painful accident. The balloon became entangled in one of the guy ropes attached to a pole; and the rope being cut the pole fell, striking Cazier's left hand where it was resting on the fence, lacerating and destroying the first finger and its support in the hand. The Drs Benedict, who attended to the case, found it necessary to remove the finger.

Deseret News
August 2, 1871

THE 24TH AT NEPHI. — The Twenty-fourth was celebrated at this place by a grand procession, music, speeches, toasts, sentiments, &c.; a dance in the afternoon for the young people, and one in the evening for the bigger people. We received a full report of the proceedings from Brother Thomas Ord.

Deseret News
August 16, 1871

ELECTION RETURNS.—The following returns were received by Deseret Telegraph to-day:

Pleasant Grove, 143; American Fork, 175; Fairview, 165; Payson, 299; Richmond 225; Logan, 330; Franklin, 165; Moroni, 131; Spring City, 142; Mount Pleasant, 338; Nephi, 372; Levan, 145; Gunnison, 165.

We understand the above votes were all polled for the regular ticket, there being no opposition.

MARRIED.

In this city by Daniel H. Wells, Aug. 9th, 1871, WILLIAM GREENHALGH of Parowan, Iron County, to ELLEN PASS, of Nephi, Juab County.

Deseret News
August 23, 1871

DIED.

At his residence, in Little Salt Creek, near Levan, on the 30th of July, 1871, of liver complaint, JOSEPH SMITH aged 4? years.

Deceased, who emigrated to this country two years ago, leaves a wife and seven children to mourn his loss. Three of the eldest children are still in England. He died in full faith of the Gospel, and was honored and respected by all who knew him.—Com,

Salt Lake Herald
September 3, 1871

[By Deseret Telegraph Line.]

ROBBERY OF NEPHI STORE.

(SPECIAL TO THE HERALD.)

Nephi, Sept. 2.—A few evenings since, our Nephi Co-operative store was entered by some persons and goods and money extracted therefrom, but through the vigilance of Sheriff Tidwell, J. Hague, and some of the Board of Directors, the thieves have been caught and about four hundred dollars in goods and money found in their possession. This was done by three boys about sixteen years old; one was an Indian boy.

Deseret News
September 6, 1871

(*Special to the* NEWS, *per Des. Tel.*)

NEPHI, Aug. 28.

A mining company was organized at Levan, on the 26th inst., to develope the mineral ledges discovered at that place.

Samuel Pitchforth has been appointed, by the county court, county recorder, to fill the vacancy caused by the death of E. Ockey, Esq.

NEPHI, Aug. 29.

A coal bed has been discovered within ten miles of Nephi, by W Zabriskie. The vein is situated in the north fork of Salt Lake canyon, and is considered very extensive and of good quality.

The grain crops of the county are very light.

Deseret News
September 6, 1871

DIED.

At Nephi, August 14, 1871, of chronic dyspepsia, Elder EDWARD OCKEY.

Brother Ockey was born at Bishop's Frome, Herefordshire, England, on the 27th of February, 1816. He was the son of John and Elizabeth Ockey. In August, 1840, he received the gospel through the teachings of Elder Woodruff. In April, 1841, he sailed in the ship *Rochester*, in company with seven of the Twelve, who were returning from missions. He was liberal with his means, assisting many of the Saints to immigrate. On arriving at New York he was married by Elder Woodruff to Miss E. Brewer. On his arrival at Nauvoo he bought a farm about four miles east of the city. He had not been long settled on it before, through the carelessness of a hired help, his home was burned and he was left destitute of nearly everything. He came to Salt Lake Valley in 1847, traveling in Gen. Rich's Company. He was one of the first settlers of the 7th Ward in Salt Lake City. He moved to Nephi in 1852, where he has held many responsible positions. He has left a large family to mourn his loss. Brother Ockey was a man much respected, for his sterling integrity, and died bearing testimony to the truth of the gospel.—COM.

Salt Lake Herald
September 26, 1871

LIST OF LETTERS

Remaining in the office at Salt Lake City, on the 25th day of September, 1871, which if not called for within one month, will be sent to the Dead Letter Office.

LADIES' LIST.

Anderson A	Hale E	Petersen A E P
Amer —	Hardy J V	Perkins A
Atchison E	Johnson M S	Parkin M
Brown C	Lewellen W	Pearce J
Brown F	Lloyd R 2	Phippen M J
Baker M	McBlane J	Phelps S L
Baker —	McFairlen J	Seiter F W
Center M	McKibbin L C	Scofield A C
Calkin S	Montgomery J	Sims P
Cash A	Morris A	Spencer H
Churchill M V	Mowlin M	Stevens W H
Cooper E	Manning J	Stevenson E J
Day F	Murphy S E	Waring —
Dening E M	Pardy A	Weston M

GENTLEMEN'S LIST.

Abbey Mining & Tunnel Co
Allen J W
Alexander G C
Andrew F
Anderson H
Anderson J
Andrews C —
Ammond G R
Ames C G
Auer C
Atkins L
Atchison J H 2
Atchison J B
Bagger C
Bancroft S D
Baker C
Barton G
Barrows A E
Barrett C
Beckman W
Bell J
Behrman J
Beesley P
Belly O
Blight W P
Blake W
Bishop H
Boyle G
Bohnemberger J
Boyde J D
Bowles J C
Burke T
Campbell J
Cady J T
Chapin H F
Clark W
Chancey W H
Claton W H
Clayton W
Coleman A
Cole F
Cone & Dunn
Conastes J
Collins D R
Conlam J
Coffall R J
Coburn S A
Coffman W H H
Cooney E
Cook W H
Crosdale B R
Cummings L A
Cushing J
Curry S T
Dawson C
Davis W O 2
Davis P
Davis D T

Debel M C
Desmond E N
Dickerson J
Dixon H
Druhot J
Duncanson D
Dunn L
Engbarg E N
Erickson N N
Everett W
Fenn A A
Gray H
Haas P
Hall E G
Hagdund A A
Hanson F
Hanson W
Hanson F
Harkins G C
Harrison P
Harvey A
Heffner S
Hoffman J
Hess J 2
Johnson J
Jones T E
Jones C
Jenagn H
Jenckes J H
Kohlhayer G
Kramer C
Levy M
Lewis J
Lota C
Lloyd J R
Lovelock E
Logwood C P
Lynch T A
Martin J W V
McDonald F
McCan J
McCullough J
McCoy & Pierce
McCarty C
McDonald J
McGinity G
McLeod T
McKeown T A
McKinney G W
McLaren J S
McNamis J
McKinney J L
McLaughlin J
J
McKim D F
Morgan H J
Mortensen S P
Moses J
Morgan C F
Morgan E H

Moses E
Merlke'ni W H
Mortensen R
Murphy J A
Myers J 3
Murphy J
Nichols —
Nichols D C
Noyes W
O'Brien J
Paterson W
Patterson A
Peterson C
Perkin L
Perkin A
Picard W G
Pinkerton S W
Phillips W J
Phelps E J
Pratt T
Randall F 2
Read S M
Rector H
Seely J W
Sawtille E P
Savage J
Sanger J
Saunderson D
Smoot —
Simmons J L
Sibley N L
Smith J B
Smith W
Smith J
Sott J
Stainforth G
Steen R 3
Stubbs & Kirkwood
Stevens J
Stewart H B
Stewart M
Thornton J B
Tillotson A
Towler D
Tyler G
Ullman J L
Vagen C D
Vinagga S C
Virgin B
Wasmer W
Ward J M
Wentworth S R
Weeist H
White C
Wayman J
Whitmore —
Whiting J
Wood F

HELD FOR POSTAGE.

Burnett J G, Wanship, Weber co, U T
Ball W, Heber city Wasatch co
Bickford D, 689 Broadway, N Y
Drake J, 808 Montgomery-st, San Francisco
Dunn J, Provo, U T
Eklund E E, Evingston, W T, box 16
Hollingdrake J, American Fork, U T
Hurlburt S E, 118 C G, Ave, Chicago
Johnson, Clark & Co, 334 Washington-st, Boston, Mass
Moulton T, Heber city, Provo valley, UT
Rose M E, North Ogden, Weber co
Stratten R, Virgin city, Kane co
Smith H M, 726 Morgan st, St Louis, Mo
Savage E, Little Cottonwood Canen, Bruner's House
Higue A & Timmins F, Nephi, Juab co
Tobin J H, under Occidental Hotel, San Francisco

Persons inquiring for the above letters are requested to state when advertised.

J. M. MOORE, Postmaster.

TERRITORIAL NEWS.

[By Deseret Telegraph Line.]

Escape of a Convict at Nephi.

[SPECIAL TO THE HERALD.]

Nephi, 27.—One C. R. Smith, a prisoner committed from Tintic to await his trial for murder at the next session of the district court to be held at Provo, broke from the Nephi cell last night by digging through the wall. He must have been assisted by persons on the outside, who furnished him tools. His description is as follows: Hight, about six feet; build, slender and trim; complexion, light, with light curly hair and blue eyes; a scar on each temple. He is a native of Virginia, from near Richmond. Officers are notified to be on the lookout for him.   THOMAS TIDWELL,
Sheriff, Nephi.

Patents for Utah Townsites.

The commisioner of the general land office has approved the applications for patenting the cash entries arising from the following townsites in the Territory of Utah: Kaysville, Springville, American Fork city, Bountiful, Centerville, Santaquin, Cedar Fort, Payson city, Mona, Ephraim city, Nephi and Levan.

Deseret News
October 4, 1871

By Deseret Telegraph.

The Nebo Coal Mining Company.

NEPHI, Sep 27, 1871.

Editor of Deseret News.—The Nebo Coal Mining Company was duly incorporated to-day, according to the laws of Utah. The principal office will be located at Nephi. The following are the officers of the company:

President, Wm. T. Matthews; vice-president, J. L. Ivie; directors, N. Jacobsen, G. Frandsen and M. Brown; secretary, W. Zabriskie; treasurer, J. Hague. This company is incorporated to work the Manhattan coal bed, situated up Salt Creek Canon. A tunnel is now being drifted.

S. PITCHFORTH.

Deseret News
October 11, 1871

DIED.

At Chicken Creek, of consumption (when?) JANE, wife of Thos. J. Irons, late of Dover, in her 58th year. Baptized at Dover, England, in 1846. Arrived in Utah, Sept. 15, 1869.

Salt Lake Herald
October 15, 1871

[By Deseret Telegraph Line.]

AN ITEM FOR COL. WICKIZER.

Fillmore, 14.—There is something wrong with our mail communication. We have had no HERALD nor *Evening News* since Saturday, Oct. 7th. Three were due up to last evening. The coach and pony arrive every day alternately, but fail to bring the right mail. One letter last evening was the total mail for Fillmore. There were also two registered letters that should have been taken out at Nephi, for Sanpete county. Our HERALD and *Evening News* are very irregular.

C. MERRELL.

Deseret News
October 18, 1871

DIED.

At Nephi, Juab County, Sept. 22nd, of inflamation of the stomach, LILLIAN BELL, daughter of William A. C. and Elizabeth Bell Bryan, aged 1 year, 2 months, and 12 days.

Salt Lake Herald
November 8, 1871

SILVER AND COAL. — Mr. John Hague, of Nephi, has handed us a very fine specimen of argentiferous galena from Mount Nebo, where there is unquestionably a large body of ore but mostly of so low a grade that it cannot at present be shipped to pay. As the railroad nears that region it will undoubtedly prove a valuable and permanent mining district.

He also handed us an excellent specimen of coal from the Aspinwall old coal bed at Weishtown, Sanpete. Mr. Hague was employed by General Aspinwall, to hunt a coal-bed for him for coke purposes, and he has succeeded in locating the mine from which this specimen was taken, which makes an excellent coke.

He says all is peace and quietness in Nephi, the people attending to their own concerns, with nothing of an excitable character occurring in that part of the Territory.

Salt Lake Herald
November 30, 1871

GUSTAVE HENRIOD, Esq., of Nephi, agent of the Juab county co-operative store, is authorized to act as agent for the HERALD, daily and semi-weekly.

Deseret News
December 6, 1871

NEPHI, Nov. 27, 12.35 p.m.—Selectman E. Taylor has expended a county appropriation in opening a new County Road

from Nephi to Sevier bridge, via Levan and Taylor's Ranch, which is by far the best route.

The Levan Co-operative Store is paying the dividend just declared for the last two months, which is twenty-five per cent. The shareholders have resolved to erect a neat store, which is already commenced.

The Nephi Co-operative Sheep Herd Association has declared a dividend of fifty per cent. for the past year. The new and commodious store of the Nephi Co-operative Mercantile Institution will be finished in a week, dedicated and opened to the public, with a full stock of goods.

Salt Lake Herald
January 5, 1872

OBSEQUIES AT NEPHI.—By a telegraphic dispatch from Nephi we learn that William Broadhead, an old and respected citizen of that place, was interred on Wednesday last.

Mrs. Andrews, treasurer of the Female Relief society of Nephi, a lady highly esteemed by all who knew her, was interred yesterday. Both funerals were largely attended.

OUR LEGISLATORS.

On Monday last the members of the Territorial Legis... ... ... for the purpose of organizing and to prepare for the business of the coming session.

The TRIBUNE in its opposition to the perpetuation of theocratic government in Utah has frequently asserted that there existed a perfect union between the ecclesiastical and legislative branches of the Mormon hierarchy, and in support of its position purposes adducing in this article some proof which may convey to the outside world an idea of the "workings" of our internal affairs. The external appearances of all pertaining to Mormonism must not be taken as an indication of its internal condition.

We also introduce the statement that all our legislators hold high ecclesiastical positions, with the view to proving that if the Mormon community had a State government its greater facilities for oppression could be exercised more in the future than in the past. That the extent to which the priesthood of Utah hold political offices is a greater evil and militates to a greater degree against the interests of non-Mormons than polygamy, is a proposition we expect to prove in this way:

That the legislators meet as a religious body.

That they are all men holding high ecclesiastical positions in the Church;

That in consequence of this they cannot enact any laws of importance to the people without the approval of the President of the Church,

That they are wholly subject to the dictation of Brigham Young;

That the enactment of important laws is suggested at meetings of the Priesthood prior to their assembling in a legislative capacity;

That they control the people in their respective districts rather than act as ~~_____~~ nomination of the head of the Church, which nomination cannot be set aside.

For the above reasons we say that the Territorial Legislature of Utah are not a body of men elected as in other Territories upon republican principles and in harmony with the spirit of the Constitution, but are chosen because they in turn control the people of the districts they represent, and are therefore better fitted to assist in building up the "Kingdom of God" than they are to represent the people of the Territory, as there exists no recognized interest outside the paramount consideration, "Are we obeying the heads of the Church?"

HOUSE.

John R. Murdock, President of Beaver; Jonathan C. Wright, a *weighty* representative of Church and State; Charles C. Rich, one of the Twelve, William B. Preston, Bishop, Silas S. Smith, President; Willard G. Smith, Bishop; William H. Lee; Samuel Pitchforth, President at Levan, Thos. Callister, President Millard Co.; Orson Pratt, John Taylor, Franklin D. Richards, B. Young, jun., Joseph F. Smith, all members of the Twelve; A. O. Rockwood, ex-warden of the Penitentiary, Enoch Reese, Geo. Peacock, Bishop Warren S. Snow, Gen. N. L., O. S. Lee

Let us understand who these legislators are and what are their ecclesiastical positions. Outsiders and sympathetic editors will thus be better able to understand the workings of a Theocratic government, from the expose.

First, we have for Speaker of the House, Orson Pratt, one of the Twelve Apostles and Mr. Young's substitute in the discussion on polygamy with Dr. Newman.

For members of the Council, Geo. Q. Cannon, one of the Twelve, and editor of the Church organ, the *Deseret News*; Wilford Woodruff, one of the Twelve, William Jennings, Mr. Young's heaviest partner in Zion's Co-op. Mercantile Institution; Joseph A. Young, son of President Young, Lot Smith, a returned missionary, and renowned for burning Government trains in 1857; Lorenzo Snow, one of the Twelve; Moses Thatcher, related to Mr. Young, A. O. Smoot, ex-Mayor of Salt Lake City and now Bishop of Provo; L. E. Harrington, Bishop of the district he represents; Orson Hyde, Prest. of the Twelve; Jacob G. Bigler, President of Nephi; Jesse N. Smith, a President's councilor; Wm. Snow, Bishop.

John Rowberry, Bishop of Tooele; A. K. Thurber, Bishop of Spanish Fork; W. B. Pace, Brigadier General of the Nauvoo Legion; David Evans, Bishop of Lehi, Abraham Hatch, Bishop of Provo Valley; Joseph W. Young, nephew of Brigham Young, and President of the Southern Mission, Lorin Farr, President at Ogden.

From the above it will be seen that there are no less than 10 out of the 12 Apostles, and 9 or more Bishops, while the rest are Presidents in their respective districts. Such are the men who compose our present Territorial Legislature, and from this it is easy to infer to what an extent the Church would infuse itself into all State Departments, if the opportunity be afforded by an unwise admission of Utah at the present session of Congress.

Salt Lake Herald
January 11, 1872

MORE MAIL DELINQUENCIES.—We are in receipt of a letter from Nephi, Juab county, which almost exhausts our patience in the matter of mail delinquencies; for we have received numerous communications on the same vexed subject from different quarters of which we have made no mention. Subscribers in Nephi to whom the HREALD is regularly mailed complain most reasonably of the non-receipt of their papers. One lady has only received four copies of the semi-weekly HERALD in about as many weeks; a gentlemen has received two copies of our daily in seven days; and so it goes. We are satisfied the missing papers have been mailed from this office; we believe they have been duly forwarded from the post office in this city, and we conclude the fault must be somewhere between Salt Lake and Nephi or at the latter place. It is to be hoped that attention being thus publicly called to the matter will have the effect of causing the grievance to be remedied; if it does not we shall be compelled to take other steps to discover where the delinquency occurs.

Bigler presented a petition from 130 citizens of Nephi, Juab county, praying for the establishment of a free school in that city to be supported by a public tax. Referred to the committee on education.

RECKLESS SHOOTING.—We are informed by a citizen of Nephi, Juab county, that a Deputy Sheriff from Cedar City, Iron county, by the name of Armstrong, accompanied by Pete Huntsman, Sheriff of Fillmore county, shot a man for whom he had a warrant at Nephi on the 23d of the present month. The ball grazed the check of the son of Thomas Schofield, taking effect in the arm of the man for whom it was intended, making a painful but not fatal wound.

According to our information, there was not the least occasion for the shooting, for though the man was accused of stealing a horse in Iron county, he was not attempting to escape from the officer at the time, nor had he about him any arms. Armstrong appears to have fired without any previous warning.

The authorities of Juab county would have arrested Armstrong if they had been wide awake and disposed to do their duty. Such rash acts should be severely punished.

THE UTAH SOUTHERN.—It is understood that this road is to be completed to Nephi by the first of July. We rejoice at the laying of every rail that goes down on this road, as the future of the Territory is in it. A railroad to Pioche will kill theocracy and redeem the Territory from isolation and poverty. It will be a saving work for the Priesthood and we urge them, by all means, to put it through, that salvation may come to them and to Israel.

DIED.

At Nephi, February 28th, 1872, of erysipelas, WILLIAM CAZIER, Patriarch of Juab County.

Father Cazier was the son of James and Elizabeth Cahoe Cazier, and was born in Woods County, Va., January 21st, 1794. His father died when he was very young, and his mother married John Dye. In 1816, Father Cazier was married to Pleasant Drake, and moved to Oldham County, Kentucky, where he continued to reside till 1840, when, with his family, he moved to Illinois.

In 1844, he was convinced of the divine mission of Joseph Smith, through seeing a remarkable vision, in which heavenly messengers bore testimony to him of the truth of the latter-day work. Himself and family received the gospel.

In 1846, they moved with the Saints West, and in 1848 he went on a short mission to his native State, also to Kentucky, bearing testimony of the truth of the gospel to his old Baptist friends.

In 1851 himself and his family moved to Utah being one of the first families which settled at Nephi, where he resided till his death.

In 1853 he was ordained a Patriarch, by the First Presidency of the Church, which office he filled with honor until his death, having blessed many hundreds.

Deceased was beloved by the Saints, being, indeed, a man of God, a father in Israel. He was noted for his kindness to the poor, the stranger never being turned from his door. He leaves a wife, seven sons, three daughters, sixty grand children, and seven great grandchildren, to mourn his loss, all of whom reside in Utah excepting his eldest son and family. His funeral took place on the first instant, and was well attended. His remains were taken to the Nephi meeting house, where suitable remarks were delivered by Elders Samuel Pitchforth, A. Love and J. G. Bigler. — [Com by S. P.]

Deseret News
March 27, 1872

NEPHI, 19.

The returns of the election held yesterday in this county, received up to this hour, for the constitution and the State ticket of Deseret, are as follows: Nephi, 272 votes; Levan, 150; Mona, 95; the returns thus far received, show no votes against the Constitution.

S. PITCHFORTH, County Clerk.

Salt Lake Herald
April 10, 1872

JUAB COUNTY.—Mr. S. Pitchforth informs us that everything is prosperous in Nephi, Levan and other parts of Juab county. Spring work is progressing rapidly, and a large breadth of land is being put under cultivation. Mr. Hague, of Nephi, is sinking on some mines in the Timmins district, Mount Nebo, with good prospects.

Deseret News
May 8, 1872

MAIL IRREGULARITIES.—The following extract from a letter, written at Mount Pleasant, Sanpete Co., April 30th, by Mr. Edward Cliff, is respectfully submitted for the consideration of the Mail Agent for the Territory. The fault is evidently in failing to make connection at Nephi, as the mail from that place to Sanpete, it appears, arrives regularly: "There are many complaints regarding the non-arrival of your valuable paper when due. Sometimes the WEEKLY does not come to hand until a week old, and the SEMI-WEEKLY the same, and then both numbers come together, causing your subscribers many fruitless errands to the post office. I do not know who is to blame; our mail from Nephi, however, arrives on time. Unless there is a change for the better soon, you will lose many subscribers. We think the mail agent should see to and rectify such mismanagement without delay."

In Glendon, Long Valley, April 12th, of congestion of the lungs and heart disease, GEORGE
SPENCER, aged 42 years.

Deceased was the son of Moses R. and Anna
Spencer: was born in Hartford Conn., Oct, 1829;
baptized by M. H. Peck, Salt Lake City, Oct 9,
1852; confirmed by J. L. Heywood on the same
day; ordained a teacher, by J. G. Bigler, Nephi,
March 5, 1853; ordained a Seventy by Joseph
Young at Kimball Creek, May 18th, 1854; started
on a mission to the States May 12th, 1871; returned
Nov 26th, 1871; took charge of the co-operative
herd and cheese factory at Upper Kanab, April
1872; here his labors were arduous, and amid the
storms he contracted a cold which terminated in
his death. He was a man full of integrity and
love for the principles of the gospel, and from
the time that he joined the church to the day of
his death he never faltered nor swerved from the
truth. He was universally beloved and esteemed; he left a large family.

FARMERS' PROSPECTS.—HOME MISSION-
ARIES.—MINES.—Subscriber, writing from
Nephi, May 15th, says:

"The prospects of the farmers and stock
raisers of Juab county, this season, are
good. Our crops look excellent and stock
of all kinds have wintered well, but, from
reports, a few of the people will have again
to contend with grasshoppers. In some
sections of the fields of Nephi and Mona
they are hatching out, but not in sufficient
numbers, we think, to do much damage.
From the appearance of the snow clad
mountains there will be a full supply of
water for irrigation purposes, and if we
are not troubled with late frosts we will
have an abundance of choice fruit, as fruit
trees of all kinds are in full bloom.

"President Grover and the 'Home Missionaries' have held meetings in Nephi,
Mona and Levan, laying before the Saints
the subjects taught at conference. On the
27th and 28th of April a conference of this
Stake of Zion was held, at which all the
authorities of the Church and this Stake
were duly presented and fully sustained.

"On the evening of May 13th we had the
pleasure of hearing from Bishop E. F.
Sheets and Elders Joseph A. and William
G. Young, who gave instructions on important subjects."

"Juab county is becoming somewhat
noted for rich deposits of minerals. The
mines in the districts of East and West
Tintic are looming up in importance and
attracting the attention of foreign capitalists. We also hear good reports from
Nebo district, formerly known as Tim-
min's district. The miners in the latter
district are developing the rich galena
deposits of Old Mount Nebo, which are
said to be very extensive and to contain
considerable silver."

FROM "DIXIE."—Brother Henry W. Miller, from St. George, called at our Office to-day. We are informed by him that the road from St. George to the quarry from which the rock for the temple at that place will be taken, is now completed. The weather has been cool and dry for a considerable time, but the extensive snow deposits in the mountains will supply water in sufficient quantity to meet the wants of the farmers for irrigation. No grasshoppers and excellent prospects for grain and fruit crops. The only grasshoppers that Brother Miller met with on his way to the City were in Juab County, between Nephi and Chicken Creek. The Canaan co-operative stock herd is prospering beyond expectation. The association recently declared a dividend of forty per cent., notwithstanding that about $3,000 had been spent by the stockholders during that period in making improvements on the ranche.

BY STAGE.

By Gilmer & Salisbury's Southern Line,
June 16 and 17.

DEPARTURES.

Robt Griffiths, M Yagr, to Pioche
E W Hitchins, G A Kenner, to Beaver.
S B Call, wife and daughter, H Wills, to Provo.
F Haight to Nephi.
Edward Robertson to Lewiston.

ARRIVALS.

C F Haywood, N Hawley, T A Buck, from Pioche.
G W Fowler from Minersville.
J Burke, R Paxton, from North Star district.
W P Hicklin, Jacob Dettelach, from Fillmore.
Harry Collins from Lewiston.
Miss Croft, Miss Hawley, Pat Swara, Chas Bassett, Mr Hosmer, J J Corrigan, mayor Harman, T Davis, Albert Grosbeck, from Springville.
Mr O Brian from Provo.

By Wines & Kimball's Ophir and Camp Floyd Stage Line.

DEPARTURES.

Mrs Benedict, A Farrington, A Reveile, S Sanders, N Densley, Thos A Jones, to Ophir.
G W Crow, H R Durkee, to Stockton.
C G Davidson to Lewiston.
M Bruneau to Tooele.
Mrs E Hasser to E T city.

ARRIVALS.

W Galligher, Mr Pardee, Mr Kiran, Mr Smith, Mrs Smith, E Richlena, Mr Wiggins, Mr Sears colonel Froiseth, Mr Brown, Mrs J D Plume, J G B Rickers, M Wheeler, John S Lawrence, Mr Trington, Mr Mead, from Ophir.
Mr Kelly, major O Keefe, Jenkin Morgan, Chris Rasmussen, from Stockton.
X X Lowery from Half-way house.
R Gill, H Stailey, T Parker, J McNeil, from Lewiston.

MORE OF THE INDIAN EXCITEMENT.

Yesterday there was a continuation, or rather a repetition, of the excitement of Saturday relative to Indian matters. Col. John L. Ivy, of Sanpete, had arrived in town, and reported that he was met in Salt Creek canyon, when in a wagon with his wife and children, by six Indians, one of them drunk, who stopped him, surrounded his wagon, and demanded if he was Jim Ivy—his brother. When he informed them that he was not, after some little time spent in talking among themselves, they allowed him to pass. He whipped up his animals lively, and got away, two of the Indians subsequently following him, but failing to overtake him. This was the groundwork for the renewed excitement. Yesterday general Cowan, assistant secretary of the Interior, who is in town, general Morrow, governor Woods and Dr. Dodge, Indian agent, held a consultation, when it was decided that Dr. Dodge should start this morning southward to have the Indians removed again to the reservation, troops to be furnished by general Morrow, if necessary, to compel the removal. This was the condition of affairs yesterday evening.

There seems a desire on the part of some to provoke, if possible, an Indian war; and the object can be accomplished, but at what cost? Suppose the policy of extermination, so strongly urged in some quarters, should be adopted; what then? Troops are sent into mountains full of lurking places unknown to them, but with which the Indians are perfectly familiar. The entire force in the Territory might be engaged in the campaign, and while they would be guarding some of the passes and following the savages into the mountains, the attacks would be made in other exposed districts. Raids would be made on settlements which the troops would be powerless to prevent; stock would be stolen as in all Indian wars; the sparsely peopled mining districts would have to be abandoned, for years, probably; and after all the white lives lost and the means expended in the effort to exterminate the Indians, bullets and bayonets would not do the work as quickly as fine flour is now doing it. And it is safe to say that ten white lives would be sacrificed for every Indian killed. An Indian war means the mining and agricultural interests seriously imperilled for years, and a great sacrifice of blood and means to accomplish what can be accomplished infinitely cheaper and easier.

The stoppage of Ivy and his family is not like an act of Indian hostilities. The aborigines do not make attacks in that fashion. They shoot first, with their victim at a disadvantage, and talk afterwards. They had been drinking, too, the liquor, it is stated, having been furnished them at Nephi. And there is no penalty authorized by law too heavy to inflict on the scoundrelly wretches who would place such an agent of evil in their hand. The authorities at Nephi should promptly use all diligence to discover and bring to strict account those who have been guilty of supplying the Indians with liquor.

But there is still another view of this Ivy matter. Jim Ivy killed an Indian a length of time ago at Scipio; shot him in cold blood, if we are correctly informed. He shot him because some time before his father had been killed by Indians. And the father had been so killed because he had also killed an Indian. In fact there is a vendetta between the Indians and the Ivys. The latter will kill Indians, and the savages will kill them. But in this Salt Creek canyon affair there was a show of justice by Te-ju-onah who was the leader of the savages, we learn; for they only wanted the man who had killed one of their number, and his life they would assuredly have taken.

Dr. Dodge is expected to start this

Dr. Dodge is expected to start this morning. We think Dr. Dodge should have gone some days ago; for it was his duty with such reports as have been flying around for some time past, to have informed himself by personal observation as to the actual state of affairs in that region of country. In another column will be found a despatch from Mount Pleasant, Sanpete County, which does not indicate anything so very serious as some excitable people appear to think exists there. Still, knowing the treacherous and uncertain character of the Indian when he gets "mad," as he expresses it, we renew our caution to all in exposed situations, to be on the alert and keep strict guard against sudden incur-

NEPHI, Juab Co., June 28, 1872.

Editor Deseret News:

On Saturday and Sunday June 22d and 23d, the home missionaries of Juab County held meetings at Mona, Prest. Grover and the following Elders were present—Jacob G. Bigler, sen., Andrew Love, Elmer Taylor, Samuel Pitchforth, John Andrews, and Andrew Kay, who spoke on the following subjects — subscribing to the Perpetual Emigration Fund for the gathering of the poor, paying tithing, building Temples, Word of Wisdom, building school houses, and the education of our youth. The Spirit of God rested upon the speakers and altogether we had a good time.

The 'hoppers are doing much damage to the crops at Mona, and also a little at Nephi.

On Thursday, by invitation, I attended the fourth annual meeting of the Nephi Female Relief Society. The meeting was well attended and the statement read by the Secretary of the society, Mrs. Amy Bigler, showed that the society had done much good, in assisting the poor, also that the institution was prospering. The foundation of a good building has been laid in a good situation on Main Street, and considerable material is on hand to finish the same, which, when erected, will be a credit to the sisters of Nephi.

The president, Mrs. A. Goldsbrough, and officers of the Nephi Relief Society have been energetic in the discharge of their duties.

Our city is alive, often, with Indians. Tabbe the chief and other bands have paid us a visit and declare their friendship. Bishop Grover has collected and sent the Indians over fourteen hundred pounds of flour and will also present them, in behalf of the citizens, some beef.

All is peace, preparing to do justice to the "Glorious Fourth."

Respectfully, A SUBSCRIBER.

NEPHI.

At sunrise the Stars and Stripes were unfurled and saluted by a volley of musketry. Capt. John S. Hawkins' brass band played the Star Spangled Banner, and other national tunes, and then serenaded the principal citizens. At 10 a.m. the people assembled at the meeting house, and after being called to order by the chairman of the committee, and prayer by chaplain Andrew Love, Thomas Ord read the Declaration of Independence, which was followed by an oration by Asa M. Abbott, Esq, of Illinois. Dr. Dodge, Indian agent, and John M. Harlow, Esq, delivered excellent patriotic speeches. Recitation, singing and music were in order till 1 o'clock p.m. At half past two the Indian agent held a conference with the Indian chief Kanosh and quite a number of Indians. They seemed well disposed and friendly. As usual the juveniles enjoyed themselves hugely in the dance. A dance in the evening, in the Social Hall, closed the proceedings of a generally well spent day.

Committee: George Kendall, Charles Sperry, Henry Goldsbrough and Kanute H. Brown. THOMAS ORD,
Reporter.

NEPHI CITY, Utah, 16th July, 1872.

Editor Deseret News:

Just before leaving Mount Pleasant, to-day, the Indian Agent, Dr. Dodge, Col. Nugent, of Camp Douglas, Major Littlefield, of the White Pine River Agency, and Mr. Geo. Bean, Indian Interpreter, arrived to have a talk with the Indians in reference to their going to the reservation.

It appeared, from what passed, that the whole proceedings were a failure, the Indians were determined not to go. Mr. Dodge reasoned with them, told them what preparations he had made for their return, the amount of beef, flour, &c., at the different points awaiting them, and promised them his future assistance. All this did not induce them to comply. After a great deal had been said at Fountain Green, yesterday, and Mount Pleasant to-day, without any apparent hope, the above gentlemen left Mt. Pleasant at 11 o'clock a.m., nooned at Fountain Green, and while there received a telegram that the Indians had reconsidered the matter. Being advised by Brother A. M. Musser and others to return to the reservation, they came to the conclusion to return immediately. Dr. Dodge, after receiving this news, purchased a number of beeves and a large amount of flour to supply their wants until they reached Strawberry Valley, where fresh supplies awaited them. A doctor will arrive here this evening by the coach to go to the various camps to administer to their sick.

I was told by citizens of Fountain Green that these gentlemen manifested a great deal of patience, treated the Indians kindly, and tried to persuade them for their good, while there yesterday.

Major Littlefield told me this evening that the Indians from the White River Agency were glad to see him, and promised to go home one moon from now. He spoke very highly of Douglass, the chief, as being a man of his word.

Dr. Dodge said he hoped we might be able to depend on this as a good peace, that the settlements may no longer be annoyed and perplexed by them.

I had quite a pleasant chat with these gentlemen and was glad to find they wished peace, and would much rather treat the Indians kindly than have difficulty.

If the above arrangements are carried out, it will take a heavy burden off the people of Sanpete.

GEO. FARNSWORTH.

At Nephi, Juab Co, Utah, June 28 1872, MARY ANN, wife of bro. Thom. Carter.

Sister Carter was the daughter of William and Harriet Goble, and was born in Boxgrove Parish, County of Sussex, England, May 2nd, 1822, was baptized in the year 1850 and emigrated to Utah in 1853, arriving in Salt Lake City October 10th. Deceased was much respected, and died bearing a strong testimony to the truth of the gospel, she leaves a husband and five childdren.—[COM.]

ABOUT INDIANS.—Bishop Moses Gifford of Monroe, Sevier County, was in town a day or two since. He stated that there were no Indians in that county when he left there. When he was at Nephi, on his way to this city, the Sanpete mail carrier, just arrived at that point from Sanpete, stated that the Indians in the latter place were feeling rather sour. A body of them at Fountain Green had been proffered three beeves and a quantity of flour by the people, and which had been refused. Brother Gifford is of opinion, however, that that did not indicate anything very serious, as they would probably change their minds in a few hours and accept the proffered gifts. Although the Indians are evidently feeling very morose, Brother Gifford, who is pretty well acquainted with the character of the red men, thinks an Indian war is improbable.

H. N. Larter writes from Moroni, July 20th. He states in his letter that Indians lately visited the houses of O. Barton, A. Scovil, — Allred and Jacob Christenson during the absence of the heads of the families, and because their demands for food, etc., were not at once and fully complied with, they became exceedingly abusive, in one instance drawing a pistol on a lady and in another spitting on the lady of the house. In still another of these cases, that of Sister Christenson, of whom they demanded a supply of beer, they, Brother Larter states, struck her with a horsewhip.

DEATH FROM MORPHINE. — The letter below explains itself. Dr. Tait used every effort to save the unfortunate man, but in vain :

NEPHI, August 5, 1872.

Editors Herald:

A stranger, who gave his name as Al. Tracy, and was left by Fred Hamilton at the Nephi House, Saturday evening, died last night from effects of an overdose of morphine administered by himself. Dr. Tait attended him.

G. HENRIOD.

NEPHI.

At 9 a.m., a procession was formed at the Bowery by the marshal of the day, Charles Foote, in the following order—martial band; Committee of Arrangements; High Council of this Stake of Zion; Chaplain, Orator and Reporter; Pioneers; Mormon battalion; high priests; seventies; teachers; Nephi Female Relief Society; twenty-four young gentlemen in black; twenty-four young ladies in white; school children; the procession moved on to the residence of Bishop Joel Grover, and, after receiving him and traversing some of the principal streets, arrived at the meeting-house at 10 o'clock, where half an hour after the people were called to order by the chairman of the committee; singing by Nephi choir, in charge of Elder William Evans, leader; prayer by the chaplain, Elder Matthew McCune; oration by Elder John Pyper; after which music, singing and recitation were freely indulged in till half past twelve o'clock.

Juvenile dance in the Bowery in the afternoon, and adult dance in the Hall in the evening.

Committee of Arrangements — George Kendall, Charles Sperry, Henry Goodsbrough, Kanute M. Brown. Reporter, Thomas Ord.

LEVAN, Juab Co., July 18th, 1872.

Editor Deseret News:

Dear Brother:—We had two days' meetings at this place on Saturday and Sunday, July 26th and 27th, which were well attended by the Saints of this and neighboring settlements. The following Brethren were on the stand; President Joel Grover; Elders A. Love, J. Andrews, J. Borman, and S. Cazier of Nephi; Bishop E. Taylor, and Elder C. Cristiansen of this place, Home Missionaries; also Bishop Kay, and Bro. Mullineux of Mona. President Joel Grover occupied a goodly portion of the time both days in exhorting the Saints to diligence, faithfulness, and punctuality in all things.

All the Elders spoke with an energetic spirit, showing that they were deeply interested in the work of God, and touched upon the following subjects; education and training of our children, tithing, emigration, and strict adherence to the keeping of God's commandments. A good spirit prevailed throughout.

Crops look well here and the settlement is in a prosperous condition, and in a fair way of becoming a beautiful place.

Yours &c.,

H. HARTLEY.

LEVAN.

Firing and salutes at daybreak from Captain C. F. B. Luybert's artillery. Unfurling of the stars and stripes at sunrise by W. Sunbridge. At 8 o'clock a.m. a procession was formed on the Public Square, by the marshal of the day, J. C. Wittbeck, as follows: Cavalry, band, choir, pioneer wagon, Sunday school scholars, representation of agriculture, horticulture, machinery, F. R. Society, mechanics and trade, to march through the principal streets, which presented a magnificent view to all spectators, and return to the bowery, where meeting was called to order by the marshal at 10 o'clock a.m. After singing by the choir and prayer by the chaplain, G. Gardener, singing, an excellent oration was delivered by E. Taylor, on the entrance of the pioneers into these valleys, followed by toasts, songs, sentiments, and speeches from C. Christiansen, G. Gardener, W. Tunbridge and J. Wilson.

At two o'clock p.m. there was a dance for the children, and amusements too numerous to mention, which lasted till sunset.

At 7 o'clock p.m. the adults met in the school house and enjoyed themselves in the dance.

Committee of Arrangements—John W. Shepherd, W. Tunbridge, G. Gardener, H. Hartley, C. F. B. Luybert, J. Francom, J. C. Wittbeck, S. H. Allred.

H. HARTLEY, Reporter.

THE DEATH OF MR. AL. TRACEY.

NEPHI, Aug. 5, 1872.

Editors Salt Lake Herald:

It is thought advisable and necessary that the following circumstance be made known, so that the friends, relations and acquaintances, of the person herein named may be made aware of his decease.

About sundown of the 3d inst., Mr. Frederick Hamilton, of Pioche, left a sick person at the Nephi House, of this town, kept by H. Goldsbrough, Esq. On the morning of the 4th he appeared to be considerably better, but about eleven o'clock a heavy, dull groaning was heard in his room, which called the attention of those in the other part of the house, when it was observed that he seemed to be laboring under the effect of some heavy narcotic. Dr. Tait being immediately called in administered the usual antidotes and restoratives, when, about three o'clock p.m., he rallied sufficiently to tell his name. He stated his name to be Al. Tracey, and that he had administered to himself some pills composed of quinine and gamboose, but upon examining his medicine case it was found that he had taken about four grains of morphine, instead. He continued to grow worse till about half past eight o'clock, when, upon making an effort to turn himself, he suddenly expired.

The same evening an inquest was held over the body by coroner Charles Sperry, and the following verdict rendered:

TERRITORY OF UTAH,
NEPHI PRECINCT,
JUAB COUNTY.

An inquisition holden at the Nephi House, in Nephi precinct, Juab county, on the fourth day of August, A.D., 1872, before Charles Sperry, coroner of said county, upon the body of Al Tracey there lying dead, by the jurors whose names are hereto subscribed.

The said jurors upon their oaths do say, that, upon the evidence presented before them, the deceased came to his death by an overdose of morphine, administered with his own hands.

In testimony whereof the said jurors have hereunto set their hands the day and year aforesaid.

Jurors { THOS. J. GUSTIN,
         JAMES MYNDERS,
         JOHN CAZIER.

Attest,   CHAS. SPERRY,
                          Coroner.

Any one interested can obtain further particulars by communicating with the coroner at Nephi.

Very respectfully,

THOS. ORD.

Nephi, Juab Co., Aug. 9.—Returns of election, as received, show that Geo. Q. Cannon received 610 votes.

Geo. R. Maxwell, 48 votes.

John Van Cott, Lewis S. Hills and John Rowberry, 597 votes each.

SAM'L PITCHFORTH, county clerk.

Salt Lake Herald
August 18, 1872

[By Deseret Telegraph Line.]

ANOTHER INDIAN OUTRAGE.

Nephi, 17.—Jerry Page, telegraph operator at Mount Pleasant, Sanpete, was badly wounded last night by an Indian as he was leaving the office going home. Just as he was opening the gate an Indian sprang on him, giving him several cuts on the head. One gash went through his skull. It is thought he will not recover. We get these particulars from his pupils.

Deseret News
August 21, 1872

LIST OF AGRICULTURAL SOCIETIES.

THE following is a list of agricultural, horticultural, and pomological societies, farmers' clubs, etc., in Utah Territory, as recorded in the books of the Department of Agriculture, June 1, 1872.

The first name after each society is that of the President and the second that of the Secretary thereof, followed by the post office address of the latter.

DISTRICT SOCIETY.

Deseret Agricultural and Manufacturing Society, Wilford Woodruff, Robert L. Campbell, Salt Lake City, Salt Lake co.

COUNTY SOCIETIES.

Agricultural—Beaver County Farmers' Club, J. R. Murdock, D. Tyler, Beaver, Beaver co.

Kane County Grape-Growers and Gardeners' Club, J Jepson, R. W. Reeve, Duncan's Retreat, Kane co.

Sanpete County Agricultural and Horticultural Society, William F. Maylet, Edward Jones, Ephraim City, Sanpete co.

Tooele County Agricultural Society, Thomas Howles, J. J. Steel, Pine Kanyon, Tooele co.

Utah County Agricultural and Manufacturing Society, D. Graves, A. F. McDonald, Provo City, Utah co.

Horticultural—Kane County Horticultural Society, L. Savage, A. L. Siler, New Harmony, Kane co.

TOWNSHIP SOCIETIES.

Agricultural—American Fork Agricultural Society, J. Duncan, W. Parman, American Fork, Utah co.

American Fork Gardeners' Club and Mechanics' Institute, J. Robinson, E. B. Lee, American Fork, Utah co.

Bellevue Branch of the Rocky Mountain Pomological Society, J. H. Johnson, J. F. Johnson, Bellevue, Kane co.

Brigham City Agricultural and Manufacturing Society, Alvin Nichols, J. Bywater, Brigham City, Box Elder co.

Cedar City Agricultural Society, F. Webster, John Urie, Cedar City, Iron co.

Domestic Gardeners' Club, G. B. Wallace, J. McKnight, Salt Lake City, Salt Lake Co.

Draper Farmers and Gardeners' Club, J. Terry, R. M. Rogers, Draper City, Salt Lake Co.

Eastern Gardeners' Club, J Proctor, W Fuller, Salt Lake City, Salt Lake Co.

Fairview Agricultural and Horticultural Society, H W Sanderson, W Christensen, Fairview, Sanpete Co.

Fayette Agricultural Society, W Miller, James Miller, Fayette, Sanpete Co.

Fountain Agricultural and Horticultural Society, N T Guymond, R Lewellyn, Fountain Green, Sanpete Co.

Goshen Gardeners' Club, W Price, J B Johnson, Goshen, Utah co.

Gunnison Farmers, Gardeners' and Forresters' Club, S Hanson, C A Madsen, Gunnison, Sanpete co.

Heber City Agricultural and Manufacturing Society, R W Glenn, Alex Fortie, Heber City, Wasatch co.

Holden Farmers' Club, I S Holman, J S Giles, Holden, Millard co.

Hyrum Farmers and Gardeners' Club, G P Ward, Charles C Shaw, Hyrum, Cache co.

Kanosh Farmers and Gardeners' Club, G Crane, Wm A Wade, Kanosh, Millard co.

Lehi Branch of Utah County Agricultural and Manufacturing Society, I Goodwin, John Woodhouse, Lehi City, Utah co.

Levan Farmers, Gardeners' and Mechanics' Club, E Taylor, J W Shepherd, Levan, Juab co.

Logan Gardeners' Club, G L Farrell, Enoch Lewis, Logan, Cache co.

Manti Home Gardeners' Club, W Anderson, J L Bench, Manti, Sanpete co.

Meadow Creek Farmers and Gardeners Club, W Stewart, A Greenhalgh, Meadow City, Millard co.

Mendon Agricultural and Horticultura Society, I Sorenson, A Gardner, Mendon Cache co.

Millville Farmers and Gardeners' Club, John King, F Yeates, Millville, Cache co.

Minersville Agricultural and Horticultural Society, Elias Blackburn, George Roberts, Minersville, Beaver co.

Monroe Farmers and Gardeners' Club, M Johnson, P Sorenson, Monroe, Sevier co.

Moroni Farmers and Gardeners' Club, L J Anderson, Geo Windons, Moroni, Sanpete co.

Mount Carmel Agricultural and Gardeners' Club, D Stark, D B Fackrell, Mount Carmel, Kane co.

Nephi Farmers and Gardeners' Club, W H Warner, M McCune, Nephi, Juab co.

Oxford Farmers and Gardeners' Club, Geo Lake, A P Welchman, Oxford, Cache co.

Paradise Farmers and Gardeners' Club, J Lofthouse, H A Shaw, Paradise, Cache co.

Paris Farmers and Gardeners' Club, James Athay, Walter Hoge, Paris, Rich co.

Parowan Gardeners' Club, T Davenport, T Durham, Parowan, Iron co.

Payson Farmers and Gardeners' Club, R Wimmer, J T Hardy, Payson, Utah co.

Pleasant Grove Farmers and Gardeners' Club, W West, J Armitstead, Pleasant Grove, Utah co.

Pleasant Vale Farmers and Gardeners' Club, S Smith, Geo Davis, Clarkston, Cache co.

Providence Farmers' and Gardeners' Club, M D Hammond, E Stratford, Providence, Cache co.

Rockville Farmers' Club, H Jennings, J C Hall, Rockville, Kane co.

Salina Farmers and Gardeners' Club, P Rasmussen, Wm McFadyen, Salina, Sevier co.

Scipio Farmers' Agricultural and Pomological Society, F W Fuller, T Memmot, Scipio, Millard co.

Shoinsburgh Farmers' Club, D A Washburn, J J Allred, Rockville, Kane co.

Smithfield Farmers and Gardeners' Club, R Meikle, F Sharp, Smithfield, Cache co.

Southern Auxiliary Agricultural Society, W H Dame, C C Pendleton, Parowan, Iron co.

South Cottonwood Farmers and Gardeners' Association, W G Young, S Richards, Union, Salt Lake co.

Spanish Fork Gardeners' Club, C H Hale, C Monk, Spanish Fork, Utah co.

Spring City Floral Club, Mrs M Commander, Mrs E Brough, Spring City, Sanpete co.

Spring City Gardeners' Club, J Schofield, George Brough, Spring City, Sanpete co.

Springville, Agricultural Society, W Mendenhall, C D Evans, Springville, Utah co.

Saint George Gardeners' Club, J E Johnson, J E Johnson, Saint George, Washington co.

Toquerville Gardeners' Association, G Spillsbury, W W Hammond, Toquerville, Kane co.

Virgin City Gardeners' and Floral Club, M E Jepson; Mrs A Isom, Virgin City, Kane co.

Virgin City Farmers' Club, G B Gardner, J Humphries, Virgin City, Kane co.

Wales Gardeners and Farmers' Club, J Midgley, H Lamb, Wales, Sanpete co.

Wasatch Agricultural and Manufacturing Society, W Foreman, A Forti, Heber City, Wasatch co.

Washington Farmers' Club, James Richey, W H Crawford, Washington, Washington co.

Wellsville Farmers and Gardeners' Club, W F Darley, W Darley, Wellsville, Cache co.

Horticultural.—Levan Ladies' Horticultural Society, A P Shepherd, N Shepherd, Levan, Juab co.

Manti Horticultural and Pomological Society, J Crawford, J P Squire, Manti, Sanpete co.

Mona Horticultural Society, M E Johnson, S W Johnson, Mona, Juab co.

Rocky Mountain Pomological Society, J E Johnson M P Romney, Saint George, Washington co.

ANOTHER INDIAN OUTRAGE.—The following, which tells of another blood thirsty outrage by Indians, at Mount Pleasant, Sanpete, was received by Deseret Telegraph, this morning, from Nephi:

Jerry Page, operator at Mount Pleasant, San Pete, was badly wounded last night, by an Indian, as he was leaving the office, going home. Just as he was opening the gate, an Indian sprang on him, giving him several cuts on the head. One gash went through his skull. It is thought he will not recover. We get these particulars from his pupils.

Salt Lake Herald
August 22, 1872

NEBO DISTRICT.—Mr. John Hague, of Nephi, half owner of the Olive Branch mine, Mount Nebo district, informed us yesterday evening that he is running a tunnel, which is now twenty-five feet in, with a hundred more contracted for, which is expected to strike the vein in a hundred and fifty feet, and to tap the Mountain Queen and other leads as well. A tunnel is also being run on the Western; and mining matters are looking up generally there. Mr. Hague took Lieut. Wheeler and his exploring party to the gypsum beds and the mines, concerning which the lieutenant expressed himself very favorably.

NEPHI.—Mr. J. Hague, of Nephi, informs us that the people of Nephi have not been troubled with Indians so far; but they have brought their stock out of the canyon and are taking means to preserve it from raids by the aborigines.

AFTER THE HOSTILE INDIANS.

Tabby and Douglass, with the Indians who met general Morrow in council at Springville last week, have left for their reservations, entertaining friendly feelings towards the whites. These Indians have long been friends with the settlers, and it would have been little short of a calamity had hostilities been inaugurated with them. We are, therefore, much pleased, as all must be who desire peace with the aborigines, that the council resulted in continued pacific relations. But there are still hostile Indians somewhere in the mountains south, and against these general Morrow now proposes to move. From a reliable source we glean the following of what is believed to be his plan of campaign: He has dispatched colonel Hough in command of the infantry to Sanpete, by way of Nephi, with instructions to guard the settlements at all points against incursions. Major Gordon also goes to Sanpete with his cavalry command, by way of Thistle valley, and his duty will be to pursue the Indians wherever seen, and follow their trails as long as their is the shadow of a chance of success. General Morrow, in person, will go with captain Deweese, Co. 2, cavalry, leaving the settlements at Spanish Fork, and striking east will scour the country right and left along the eastern base of the Wasatch mountains. Thus if major Gordon or colonel Hough start any Indians, these latter will be likely to push back over the mountains towards Green river, and may fall into the hands of the force directly under the general's command. It is desirable that the troops may meet the marauding bands of savages and give them a chastisement that they will remember. General Morrow, we learn, expects to come into the settlements again somewhere in the neighborhood of Salinas, in the Sevier country, probably in ten or twelve days; though he may be longer, for should he fall in with the Indians he will likely pursue them to Green river and beyond it, if there is any prospect of teaching them a salutary lesson. After the Sanpete country is cleaned out of the hostile Indians, general Morrow will proceed farther south should he hear of others in that direction; and will probably leave a force of cavalry in Sanpete to punish any Indians that might attempt to repeat their outrages during the present season.

The plan of the campaign is a good one, and should the troops come in contact with the Elk Mountain bands, that well deserve chastisement, they will no doubt receive their deserts. But while these efforts are being made to find and punish the guilty, those who have charge of the friendly Indians on the reservations should see to it that justice is rendered them, and that the promises made are kept sacred, that they may have no just cause for discontent and hostile feelings.

Deseret News
August 28, 1872

Correspondence.

PROVO CITY, Aug. 21, 1872.

Editor Deseret News:

Sir:—I started this morning in company with Prest. Smoot and Gen. Pace for Springville. At 11 o'clock the Indians commenced to arrive. At half past 11 the talk commenced, L. S. Woods, Esq., having made the necessary arrangements in front of his residence. Present—Gen. Morrow, Col. Heath, Supt. Dodge, Major Critchlow, Prest. Smoot, Gens. Pace and Thurber, Bishops W. Miller, W. Bringhurst, and M. Tanner, also Messrs. Jos. Tanner, —— Grover of Nephi, Chas. D. Evans, L. S. Woods Interpreter, and your correspondent; of the Indians, Tabby, Douglass, and Judge of White River Indians, Antero, Togo-woona, son of Sowiet, Waundaroads, son of Peteetneet, Joe of Payson, John of Kanosh Band and some 200 others.

Gen. Morrow said, "I am glad to meet so many of my Indian friends to-day. The Utes and the white people have been together and at peace so long, that they should by this time feel as one people. The Great Father has heard that this portion of his children have cause of complaint. He does not know what it is for, and he has sent me here to have a council with you. I want you to tell me all your troubles. The Great Father is standing with open ears to hear all you say. All you tell me shall be reported word for word to the Great Father. The country below here has bad Indians in it. I want these good Indians round here to return to the reservation, so that they may not be confounded with the bad Indians. The stores for Douglass have been for some time at Fort Steel, and they are now waiting for him until it is known whether he will return to the Reservation or not. So far as Tabby is concerned, we have already sent cattle and flour for him. After you have told me all your complaints, which I want you to do, in an open manner, not to keep anything back, then, if you want to send any of your leading men to Washington, I will see that they go, and if you want me I will go with them. I will give you all rations of flour and beef to help you to get to the Reservation, and those who are to go to Washington, if they will go to Camp Douglas, I will provide for them until I return and then go back with them to Washington, or you can all go home and then come to camp afterwards, if it suits you best. I would advise you, by all means, and these men now here will all advise you, to send some of your leading men to Washington, so that you can tell the Great Father himself. This is all I have to say, and now I want to hear you talk."

Douglass said, "A long time ago we had among us big chiefs who made many good treaties with the Americans. I with these Indians desire to live with the whites as friends now, to be friends while we live and be friends hereafter. Would like that the earth should be white all the time, no blood to run on it, that all should travel and live in peace. I want the General, Bishops, Captains and the boys to see that a good peace is now made, and that it be not broken. The Indians do not want to be crowded and as it were tied down, but so that they can live, associate and laugh together. They want Brigham and Washington to feel and know that there is nothing hidden under their feet. There is a good deal of talk at Bridger and other places that makes them feel bad, and they do not receive what Washington sends to them. They have heard that Washington has bought lands from other Indians. They do not want to sell their lands. It makes them feel bad to think of selling their land. This (the General) is a good man, he is getting gray, he has come a long way to do us good. The agents at the Reservation have not treated the Indians good, but now this man will see that they have good agents. An agent at White River, named Adams, would take the papers sent from Washington and would not let the Indians have them, but would bury the papers in the ground so they could not get them. They have heard that papers have been sent from Washington in their favor, that have lain in the ground so long they could not be read. Now the women and children will feel glad at this peace. We have come in with our squaws and have no desire for fight. Tabby has always advised the Indians not to steal or kill anybody, but during the last moon there has been some trouble in Sanpete, and he (Tabby) is ashamed of it. I do not know of any Mormons being killed, but maybe some of the others do. It is not Indians who have horses that steal and kill, but they who are poor and like squaws. They live in the south and there are not many of them. All the land, with the exception of a small piece near Salina and east of Sanpete, is at peace.

Joe said. "I think there has not been much blood shed in Sanpete, and that has been done by Piutes from the other side of the Colorado river. Want that no blood shall be shed in Sanpete, that it shall be all right. Do not want the General to anker after Indian meat too much. It is only a few mean Indians and their dogs who do this killing. Do not want the good Indians, who may be hunting in the mountains for deer, to be killed. There are some good Indians also hunting in the mountains near Fish Lake, and north-east of Sanpete, in Pleasant Valley. We are poor. You can see we are poor. Washington says, do not steal. Have heard there has been sent from Washington for the Indians a large amount of money, but the Indians do not get it. May be the agents have put the money in their pockets and it has not been given to Washington's boys, the Indians. I want that no blood shall be shed. Do not want a big mad. There has only been a few killed and it is not so bad as it may have been told. Am glad that the General is here. He can see we are poor. We have brought our squaws and children. We all look alike, we want to live in peace with the Mormons, Americans, and all together.

Tabby, on seeing Superintendent Dodge writing at the table, asked the General if he was writing good. The General said he was. Tabby said that when they met at Fairview he talked too harsh to them and made their hearts cry. If he now feels better towards them all right. They formed a very unfavorable impression of him. When they are at the Reservation and have something to eat and are treated right they like it very well, and if the Doctor feels better to them now, all right. "I have not thrown up going to Uinta. Am here on a visit. When did I throw any of you away? When did I steal from you? I have not given up my country. I like it. I always feel well. My heart is good towards all mankind. I consider all mankind are of one flesh, and should have feelings alike. Whom have I lied to? When have I hidden anything from you, or deceived any of you? I have not done it. The boys and all have heard the General talk, and they now feel well. I do not lie, and I believe the General talked as I now am talking. I desire that all the Mormons, miners and everybody shall travel these mountains in peace, work and lie down in peace. We do not know anything about the minerals. We want the deer and game and want the miners to get the minerals, and do not want any trouble on the roads in or to and around this country. In Sanpete is all the trouble, but none have been killed in my land at any time. The Indians down there do not have many old men among them, they are all young. As to going to Washington, I do not know what to think about it. We will have to have a meeting about that. Suppose we will go by the iron road. We have some Indians out hunting. I am glad to receive blankets, provisions, etc., given by the government, yet some do not feel well in receiving them, as they think it is for their land. A long time ago the whites came to this country and traded for furs, etc. Brigham came and has dealt with them. Indians did not think of killing whites until after the whites killed the Indians. But now the General has talked and we believe him. He has talked good and our hearts are one. Want the General to give some of the chiefs a recommend, that they have attended this meeting, and they are good. I suppose the Bishop got scared and had reasons for bringing out the cattle from the mountains, but I do not know of any reasons. If Agent Dodge had come here alone, the Indians would have all left the country, but now the General has come it is all right. I feel well that these bishops are here to hear what the General says, and if the Agent has any powder to give us, all right; if not, all right.

Joe said, the Indians had good instructions and everything they should have in the country on the other side of Green River, near Denver, and the Indians wanted it to be so in this country.

Douglass wanted General Morrow to send word to agent Thompson at Denver, that he is good, and attended this meeting. He is now travelling with Tabby; will soon come home. Some of the Indians have gone home.

General Morrow said, "With the whites, we say it is good to settle one thing at a time, where we have more than one thing to do. Then we pass that. We have made arrangements to have provisions meet you at Strawberry Valley, and more from Heber City as you proceed. When will you be ready to start, so that we can make the necessary arrangements? When will Douglass be ready to start with his men?"

Douglass said he did not know.

General Morrow, "When will Tabby be ready to start with his men?"

Tabby, "In three days, but we want something to eat now."

Gen. Morrow, I "will get you something to eat. Can you not go the day after to-morrow?"

Tabby, "Yes."

Gen. Morrow, "You shall have beef and flour to last you to Strawberry Valley. Then you shall have more as you go along. But all must go. I do not want to confound these Indians with the bad ones. This being settled, we want you to talk of your grievances, or of sending your Indians to Washington. If you do not conclude about going to Washington now, you can talk it over when you get to the agency. If you conclude to send them, let them come to my friend, Bishop Smoot, and he will send them down to Camp Douglass."

Tabby said they would wait till they got to the agency to talk this over. He asked Gen. Morrow to obtain authority from Washington for them to go to Washington, so if they concluded to go it would be all right.

General Morrow said, "While you are consulting at the agency I will write to Washington, and on receiving an answer I will send to you at the agency, so that you need not come to Bishop Smoot until after hearing from me,"

Antero said he felt good and would go to Washington.

The General said he wanted Tabby to go.

Tabby answered he must stay at home and take care of his men.

Waundaroads wanted to go and on the way visit his brother at school in Chester Co., Pennsylvania.

General Morrow said he heard the Indians claimed this land and wanted rent for it, that he also heard that a treaty had been made at Spanish Fork, which was not satisfactory, and "you should tell all about it to the Great Father," also heard that Uinta was not a good place for farming,

Waundaroad said it was.

Tabby said that at the Spanish Fork treaty Col. Irish told them that if they would go to Uinta, he would give them beef, flour, guns, powder, shirts, and everything they needed. "We went over and I have been on guard ever since, some three or four years, but I have not seen it come yet. You need not take my word for this. There are many here now who heard it and I know I tell the truth. It has been so long ago we have almost forgot he told us, but it was big lie."

The General remarked they would probably find it when they got back.

Tabby said, "No. All that Irish said has gone to the grass. We do not want to remember it," and that he would send the most of the Indians to camp, and he and some others would remain and meet the General in the morning.

Supt. Dodge having prepared a repast, the Indians sat down to bread, beef, coffee, etc.

At 2 p.m. council adjourned till 10 a.m. to-morrow.   Respectfully,
                                    L. JOHN NUTTALL.

LETTER FROM SANPETE.

SANPETE, Aug. 29, 1872.

Editors Herald:

The modern Jehu, as he gathers up his lines, gives the swinging whip its force, with foot artistically placed on the brake, and sees the great innovator, the "iron horse," steadily progressing to a complete absorption of his domain, can only look forward to some remote region for the exercise of his peculiar functions.

It is a positive pleasure on a stage-box, seated by the side of a communicative driver, to see the beauties of the country through which you travel; to hear a driver's yarns—for they have yarns—of hair-bredth escapes, the very near upsetting of the coach, road agents, the qualities of his team, &c., and feel the enthusiasm of a spanking four in hand.

Such was my pleasure as we emerged from the cars the other day at the point of the mountain, as at the word "all aboard" we sprang to seats inside and out and Gilmer & Salisbury's well equipped coaches conveyed us on our road; through towns and cities embowered in nature's beautiful green; through waving fields of grain, whiling away the time by scenes pleasing to the eye and mind, while Jehu told us his experience of day and night coaching. You can always count on a splendid New England dinner at Mrs. Groen's; it is a true pleasure to forego even your city breakfast to eat her substantial meal. You bowl along from there to Payson, to find at the California House the counterpart of Mrs. G's. Here night lets down her sable mantle, and by nods, bits of sleep, and sundry thumps, you arrive at Nephi; a quiet, unostentations town, and find mine host Gouldsborough ready to receive you if you diverge, stop, or travel on. If to Bullion, and you are inclined to see the Sevier mines, here the Farmer and Gifford line meets you in new and ample conveyances, and at cheap rates they bowl you along through canyons and defiles, over divides and through the thousands of acres of most excellent grain. You feel for your scalp, perhaps, but you come out safe. Sanpete is now destined for a day of rest from her watching and her cares. Colonel Hough is pleasantly located on Pleasant Creek, while major Gordon passed on with the agreeable Dr. Vollum by his side, to look the valleys and hills through for "poor Lo!" J. L. Ivie, of Mount Pleasant, is the guide of the cavalry; a better one it would be hard to find. In fact, both of the contracting parties are fortunate. Ere the advent of the "boys in blue," the Indians protested their ability to whip any force sent against them; but discretion is the better part of valor—they have left.

Something should be done to make the Sanpete mails, destined for the north, connect with the Gilmer & Salsbury route. You lose twenty-four hours in this fast age.

DATA.

Deseret News
September 25, 1872

DIED.

At Nephi, August 28th, 1872, of inflammation of the bowels, JAMES SINCLAIR, aged 16 years and 24 days. The saints of Nephi sympathize muc with Bro. Mathew Sinclair, in the loss of his only son, who was a promising and obedient boy. [COM.

Mill. St r. please copy.

INDIAN MATTERS IN SANPETE.

Correspondence Between Gen. Morrow and Dr. Dodge

HEADQUARTERS, Military Dist.
of Utah, Mount Pleasant,
September 7th, 1872.

Dr. Geo. W. Dodge, Special Indian Agent, Salt Lake.

Dear Sir—All the facts I have been able to collect, and they are many, point conclusively to the Utes, from the Uintah and White River agencies, as having been the principal, if not the exclusive, agents in committing the depredations in Sanpete and the adjoining counties. These Indians came to the settlements early last spring, and remained in them until I arrived with troops. Their conduct towards the citizens was arrogant, domineering, and dictatorial. Indeed, it assumed finally the air of a conqueror towards a subjugated community. They entered private dwellings at all hours of the day and night, and compelled the women to cook meals for them "at all hours," often prescribing the dishes they wished served. In addition to this they were impudent beggars. I am not sure but it would be more proper to say they were impudent *robbers*, for their demands for food and presents were usually made with weapons in their hands to compel obedience to their exactions. After plundering the people in their homes, they entered upon a systematic course of horse and cattle stealing, which resulted in the loss, to the inhabitants of Sanpete alone, of more than 200 head of horses and as many head of cattle. To prevent this, an attempt was made to guard the herds more closely. This was not to be submitted to by the Indians, who killed two of the herders, and wounded several others. This state of things had gone on until one of the highways of travel between Sanpete county and the settlements on Utah Lake had to be abandoned, and people went armed to their fields and about their villages. Patrols were established, and when Col. Hough, of my command, arrived at Mount Pleasant, he found almost a reign of terror among the people, who welcomed his soldiers as deliverers. I think I may say with truthfulness, that there is not another American community in the nation which would have endured half the outrages these people endured, before rising up as one man to drive out the savage invaders at the point of the bayonet. On any principle of self-defense, they would have been justified in doing this.

Now, sir, I have given you a plain statement of facts, and I desire to invite your attention, and through you the attention of the Indian Department, to the justice and propriety of making this people some recompense for their losses. This may be done, I believe, from the appropriation made by Congress for these tribes. It is only an act of simple justice to the poor people who have suffered so severely that it should be done. It is some time since I had occasion to examine the subject, but I believe there is a law of Congress, of 1834, which authorizes compensation to be made in cases like the present, and prescribes the manner in which it shall be done. If this course is pursued now, it will not only be proper in itself, as an act of justice to the people, but it will also teach the Indians that they cannot commit depredations with impunity.

I am, sir,
Your obedient servant,
HENRY A. MORROW,
Lt. Col. U. S. Army,
Commanding.

OFFICE U. S. S. IND. AGT.,
Salt Lake City, Utah,
Sept. 16th, 1872
Lieut. Col. H. A. Morrow, Comdg. Military Dist., Utah.

Dear Sir:—Your letter of date "Mount Pleasant, Sept. 7th, 1872," is before me and contents carefully considered. Bodily ills and official duties have prevented an earlier reply. I fully concur with you in all the statements you have therein made. I have for a long time been satisfied that the Indians of the Uintah and White River reservations were the *principals* or largely concerned in the depredations in Sanpete and adjoining counties this summer. I feared such results in their first appearance in May last.

Both myself and the Hon. Sec. of Interior, who was in Salt Lake about that time, deemed it of the greatest importance that they should be returned to their respective reservations as soon as possible. Certain charges made to him against the Uintah agent, caused him to order me to visit the camps of these Indians as soon as practicable, and ascertain the cause of their leaving their agencies, and to request them to return. I held a council with them the 5th and 6th of June, at Fairview, Sanpete county, at which they gave the following as the reason for leaving their agencies:

1st—To visit their friends, the Mormons, to exchange friendly greetings, and trade with other Indians; to worship the Great Spirit near the resting place of their fathers; and to receive compensation for the use of their lands, now occupied by Mormons and miners.

2. The Uintah Indians urged still farther that they had no means of subsistence at the Agency.

3. That the Agent and his employees treated them harshly, even preventing them from laboring when they asked the privilege.

4. That the Agent did not give them the goods and provisions that government provided for them.

5. That the government had not carried out the promises made to them in the Spanish Fork treaty

I made a minute of all the proceedings of this council, and assured the Indians that their statement of grievances would be forwarded to Washington as soon as I returned to Salt Lake; and that I would furnish them provisions to enable them to return at once to their agencies. I gave my official order to Amasa Tucker, Bishop of Fairview, to issue to them 4,000 pounds of flour and 2,500 pounds of beef. The Indians assured me that they had not finally abandoned the agencies. They only wished the assurance that they would be kindly treated and fairly dealt with and they would return, though they desired to visit for a few months before they returned. I could not consent to this, but promised to do all in my power to have their wants supplied in the future. I also issued a quantity of ammunition and a few articles of

tity of ammunition and a few articles of clothing. Having done all that was immediately necessary for them, I left, hoping they would return to their Agencies and give the government and settlements no farther trouble this season. However, on my return to Salt Lake, about the middle of June, I found they were still in Sanpete Valley, and that they did not intend to return to their Agencies until Autumn. I therefore sent an official order to them, through Bishop Tucker, to return to their Agencies at once, renewing my assurance that government would do everything consistent with right to redress their grievances. This order was issued June 20th. The Indians declined to obey.

The first day of July a council was held in my office in Salt Lake City, composed of Gen. B. R. Cowen, Asst. Sec. Int., Hon. John S. Delano, Chief Clerk Int., Hon. J. N. Turney, Civil Comr. Ind. Affairs, Geo. L. Woods, Governor of Utah Territory, Hon. J. B. McKean, Chief Justice, and Hon. C. M. Hawley, Associate Justice U. S. Court, Utah Ter., Lieut. Col. H. A. Morrow, Commanding Military District of Utah, and myself, at which the condition of Indian affairs in this Territory was fully discussed; the result of which was, the issuing of instructions to me to proceed at once to the Indian camps and make provision for their "immediate return to their Agencies, peaceably if possible, otherwise to call on the military to force them back." The next morning (July 2d) I started again for the scene of trouble, and succeeded in holding a council at Nephi, on the 5th, with Tabby and Douglas, with several of their counsellors, at which I was assisted by Judge George Bean, of Provo. Every argument that I urged to induce them to return to their agencies was stoutly resisted, they stating, in addition to the reasons already assigned, that, as the Spanish Fork Treaty was never ratified, therefore, the land of Utah, occupied by them before the coming of the white man,

was theirs, and that the white man was only occupying the same by their permission. They also urged that they had, the night previous, received a revelation from the Great Spirit, that they might remain away from their agencies two months longer, when the "Voice from the West" would appear to them, and give instructions about their future course. Of course I could not admit these reasons, and to conclude the matter at once, I gave them ten days to prepare to comply with my request, giving them 1,500 pounds of flour and two beeves at the same time. I also promised to subsist them at the Agency until the agent could stock the same with his winter's supplies. They agreed to these terms. I at once returned to Salt Lake City, and contracted with Mr. Chas. Popper to send forward 100 beef cattle and 50,000 pounds of flour. All the cattle were at Heber City, the point agreed upon with the Indians, within one week from this time; also 6,000 pounds of flour. Soon after 10,000 pounds more were in readiness for distribution. On the 14th of July I visited the Indian camp again at Fountain Green, that I might make every provision for their return trip. This time I was accompanied by Capt. Nugent, of your command, agent Littlefield, of the White River agency, and Judge Bean of Provo. The 15th the Indians met us in council, when they manifested decided hostility to any arrangement whatever for returning to their agencies. The Indians returned to their camps very angry. The 16th we met a large band of Elk Mountain Utes, Navajoes and Kapotas, who were so insolent that I found it necessary to issue an official order forbidding the citizens furnishing them any supplies whatever, hoping they would thus be compelled to leave, but no! They all interpreted the presence of a military officer with me, as a declaration of war against them and they determined to resist. We turned back from here, feeling that we had no alternative but to turn them over to the military. At Fountain Green I was overtaken by a telegram from Bishop Seeley, of Mount Pleasant, stating that Tabby and Douglas had concluded to start at once for their agencies. This fourth promise they did not carry out.

The most of these bands became more and more insubordinate, until the chiefs gave notice that they could no longer control their people. Telegrams to this effect were immediately sent by the Bishop to Mayor Wells, to you and to myself. There was, evidently, but one course to pursue, which was to call for the military to protect the citizens, and compel the Indians to obedience. I at once took the necessary steps to hasten the preparations for this new departure, telegraphing to the Hon. Secretary of the Interior to call on the War Department for the necessary order for employing troops; also making a requisition upon Gov. Woods for the same, and communicating my action in the premises to you at the same time. The results are well known to you. The promptness on the part of Government, and your own decisive and politic course, have brought the Indians to accept the terms of the government without bloodshed. I can but congratulate you, sir, the government, the citizens and myself, on the success of your expedition and negotiations. I beg you to accept my grateful acknowledgment for so cheerfully undertaking, and so successfully carrying out, that part of the programme belonging to me. I should not have imposed this upon you, but for my serious illness at the time. I most heartily join you in recommending that a deputation of the most able of these Indians be allowed to visit Washington, for the purpose of laying their grievances before the President and Indian Bureau. I trust this will be granted, and that the President will permit persons who comprehend the condition of Indian affairs here to accompany them.

Your reference to the great losses on the part of the citizens of the disturbed district, is eminently just, and I shall do everything in my power to bring such relief to the sufferers as the law will allow. Those who have met with losses should lose no time in laying before the agent all the facts in the case. They should not only give their own names clearly; the number of horses or other stock they each have lost; the amount and kind of other property stolen or destroyed, but should obtain the certificate of two or more responsible persons, of known veracity, who are not party concerned, to the effect that their claims are just and true, and that they have sustained such losses at the hands of certain Indians, giving *their individual names*, and the names of their tribes or bands; as government requires *specific* and not *general* statements in such cases. Simple justice requires that they should receive back their property in good condition, or its value. It is also simple justice, that the government should only be required to pay the losses that are clearly proven to come under the laws made and provided for such cases. Where there are annuities due such Indians as have committed these depredations, sound policy would dictate that the portion of goods properly due the depredators, should be taken to pay such losses, and thus they be taught that they cannot commit such acts with impunity.

No efforts will be spared on my part to make good our mutual promises to the Indians and citizens. Though still needing rest, I am ready to move as soon as your forces can accompany me, to make an effort to recover the stolen horses, and to apprehend and bring to justice the thieves.

I have carried this reply to your letter much beyond what I desired. However, the peculiarity of the circumstances seem to necessitate all I have written. I trust the publication of your letter with my reply, will remove from the minds of the people any impression they may have entertained, either of neglect on the one hand, or too great severity on the other hand, on the part of the Indian Agent of this district, or of any other government official, who has acted a prominent part in these matters. The Agent has not been indifferent, nor idle, but has worked indefatigably. *No! let me not say that.* He has worked to weariness and sickness, and worked *when weary and sick,* as you very well know. If peace and prosperity is the result, his joy will abundantly compensate for all this.

I remain, dear sir, very respectfully,
Your obedient servant,
GEO. W. DODGE,
U. S. Special Indian Agent.

Correspondence.

SPRING CITY, Sept. 27, 1872.

Editor Deseret News:

We are pained to chronicle another Indian raid and murder. Brother Daniel Miller, of Nephi, had been logging in Oak Creek Cañon, about a week, and yesterday morning left B. Snow's mill with a load of lumber for home. He was accompanied by his son, a boy about twelve years old. They had proceeded about a quarter of a mile, when they stopped to tighten the binder, and got upon the load to start, when they were fired upon by five Indians in ambush. One ball struck Brother Miller in the centre of the abdomen, passing through his body; another struck the boy, passing through his hand and wrist, also through his thigh near the hip. His father told the boy to run to town, which he did, and reported the occurrence. Colonel Allred, with a company of armed men, proceeded to the spot. Brother Miller told them that he was fatally wounded, and did not wish to be moved, as he could not live long. After the boy ran away the Indians came out in sight and shot again at Bro. Miller, the shot passing through his arm and shoulder. They then cut the harness of his mule, but finding one was very thin in flesh, they turned it out. Bro. Alma Bennet, of Mount Pleasant, was going to the mill for lumber, and it is supposed the Indians must have heard him coming, which probably accounts for the miraculous escape of the boy. A litter was constructed by Col. Allred and company, and the wounded man placed upon it, but they had not proceeded more than a few hundred yards when he expired. His body was conveyed to Col. Allred's, where his wounded son was receiving medical assistance from Dr. Christensen of Mt. Pleasant, who had been telegraphed for as soon as the boy reached town. Dr. C., while coming to this place, between Cedar Creek and Oak Creek, was pursued by the Indians, who tried to get in ahead of him. Nine Indians were seen, some of them being on foot, and only for the fleetness of his horse did he escape them. He reported the circumstance on his arrival, and a company of men went out who found the tracks of Indians, but could not find them.

The friends of Br. Miller arrived from Nephi last evening, and took the body this morning to Nephi. His wounded son remains at Col. Allred's, it not being deemed wisdom to move him at present, although his wounds are not considered dangerous at present.

On the night of the 25th a span of horses were taken out of the corral of Br. Joseph P. Allred, and the stable of your correspondent was entered by a small door, and two horses of Bp. T. Taylor, of the 14th Ward, Salt Lake City, and two of mine were enticed from the rack, and the halters taken off; but the two large doors being locked they could not get the horses out.

The danger from Indians at present seems greater than at any previous time this season, although I am happy to state that most of our grain is hauled out of the field.

A machine arrived yesterday, and thrashing commenced this morning in earnest. Crops are good and a very large amount of grain is raised in this place. Another machine is expected in a few days. Yours in haste,

GEO. BROUGH.

OBITUARY OF D. M. MILLER.—The appended obituary of the late Daniel M. Miller, of Nephi, who was killed by Indians in Sanpete County, September 26th, has been forwarded to us by brother Samuel Pitchforth, with a request to publish. An accompanying note from brother Pitchforth informs us that the son of the deceased, aged 12 years, who was with his father when the attack was made, and who received two wounds at the same time, says that he recognized three of the attacking Indians as persons who dined at his father's house on the 24th of July, when the Indian Agent was there:

Daniel Morgan Miller, son of Josiah and Amanda Miller, was born Nov. 20, 1820, in the town of Murray, Genesee County, State of New York. In 1831 his parents were baptized into the Church of Jesus Christ of Latter-day Saints, and moved, with their family, to Kirtland, Ohio, where they resided until the Saints migrated West, keeping with the Church.

On the 16th of July, 1846, Brother Daniel was baptized, at Council Bluffs, by Elder A. Love, and ordained an elder by Presidents B. Young and Geo. A. Smith. The same day he joined company E of the Mormon Battalion, and traveled with it to Santa Fe.

At the latter place he was taken sick and could not proceed with the company, where his brother Miles left him to go on with the battalion to the coast. The latter did not expect ever to see his brother again; even Daniel had little hopes of his own recovery, he became so far convalescent, however, as to be able to travel with Capt. Brown's company, the members of which, after receiving their discharge came to Salt Lake Valley, arriving soon after the pioneers. He resided in the 4th and 7th Wards until 1852; when he moved to Nephi, Juab county, where he remained until his death. He was a member of the 22nd Quorum of Seventies till Sept 24, 1865, when he was ordained one of the Presidents of the 71st Quorum.

Deceased was much respected by all who had the pleasure of his acquaintance. He leaves a wife and eight children.

His funeral took place on Sunday, Sept. 29th, and was the largest ever seen in Nephi. A subscription list has been started to raise means to erect a suitable tombstone to his memory.

DIED.

At Levan, Juab Co., Oct. 8th, ALBERT JOSEPH CRANDALL, of old age.

He was born in Duchess Co., N. Y., July 22nd 1801, emigrated to Nauvoo the fall previous to the Saints being driven, and wintered at Council Bluffs. He came to Salt Lake City the year after the pioneers. He was ordained a High Priest and labored many years, bearing testimony to the truth of the Latter-day work, and died in full faith of the gospel.—[COM.

DIED.

At the residence of Lyman Hubbard, Mona, Juab Co., Nov. 24th, RICHARD EDWIN, son of Richard and Marinda Sides, aged 3 years, 4 months and 3 days

Deseret News
December 25, 1872

Per Deseret Telegraph.

NEPHI, December 16, 1872.

President Young and party laid over here yesterday. The meeting was largely attended. The speakers were Elders L. D. Young, W. C. Staines and A. M. Musser. We go to Scipio to-day. The weather is fine, roads dry and dusty. Hundreds of freight teams line the road loaded for Pioche. A. M. M.

DIED.

At Nephi, Dec. 3, 1872, from the effects of injuries received at a Sanpete coal bed, on Dec. 30, 1872, BENGT SVENSON, born at Saoreby, Sweden, June 23, 1826.

Scandinavian Star, please copy.

Deseret News
January 1, 1873

Names of the passengers pr steamer "Manhattan" from Liverpool, Dec. 5, 1872:

Helen Hendry; Helen Jackson; William, Ellen, Nephi, Edward, David, Benjamin, and Eleanor McCleery; Phoeby and Agnes Bradshaw; Thomas, Sarah, Sarah, Hugh and infant McKenna; Thomas, Mary A., Mary, Robert, James and Stephen Cordner; Thomas, Priscilla, Thomas, Heber, Elizabeth, Annie and Sarah Sparks; Daniel, Ann, Christina, Catherine, Anna and Margaret Kennedy; John and Grace Holden.

Salt Lake Tribune
January 6, 1873

The Juab, San Pete and Sevier Railroad,

Organized in September, 1872. Capital stock, $1,500,000. Track, three foot narrow gauge. Officers, Brigham Young, president; David McKenzie, secretary; Joseph A. Young, superintendent and chief engineer; O. L. Ericsson, assistant engineer.

The road will connect with the U. S. Railroad at Nephi and go through Salt Creek canyon, thence in a south-easterly direction with branches to the different coal beds in the vicinity. The total length, including branches will be about 150 miles. Nearly the whole length has been surveyed and located. Contracts for grading and ties have been made and work will be commenced early in the spring.

Deseret News
January 8, 1873

Per Deseret Telegraph.

St. George, Jan. 2nd.

Singularly enough we have not seen an Indian South of Nephi City clothed in the habiliments of Uncle Sam's annuities. Almost every one had a small Navajo and not a U. S. blanket around his shivering frame.

There is a constantly increasing demand for a money order office and a Wells, Fargo & Co's Express agency, at this point.

The late southern mission conference was attended by people from Kanab, Beaver, Panacca, and the intermediate settlements, and was held in the main hall of the new Tabernacle. President Young, whose health is gradually improving, spoke three times during the conference. Much valuable instruction was given by the several speakers.

For a past number of days and nights copious rain falls have quenched the earth's thirst. At this writing the weather remains threatening.   A. M. M.

Deseret News
January 15, 1873

INFORMATION WANTED.—Silas L. Jackson, of Nephi City, Juab Co., wants to know the whereabouts of Thomas Warwick, who came to this Territory about two years ago, and some time since was living at North Ogden. Address as above.

DIED.

Elder THOMAS PARDINGTON died in Mona, Juab County, on the 16th day of December, 1872.

He was born in Ashton, Macclesfield, England, where he embraced the gospel. He emigrated to Utah in 1862. He was a faithful Saint and a kind father. He leaves a widow and children.

Salt Lake Herald
March 12, 1873

Juab County Items.

The unusual hard winter has caused many cattle in Juab county to die, and hundreds more cattle and sheep will surely perish unless the snow soon disappears.

County road commissioner Thomas Wright has located, under instructions of the county court, a road to Tintic via Dog and Turner valleys. When completed the road will be the best and nearest route from the line of the U. S. R. R. to the Tintic districts, bringing them within twenty miles of Nephi on an easy grade.

The Salt trade is looming up in Juab county. Jenkins, Booth & Co., have erected a mill at Nephi for crushing the native rock salt.

Miners are at work developing some of the valuable prospects in Levan district.

The people are anxiously awaiting the time when the Utah Southern will run through Juab Valley.

We learn the above from a letter from "Nephi."

SMALL POX AT MILL CREEK.

Our readers will remember that the HERALD of last Sunday called attention to the fact of a man—whose name is Hans Christiansen — recklessly promenading the streets of the city with his face covered with small pox scabs. From Dr. J. M. Benedict, we learn further particulars in regard to this case, which the doctor has investigated, supposing it might come within the city jurisdiction. Christiansen resides at Mill Creek ward, a short distance this side of Mill Creek. Opposite him lives Andrew Jensen, whose sister resided some time in the 11th ward in the house where the Canuteson small pox cases occurred. This sister married and started for Levan, stopping en route, at Jensen's house, opposite Christiansen's. Shortly after she left Mill Creek, Jensen was taken sick and broke out with small-pox pustules, Christiansen staying with him several nights while he was in the worst stage of the disease. As a consequence, and one step more toward extending this loathsome contagion, in a little while Christiansen was completely covered with small-pox which proved so severe that for four days he was utterly blind, and yesterday, when visited by Dr. Benedict, his face, head, limbs, and body were covered with scabs. His having been vaccinated probably alone saved his life. There seemed to be in the neighborhood no conception of the danger of the disease, or else the utmost recklessness in regard thereto, Christiansen having visited at will the dozen or so neighbors, and they having called upon him, one youngster standing carelessly about in the doorway of the house as Hans talked with the physician who remained outside on horseback, the smell from the house proving strong enough to surfeit all desire for nearer approach. As the case proved to be beyond the jurisdiction of Dr. Benedict, he, upon his return to Salt Lake, made a report to judge Smith, of the county court, from whom he awaits instructions preparatory to a perfect overhauling and cleaning out of this pest house. It will probably cost the county $100 to put the place in proper condition.

It appears that Christiansen had no realization of his condition, a physician whom he had consulted having assured him that the disease under which he suffered was not small pox. Two or three persons at Mill Creek are now sick, probably with the disease, and it is likely others will be attacked. The brother of the woman, who undoubtedly carried about in her clothing seeds of the contagion from the Canuteson house in the 11th ward, to Mill Creek, has lately had a letter from her from Levan, saying that she had broken out with an eruption, as also had others. Thus one person through culpable carelessness, or ignorance, has succeeded in spreading the small-pox from Salt Lake into Juab county. It is perhaps proper to state that a physician who ought to have notified the officer having jurisdiction so that proper quarantine might have been enforced, neglected to do so. Mill Creek needs prompt and thorough action to arrest the extended spread of small pox.

LETTER FROM JUAB COUNTY.

Amusements at Nephi— Educational Matters.

Editors Herald.

Our winter has been passed as usual, with amusements of various kinds, such as theatrical performances, dancing, &c. But the greatest feature of the season was an exhibition given by the pupils of our friend and teacher, T. B. Lewis, Esq., in the social hall last evening. The entertainment was gratuitously offered to the public and the doors opened to all. Your correspondent fails to remember having ever before witnessed such a crowded house. It was with regret that a great number of the people were obliged to return to their homes, being unable to get in, to witness the efforts of the young students who assisted in the performance. The programme was attractive and well selected by the teacher. The pieces in declamation, elocution, dialogues, &c., were rendered with good effect and surpassed the expectation of all present. The rhetorical readings, although not delivered with "stentorian and sonorous voices," fell most harmoniously and musically on the ears of the audience, and indicated excellent training on the part of the teacher. They were all greeted with applause.

There was quite an amount of talent exhibited by the young pupils, nearly all of whom made their *debut* upon the boards last evening. Great praise is due to T. B. Lewis, Esq., for his indefatigable labors in getting up and presenting this novel exhibition to the public, although it is no more than he accomplishes daily in the schoolroom; but the demonstration of this fact is brought out more forcibly and vividly when presented in one evening's bill as it was last night. The Nephi choir, string band, and some excellent singing with accompaniments on the organ largely contributed and pleasantly added to the evening's programme.

Education has a good foundation laid in this city, and it is due to our inhabitants to say, that they fully realize its powerful influence and moralizing tendency with the young. We firmly believe that a population well educated with well drilled and trained minds, is worth at least as much as a population who rarely educate and grovel in ignorance. Educated nations are easier governed and have better forms of governing than those that are unlearned.

G. H.

PRESIDING
ELDERS AND BISHOPS

Of the Church of Jesus Christ of Latter-day Saints, in Utah Territory and adjacent Settlements.

Bennington, J. W. Moore, Oneida co., Idaho
Montpelier, John Cozzens, „ „
Ovid, N. C. Edlefsen, „ „
Liberty, E. N. Austin, „ „
Paris, H. N. Horne, „ „
Bloomington, George Asmond, „ „
St. Charles, John A. Hunt, „ „
Fish Haven, Hugh Findley, „ „
Lake Town, alias Ithica, Ira Nebeker,
  Rich co., Utah
Meadowville, Josiah Tufts, „ „
Randolph, Randolph Stewart, „ „
Woodruff, Henry Lee, „ „
Evanston, alias Alma, Samuel Pike,
  Wyoming Territory

WILLIAM BUDGE is Presiding Bishop over the above Wards.

Oxford, George Lake, Oneida co., Idaho
Clifton, Wm. Pratt, „ „
Bridgeport, N. W. Packer, „ „
Franklin, L. H. Hatch, „ „
Weston, John Maughan, Cache co., Utah.
Clarkston, Simon Smith, „ „
Newton, W. F. Littlewood, „ „
Lowiston, W. C. Lewis, „ „
Richmond, W. W. Merrill, „ „
Smithfield, Samuel Roskelly, „ „
Hyde Park, Wm. Hyde, „ „
*Logan, W. B. Preston, „ „
Providence, M. D. Hammond, „ „
Millville, G. O. Pitkin, „ „
Hyrum, O. N. Liljenquist, „ „

Paradise, David James, „ „
Wellsville, Wm. Maughan, „ „
Mendon, Henry Hughes, „ „

WM. B. PRESTON is Presiding Bishop over the foregoing eighteen Wards.

*Malad City, Daniel Daniels, Oneida co., Idaho
Samaria, Samuel Williams, „ „

DANIEL DANIELS, Presiding Bishop over the two last named places.

Portage, O. C. Hoskins, Box Elder co., Utah
Deweyville, J. C. Dewey, „ „
Calls Fort, Thomas Hasper, „ „
Bear River City, Wm. Neeley, „ „
Mantua, H. P. Jensen, „ „
*Brigham City, Alvin Nichols, „ „

A. NICHOLS, Presiding Bishop over the six last named Wards.

Willard City, G. W. Ward.

WEBER COUNTY, UTAH.

L. J. HERRICK, Presiding Bp.

*Ogden, L. J. Herrick.
North Ogden, Henry Holmes.
Plain City, L. W. Shirtliff.
Mound Fort, David Moore.
Bingham Fort, Robert Biard.
Slaterville, Thomas Richardson.
Rawson, David Rawson.
Marriat, S. P. Halverston.
West Weber, John Hart.
East Weber, A. Spaulding.
South Weber, John Cook.
River Dale, Sanford Bingham.
Eden, Richard Ballantyne.
Huntsville, F. A. Hammond.
Hooperville, Gilbert Belknap.

DAVIS COUNTY.

Kaysville, Christopher Layton.
*Farmington, John W. Hess.
Centreville, Wm. R. Smith.
Bountiful, John Stoker.

MORGAN COUNTY.

Mountain Green, Eli Spaulding.
Weber City, C. S. Peterson.
Enterprise, Jesse Haven.

C. S. PETERSON is Presiding Bishop over the three last named Wards.

Milton, L. P. Christiansen.
Littleton, W. G. Smith.
Richville, John Seaman.
Porterville, Alma Porter.
*Morgan City, Richard Fry.
Round Valley, Samuel Carter.

W. G. SMITH is Presiding Bishop over the six last named places.

Croyden, Ephraim Swann.

SUMMIT COUNTY.

Henneferville, Chas. Richens.
Echo, Elias Hasper.
*Coalville, W. W. Cluff.
Unionville, Alonzo Winters.

WM. W. CLUFF presides over Morgan County and the above four Wards in Summit Co.

Wanship, G. G. Snyder.
Rockport, Edwin Bryant.
Peoa, Abraham Marchant.
Morell, John K. Lemmon.
Kamas, W. S. Harder.
Parley's Park, Ephraim Snyder.

SAMUEL F. ATWOOD, Presiding Bishop over the above six Wards.

WASATCH COUNTY.

ABRAHAM HATCH, Presiding Bishop.

*Heber City, Abraham Hatch.
Midway, Henry S. Alexander.
Charleston, John Watkins.
Wallsburgh, Wm. E. Nuttall.

SALT LAKE COUNTY.

1st Ward, S. L. City, Jos. Warburton.
2d   ,,   James Leach.
3d   ,,   Jacob Weller.
4th   ,,   Thomas Jenkins.
5th & 6th, W. H. Hickenlooper.
7th   ,,   Wm. Thorn.
8th   ,,   E. F. Sheets.
9th   ,,   S. A. Woolley.
10th ,,   John Proctor.
11th ,,   Alex. McRae.
12th ,,   L. W. Hardy.
13th ,,   E. D. Woolley.
14th ,,   Thomas Taylor.
15th ,,   R. T. Burton.
16th ,,   Frederick Kesler.
17th ,,   Nathan Davis.
18th ,,   L. D. Young.
19th ,,   A. H. Raleigh.
20th ,,   John Sharp.
Sugar House Ward, W. C. A. Smoot.
Brighton, A. H. Raleigh.
Big Cottonwood, David Brinton.
Mill Creek, Reuben Miller.
South Cottonwood, J. S. Rawlins.
West Jordan, Archibald Gardner.
South Willow Creek, L. M. Stewart.

[Capital of Ter. and co. seat S. L. Co.]

TOOELE COUNTY.

JOHN ROWBERRY, Presiding Bishop.

E. T. City, G. W. Bryan.
Pine Kanyon, Moses Martin.
*Tooele City, John Rowberry.
Grantsville, T. H. Clark.
St. Johns, G. W. Burridge.
Centreville, James Jordan.
Vernon, Hyrum Bennion.
Deep Creek, Edwin Tadlock.
Skull Valley, B. F. Knowlton.

UTAH COUNTY.

Lehi, David Evans.
Cedar Fort, H. F. Cook.
Fairfield, John Carson.

DAVID EVANS, Presiding Bishop over the three last named places.

American Fork, L. E. Harrington.
Alpine, T. J. McCullough.

L. E. HARRINGTON, Presiding Bishop over the two last named places.

Pleasant Grove, John Brown.
*Provo, A. O. Smoot.
Springville, Wm. Bringhurst.
Spanish Fork, A. K. Thurber.
Salem, *alias* Pondtown, Robt. H. Davis.
Payson, J. S. Tanner.
Santaquin, D. H. Halliday.
Spring Lake Villa, B. F. Johnson.

J. S. TANNER is presiding Bishop over the four last named places.

Goshen, Wm. Price.

JUAB COUNTY.

JOEL GROVER, Presiding Bishop

Mona, Edward Kay.
*Nephi, *alias* Salt Creek, Joel Grover.

ADDRESS OF CHURCH EMIGRATION AGENT:—Mr. William C. Staines, Box 3957, P. O., New York City.

Salt Lake Herald
March 25, 1873

THE NEPHI SMALL-POX CASES.—The following has been received, and claims space:

Nephi, March 21st, 1873.

Editors Herald:

Gentlemen, in your issue of Wednesday last, a correspondent writing from Nephi says, "Two cases of small-pox; and, from appearances, likely to have 150 in a few days here." Also, "It is said that Nephi received the contagion from the 11th ward of Salt Lake City."

Now, the facts are these: We have only had the two cases above referred to, and from present appearances not likely to spread at all; and, further, Nephi did not receive, as here asserted, the contagion from Salt Lake City, but from Moroni, Sanpete county; consequently the remarks of your correspondent for Nephi are rather unnecessarily of an alarmist character.

Auld Reekey.

A gentleman from Nephi informs us that the two cases referred to were all that had occurred in that place, and that the disease has disappeared; one having recovered and the other died; although, our informant adds, the fatal case was mild, and there was matter for surprise in that it terminated as it did. It would be wise now to take the necessary steps for preventing the contagion spreading from the clothes or other surroundings of those who had the disease.

Salt Lake Herald
April 26, 1873

PERSONAL.—C. W. Penrose, Esq., editor of the Junction, was in town yesterday, and dropped in fraternally.

G. Henriod, Esq., of Nephi, also favored us with a brief call. We were pleased to see friend Gustave well and hearty.

Salt Lake Herald
May 2, 1873

SERIOUS FIRE. — The following reached us by Deseret Telegraph yesterday:

Nephi, 1.—Fort Birch grist mill burned last night. The cause of the fire is not known. Loss about fifteen thousand; no insurance.

Deseret News
May 7, 1873

DIED,

At Fountain Green, on the 14th of April, at five minutes past 10 o'clock a. m., of consumption, JAMES WARNER BOSNELL.

He was confined to his bed four weeks, gradually wasted away and died without a struggle. He was born January 9, 1803, and baptized December 25, 1847; emigrated from England, January, 1849, and came to Council Bluffs, where he stayed one year. He came on to Salt Lake City and stayed there one year, after which he was sent, by President Young, to Iron County. He labored on the Iron Works, built a grist mill, in connection with Erastus Snow, at Cedar City, labored hard to help to build Cedar City and the Iron Works, for a number of years. When the Iron Works stopped he moved north; labored at Camp Floyd, on the mail route, for two years. He then settled at Nephi; which place he left and came here in 1867. Early in the Spring of that year he joined with Samuel Jewkes and built a saw mill, which has been in operation nearly five years. He also built and remodeled several grist mills in the county, and nearly completed putting in the machinery for a grist mill in connection with the saw mill here. His funeral took place on the 15th of April at 4 o'clock, p. m. Nearly all the citizens attended his funeral. He leaves a family.—COM.

Deseret News
May 14, 1873

SPANISH FORK, May 7th, 1873.
Editor Deseret News:

There are four cases of small-pox at Salem City (Pond Town) in the family of Nathaniel Hamchett. The disease was taken there by the children of Brother Huggins, who died, of small-pox, at Nephi, and after it was supposed that there was no danger of infection. All the cases reported are doing well. The residence of Hanchett is quarantined. Respectfully,

WILLIAM CREER.

Deseret News
June 25, 1873

NEPHI, June 16, 1873.
Editor Deseret News:

Pursuant to an appointment made by Supt. R. L. Campbell on his recent visit South, a large number of the citizens of Juab county met at this place on the 15th inst., in the meeting house, for the purpose of organizing a Teachers' Institute. A preamble and constitution similar to those drafted for other counties of the Territory, were subscribed to and a permanent organization was entered into by a number of those present.

The following officers were elected—T. B. Lewis, president; Thomas Ord, vice president; Wm. May, recording secretary; Wm. A. C. Bryan, corresponding secretary; Wm. Newton, of Mona, asst. recording secretary; Heber Hartley, of Levan, asst. recording secretary; Martha J. Lewis, asst. corresponding secretary; Edwin Harley, treasurer.

A marked interest was felt, although we were disappointed in not having Supt. R. L. Campbell with us, business having called him away.

Juab county is small as regards numerical strength, but she is big with interest for all that pertains to building up the commonwealth. She is especially energetic in the discharge of the duties required of her, and is wide awake upon educational interests.

We now have two schools, one of which has one hundred and twenty-five pupils enrolled for summer.

T. B. LEWIS,
Sec. Pro tem.

Deseret News
December 17, 1873

DIED.

At Mona, Juab Co., Utah, J. M. DAVIS, Esq., M. D., in the 67th year of his age; formerly of Ohio.

Wednesday morning, the deceased was taken very suddenly with a violent cramp in his bowels, which resulted in "inflammation of the colon." Every attention was bestowed upon him and every remedy tried, but without success. He lingered three days and expired.

The death of this excellent man has cast a deep gloom over our town, endeared as he was to all by his amiable disposition, urbane manner and upright conduct. Although almost a stranger, having resided scarcely a year in Mona, yet few could rejoice in warmer friends, none better deserve them. He was possessed of fine intellect, was a skillful and scientific physician, was also mild and courteous, and was animated in every action by an exalted sense of honor. From the first hour of his sickness he said he was very confident he would not recover, yet he was perfectly resigned, and said he trusted all to the mercy of an overruling and all-wise Providence.

Ohio papers, please copy.

P.S.—Dr. Davis was not a member of the Church of Latter-day Saints, but he was all that the above represents him to be. He came to Utah for his health. He has a large circle of relatives and friends in the East, and I write this on their account.

SUSIE E. TIBBS.

Mona, Juab Co., Dec. 4, 1873.

Deseret News
January 14, 1874

Holiday Parties—Schools.

NEPHI CITY, JUAB COUNTY,
Jan. 1, 1874.

Editor Deseret News:

The annual party for the Sunday School children of this city came off on Tuesday last, under the management of Superintendent Wm. H. Warner, and his Councilors, Abraham Orme and Langley A. Bailey.

The children under twelve years danced in the afternoon and those over twelve in the evening, and on both occasions the hall was filled with a delighted assembly. The little dancers in the afternoon were instructed by their teachers. Our excellent musicians made beautiful melody free of charge. Our stores donated liberally of candy, raisins and nuts, which the children enjoyed hugely.

On New Year's Day the pupils of Bro. T. B. Lewis and Sister Grover's day schools, enjoyed themselves in the dance. Thus while the "old folks" were celebrating the passing away of the "old year" and the introduction of the new, the "young folks" were also remembered, and had an opportunity of enjoying themselves. Thus the holidays have passed away agreeably and orderly. I am happy to say that our Sunday School is reviving, the teachers are attending better and several experienced brethren have begun to attend, taking charge of the older boys, which is quite a help.

THOMAS CRAWLEY.

A Numerous Family.

LEVAN, Jan. 1, 1874.

Editor Deseret News:

Christmas and New Year's day passed off very quietly and pleasantly, the weather is cold, with considerable snow. Health and peace prevail. We have a good Sabbath and day school, well attended. The subject of education seems to be on the increase.

On the 26th ult., I had the pleasure of attending the birthday party of Brother Martin Taylor, at Taylor's Ranch, five miles south of Levan. There were present the aged father and mother, who had eleven living children at last accounts, eighty grandchildren, and three great-grandchildren. Four of the brothers and three of the sisters were present on the occasion, and seventy in all of the name of Taylor, besides several of their relatives of other names. The day and evening were spent in partaking of a sumptuous dinner, dancing, singing songs, etc., and in a general time of rejoicing till a late hour.

ELMER TAYLOR.

Salt Lake Herald
March 12, 1874

Juab County Items.

The unusual hard winter has caused many cattle in Juab county to die, and hundreds more cattle and sheep will surely perish unless the snow soon disappears.

County road commissioner Thomas Wright has located, under instructions of the county court, a road to Tintic *via* Dog and Turner valleys. When completed the road will be the best and nearest route from the line of the U. S. R. R. to the Tintic districts, bringing them within twenty miles of Nephi on an easy grade.

The Salt trade is looming up in Juab county. Jenkins, Booth & Co., have erected a mill at Nephi for crushing the native rock salt.

Miners are at work developing some of the valuable prospects in Levan district.

The people are anxiously awaiting the time when the Utah Southern will run through Juab Valley.

We learn the above from a letter from "Nephi."

Deseret News
March 18, 1874

Mail Contracts.—The contracts to carry the U. S. mails between Salt Lake City and Ophir, and Salt Creek or Nephi and Bullion, have been awarded to Mr. Leonard I. Smith. For the first named route he will get $1790 a year and for the second $3,490 a year.

Mr. Wheeler has been awarded the contracts to carry the mails between Lehi and Eureka, Tintic District, and Payson and Eureka. For the first he will get $1,200 and for the second $800.

The parties above named are expected to commence filling the contracts on the first day of July.

Salt Lake Tribune
March 27, 1874

Correspondence Tribune.]

NEPHI CITY, March 22, '74.

Last Tuesday, the Bishop of this place received a dispatch from Brigham Young and George A. Smith, of which the following is a copy:

"If you and the People of your ward want to receive the Order of Enoch, let me know, and I will stop on our way up and give you a temporary organization."

Upon the receipt of this, a two-days' meeting was ordered, which came off on Saturday and Sunday last, largely attended on both days.

Twelve persons were called to the platform to

President Young's Party.

The following programme of the journeyings, meetings, etc., of President Young's party, on its return from St. George, we take from last evening's *News:*

Leave St. George on Monday, April 6th, hold meeting at Belleyue at 4 p. m., and stay there all night.

Tuesday, 7th.—To Kanarra, and hold meeting at 2 p. m.

Wednesday, 8th.—To Cedar City, and hold meetings at 11 a. m. and 3 p. m.

Thursday, 9th.—To Parowan, and hold meeting at 2 p. m.; tarry there Friday and hold meetings at 10 a. m, and 2 p. m.

Saturday, 11th.—To Beaver, hold meeting at 6:30 p. m.; tarry over Sunday, 12th, and have meetings at 10 a. m. and 2 p. m.

Monday, 13th —To Cove Creek.

Tuesday, 14th.—To Fillmore, hold meeting at Kanosh at 12 m. on the way.

Wednesday, 15th.—Tarry at Fillmore, and hold meetings at 10 a. m. and 2 p. m.

Thursday, 16th.—To Scipio, hold meeting at 12 m. on the way at Cedar Springs, and Scipio at 6:30 p. m.

Friday, 17th.—To Nephi.

Saturday and Sunday, 18th and 19th.—Hold meetings each day at 10 a. m. and 2 p. m.

Monday, 20th.—To Provo.

BENDER IS BENDER.

THE OLD MAN IDENTIFIED AS THE PATER FAMILIAS OF KANSAS BUTCHERS.

He Becomes more Communicative.

The Junior Bender also Captured and will be Brought to this City.

Yesterday the scene around the city jail was one of intense excitement and clamor, the object which drew the crowd to that point being the supposed old man Bender. At early morn people began to flock to the city hall, and by 10 a m. the importunities of the crowd to see the greatest murderer of modern times became so great that the jailer to quiet and gratify them threw open the jail and exhibited the accused. The curiosity to see the author of so many crimes was not confined to the male portion of mankind only, as the ladies were seized with the same desire and during the day dozens of the weaker sex called at the classic establishment and gazed at the man—if he be Bender—who has done enough in this world to entitle him to a front seat during a portion, at least, of eternity, in the dominions of his Satanic Majesty.

The old man was calmer yesterday than on the day previous and talked with greater freedom and could be better understood than on the day of his arrival. He stated to a German who was in the cell with him for some time that he had been engaged in farming in Kansas; but said nothing else that would indicate that he was Bender. During the day two gentlemen visited him who had known him in former years, and they both recognized him as being the much sought after Kansas butcher. One gentleman, who was in the Pike county (Ill.) clerk's office in 1866-7, immediately recognized the accused as being the man who had taken out letters of administration in Pike county, in the name of John T. Bender, on the estate of his brother-in-law, one Schmidt. The gentlemen above made out the papers and saw Bender frequently during that year, 1867, after which the latter moved to Kansas. A former Indian agent of Kansas, who formerly knew Bender, says the right man is captured. With this strong evidence it can scarcely be doubted that the great criminal, who has eluded officers and detectives for the past year, has at last stumbled into the clutches of the law, and is now a prisoner in the city jail.

One day, when the old man was in the Manti jail, Sanpete county, another strange-looking German appeared there and asked permission to see the accused. His request was granted, and the two had a long and confidential interview. The sheriff who had charge of the jail said the meeting of the men was most cordial and that they appeared to talk freely on a subject with which they were both acquainted. The German left town next day as mysteriously as he had appeared in it. The circumstance of his visit having reached the ears of one of the deputy sheriffs of Sevier County, the latter concluded that the German stranger was young Bender, and started in search of him. He followed him to Nephi in Juab County, where he overtook and arrested him. He is now there, and this morning Deputy Sheriffs Farnsworth and Foutz, of Sevier County, go to bring him to this city. They expect to return on Saturday or Sunday.

Should these two Germans be the male portion of the Bender family, it would not be an improbable occurrence if the female members of the murderous quartette were discovered ere long in the vicinity.

Salt Lake Herald
April 14, 1874

"John T. Bender."

The man arrested at Nephi and brought to this city on suspicion of being John T. Bender, the "son of his father," is another man entirely. On Sunday Major Gordon, of Camp Douglas, came down and recognized the supposed Kansas notoriety as his former bugler, who deserted last Spring. The Major says that while he can vouch for his bugler as not being Bender, he has frequently known him to be on a "bender." We understand the prisoner, upon being arrested, told who he was, prefering the stigma of desertion to being thought a Bender. He was removed to Camp Douglas, and will probably be taken from there to the penitentiary, this being the second time he has deserted the United States army.

Salt Lake Herald
April 19, 1874

Meetings at Nephi.

By private dispatches, received here yesterday, we learn that the meetings being held at Nephi by President Brigham Young and party were very largely attended, so much so that the meeting house was found too small to accommodate the congregations. Besides a general gathering of the inhabitants of Juab county, many from San Pete and Utah county were present, and great interest was manifested in the preaching of the Elders.

The party are expected in this city on Monday afternoon.

President Young and Party.— President Brigham Young and party are expected to reach Nephi, Juab County, to-morrow evening, and President D. H. Wells, a number of the Quorum of the Twelve Apostles and others will leave this city to-morrow morning, for the purpose of reaching Nephi in the evening, in order to take part in two days meetings, to be held there on Saturday and Sunday.

PROVO, April 20.—At the meeting at Nephi, on Saturday afternoon, the speakers were Elders A. M. Cannon and Milo Andrus, and Presidents Geo. A. Smith, B. Young, and Orson Hyde. The meeting in the evening was addressed by Elders Erastus Snow and B. Young, Jr. On Sunday morning President D. H. Wells and Elder John Taylor preached. In the afternoon a branch of the United Order was organized, over four hundred residents of Nephi and four hundred from other places being enrolled. Addresses were made by President Geo. A. Smith and Orson Hyde, and Elder John Taylor.

The party left Nephi at three o'clock on Sunday afternoon and drove to Payson, where a crowded house was addressed by Elder B. Young, jr., Milo Andrus, Erastus Snow, and John Taylor. The subject discoursed upon at all the meetings by all the speakers was the United Order.

The President and party left Payson about twenty minutes to eight this morning, and reached Provo at eleven o'clock, driving through a storm of snow and rain the whole distance; the storm still continues. The party leaves for Salt Lake at half past 12.

Notes From Utah Territory—The Co-operative Feature.

One of the peculiarities of the Mormon settlement in Utah has been, from the very commencement, that its inhabitants, from the beginning, located themselves in villages for mutual support and protection against the Indians, wild beasts and all enemies from without, many of which villages, as Salt Lake, were inclosed with adobe walls encircling them; and then occupied the out-lots in common, for pasturing and agriculture. In this respect they followed the customs and usages of Mexican people, who always settle in this manner, and, by this means, the great principle of co-operation became developed. To its practical results is Brigham Young indebted for his wonderful success.

Ogden, Salt Lake, Provo, Manti, Parowan, Cedar City, Lehi, Fillmore, Nephi, City of Springville, American Fork City, Pleasant Grove City, Spanish Fork City, and numerous other cities, were incorporated even in 1852, and are strung along from north to south, over 300 miles, down to St. George in Dixie, where cotton and tropical plants are grown, and where the climate is like that of Florida. All the spaces between these cities are filled up with farms, and stock,and all the developments of gardens, ranches, mills and other improvements; and thus each small town is a support and an aid to every other.

Over all this surface of land, this one people, having one head, President Young, one form of government and religion, one bond of brotherhood, one home, one territory, one destiny, have grown up by large yearly accessions from Europe, of 2,500 imported each year, and a very large increase by native born births, until they now count at least 130,000 people, and their estates at least twenty-five millions of property. Over all this region there are now schools, churches, universities, manufactories, and all the accompaniments of religion, cultivation and comfort. Such has been the work of one man in a quarter of a century.

The question naturally arises, how has Brigham Young kept the people together? How has he defended them against want, starvation, the attacks of Indians, the loss of crops and all the incidents of a new territory? The answer is to be seen here, everywhere, in the coat of arms of this people, and the one grand chain that binds them all together. Before me lies in that coat of arms the great secret of Mormon success. In its center you behold the Beehive, indicative of an industry that never tires, of provision in Summer against the cold and storms of Winter; of driving out all drones and idlers, and subjecting every inhabitant to the order and direction of the king bee.

Over this bee hive and enclosing it within its rays of light is the Eye of God; reminding this people that, at all times, in all places, in all seasons, by night as by day, in Summer and Winter, the great Father of Industry is watching over them, and that His eye will see "that as each man shall sow so shall he reap" and that no one of his chosen people shall ever turn their backs upon duty, virtue, industry, and go downward to hell, through the temptation of intemperance, gaming, idleness or debauchery. Across the face of the hive, in great letters of virgin gold, is inscribed those magic letters, "Z. M. C. I." which, like those other wondrous letters, "I. H. S.," written upon the altars of Christ, are the inspiration of this people, and the talisman of success. Zion's mercantile, manufacturing and mining co-operative associations are, day by day, adding quietly but steadily to the wealth, the culture and happiness of this people, and are building up their waste places, opening these mines, sowing these vales and penetrating these mountains. Here you will see what a body of growing people can do by a unity of labor, capital, heads, hearts and minds, all bound together by one common religion, marching day by day under one great leader, keeping tune and time to the music of one great anthem, sung in chorus by a whole people. What other nations have tried in vain to do, in fragments and fractions, Brigham Young has done with this whole people, viz., to make each and every man, woman and child a co-operator with each other, so, like the bundle of sticks, to make the whole invincible, while in parts there would be nothing but weakness.

Whoever comes here and studies carefully the characteristics of Utah, will find that it is this co-operation of prayer, religion, industry, prudence, economy and benevolence, alone, that has enabled them so to triumph and succeed; and that no other people on earth could ever have conquered this desert, and made happy homes here in this valley. At the time they first entered it, so long as they were here alone, four months' journey from the Missouri, and two months' from the Pacific, their number increased, their daily strength grew, and they bade fair, as things then were, to become a mighty, mighty people. But time, that changes all things, and man more than all other things, is now changing Utah and its people. The railroads, telegraphs and daily newspapers are here; the Gentiles are here, and with them have come the drinking hells, gambling rooms, bawdy houses, fashion, extravagance and all the crimes that, of late years, make up the daily record of our people; and they are all united combatants and in active co-operation to make the Mormons destroy their Bee-hive, put out the Eye of God, and scatter to the winds their former habit of life. In addition to this, the Federal Government has sent here a parcel of officers, "clad in a little brief authority;" scurvy politicians, (most of them) who play such high, fantastic tricks before high Heaven as make angels weep. But more anon.

GEO. C. BATES.

—*Western Rural.*

Deseret News
May 27, 1874

JUAB COUNTY.
JOEL GROVER, *Presiding Bishop*
Mona, Edward Kay.
*Nephi, *alias* Salt Creek, Joel Grover.
Levan, Elmer Taylor.

Salt Lake Tribune
June 3, 1874

An Inquiring Saint.

We saw a Saint yesterday, from Juab County, who had come to the city to inquire into the merits of Enoch. He owns a good farm, of eighty acres, well improved, with a herd of thrifty cattle. As he left home, he tells us, the Enochites had begun to brand the cattle turned over to the Order, and his brother Saints were going in quite lively. The brand in Nephi, is U. O. N., (United Order, Nephi,) upon the horn, and "U. O." with a semi-circle, upon the shoulder. Three hundred cattle were corralled, for branding, and a number of horses were being gathered up for the same purpose. The Enoch swindle, he tells us, prospers from Juab County southward; but on his road, north from there, he found the old bilk had few supporters. He wanted to do some trading here, he says, as a color for his visit, but his real object was to inquire somewhat into the history and character of U. O. He has concluded to go it alone awhile longer.

Salt Lake Tribune
June 19, 1874

Correspondence Tribune.]

Nephi, June 16, 1874.

As some time has elapsed since you have been informed of the existence of this place, and fearing you might think that we had arisen, Enoch-like, from these sage brush plains, I concluded, having a few spare moments at my command, that I would inform you of our prosperity in the new Order, in these "last days in the fullness of time." Since my last letter, we have had a "right smart chance" of the spirit shed abroad in our hearts. Nearly all the good folks of this place came into the Order with their names and those of their families; but as the day came for our beloved people of the "valley of the mountains"

Deseret News
July 1, 1874

Outrage at Nephi.—We have received a communication from Nephi, dated June 22, and regret that we cannot publish it because it is anonymous. It appears that on the 20th three drunken persons assaulted two or three others, and used exceedingly insulting and abusive language, defying the police, endeavoring to rescue prisoners, and one person taking a rifle to the jail and offering to liberate a prisoner therefrom. The three persons are reported to have been subsequently fined $25, $15, and $7 and costs.

NEPHI GATHERINGS.

How Changed My Brethren—Dawning of a Better Day—Retraction—Late Quotations, Etc.

Correspondence Tribune]

Nephi, July 7, '74.

Since my last, quiet reigns in Nephi, but Sol is making it hot for us all—he makes no distinction between Saint or sinner, but cremates us alike.

A LITTLE COMMON SENSE

has been distilled into the noggen of the Bishop here, since the late unpleasantness, of which mention was made in The Tribune, and we have no more long and abusive harangues. The Priesthood have learned that the people have rights, and those rights must be respected. The times have indeed changed in a wondrous degree, and in an exceeding short time. In the good old days of Blood Atonement the command was, "you *shall* do our bidding." To day it is changed to—"Will you, if you please." For my part, I don't think I wi'l. We have The Tribune, the mines and railways to thank for this modified and pleading language. We yet have those among us who sigh for the past, but there are very many who welcome the change, and hope the bloody record of the past may be buried forever.

THE NEW LAW.

Since the passage of the Poland bill, there are many expressions of joy, and a fervent wish that it had clothed the courts with greater and surer power. The people of the interior have heretofore lacked faith in the power of the Government to shield them from the knife of their assassin leaders, but their eyes are opening, and those who but one short year ago, dare not speak their minds, are to-day openly asserting their rights as citizens of a free and independent Government.

There is scarcely a day passes but we hear of some one being dissatisfied, and openly cussing the Order. Consecrating property has ceased. Out of a population of over 1,500 persons, I think not over 100 are in the Order.

RETRACTION.

I see by your paper that a woman by the name of Beal, has become wrothy at her name having been mentioned in the paper. But what she most objects to, is that your correspondent said she was knocked down with a rock while at prayers. I have investigated further, and find that I was mistaken. I therefore retract this much: She couldn't have been knocked down, and tho the weapon used was not a rock, but a lump of dirt or a lobe; and to say that she was at prayers is an insult to the Deity; she is not a praying woman.

STOCK REPORTS.

I suppose your readers would be glad to see a report of stocks from these parts. The Nephi Board reports as follows for the month of June,

Brigham's Enoch Salvation Company—Worthless, with a downward tendency.

Blood Atonement and Danite Consolidated Savings Company—No takers.

To Hell Across Lots—Entirely disappeared from the board, although believed by some to be under repair.

Half-worn Endowment Garments—Plenty but no sale.

Anointing Oil, extensively used in making soap—Good demand.

On account of the Poland bill,—cradles and trundle beds have declined.

Blessings—Cheap.

Cursings—Can be had for nothing.

Fish market—suckers and sardines—Much sought after by the Order, but few in the market.

I. C. At L.

Deseret News
July 15, 1874

Levan, Juab County.

The 4th was saluted at daybreak with firing of guns by Capt. Wm. Tunbridge and his men, and the unfurling of the stars and stripes. The cavalry and Sunday school marched through the principal streets to the meeting house, where were reading of the Declaration of Independence by George Gardner, saluted by the artillery, singing by the choir, songs by Chas. Olsen, George Gardner, and Joseph Goodwin, speeches by Bishop E. Taylor, and by John C. Witbeck and Eli Curtis, toasts, string band music.

In the afternoon the Sunday school scholars participated in the dance and other amusements, and in the evening the adults also tripped the light fantastic and had a good time.

Good health and laboring in the "United Order" is the occupation of us here at present.

John W. Shepherd, C. F. B. Tybbert, H. Harris, Committee of Arrangements; D. Harris, Marshal of the day; Chaplin, Eric Peterson.

HEBER W. HARLEY,
Reporter.

Nephi.

July 6.

We had a good time here on the 4th. In the morning the people met in the meeting house. The exercises consisted of singing, toasts and recitations, an oration by Bro. Chase, a speech by John Borrowman, reading of the Declaration of Independence by Thomas Ord; Bro. Timothy Olt chaplain. The meeting house was decorated with green boughs. Over the stand were the photographs of President Young, George Washington and Abraham Lincoln. We had two choirs, that of Bro. Evans, and the Sunday school choir, led by Bro. Miller, also a string band and a brass band.

At half-past one there was a dance for the children, and in the evening another for the adults, both of which went off in good order.

There were also horse racing and a foot race.

Committee of arrangements—Henry Goldsborough, T. S. Brown and Samuel Cazier.

William Tolley has commenced the railroad in Salt Creek canyon, which will connect with the Utah Southern Railroad. It will be a narrow-gauge road.

A pretty good feeling prevails here, and the majority of the people are on the right track. The United Order is getting on first-rate. We have gone into stock-raising, farming and salt-making, and we have opened a butcher-shop belonging to the Order.

SILAS L. JACKSON.

Salt Lake Tribune
July 30, 1874

NEPHI CITY NOTES.

Skinning the Newly Arrived Scandinavians—Election, &c.

Correspondence Tribune.

NEPHI, July 26, 1874.

Saturday a company of Scandinavian emigrants, newly fledged, arrived here— that is, what was left of them— as their pockets had been rifled, and they looked upon Zion and her solemnities with pitiful eyes. They were on their way south to Saint George and vicinity. These poor duped disciples of the Prefit were like Geo. A. Smith says the Mormons were who left their homes in the East to come to this salt and barren land, and do the will of God by making the desert blossom as the rose. They did it willingly, because they were obliged to.

POVERTY IS NO DISGRACE,

but is very inconvenient, and if the pockets of the poor Danes had not been rifled, they would have chosen a land of their choice, more than the barren sands of Southern Utah.

KEPT SECLUDED.

One of our liberal-minded free-thinkers went to visit his friends and former acquaintance from his native land, before they left for the South, but the fear of the Lord, (Brigham) fell upon the Bishop, and he, with more than the power of a Cromwell, dissolved the session in the Nephi Hall. Still the already disaffected Danes wanted to hold another interview with their friends and fellow-countrymen, but being already ordered to the street by our beloved Bishop, who feared that they might partake of the forbidden fruit, and become wise like other men, ordered the old man of counsel and good sense, from the street, as he might overthrow the Kingdom which needs so much care and attention to keep it in the narrow path.

It takes all the stump speeches and rallying of forces, with now and then a smell of fire and brimstone to keep the Saints from using the privileges guaranteed by the constitution of the great Republic.

Our saintly politicians begin to smell hell through a quill, and are providing us with officers for the next term. There is no sense in the Saints here to choose a judge for this county, so George A. Smith demands his brother-in-law to fill that office at the expense of the people. This one man's choice is called the People's ticket!

The Nephites voted to a man for Joel Grover for Representative to the Legislature, with the view of having a new Judge; but Joel has the office, and the first thing he did was to appoint the same old brother-in-law, in obedience to George, who ever remains loyal to the constitution of the Profit, and fattens on it, so the ticket is well greased. As the weather is hot, most of the grease may melt off George Ass's ticket; so the people who have brains to use without using the borrowed material, have provided themselves with a judge who has brains of his own in case the other fails. We are not very particular, if the majority prevails; while the *Liberal Mormons* are not particular if one man can do all their voting.

P. B. PUBLICO.

Salt Lake Tribune
July 31, 1874

TALKING PROHIBITED.

A Tribune correspondent writes from Nephi to complain of the arrogance of one of Brigham's episcopal satraps performing vice-regal functions there. A number of newly arrived Danes on their way south—to work on the temple at St. George, most probably—rested at Nephi over night. Their fellow countrymen living there, who had learnt the ropes, thought it would be an act of kindness to these inexperienced Saints to tell them some of the ways of Zion.

Accordingly the former repaired to a hall, built and supported with the public money, and invited their new friends to spend an evening with them. The Bishop ordered the whole party into the street. This command was complied with, and the oppressed Danes began conversing with each other in the open air. Fearing that this also might result in mischief, the episcopal bully again appeared and ordered his recalcitrant subjects to their homes. Our correspondent fails to mention whether any of these outraged freemen knocked the brutal ruffian down, and kicked him well as he lay prostrate. Such instances as these lead to the natural inquiry how long can a decaying system be bolstered up, when it is considered dangerous to its existence to allow private citizens to talk quietly together?

NEPHI ITEMS.

None but Officers Left to Run the Order—Water Troubles—Belligerents and Justice.

Correspondence Tribune.]

Nephi, July 29, '74.

Our Order, as you are well aware, started with the hope of the grandest results, which hope has been realized beyond the expectations of the most sanguine. It has succeeded in busting. I would not have you think that it was the fault of the Order; the Order is well enough, but the people have not prepared themselves to take the onward step, as Brother Brigham says, especially when that step would lead them from their worldly trash. The burst came about in this way: There were many officers and few workers in the start; all the workers threw up the sponge and left; the work to be done by the officers. Such a state of things could not last long—the brethren saw it. Bro. V. was determined the Order should prosper, so he and his son worked day and night.

HE HAD THE PRAYERS OF US ALL,

but a man can't live on prayers in these days, and as the Lord didn't want any of the cattle that were branded with the U. O. N. killed, he was forced to yield to hunger and the want of muscle, so one morning, not long ago, the brother was seen sitting upon a door step on Main street, ruminating upon some weighty subject.

All who saw him with his head bowed down, exclaimed,

"BUSTED!"

Orders have been given for all who have hay ground in the Order to cut and haul it, as the Order couldn't do it. They were, of course, to haul it for the Order; at least one tenth was to go to the Lord—which is very kind of the bishop, and I think it is a miracle that the hay was not allowed to rot in the field. The grain land is also to be taken care of in the same way.

The cattle and horses are to remain in possession of the Lord, as it would be ungenerous to give them and then take them back.

TROUBLE IN THE AIR.

I am sorry to say that our city has been the stage on which has been enacted some strange scenes of late. The water becoming scarce, and some of the brethren wishing to use more than their share, attempted to do so by force. Some cases came before a justice of the peace. He is a man who has acquired more illegal ability during his life than any man I have ever known. I will not go into detail, but give some of his decisions. One man was fined one dollar and costs for stopping the water from a sister, which she wanted for her flowers. A woman, man and dog were fined ten dollars for whipping a man, and a woman built an artificial head on another woman, and for so doing; the belligerent woman had her arm broken. The one that had the broken arm swore out a warrant. The case came off, and the learned judge would not allow the prosecuting witness to testify, as she was an interested party. The decision was reserved, but it is understood that he will eventually find for the plaintiff.

I. C. ALL.

Salt Lake Herald
August 4, 1874

THE ELECTION AT NEPHI.

[Special Dispatch to the Herald.

NEPHI, Aug. 3d.

The legal voters of Nephi have been alive to-day in voting the "People's Ticket." Last report from the polls, 430 votes cast. Very few liberals are to be seen or heard. S. H. Gilson made himself conspicuous in contesting votes, which aroused the energies of the citizens, and has done good. From all reports Juab County will give a large majority for the "People's Ticket." The election has thus far passed off peaceably. Capt. Darton's band has been on duty all day. Our streets have been alive with carriages travelling to and from the polls.

Twenty-fourth at Nephi.—This morning we received an account of the 24th at Nephi, from "Thomas Crawley, Reporter." With daily newspapers it is usually first come first served, and as we published a report from Nephi three days ago, we are obliged, though reluctantly, to omit this later report.

Nephi.

A grand jubilee of the school children of the county was held in this city on the 24th. The meeting-house was decorated with grape vines and flowers.

We had three choirs—that of Bro. Evans, and the Sunday School choirs of this place and Levan, also a string band led by C. H. Sperry, and a brass band led by C. Hudson.

Mrs. C. Bigler, John T. Chase, and Misses Bigler, P. Pickston, Garrett, Borrowman, and Keinke, R. Pay and John W. Shephard gave recitations.

Mrs. M. A. Andrews and Miss L. Evans and two sisters sang songs. There was a solo by Joseph Darton, Gustave Henrold accompanying on the organ. Several anthems, &c., were sung by the juveniles under the superintendence of Bro. Evans. A dialogue was read by Miss Bigler and Miss Ord. Seth Ollinton delivered a speech on the training of children in the right way. The choir sang, "The Jubilee."

In the afternoon the children marched in procession from the meeting-house to the city hall, where they enjoyed themselves in dancing, and the adults enjoyed the same privilege in the evening.

Samuel Pitchforth., Superintendent of the Schools.

SILAS L. JACKSON,

The Accursed Nephites.

One hundred and ten illegal votes were cast on election day at Nephi, a small hamlet in Juab county. That batch of criminals will hereafter be of use to the Territory when the U. S. Marshal gets them corraled in the penitentiary. We suggest that they be organized after conviction into an association of co operative shoemakers. A list of their names has been presented to the District Attorney for his perusal.

Salt Lake Herald
August 16, 1874

Fire at Nephi.

A communication from Nephi, Juab County, says that a fire broke out at that place, in the barn yard of Mr. Charles Sperry, at about a quarter past 12 on Thursday afternoon; but that, through the exertions of H. Goldsborough it was extinguished before much damage was done.

Deseret News
September 2, 1874

DIED.

At Nephi, Juab Co , August 15th, ANNIE OSTLER, wife of David Ostler, of consumption, aged 32 years.

She leaves a husband and seven children and a large circle of friends to mourn her loss. She was born in Hampshire, England, August 14th, 1842, and emigrated with the Saints in the fall of 1861, and has proven herself faithful to the truth.—Com.

Millennial Star, please copy.

Hay-stack Burned at Nephi.— Silas L. Jackson writes from Nephi, 25th—

"There was a hay-stack burned here on the 23rd, belonging to Charles Price. The stack contained twenty-four loads. It was first discovered by several young ladies, who did all in their power, by pulling down the fence, to prevent the fire from spreading. Miss Georgia Parks sprained her wrist in lifting a pole from the fence. By that time plenty of help came, and prevented the fire from doing any more damage. Luckily the wind was the right way, or it might have done a great deal more damage.

"Harvesting is nearly all done here, but the weather is stormy, which makes it bad under foot.

"The general health of the people is good. We have had a few cases of scarlet fever, but it is all gone now.'"

From Juab County.

Hon. Samuel Pitchforth, of Nephi, Juab County, with his wife and daughter, arrived in the city yesterday.

The gentleman reports the grain in that county has been harvested, and while the yield has been a good one, it is not so large as usual.

A new saw mill has been erected and put in operation by Mr. W. R. May, a few miles up Salt Creek Cañon. The mill is turning out large quantities of lumber, and there is plenty of timber to keep it running for some time.

Mr. A. G. Sutherland, of Silver City, Tintic, who was placed on both tickets as a candidate for selectman, at the recent election, and who was consequently elected, appeared last Monday and filed his bonds, when the county court was fully organized. During its session school and road districts for the Tintics, were organized.

Everything was moving along quietly in Juab.

A NEW TRICK.

How the Temple is Built in St. George.

EDS. TRIBUNE:—The law of the Lord came forth from Zion that the Temple at St. George must be finished this fall or it would not be accepted.

The Saints of Nephi have been called to the rescue. For this purpose the Profit imposes a tax of nine dollars per head upon every man of family, increasing the assessment according to the tax pay roll. One half of this tax is to be paid in cash, the other half in grain and other produce. Twenty men are called to labor six months in the Lord-able undertaking. All bachelors are taxed nine dollars per head. The balance, in proportion to their taxable property, all being on an equal footing. Thus, James B. (a bachelor) pays eighteen dollars. Mr. L., (married) owning twice the amount of Mr. B., pays nine dollars. Now this is on the principle that twice nine are four and a half. It is said that figures will not lie. If these figures do not lie, who does lie?

Mr. H. owns, say $1,500, and pays a tax of $100. Mr. V. owns $3,000, and is required to pay sixty-five dollars. How equal! At the same ratio $10,000 will be required. The cost of twenty men's labor for six months, at twenty dollars per month, is $2,100, leaving a balance of $7,600. Where does this go? Ask the Royal family in Salt Lake. Ask the lawyers now in the employ of Brigham.

"ARO SRO."

NEPHI, Sept. 21, 1874.

Salt Lake Herald
October 29, 1874

From Nephi.

We received a call last evening from John Hague, Esq., of Nephi, who arrived in town yesterday. He reports everything as peaceable in Juab county. The fruit crop of this season was good, but the grain and vegetable crop would fall short of the average of other years at least one fourth; and many who are now selling grain will, before another harvest, be forced to buy it back at an advance or suffer for bread. This latter is not good policy; every farmer should save sufficient grain to bread his family and supply seed for another season's sowing. Mr. Hague reports the grain crops of Sanpete as also being light. Our people should be cautious about disposing of their grain for exportation till they know what the home demand will be.

The people of Sanpete and Juab are anxiously looking for the extension of the U. S. R. R., to afford them a means for transporting the coal and coke of the former and the ores (gypsum) of the latter to an available market. There is lots of trade for the railroads in that direction.

Salt Lake Tribune
November 8, 1874

SECOND DISTRICT COURT.

Associate Justice Emerson Presiding.

The Second District Court, at Provo, adjourned sine die on the 5th instant, after hearing and receiving reports of the Grand Jury on the condition of jails in that District. By these reports it was ascertained that most of the prisons are damp, filthy, and unfit for the use of human inmates. The Provo County jail is among the worst, having unventilated cells, stone floors, swarms of vermin, and altogether uninhabitable. No bunks for the prisoners to sleep on, but the Sheriff wants a supply of irons for the incarcerated wretches. Handcuffs and shackles are hardly the things to keep them warm in winter. The

Sanpete, Millard and Juab jails are a little better; that at Fillmore being in the basement of the State House which Congress paid for, but the rest of that building is used for tithing offices, Blood Atonement war dances, and a Co-op. store, though the Committee omitted to mention these facts. That at Nephi is a veritable black hole, having neither air or light, utterly ruinous to the health of prisoners, and condemned by the jurors. The report from which we condense is evidently not the composition of a schoolmaster, though the gloomy facts rise to the surface of the document. After the reading of the report, the Grand Jury was discharged from further service.

Gone to St. George.— Bro. Silas L. Jackson writes from St. George, November 2, concerning the company who went from Nephi to work on the Temple at the former place. They left Nephi Oct. 20, and went as far as Little Salt Creek that day; 21st to Scipio; 22nd to Fillmore; 23d to Baker's Pass; 24th to Wild Cat Canyon, severe snowstorm; 25th to Beaver; 26th to Paragoonah, wet night; 27th to Parowan, heavy snowstorm; 28th to Cedar City; 29th to near Bellevue; 30th to Washington; 31st to St. George.

The company was organized as follows—Andrew Love, president; George B. Reid, commissary; Silas L. Jackson, secretary; Wm. Bird, chaplain; Samuel Tolley, George Read, Edwin Scott and Sister Scott, cooks.

The following are the names of the brethren gone to work on the Temple—G. B. Reid, J. Adams, W. Bird, S. L. Jackson, J. G. Bigler, jr., J. Foutz, E. Scott, S. Tolley, E. Shepard, H. Mangrum, G Read and D. Bigler.

COURT PROCEEDINGS.

FIRST JUDICIAL DISTRICT OF THE TERRITORY OF UTAH.

Hon. P. H. Emerson, Judge Presiding.

Provo City,
November 4, 1874.

Court convened at 10 a.m.

No particular cases were before the court, and after a few cases of law motions, the grand jury appeared, and by their foreman, presented the following reports of the prisons in this district:

Gentlemen of the Grand Jury:— We the undersigned committee, having been appointed to visit the county jail, at Provo City, Utah Territory, and find it in the following condition: There is one passage-way running east and west six feet wide by fifteen long, with iron grating door, and an outside heavy batten door on the east, and window for ventilation about three feet high and one foot wide with shutter to close against storm; and one stove in poor condition; with rock floor. On the north is one room for the use of prisoners through the day, it is fifteen by twelve, with three ventilators three feet by one, with iron grating about six and a half feet above the floor, said floor is all rock flag, about the level of the outside ground, which is a very good room. On the south is three cells, one seven and eight-twelfths feet long by four and five-twelfths, with no ventilation, only one four inch square hole, and no light comes in said cells, with solid rock walls about two feet in thickness between each cell, and open iron grating doors, a little or no ventilation in them, and no bunks, the bedding is laid on a rock floor and said floor will not add any to the comfort of the prisoners; we do believe these cells are kept free from all body-lice, but mice, we are informed, are by the hundreds.

Treatment of the prisoners is as follows: They have bread, butter, meat and tea and potatoes, and all they want as far as necessary can be obtained by the sheriff; and we do think that the said sheriff treats the prisoners in a gentlemanly way, said Mr. Rogers, sheriff, says that he has not a complement of irons, that is necessary for his use, that is furnished by the county officials.

And we do hereby certify that the cells are in a very unhealthy condition, and no ventilation whatever, and not fit up with bunks, etc., for the use of prisoners.

HENRY H. BOLEY, } Grand
JOHN W. DEAL,   } Jurors.
PAUL JONES,   }

Report accepted and adopted by the Grand Jury, October 3rd, 1874.
STEPHEN B. MOORE,
Foreman.

Gentlemen of the Grand Jury: We the undersigned committee appointed by your honorable body to visit the county jails of Sanpete, Millard and Juab counties, having given the jails a thorough inspection, and inquired into the treatment of prisoners when in custody.

Manti, jail, Sanpete county, was visited by Henry N. Larter, Saul Norman and Harrison Edwards, on October 14, 1874. Found the present jail filled almost with building material, lime, etc. Front room is 16 by 21 feet, well ventilated by two twenty light windows; walls are 2½ thick, of rock, iron bars across the windows, plank floor, this is for the use of the prisoners through the day, and at night they are put into cells; these cells, three in number, are six feet wide, 12 feet long, 9 feet high with 3 inch plank thoroughly doweled together and fastened strongly to the rock work; good solid doors of the same material three feet above the level of the ground, and the prisoners are kept from all damp, and good bunks with good bedding worth $40; the present fare is good and all prisoners are treated well, furnished with writing materials and books to read.

The new jail is of the same size, built of red rock block work, with two large windows fronting east, four feet from the ground; the large room is 16 by 21 and 10 feet high; the cells are 6 by 12 and 10 feet high, with a good ventilation running through north and south with small spouts running through the walls of the cells to urinate in, by this method will keep said cells from so much stench; these cells are to be lined with 3 inch red pine wood strongly doweled together, the sleepers for floor are one foot above the level with rock fitted in a compact way and grouted with cement, then a floor of 3 inch red pine, with bunks, a yard 24 feet square 12 feet high, of rock block work, will be built for the benefit of the prisoners, so they can have the benefit of the sun; the doors of the cells are to be iron grating made in Chicago; also a room is in progression for the jailor; when completed we think it will be a very good, strong and healthy jail and will pass inspection. The sheriff has got a good complement of irons and fastenings of all description that is necessary; splendid record books, so it can be seen when a prisoner is brought there, when away, or set at liberty, the crime, etc., etc.

Visited Fillmore jail on the 17, 1874; the jail for present use is under the State House, four feet below the surface, with a four foot window with iron grating of ⅜ round iron, no glass or shutter; the cell is all rock, about twelve feet square, rock floor and liable to be very damp, no bunk, and not very safe, in fact it is like the State House, getting dilapidated and not fit nor safe for prisoners.

The new jail is under the Court House, there is three cells 6 by 9 and seven feet high, rock sides and floor with sheet iron over head, iron grating doors are to be used, no large room, and three feet below the surface looks quite damp, and in fact, in our opinion, we think it is not a fit place to put prisoners in on account of too much dampness and too much confinement, in fact we, the Committee, have condemned the said jail. The sheriff is much of a gentlemen and does all he can for the benefit of those who have charge over them; and bad ventilation. This jail is in an unfinished condition.

Visiting Nephi jail on the 20th day of October, we found it situated under the Court House that is in erection, they have one large room 33 by 21 with two windows for ventilation, 9 feet from ground, 2½ feet long by 1½ with grating in front; the cells are three in number, 7 by 9 feet, with arching roof, all rock, about eight feet high in the centre and near six feet at the sides, there is a small hole in the centre of the arch for ventilation, but when the floor is laid all ventilation is stopped; iron grating doors. Prisoners fare is good; no bunks; walls are two feet thick, all rock and rock floor, and six or seven feet below the surface, it is a very unhealthy place, in fact we, the undersigned, consider it no jail, but a thorough dungeon, and not a fit place to put men in and we condemned the same. When the covering or floor is over the large room it will cut off more light and less ventilation. The cells are entirely without fresh air.

Very respectfully,
HENRY N. LARTER,
SAUL NORMAN,   } Grand Jurors
HARRISON EDWARDS,
EDWIN HORLEY.

Report accepted and adopted by the Grand Jury, Oct. 2nd, 1874.

S. B. MOORE, Foreman.

After presenting the above report the grand jury were discharged from further service.

Court adjourned till 2 p.m.

2 p. m.

Court resumed its session, and after disposing of some law motions adjourned *sino die.*
—*Utah County Times, Nov. 5.*

Deseret News
December 2, 1874

Pueblo and Salt Lake Railroad.

The Denver *News* gives an account of a large colony forming in Illinois under the leadership of a Mr. Shirts, and backed by Senator Logan, which is to be settled in Western Colorado, near the junction of the Green and Grand rivers, A large body of fine land is said to lie in the fertile valleys of this locality, and it is expected that from five hundred to a thousand families will settle in them next spring.

This is a matter of interest to us, since the location named is directly on the line of the Pueblo and Salt Lake Railway west of the Tennessee Pass, and lies partly in Colorado and partly in Utah. We have always contended that the country from the head of the Arkansas all the way across to the Salt Lake basin is desirable for settlement, and is rich in agricultural, pastoral and mineral resources, and will be rapidly developed as soon as railroads are made to penetrate that country.

The railroad from Provo south is now being pushed to completion (nearly) to Nephi, making about one hundred miles of railway south from Salt Lake City, and this is the same as one hundred miles of the Pueblo and Salt Lake road at the western end which will be finished by next Spring. We have the utmost confidence that if the Atchison and Topeka Railroad company join with the Pueblo and Salt Lake Company in pushing this enterprise hereafter, in five years from this time we will see a complete line of road from Pueblo west to Salt Lake City, and through a country which will furnish a paying business the whole distance and which will add untold wealth to Colorado in the development of our southwestern regions.—*Pueblo, Col., People, Nov. 14.*

DIED.

Of general debility at Nephi, Juab Co., U. T., November 9, SALLY, relic of Elder James Randall.

Sister Randall was the daughter of George and Betsy Carlisle; was born in the town of Westmoreland, County of Cheshire, State of New Hampshire, May 26, 1805; was baptized a member of the Church of Jesus Christ of Latter-day Saints, by Elder John P. Green, in the town of Warsaw, Genesee County, New York, in June, 1832. Sister Randall, together with her husband and children, resided in Kirtland, Missouri, Illinois and Iowa, enduring, in connection with the Saints, all the privations and persecutions in their travels from Kirtland to these valleys in the mountains. having emigrated to Utah in the Fall of 1852, locating at Nephi, where she continued to reside until her death. Since her husband's death, which took place thirteen years ago, she has resided with her son, Elder Eld Randall. Sister Randall was one of our oldest and most respected citizens; for many months she was a great sufferer, and longed for the time to come when she would be permitted to join her beloved and much respected husband and son. She was noted for her faith and integrity in the truth of the gospel as revealed by Joseph Smith. She left a son, daughter-in-law, four grandchildren and many friends.—COM.

At Levan, Juab County, Nov. 19, of asthma, after suffering a long illness, WILLIAM DYE, formerly a resident of Salt Lake City.

Deceased was born May 28th, 1818. It is said by all who knew him that he was an honest, upright man, a man that had kept his covenants. He died without a struggle, in full faith of the gospel; leaves a wife and two grown children and numerous friends and relatives.—COM.

At Levan, Oct. 27, of dropsy, after an illness of three months, CARN MARGRETHE MARCFIL.

Deceased was born on Bornholm, Denmark, May 21, 1811; emigrated to Utah in 1857; was a faithful Latter-day Saint, and died in peace, leaving a husband and many friends behind her.—COM.

Salt Lake Herald
December 17, 1874

Sanpete Calling for the Railroad.

MT. PLEASANT, Dec. 10, 1874.

Editors Herald:

It seems to be a foregone conclusion that the U. S. railroad company will build the grand trunk line through the heart of southern Utah, leaving others who may desire to feed the trunk to do so by branch lines. Hearing of Gen. Clark's arrival with engineers, etc., to survey the route of a railroad from Nephi to Manti, I paid a visit to the headquarters of the Sanpete coal and coke company, in which enterprise the general and some of your townsmen are interested. The feasibility of the railroad and its necessity as compared with any county south of Utah is unquestioned, for the development of this county has scarcely commenced. Here are unlimited fields of coal, and mountains of fine, white building rock, besides the many other items that are awaiting capital to bring them into use. Then we have one of the finest mineral regions in the country, and our agricultural resources are not excelled in the territory.

The proposed railroad will necessarily have to be a narrow guage with probably such appliances as are necessary to overcome the steepness of the grade. After gaining the valley proper, all difficulties would be overcome, especially on the west side of Sanpitch river, the proposed route. We all hope that the road may be pushed forward to Nephi with celerity, certainty and dispatch, for the action of the U. S. company control the Sanpete, Sevier and Castle Valley railroad company who must necessarily wait on the movements of the former.   D. C.

NEPHI ITEMS.

New Railroad Project—A Priest who is Afraid of the Light of Day.

Correspondence Tribune.]

Nephi, Dec. 16, 1874.

As the people are beginning more than ever to take an interest in THE TRIBUNE, and as it is often remarked here, that it is the only newspaper published in Utah, I thought it not amiss to lend a hand in noting events as they pass in Nephi. There are a number of your papers taken in this place, which are doing much good. It comes like a gleam of sunshine to us benighted Nephites, dispelling the clouds that have so long settled around us.

RAILROAD.

We have in our midst Gen. Geo. W. Clark and staff, who are surveying and locating a railroad from this point to the coal fields of Sanpete. General Clark has informed me that he intends letting some contracts immediately and have the work pushed ahead as fast as possible. The company is a staunch one and there is no doubt that the Sanpeters will be ready with their coal and coke when the Utah Southern railroad reaches that point.

LYCEUM.

The young men of this place organized a lyceum, and repaired to the trustee who had the hall or school house in charge, and asked the privilege of meeting therein. This worthy officer (whose initials are K. H. Brown) refused, saying it would look bad to introduce such things amongst the Saints; that they had always been contented, happy and virtuous(?) before the Gentiles came, and he would not lend a hand to tear down what it had taken so long for the Church to build up. In vain they plead, acquainting him of the nature of a lyceum, but he was firm, and was determined that no "secret organization" should be held in that school house.   I. C. ALL.

For St. George.— A dispatch, dated at Nephi, Dec. 26th, to President D. H. Wells, states that, on that same day, a train of thirty-two yoke of cattle and seven wagons, left that place for St. George, to haul lumber for the Temple. The wagons were loaded with ninety-five sacks of flour, three tons of wheat and three and a half tons of barley and oats; a complete outfit for teams and men. The train was in charge of Alma H. Bennett, of Mount Pleasant.

Fatal Accident at Nephi.

(Special Dispatch to the Herald.)

Nephi, 9.—A sad accident occurred about 4 o'clock this p.m., which cast a gloom over our city. While one of our citizens, George Ostler, accompanied by his little daughter, aged 10 years, was riding on a wagon loaded with chaff and coming down in a hollow, the father slid off from the load and fell immediately behind the horses, one of the wheels passing over his leg and bruising it severely. The little girl seeing her father fall, leaned over towards him and also fell off, one of the wheels passing over her shoulder. It is believed that her neck was broken in the fall as she expired almost immediately.

Nephi 9.

A sad accident occurred about 4 o'clock this p.m., which cast a gloom over our city. While one of our citizens, George Ostler, accompanied by his little daughter, aged 10 years, was riding on a wagon loaded with chaff and coming down in a hollow, the father slid off from the load and fell immediately behind the horses, one of the wheels passing over his leg and bruising it severely. The little girl, seeing her father fall, leaned over towards him and also fell off, one of the wheels passing over her shoulder. It is believed that her neck was broken in the fall, as she expired almost immediately.

Railroad into Sanpete.

Hon. William Jenhings and Bishop John Sharp, of the Utah Central and Southern roads, returned last evening from a business visit nnd tour of inspection to Sanpete valley, in connection with the extension of the railroad. The company organized recently for building a narrow guage through Salt Creek cañon from Nephi into Sanpete, has a force of laborers at work grading for the road. As soon as spring opens the grading of the Utah Southern to Nephi will be energetically prosecuted. Ties are being purchased for the extension, and the intention is to have it completed, and the cars running early in the coming summer. If the builders of the Sanpete valley road hurry up with their line, the summer will not pass before the iron horse makes himself heard in that productive region.

The Sanpete Railroad.

The Sanpeters are growing more jubilant every day, as the work of grading for the narrow-gauge railroad from Nephi to the Sanpete valley progresses. From Nephi to the coal beds is twenty-five miles, and we understand the narrow-gauge company propose to have the line graded, ready for the iron, by the time the Utah Southern extension reaches the former place.

Another Railroad.

It is talked in financial circles that the people of Utah county will build a narrow gauge railroad from Springville through Spanish Fork cañon to the Sanpete valley coal fields. If the rumor be correct Sanpete will have two railroads, as the line from Nephi through Salt Creek cañon is being crowded ahead. Utah leads the van in the matter of railroad building in the far west.

President Young's Party.

Presidents Brigham Young and Geo. A. Smith, and party, arrived at Nephi, Juab county, last evening, and remained there during the night. This morning they will drive to the terminus of the Utah Southern railroad, where they will be met by a special train, with a party of ladies and gentlemen from this city on board. The company will reach the city about 4 o'clock this afternoon.

Telegraphic.—Yesterday, by the enterprise of the Deseret Telegraph Company, we were enabled to send a dispatch to this city from York, at which place there is no office. Wm. Bryan, the operator of the line at Nephi, came up to the end of the track, carrying with him a pocket instrument, by means of which the message to the NEWS was sent over the wires.

NEPHI NOTES.

NEPHI, March 12, 1875.

EDS. TRIBUNE :—A few days ago, I noticed in the Church organ a letter from "Camera," announcing in very flattering words the doings of three or four of our good Saints in Nephi. The effect that it produced was equal to that of a shot fired among a flock of geese, the wounded birds coming off second best, with a head put on them.

One "re-Probate" dignitary and one sap-head missionary were heard from in loud and vociferous expressions, denouncing the "calumnies" so heaped upon them, and these "tissues of falsehoods" were hurled at the walls of the meeting house and Co-op store with such force that it was really surprising to find both edifices still standing where they stood before. My advice to "Camera" is, that if he ever moralizes again about this place, to be sure and not hit so closely on facts, as truth cuts like a double edged sword.

Our good Saints are about to re-organize the United Order once more; this time with more spirit than previously. We have three spirituous halls to encourage the brethren on to success. These three proprietors still persist in dealing out the spirit to their fellow laborers who are thirsting after it. What will become of these wicked dealers of beverage, if they do not listen to counsel, repent of their sins and apply to Bishop Axtell for pardon? By the bye, is he coming to give us a sermon?

The Nephites anticipate lively times next summer, as the railroad advances south.   A NEPHITE.

Daily Mail—For the benefit of the public we have been requested to state that a daily stage, for the conveyance of mails and passengers, runs between Nephi, Juab Co., and Richfield, Sevier Co., passing through Sanpete.

ESTRAY NOTICE.

I HAVE in my possession the following estray, which, if not claimed, will be sold at my corral on Friday, April 2nd, at 10 o'clock a.m., as the law directs:

One red STEER, about three years old, half circle and underbit in right ear, underbit in left, branded W G on right hip.

THOMAS WRIGHT, Sen.,
District Poundkeeper.

Nephi, March 18, 1875.   d&w

NEPHI CITY,
March 19th, 1875.

Editor Deseret News:

Winter, our faithful friend, still lingers around us and seems unwilling to give way to its successor. Spring appears timid, and, annoyed at the long stay of the stern and cold monarch, modestly refuses to contest for her ground. But, as the season for farming is approaching, I would beg of the intelligent farmers to pardon me, if, with your kind permission, I advance through your columns a few ideas upon a subject concerning their future benefit.

Our farmers complain of the presence of smut in their wheat fields, and, as many devices have been proposed for the prevention of this evil, it may not be considered out of place to suggest another experiment. Scientific discoveries have demonstrated beyond doubt that smut is produced from the seed that is sown and not from the influences of the elements that regulate its growth, nor the time of sowing. For years the American farmer has imported (at a high price) a foreign wheat said to be free of smut the first year. It does not prove so any longer after being sown on our soil subsequently, but becomes no better than that of our own raising. This imported seed wheat is thrashed by the hands of the poor peasants of Russia (not by machine) and when closely examined is found to be perfectly sound, none of the grains having been broken, cracked or injured, as is that which has passed through the machines.

It may be argued that good and healthy seed wheat may accidentally produce unhealthy plants, but in no case can diseased or impotent seed produce healthy wheat.

The grain that has been cracked or partially damaged (although invisibly to the eye) may germinate in the earth and attain to a certain growth at which it should form itself into grains or heads of wheat, but instead of which it proves an abortion, not being capable of attaining to a complete state of maturity, hence smut, which is the result of this abortion, and the consequence of imperfect seed.

The farmer has noticed that self-sown, or what is commonly called "volunteer wheat" is free of smut, this rather favors my theory, for this wheat has not passed through the breaking up process of the thrashing machine, or that of tramping out, therefore is sound and uninjured and produces no smut, except, however, what few grains have been damaged by wagon wheels when clearing up the crop.

Winter wheat is less liable to smut than Spring wheat. From this I conclude that the imperfect and sickly wheat that would have produced the smut has been killed, being weaker and unable to stand the Winter, whereas healthy germs survive and ripen. It is a good preventive to wash seed wheat in a solution made of blue vitriol or strong brine, and the sound and perfect grains of wheat will sustain no injury thereby, while the broken and cracked grains will be so affected that their vitality or germ will be destroyed, hence they cannot germinate.

Smut is not contagious. Keep your seed wheat healthy and sound, and I will insure your grain free of smut. Try the experiment, it costs but little. Thrash a few quarts of your best wheat by hand (not your whole crop) and sow it at the same time and on the same land as that thrashed by machine, then wait and watch the result.

Correspondence.

Free Schools — Normal Schools —
Mount Pleasant — Spring City —
Ephraim — Manti — Gunnison — Sa-
lina — Richfield — Swarms of Chil-
dren — Prattville — Cove Creek —
Levan — Nephi — Fillmore.

FILLMORE, Millard Co.,
March 19th, 1875.

Editor Deseret News:

Territorial Supt. of Common
Schools O. H. Riggs and myself arrived here this morning from Cove
Creek, Millard Co., after visiting
the schools throughout Utah, Sanpete and Sevier Counties. In
almost every settlement, we found
the schoolhouses inadequate to the
great number of children in attendance, many of the schoolhouses
being unfit for school purposes,
badly ventilated and seated, and
with regular back-breaking and
spine-curving seats of the roughest
kind, without maps, charts, globes,
or black-boards.

Springville, Payson, Nephi, and
Fairview have tolerably good
schoolhouses. Of Utah County
schoolhouses Supt. Riggs has already informed you.

The great cry throughout the
country we have passed over is,
give us free schools, and good
qualified teachers. Good teachers
are scarce and there are but few
teachers in Utah to-day who
thoroughly understand their business.

We need a normal school for the
manufacturing, if you please, and
training of teachers. To supply
this great want in our schools to-
day, we hope something will be
done next Winter in the Legislature, in the way of getting a normal school started, and we believe
there is no greater want in our
Territory to-day. The Educational
Bureau is written to frequently to
supply good qualified teachers.
Our reply is, we have none to send,
and the people have to put up with
the best material they can find
among themselves in the shape of
teachers.

At Fairview we found a tolerably
good school-house, supplied with
good maps, &c., but tough benches.
This school is well attended. The
teacher, Miss Mary Jones, is the
daughter of our well known townsman, Dan Jones, the saddletree
maker. Miss Jones drilled her
classes in a most creditable manner,
and her pupils were well posted in
their studies. Wm. Christianson,
also one of the day school teachers,
has a large class in the upper room
of the school-house, and is superintendent of the Sunday school,
which we found to be in a flourishing condition under his able management, and he is a live man.
Bishop Amasa Tucker and the
whole people of Fairview are live
people, and are bound to succeed,
and we wish them God speed.

We found at Mount Pleasant one
of the best Sunday school attend-
ances we have seen. The school is
presided over by Supt. Tidwell,
and a corps of efficient teachers,
who are thoroughly interested in
Sunday school matters, and I wish
the same could be said of other
settlements. There are 170 pupils
enrolled.

The school-houses we visited at
Mount Pleasant are entirely too
small for the number of children in
attendance, and are without comfortable seats, desks, maps, charts,
or globes. The school-house Joseph
Page was teaching in was too
crowded and poorly ventilated.
The school-house Mrs. Wheelock
and Miss Hilda Dehlin was teaching in could be made a good one by
having it furnished with comfortable seats and desks and a few
maps hanging on its bare walls.

The above named ladies are hard workers, and they exhibited considerable vim and snap in the art of teaching. Our friend David Canldland's school we did not visit, as the term expired the day we arrived there.

We hope to soon hear of a good graded school-house being built at Mount Pleasant for the accommodation of its numerous and intelligent looking children, worthy of the enterprise and intelligence of the people. Bishop Seely and those associated with him are alive to the need of educational facilities at Mount Pleasant, and they showed their appreciation by getting us up two good rousing meetings. The Sunday school choir was in attendance and sang very sweetly.

At Spring City we met with President Orson Hyde and the good people of that place, who were pleased to see us. The School-house, like many others we visited, was too small, and Bro. Hyde and the people felt ashamed of it, so that we did not see the inside of the School-house at all. The examination was held in the Meeting-house, and at the close of the exercises, Pres. Hyde made a proposition to the people to go into the U. O. long enough to build them a good, substantial school-house, and he would give as much towards putting up a good one as any other man in the place. His proposition was seconded and no doubt Spring City will soon have as good a school-house as any in Sanpete Co. Pres. Hyde sees the great necessity of having good school-houses and qualified teachers in every settlement, and Spring City can boast of having as good a teacher as there is in Sanpete Co. Bro. Alred, the present teacher, knows how to keep good order. His students are well drilled in grammar, arithmetic, reading, and other branches.

Bishop K. Peterson, of Ephraim, is also alive to educational matters and he too showed his interest by giving us two good audiences in his new meeting house, which is a credit to the people of Ephraim. The house contains three splendid chandeliers, with cut glass pendants, exquisitely finished, which were purchased in New York at a cost of $525. We visited two schools at Ephraim, one being taught by Wm. W. Willis, the other being taught by Miss Emma Thirstrup, a talented young Danish lady. She understood her business, and her pupils were well up in their studies.

At Ephraim we were met by Judge Peacock of Manti, who brought his carriage to take us over in. The judge is very much interested in educational matters. He and county superintendent Wm. F. Reid were not behind in extending to us the hospitality of their homes, and they made us feel perfectly at home. Manti has the best appointed schoolhouse south of Salt Lake City, being situated in the first story of the new court house. It is comfortably seated with the celebrated Triumph seats and desks, which were furnished by the Utah Educational Bureau. The walls are adorned with first-class outline maps, charts, globes, &c. All that the people of Manti want now is a good qualified teacher, to make that school a success, and I have just learned with pleasure that want is already supplied in the person of T. B. Lewis, of Nephi, who is county superintendent of Juab Co. Bro. Lewis understands the science of teaching, and will no doubt make the school of Manti a grand success. He traveled with us through Sanpete Co. and his instructions to the people on education were excellent. Manti is a substantial place, and her citizens are enterprising. They are building a good substantial rock meeting-house, which, when finished, will be an ornament to Manti, and a credit to the people. Several other fine public buildings are in contemplation, which will add to the beauty, prosperity and solidity of Manti. If Manti succeeds in getting a good high school established, with other contemplated improvements, it will yet become the most desirable place in which to locate in Sanpete county.

At Gunnison we found Bishop Horn teaching school in the Meeting-house; he is a hard worker in the cause of education. We found the bishop pretty well posted and doing the best he could under the circumstances. Our friend, Bro. Madsen, sent his son and team to take us to Salina, Sevier Co., where we arrived in good time, thanking Capt. Madsen and son for their kindness.

On arriving at Salina we were informed by our friend, Bishop Spencer, that the school in that place was at a discount for want of a good teacher, and that class of teachers could not be found in the county.

We arrived at Richfield, Sevier Co., on the 13th inst., and for a new place we were more than surprised to find Richfield so large a place. The people of Richfield, and in fact almost all the people in the county, are working in the U. O., and, as far as we could see, were all working harmoniously, and going ahead in a most surprising manner in every branch of industry. Joseph A. Young, who presides over the people of Sevier Co. and adjacent settlements, is much esteemed by the people, and is accomplishing a good work in organizing and working with the people in building up that country. The great improvements made in so short a time are perfectly surprising. The people have the most abiding confidence in Jos. A.'s ability and business tact to lead them to success and prosperity.

For such a new place as Richfield they have a very good meeting-house, in which the day and Sunday schools are held for the present.

Jos. A., Bishop Segmiller, and others are much interested in educational matters in the settlements of Sevier, and in a short time Sevier County will have as good schools as any other County in the Territory. On the morning of the 14th inst., we visited the Sunday school, and were surprised to see such a large attendance of intelligent looking children. It speaks well for those teachers having it in charge. The day school is also well attended. But it is in charge of a young man who had never taught school before, and he was the best they could get in the settlement. So you see the people in most of the settlements are actually suffering for the want of good qualified teachers. The whole country swarms with children, and their natural qualifications cannot be surpassed in any country. I never saw a brighter and more intellectual looking set of children in my life.

Now what shall be done with these children? Shall they be allowed to grow up in ignorance in those settlements for the want of good teachers? Shall they be crammed into poor miserable school-houses, without ventilation and good comfortable seats, and be presided over by a teacher or teachers who do not understand their physical, mental, and moral composition? The remedy for this is the establishment of a normal school, and we are glad to say that the

people and leading men in every settlement see the great need of such a school.

We visited the school at Prattville, Sevier Co., and found, in the person of Miss Bean, Judge Bean's daughter, of Provo, a very good teacher. The children in her school were the cleanest and best dressed of any we had seen, and were well up in their studies. Prattville is a new enterprising place, situated almost half way between Richfield and Glenwood.

The school is held in the Meeting-house at Glenwood, but I cannot say much in favor of the mode of instruction in that school.

At the school at Munro, the last place we visited in Sevier Co., we found a very large attendance. The school was supplied with a set of Camp's outline maps, and the students were getting along tolerably well under their present teacher. From 80 to 90 pupils is the average attendance at this school. The Sunday school is also well represented, having over 140 pupils enrolled, and is presided over by a corps of good live teachers, under the superintendency of S. Semmersan, who is also a live superintendent.

We are under many obligations to Jos. A. Young, for placing teams at our disposal. County Superintendent Miller and ex-Judge Morrison accompanied us in visiting the schools throughout the county. After we got through visiting Sevier county, at Jos. A.'s instance, Bro. B. Lewis, of Joseph settlement, had a fresh team ready to take us out of the county to Cove Creek, in Millard county, a distance of twenty-three miles.

We are also under obligations to Brother K. H. Brown, of Nephi, who placed himself and team at our service and drove us all through Sanpete county, and said he was well paid for his time and trouble in listening to the lectures on education by Superintendent Riggs, T. B. Lewis, of Nephi, and others. On our return trip to Nephi, Bro. Brown met us at Levan and brought us to Nephi with his team.

We found, in almost all the schools we visited, from six to eight different kinds of school books used, instead of having one uniform series, which must be a great expense to the parents of the pupils. I hope, when we get a school law, a stop will be put to this idea of using so many different text books in our schools.

We arrived at Fillmore on Friday morning, the 19th inst., and met with a warm reception from Prest. Callister and the good people of Fillmore, whom we found to be thoroughly interested in the cause of education. The schools were having a two weeks' vacation, so we did not see any of the exercises of those schools, except of a private one, taught by Mrs. Olsen, whom we found to be a lady of considerable tact and well posted in the art of teaching. Her pupils answered all the questions put to them in a most creditable manner. We visited two district or ward schoolhouses and found them very comfortably seated with nice homemade seats and desks, with good maps, black-board, &c. There is a large two story brick schoolhouse in course of erection, and when completed will be an ornament and a credit to the people of Fillmore. Wherever we found good school-houses and competent teachers, we found a corresponding elevation in the character and intelligence of the people. And I am satisfied that Prest. Callister with the good people of Fillmore, are doing their best to elevate the character of their schools. The two district schools now closed are presided over by the Misses Millie and Mary Callister, who, from what we could learn, are very good teachers. There is an air of solidity about Fillmore that I like. The co-operative store is in a flourishing condition, and the goods on the shelves look as though those having it in charge know how to keep store. We visited the Fillmore Atheneum Library and found most of the books were taken out to be read by the enterprising young ladies and gentlemen who are interested in storing their minds with useful knowledge. We hope Prest. Callister will be successful in establishing at Fillmore a graded high school.

When we take into consideration the circumstances of the people and what they have done, we often wonder that there are any schools at all. We consider the people have done the very best they could, and we hope the time is not far distant when every settlement in Utah will have good, comfortable schoolhouses and well qualified teachers.

We have received the kindest treatment and generous hospitality from the people in those settlements where we have been visiting, for which we tender to one and all our grateful thanks.

Respectfully yours, etc.,
JAMES DWYER.

Business Manager Utah Educational Bureau.

Sanpete Coal.

We understand some of the Sanpete coal has been tested in the engine that runs the construction at York, on the Utah Southern, and that it has proved superior in every respect to any other coal which has been used on the line. The narrow guage railroad from Nephi through Salt Creek cañon into the Sanpete coal regions will surely be constructed by the time the Utah Southern reaches Nephi, the date for which event it is to be hoped is not far distant, and then new life will be injected into the southern district, while Salt Lake, also, will reap largely of the benefits in the shape of cheaper fuel.

RAILWAY EXTORTION.

A Nephi correspondent, whose letter appears in another column, complains of the extortion practiced upon the Utah Southern Railroad. His statement is confirmed by a second correspondent living on that line who is hindered from sending his farm produce to town because of the prohibitive freight tariff. From Draperville to Salt Lake, a distance of eighteen miles, the charge upon vegetables, grains and other crude products, is half a cent a pound, or ten dollars a ton. This no farmer can afford to pay, and accordingly he gives but slight attention to kitchen gardening, and what goods he brings in are carried in on his wagon. The first essential to the growth of a city is an abundant market, which secures cheap living. But the Mormon leaders do not want the city to grow, and our industrial interests to thrive and extend; that would be too much like American life, and Apostle Cannon declares he does not want Salt Lake to resemble Babylonian cities. Railroads are said to be great civilizers, but in the blighting hands of the priesthood, their usefulness is sadly impaired. What an insreperable bar to all progress is this divinely appointed government!

Deseret News
May 19, 1875

DIED.

At Mona, Juab County, March 26, MARY, relict of Walter Smith, aged 83 years, one month and twelve days.

Deceased was a kind and faithful mother and true to all the trusts of life. She joined the Church of Jesus Christ of Latter-day Saints in Hancock County, Illinois, in 1841, and never wavered in her faith for one moment. She passed away like one asleep.

Salt Lake Tribune
May 26, 1875

THE SAN PETE COAL FIELD.

Railroads are regarded as the pioneers of civilization. Not only do they promote intercourse between communities remote from each other, and thus diffuse the thought and discoveries of the age, but the facilities they afford for the transportation of commodities, extend the field of industry, reduce expense and add to the sum of human enjoyment. It is a recognized fact that in Utah, the deficiency of railroad lines reaching to all parts of the Territory where valuable mineral products abound, seriously retards development and burdens the producing community with such a load of expense that the value created by the labor and capital employed in our mines is almost totally absorbed, and no increment is gained; wherewith to extend our operations.

Railroad extension being the great need of Utah, we hear with unalloyed satisfaction of the work now being performed by the San Pete Valley Railway Company, whose objective point is the inexhaustible coal region in the valley above named. This road is designed to start from Nephi, fifteen miles south of York Station, the present terminus of the Utah Southern railroad, and run east and south, a distance of 27 8 10 miles, until it reaches the San Pete coal field. We learn from Mr. M. T. Burgess, who has been engaged upon the survey of this important branch or feeder, that the location has been made, and the work of grading through Salt Creek Canyon is now being rapidly prosecuted. Gov. Clark is president of the company, and from the energy with which he is pushing the work, it is reasonable to believe that the construction of the road will be proceeded with, with all possible diligence.

To connect this feeder with the trunk road, a new company has been formed, called the Utah Southern Railroad Extension company, of which Messrs. William Jennings, John Sharp and Feramorz Little are the most prominent members; and the design of these enterprising gentlemen is to carry the Utah Southern road on to Nephi and thence to the Iron Mountains. The road is already graded to Nephi, a contract for ties is now being filled, and it is expected that the rails will be on hand by the time the ties are in place. The value of this unsurpassed coal deposit to our mining interest offers an immense inducement to active labor, and that the advantages to accrue from this railroad enterprise may be fully appreciated, we will proceed to give a few figures to bring the matter within the comprehension of the reader.

The amount of coke used in the reduction of ores in Utah and eastern Nevada last year, exceeded twelve thousand tons. This was all brought from Pennsylvania, and cost when delivered at the various smelters an average of $34 per ton. Here is an expense of $408,000 imposed upon the community for an article of fuel, nearly the whole of which sum is sent to an Eastern State, while we have the means of procuring equally as good an article at our own doors. In proof of this we may mention that last summer the San Pete Coal Company with such crude machinery as they could improvise for the purpose, baked a small quantity of coke (fifteen tons) which was used in the Germania smelters, and was found to be fully equal in every respect to the coke brought from Connellsville, Pennsylvania. And anticipating the early completion of the railroad to the coal region, the San Pete Coal Company have procured the necessary machinery for the manufacture of coke, which was shipped from this city on Monday last. As is already known to our readers, San Pete coal, hauled in wagons a distance of forty miles to the end of the Utah Southern track, is now used in the Salt Lake gas works and in a number of city forges, and although the price is three dollars per ton in excess of other native coals, it is preferred on account of its superior illuminating and coking qualities. With through railway carriage it is expected that the San Pete coke can be furnished to the smelters at from $15 to $17 per ton, a saving of fully one-half of the present cost; and in addition to the considerable saving to be effected, the further advantage will be afforded us of expending the money among our own people; thus benefiting our home trade and increasing the demand for farm products.

The continued use of charcoal for smelting purposes is found to be impracticable. Each smelter consumes six hundred bushels of charcoal daily, and to supply this immense demand the denudation of the timbered canyons is proceeding at so rapid a rate, that in a very few years, the Territory will be entirely stripped of timber. The San Pete coal field is pronounced inexhaustible; one vein of five feet ten inches is now being worked, and four other veins of less extent have already been uncovered. Our entire mining interest is vitally interested in having this valuable coal supply made instantly available, and we trust that no financial difficulties will be allowed to stand in the way of completing the railroad lines as above briefly sketched, so as to utilize the advantages which Providence has placed in our hands.

Salt Lake Herald
May 26, 1875

A Scoundrel Caught.

There is good evidence for the belief that Nephi Vaughan is one of the human brutes who has been engaged in the recent midnight outrages which have so exercised the good people of the city. On Monday night, Mrs. Heath, a lady 82 years of age, who resides in the 10th ward, was aroused from her slumbers, and on wakening discovered that a man was in bed with her. The old lady immediately commenced screaming and this alarmed Mrs. Rance, who was sleeping in the adjoining room. The scoundrel Vaughan—for so he afterwards proved to be—sprung from the bed and attacked Mrs. R., when a severe struggle ensued, the little children of Mrs. R. taking part with their mother. Finally Vaughan left without accomplishing his hellish design, and was fortunately captured a short distance from the house by the night watchmen, who had been attracted to the spot by the screams of the ladies. The villain was conducted to the city jail, and yesterday had an examination before justice Pyper. The evidence was most conclusive against the rascal, who was bound over to the district court for trial in bonds of $1,500, and failing to give which he was committed to the county jail to await the action of the grand jury. Vaughan is a depraved wretch, who has been a resident of the city jail several times.

ESTRAY NOTICE.

I HAVE in my possession:
One red and white two-year old STEER, branded something like J K on left side, the same on left hip, crop off left ear.

One red two-year old HEIFER, white under belly grizzly tail, brands resembling G with circle round it on right side, W on right hip, crop off right ear.

One red two-year old HEIFER, white under belly, white spot in face, no brands visible.

If not claimed they will be sold on Saturday, June 19th, 1875, at 10 a.m.

LANGLEY A. BAILEY,
District Poundkeeper.

Nephi, June 8th, 1875.   ds&w

Correspondence.

School Children's Jubilee.

LEVAN, June 3rd, 1875.

Editor Deseret News—

We celebrated the birthday of our beloved President Brigham Young, in a jubilee given by our Sunday Scholars. At 8 o'clock a. m. the juveniles and all associated with our Sunday school, together with the brethren and sisters, assembled at the meeting-house and rode from there to Chicken Creek Canyon in wagons and on horseback, where they alighted and seated themselves in the bowery, prepared for the occasion, under a large rock cavation, but the day being one of unusual coldness it was deemed necessary to move out on the small plain where the sun shone warmly.

The congregation were called to order by the Supt., and the meeting was opened with singing and prayer. Songs, pieces, recitations and short speeches followed, and were received with pleasure by all present.

After the close of the proceedings, the party retired to their pic-nics and enjoyed a sumptuous dinner. The day being so cold the party then returned home.

In the afternoon a dance was given to the juveniles, which they enjoyed very much, besides receiving presents.

In the evening the adults assembled in the School-house and had their dance until time for all to retire.

Altogether the day was well spent in amusement and plenty of rejoicing and will be remembered here.

The health of the people is good, grain prospects are very favorable, and the Saints are feeling pretty well.
JOHN N. SHEPHERD.

Salt Lake Herald
July 10, 1875

Juab County Taxpayers.

County clerk Pitchforth, of Juab county, publishes an official notice in this morning's HERALD to the effect that an adjourned session of the Juab county court will be held in Nephi, on July 26th, for adjusting the tax assessment roll for 1875.

Deseret News
July 14, 1875

LEVAN, June 30th, 1875.

Editor Deseret News:

We were yesterday favored with a call and visit from Sisters E. R. Snow, Horne, Howard, and Barney on their return from a tour through Sanpete County. The R. S., on hearing that they were coming here, arranged and made preparations for a meeting at 4 o'clock p. m. They arrived here about 5 o'clock p. m., consequently they were *hurried* to meet at the appointed hour, and were punctual in meeting, which was well attended by the members of the R. S. and brethren and sisters; Sister Snow having sent out a special invitation to all who felt like meeting.

The meeting was called to order at the appointed hour by the President, N. Hartley, and opened with singing and prayer. The President introduced these worthy sisters to the assemblage of Saints, and Sister Snow made the opening remarks, which were kind, cheering, comforting, and full of love for all those whom she is associated with. She showed the object of the "Relief Societies," and what God had called them to be. The remarks were listened to with much pleasure by the crowded audience and were very impressive. She gave some excellent instructions to the young girls and counseled them to organize themselves in retrenchment and other good societies, in accordance with the gospel and the commandments of God. She was followed by Sisters Horne, Howard and Barney, who all spoke with great credit to themselves, and the religion we profess. Their remarks were very appropriate in and applicable to our situation and feelings as a people, and I think will leave a lasting impression on the pure in heart, and those who are seeking to love God and keep his commandments. I think it was one of the best meetings I ever attended in Levan, and was highly appreciated by all present. These sisters left here this morning in good season and we wish them a safe return to their respective homes.   Yours, etc.,

BRANCH CLERK.

THE TWENTY-FOURTH IN THE COUNTRY.

Nephi.

July 25th, 1875.

As day dawned on the morning of the 24th, the report of "guns" burst forth upon the air, disturbing the quietness of the clear, calm morning. At sunrise twenty-four guns were fired in honor of the day. Just as old Sol's rays tipped the western mountains the flag was hoisted, amid the stirring strains of the "Star Spangled Banner," played by Capt. Hawkins' newly organized and most excellent brass band.

The band discoursed some of their music through town.

At 8 o'clock a procession was formed under the bowery by Marshal Walter P. Reed, marshal of the day, attended by the brass band. Conspicuous in the procession were the Relief Society; Twenty-four young ladies, selected from the "Young Ladies' Association;" Twenty-four young men, from the "Young Men's Association," and the Sunday School, with their banners bearing beautiful and appropriate mottoes.

After marching through several streets, the procession passed under a splendidly arranged arch into the meeting-house, which was soon filled. The exercises were opened with a song by Nephi's popular and "far-famed" choir.

Prayer was offered by the chaplain, Elder J. G. Bigler.

A minutely descriptive oration was delivered by Bro. Saml. Pitchforth and was listened to with much interest.

Appropriate remarks were made by Bp. Grover and Elder M. McCune. The brass band and Capt. Darton's popular string band were in attendance and filled the house with their musical and concordant sounds whenever called upon.

The Church and Sunday School choirs also charmed us with their sweet music. Songs, beautiful and appropriate, were sung by members of the choir. A recitation and toasts were also interluded with effect. Among the toasts were some in honor of Prest. B. Young, Hon. Geo. Q. Cannon and the U. S. and S. V. R. Rs.

At 2 p.m. the children danced under the bowery prepared for them.

At 7 our stately matrons, attended by their "liege lords" and many of our fair young ladies with their gallants, went forth in a dance in the social hall, which was kept up with lively interest and good order, until the faithful timepiece warned them not to break in upon the sacredness of that day which God has commanded all men to "remember and keep holy." Good order prevailed throughout the day.

The committee consisted of Saml. Cazier, T. B. Lewis, Edward Sparks, and Lyman Hudson.

Organization of U. O.

MOUNT CARMEL, Kane Co.,
July 31, 1875.

Editor Deseret News:

July 11th, Brother Joseph A. Young was here and organized the brethren here in the United Order. Joseph A. Young was appointed chairman and the business carried so far as should be in the first meeting.

The next meeting was held on the 19th of July, W. B. M. Jolley, chairman, when the following named persons were unanimously elected directors of the United Order—Henry B. M. Jolley, Wm. J. Jolley, Robert Monceur, Nephi Jolley, Williamson N. Jolley, Rasmus M. Engelstad, John W. Reed, William H. Worthen.

The third meeting was held at the County Courthouse, Toquerville, July 23, where the directors qualified before the Probate Judge, and gave the required bonds. The directors then appointed a committee of three to nominate officers, who returned and nominated H. B. M. Jolley President, W. J. Jolley 1st Vice-President, R. Monceur 2nd Vice-President, R. M. Engelstad Secretary, Nephi Jolley Treasurer. All, one by one, were unanimously elected, all elections being viva voce. The officers then took the oath of office and gave the required bonds.

Your Brother in the gospel,
R. M. ENGELSTED,
Secretary U. O.

Salt Lake Herald
August 26, 1875

From Juab.

John Hawkins, from Nephi, reports that the crops in that region never looked better than this year, and a bounteous harvest is anticipated.

A considerable force of men are working on the grade for the narrow-gauge railroad from Nephi into Sanpete valley. Gen. Clark has recently been to the Wale's coal beds and tested the quality of the coal there, which he ascertained coked easily.

The Nebo mines are again attracting attention, and are to be worked by capitalists.

The Nephites believe that when the railroad run into their town it will take rapid strides towards eclipsing Provo as the largest city south of Salt Lake.

Salt Lake Tribune
September 10, 1875

THE SAN PETE COAL BEDS.

A Coke Supply for Utah and Nevada

Much has been said and written about the necessity of a cheaper fuel supply in Salt Lake, and especially upon the desideratum of a good quality of coke made from Utah coal. To day we have good news from the South. The San Pete Coal and Coke Company, after much time and money spent in experimenting, have achieved a gratifying success, and are actually supplying one furnace with coke which gives entire satisfaction. For two years this company have been steadily at work with this end in view. The time and expense required in properly opening a coal mine takes energy and capitol. This much has been done, and in addition ovens built. The first attempt at making coke proved a failure. The impurities left in the coal rendered the coke unmerchantable. This caused further delay, and entailed additional expense. Machinery for crushing the coal and properly cleaning it was procured. Various kinds of ovens were also built with a view to ascertain which was the best. This ascertained, a sufficient number was built, and are now in operation to produce two car-loads of coke a week. Mr. Billings of the Germania works is receiving, and using this, and, we understand, is entirely pleased with its quality. He has contracted for all the coke these ovens will produce.

The ranch ground is thus thorough-

This much ground is thus thoroughly secured. Now, the ambition of the company is to strike out further. They have machinery on the ground, capable of preparing for coking one hundred tons of coal a day. Their next purpose is to build more ovens as rapidly as possible, and this will be proceeded with forthwith. In ninety days from date, we are assured they will be ready to furnish the smelting companies with coke at little more than one-half the price now paid for an Eastern article; and by six months they expect to be able to supply all Utah and Nevada. The coal supply at San Pete is said to be inexhaustible.

This growing industry will require increased facilities of transportation. At present the crude and prepared products of the mines are hauled in wagons forty miles to the end of the Utah Southern railroad track at York. A railroad must be built to the mines.

A railroad must be built to the mines. The enterprising coal company design building a narrow gauge feeder to connect with the main line at Nephi. Eight miles of the heaviest grading has already been done through the canyon, and Gen. Clark, the president of this railroad company, is now East to make the purchase of iron and rolling stock. As soon as the purchases are made, the Utah Southern Extension Company, composed of a number of responsible men, have engaged to set to work upon carrying their road from York (its present terminus) to Nephi, fourteen miles, with the least delay practicable. But the completion of both these lines to San Pete, we do not look for till next summer.

The miners are now furnishing the Utah Southern Company with all the coal they use on their locomotives, which for generating steam they pronounce superior to any other native coal. And for blacksmith's use the washed coal has proved to be equal to the celebrated Cumberland coal. It is now in use all through the Territory, and along the line of the Central Pacific Railroad at points in Nevada and elsewhere. We regard the success of this company as vital to the best interests of the Territory, and wish them continued success and further progress in the direction sought.

Deseret News
September 15, 1875

SPRING CITY, Aug. 31, 1875.

Editor Deseret News:

Our mail stage runs as regularly and as faithfully as we could ask, but unfortunately does not bring us the NEWS punctually. Three or four times of late my papers have not reached me by due course, and after the news becomes stale I get my papers all at once. I do not wish to accuse any of the P. M's. on the line, yet it sometimes happens that mail matter that should go south from Nephi comes round into Sanpete and has to be sent back. In these stirring times it is not a little annoying to endure these irregularities, and it might be well for those who have the authority to look after the neglect and inattention of P. M's. between Nephi and Salt Lake City.

A gentle rain last night, which has laid the dust, did some little good and no harm. The health of the people is generally good and we all have reason to be thankful for the kindly providences over us.

Respectfully,

O. HYDE.

Salt Lake Herald
September 26, 1875

Suicide.

A special dispatch from Nephi, Juab county, brings news of the suicide of Mrs. Elizabeth Henriod, wife of Gustave Henriod, of that place, which sad event occurred yesterday morning. At 9 o'clock she was found hanging behind her bedroom door, and life was extinct. About an hour before the discovery, the lady was seen alive.

Justice T. B. Lewis, of Nephi, was preparing to hold an inquest when the dispatch was sent.

Deseret News
September 29. 1875

ST. GEORGE, Utah,
December 4, 1874.

John Codman, Esq. Salt Lake City:

Dear Sir: Your letter of November 20 is received, and also your book entitled the "Mormon Country." I have hastily read it with great pleasure, as I had never had the privilege of doing so before. I should have been pleased if you could have visited this country. I was glad to learn that your tour through Sevier, Millard and Juab counties was agreeable and instructive.

You ask for information respecting railroad routes to connect the Union Pacific with the Southern Pacific. There are two natural routes from Santaquin. The road should go by Tintic mines, if the divide is not too high. If this is impracticable, the road should go by Nephi, Chicken Creek, and the lower Sevier Valley, passing through

Star and other mining districts, on the desert to Panacca, Lincoln county, Nevada; thence down the Meadow Valley Wash and Muddy Valley, down the Rio Virgen to where it empties into the Colorado. There is a good place to cross the Colorado, and an easy grade to get out on the other side. Then skirt the west side of the San Francisco Mountains through to Prescott, and connect with the southern road. The advantages of this road are, that it connects with the rich silver, lead, copper and iron mines of western and southern Utah and southeastern Nevada.

The other route, and in some respects more preferable, would be through Salt Creek Canyon, Juab County, to the coal and iron mines of Sanpete, taking in the lead and salt mines at the base of Mount Nebo, and through the rich grain fields of Sanpete and Sevier valleys; thence up the Sevier to Panguitch and up to the rim of the basin, which, I think, can be crossed without a tunnel, through immense forests of pine timber, and on a gradual descent to the Ki Babbi, or Buckskin Mountains, where Major Powell discovered an excellent place for a suspension bridge across the Colorado, where the river runs in a narrow, deep canyon, and the bridge would be very high above water; skirt the San Francisco Mountains on the east, and connect with the Southern Pacific. The advantages of this route would be to develop the stone quarries, coal fields, iron and copper mines, and grain and lumber regions, and grazing lands of Sanpete and Sevier valleys and Upper Kanab. I believe there is no difficulty on this route but what can and will be easily overcome with time, labor and capital. I understand these to be substantially the routes designed by President Young for the Utah Southern road.

I believe another feasible route, and in some respects superior to either of those mentioned, would be to leave the Sevier at Fort Sanford, crossing the Wasatch range, up Bear Creek and down Fremont's Pass, through Little Salt Lake Valley, passing near Paragoonah and Parowan to Iron City. From Iron City through Mountain Meadow Pass, down the Santa Clara to St. George. From there in a southerly direction, to the mouth of the Grand Gulch, where there is a good crossing of the Colorado; thence out on the plateau described by Lieut. Wheeler, who describes the route from St. George south on page 74 of his book of explorations for 1871. The advantages of this route are that it will pass through one of the greatest iron, coal and copper regions in the known world, which has not been successfully worked yet to any great extent for want of railroad facilities.

You say in your letter: "I send you a copy of that (book) with the request that, although we cannot be expected to agree on religious matters, you will kindly set me right as to the facts where I am in error." Page 4 reads: "The former policy of this people was seclusive, and consequently strongly opposed to all railroad enterprises; but when inevitable fate pushed the Union

Pacific and Central Pacific lines across the continent, directly through their territory, they wisely concluded to make the innovation profitable, as it was unavoidable." This declaration somewhat surprised me. If you will read the memorial to Congress, approved March 3, 1852, you will learn that Brigham Young, then Governor of Utah, and the Legislature of Utah, were the first legislative body who took action concerning a railroad across the continent. The memorial will be found in the first volume of Utah laws. The original was signed by Brigham Young, Governor, as well as by the officers and members of the Assembly. It reads as follows:

"MEMORIAL TO CONGRESS FOR THE CONSTRUCTION OF A GREAT NATIONAL CENTRAL RAILROAD TO THE PACIFIC COAST. APPROVED MARCH 3D, 1852.

To the Honorable the Senate and House of Representatives of the United States, in Congress assembled:

"Your Memorialists, the Governor and the legislative assembly of the Territory of Utah, respectfully pray your honorable body to provide for the establishment of a national railroad from some eligible point on the Mississippi or Missouri river to San Diego, San Francisco, Sacramento or Astoria, or such other point on or near the Pacific coast as the wisdom of your honorable body may dictate. Your memorialists respectfully state that the immense emigration to and from the Pacific requires the immediate attention, guardian care and fostering assistance of the greatest and most liberal government on the face of the earth. Your memorialists are of the opinion that not less than five thousand American citizens have perished on the different routes within the last three years, for the want of proper means of transportation. That an eligible route can be obtained your memorialists have no doubt. Being extensively acquainted with the country, we know that no obstruction exists between this point and San Diego, and that iron, coal, timber, stone and other materials exist in various places on the route, and that the settlements of this territory are so situated as to amply supply the builders of this road with material and provisions, for a considerable portion of the route; and to carry on an extensive trade after the road is completed.

"Your memorialists are of opinion that the mineral resources of California and these mountains can never be fully developed to the benefit of the people of the United States without the construction of such a road; and upon its completion the entire trade of China and the East Indies will pass through the heart of the Union, thereby giving our citizens the almost entire control of the Asiatic and Pacific trade; pouring into the lap of the American states the millions that are now diverted through other commercial channels; and last, though not least, the road herein proposed would be a perpetual chain or iron band which would effectually held together our glorious Union, with an imperishable identity of mutual interest, thereby consolidating our relations with foreign powers in times of peace, and our defence from foreign invasion by the speedy transmission of troops and supplies in times of war. The earnest attention of Congress to this important subject is solicited by your memorialists, who in duty bound will ever pray."

When this memorial was presented to Congress by Mr. John M. Bernhisel, Utah's delegate, he was told by the members that we were one hundred years ahead of the age. He humorously invited them, when the road was done, to come and see him, and some of them have done so, twenty years afterwards. The legislature have repeatedly sent memorials to Congress, keeping the subject continually before them, until they enacted a law on the subject. The memorials of 1855-56 point out the Bitter Creek route, but recommended the Timpanogas Pass, or Provo route, instead of the Weber. In the spring of 1856 a mass meeting, held at Salt Lake City, passed resolutions urging the necessity of immediate action of Congress for a national railroad. So far, then, from our people being opposed to railroad enterprise, they were among the first to bring the question before Congress, and kept continually calling their attention to the subject until it was made effectual.

I crossed the plains with Brigham Young on his pioneer journey in 1847. We were looking for a railroad route as well as a wagon road, and in company with him I made many a detour from the wagon road to find passes where a railroad could be constructed through the mountains. We then expected that ten or fifteen years would be sufficient to complete the road. The memorial of March 3, 1852, is almost prophetic. Brigham Young's and the people of Utah's efforts were probably the cause of his being appointed one of the original directors of the Union Pacific road.

I was reared rigidly a Presbyterian. Our people have never been, in any particular, as seclusive as my Presbyterian ancestors were. This may be somewhat singular, considering the rigid modern Christian training that our people have received since the organization of the church, embracing forty-seven vexatious lawsuits against Joseph Smith; and notwithstanding any amount of perjury, not one of them were successful, though it cost more than one hundred thousand dollars to defend them.

Joseph Smith and his counsellor were tarred and feathered, in the spring of 1832, as a piece of modern Christian discipline, two Christian (?) ministers presiding on the occasion. A child sick with the measles *died from the exposure caused by breaking into the house and tearing* Joseph Smith out of bed. In 1833 the Rev. Isaac McCoy, a Baptist clergyman, and the Rev. D. Pixley, Presbyterian, were *foremost* in administering Christian discipline to the Latter-day Saints in Jackson county, Missouri, aided by lesser lights in the Christian faith, tore down houses, destroyed printing offices, pillaged goods, whipped, tarred and feathered; killed, wounded and drove fifteen hundred people disarmed and destitute to perish in the wilderness; burned two hundred and sixteen of their houses, which stood upon lands for which they had paid their specie to the *United States treasury*. The same Christian *discipline, in a milder* way, was again administered *in* Clay county. They were driven to the naked, uninhabited prairies of Caldwell county, their enemies ever-declaring that it was such a *worthless country*, and so destitute of timber, that the Mormons were welcome to it. Two years of industry and enterprise, with great faith on the part of our people, made Caldwell one of the most flourishing counties in that State.

Here the Rev. Sashael Woods, a Presbyterian minister, and the Rev. Samuel Bogard, a Methodist, assisted by ministers of other denominations, and their aiders and abettors, renewed the system of religious tyranny by beating, stabbing, robbing, plundering, house-burning, ravishing, and finally exterminating and driving about five thousand people from the State of Missouri in midwinter. Every one of them that was driven was repeatedly urged, and many solicited to stay, if they would renounce their religion—not polygamy, for we were then rigid monogamists, but our church organization. Major General John W. Clark, a Methodist, in enforcing the exterminating order, said: "You must not meet in council meetings or in conferences; and if you ever organize again with bishops and presidents, the people will be upon you, and you utterly destroyed." Our benevolent Christian friends of Missouri followed many of those exterminated people with vexatious demands upon the Governor of Illinois for extradition for violation of Missouri laws. I believe that a record cannot be found in the State of Missouri wherein a criminal judgment is entered against one of our people, though the administration of the law was entirely in the hands of our enemies. One especial lesson in Christian charity was administered at the meeting ground near the missionary camp, where several women were lashed to benches and * * * * . While Joseph Smith and his fellows were in prison and in chains, they were told that a party of these men had gone for the purpose of administering the same Christian training to their wives, but they returned without accomplishing their purpose, as they found the families so well guarded as to make the attempt unsafe.

In 1844 a handsome city had grown up in Hancock county, Illinois, called Nauvoo. A charge of treason against Joseph and Hyrum Smith caused their arrest. Knowing the intention of his persecutors to murder him, Joseph Smith obtained from the Governor of the state a pledge of the faith of the state for his protection from all violence, and a fair trial; but he and his brother were murdered in jail, while awaiting examination, by a party of men with blackened faces, led by a Baptist minister; ministers of other denominations taking part. In 1845 one hundred and seventy-five houses were burned in different parts of Hancock county by parties led by Christian ministers; and culminated in driving the entire people in winter, numbering many thousands, homeless and destitute, into the wilderness, leaving the hard toil of six years, their magnificent temple, mills, factories,

farms and neighboring villages a prey to their Christian tutors. But they faithfully promised that the few helpless and destitute might remain in the city. The Rev. Thomas Brockman, and about fifteen hundred of his pious confederates, after several days' siege, and three days' bombardment with artillery, succeeded in setting across the river the last six hundred men, women and children, helpless and destitute. A description of this suffering camp was given by Colonel Kane, who visited them. He says, "Dreadful, indeed, was the suffering of those forsaken beings, bowed and cramped by cold and sunburn, as each alternate day and night dragged on. It was the fourth week of September, 1846." (For extract from Colonel Kane's description, see Answers to Questions, page 12.) This short reference to points of our history would be sufficient to satisfy the kind, generous and impartial historian, that when added too by the years of hardship, toil and suffering incident to forcing our way into these mountains and contending with Indians, wild beasts and the sterility of an unknown desert, solely for the enjoyment of religious liberty, the whole Mormon people ought to have become, in the most eminent degree, thoroughly possessed of all the meek, quiet, peaceful, humane and liberal principles of true Christianity.

We fed the Indians; we fed the emigrants who came here hungry by the thousands; dug them out of the snow in the mountains, and nursed them when sick; and although thieves and robbers among them plundered our ranges of the most valuable cattle and horses, we extended to them the protection of our laws. Some of them were taken, tried and imprisoned, were reprieved by Governor Young in the spring and aided on their journey. The rights of no apostate or stranger were compromised while he was governor. We had successfully contended with two grasshopper wars, far more destructive than the present one in Kansas, and one cricket war, till on the 24th day of July, 1857, the news arrived, while we were engaged celebrating that memorable day at Big Cottonwood Lake, that Brigham Young had been removed from being Governor; that 2,500 infantry, two regiments of cavalry and two batteries of artillery were ordered to Utah; and that their outfit was the most complete ever furnished to an American army; the command to be given to General Harney, who was known in Utah by the name of "Squaw

Killer," and whose very name carried with it among our people a feeling of horror; and what was more significant, all the administration papers and many others were filled with threats of extermination, blood and slaughter. Even our old friend Senator Douglas, in a speech, requested the administration to cut out the loathsome ulcer, meaning Utah; and what was even more significant, the United States mail was stopped. The people struggling with the desert said in their hearts, "This means bloodshed." When the mob began operations in Jackson county the United States mail was stopped. When like operations commenced in Clay county the United States mail was stopped. At the commencement of mob interference in Caldwell county the United States mail was stopped. As soon as the disturbance began that brought about the assassination of Joseph and Hyrum Smith, the mail was stopped. The commencement of house burning in Hancock county in 1845 was simultaneous with the stoppage of the mail; and if the government has stopped the mail, we need ex-

pect no mercy, "judging the present by the long and bitter past." Some Utah people had the contract for carrying the mail. One hundred thousand dollars had been expended in stocking the road, which was all lost.

In the spring of 1856 I went to Washington with a petition to ask for the admission of Utah into the Union. It was well known in the States that the people of Utah had lost their crops the previous year through grasshoppers. We had, indeed, lived on half allowance of bread for a year, and it was believed that we must inevitably starve; and they seemed disappointed to find us in good health and applying for admission into the Union. The press of both parties commenced a universal tirade of abuse and falsehood concerning the people of Utah. We were unable to get any paper of prominence to correct these falsehoods, or publish anything that was reliable.

I returned to Utah on May 25th. For almost a year not a single package was brought into Salt Lake by the mail from the east. When it did come everything that had not been plundered had been opened. I have no doubt but the bloody extermination of our people would have been carried out, had it not been for the humane influence of General Sam Houston, of Texas, and Colonel Thomas L. Kane, of Pennsylvania, or some other miraculous intervention on the part of the Almighty. Brigham Young sternly and continually instructed, in all of his speeches and proclamations to the people and orders to his men, that no blood should be shed, and assured them if they would implicitly obey his orders that they should come off triumphant. Nearly all the desperate acts charged against the people of Utah occurred during this period.

Imagine the feelings of a people: the mail stopped; the best appointed army ever sent out by the United States headed, so reported, by a bloodthirsty "squaw killer," on the way to cut out the "loathsome ulcer." We had few men, and they were without arms and ammunition. This was decidedly one of the tightest places I ever saw in Mormonism. It was therefore determined to seize the hand that held the bowie knife, and hold it until the knife could be taken away; and this was done in a wondrous manner, without bloodshed. It appears, however, that in some of the distant setttlements some men, acting under the spirit and influence of the Christian lessons they had received, were guilty of acts of violence. All these were magnanimously cancelled by a general pardon of the President of the United States, and a special pardon of the Governor of Utah, for all crimes and offences growing out of the difficulties; and there has not since been, so far as I know, the least violation of faith on the part of the people of Utah; although the federal authorities have not invariably maintained good faith on their part, but have, and are still endeavoring to disturb the peace of the community with difficulties of that period. Even your book, written with such apparent fairness, bases upon the extreme utterances of men, many of them extremists, a faith almost as brutal as that practised upon us by our religious trainers, the Christian clergy, and their assistants in the United States. Page 156 of your book says: "It is scarcely pretended that Brigham Young gave the order for the 'Mountain Meadow Massacre,' but he took no steps to bring the murderers to justice."

Now the facts of this are, President Young, who had been superseded as Governor by Alfred Cumming, requested him and United States District Attorney Wilson to investigate this matter. He offered to go with them; guaranty their protection, and use his influence for the arrest of every party desired; and that a fair trial be had. This was refused by the judiciary, notwithstanding it was urged by the Governor and Attorney, as an investigation of this subject would not bring the guilt upon those whom political and religious intriguantes wished to criminate. We are still desirous for a fair investigation of this subject, but do not want it investigated before a religious bigot or political trickster. Let the officers who handle this matter be just, high-minded men.

On the same page your book refers to the Morrisites. Morris had gathered around him some idlers, who had stopped work, and were living from cattle on the range.

One of their number had apostatized from them, and had been sentenced by them to die. His friends, in terror, appealed to the United States Chief Justice of Utah to save his life, as he was imprisoned in Kington Fort, held by the Morrisites, and would be killed immediately. The Chief Justice issued a writ of *habeas corpus*. The officer was resisted, his life threatened, and he forbidden to return on pain of death. The Judge, John F. Kinney, called upon the Governor for a posse, which were accordingly ordered. Mormons being the citizens, were of course called upon. Brigham Young, on hearing of this, visited the Chief Justice and remonstrated against this proceeding, and the Judge insisted that the majesty of the law must be preserved. President Young urged that they were a band of fanatics entrenched in a fort, who would

fight, and probably many lives would be lost; but if they were left alone, in a short time, with their idle habits, they would scatter. But *the Judge still persisted* that the dignity of the court must be maintained. I visited the Chief Justice myself, not knowing of President Young's visit, and *insisted that the move was ill-timed and wrong; and further, that it would be construed* by our enemies as a persecution of the Morrisites by the Mormons, and was calculated to do us immense injury. The Judge insisted that this could not be; but the majesty of the law must be maintained. He could not allow those people to kill their prisoners, or threaten an officer of the court. It is therefore an injustice to construe this as a Mormon persecution. I am satisfied your reference to Burton is untrue.

Your account of the Mormon doctrine of blood atonement is, to me, entirely new. I have been in this church forty-two years, and have been acquainted forty-four years with its founders. We have had some extremists and some extreme men, but I never heard any one advocate the extreme doctrine you impute to us. The beautiful woman you describe as being killed by her husband I never heard of; she must have been a myth. We believe in the death penalty. Our territorial laws were enacted in accordance with our faith. Give the murderer his choice to be hung or to have his blood spilled on the ground. Utah jurors have refused to hang men who had killed the seducer of their wives or daughters. On page 140 you say, "Polygamy was revealed to Smith to meet some difficulties of a social character with which he found himself embarrassed." It is not so. It should read, The revelation of plurality of wives caused Joseph Smith to be embarrassed with some difficulties of a social character. He was a rigidly moral, virtuous and pure man, and nothing but a sense of the awful responsibility of disobeying the Almighty caused him to teach or practise a principle which increased manifold the responsibilities and burdens of men.

The Spaulding story is a myth, and exceedingly shallow. I am ashamed of the credulity of my fellow-men who believe it.

Murders have been committed in Utah; but on investigation these troubles invariably prove to be individual difficulties, and not unfrequently growing out of cattle and horse-stealing enterprises.

Had you travelled all over Utah during the exciting year of 1857, in the same kind, gentle and peaceful manner that you have done in the past two years, you would not have been molested.

I thank you for sending me the book. The references I have made have been very hasty, and in the absence of my library and journals. On page 91 of your book you accuse us, like the Puritans, of persecuting other sects. From the foundation of the church to the present, ministers of all denominations have been invited to preach in our pulpits. Men of all persuasions have done business in our settlements without interruption. When some of these business men whom we have made rich with our trade used that means and influence to induce the country to shed our blood, we withdrew our trade from them; and all the acts of violence that occurred during the war of '57 were done under a firm conviction, on the part of our people, that the nation had decreed our extermination, and not from a spirit of persecution.

My reference to preachers is not intended to apply to all, as I have reason to believe that some chrisian ministers deprecate these acts of persecution, though I have no knowledge of any of them speaking out, either in public print or in the pulpit, against them. We have had professors of religion of different denominations as federal officers in the territory, who have been impartial, and not disgraced themselves and their professional honor by trampling the law under foot to injure the people; though as a rule the federal officers of the territory, I believe, have been bigoted tricksters, unworthy the confidence of their neighbors, and probably sent to Utah to get rid of them. You say, page 96: "I find it hard to believe that any educated man can have or have had a real faith in the inspiration of Joseph Smith or Brigham Young." What other motive than real faith could have prompted men to endure the persecution and suffering which this faith inevitably brought upon them? I find it hard to believe that any educated, honest man, with the evidence which exists before his eyes of its truth, can reject it. I believe that many who entered the church with a firm conviction of the truth have been induced to abandon it through persecution.

You certainly have as good a right to your belief on this subject as I have to mine. Not a single criminal connected with tarring and feathering, burning hundreds of houses, murdering men while trying to put out the fire of their burning building, the bloody scenes of the Blue, Haun's Mill, Crooked River, Goose Creek, the boasted ravishings of Mormon women at their meeting grounds, the murder of their prophets, the driving of tens of thousands of people into the wilderness and robbing them of nearly all they possessed—I have never known of a state or national court bringing one of those criminals to justice, but do know of instances where a Mormon court, Mormon jury, and Mormon officers have executed a Mormon for killing an outsider. Thomas Ford, then Governor of Illinois, in a letter to my father and myself, in 1844, said many of the people of the state regretted the manner in which Joseph and Hyrum Smith were killed, but were glad they were dead. Their murderers were admitted to bail for $1,000 each, allowed to go security for each other, and of course were acquitted.

The weather is fine. There are one hundred masons and tenders, with seven carpenters, at work on the Temple building here. Ninety five quarrymen and twenty-five stone-cutters are at work in the quarry. More than fifty tons of rock are daily laid in the walls. Lime burners, wood, lime, stone and sand haulers and road-makers, lumbermen and lumber haulers amount to one hundred and twenty men more. The lumber and timbers are hauled sixty-five miles across a desert, forty of which are without water.

A portion of the road is now almost impassable from mud. The walls of the building are about forty feet high.

GEO. A. SMITH.

—*New York Post.*

Correspondence.

Suicide of Mrs. Henriod.

NEPHI, Sept. 25, 1875.

Editor Deseret News:

According to my telegram to-day I will now give the particulars of the death of Elizabeth Henriod, wife of Gustave Henriod, of this place. T. B. Lewis, Esq., justice of the peace, at 12:20 p.m. to-day, held an inquest over the body of the deceased, which occupied the most of the day.

From the evidence given before the inquest, it appears that the deceased cooked breakfast for the family and appeared cheerful. Nothing transpired to excite any suspicion or give any hint that she intended to destroy herself. Bro. Henriod was in the garden, paring peaches, and saw her go to the cellar several times, as it was her custom when putting the milk away. Between nine and ten o'clock her little girl, a child five years of age, came running from the house, crying and said that her mother was hanging dead behind the bed-room door. He immediately ran into the house and found the bed-room door a little open, and on entering saw his wife hanging by a small hair rope, which was fastened to some hooks, such as people hang hats or coats on, her feet touching the floor. He in an instant cut the rope, caught her in his arms, and laid her on the bed, but life was extinct. Bro. T. B. Lewis, who was passing by, on hearing the cries of the children, ran to the house and examined the deceased, but she was nearly cold, and the vital spark had flown. From the evidence given before the jury, we learn that she had been seen and spoken to within half an hour before she was found dead.

The following is the verdict of the jury—

"Territory of Utah, } Nephi Precinct.
County of Juab, }

"An inquisition holden at the house of Gustave Henriod, in the town of Nephi, Precinct of Nephi, County aforesaid, at 12.30 a.m. of the 25th day of September, A. D. 1875, before T. B. Lewis, an acting justice of the peace in and for the county aforesaid, Nephi Precinct, upon the body of Elizabeth Henriod, wife of Gustave Henriod, there lying dead, by the jurors whose names are hereunto subscribed. The said jurors upon their oaths do say that the deceased Elizabeth Henriod came to her death by hanging by the neck with a hair rope, attached to a clothes hook on the wall of her bedroom, said act being performed by her own hands while in a fit of temporary insanity.

"In testimony whereof the said jurors have hereunto set their hands the day and year aforesaid.

"JACOB G. BIGLER, SEN.,
"ELI RANDELL,
"C. H. BRYANT.

"Attested this 25th day of Sept., A. D. 1875. T. B. LEWIS,
"Justice of the Peace."

Mrs. Henriod has left a family consisting of six boys and one girl, the youngest about thirteen months old. She has also left an aged and respected father, two brothers and two sisters to mourn her loss. She was much respected, and all come to the conclusion that she must have had a fit of temporary insanity, or she would not have committed the rash act which has deprived her husband, children and friends of the pleasure of her society.

SAMUEL PITCHFORTH.

Salt Lake Herald
October 10, 1875

Robbing the Mail.

A gentleman of this city informs us that he recently sent two letters containing money to a party in Nephi, Juab county, but they both failed to reach their destination. It is also said there are other instances of stealing valuable letters somewhere between Salt Lake and Nephi. The matter should be looked into and the thief guillotined.

Deseret News
October 27, 1875

Big Apple.—Here comes a big apple from Nephi, Juab Co. It is of the King of Tompkins County variety, is fourteen inches in circumference, and was grown by Thomas Boles. Every inch a king

Deseret News
November 3, 1875

Amputation.—A few days ago a young married man, named Francis Sells, came up to the City from Nephi, his place of residence, to obtain surgical relief for a disease that he had contracted in the knee joint of his right leg. He was attended by Dr. W. F. Anderson, who performed an operation upon the young man, but, in doing so, discovered that the bone was in such an advanced state of decay that nothing but amputation of the limb could be done for the relief of the patient, and consequently, he consenting, the leg was amputated some distance above the affected joint, the operation being successfully performed by Dr. Joseph Richards, and the patient has been doing very well ever since, all the symptoms being favorable to his recovery. Drs. W. F. Anderson and Heber Richards were present on the occasion.

The patient is staying, until able to remove to his home in Nephi, at the house of Mrs. Macdonald, in the 13th Ward, where he is well cared for. His having, unexpectedly to himself, to undergo the operation of amputation, involving a somewhat prolonged stay in the city, necessarily brings a considerable amount of expense, beyond his present ability to meet, and his case is one that is worthy the attention of the benevolently inclined, his present circumstances presenting a good opportunity for any of his friends so disposed to render him some assistance pecuniarily. He is a respectable young man, who has been in the Territory nine years, having come to this country in the company which crossed the ocean in the ship *American Congress*, in 1866. Subscriptions can be left for him with John Nicholson, at this office, or parties disposed to aid him can call at his boarding house, near the residence of Mr. Joseph E. Taylor.

Deseret News
November 24, 1875

NEW YORK, Nov. 9, 1875.

Editor Deseret News:

We are all on the *qui vive*, getting ready to go on board the *Wisconsin* by 12 o'clock m.

Brothers W. M. Evans and John S. Hawkins, of Nephi, joined us yesterday, which makes our party nine in number. Brothers Jeremy and Llewellyn have not yet arrived, and if they do not come soon they will not be able to sail with us.

Brother Evans got robbed on the way from Omaha to Chicago, and Brother Hawkins had to lend him money enough to take him to this city.

Bros. John W. Young and Rudger Clawson paid us a visit yesterday at our boarding house; we were very happy to see them.

As soon as Bro. Young became acquainted with Bro. Evans' misfortune, he, without being asked, very generously handed over to Bro. Evans enough money to pay his passage to Liverpool and his expenses here God bless him for the good deed.

In my last I sent you the names of all who were then here, and in this you have two more names for Europe.

Your Brother in the Gospel,
J. C. SANDBERG.

DIED.

At Levan, Juab county, November 2nd, LOUISE MARIANE CHRISTIANSEN.;

Deceased was born October 27th, 1821, at Loutrup, in Randers, Denmark; received the Gospel in 1854; emigrated in a hand cart company in 1856; was a faithful Saint; she was a mother to one girl, who died in 1865. She died with a stroke of apoplexy.—[COM.

Scandinavian Stjerne, please copy.

At Nephi, Oct. 30, of chronic bronchitis, ELIZABETH BESSAE, wife of Timothy B. Foot.

Deceased was born in Tioga county, New York, July 5th, 1813; baptized into the Church of Jesus Christ of Latter-day Saints in Dayton, Ohio, by Elder Andrew L. Lamoreaux; soon after moved with her husband, Joseph M. and, to Nauvoo, Illinois; was a member of the first company that came to Utah, and consequently was subjected to all those trials and hardships so rife in the history of this people in their exodus from Nauvoo and their subsequent pilgrimage, all of which she endured with a fixed purpose and a steadfast faith. Even in the darkest hour of her sorest trials she clung to her faith, and preferred to live and die with the people she had chosen as her people. She was of noble ancestry. Her grandfather Bessae was an officer in that noble band of heroes who came from France under the illustrious Lafayette, to assist America in establishing constitutional liberty, protected by law. In 1857 she came to Nephi, and was married to T. B. Foot. For a number of years she has been afflicted with the disease that took her life. Everything was done that could be done by fond children and kind friends, but of no avail. She died surrounded by them, strong in the faith and the hope of a resurrection and a reunion of her family.—[COM.

Deseret News
December 22, 1875

Beaver *Enterprise*, Dec, 14—
On Sunday, Sheriff Coombs overtook and arrested John Christiansen, of Levan, at Round Valley, he
having stolen a set of harness at
Greenville. The Sheriff found the
property in the prisoner's possession, which, with everything else
he had with him, was brought to
Beaver yesterday. A hearing will
be had to-day. Sheriff Coombs is
making a good record as an efficient officer.

Salt Lake Tribune
January 1, 1876

UTAH COKE.

Developments by the San Pete Coal & Coke Company.

The question of smelting Utah ores at home, rather than in Omaha, Chicago or St. Louis, is at last settled. It has been a question in the past whether to ship ores East, at a cost of $25 per ton, or bring Pittsburgh coke from Chicago at the same cost. For more than three years it has been known that the coal in Southern Utah would make good coke. The San Pete coal mine has been developed more or less for the last fifteen years. It was taken up by some settlers from the coal fields of Wales. Being unable to develop it, the parties comprising the above company were interested to under-take its development. Thorough tests were made as regards its cooking properties, both in this country and in London. The result being satisfac-tory, work was commenced about two years ago. Two or three ovens were built at first, and the coke thoroughly tested by the Germania works, eight miles south of Salt Lake City, run-ning several days upon it. Fire brick, engines and all the freight necessary for their works had to be taken from from Salt Lake City. This had to be hauled by teams from the terminus of the Utah Southern Railroad, some forty miles. Coal and coke were freighted back the same distance.

They have expended in their de-velopments, machinery and buildings, over $75,000.

They have about 4,000 feet of tun-neling, the deepest being 1,200 feet. This coal crops out in the foot hills on the west side of the San Pete Valley, twenty-five miles south of Nephi, and 125 miles from this city.

The Company have now twenty-five ovens of the improved Belgian patterns, which were fired up on December 27th. These ovens are the best known, and are expected to discharge about twenty tons per day.

They are also constructing a narrow gauge railroad from Nephi to the mine, a distance of twenty five miles. This has been surveyed, and the most difficult part graded, under the direction of chief engineer Burgess of this city.

The President, Gen. G. W. Clark, of Des Moines, is now East, negotiat-ing for iron and rolling stock. This done, and the Utah Southern com-pleted to Nephi, and Utah will say good by to shipping ores East, or bringing coke from Pittsburgh and St. Louis; the reduction of ores very much lessened, and large sums of money retained in Utah.

PRESIDING ELDERS AND BISHOPS

Of the Church of Jesus Christ of Latter-day Saints.

EDWARD HUNTER
Presiding Bishop of the Church.

WILLIAM BUDGE Presiding Bishop.

Georgetown, Henry Lewis, Bear Lake co, Idaho
Bennington, J. W. Moore, " "
Montpelier, Charles Robinson, " "
Preston, H. H. Dalrymple, " "
Ovid, Peter Jensen, " "
Liberty, S. N. Austin, " "
*Paris, H. J. Horne, " "
Bloomington, George Osmond, " "
St. Charles, John A. Hunt, " "
Fish Haven, Hyrum Rich, "
Lake Town, Ira Nebeker, Bear Lake co, Utah
Meadowville, Josiah Tufts, " "
*Randolph, Randolph Stewart, " "
Woodruff, Henry Lee, " "
Almy, Samuel Pike, Wyoming Territory
Evanston, Wm. G. Burton, " "

WM. B. PRESTON, Presiding Bishop.

Soda Springs, Joseph G
    Fokman,   Oneida co., Idaho.
Oxford, George Lake, " "
Clifton, Wm. Pratt, " "
Bridgeport, N. W. Packer, " "
Franklin, L. H. Hatch, " "
Willow Springs Branch, J. D. Jones, "
Weston, John Maughan, Cache co., Utah.
Clarkston, Simon Smith, " "
Newton, W. F. Littlewood, " "
Lewiston, W. H. Lewis, " "
Richmond, M. W. Merrill, " "
Smithfield, Samuel Roskelly, " "
Hyde Park, Robt Daynes, " "
*Logan, W. B. Preston, " "
Providence, M. D. Hammond, " "
Millville, G. O. Pitkin, " "
Hyrum, C. N. Liljenquist, " "

Paradise, Henry C. Jackson, " "
Wellsville, John Jordine, " "
Mendon, Henry Hughes, " "

DANIEL DANIELS, Presiding Bishop.

*Malad City, Daniel Daniels, Oneida co., Idaho
Samaria, Samuel Williams, " "

A. NICHOLS, Presiding Bishop.

Portage, O. C. Hoskins, Box Elder co., Utah
Deweyville, J. C. Dewey, " "
Calls Fort, Thomas Hasper, " "
Bear River City, Wm. Neeley, " "
Mantua, H. P. Jensen, " "
*Brigham City, Alvin Nichols, " "
Willard City, G. W. Ward.

WEBER COUNTY, UTAH.
LORIN FARR, Presiding Bishop.

1st Ward, Ogden, F. A. Brown.
2d   "   Robert McQuarrie.
3d   "   Joseph Parry.
North Ogden, C H Wheelock,
Plain City, L. W. Shurtliff.
Mound Fort, David Moore.
Lynne, Daniel Thomas.
Slaterville, John Allred.
Harrisville, David Rawsen.
Marriat, John Halverston.
West Weber, John L. Hart.
East Weber, L. Spaulding.
South Weber, D Cook.
River Dale, Sanford Bingham
Eden, Joseph Ferrin.
Huntsville, F. A. Hammond.
Hooperville, Gilbert Belnap.

DAVIS COUNTY.

Kaysville, Christopher Layton.
*Farmington, John W. Hess.
Centreville, Wm. R. Smith.
Bountiful, Anson Call.

MORGAN COUNTY.

C. S. PETERSON, Presiding Bishop

Mountain Green, Eli Spaulding.
Weber City, C. S. Peterson.
Enterprise, Jesse Haven.

W. G. SMITH, Presiding Bishop.

Milton, Jens Hansen.
Littleton, J. H. Giles.
Richville, Glaspie Waldron.
East Porterville, Alma Porter.
West Porterville, Thomas Brough.
*South Morgan Richard Fry.
North Morgan, Charles Turner.
Croyden, Ephraim Swan

SUMMIT COUNTY.

Henneferville, Chas. Richens.
Echo, Elias Asper.
*Coalville, W. W. Cluff.
Unionville, Alonzo Winters.

WM. W. CLUFF presides over Morgan County and the above four Wards in Summit Co.

SAMUEL F. ATWOOD, Presiding Bishop.

Wanship, Jared C. Roundy.
Rockport, Edwin Bryant.
Peoa, Abraham Marchant.
Morell, John K. Lemon.
Kamas, W. Harder.
Parley's Park, Ephraim Snyder.

TOOELE COUNTY.

JOHN ROWBERRY, Presiding Bishop.

E. T. City, W. F. Moss.
Pine Kanyon, Moses Martin.
*Tooele City, John Rowberry.
Grantsville, William Jeffries.
St. Johns, G. W. Burridge.
Centreville, James Jordan.
Vernon, Hyrum Bennion.
Deep Creek, Edwin Tadlock.
Skull Valley, B. F. Knowlton.

WASATCH COUNTY.

ABRAHAM HATCH, Presiding Bishop.

*Heber City, Abraham Hatch.
Midway, Henry S. Alexander.
Charleston, John Watkins.
Wallsburgh, Wm. E. Nuttall.

SALT LAKE COUNTY.

1st Ward, S. L. City, Jos. Warburton.
2d " James Leach.
3d " Jacob Weiler.
4th " Harrison Sperry.
5th & 6th, W. H. Hickenlooper.
7th " Wm. Thorn.
8th " E. F. Sheets.
9th " S. A. Woolley.
10th " A Speirs,
11th " Alex. McRae.
12th " L. W. Hardy.
13th " E. D. Woolley.
14th " Thomas Taylor.
15th " R. T. Burton.
16th " Frederick Kesler.
17th " John Henry Smith.
18th " L. D. Young.
19th " A. H. Raleigh.
20th " John Sharp.
Sugar House Ward, W. C. A. Smoot.
Brighton, A. H. Raleigh.
Big Cottonwood, Wm G Young,
Mill Creek, Reuben Miller.
South Cottonwood, J. S. Rawlins.
West Jordan, Archibald Gardner.
South Willow Creek, L. M. Stewart.

UTAH COUNTY.

A. O. SMOOT, Presiding Bishop.
*Provo.

First Ward, J. P. R. Johnson,
Second Ward, A. H. Scott,
Third Ward, Myron Tanner,
Fourth Ward, H. H. Cluff.
Lehi, David Evans.
Cedar Fort, H. F. Cook.
Fairfield, John Carson.

DAVID EVANS, Presiding Bishop
over the three last named places.

American Fork, L. E. Harrington.
Alpine, T. J. McCullough.

L. E. HARRINGTON, Presiding
Bishop over the two last named

places.

Pleasant Grove, John Brown.
Springville, Wm. Bringhurst.
Spanish Fork, Geo D Snell,
Salem, alias Pondtown, Robt. B. Fa
Payson, J. S. Tanner.
Santaquin Ward, George Halliday.

J. S. TANNER is Presiding Bishop
over Payson and Salem.

Goshen, Wm. Price.

SANPETE COUNTY.

Fountain Green, R. L. Johnson.
Moroni, G. W. Bradley.
Fairview, Amasa Tucker.
Mount Pleasant, W. S. Seeley.
Spring City, Frederick Olsen.
Ephraim, Kanute Petersen.
*Manti, John B. Maiben.
Gunnison, J. S. Horne.
Fayette, John Bartholomew.

JUAB COUNTY.

JOEL GROVER, Presiding Bishop.

Mona, John W. Haws.
*Nephi, alias Salt Creek, Joel Grover
Levan, Elmer Taylor.

SEVIER COUNTY.

**E. K. THURBER and W. H.
SEEGMILLER. Presiding.**

Salina, Franklin Spencer,
*Richfield, W H Seegmiller,
Monroe, J T Lisenbee.
Annabelle Springs, H D Lisonbee.
Joseph, A. L. Farnsworth.
Prattville, Jos. L. Rogers.
Glenwood, P. T. Olroyed,

MILLARD COUNTY.
THOMAS CALLISTER, Presiding
Bishop.

Scipio, Daniel Thompson.
Cedar Springs, alias Holden, David
Stephens.
*Fillmore, Edward Partridge.
Meadow Creek, W. H. Stott.
Oak Creek, P. D. Lyman.
Kanosh, Culbert King.

BEAVER COUNTY.

JOHN R. MURDOCK, Presiding
Bishop.

*Beaver, John R. Murdock.
Minersville, James McKnight.

IRON COUNTY.

Paragoonah, S. S. Smith.
*Parowan, W. H. Dame.
Summit, S C Hulet

W. H. DAME, Presiding Bishop
over the three last named places.

Panguitch, G. W. Sevy.
Cedar City, Henry Lunt.

KANE COUNTY.

Kanarra, L. W. Roundy.
Harmony, W. D. Pace.
Bellevue, J. H. Johnson.
*Toker, Wm A Bringhurst
Virgen, John Parker.
Duncan's Retreat, Moses Gibson
Rockville, C. N. Smith.
Long Valley, Howard O Spencer,
Glendale, James Leathead,
Mt Carmel, Israel Hoyt,
Kanab, L. John Nuttall.
Johnsonia, Sextus E Johnson,
Paria, A V Smithson

WASHINGTON COUNTY.

Leeds, Solomon Angell
Harrisburg, Willis D Fuller,
Washington, J. W. Freeman.
*St. George, D. D. McArthur.
Santa Clara, Edward Bunker.
Pine Valley, Wm. Snow.
Pinto, Richard Robinson.
Hebron, G. H. Crosby.

LINCOLN COUNTY, NEVADA.

Clover L L Wood,
Panacca, Luke Syphus
County Seat

Salt Lake Herald
January 22, 1876

The Storm.

The snow storm which set in about midnight on Thursday, was one of the heaviest that has occurred in this valley for years. Yesterday morning the snow, on the level, was thirteen inches in depth. The storm, we learn by telegraph, was pretty general throughout the territory. The Deseret line reported the depth of snow at different points, as follows: Paris, 18 inches; Logan, 20 in.; Brigham city, 12 in.; Ogden, 6 in.; Alta, 14 feet; Bingham, 5 in.; American Fork, 5 in.; Provo, 5 in.; Nephi, 12 in.; Manti, 3 in.; Fillmore, 5 in.; Beaver, 5 in.; Hebron, 2 inches and still snowing.

Deseret News
January 26, 1876

Our Mail Facilities.

LEVAN, Jan. 8th, 1876.

Editor Deseret News:

Last spring this place was published in the mail route from Salt Lake to Pioche to receive a daily mail, which we need very bad. Well, the stages ran through here about six months, and then Hugh White moved his station down to his quarter section, below this place, about three miles west, and since then we have had no regular mail to depend upon. That is the reason we do not get our papers regularly. Our mail is sorted out at Nephi and brought to us sometimes, and when a letter goes from here it has to stop at Salt Creek, and the same way with the north mail.

Yours, &c.,

OBSERVER.

Salt Lake Herald
January 29, 1876

JUAB COUNTY.

The People Object to Dividing their County with Utah—Cold Weather Killing Stock.

NEPHI, JUAB COUNTY,
January 27th, 1876.

Editors Herald:

We were much surprised yesterday by hearing a rumor that a mammoth petition had been presented to the legislative assembly from the counties of Salt Lake, Weber, Davis, Summit, Wasatch, Sanpete, Juab and Millard, asking that the aforesaid counties be immediately attached to Utah county, the grand head centre to be at Provo. We waited anxiously for the HERALD, and felt much relieved to learn that our kind neighbors, without the permission of Wasatch and Juab, had petitioned for a portion of our little possessions. Have the citizens of Utah county, in the day of their prosperity, become greedy, that they want to rob their poor neighbors; or is this the invention of some member of the assembly, as a bid for his re-election? If the petition had originated from the citizens of Wasatch and Juab we should have liked its appearance much better. Several years ago a portion of Utah county thought it to their interest to petition the legislative assembly of Utah to attach them to Juab county. This petition was not granted even when it came from the people themselves, and we cannot believe for a moment that the petition of Utah county will be given a favorable consideration, or there would be a strong remonstrance sent from Juab. Perhaps our kind neighbors want a portion of our county for a sheep pasture or herd ground. If this is their object, the lines need not be changed, for we have for years fed their flocks and herds. But enough on this subject, as our friends must be only joking.

The winter is extremely severe. The snow being unusually deep, our stock are in a critical situation. Hay is scarce, and what to do to save the cattle, horses and sheep is the question of the day. Report says that our sheep are dying at the rate of twenty-five a day. If the weather does not moderate immediately a large amount of stock will be lost.

The Nephi dramatic troupe gave a performance last evening, and made lots of fun, if it was "home made."

On Friday evening the Nephi Young Men's Mutual Improvement association will give a grand social party in the Social hall, as a compliment to those going from Juab county on the Arizona mission. We expect a pleasant time.

A CITIZEN OF JUAB COUNTY.

Salt Lake Tribune
February 24, 1876

That County Convention.

EDS. TRIBUNE: Pursuant to notice, the Republicans of Juab county assembled at the school house in Nephi on the 16th of February, for the purpose of electing delegates to the Territorial Republican Convention to be held at Salt Lake City.

The meeting was organized by placing Alma Hague in the chair and N. E. Britt, secretary.

Mr. B. Bachman, of Provo, being called upon to address the meeting, stated its object in a few appropriate remarks, after which the following named gentlemen were elected delegates: W. G. Seely and Alma Hague. The meeting was well attended, good feeling prevailing throughout.   N. E BRITT,
                    Secretary.

NEPHI, Feb. 22, 1876.

Deseret News
May 10, 1876

Returned Missionaries. — Elder W. A. C. Bryan, of Nephi, called this morning. He left Utah about a year ago on a mission to England, and left Liverpool on his return April 12, arriving in this city on Tuesday evening. Elders Arnold Goodliffe, of Malad, and Shadrach Empey, of Lehi, missionaries, returned with him. They all left England sooner than they had expected, in consequence of poor health while there. On the journey home the health of all improved considerably,

Elder Bryan labored in the Not-tingham Conference while on his mission. He reports good prospects in the mission, better than for many years past.

Salt Lake Tribune
June 21, 1876

JUAB COUNTY.

A Look Among the Brethren—New Mexican Colonization—A Brute Living His Hoggish Religion.

Correspondence Tribune.]

Provo, June 20, 1876.

Having occasion to visit our brethren in Juab county, we took some note of passing events. Near Nephi we had verified the assertion of THE TRIBUNE, that the Saints have intended to colonize New Mexico. A number of families are making preparations to migrate at an early day to the promised land. The settlement is to be made near the Rio Jo Chico. The proposed migrators confidently assert that they can control the politics of that Territory by the numbers who are now contemplating the hegira, and absolutely mould the destiny of that hybrid country. The flocks, herds, and female appendages under lechery, are to take up their line of march in the early fall months, so that they can reach their new Zion in time for early planting. The Prophet talks of having his dupes who start from Europe late in the season, come by way of New Orleans, and from thence go direct to New Mexico, where old Enoch will appear and reign in his glory.

LIVING HIS RELIGION.

A shyster of Salt Creek by the name of Wm. May, has lately been at Salt Lake to be sealed to two of Brother Pitchforth's daughters. The sealing took place, and May is now basking in the caresses of his harem mistresses. He tries to keep secret his alliances, but the public are fully advised of his having been sealed. This criminal appears as prosecutor in the courts of Juab.

Surprise was expressed to us by a number of citizens that no effort is ever made to indict the murderers of the Aiken party. Witnesses of the assassination are said to be easily obtainable. The old man Foote yet has, or lately had, the pistols he took from the murdered men.

THE CROPS

of this county are looking well and promise to yield richly to the husbandman. The mountain streams are affording abundant water.

The Nebo mines are being prospected with flattering indications. The ores are low grade galena, but we are of opinion that the yield will be in large quantities after a time.

FACE TUA

The Sanpete Mail.

EPHRAIM, SANPETE Co., }
July 27th, 1876. }

Editors Herald:

Day before yesterday the thing called a mail did not reach here until after dark. I asked the postmaster why the mail was so late? He replied, "They could not catch their horses." Yesterday was just the same—after dark—before the mail arrived. In the morning I repeated the question, and the answer was, "One horse was sick." I concluded that the horse had something to eat the day before and it made him sick. I went to the office to-day and asked for my mail matter. The reply was, "There was no Salt Lake mail, as the driver did not go any further than Fountain Green"—fourteen miles from Nephi, his destination! In the latter part of the winter we had a mail once in a while, and the delay, most of the time, was just simply because the teams were so poor they could not travel: in fact, they were the poorest brutes I ever saw hitched to a wagon.

I can give no reason why the present contractor persists in keeping such poor teams and rickety wagons or carriages, or whatever he may call them—for I must confess that I do not know what name to give them—upon the mail line from Nephi to Manti, but of one thing I am certain, it is an imposition upon the residents of this county. The people of this county must be deprived of all their mail matter because an old crow bait of a horse gives out, or an old clap-trap of a wagon breaks down. I have lived in this county for twenty years, but have not seen such an outfit for carrying the mail as the present contractor indulges in keeping upon the line. I would not like to do anything that would injure the contractor, but I do not believe he is doing as well as he should do, or as well as he can in the matter.
A.

Go and Do Likewise.

Edwin Booth subscribed for the HERALD yesterday. He resides in Nephi, and is not the great tragedian.

The Larson Case.—We have received a communication, signed by about sixty residents of Nephi, affirming, from their knowledge and belief, that the late Ephraim Larson had a good reputation for industry, truthfulness, sobriety, etc.

As the case connected with the death of Larson is now in the hands of the courts, and in the course of its adjudication all the pertinent facts pertaining thereto may be expected to be presented, it does not appear to be judicious to encourage a discussional investigation of the merits of the same through the newspapers, and thus forestall the action of the courts therein.

Correspondence.

COUNTY CONVENTIONS.

JUAB.

On the 29th of Sept., 1876, a People's County Convention for Juab County was held in Nephi, for the purpose of electing three delegates and three alternates to represent said county in the People's Territorial Convention, to be held in Salt Lake City, October 7th, 1876, to nominate a candidate for delegate to Congress.

On motion Mr. Wm. Knight was elected temporary president, and Mr. Thos. Ord temporary secretary.

Messrs. Charles Sperry and Charles Foot were appointed a committee on credentials, and reported the following named gentlemen entitled to seats, to wit, from Nephi precinct, William Knight, Charles H. Bryan, Thomas Ord, John Andrews, Charles Foote, Charles Sperry and Jacob G. Bigler, senr.; Mona precinct, John M. Haws, William Somerville; Levan precinct, Seth Ollerton, C. F. B. Lybbert.

W. Knight was elected permanent president and Thomas Ord secretary.

On separate motions the following named gentlemen were duly elected delegates—J. Grover, J. M. Haws, C. Foote; Alternates, Elmer Tayler, John Pyper, Thomas Midgley.

The following were passed—

"Resolved, That the Hon. George Q. Cannon, having proved himself the true friend of the people of Utah Territory, it is the sense of this Convention that the delegates from this county vote for that gentleman as a candidate for Delegate to Congress, subject to the vote of the Territorial Convention.

"Resolved, That Messrs. J. Grover, C. Foote, W. Knight, Thomas Ord and Edwin Harley be a central committee on elections for this county, for two years and until their successors are elected.

"Resolved, "That a synopsis of the proceedings of this Convention be sent to the DESERET NEWS and Salt Lake Herald offices for publication.

WILLIAM KNIGHT,
President of Convention.
THOMAS ORD, Secretary.

Salt Lake Herald
October 18, 1876

Sudden Death.

Miss Catherine Pyper, daughter of John Pyper of Nephi, died suddenly at the residence of her uncle, Judge A. C. Pyper, yesterday. Deceased was an interesting young lady, 20 years of age. She was residing temporarily in the family of her uncle, and being afflicted with what was supposed to be only a cold, the doctor was called in, and prescribed for her, but without beneficial results, as she retired to bed, and soon was asleep in death. We sympathize with the family and friends in their great loss.

Salt Lake Herald
October 21, 1876

The Sanpete Mail.

Leonard I. Smith, who carries the mail from Nephi, through Sanpete, into Richfield, Sevier county, says the complaints on that route cannot be attributed to him, the fault, if any, lying in the postoffices. He asserts that the mail is carried regularly according to schedule time, except on occasions of a breakdown, when he may be hindered an hour or so. We hope Mr. Smith is correct in this matter, but if he is his stock gets a good deal of hard "cussing" to which it is not entitled.

Special Deputies.

United States Marshals and their deputies are conservators of the peace on the 7th day of November. At the polls in the Fifth precinct, the police have pursued a bullying course towards non-Mormons on election days. Two years ago Gen. Maxwell, the United States Marshal, appointed a force of deputies to stop this, and the result was a collision between them and the police. But we understand, because the appointment of the deputies was irregular, nothing could be done with the police, who were the assaulting parties, and obstructed the Marshals in the performance of their duties. The law requires the Marshal to appoint his special deputies several days before the election, and to this end would it not be advisable for the central committee to wait upon Marshal Nelson as soon as he arrives in the city? Special deputies are needed at Ogden, Logan, Salt Lake, Nephi and other places.

NEPHI.

Who Has a Right to Vote in Utah.

EDS. TRIBUNE: I trust a few questions on the important matter of the election may not be regarded as untimely. There are many here who have a just right to vote, but do not for good reasons; they know that the ballot-box in the hands of the Mormons is a fraud from past experience. The votes of outsiders may be cast, and as the same are numbered, and of course the ungodly Outsiders and Apostates are known, as their ballot is taken by a Mormon priest and receives the *mark* of the *beast*. The first question is, what becomes of his vote? Second, Is it cast into "otter darkness?" Third, Can a resident of one settlement, while necessarily away from home, cast his vote in any other place where election day may find him? Fourth, Have the legal wives of the ungodly outsiders a right to vote at the coming election?

There should be some trusty person appointed to take charge of such votes on election day, and, a true report obtained, or many persons will not vote, for they say among themselves, what is the use of voting? It is a positive fact, that if the Liberals of Juab county would make an entire turnout and vote, their number would exceed the legal vote of the priesthood. Of course this does not include the votes of the concubines, as they might rule Zion if they would turn out to a unit.

Brigham says if he and his people go to hell they will make a heaven of it. Question: Will it not be a hell of a heaven? It will be just such a heaven as Brig will make for Gentiles, Apostates, Liberals, miners and all, if Utah becomes a State. Let every Liberal in Utah vote.

LIBERAL.

Salt Lake Tribune
November 7, 1876

NEPHI LIBERALS.

The Cause Strengthened by the Voice of Freemen.

Ed. Tribune! The 'Liberals' of Nephi were treated to a meeting last evening, the first of the kind ever held in the town. It was called to order by Mr. W. G. Sealy, and Mr. Alma Hayne was elected to the chair, with M. P. Bulger secretary.

A. G. Sutherland, Esq., of Tintic, was first introduced, and proceeded to deliver an interesting address on the rights of the people to choose for themselves a representative to Congress.

General Maxwell made a few brief remarks on the issues of the canvass, and declared the right of every man to free speech, free ballot, free schools and the enjoyment of American principles.

Rev. W. Carver was called for and held forth for half an hour on the history of different nations, showing that the union of Church and State never had been a success and never could be.

The meeting then adjourned, every one concurring that the Liberal cause in Nephi had been greatly strengthened by the voices of freemen.

M. P. BULGER.

Salt Lake Herald
November 8, 1876

The Election.

The election for delegate to congress from this territory, passed off quietly yesterday. So far as reported not the slightest disturbance occurred. In Salt Lake not a solitary arrest was made. Less drunkenness and disorder were observed than on an ordinary occasion. The supervisors and judges worked together harmoniously, and the deputy United States marshals deported themselves most gentlemanly, receiving the commendation of all parties. The marshal had appointed a different class of men to do this duty at the polls than those who officiated two years ago. It is a matter of congratulation that the election was harmonious. The vote was not large, Salt Lake polling only 4,085. However, there was less illegal voting than usual. As regards this city, with trifling exceptions, those who were not clearly entitled to vote did not make the attempt. Both parties exerted themselves to get people to the polls. Following are the returns of the city, and other parts of the territory, so far as heard from:

SALT LAKE CITY.
First Precinct.

SALT LAKE CITY.
First Precinct.

Cannon	580	Baskin		136

Second Precinct.

Cannon	832	Baskin		305

Third Precinct.

Cannon	706	Baskin		44
C. W. Bennett	2			

Fourth Precinct.

Cannon	413	Baskin		26

Fifth Precinct.

Cannon	633	Baskin		406

Total	3,164	Total		917
C. W. Bennett	2			
Cannon's majority				2,237

SUGAR HOUSE PRECINCT.

Cannon	152	Baskin		6

Cannon's majority, 146.

BIG COTTONWOOD PRECINCT.

Cannon	126	Pat Lannan		1

Cannon's majority, 125.

DRAPER PRECINCT.

Cannon	122	Baskin		3

Cannon's majority, 119.

BRIGHTON PRECINCT.

Cannon	23	Baskin		0

(Special Telegrams.)

BRAVE LITTLE SANDY.

Sandy, 7.—The election passed off very quietly. There was no disturbance and no bad feeling existed. This precinct polled 114 votes, giving Geo. Q. Cannon a small majority.

WHERE DID BINGHAM FIND THEM?

Bingham, 7.—The election was unusually quiet. There was considerable illegal voting on the part of the "liberals." Baskin received 470 votes; George Q. Cannon, 6.

NEPHI INCREASES CANNON'S MAJORITY.

Nephi, 7.—There was no disturbance at the election to-day. Number of votes polled in Nephi precinct, 363, of which 340 were for George Q. Cannon. Juab county will give Mr. Cannon a handsome majority.

Salt Lake Tribune
November 11, 1876

NEPHI ELECTION.

How the Priesthood Prevent Liberals from Voting.

Eds. Tribune: I wish to inform the Liberals of Utah through your paper, of some of the tricks of the priesthood to bar Gentiles from voting. In this place, at the peep of day, every one in the place was awakened by the thundering of blacksmith anvils, and the tooting of horns, and at sunrise the streets were alive with the serfs of Brigham. Wagons were running to and fro gathering up the Female Roosters, the drivers being very careful to avoid all houses where the occupants were supposed to be Liberals. At noon I wended my way to the place of voting, in company with another ungodly cuss, to do our mite toward free speech, free schools and free ballots in Utah. Arriving there, we found the judge sitting at a table with the precious box on one side of him and a whiskey bottle on the other side. I proceeded to fold my ballot and hand it to the judge, when I was accosted by a foreigner, with a wart on his right eye, and murder in the left.

Said he, "Are you a local voter?"

"I suppose so; was born in the United States, twenty-seven years ago, and have managed to steer clear of the Penitentiary and Mountain Meadows."

"But, haf you paid taxes?"

"No; but I have been assessed by the assessor."

To the Judge: "Yoost you look on dose book and see if he have got his name."

At this suggestion, the Judge went for his pocket and drew out a book After looking through it he decided my name was not in the book. Consequently I could not vote.

The Judge goes to the polls armed with a memorandum book containing the names of all the tax-payers in his precinct; but in making out the list he is careful to leave out the names of Liberal tax-payers; and when a Liberal steps up to vote, he is stopped by some officious elder, who inquires as to his tax. The Gentile says he is a tax-payer; the Judge looks for his name, and as a matter of course does not find it. The Judge quietly tells him he cannot vote unless he finds the assessor, and gets a certificate that he is a tax-payer. Mr. Gentile takes a walk to find the assessor, congratulating himself that he will yet outwit the elder.

But O, ye innocent Babylonians, if you but knew that the assessor had been too well drilled to be caught in such a trap, you would have remained at home, meditating the probable result of the election. The assessor cannot be found; you go to his house, and you are informed that he is at his office; you depart for his office. Arriving there you are informed that Mr. Assessor is down at the sorghum mill, three or four miles away. On going there, you find he has not been there for a month.

On returning to the polls, I found the foreign elder aforesaid interrogating Mr. Wm. Leverich, an ungodly Gentile, as to his right to vote. Mr. Leverich is a native born citizen, has been paying taxes for the last thirty years, has taxable property now in Utah to the amount of thousands of dollars, but owing to the negligence of the assessor, it has not been assessed, and Mr. Leverich loses his rights as an American citizen.

A Mormon was allowed to vote, who never owned a single cent's worth of property in his life, and never was assessed or taxed for anything.

Last evening I interviewed him as to his voting. He said he had voted, but did not know whom he voted for. I suggested the name of Perkins. "Yes," he said, "that was the name of the man I voted for;" and when asked what office the man was aspiring to, he said he did not know. I suggested the Supreme Judge of the United States. "Yes," said he, "that's the office." All he knew about it was, that Brother Knight gave him a big ticket and he voted it.

After refusing to let Mr. Leverich vote, they called on him for his taxes. Mr. L. informed them that they would find his taxes at the office, or saw mill.

These are facts, and can be proven beyond controversy.

Twenty-three white votes for Baskin were cast here.

M. P. Buroer.

Nephi, Utah, Nov. 8, 1876.

Deseret News
November 15, 1876

NEPHI.

Nephi, 7.—There was no disturbance at the election to-day. Number of votes polled in Nephi precinct, 363, of which 340 were for George Q. Cannon. Juab county will give Mr. Cannon a handsome majority.

Salt Lake Herald
November 19, 1876

The HERALD is looked for very anxiously every day, as it gives us so many more hours later news than an evening paper. To the credit of Leonard I. Smith it must be said, although his team, wagon and general outfit for carrying mails are not of the Gilmer & Salisbury touch, yet he arrives at this postoffice pretty punctual. I believe his arrivals and departures are right. If so, no just cause of complaint can lodge. However, from positive knowledge some causes of serious complaint in connection with York terminus to Nephi could be made to stick against the great southern route, which seriously affect our newspapers, etc., being duly received.

D. C.

Salt Lake Tribune
December 8, 1876

NEPHI.

Our Carrot Crop—Rounding Up the
Sisters on the Famine Corner—A New Bishop.

Correspondence Tribune.]

Nephi, Dec. 3, 1876.

Believing it to be the duty of every good citizen to keep the public acquainted with the doings of the brethren in all parts of the Territory, and as I live in a place where we produce more Saints for the amount of honesty than can be found in any other part of the Prophet's dominions, I consider it my duty to bear my testimony to the work of these Latter-days.

The Methodists are erecting a church and school house at this place, and will have it ready for use by the first of the year.

OUR CROPS.

Our grain is threshed and garnered. The crop was light, owing to the stiff-neckedness of the people in refusing to join the Holy Order, but the carrot crop is unusually large, which is being hoed up to meet the contingency of God's universal corner on wheat, which is now beginning.

ROUND DANCING

is receiving a good deal of attention at present. The young men of this place had a party the other night, and were enjoying themselves nicely, when the Bishop made his appearance and ordered them to go home or he would cut them off the church. But somehow the cutting process has no terrors for the boys now, and on went the dance and out went the Bishop just in time to avoid being dropped off the toe of II—a Fifteenth Amendment. The boys were about to have the Bishop arrested for disturbing a public gathering, but learning that he and his counselors are a little "off," concluded to let the matter drop this time, they agreeing not to molest the dancing any more.

TEMPLE.

They preach a great deal here about a Temple to be built at Manti, in San Pete. They say that if every one would bring a stone apiece, the Temple could be built immediately, but no one is willing to cast the first stone.

THE FAMINE.

There has been a Female Rooster by the name of Horne, through the settlements, preaching God's corner on wheat and the "famine," exhorting all to save their grain and deposit with the Lord's anointed until a bushel of grain will bring a bushel of gold. She also wanted the Sisters to donate for the purpose of publishing the Lives of Mormon Women. She said that the outside world seemed to take a great interest in everything that was written against polygamy, and she thought they would take the same interest in reading the facts in relation to the lives of those women who were happy in the practice of it. In one of the settlements, a lady suggested that the true lives of the Sisters in polygamy might be a serious blow to the "Divine" ordinance. Whereupon Sister Horne waxed warm and declared that the women of Utah had lives, and 'good lives' at that, and the world wanted to know it. Quite a discussion followed on the probability of Mormon women having lives, some contended that they were only here for the benefit of man, and their lives would only commence when they left this tabernacle and because-quisons in the next world. Sister Horne insisted that if they would only donate the sum of $3,000, she would prove to them that they had lives, to which proposition she clung as close as a polygamous wife to the saving power of a Mormon elder.

STARS IN HIS CROWN.

C. Christensen of Levan, the man who built his house on the grave of an emigrant child, is elected bishop of that place, in the place of E. Taylor, and of him I must now speak. There having been some mutinous language used by the women of Levan in relation to the unclean practice, Bishop Christensen attempts to show the distressed sisters that the men suffer alike with the women, and he speaketh truly:

Ve know dot de sisters in boligamy haves a arde dime, but der vomens mit der varied haves a arder dime, bekaus de mens are arder day snot get der have of der older in Zion, yaw we dot by der reason dot day dont vant to dake do vemens to der preat unt own der obilder; but sisters der mens of Got have a arde dime doo, I dell you vot a ard dime I ave ad in boligamy, I dakes doo vomens de mine preat vone dime, vone of dem vash oldt vomen, dot oldt voman got some litte broperty, I tinke dot oldt voman con't live moren as von year; de oder voman is a Yank voman. I tink dat Yank voman makes a goot many stars unt the grown of mine glory.

Vel I laves dot youngt vomen, but she don't got me no stars, unt she tie in von year, unt dot oldt voman live fifteen years. No sisters don't dot druble in boligamy, tho a slers seems to be convinced and they intend to round up and beat tho cross. Yours truly,   I. C. ALL.

Salt Lake Herald
December 8, 1876

PERSONAL.

Mr. S. W. Sears has got back from San Francisco.

Mr. John Hague, one of the solid men of Nephi, is in town.

Sheriff Hinton of Evanston came down on last night's train.

Mr. Charles Smith, agent and correspondent of the Omaha Republican, made us a fraternal visit yesterday.

Hon. Barbour Lewis of Tennessee, the recently appointed register of the land office in this city, is *en route* for this place, and is daily expected to arrive.

Captain G. S. Carpenter, 14th infantry, who has been stationed at Medicine Bow for some weeks, arrived last night, to make preparations for removing to one of the frontier forts for the winter.

Salt Lake Tribune
November 11, 1876

NEPHI ELECTION.

How the Priesthood Prevent Liberals from Voting.

Eds. Tribune: I wish to inform the Liberals of Utah through your paper, of some of the tricks of the priesthood to bar Gentiles from voting. In this place, at the peep of day, every one in the place was awakened by the thundering of blacksmith anvils, and the tooting of horns, and at sunrise the streets were alive with the serfs of Brigham. Wagons were running to and fro gathering up the Female Roosters, the drivers being very careful to avoid all houses where the occupants were supposed to be Liberals. At noon I wended my way to the place of voting, in company with another ungodly cuss, to do our mite toward free speech, free schools and free ballots in Utah. Arriving there, we found the judge sitting at a table with the precious box on one side of him and a whiskey bottle on the other side. I proceeded to fold my ballot and hand it to the judge, when I was accosted by a foreigner, with a wart on his right eye, and murder in the left.

Said he, "Are you a legal voter?"

"I suppose so; was born in the United States, twenty-seven years ago, and have managed to steer clear of the Penitentiary and Mountain Meadows."

"But, haf you paid taxes?"

"No; but I have been assessed by the assessor."

To the Judge: "Yoost you look on dose book and see if he haf got his name."

At this suggestion, the Judge went for his pocket and drew out a book. After looking through it he decided my name was not in the book. Consequently I could not vote.

The Judge goes to the polls armed with a memorandum book containing the names of all the tax-payers in his precinct; but in making out the list he is careful to leave out the names of Liberal tax-payers; and when a Liberal steps up to vote, he is stopped by some officious elder, who inquires as to his tax. The Gentile says he is a tax-payer; the Judge looks for his name, and as a matter of course does not find it. The Judge quietly tells him he cannot vote unless he finds the assessor, and gets a certificate that he is a tax-payer. Mr. Gentile takes a walk to find the assessor, congratulating himself that he will yet outwit the elder.

But O, ye innocent Babylonians, if you but knew that the assessor had been too well drilled to be caught in such a trap, you would have remained at home, meditating the probable result of the election. The assessor cannot be found; you go to his house, and you are informed that he is at his office; you depart for his office. Arriving there you are informed that Mr. Assessor is down at the sorghum mill, three or four miles away. On going there, you find he has not been there for a month.

On returning to the polls, I found the foreign elder aforesaid interrogating Mr. Wm. Leverich, an ungodly Gentile, as to his right to vote. Mr. Leverich is a native born citizen, has been paying taxes for the last thirty years, has taxable property now in Utah to the amount of thousands of dollars, but owing to the negligence of the assessor, it has not been assessed, and Mr. Leverich loses his rights as an American citizen.

A Mormon was allowed to vote, who never owned a single cent's worth of property in his life, and never was assessed or taxed for anything.

Last evening I interviewed him as to his voting. He said he had voted, but did not know whom he voted for. I suggested the name of Perkins. "Yes," he said, "that was the name of the man I voted for;" and when asked what office the man was aspiring to, he said he did not know. I suggested the Supreme Judge of the United States. "Yes," said he, "that's the office." All he knew about it was, that Brother Knight gave him a big ticket and he voted it.

After refusing to let Mr. Leverich vote, they called on him for his taxes. Mr. L. informed them that they would find his taxes at the office, or saw mill.

These are facts, and can be proven beyond controversy.

Twenty-three white votes for Baskin were cast here.

M. P. Buider.

Nephi, Utah, Nov. 8, 1870.

Deseret News
November 15, 1876

NEPHI.

Nephi, 7.—There was no disturbance at the election to-day. Number of votes polled in Nephi precinct, 363, of which 340 were for George Q. Cannon. Juab county will give Mr. Cannon a handsome majority.

Salt Lake Tribune
December 8, 1876

NEPHI.

Our Carrot Crop—Rounding Up the Sisters on the Famine Corner—A New Bishop

Correspondence Tribune.]

Nephi, Dec. 3, 1876.

Believing it to be the duty of every good citizen to keep the public acquainted with the doings of the brethren in all parts of the Territory, and as I live in a place where we produce more Saints for the amount of honesty than can be found in any other part of the Prophet's dominions, I consider it my duty to bear my testimony to the work of these Latter-days.

The Methodists are erecting a church and school house at this place, and will have it ready for use by the first of the year.

OUR CROPS.

Our grain is threshed and garnered. The crop was light, owing to the stiff-neckedness of the people in refusing to join the Holy Order, but the carrot crop is unusually large, which is being holed up to meet the contingency of God's universal corner on wheat, which is now beginning.

ROUND DANCING

is receiving a good deal of attention at present. The young men of this place had a party the other night, and were enjoying themselves nicely, when the Bishop made his appearance and ordered them to go home or he would cut them off the church. But somehow the cutting process has no terrors for the boys now, and on went the dance and out went the Bishop just in time to avoid being dropped off the toe of H—a Fifteenth Amendment. The boys were about to have the Bishop arrested for disturbing a public gathering, but learning that he and his counselors are a little "off," concluded to let the matter drop this time, they agreeing not to molest the dancing any more.

TEMPLE.

They preach a great deal here about a Temple to be built at Manti, in San Pete. They say that if every one would bring a stone apiece, the Temple could be built immediately, but no one is willing to cast the first stone.

THE FAMINE.

There has been a Female Rooster by the name of Horne, through the settlements, preaching God's corner on wheat and the "famine," exhorting all to save their grain and deposit with the Lord's anointed until a bushel of grain will bring a bushel of gold. She also wanted the Sisters to donate for the purpose of publishing the Lives of Mormon Women. She said that the outside world seemed to take a great interest in everything that was written against polygamy, and she thought they would take the same interest in reading the facts in relation to the lives of those women who were happy in the practice of it. In one of the settlements, a lady suggested that the true lives of the Sisters in polygamy might be a serious blow to the "Divine" ordinance. Whereupon Sister Horne waxed warm and declared that the women of Utah had lives, and good lives at that, and the world wanted to know it. Quite a discussion followed on the probability of Mormon women having lives, some contended that they were only here for the benefit of man, and their lives would only commence when they left this tabernacle and became queens in the next world. Sister Horne insisted that if they would only donate the sum of $3,000, she would prove to them that they had lives, to which proposition she clung as close as a polygamous wife to the saying power of a Mormon elder.

STARS IN HIS CROWN.

C. Christensen of Levan, the man who built his house on the grave of an emigrant child, is elected bishop of that place, in the place of E. Taylor, and of him I must now speak. There having been some mutinous language used by the women of Levan in relation to the unclean practice, Bishop Christensen attempts to show the distressed sisters that the men suffer alike with the women, and he speaketh truly:

Ve know dot de sisters in bolygamy haves a arde dime, but der vomans mit der varied haves a arder dime, bekause de mens are arder day haent gat der have of der older in Zion, yow we dot by der reason dot day dont vant to dake de vomens to der prest unt own der obilder; but sisters der mens of Got have a arde dime doo, I dell you 'vot a ard dime I ave ad in boligamy, I dakes doo vomens de mine prest vone dime, I go a dunder voman dot dime, vone of dem vash oldt voman, dot oldt voman got some litle broperty, I tinke dot oldt voman con't live mores as von year; de oder voman is a Yank voman, I tink dat Yank voman makes a goot many stars unt the growa of mine olory.

Vel I loves dot youngt vomen, but she don't got me no stars, unt she tie in von year, unt dot oldt voman live fifteen years. No sisters don't dot druble in boligamy, the sisters seems to be convinced and they intend to round up and bear the cross. Yours truly,   I. C. ALL.

Cattle Stealing and Recovery.

Mr. John Paul, of Salt Lake City, had quite an adventure, in driving Mr. Jennings' cattle from Salina to Salt Lake City last week. On Friday he arrived at Nephi with fifty-three head of cattle, of pure Devon and Durham breeds, in the best possible condition for the eye of the butcher and the palate of the epicure. As he was putting them in a corral in Nephi, remarks were made by a couple of men of noted character that they would have some of the herd, before it left that place. Mr. Paul was informed of the remarks, and advised to guard his cattle all night, which he did until about four o'clock in the morning, as well as having the gate locked. At daybreak he returned to the corral, and there discovered that during his short absence the whole herd, except two or three, were driven away and were out of sight. Mr. Paul sent his men out north, south, east and west in search but without effect. He had the two men arrested that had expressed themselves so covetously about the cattle, and tried before a justice of the peace. They acknowledged saying as stated, but denied the robbery, and there being no evidence sufficient to hold them, they were released. Search was again made, but no tracks or clue could be found, although a large corral some miles west from Nephi, in a secure and secluded position, was discovered, which evidently was made and used for keeping cattle under such circumstances. It is well understood that there is a gang of thieves in that vicinity, well acquainted with every resource and resort to make these raids successful. As one of the herdsmen was looking around, an individual approached him, and stated that he thought he could find the cattle, and if he would give him $20 he could find twenty or thirty head. Mr. Paul was informed of the proposition, and visited the party, but told him that no $20 would be forthcoming, but if the animals were not returned soon he would not be overlooked. Next morning, about three miles from Nephi, the whole number save one were found, and they appeared to have been driven hard and pretty far, as they were in a lather of sweat. They were then taken to their place of destination, passing through Provo on Thursday morning, and fine specimens of cattle they were.—*Provo Enquirer, Dec. 16th.*

Deseret News
January 17, 1877

ESTRAY NOTICE.

I HAVE in my possession:

One blue STEER, about four or five years old, underslope in left ear, crop and underbit in right. No brands visible.

One red and white spotted five or six year old COW, brand resembling ∩ on left hip, 6 on right shoulder, also on right ribs.

One red and white COW, three or four years old, branded (暴) on left side of body, brand resembling)—C on left hip, slit and upperbit in left ear, underbit and bit out of end of right.

If the above described animals are not claimed they will be sold on Saturday, Jan. 20th, 1877, at 1 p.m., at my corral.

L. A. BAILEY,
District Poundkeeper,

Nephi, Jan. 16, 1877. d&w

Salt Lake Tribune
January 20, 1877

BEAVER.

Scattered Items Along the Southern Line—How Prospers This People

Correspondence Tribune.]

BEAVER, Jan. 15, 1877.

Thinking that you may be pleased to hear of the doings in Southern Zion, I write a few items that have fallen under my observation on my way to the Southern Temple.

At Springville Saints and Sinners were recovering from their New Year's war. The battle was drawn and the police were repairing injured mansoles. The fight will be renewed at the next general holiday.

I found Santaquin encased in ice, waiting for Enoch's bugle.

Times at Nephi are very dull. McCune's tangle foot is so nearly exhausted, that the boys no more break in to steal. They now steal anvils and vices. A town is hard up indeed, when nothing better than an anvil or a vice is available to thieves. One of May's two-ply has presented the overjoyed parient with a child.

Old Enoch died at Round Valley, about four weeks ago. His funeral was thinly attended. His coffin was of the simplest kind, the boards were native and knotty. The old man's limited estate has been administered on by the priests and undertakers. There will be little, if any property, to go to the heirs after paying the debts. The orphans are left in an unfeeling world, penoi less, to rustle for grub. It would be a blessing if they could be called to rest with their father.

Fillmore is quiet in bus'ness, but on the quivive for the advent of Methodism. Brother Carver has sent his advance sheet notifying the people of his coming. Like historic Nasby, good old Henry is in trouble. He has been superseded in his post office. The government is ungrateful to this faithful servant. He has faithfully served Zion as postmaster for nine long years, and now, in his old age, is rewarded with dismissal. Republics were always ungrateful.

A snow storm caught me at Cove Creek, so did Bishop Thurber of Legislative renown. The Bishop is on his way to worship at the Temple.

Beaver is quietly contemplating the snow.

Jack Gilmer is regulating his stage line between here and Leeds.

JAMES.

Correspondence.

A Woman Lost, and Found Dead.

NEPHI, Jan. 19th, 1877.

Editor Deseret News:

A sad gloom came over the inhabitants of this place on Sunday, 14th instant, on hearing that Sister Elizabeth Betts was missing. She was inquired for all over the settlement. A party started that night in search of her. Some snow had fallen during the day. They returned without any success. Men were out on horseback and foot every day until Thursday, the 18th, when Wm. Gace, who had been hunting his horses, found her dead. He made signs to the hunters, who were not far away, and they soon reached the spot. A team and sleigh were in the company, and she was conveyed to her son-in-law's, D. Broadhead's. A man rode into town and t. ld the news. The School-house bell rang and some shots were fired off to let the hunters and inhabitants know she was found.

The deceased was born in Staffordshire, England, in 1807. She emigrated to this Territory seven years ago. Sister Betts has been in a delirious state of mind for some time past. On Saturday morning she told her husband she would take a walk out for her health. She called on her two daughters and said she was going north to Brother Ringrose's, an acquaintance of hers. Reaching there she took dinner. He gave her some butter and meat. She returned as if going home, but she was seen about four p. m. going in a south-east direction towards the mountains. She traveled until she come to Cedar Point, a little over two miles south of this place. She broke off some small cedar limbs, put them in her sack, and no doubt became weary and cold, and fell asleep and expired. Her butter and meat fell out of her sack and lay under her head. No birds or beast had molested her during the five days. She was a woman of large stature, had fifteen children, some living in England, some in the States, and her husband and two daughters living here. She was a kind mother and a good wife, and lived the life of a Saint. Her daughters are good citizens and have large families, all of whom feel grieved at the way she came to her end.

L. A. BAILEY.

At Nephi City, January 5, 1877, of Bright's disease of the kidneys, WILLIAM M. EVANS, aged 51 years and 10 months.

Elder Evans was born in Liverpool, England, March 12, 1825; was baptized into the Church of Jesus Christ of Latter-day Saints, November 28th, 1841; was ordained to the office of a teacher, January, 1842; was a member of the choir in Liverpool until May, 1848, at which time he emigrated to New York; from there he worked his way west, arriving at Kanesville in June, 1850; left there in 1851 for Salt Lake City, arriving in the fall of the same year. Soon afterwards he was ordained a member of the 29th Quorum of Seventies. In 1853 he went to Nephi and became a member of the choir; was afterwards appointed leader of the same, which position he has held for over twenty years; was ordained to the High Priests' Quorum and became a member of the High Council of that stake of Zion in 1869. At the October Conference, 1875, was called on a mission to England, where he was traveling Elder in the Liverpool Conference, and subsequently President of the Bristol Conference, until released to come home, arriving with the last company of Saints, Nov. 12th 1876.

His funeral took place on Sunday, January 7th, his remains being carried from his late residence to the Meeting-house by the members of the High Council, the Nephi brass band, of which he was a member, playing a funeral march. The large Meeting-house was filled to overflowing, and his remains were followed to the cemetery by a large concourse of citizens, over seventy teams being in the cortege. While his remains were being deposited in the grave the choir sang a favorite hymn. On his death-bed he bore a strong and faithful testimony to the truth of the principles of the gospel of Christ, in which he died in full faith.

He leaves a wife and nine children and numerous relatives and friends to mourn his loss.—[Com.

Millennial Star, please copy.

Deseret News
January 31, 1877

Weather and Health—Things Dramatic, Etc.

NEPHI, Jan. 22nd, 1877.

Editor Deseret News:

As usual the snow king has not slighted us Nephites this winter, but we have had beautiful weather as a general thing. The health of the people is very good indeed, for which we have every reason to thank our heavenly Father, and I think the spirit of the people is to give praise to him on high.

We have had pleasant entertainments here this winter. Among the foremost are those given by our dramatic troupe, which I think I am safe in saying are excelled by but few if any in the Territory. They have an entire new fit out of beautiful scenery, and it is a credit to the artist, Mr. Lambourne, of Salt Lake City, and the troupe. Mrs. W. A. C. Bryan is our leading lady. Her name draws full houses. Mr. Walter Read, our leading gentleman, is one that pleases long and pleases many, and there are many others in the troupe who render their parts in a very pleasing and creditable manner.

AN OBSERVER.

TROUBLE IN NEPHI.

A Woman at the Bottom of It—A Nasty, Polygamous Wife-Beater the Cause of It—and Mr. S. Gilson Indicted Through It.

EDS. TRIBUNE: To-day this little, quiet burg was thrown into commotion by the "fruits of the spirit of lust." Some time has passed since any mention has been made in your paper of the Painter-Brooks divorce case. This candidate for celestial glory, you may doubtless remember, conceived a love (?) for his wife's sister, who was then the wife of another polygamist, sealed, of course, to all eternity and a queen among the gods.

THE FACTS

are these: Mrs. Brooks, first wife of John Painter, having suffered untold miseries from the brutality and ill treatment of her husband and sister-usurper, became subject to severe fits, and the sight of her faithless wretch would cause her to shudder, shrink and fear and fall to the ground in these fits. Wearied of her life she sued for a divorce and obtained one, but her miseries did not end. After months of importunity at the feet of the Gamaliels of this Latter-day fraud, the poor woman sought in vain for needed help. She frequently implored Mr. Gilson for help, knowing him to be a good man and a friend to the helpless. Although a Gentile of note, he is known to be a good citizen, quiet, peaceable and benevolent.

This morning, while working in a blacksmith shop, Mr. Gilson was informed by his little son, with tears in his eyes, that Painter was beating his wife and would kill her. Of course, no time was lost in repairing to the spot, a few steps from the shop. Mr. G. thrust his fist in the back of Painter; and calling him a "dirty polygamist," went through him like a saw-mill.

No time was lost in scouring the defender of the helpless women and bringing him a prisoner at the bar. Had this been fifteen years ago, he would have been meat for the fowls of heaven for usurping the rights of the Blood Atoners. As it was, the limbs of the law ripped, tore, snorted and swore. They fought bravely to find the noble defender, quietly and immure him in a felon's cell. Yes, they fought more to do a good man injury than they ever fought to do the poor woman good. Had it not been for the Poland bill, Mr. Gilson would have had a cold breakfast this morning in a cool place. Mr. Gilson was a whole branch of the law, and appealed the case to the District Court.

The prisoner was fined $25 for *salt* and $50 for battery, with imprisonment until the fine was paid, but the salt was too fine and the battery being a 13 pounder, was far too light.

NEPHI.

NEPHI, Feb. 2, 1877.

Salt Lake Herald
February 13, 1877

Postal Changes.

The following postal changes have been made in this territory:

A new postoffice has been established at Silver Reef, Washington county, Benjamin H. Paddock, postmaster. The following postmasters have been appointed: Nymphus O. Murdock, Charleston, Wasatch county; Elmer Taylor, Levan, Juab county, Utah.

Salt Lake Tribune
February 23, 1877

NEPHI.

Trying to Bulldoze the Ungodly Tribune Into Silence.

NEPHI, Feb. 19, 1877.

There has been a series of articles published in your paper in regard to Bros. Painter, Darrowman, Scofield and other brethren whom we can testify are trying to live their religion in accordance with the teachings they have received from the Profits and teachers of this people. Now, in regard to the matters that have been published, we do not intend to deny any of them, but we beg of you as a favor not to publish any more communications to you regarding the brethren. As we said before, it is not our intention to deny or admit any of the charges that have been made, but we beg of you to desist from publishing any such communications.

Supposing that Bro. Ord was horsewhipped home last Fourth of July, what interest can that be to the outside world?

One thing in particular we wish you to correct. I. C. All stated in his correspondence that Judge Darrowman imposed a fine of $2 on a man for knocking his wife down and shooting at his father-in-law. Now, to our certain knowledge, this is not so. The man was let off without any fine. And in regard to the alimony of Mrs. Painter, I. C. All forgot to mention all the property which was set apart for Mrs. P. Bro. Painter let her have a pine table 3x3 feet, and only charged her $7 for it. He let her have two sad irons at $1.25 apiece, and you cou'd not get them in any store for less than 60 cents apiece; yet I. O. All complains of the alimony not being paid.

But to the point, we ho'd these things as not fit matter for publication. A man can't meet his neighbor's wife wi hout the whole world knowing it. We suppose the next thing we shall see in THE TRIBUNE will be that Billy May's concubine has another child, and that the bishop and council cut twenty-seven of the brethren off from the Church last Sunday.

We suppose that you will have to let the whole world know that Brother Painter offered Drs. Gustin and Bryant $2.50 each, if they would swear that S. H. Gr's'n broke three of his (Painter's) ribs. As a matter of course you will not say anything about what I have confided to you.

Yours,　T. ORDER.

NEPHI.

Another Outrage on a Square Gen. tile in a Mormon Community.

EDS. TRIBUNE: It has been my privilege to witness one of the most glaring frauds ever enacted under the guise of a court of justice. I judge most of your readers are acquainted with the subject matter of the case (the Gibson-Painter case), so I will not repeat it, further than to say that several weeks since as S. H. Gibson was entering the store of Jennings & Sons, of this place, he caught one John Painter in the act of abusing his cast-off wife. Mr. Gibson proceeded then and there to chastise Brother Painter in a manner that he will not soon forget. Painter had Gibson brought before one of the priestly magistrates for an assault and battery. It is needless to mention here how that certain members of the jury (not all) took repeated naps during the proceedings of the trial, and, after being wakened, retired for a few moments and returned with a verdict of guilty of one offense, and how the court imposed fines for two separate crimes. Mr. Gibson did not see fit to submit to such an insult, and took an appeal to the First District Court. At the sitting of that court it was decided that the aforesaid priest had no right to sentence a man to imprisonment for life, and his judgment was vacated.

But the scavenger of the Mountain Meadows butcher shop was not satisfied to be outwitted in that manner, and yesterday Gibson was araigned the second time on the same charge, adding the crime of mayhem. Gibson gave the Justice the names of the persons he wanted as witnesses for the defense, and the Justice informed him that he could not have any of them.

Yesterday at 11 A. M. the court room was crowded to witness the trial.

Borrowman arose and informed the spectators that there would not be any trial (the only truth he told), but merely an examination of the witnesses for the prosecution to see if there were sufficient grounds for binding the defendant over to appear before the next Grand Jury.

Mr. Gibson arose as one of the bystanders, and asked what case he was going to investigate? He was ordered to shut his mouth and sit down or he would be fined $10 for contempt of court; at the same time informing him that the court was not opened yet. The Justice then proceeded to read the charge to the defendant, and asked him if he was guilty. The prisoner pleaded not guilty, and asked the court if his witnesses were in court. He informed the ex-Marshal that he could not have any witnesses. Gibson then demanded to be sworn, as he wished a change of venue. The court refused to administer the necessary oath, and Gibson then swore himself, and read his affidavit to the court. He was informed that his request would not be granted, as the court did not intend to be bulldozed into anything.

The Judge then examined the witnesses for the prosecution and bound the defendant over to appear before the Grand Jury at its next sitting. The bond was fixed at $500. The prisoner informed the Court that he could not give bonds, at which there was a big smile came over the Justice's face, for if there is anything that would please the Saints better than seeing old Brig, the butcher, President of the United States, it would be to see Sam. Gibson in jail, and they were gratified. He was taken down to the basement of the court house and put into a dirty, dark and damp hole—it was not fit for a dog kennel—and thus a free-born American citizen was denied the ordinary privileges of a sheep-killing dog.

Some of Mr. Gilson's friends applied to the Judge for the bonds to be made out, and it took the old fool from 1 p. m. until 7 to perfect the bonds and order for his release. He wanted to keep the ex-Marshal shut up as long as possible.

The bonds were signed by Messrs. Carlos A. Gregory and Edward Mc-Can, who did not stop to consider the effect it might have on their future financial prospects in this part of Utah. Mr. McCan was cut off from the Church, a few days since, for daring to sign Mr. Gilson's bonds on a former occasion. T. OGDEN.

Nephi, March 2, 1877.

Salt Lake Tribune
March 8, 1877

NEPHI.

A Chance for the Plundering Priests to Explain.

EDS. TRIBUNE: At the last sitting of the Grand Jury at Provo, a proposition was made by a wide-awake member of that body to examine into the county books of Juab county. The idea was acted upon, and a committee was appointed to call on the brethren of Nephi to see how matters panned out. The result is not known, but perhaps the saintly stray pound-keepers will have an opportunity to explain where the proceeds have gone of about $10,000 worth of stray stock which has been sold in the county in the last few years.

At the last sitting of the county court there was a committee appointed to investigate the books for the satisfaction of the county officials. The investigation was made. Whether it panned out to the satisfaction of the county papers or not I cannot say, but I understand from one of the committee, that they could do about as much with the works of Confucius or the Deseret alphabet, as they could with county book. Since it has become patent that the books are to be examined, there is considerable nervousness being manifested among the officials, and from what I can learn, I think there is an excellent opportunity for certain priests to figure up the accounts with his nose on an iron black board. T. OGDEN.

Nephi, March 4, 1877.

Deseret News
April 4, 1877

NEPHI, March 26th, 1877.
Editor Deseret News.
On the 5th day of March, 1877,

under the auspices of Bros. W. G. Young and John Young, an improvement society was established here, called the Young Men's Mutual Improvement Association. Our worthy bishop, Joel Grover, and his council were appointed a committee to suggest officers. They reported Lyman Hudson for president; James Jenkins, Jr., 1st counsellor, Thomas Belliston 2nd counsellor; with a secretary and treasurer, a corresponding secretary and librarian to be added when necessary.

We have been waiting for constitution and bye-laws. We have received great assistance in our rules from Bro. Junius Wells, President of the Y. M. M. I. Association, Salt Lake City.

On Saturday evening, March 24, 1877, we had a visit from several of the brethren of Salt Lake City, amongst whom were President D. H. Wells, Elder Geo. Q. Cannon, Elders Woolley, Junius F. Wells, and George Burton.

The meeting was addressed by Elders George Burton, — Woolley, Junius F. Wells, and James Jenkins, Jr. We had a good time, and the spirit of the Lord was felt by many present, and will be the precursor of much good in Nephi.

Respectfully,

GEORGE CARTER,
Secretary Y. M. M. I. A.

Salt Lake Tribune
April 7, 1877

NEPHI.

How the Rural Saints Take the Execution—A Dirty Dog

Correspondence Tribune.]

NEPHI, April 4, 1877.

It has been some time since I communicated my last tidings of the Saints and their doings in this stake of Zion. I suppose they thought that Tommy Ord had effectually squelched me by his threat to THE TRIBUNE, but such is not the case. "Richard is himself again," but "Tommy" is insane. He thinks he is to be executed with John D. Lee, and I should not wonder, if he had justice, he would have been. The brethren here—that is the better class—are satisfied with the execution and the confession. It has done good work. It has caused them to turn over the blackened pages of their past history and to ruminate on what is written there. They see their folly in being blindly led by the crime-stained priesthood, and are now willing to aid in removing the odium that has so long been attached to them. There are others, however, who still adhere to their oath, and will not admit facts that are proved, but this class is in the minority. The class which flows with the tide of civilization asks of those who are oath-bound these two important questions:

1st. If Brigham is innocent and had no connection with the murderous combination of Mormon Danites, why was a messenger sent to him from the bloody field of the Mountain Meadows?

2d. Why did Lee report to Brigham unless he was satisfied that Brigham would sanction this act?

These questions remain unanswered here, and are what will have to be answered before the honest portion of the Mormon community will be satisfied that Brigham is the good man he represents himself.

That brute, John Koby, mentioned in a former letter as having married a woman and left her, she marrying another man and raising a family of girls, and he again marrying the woman and one of her daughters, has taken a second daughter, aged 13 years, to St. George to become his fourth. There are two more left, aged nine and eleven, whom he intends to take as soon as possible. He believes in Brigham's innocence of the Mountain Meadows Massacre. And of such is the kingdom, at present.

Chief Justice B., of this place, has not rendered any of his decisions lately, but will soon have to render an account to the Grand Jury at Provo, and shortly after have the privilege of answering the question, guilty or not guilty.

When the Apostles went south, they spoke here about the prophecy of civil war. They said the reason it did not come was that the Saints were not self-sustaining, and the Lord had averted it until they were; and if the brethren would only be faithful, it would come soon.

As John W. went through, he to'd the brethren in a harangue at Gunnison, that the President wanted them to drill, as there was going to be a war in the States, and the Mormons must be ready to take charge of the Government. They were out three times. When Hayes took his seat, they concluded to stop training. Johnny told them that if he wanted, he would go to Salt Lake and take a company out to drill and defy arrest; but I guess Johnny don't want to.

There is a rumor in circulation here which has many believers, to the effect that Geo. H. Smith is not dead, but has gone to New Mexico. Several persons assert that they saw him after his supposed burial, on the road thither.

Give 'em hell. THE TRIBUNE is doing more good than everything else combined.　　　　　I. C. ALL.

Deseret News
April 11, 1877

ESTRAY NOTICE

I HAVE in my possession:

One white speckled 5 year old OX, has a blotched brand on left thigh, underbit in each ear, crumpled horns.

One brindled 5 or 6 year old COW, square-crop off both ears, no brands visible.

One red COW, about 3 or 4 years old, under half crop in right ear, swallow fork in left ear, no brands visible, has a young calf.

If the above described animals are not claimed they will be sold on Thursday, April 12th, 1877, at 9 a. m. at my corral.

L. A. BAILEY,
District Poundkeeper.

Nephi, April 2nd, 1877.

Salt Lake Herald
April 14, 1877

DIED.

GREENHALGH—At Nephi, Juab Co., April 13th, 1877, John Samuel, son of William and Ellen Greenhalgh, aged 1 year and 5 months.—Mill. Ster please copy.

Salt Lake Tribune
April 25, 1877

ANTI-MORMON.

Proceedings of the Finance Committee at Their Last Meeting.

The Finance Committee, appointed at the anti-Mormon meeting, on the 14th inst., met at the office of Judge Hemingray, at 11 a. m. Present: M. K. Harkness, Henry Simons, Dr. A. K. Smith, Dr. O. F. Winslow, and Col. R. A. M. Froiseth; two members were absent, L. U. Colbath and J. C. Young—out of the city.

M. K. Harkness was selected as Chairman and Henry Simons as Secretary of the Committee. The object and business of the Committee were stated in a clear, concise manner by the Chairman. The Committee was authorized to appoint sub-committees in every part of the Territory, to collect funds to pay the necessary expenses of representatives to Washington, for the purpose of procuring such legislation as is required for the future welfare and protection of the business interests of Utah Territory.

The Committee proceeded to form the committees named as follows:

Park City.—W. J. Montgomery, with power to add associates.

Bingham.—Isador Morris, Maurice McGrath and Henry Thompson.

Little and Big Cottonwoods—J. M. Orr, Justice Bateman and J. S. Johnson.

Sandy.—Gibson Clark, Dan Hutcheson and Chas. Jonson.

South Cottonwood.—Andrew Cahoon and Vincent Shurtliff.

Tooele.—Thomas F. Potts, D. W. Mitchell and E. bird.

Stockton—J. D Brown, Judge Warren, P. L. Shoaff, D. G. Alston, C. W. Ellis.

Rush Lake—J. J. Greenwald, W. S. Godbe, M. P. Minor.

Dry Canyon—J. T. Spangler, Cal Kirk, Hiram Lael, H. Clay Callahan.

Ophir—Horace Blies, Jas. Lawrence. F. L. Crabbee, James Shields.

Martinsville—Nelson Bennett.

Camp Floyd—O. D. Thompson, B. Frank Shaw.

Homansville and Eureka—Thos. L. Clohecy.

Diamond and Silver City—O. D. Johnson, Chas. Poynter, A. D. Sutherland.

Provo—Rev. Mr. Smith, M. V. Ashbrook, C. W. Emerson

Mount Pleasant—Rev. D. J. McMillan.

Spring City—Jacob Johnson.

Ephraim City—C. A. Larson.

Moroni—N L. Eliason.

Nephi—Sam Gilson

Farmington—Hiram Shurtliff.

Ogden—M. H. Beardsley, Dr. A. S. Condon, Jas Horrocks.

Corrine — Fred Kersel, T. W. Black, P. M., F. H. Church.

Kelton and Terrace—H. M. Ellsworth, A. Riley.

Logan—Rev. W. H. Stoy.

Echo and Coalville—Wm. Lawder.

Morgan County—L. P. Edholm.

Dr. A. K. Smith, a member of this committee, who is about to proceed to the Southern portion of the Territory, was selected to appoint suitable persons as sub committees at all places south of Beaver, and report said appointments to headquarters of this committee, in Salt Lake City.

That George F. Prescott was duly authorized to receive all sums of money from all persons who desire to contribute to the advancement of the anti Mormon cause, at the office of THE SALT LAKE DAILY TRIBUNE.

All moneys collected by this committee are to be placed on deposit at the banking house of Wells, Fargo & Co., in this city, as a special deposit, subject to the order of the chairman, for the purposes specified.

It was resolved that the proceedings of this committee be published in THE SALT LAKE TRIBUNE and the Utah *Skandinav*.

It was resolved that the chairman have power to call meetings of this committee during recess.

The chairmen of all sub-committees will report direct to M. K. Harkness, chairman of the general committee on finance, all sums of money collected as early as possible.

It was resolved that it is the sense of this finance committee that all persons favorable to the anti-Mormon cause in Utah, be requested to contribute at least one dollar, as that amount is within the reach of every person opposed to the Mormon priesthood; and that all lovers of free institutions and the separation of fanaticism and politics, are requested to assist at this time.

Additional appointments of local committees at distant points will be made, and announced at an early date.

The committee adjourned to meet at the call of the chairman.

MARTIN K. HARKNESS, Ch'n.
HENRY SIMONS, Sec.

Deseret News
April 25, 1877

ESTRAY NOTICE.

I HAVE in my possession:

One brown MULE five or six years old, branded on left shoulder with a wine glass vented on thigh, Spanish brand on left thigh, has a deformed hind leg.

One sorrel pinto MARE about 10 years old, branded JN combined, on left hip, vented on left shoulder.

One brown three year old MARE, branded Z on left shoulder.

One red and white cow, five or six years old, brand resembling a large door key on left hip, underbit out of left ear, end broke off right horn, has a young calf.

If the above described animals are not claimed they will be sold on Saturday, April 28th, 1877, at 9 a. m. at my corral.

L. A. BAILEY,
District Poundkeeper.
Nephi, April 18th, 1877.   d 137

DIED.

Also at Nephi, Juab County, March 5, 1877, MINNIE ALICE, daughter of John W. and Mary A. M. Ellison, aged 1 year, 9 months and 11 days, grandchild of the above James Ellison.

At Mona, Juab County, Utah, March 26, 1877, of diphtheria, NANCY ALTHERA, daughter of John and Nancy Harrison, aged 3 years, 2 months and 6 days.

Deseret News
May 2, 1877

DIED.

At Mona, Juab County, Utah, March 28, 1877, NANCY ALTHERA, daughter of John and Nancy Harrison, aged 3 years, 2 months and 6 days.

Salt Lake Tribune
May 23, 1877

ts History, Prospects and Development — Mines, Districts and Towns, etc. etc.

[Correspondence Tribune.]

OURAY, COL., May 5, '77.

Your correspondent left Salt Lake on the 17th day of last February, for what is called the San Juan mining country. Our route was south from the city through the several settlements, until we reached Salina, crossing the Wasatch pass at that place, striking Castle valley at John Wilson's horse ranch, and continuing for sixty miles up that barren and sterile valley until we reached the Book mountains, thence taking an eastward course for ninety miles, until we strike Grand river, but in the meantime having crossed the Green river.

Upon reaching Grand river we came upon what was supposed to be friendly Indian country, but were greatly disappointed, having heard, through Mr. Chris Taylor, of Nephi, of the scalping of the two Green brothers, and after that we used all the precaution necessary in that kind of a region, until we had traveled some eighty miles, when we knew that we were through the dangerous red man's country. Fearing that you may not have space enough to allow the publication of a lengthy letter, I will try and give truly the facts relative to the

SAN JUAN MINING COUNTRY.

That region of country now widely known to the world as the San Juan, situated in the southwest portion of Colorado; comprising the counties of Ouray, La Plata, Hinsdale, La Pauche and portions of Conejos, Costilla and the Rio Grande, embracing an area of 15,000 square miles.

Ouray county lies west 35 miles across the range from Lake City, and is in the very center of one of the richest mineral belts known on the western slope, and has in itself all the accessories necessary to future development. It is one of the best timbered and watered regions in the United States, the timber being suitable for fuel, lumber, tunnels, shafts and other mining purposes; but at the present date the country known

Deseret News
May 23, 1877

A Romantic History—Baptisms and Emigration.

NEPHI, May 4th, 1877.

Editor Deseret News:

In the summer of 1875 I baptised L. M. Petersen and his wife and their Spanish muleteer, in company with many others at Manti, who at that time were renewing their covenants. The three named were visitors from the southern border of Colorado, and enquirers after truth.

There is a bit of romance connected with this man, Peterson, not altogether devoid of interest. He was a Scandinavian by birth, but Spanish-American by education. When eleven years old, in the summer of 1854, he strayed from a camp of the Saints near Kansas City, Missouri, while they were waiting for William Empy, our emigration agent for that year, to procure their teams and outfits for Utah.

His father and mother had both died during the voyage to America, and the rest of his family and friends, after many a fruitless search, gave up young Peterson as lost to them forever and wended their way to Utah, while the lost boy fell in with some Spanish traders from New Mexico, who enticed him home with them, where he subsequently became quite proficient as a Spanish and English scholar, married a Spanish woman, was elected a county recorder, and while serving in that capacity he commenced corresponding with the recorders of Utah, which resulted in finding the whereabouts of his elder brother in Manti, and paying him a visit with his family, where they also embraced the gospel and provided themselves with our church works, and he being ordained an Elder returned to his former home and commenced a quiet missionary labor amongst the Spanish Catholics. He translated into Spanish some choice selections from our works, and with the aid of these and the Spanish translation of the Book of Mormon, he succeeded in baptizing about forty persons and awoke the wrath of the Spanish priests and editors.

He writes from Las Tjeras, Col., April 14th, 1877, to his brother in Manti, that he expects to start about the 20th to the 25th of April, with his new converts, in twelve or thirteen wagons, *via* Albuquerque, for the Little Colorado, Arizona, where they intend locating with our new colonists. He hopes to reach there about the last of this month.

I trust they will find Elders Hatch, Burnham, Lake, Allen and Lot Smith, to whose care and further instruction Brother Petersen and his new colonists are earnestly commended, hoping and praying also that they may prove valuable aids among the Spanish speaking natives and citizens of that region.

Respectfully, &c.,

ERASTUS SNOW.

Salt Lake Herald
May 30, 1877

All Thief.

The man who was fined Monday for stealing the beer from Mr. Pitts' brewery has considerable notoriety. He went to the brewer about two months ago and pleaded poverty so that Mr. Pitts relieved his wants, paid for his board at a hotel, which he promised to work out, but the first work he has done was to steal from his benefactor. He is working out a thirty days' fine now with the city. When that is finished he will have to face a charge of stealing from Camp Douglas. He has been run out of Nephi and Provo cities for stealing, and should be run out of this city as soon as his accounts with the corporation are settled.

Salt Lake Herald
June 24, 1877

From Juab County.

Editors Herald:

Our farmers are in full expectations of an abundant harvest. At one time this spring it was thought that our supply of water would be very limited, but the storms in April and May left a liberal deposit of snow.

The health of the people, as a general thing, is good, and irrigating land, hauling timber, poles, preparing to build, fencing, etc., is the order of the day. But few have time to loaf or drill.

A company has been organized for the purpose of erecting a coöperative flour mill to be situated near the mouth of Salt Creek cañon. Considerable stock has been subscribed and men are getting out the timber needed in the erection of the mill.

We are pleased with the prospect of being better supplied with lumber as a steam sawmill will in a few days start in North cañon. Five hundred thousand feet of logs are cut and being hauled in to commence with, and more are contracted for. NEPHI.

Salt Lake Tribune
June 24, 1877

THE RAILWAY MONOPOLY.

The letter we published yesterday from a well informed correspondent, who signs himself "A Wagon Dealer," contains so many useful reflections that we deem it profitable to refer to it awhile. The writer very ingeniously traces the limits of the ring which encompasses the ungodly in Zion, whose links are Brigham with his facile instruments of oppression and the Union Pacific railway directory. It was evident that Dillon and his little clique had a bias against the Gentile interest, and evinced a hostility rather than a disposition to oblige and foster a growing industry. It is no use charging Jack-Mormonism against these railroad men, because they are incapable of indulging a sentiment—albeit a perverted one—and they care no more for Brigham Young than they do for Confucius or the Blessed Saviour. Their object is gain, and to accomplish this they would sell their country and their God to the highest bidder. But Brigham has a hold upon them in his power to phlebotomize the company by means of a tax upon their property in this Territory. A bill to this end was introduced in the last Legislature, but was defeated by the influence of Bishop Sharp, who as director of the Union Pacific and member of the Lord's parliament, was enabled to appease the prophet's greed by the promise of some future advantage. That there is some community of interest between the Lord's anointed and these railroad sharps, is evident by their very perverse conduct during their stay in Salt Lake.

Common business sagacity would suggest to these men the advisability of extending, without delay, the Utah Southern road to the Beaver mining district. The portion that is now constructed lends nowhere, is worked at excessive freight and passenger rates and is of merely local utility. If it were extended a hundred or more miles it would open up the rich San Pete coal region, it would bring the extensive mineral wealth of Beaver county within reach of the world, and it would be so much nearer to the vast iron deposits of Southern Utah. The people of that section are begging for a railway, would give prodigally to aid the work, and the profit of such an enterprise is not open to question. Then why did these railway men not look into the question while in Utah? Look over the ground at least, and see what business is awaiting them whenever they shall conclude to reach after it? Because the extension of this road would break the monopoly by which these plutocrats holds us remorselessly to inflated prices and non progression. We understand that one or two Eastern capitalists one time thought of buying the San Pete coal property, and in order to see what use it would be to them, called upon Messrs. Dillon and Gould to enquire about the extension of the road to Nephi, and their rates upon coal to Salt Lake. But they received no satisfaction. These two chiefs informed their visitors that they would not carry coal over the Utah Southern to Salt Lake, because it would be destroying their own coal trade on the Union Pacific. They could bake coke and the company would furnish cars to carry it at fair rates to the smelters in Sandy; but the coal trade was their own special franchise, and they would admit no others to divide the profits. Of course, the proposed investment in San Pete coal lands was abandoned.

Can we wonder that development is retarded in Utah under such a monopoly? With inflated prices, we cannot compete with communities who work at less cost. Abundant and cheap coal is the very basis upon which all manufacturing industry is founded, and there is no reason in the world why coal and coke should not be furnished to smelters, and and smithies and our private homes at as low rates as anywhere on the continent. But the Union Pacific directors want to make money. They have not the sagacity to make it by honest and liberal enterprise, by aiding development, attracting hitherward population and capital, and taking tribute from the good they have diffused. They must play the tyrant, abuse opportunity, crush out progression, monopolize advantages and, Shylock-like, have their pound of flesh.

Such a policy suits Brigham Young, because a part of his prophetic mission is to drive out unbelievers, and whether Enoch or railway monopoly accomplishes the work makes slight difference to him. Bishop Sharp seems to be the go-between for the two parties. His divine master wants to get rid of Outsiders; the d—d, cussed hounds of the law would not make themselves so annoyingly familiar if he could have this land to himself. And the Union Pacific directory refer pretty much all the business relating to Utah to the resident director. It is to see that this is a baleful configuration. Men antagonistic to the best interests of the Territory have the drop on us. And our producing and business classes must find a way out. This circular combination must be disrupted. It is a matter worth studying over, and the man who has the most useful suggestion to offer, is the one we want to hear from first. President Dillon says "reduce your workmen's wages," which sounds so much like inspiration, that we are morally certain he must have obtained it from Brigham. But human reason would prefer to strike at monopoly, which, like Victor Hugo's devil fish, holds us all fast bound in its unyielding antennæ. Let us break the Church ring and the concentric railroad ring by properly directed efforts; then we can look for progress, then we can come down to the solid basis of low prices, and then we can talk of reducing wages, if such a resort should be necessary.

Deseret News
July 4, 1877

ESTRAY NOTICE.

I HAVE in my possession:

One bay MARE, about six or seven years old, branded P with an extension to the left, and a mark resembling an 8 at the bottom, connected to the P, on left thigh; has a colt.

One sorrel MARE, about five or six years old, branded N, with two bars above, on left shoulder; has a colt.

One red COW, about three years old, branded H B on left hip, square crop off left ear, slit and under half crop in right.

One red HEIFER, about three years old branded ϖ on left side of body, and under-bit and hole in right ear.

One brindle three or four year old STEER, branded ʌ1 on left hip, illegible brand on left thigh, upper slope in right ear.

One dark red STEER, about two years old, branded E on right shoulder, white tail, upperbit in right ear, crop and under-bit in left.

If the above described animals are not claimed, they will be sold on Wednesday, July 11th, 1877, at 9 a. m., at my corral.

L. A. BAILEY,
District Poundkeeper.
Nephi, Juab County, July 1st, 1877.
d s & w

Salt Lake Herald
July 21, 1877

DIED.

McCune—In Nephi, July 17, 1877, Sarah Elizabeth Caroline Scott, wife of Dr. Mathew McCune; born in London, December 28th, 1812; married M. McCune July 11, 1835, and sailed with him immediately thereafter for Calcutta; spent twenty-two years in the East Indies, and bore a family of seven sons and one daughter while there. Baptized with her husband in the Church of Jesus Christ of Latter-day Saints in 1845 at Ackra farm, near Calcutta, the country seat of the late Dr. J. P. Meeks of Salt Lake city, by Elder Joseph Richards, then on a mission to India. During the last Burmese war, after the taking of Rangoon by the East Indian company's forces, she joined her husband there with her family, and spent there the last four years of their residence in India.

Her house and purse were ever open to the elders there on missions from the valley. Left India in 1856, arriving in Utah the fall of 1857, having traveled 4,000 miles. Came with her family to Utah to learn to sustain herself by the labors of her own hands, which she had never done in her life previously. She was a faithful wife and a devoted mother; lived a most exemplary life and sacrificed home and wealth to gather with her family to Utah. Her loss to her husband and family is irreparable.
—[Com.

Salt Lake Tribune
July 22, 1877

Late Arrival.

The daughter of Mrs. and Mr. M. P. Bulger, arrived at Nephi, the 19th ult., on the 11:30 o'clock train. She is a nine pounder. All parties are doing well.

Salt Lake Herald
July 31, 1877

The Sanpete Mails.

Following is one of many similar letters received at this office. The papers are mailed regularly, and if subscribers do not receive them, the fault lies with postmasters:

EPHRAIM, SANPETE Co.,
July 27th, 1877.

Can you tell me why my paper comes so irregularly? Do you mail it regularly, or is the fault with the postmasters? While the mail runs regularly in this county I receive my papers two or three at a time, instead of every day. Some of the postmasters say it is the fault of the postmaster at Nephi, who is said to be very careless at times. How that may be I do not know, but that we are perplexed with poor mail outfits all of the time is certain. There was no mail to-day, because one of the carrier's horses balked, and he did not go to Nephi yesterday. There is first one trifling excuse and then another for keeping the entire mail of the county behind time. If the postmasters are at fault they should be made to wake up to the performance of their duties. The mail running into this county is bad enough, without postmasters helping to delay the mail matter.

NEPHI.

How the Ungodly Saints Ran the Election.

Correspondence Tribune.]

Nephi, Aug. 7, 1877.

Business opened here this morning with the usual amount of tooting of horns and the running to and fro of teams collecting the mothers in Israel to do their part toward redeeming this people and preparing for the exodus to Jackson county. Everything went off quietly, if not satisfactorily. Brother Knight was at his usual place at the polls, challenging American citizens who were born long before the Mormons whipped the United States. By the way, Brother Knight is one of the most obliging elders in all Israel. One would imagine that the chair he sat upon would have corns on it, he has been upon it so long. He is one of the best drilled Saints in the kingdom. It is the duty of this brother to sit at the place of polling and see that no Gentile defiles the ballot box with his vote. When the sisters walk up to the table to vote, Brother Knight comes to their rescue with the remark, "This is the ticket, sisters; this ticket has the bishop's name on it for selectman; the other has the name of A. G. Sutherland—he who denounced this people last fall in this very 'ouse." This was enough, and the sisters would make a fearful rush for the ticket.

We were amused at an old Danish sister who read, or rather pretended to read, the ticket up side down. At the suggestion of Brother Knight who turned the ticket over with a grin, folding the same and passing it to the judge.

The parties in charge of the box were over anxious to see how the voting was going on, and at about 1 o'clock, they opened the box and were examining the contents, when W. G. Sealy appeared upon the scene and demanded to know what they were doing. They explained the matter by saying there was a mistake in some of the numbers.

Mr. John W. Casur, who was born, twenty-eight years ago, in the United States of America, was not allowed to vote, simply because Bro. Pitchforth neglected to assess his property, or rather because he wanted to vote for A. G. Sutherland. Mr. Casur said he had taxable property and wanted to swear his vote in, but the Judge informed him that he could not bulldoze that court, and Mr. Casur vented his spite on the Judge by reminding him of the good old days of Robinson and Yates, when the Saints used to cast a vote for every mule they owned and vote for their children. The Saint smiled and said: "Well, Johnny, let bygones be by gones."

The ways of the Lord are wondrous.   T. OGDEN.

"Ben" Tasker Captured. — Ben Tasker, the notorious horse thief, who has been so often seized by the officers of the law, and has as frequently succeeded in eluding the just reward of his misdeeds, is once more in custody. As previously mentioned in the NEWS, he has lately been making the southern part of the Territory the base of his thieving operations. In consequence, the officers in that part went after him a day or two since. In their search they visited the camp of Taylor, of Bingham, on the Sevier, who it is alleged denied having any knowledge of Tasker's whereabouts. The officers were satisfied, however, that he was hiding in the vicinity, and took the novel plan of getting the fox out of his den by setting fire to the willows. By this means the place was made too hot for Tasker and

he got out and ran, pursued by the officers. However, he found another hiding place, but, after some careful searching, one of the men in pursuit saw between two clumps of willows, Tasker's wolf-like face, just barely visible above water, the whole of his body being submerged. Leveling his pistol on that face the officer commanded its owner to come out of there, and he did.

The prisoner was taken to Nephi, and from there to Round Valley, at which latter place he was to undergo an examination on a charge of horse-stealing.

Since the above was in type we learn by letter from Nephi that the party who captured Taylor and Tasker, the former calling himself Thomson, was composed of Messrs. Richard Jenkins, Alex. J. Pyper, D. J. Bigler and P. Tidwell of Nephi, and that it is pretty evident that there are persons through the southern settlements who are in league with Tasker and his associates.

DIED.

At Nephi, Juab County, Saturday, Aug. 25th, 1877, of cholera morbus, MARGARET GARDINER, wife of George B. Reid.

Deceased was born in Edinburgh, Scotland, on the 12th of March, 1826; embraced the Gospel on the 27th of December, 1840, baptized by Geo. D. Watt; was married to Geo. B. Reid on the 3rd of August, 1847; emigrated to America in September, 1848; wintered in St. Louis, and arrived in Salt Lake City on the 16th of October, 1849. She moved to Nephi in September, 1856, where she resided until her death. She was the mother of eight children and grandmother of two. Seven children are still living, and who, with her husband, grandchildren and a host of friends, are left to mourn her departure. She was an exemplary wife and mother, firm in the faith, and died in the hope of a glorious resurrection. Her funeral was largely attended. Consolatory remarks were made by Elders Allen, Grover, Andrews, Kendall and Teasdale. Blessed indeed are those who die in the Lord.— COM.

Millennial Star, and Edinburgh papers, please copy.

Deseret News
September 26, 1877

ESTRAY NOTICE.

I HAVE in my possession:

One red 3 or 4 year old STEER, has a little white in face and under belly, illegible brand on right hip, upper slope in right ear, underslope in left.

If the above described animal is not claimed he will be sold on September 29th, 1877, at 8 a.m. at my corral

L. A. BAILEY,
District Poundkeeper.
Nephi, Juab Co., Sept. 19, 1877.   d&w

Salt Lake Tribune
September 30, 1877

On Friday last, a little girl by the name of Harriet Eliza Brough, aged between five and six years, residing at Nephi, fell off an ox team and broke her neck, causing almost instant death.

Salt Lake Herald
October 9, 1877

Andrew Hendrickson of Levan was given permission to go to Scandinavia to preach to his friends and settle some business.

The Nephi Horse Thieves.

The two horse thieves from Nephi who were recently captured near St. George, having been returned to Juab county, on Saturday, 13th, had an examination before Alma Hague, J. P. The justice bound them over to await the action of the grand jury in bonds of $500 and $600. In default of bail, both were committed to prison. The fellows give their names as Allen and Hawkins, and they appear to be a hard pair. It appears that on their trip south, after stealing the horses and saddles, they killed a pig on the Sevier, and carried the hams with them. The particulars of their capture, one on the Clara, and the other in Leeds, have already been published in the HERALD. They were brought to Nephi by Mangrum and Whitmore, and had with them a black horse, white stripe in the face and hind feet white; branded C M or G M on the left thigh, and figure 2 on right thigh. The animal is believed to have been stolen.

to have been stolen.

The fellows appear to be well acquainted with the country and seem hardened wretches. When asked their names in the court they said they had about fifty aliases and hardly knew which to give. No one in the vicinity of Nephi seems to know them or whence they came. One is about six feet high, has a very coarse, gruff voice, is red-headed, and is about 25 years of age. The other is a short, thick-set chap, dark complexion, and is about 22 years old.

Juab Items.

John Hague's flouring mill is running to its full capacity.

The grain crop this season was excellent, but the potato yield was slim.

Henry Goldsbrough runs a daily stage between Nephi and York; fare, $1.

There is a prosperous Sunday school in Nephi, attended by about 300 children.

William Jennings' store, which is being managed by John Hague, is also doing a good business.

A large coöperative grist mill is being erected near the mouth of Salt Creek cañon. It is the intention to have it completed this fall.

John Ostler is running a small tannery and producing a very fair article of upper leather. He expects to manufacture sole leather when he obtains suitable bark.

The coöperative store, under the management of Charles Foot, is doing a good business. Before Mr. F. took it in hand the store had run behind somewhat, but it is now paying fair dividends.

Deseret News
October 24, 1877

ESTRAY NOTICE.

I HAVE in my possession the following described animal:

One red two year old HEIFER, branded resembling a wine glass on right hip, upper and under bit in right ear, slit in left.

If not claimed she will be sold on October 25th, 1877, at my corral, at 8 a. m.

L. A. BAILEY,
District Poundkeeper.

Nephi, October 15, 1877.

Quarterly Conferences. — To-morrow and Sunday the regular quarterly conferences of Weber and Juab Stakes of Zion will convene at Ogden and Nephi respectively. Of the Quorum of the Apostles, President John Taylor and Elders O. Pratt, F. D. Richards, Joseph F. Smith and D. H. Wells expect to attend the meetings at Ogden, and Elders W. Woodruff, O. Hyde and E. Snow those at Nephi.

Deseret News
October 31, 1877

PRESIDENT GEORGE TEASDALE

testified to the willingness of the priesthood and members of the Juab Stake of Zion to sustain true principle and the pleasure he had enjoyed in his labors, exhorted the Saints to purity of life, and presented the church authorities, which

were unanimously sustained, also the local authorities as follows:

George Teasdale, President, Joel Grover and Kanad H. Brown, Counselors.

High Council—George Kendall, Timothy S. Hoyt, Wm. H. Warner, Samuel Cazier, David Cazier, Jacob G. Bigler, Jr., John Vickers, John Kinke, Thomas Ord, Abraham Orme, Charles H. Bryan and John D. Chase.

Patriarchs, Jacob G. Bigler, Sen., Samuel Pitchforth.

Andrew Love, President of the High Priests' Quorum, Robert H Scott and James T. Belliston. Counselors.

John Pyper, Clerk of Stake.

Bishop of Nephi, First Ward, John Andrews, Edwin Harley and Wm. A. C. Bryan, Counselors; Second Ward, Charles Sperry, Bishop, Wm. F. Felley and Chas. D. Cazier, Counselors.

Levan — Niels Aagaar, Bishop, Eimer Taylor and Eric Petterson, Counselors.

Mona — John M. Haws Bishop, William Newton and John W. Bell Counselors.

Choir sang—

Earth is the place where Christ will reign.

Benediction by President Petterson.

Adjourned till 7 p.m.

7 p.m.

Choir sang:

Joy to the world, the Lord will come.

Prayer by Elder John B. Maiben. Choir sang:

God moves in a mysterious way.

On motion of President Teasdale, the following committee were sustained to employ and arrange with the laborers on the Manti Temple from Juab County—George Teasdale, Joel Grover, Knud H. Brown, John Andrews, Chas. Speery, Niels Asgaard and John M. Haws.

Salt Lake Herald
November 2, 1877

LIST OF AGENTS

Authorized to take subscriptions for SALT LAKE DAILY and SEMI-WEEKLY HERALD:

O. B. Robbins,	Logan
John Pynim,	St. George
S A. Wixom.	Beaver
Jourdon Davis,	Springville
Walter Walker,	Farmington
W. L. Watkins,	Brigham City
Jos. U. Eldredge,	Meadowville
J. W. Clarke,	Grantsville
John Boyden,	Coalville
Charles Foote,	Nephi

Salt Lake Herald
November 10, 1877

Southward.

Mr. J. S. Lindsay, the author-actor, contemplates taking a company south in about a week, to play his successful drama, "Under One Flag." American Fork, Provo, Payson, Nephi and maybe one or two other towns will be visited. Good luck.

Deseret News
November 14, 1877

From Nephi.—To-day we met with Mr. John Hague, of Nephi. He reports everything prosperous in that part of Utah.

Salt Lake Herald
November 17, 1877

Southern Notes.

Farmers are busy plowing for fall crops; some wheat is up and looks pretty. Lucerne is increasing the area of pasture land greatly.

Machinery is passing over the roads to the San Francisco and Tintic districts daily.

The Nephi coöp. is increasing its storage room, and is doing a good business.

J. O. Swift & Co., with their steam saw mill, are turning out plenty of fine-looking lumber in Juab county and planting it at York.

The northwest bench at Provo is being freely cultivated. Mr. Joshua Davis said he grew a radish on that soil this year three feet four inches in length.

Henry Goldsborough is running an express from Nephi to York for $1. He gets so much patronage that he feels he can "buck" against the railroad company as well as the stage company.

Some parts of the bench at Provo have been luxuriating in green melons up till last week, the frost not having reached them until then.

S. Pitchforth, Esq., of Nephi, returned home on Tuesday, reduced in strength, after having been in Salt Lake city for six weeks, undergoing a surgical operation.

Ore and bullion seem plentiful at York, Santaquin, Bingham junction and Sandy.

The Nephi tannery is turning out a good quantity and quality of leather.

Provo is rejoicing over having graveled sidewalks.

The citizens of American Fork are extending the size of one of their ward houses, by making a large addition thereto.

Salt Lake Tribune
November 20, 1877

Attempted Escape.

The two men indicted for stealing horses at Nephi, recently, and confined in the Juab county jail, were taken to Provo, yesterday, for trial. One of them created considerable excitement on the train by twice trying to escape. He was handcuffed, shackled and his feet fastened to the other prisoner, which, however, he did not know. In this plight, while the train was in motion between York and Payson, he leaped from the car window and hung with his head down, until sheriff Reed, of Juab county, who had them in charge, could pull him back into the car. The second attempt consisted of a sort of insane rush for the car door, but it proved a futile effort. The performances of this prisoner were thought to be prompted by a desire to commit suicide, though it is more probable he was playing for public sympathy.

Salt Lake Herald
November 28, 1877

Salt Lake Herald
December 23, 1877

Fire at Nephi.

By telegram received yesterday, we learn that a fire was discovered on Friday night in the harness shop of W. P. Reid, Nephi, which burned the building and contents, valued at about $2,000. The exact cause of the fire is unknown, but it was supposed, by a gentleman up from there yesterday, that a cigarette, carelessly thrown away, had dropped through an opening in the floor and smouldered until the fire broke out. Of course, this is but a supposition, but such cases of carelessness by smokers are altogether too common, and a warning should be taken by thoughtless persons and they should learn that playing with fire is too dangerous a pastime. The wind was not blowing at the time, or the fire would undoubtedly have communicated to the adjoining buildings. The citizens turned out and labored diligently to save property. Donations for Mr. Reid were being freely made yesterday and it is thought his loss will be partially repaired in a short time.

Salt Lake Tribune
January 1, 1878

SAN PETE.

Proposed Work of the San Pete Coal and Coke Company.

A New Narrow Gauge Railroad to be Built to the Connelsville of Utah.

The San Pete coal fields were discovered twenty-five years ago, by John E. Rees, an experienced coal miner from Wales. Under the excitement prevailing then in Utah for setting God's heritage, he, with three others, went into San Pe e Valley to assist in setting up that most fertile grain country of the Territory. Soon after arriving there his attention was called to this coal by some Indians with whom he came in contact. He at once said that it would soon become valuable; hence he and his companions set about developing it. The seam was opened in the most convenient and accessible places, and the country around at once supplied with coal. Subsequently explorations were resumed and the coal was traced for the distance of six to eight miles.

As the country grew up the demand for coal increased until thousands of tons were sold every year. The price at Salt Lake City ranged from $30 to $35 per ton, and sold at the mine for $4 per ton. Soon after its discovery it was found that it made good coke. Rude ovens were erected and coke manufactured to supply the demand in the Territory. It was hauled to Salt Lake City at $60 to $70 per ton.

Some four years ago this immense property was sold to the San Pete Coal & Coke Co., who soon commenced its development upon a more extensive scale than had been done before. The mine was opened by driving main entries, turning rooms, putting down roads, tramways and such other improvements as was deemed necessary to insure its profitable working. Wagon roads were graded up the canyons, so that heavily loaded teams could pass from the mines with safety. A large mill was built with crushing and washing machines of the most approved style for crushing coal, and extensive coke works were erected. Finally, under a promise from the Utah Southern Railroad that they would by 1875, extend their road to Nephi the Coal & Coke Company surveyed and located twenty-eight miles of narrow gauge road from Nephi to the coal fields, and graded some seven miles of it, under the belief that the Utah Southern people really meant what they said and would as soon as possible build their road on to Nephi. But no; there was no such good luck in store for these hardy rustlers for Utah's best interest.

The panic of 1873 crushed all railroad enterprises, and even the Utah Southern could not comply with their promise, and were compelled to delay their proposed work of extending the road.

This of course threw a damper over the operations of the San Pete company. The company has gone through bankruptcy and the entire property was bought by C. W. Bennett, Esq., of this city, and is now being worked quite successfully under the superintendency of Mr. S. Bamberger.

They have added to the concern the manufacturing of fire brick, and are making from the large beds of clay that surround the coal as good a quality of fire brick as can be found in the West. This, with the coal and coke, enables them to drive quite a business with the road even at York, the present terminus of the Utah Southern Railroad, which is expected to reach Nephi in the early spring.

We understand from good authority that Mr Bamberger is now negotiating with the people along the line of their narrow gauge for grading and ties, so as to get this road in operation as early in the coming summer as possible. With this road completed to Nephi, so that our smelters can be supplied with this excellent steam coal and coke, just now, where he mining interests seem to be looking up all over the Territory, will add more to our permanent prosperity than all the things yet done in Utah, and we we cannot help but think that this San Pete narrow gauge road is the entering wedge for a competing railroad, which is the only thing that can give us real prosperity, and put our grand mining interests in a position to attract that attention from abroad they are entitled to. Parties in the interest of the Rio Grande narrow gauge road, now this side of the Santa Christo Pass, have already been prospecting the feasibility of the route from the San Pete coal fields, via Selina Canyon through Thistle Valley, and on across the Colorado, via Ouray through the San Juan mines, with a view of extending their road to Ogden City at an early day.

Every man in Utah should lend a helping hand to this enterprise, so that our various interests may be subserved by two roads, instead of one, whose policy has always been to crush out rather than build up this country.

The San Pete narrow gauge and the immense coal, coke and fire brick interests must of necessity cut an important figure in this enterprise, besides over a million bushels of surplus grain raised in San Pete county per annum, will find a profitable market.

We from our hearts bid them God speed, and will listen with eagerness and some degree of impatience, for the first narrow gauge whistle coming to us from the south, by which we will be introduced to the Bonanza men of the Beaver county mines, the iron men from Iron county and all of Southeastern Nevada and Southwestern Colorado,

DIED.

December 21st, 1877, at his residence in Nephi, Juab County, Utah Territory, SAMUEL PITCHFORTH, son of Solomon and Ann Pitchforth.

Deceased was born November 23d, 1826, in Halifax, England; and was the first person to offer himself for baptism into the Church of Jesus Christ of Latter-day Saints on the Isle of Man, being baptized by Elder John Taylor in September, 1840. He emigrated to Nauvoo in the spring of 1845, and on the 9th of April of the same year was ordained into the 24th Quorum of Seventies, and participated with the Saints in the drive from Nauvoo, his mother dying from exposure on the road, leaving him with a frail constitution at the age of 19 with a wife and three sisters, the youngest being only four years old. He crossed the plains in Elder John Taylor's company in 1847; resided in Salt Lake City until the fall of 1852, when he moved to Nephi, where he continued to reside until his death and where he took a most active part in all the responsibilities incidental to the development of a new country. Was ordained a president of the 49th quorum of Seventies on the 18th of May, 1857, and a patriarch in July, 1877. Was also superintendent of Sunday schools for many years. He was a member of the Legislative Assembly of Utah for five consecutive sessions, and assistant clerk of the House for two years, was also recorder and assessor and collector for Juab County during many years. He leaves behind him two wives, seven children, one adopted son and two grandchildren. With a name unsullied he literally wore out his body by a life of useful and active labor in all that pertained to the building up of the cause which he had espoused.—COM.

Salt Lake Herald
January 8, 1878

Murder at Sevier.

[Special Dispatch to the HERALD.]

NEPHI, UTAH, Jan. 7, 1878.

G. F. Sibbley, storekeeper at Sevier bridge, shot and instantly killed Joseph R. Ivie, on the 5th instant. Sibbley surrendered himself and is now at Nephi, awaiting his trial. The trouble was caused through intoxication. Ivie leaves a wife.

Deseret News
January 9, 1878

Deseret Museum — We were shown, to-day, a relic of the *Mayflower*, an old pepper-mill brought over with the Puritan Fathers by a maternal ancestor of Sister Hannah Grover, of Nephi City, Utah. Sister Grover justly prizes this curious relic and, in 1870, she deposited it in the Deseret Museum, by recommendation of the late President Brigham Young, at which time she refused to sell the mill. We learn now that Sister Grover has finally concluded to part with the treasure, and has wisely donated it in perpetuity to the Museum. The relic is to be restored carefully to its original shape, so as to still retain its antiquated appearance, in which condition it will be seen in the Museum cabinets among a large collection of ancient curiosities.

Deseret News
January 16, 1878

ESTRAY NOTICE.

I HAVE in my possession:

One red 3 or 4 year old COW, branded on left hip JH, combined, crop off left ear, underbit in right.

If not claimed, the above will be sold on January 14, 1878, at 9 a. m. at my corral.

L. A BAILEY,
District Pound-keeper.

Nephi, Juab Co., Jan 4, 1878.   d&w

NEPHI POLYGAMY.

A List of the Brethern who Are Living Up to their Privileges.

EDS. TRIBUNE: Several circumstances that have and are taking place here, call for this communication, so that a protest may be on record against dirty polygamists.

Thomas Grover, alias Tommy Dawdle, is one of those kind of men who experience supreme gratification in the fact that "I was bred and born in the Church. I know nothing else, and I don't want to know anything else, either." These are his own words, which he uttered from the stand last Sunday, after his return from the sink hole. But, in the allwise providence of God, he will know something else. A few years ago this man was called by God through his servant Brigham, to settle in Southern Utah. He returned financially prostrated, and his wife physically so. But, "I was bred and born," etc., and now instead of protecting the wife of his youth, he violates the exclusiveness of his first love by taking a concubine in the person of Louie Piston.

Edward Sparks has a wife of whom any man would be proud, except those who have an unnatural development of the cerebellum. Ed. is such an one. He has taken a concubine in the person of Emily Harley. His residence consists of one room.

In delivering a sermon on polygamy, a few years ago, at this place, he said, "You say, I believe in polygamy, but my circumstances will not admit of my taking another. Never let that stand as a barrier from fulfilling God's law. Why, how do you suppose I was situated when I took my second? I only had one room, three plates, three cups, three knives and forks and one bed, my trunk for a table, etc. You ask, Did you all sleep in that bed? Yes. Was there anything wrong about it? No. Then my advice is, go into polygamy, brethren."

This man Sparks has taken the girl against her father's consent, but this only proves that God is on the young man's side, and the father had better withdraw his objections for fear the Lord will visit him with a terrible curse.

Bro. Teasdell, president of this stake, is making a good record, preparatory to going behind the "vail." It is well known that his wife will not move down here, and his royal highness is indispensable to this part of the Lord's vineyard. He is going to take as a second one Miss Tilly Victor.

The reformation is becoming stale, but the leaders have that for which they fought. They have netted a vast amount of their dupes' hard earnings.   EPHRAIM.

NEPHI, Jan. 12.

Deseret News
January 23, 1878

Admitted to Bail.—George Sibley, proprietor of the store at the Sevier Bridge, who shot and killed Joseph Ivie, at that place on the 5th instant, recently had an examination, before a justice of the peace at Nephi, by whom he was held to answer to the grand jury in bonds of $2,500.

It appeared at the examination that Ivie had been very boisterous, noisy and quarrelsome on the day he was killed. Samuel Lutz, employed at the store, remonstrated with him, whereupon he attacked him, and seized Lutz by the cheek with his teeth. Ivie was finally ejected from the building, but subsequently burst in the door and dragged Lutz out upon the road, when the proprietor of the place, Mr. Sibley, fired at and almost instantly killed him.

Conference.—The holding of the regular quarterly Conference of the Nephi Stake of Zion commenced this morning. Some members of the Quorum of the Twelve Apostles are attending it.

Salt Lake Herald
January 29. 1878

Bilks.

Bilks are a scourge to any community and the scarcer they are the better off are honest people and industrious citizens. The southern country recently has been the "stamping ground" of one of these plagues of society whom it would be well to "spot" and give the go-by. Mr. Norman Taylor, who resides at Taylor's ranche, a short distance south of Levan, Juab county, informed us yesterday that a number of people in that county and several north and south of it had been imposed upon by an aged individual, with long hair and a number of *aliases* and that people might be put upon their guard against his winning ways and importuning manner, desired the publication of a few items concerning him. His name is James Rice, *alias* John Rice, *alias* Dr. Rice, *alias* "Baldy" Rice. He has made repeated representations and obtained clothing, sustenance and traveling expenses upon his word that he was well-connected and was related to a Mr. Rice at Leeds. The last-named gentleman was telegraphed to a short time ago, when he replied that he had no such relative. A contract for between 1,200 and 2,000 sheep was made at his suggestion and the flock driven up and left on the hands of the contractor.

Nephi is doing a thriving business and keeping pace with the neighboring towns of Juab, Utah and Sanpete counties. The people are in good spirits and general good health prevails.

DIED.

At Mona, Juab County, January 26th, 1878, NANCY, wife of John Harrison, aged 37 years, 2 months and 3 days.

Deceased was born in St. Helens, Lancashire, England. She had a very amiable disposition and has left a husband and five children and numerous friends to mourn her loss.—COM.

HOUSE OF REPRESENTATIVES.

REPRESENTATIVES' HALL,

Feb. 9, 1878, 10 a.m.

House met as per adjournment.

Roll called. Quorum present.

Prayer by the chaplain.

Mr. Brown reported H. F. 21, "to provide for the licensing of auctioneers, traveling merchants, etc." Read first time and ordered printed.

Mr. Pace reported adversely on C. F. 17, "changing the boundary between Sevier and Piute counties." Report adopted and the bill rejected.

Mr. Birch presented a petition of G. M. Hudson and 302 others, accompanied by H. F. 22, "to disincorporate Kaysville city, Davis county," which was read first time and referred.

H. F. No. 20 was read first time and ordered printed.

H. F. No. 19 was taken up on its second reading by sections.

Adjourned till 2 p.m.

2 o'clock, p m.

House convened as per adjournment.

Roll called. Quorum present.

H. F. 19 was taken up on its second reading, and the motion to read it the third time by its title was lost.

Mr. Milner presented a claim of Jerome P. Cross for $615, for services for the territory, which was referred to the committee on claims and appropriations.

Mr. Milner presented a petition of the inhabitants of Spanish Fork city, asking for amendment to the city charter. Referred to committee on municipal corporations and townsites.

Mr. Preston presented a petition from William Howard, ex-assessor and collector of Rich county, asking remittance of territorial taxes. Referred to the committee on claims, etc.

Mr. Milner presented a petition from G. W. Jacques et al., for removal of a dam in Jordan river. Referred to the committee on judiciary.

Mr. Grover moved that the committee on municipal corporations, etc., be instructed to include in their report on the Kaysville petition the propriety of repealing the act incorporating Nephi city. Carried.

Mr. Murdock presented a petition of E. Tolton and 630 others, for an appropriation for the establishment of a preparatory school for teachers for Beaver county. Referred to the committee on education.

Mr. Pace reported favorably on the petition of W. H. Lee and 362 others for a change of boundary lines between Rich and Summit counties, and submitted a bill H. F. 23, for an act amending section 163 of the compiled laws of Utah and recommended its passage.

The bill was read the first time and laid on the table till called for.

Mr. Farr reported back, amended, H. F. No. 12, on chattel mortgages. Amendments read and concurred in and the bill ordered printed.

A message was received from the council accompanying the resolutions of respect to the memory of the late Hon. Brigham Young.

The resolutions were then read and unanimously concurred in.

H. F. 23 was taken up on its second reading, amended, and read the third time by its title, the bill passed and the title was amended to read, "amending section 163 of compiled laws of Utah," and changing the boundary line between Rich and Summit counties.

Mr. Rockwood reported as follows on the following petitions:

Adversely on that of John Sharp for passing Marshal Nelson and others over the U. C. and U. S. R. R., $525.55. Adopted.

Adversely in regard to that of Josiah Rogerson, for $100 for reporting ten days in the Second district court. Adopted.

Adversely on Presley Denny's petition for $1,500 for services as assistant district attorney. Adopted.

The petition of Auditor Clayton recommending an appropriation of $20,000 for juries and witnesses for 1876-7. The committee recommend $18,000 to be appropriated. Laid over.

In regard to the petition of B. H. Norris and others, and of Ashton Nebeker, the committee reported their claims were included in the $18,000 recommended above. Accepted.

The sum of $240 for Jesse W. Fox, for rent of office, was recommended to be placed on the appropriation bill. Adopted and allowed. Also $22.48 for the relief of Joseph S. Gyles.

The committee recommended that the presenters of petitions, reported on adversely, be allowed to withdraw them from the table.

House adjourned till Monday morning at 10 o'clock.

Benediction by the chaplain.

Salt Lake Herald
February 19, 1878

MARRIED.

HYDE-HAGUE.—On the 14th of February, by Alma Hague, at the residence of the bride's father, J. Alonzo Hyde of Salt Lake City to Miss Ada Hague of Nephi.

Deseret News
March 27, 1878

DIED.

At Washington, Washington County, March 18, 1878, from the effects of an accident while wrestling, DAVID, son of David and Mary Ann Helden Cook, born March 13, 1854, at Nephi, Juab County.

He died a member of the Church of Jesus Christ of Latter-day Saints.

Deseret News
May 1, 1878

DIED.

At Nephi, April 14, 1878, WM. LORDON, aged 31 years and 4 months
He was a native of Lackmo, Canada. West. He leaves a young wife and three small children.—COM
Canada papers, please copy.

Deseret News
May 8, 1878

JUAB STAKE CONFERENCE.

Minutes of the Quarterly Conference of the Juab Stake of Zion, commenced at the meeting house in Nephi, April 20th and 21st, 1878. Present on the stand, President George Teasdale, Joel Grover and K. H. Brown, of the Presidency of the Stake, and the whole of the officers of the Stake. After singing and prayer, the bishops of the several wards gave a very flattering report of the condition of their respective districts, and that an excellent spirit prevailed throughout the settlements, and through the assistance of the several societies and the teachers in the Sunday Schools, they hoped to make a better showing by next conference. The general instructions were, that the people should see the necessity of aiding the forwarding of the Temple at Manti.

Singing and prayer.

2 P. M.

Elder Joel Grover addressed the congregation on the necessity of prompt action in all their movements and to live so that every man and woman know for themselves by the spirit that they are doing the will of the Almighty.

Elder K. H. Brown bore testimony to the work of God, and said that if we would take the councils of the servants of God and be united, as the heart of one man, the blessings of the Father would be and abide with us. God is no respector of persons and he will answer all who will give heed to the whisperings of his spirit.

Sunday morning, 10 a.m.

Singing and prayer.

Brother Elmer Taylor, of Levan, exhorted the people to live so that whatsoever might transpire they would be prepared for every event, and showed the necessity of our laboring, not altogether for this life, but for eternity.

President Teasdale read a dispatch from the city, stating that owing to the press of business none of the Twelve would be with us.

Choir sang an anthem.

Adjourned.

2 p. m.

After singing and prayer President Joel Grover being the first speaker, said that we all should live so that when the servants of the Almighty were called to address us they could feed us with the bread of life; and then gave some very excellent instructions on the principle of sustaining ourselves.

President Teasdale then presented the general authorities of the church as they were presented at the General Conference, who were sustained without a dissenting vote; also the Stake and Branch authorities which were also unanimously sustained, after which he read from the Bible and gave an interesting discourse on the glories to be obtained by keeping the commands of the Almighty and living so that we can commune with God the Father.

We had an excellent time and a good spirit prevailed throughout the whole of Conference and the people from all parts of the country felt happy.

JOHN PYPER,
Clerk of Conference.

Deseret News
May 15, 1878

The Nephi Accident.—By letter from Brother L. A. Bailey, we have further particulars of the disaster that occurred at Nephi, during the wind storm of Sunday night. When the adobie house of W. D. Norton was blown down, the family were in bed, the incident occuring at ten o'clock. While Brother Norton was exerting himself to rescue his children, one of whom was killed, the wall fell in upon him, burying him in the debris. Sister Norton, with a child in her arms, by great exertion, removed the rubbish from and released him. He was badly injured in the back. The little girl who was hurt is expected to recover.

At Franklin Meadows, Oneida Co., Idaho April 6, 1878, of lung fever, ANTON LIND, aged 55, formerly of Levan, Juab Co., Utah.
Deceased leaves a wife and seven children.

Salt Lake Herald
May 16, 1878

A SOUTHERN JAUNT.

Notes and Jottings by the Way.

MANTI CITY, SANPETE CO.,
May 9th, 1878.

As intended, I left Salt Lake City on the morning of the 4th instant, and wending my way southward soon reached the pleasant settlement of Battle Creek or Pleasant Grove, where I and party were kindly received and hospitably entertained by Justice D. West. In conversation with him I find the residents of that settlement, especially those engaged in agriculture, are alive and wide awake to their own interests. There is a much greater breadth of land planted this season than ever before. Indeed, there seems to be a spirit of industrial enterprise among the people of the various settlements so far as I have gone, never before witnessed. Large tracts of land have been taken up, cleared and laid under cultivation and from present appearances it will be a long time before any dearth can happen in Utah from an insufficient average of any given product being planted. The hint that appeared in the HERALD some time since on the potato question is germinating and no doubt there will be a considerable addition to the supply of this article of food.

Proceeding next morning I interviewed the manufacturing emporiums of the south Provo. Considerable additions and alterations are in progress in this thriving city, although slow. The energetic and bustling superintendent of the factory blew his whistle last Monday morning calling his assistants to his aid and started in full life and vigor once more; and no doubt the indefatigable Dunn will soon be heard from with something new to entice both males and females to purchase and paterfamilias to foot the bill.

Proceeding onwards, we passed through Springville and Spanish Fork, bringing up and camping in Payson. Here, as elsewhere, everything is in an onward and upward path. Several new stores have been built and opened, all doing a steady trade, among which we may mention that of Pomeroy & Greer as apothecaries and druggists, and the new branch coöp. Dr. Greer reports the health of the city as good, with an entire absence of any epidemic. Mr. Hancock has also fitted up an excellent little theatre over his store. It is a marvel of neatness and compactness combined, capable of seating about 250 persons.

Salt Creek and Nephi we visited on Sunday night, with the severest wind storm that has visited that settlement for the last twenty years. About 10 o'clock it had reached its full force, and striking the adobe residence of Mr. Wm. D. Norton, blew it down, killing one child instantly and severely injuring the remaining members of the family. What even adds to the distress attending this accident is the fact that Mr. Norton had been of weak intellect for some time, and it is feared that this calamity will upset reason altogether. Influenza is very prevalent in Nephi. The fruit crop will be an entire failure, owing to the severe frost.

Leaving Nephi we passed through Salt Creek cañon and entered that magnificent home of agricultural industry—Sanpete valley—proceeding through it southward by way of Fountain Green, Moroni, Ephraim and this city (Manti), with Mount Pleasant, Spring city and Wales a little way off, the eye is gladdened and the heart made to rejoice at the indications of a plenteous and bountiful harvest. In all other respects the same improvements are to be seen, in fact, Utah in general is arising from her lethargy and will soon show what she can do in the future to supply the demand of the export market. Of Manti and its temple and prospects generally in my next. McE.

Deseret News
June 19, 1878

Coins.—Bro. Canute H. Brown, of Nephi, has presented a collection of silver and copper coins of Denmark to the Museum.

Salt Lake Herald
June 21, 1878

Sad Death.

The wife of Mr. John Pyper died at their home, in Nephi, early Thursday morning, leaving a sorrowing husband, mourning children and regretting friends. The family have our sincere sympathy in their sad bereavement.

DIED.

PYPER.—In Nephi, Juab county, Utah, at 3.30 a. m. Thursday, June 20th, of dropsy Madelina, wife of John Pyper, aged 47 years. Funeral at Nephi, to-day, Friday.

Deceased was baptized in the church of Jesus Christ of Latter-day Saints, in Edinburgh, Scotland, 1840; emigrated to Nauvoo, Illinois, 1844, and came to Utah 1849. She was highly respected in the community, and deeply loved and appreciated by her husband and children.—Com.]

Nephi Notes.

NEPHI, June 20th.

Editors Herald:

Business in Nephi seems to be better than in some other towns. There is a good deal of travel and traffic from Frisco, Silver Reef and Pioche, and much of the supplies for those places are obtained here. As an evidence of this the coöp. store, superintended by C. Foote, has handled and turned over during the year ending June 15th, about $54,000 worth of goods, and this has been done by three persons. They declared a dividend of 20 per cent. for the year and reëlected the same officers, and are now doing a big business. They sell goods as cheap as they can be got in Salt Lake.

The new coöp flouring mill is doing a good business, and turning out a first class article of flour, the finest I have seen in this country. It seems that a good deal of the flour used at the camps is supplied from California but they think here, with the brand of flour they are now making, they will be able to get the trade.

Quite a tragic affair took place on the 17th at the Sevier bridge, about twenty miles south of Nephi. It seems that Francis Caldwell, from Scipio and a half breed named Parshinely Purblo, met in a saloon and did some shooting. Caldwell accused Purblo of trying to take his girl away from him; this Purblo denied, but Caldwell said he was determined to kill him any way, and raised his rifle and blazed away.

Three shots were exchanged. All of Purblo's shots took effect, one in the wrist, another in the hip, and the third in the back, as C. attempted to retreat after firing his last shot. Caldwell died the same night. Purblo underwent an examination on the 18th before Justice Borrowman of Nephi. The testimony of all the witnesses went to show that it was purely in self defence that he shot, and that he stood a great deal of provocation and threatening. He was consequently discharged.

The visit of the railroad men was quite an event, Mr. Hawkins, leader, got out the Nephi brass band and serenaded them, and made the town lively with their sweet strains of music.

Miss Eliza R. Snow and Mrs. Zina Young, who are traveling in the interest of the Ladies' Relief societies, were at Pleasant Grove on Tuesday, Mona on Wednesday, and have a meeting here on Thursday.

The prospects here, as in Utah valley, are for large crops.   D.

Deseret News
June 26, 1878

Demise.—Judge A. C. Pyper has received a dispatch from Nephi, Informing him that Madeline, the wife of his brother, John Pyper, died, this morning, at that place. Deceased leaves a large family of small children. She was the daughter of the late Mrs. Gardner, formerly of Edinburgh, Scotland.

Utah Southern.—The railroad party that visited Nephi the other day did not come to a definite decision in relation to the future terminus of the road. However, a point about one mile south of Mona, known as Robert's Spring, was considered the most favorable. This spot is seven miles this side of Nephi, and has good advantages for water. It is probable that the line will be completed to that place this summer.

Deseret News
July 17, 1878

Nephi.

NEPHI, July 5th, 1878.

At daybreak a salute of 13 guns informed the inhabitants of Nephi another anniversary of the nation's independence had dawned upon the nation.

At sunrise another salute, the hoisting of the national flag and the stirring notes of the brass band, under the leadership of Captain John S. Hawkins, filled the air with melody and joyous sounds.

At 9.30 the county officers and citizens were formed into procession, headed by the brass band, by David Cazier, Esq., marshal of the day, marched from the Social Hall to the meeting house, Timothy B. Foot, Esq., an old veteran, aged 79 years, who had fought under Col. Forsythe in the revolution, marching at the head of the procession.

At the meeting-house the marshal called the assembly to order. The choir, under the leadership of Professor James B. Darton, sang a hymn.

Prayer by the chaplain of the day, Patriarch Jacob G. Bigler, Sr. Music by the brass band.

The reading of the Declaration of Independence by Thos. Ord, Esq. A song, "For all and forever the flag of the free," by Mrs. E. Grace; an oration by the Hon. Joel Grover, the orator of the day. The "Star Spangled Banner" was sung by Mrs. John Andrews, full chorus by the band and choir; followed by music from the band. A song from George Kendall, Esq. (encored); a stirring recitation, "My own, my country's flag," by Mrs. John Andrews; a duet, "Beautiful Gates Ajar," by Mrs. C. Adams and Bird. A speech from George Teasdel, Esq. "The blessings of freedom;" a stirring song, "The Valley for ever," by Mrs. E. Grace; followed by toasts and sentiments. Mrs. John Andrews sang a comic song, "Father will settle the bill."

A vote of thanks to the committee, Messrs. Knud H. Brown, Samuel Cazier; David K. Udall and [...] of the day, the band, choir and all who had taken part in the celebration, and the vast assembly was dismissed by the chaplain.

A dance for the children in the afternoon at the Social and Nephi Halls, and one for the older folks in the evening, was the way "Independence Day" was celebrated in Nephi. We had a good day and enjoyed ourselves well.

ASHER.

Salt Lake Herald
July 21, 1878

NEPHI, UTAH, July, 19, 1878.

Having seen the Osborne Self-binder in the field, on the farm of Judge Tolley, we take pleasure in saying it did excellent work, although the ground was very rough and the grain, in places, light and badly tangled. The work was in all respects far better than we expected, under the circumstances, and we pronounce the Osborne Binder a success.

John Painter, — Goldsboro,
C. Andrews, P. Christison,
David Salisbury, John Fouks,
Carlos Higgins, I. Neulon,
C. E. Abbott, Judge Wm. Tolley.

Deseret News
July 24, 1878

Fatal Accident.—The following special to the NEWS has been received per Deseret Telegraph Line:

NEPHI, Utah,
July 18, 1878.

A fatal accident occurred yesterday, about 6 p. m. Frederick Winn, aged 11 years, son of George and Emily Winn, was killed while playing beneath the bank of the Big Hollow. He and several other children were playing, when the bank gave way, completely burying him. Assistance was rendered immediately, but before he could be dug out, life was extinct. The funeral takes place at 5 p. m. to-day.

Deseret News
August 21, 1878

In this city, Aug. 13, 1878, of consumption of the bowels, DAVID THURWELL, son of Isaac and Elizabeth Sowby, aged 24 years.

Deceased was a resident of Nephi, but was brought to this city a few weeks ago, by his parents, to receive medical treatment. He has been a sufferer for years with the above disease. He was respected by all who knew him, and died in the faith of the gospel.—COM.

Millennial Star please copy.

Deseret News
September 18, 1878

NEW YORK CITY,
September 9, 1878.

Editors Deseret News:

The following missionaries, who left Salt Lake City, Sept. 3rd, are here all well: G. Hogan, from Orderville; Lars Svensen, Moroni G. Frandsen and Christian Jensen, Mount Pleasant; N. P. Rasmussen, Levan; John Halvorsen, Salt Lake City; N. M. Andersen, Ephraim; and we expect L. M. Olsen, from Ephraim, to join us to-day, and to leave on the steamer *Montana* for Liverpool, England, Sept. 10th, at 3 o'clock p.m.

We have had a quick and pleasant journey thus far, and trust we shall have across the ocean. Feel well in body and spirit, and send our best respects to our friends in Utah.

Respectfully yours,
N. P. RASMUSSEN.

Salt Lake Herald
October 10, 1878

BORN.

PEPPER.—In this city, October 8th, to the wife of W. Pepper (residents of Nephi), a son. Mother and child doing well, and the father happy.

Salt Lake Herald
October 26, 1878

Nephi Notes.

A large, two-story addition is being made to the meeting house for a vestry and stand, at the east end of the structure. They intend cutting out the end of the building in the form of an arch, and have the stand in the part now being erected. Having taken out the partition in the west end, they will have, when completed, a very fine hall. It is observed by the plan that they contemplate adding a piece to the front or west end, and putting up a very handsome spire.

Considerable building is going on of small stores on Main street and dwelling houses in different parts of the town.

MOLASSES.

Molasses-making seems to be the great sensation of the season. One can smell treacle several miles outside of the town. Six mills are converting the juice of the sugar cane into molasses.

FARMING

In this locality has been very successful, so far as grain is concerned. John Vickers, as usual, has made a very good showing, although not so heavy as last year. He cultivates thirty nine acres, on which he raised 2,184 bushels of wheat, barley and oats—an average of fifty bushels to the acre. He had a small patch of four and a half acres, on which he raised the incredible quantity of eighty six bushels to the acre. He is a farmer. Potatoes are scarce, so also are greenbacks; silver coin is a medium crop.

The Nephi coöp. is still in a prosperous condition, and doing a big business with Charles Foote as superintendent.

E. Williams does quite a snug business, also in general merchandising.

Nephi has a large flour trade. The new coöperative flouring mill, and John Hague turn out a fine quality.

There is a continual stream of wagons on the road going and coming to and from York, loaded with goods for different camps. Somebody must be doing big business in that southern country.

Diphtheria has made its appearance. Two children died from it on Thursday.

Goldsbrough, with his coal black steeds and handsome carriage, is still carrying passengers between York and Nephi, for the small sum of 50 cents, and all his jokes thrown in.

Deseret News
November 6, 1878

DIED

At Nephi, October 23rd, 1878, of diphtheria, BESSIE LIZETTE, daughter of Edward and Bessie Sparks, aged 7 years, 1 month and 26 days.
Millennial Star please copy.

Salt Lake Herald
December 15, 1878

Saw Mill Burned.

The saw and chopping mill of Bishop John Andrews, of Nephi, was burned on Friday night. The fire took place at 12 o'clock, and is presumed to be the work of an incendiary. The loss is estimated at $1,000.

Deseret News
December 18, 1878

A Lucky Strike.—We had a call to-day from Brother John Rowley, of Nephi, who gives us the following interesting account. A few years ago he took up a farm in a dry region near Nephi, and for several seasons, in addition to the jeers he had to undergo for attempting to utilize so barren a piece of land, was forced to hire water from a creek to irrigate a small portion of it, and leave the other part to the chances of dry farming. A year ago last spring, he bought a piece of swampy ground up in the mountains above Nephi, and was induced by the hope of eventual remuneration, to develop its latent resources. About 40 or 50 small springs oozed forth from the surface, but their waters merely soaked down the hill a distance of about 200 yards and disappeared. Brother Rowley first dug a cut through the swamp, down the hill parallel to the course of the trickling stream, and by this means tapped most of the minute springs and united their waters. He then began about 30 feet below the highest source, and tunnelled, on a level beneath, into the mountain. When he had reached a point even with the highest spring, only a slight seepage was noticeable, and further investigation, above, showed that the spring arose along a slant of about 50 degrees. Returning to his work he continued digging, and one morning, on going to resume labor, he found that the water had broken through and quite a stream was running down his tunnel. This arrested the flow of the springs effectually. The enterprising settler then continued his trench for three-quarters of a mile, to another spring further down, and uniting their waters conducted the stream to his farm. He now waters 25 acres of his land with it, and will leave the hiring of water hereafter, to those who can better afford it, and are less lucky in making a strike similar to his. When he began work, the water in the swamp was foul and brackish, now at his farm it is perfectly pure and healthy. We congratulate our friend on the success which has crowned his perseverance and industry.

Salt Lake Herald
December 27, 1878

DIED.

BLACKETT.—At Nephi, at the residence of his son-in-law, Thomas Pace, December 19, 1878, of old age, Robert Collingwood Blackett.

Deceased was born in London, November 5, 1807, embraced the gospel in 1859, emigrated in 1856. Was a member of the High Priests' quorum. He leaves a wife, six children and twenty-eight grandchildren to mourn his loss. He died in full faith and fellowship.—[Com.

Deseret News
January 8, 1879

Correspondence.

Christmas at Nephi.

MOUNT NEBO, Juab Co., Dec. 25th, 1878.

Editors Deseret News:

From my lofty height I gazed down upon my children dwelling at my feet in the town of Nephi, and saw a sight that pleased me. In my time I have gazed upon many many scenes, have dwelt in solitude when the hum of life and industry was hushed, and silence, almost painful, ruled. But now the scene is changed, and has been since my peaceful vales have been inhabited by the worshippers of the living God.

For a few days I noticed a busy work going on in the Nephi Meeting House. Young men with teams came up my slopes and bereft me of some fine young pines which were taken to decorate and beautify that building. Pictures, flags and banners emblazoned with appropriate mottoes were tastefully hung around. Two of the pines on each side of the stand were converted into Christmas trees upon which a number of curious articles were made to appear to grow. Busy folks sat at a table writing names in books, on cards and pictures, working as diligently as if they were to receive the greatest reward for their labors. This morning, a real Christmas morning, everything was covered with snow, there poured forth a stream of life to that meeting house, teachers and scholars, all in joyful anticipation. Being seated the services commenced.

The Sabbath School choir sweetly sang, "Give us room that we may dwell." The Patriarch Jacob G. Bigler, sr., invoked the divine blessing. The Nephi brass band arrived, and accompanied the school, who sang "Jesus mighty king in Zion." Counselor Joel Grover expressed his joy at seeing so many smiling, happy faces; encouraged and blessed the children. School sang "We thank thee O God for a prophet."

Counsellor K. H. Brown gave instructions on the birth of our Savior and the benefits resulting therefrom.

The school sang, *"Oh, my Father."*

Superintendent Wm. H. Warner addressed the school expressive of the joy and satisfaction of this joyous meeting.

County Superintendent George Teasdale moved a vote of thanks to the committee on decorations, Bros. L. A. Bailey, B. Riches, T. Belliston, and Sisters A. C. Bigler, Kate Love, Mary Udall, and assistants.

School sang, "Mid scenes of confusion."

Sister Amelia Goldsborough addressed the school in a very feeling and affectionate manner.

Music by the band.

Sabbath school choir sang, "My God the Spring of all my joys."

A recitation by Sister A. C. Bigler, "Let us try to be happy."

A comic song from Bro. S. Shaw, greatly amused the children, followed by an interesting address by Sister Hannah Grover.

The school sang "Our Own Sabbath School" with band accompaniment,

Bro. Geo. Kendall spoke encouragingly to the children.

School sang "The Standard of Zion."

Patriarch J. G. Bigler, Sr., invited the children to visit his family Christmas tree at home and blessed the children.

Bro. A. Orme moved a vote of thanks to Supt. G. Teasdale for his labors in behalf of the Sabbath Schools.

A vote of thanks was given to Bros. G. Kendall, T. Crawley, Wm. Ostler, Mary Udall and Kate Love, committee on finance.

Supt. Teasdale expressed his pleasure at this happy meeting, and blessed the children.

The teachers were then supplied with the presents for the children, who received them with great joy.

The band enlivened the occasion with their fine music.

Packets of candy were then presented to all the school, and the County Superintendent made a few encouraging remarks with regard to the future labors of the school. Congregation sang, "The Spirit of

God like a fire is burning,', all standing, with band accompaniment, and were dismissed with prayer and *blessing*.

With light hearts and radiant faces, the happy children hastened home to display their presents to their parents and to tell of the happy time spent at our "Nephi Sabbath School."

Happy are thy children, O Zion: Whilst distress and calamity are overtaking the nations, peace and prosperity are within thy borders. Surely thy inhabitants should be grateful for so many blessings from the bountiful hand of thy glorious redeemer, whose praise was so celebrated, this happy, long to be remembered day.

NEBO.

Deseret News
January 22, 1879

From Nephi.—A correspondent at Nephi writes to us that a number of young men have employed themselves in hauling wood to give to the poor, and that as a mark of appreciation of these benevolent actions, the members of the Young Ladies' Improvement Association tendered the benefactors a complimentary dinner and dance. Some sense in the Nephi folks.

Sad Affair.—Our Nephi correspondent sends us particulars of an operation performed in that city on the 14th inst.

It appears that Andrew Swensen started on the third inst., in company with two others, for a deer hunt, in the mountains east of Nephi. The three hunters separated, agreeing not to get so far apart as to be out of hearing of each other. After some time, his companions, finding he did not answer their calls, went home, supposing that he had become tired and had also gone home. One finding that he had not been seen or heard of since he started on his hunt, a number went the next morning in search of the unfortunate man. He was finally found wandering about, 15 miles up Salt Creek Cañon, and was placed on a horse and carried to the nearest house, where he received every attention. It was found that his feet were badly frozen, but at that time it was not thought that any serious consequences would follow. It was finally seen, however, that to save the man's life, amputation of the injured mem-

bers would be necessary, and accordingly, on the 14th instant, the operation was performed, one foot being taken off just above the ankle, the other just below the knee. He seems, at last accounts, to be a little deranged, but is well cared for, and hopes are entertained of his speedy recovery.

He is lately from Sweden, where he has a wife and three children, and is unable to talk English, so that his situation at the present time is particularly distressing.

Dead.—The unfortunate man, Andrew Swensen, concerning the amputation of whose feet we wrote in last evening's NEWS, died from his injuries on the 16th inst. So we learn by letter from Nephi.

DIED.

In Nephi, Juab County, January 9th, 1879, of lung fever, THOMAS W., son of Francis and Priscilla Sells, aged 3 years and 6 months.

Also January 10th, 1879, of lung fever, EDWARD HIGBEE, son of Francis and Priscilla Sells, aged 6 years and 9 months.

Millennial Star, please copy.

Salt Lake Herald
January 24, 1879

PERSONAL.

Mr. John E. Cowles, of New York, arrived last night.

Mr. O. H. Lashbrook, the Bingham merchant, is again in town.

Mr. Foot, superintendent of the Nephi coöp., is in town, and states that diphtheria has been very prevalent there for a couple of months past, and that quite a number of children have died from the fatal disease.

Deseret News
January 29, 1879

DIED.

At Nephi, of diphtheria. Jan. 19, 1879- ANNIE MARIA SELLS, aged 6 years and 6 months, daughter of Priscilla and Francis Sells.

Millennial Star, please copy.

Deseret News
February 5, 1879

DIED.

At Nephi, Juab County, Utah, January 3, 1879, of diphtheria, JOHN THOMAS, eldest son of John and Eliza Chapman, aged 11 years and 19 days.

Also at Nephi, Juab County, Utah, January 27th, of lung fever, SILAS HENRY, son of John and Eliza Chapman, of Hayes, England, aged 9 years, 10 months and 24 days.

Millennial Star, please copy.

Salt Lake Herald
February 18, 1879

Judge Tolley, of Nephi, is in his usual activity, running around this city on railroad business.

Our old friend, John Hague, of Nephi, is doing the metropolis. He looks hearty and well, and says Nephi is away up.

Salt Lake Herald
February 22, 1879

LIST OF AGENTS

Authorized to take subscriptions for SALT LAKE DAILY and SEMI-WEEKLY HERALD:

Hammond, Brown & Co.,   Cache Co.
John Pymm, - - - St. George
S. A. Wixom, - - - Beaver
W. O. Creer - - Spanish Fork
Walter Walker, - - Farmington
W. L. Watkins, - Brigham City
Jos. U. Eldredge, - - Meadowville
J. R. Clark, - - - Grantsville
John Boyden, - - - Coalville
Charles Foote, - - - Nephi
John C. Stevenson, - - Provo
Thos. Wallace,   Ogden and Weber Co
J. E. Johnson, - - Silver Reef
Edw. Reid, - - - Payson
A. W. Babbitt, - Spring Lake and Santaquin
J. B. Darton, - - - Nephi
Isaac Duffin, - Tokerville, Kane co

John Shields, - - Tooele City
Wm. Rich,   Montpelier, Bear Lake
Wm. Hulme,   Bloomington, Do.
W. Hodge,   Paris,   Do.
W. L. Webster, - Franklin

The HERALD is also supplied by the following Newsmen:

Jas. Dwyer, - - Salt Lake City
Miller, Shelton & Fleming,   Do.
R. Carter, - - - Do.
Walker House do. - Do.
Townsend House do - Do.
R. Deighton, R. R Depot,   Do.
Low & Bro., R. R. Depot,   Ogden
J. G. Chambers, - - Do.
L. Johnson, - - U. S. R. R.
Barkelow Bros., - - U. P. R. R.
G. Marriott,   Sandy and West Jordan
W. Grant, - American Fork
E. Hill - - - Bingham
J. C. Winslow, - Evanston

Deseret News
February 26, 1879

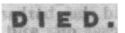

In this city, Feb. 16th NIMSHI SMITH, son of Nimshi and Emily Smith, aged 10 months and 16 days.
Millennial Star, please copy.

Deseret News
March 19, 1879

DIED.

In Nephi, March 12, 1879, of diphtheria, HARRY, son of T. P. and Jane Stephenson, born Feb. 20, 1877.
Millennial Star, please copy.

Deseret News
April 2, 1879

DIED.

At Nephi City, March 25th, 1879, MARY
ANN B KTON, wife of James M Pyp r.
aft r a short illness of 2 hours, aged 31
years and 7 months She leaves four young
children and numerous friends.

Salt Lake Herald
April 15, 1879

THE MANTI TEMPLE.

The Dedicatory Services and General Ceremonies.

[Special to the HERALD.]

Manti, April 14.—At about 11.30
a.m. to-day, a vast number of people
assembled near the temple site and
formed into procession in the follow
ing order: The Nephi brass band,
quorum of the Twelve, patriarches,
presidents of stakes, high council,
seventies, high priests, elders, presid
ing bishops and counselors, bishops
and counselors, lesser priesthood,
mayor of Manti city and council,
judge and county officers, ladies'
relief societies, superintendent,
teachers and Sunday schools, Manti
choir and Manti martial band.
Marshal of the day, General W.
S. Snow. They then marched
up to the temple site to the
southeast corner. President Taylor
called the congregation to order. The
opening prayer was offered by Apostle
Rich. An oration was delivered by
Apostle E. Snow. Master Mason
E. L. Parry and Architect W. H.
Folsom laid the chief corner stone.
President Taylor pronounced it
properly laid and Apostle Lorenzo
Snow offered the dedicatory prayer.
Bishop Hunter laid the southwest
corner stone and Bishop Hardy pro
nounced the dedicatory prayer. F.
W. Cox, president of the high priests'
quorum, Sanpete stake, laid the
northwest corner and President Peter
sen offered the dedicatory prayer. H.
S. Eldredge, president of the first
quorum of seventies, laid the north
east corner and the dedicatory
prayer was offered by John
VanCott. The ceremonies lasted
about two hours, after which the con
gregation was addressed by Apostles
F. D. Richards, B. Young, J. F.
Smith, A. Carrington, Moses
Thatcher and President Taylor, with
the benediction by Bishop Hunter.
The Manti choir and Nephi brass
band rendered singing and music for
the occasion. No accidents hap
pened. Between 3,000 and 4,000
people were present. Showers of rain
fell before and after the exercises.
Harmony and goodwill prevailed.
The stars and stripes were unfurled
to the breeze upon the site and else
where.

Correspondence.

Another Veteran Gone.

MINERSVILLE, Beaver Co.,
March 31, 1879.

Editors Deseret News:

Jehu Blackburn died at Nephi, Juab County, at one o'clock a. m., on Wednesday, 19th inst., of lung fever, after an illness of nine days. Was born December 25, 1824, in Bedford County, Pennsylvania; was the son of Thomas and Elizabeth Blackburn; moved to the State of Ohio in 1835, and to the State of Illinois in 1841; was baptized into the Church of Jesus Christ of Latter-day Saints in 1842, by Bishop David Evans, shared the expulsion of the Saints at Nauvoo in 1846; arrived in Salt Lake Valley in 1848; helped to build the Old Fort in Salt Lake Valley in 1849; pioneered and helped to build the

fort in Provo, and in 1853 was called by President G. A. Smith to strengthen the southern settlements; helped to build up Fillmore City, and in 1856 built a mill in Pine Valley, and in 1859 helped to found and build up Minersville, Beaver Bounty, and in the Spring of 1876, pioneered and founded the settlement in Fremont or Rabbit Valley, Piute County, and at the time of his death was building a mill at that place.

He was the husband of four wives and the father of 21 children, 15 boys and six girls and nine grandchildren. He leaves a large family and a large number of friends to mourn his loss. Died in full faith of a glorious resurrection. Respectfully, etc.

E. H. BLACKBURN.

JUAB STAKE CONFERENCE.

The quarterly conference of the Juab County Stake of Zion, was held Saturday and Sunday, April 19th and 20th, 1879.

Saturday, April 19th, 10 a.m.

Present on the stand, President John Taylor; Elders A. P. Rockwood, John Van Cott and Wm. W. Taylor, of Salt Lake City.

President George Teasdale and Counselor K. H. Brown, Patriarch Jacob G. Bigler, sen., Members of the High Council, the bishops of the several wards and their counselors.

After singing and prayer, the clerk read the statistical and Sunday School reports, and the Bishops reported their various wards in favorable condition. President Teasdale remarked that notwithstanding the local improvements by way of a vestry added to the Tabernacle, and the building of a co-operative mill, amounting to nearly $15,000, there had been no decrease in tithing, the faith of the Saints being demonstrated by their works.

President John Taylor was pleased to hear the good reports given by the President and Bishops of the Stake. Instructed the officers of the Stake in their duties, exhorting them, by fatherly kindess, humility, and love to unite the Saints together, and if there were any who were inclined to go astray, to endeavor by longsuffering and kindness to show them the right way and keep them within the fold. Exhorted the Saints to prayerfulness, that they might have the Spirit of the Lord among them, to have no hard feelings one against another, but to promote harmony in all their dealings. Portrayed the duties of the officers of the Church, from the the greatest to the least, showed that all were necessary in order to form the perfect body of the Church, and that each should be honored and respected in their place and authority.

2 p.m.

After devotional exercises, Elder John Van Cott addressed the conference. Showed the beauties of the organization of the church and kingdom of God, the advantages that the Latter-day Saints had over the people of the world, the Latter-day Saints being taught by those who are inspired of God, etc.; the responsibilities of parents to teach their children correct principles; eulogized the Nephi brass band on their sweet and soul-stirring music at the laying of the corner stones of the Manti Temple and also during this conference; exhorted the Saints to cultivate the spirit of union, that they may eventually become prepared to enter into the United Order.

President Teasdale then presented the general and local authorities of the Church, which were unanimously sustained.

At noon the dedication of the Tabernacle vestry took place.

There were present during this service—President John Taylor and visitors, the Presidency of the Stake and the High Council, Patriarch and Presidency of the High Priests, the Bishops and representatives of all the Quorum and Societies and Associations in the ward. The services consisted of singing, and remarks by President John Taylor, who also offered the dedicatory prayer.

Elder William Jennings spoke on co-operation; showed that it had proven a success and had been a great benefit to the people; also of the advantages the young people have to-day in being instructed in the principles of righteousness.

President John Taylor demonstrated how the people had been blessed by co operation at various times and under various circumstances; spoke at some length upon the Board of Trade and encouraged the Saints to become self-sustaining.

Sunday, April 20th, 10 a.m.

After the usual exercises, Elder A. P. Rockwood impressed upon the minds of the Saints that the coming of the Son of Man is near at hand, and the necessity of the gospel being preached in all the world; showed the duties of the Seventies, and exhorted the young to study the Scriptures and all good books, preparing themselves for the ministry, etc.

Elder Wm. Paxman, of American Fork, spoke of the different circumstances under which the Saints had heard and received the gospel, and the intelligence which they had received through obedience.

2 p.m.

After singing and prayer,

President Teasdale read from the Doctrine and Covenants, commencing at page 283 to end of section, during which time the Sacrament was administered.

President John Taylor occupied the afternoon on the dispensation of the fulness of times; referred to the first vision of Joseph Smith, the visitation of Moroni, John the Baptist, Peter, James and John, Moses and Elijah, with the keys of the Priesthood they held, and referred to the experience of the Elders since the restoration of the gospel, their experience proving the correctness of the promises given therein; spoke very encouragingly to the Saints and exhorted them to live and practice the principles of righteousness, magnify their callings and sustain every correct principle; referred to the labors performed on the Manti and Logan Temples and the increase of faith manifested by the works of the Saints; exhorted the Saints to live in love and union in family and social relationships, and invoked God's blessing upon them.

Benediction by President George Teasdale.

WM. A. C. BRYAN, Clerk.

Nephi, April 22nd, 1879.

Salt Lake Herald
May 18, 1879

Stabbing.

A gentleman up from Nephi states that a few days ago a difficulty occurred between two men in Salt Creek Cañon, at what is called Tidwell's ranch. The parties were Henry Hoyt and Thomas Tidwell. The cause of the difficulty is unknown, but Tidwell stabbed Hoyt in the ribs. Hoyt managed to get home, but upon arriving there he fainted, and examination proved that the injury was more serious than at first believed.

Railroad Matters.

The track of the extension of the Utah Southern Railroad is now laid beyond Nephi, and is expected to be completed as far as Chicken Creek, the final destination of this road, by the 1st of June. There is an abundance of ties, rails, nails, etc., on hand, and nearly every day sees car loads of truck taken south. The work is being pushed ahead with all possible expediency and the running of cars and construction engines over the new road, it is expected, will have so far settled the bed of the road that it will be in condition for trains to run over almost as soon as completed.

Bishop Sharp states that contracts have been let for grading the road of the Utah Southern Extension, which commences where the Utah Southern leaves off—Chicken Creek—as far as what is known as the Church House, a distance of sixteen and a half miles, which will take it through the Sevier Cañon. All the contracts are to be completed within thirty days. So it will be seen that business is the intention.

Salt Lake Herald
June 15, 1879

RELIGIOUS SERVICES TO-DAY.

CHURCH OF JESUS CHRIST OF LATTER-DAY SAINTS.—Services in the Tabernacle at 2 p.m. and in the ward meeting houses in the evening.

TWENTIETH WARD.—Elder George Teasdale, of Nephi, will preach this evening at 6.30 o'clock.

SCANDINAVIAN SERVICE in the Council house every Sunday at 6 p.m.

GERMAN SERVICE.—Service in German at the City Hall, every Sunday at 10 o'clock. German and Swiss are cordially invited to attend.

ST. MARK'S CATHEDRAL—Evening service, 7.30 o'clock. Sunday school, 9.45 a.m.

ST. PAUL'S CHAPEL, corner of Fifth South and Second West streets.—Sunday School 2 30 p.m. Evening service at 7.20 o'clock.

METHODIST EPISCOPAL CHURCH.—First Church.—Rev. J. McEldowney, pastor. Rev. J. H. Vincent will preach at 11 a m.

CATHOLIC.—Church of St. Mary Magdalene, Rev. Father Scanlan, Pastor. Mass and Benediction at 11 a.m.; Vespers and Benediction at 7.30 p.m.

CATHOLIC SERVICE at Camp Douglas the second Sunday of each month at 10 o'clock a.m.

PRESBYTERIAN CHURCH.—Preaching at 11 a.m. by the pastor, Rev, R. G. McNiece. Sabbath school at 9.20 a.m. Young People's Prayer Meeting at 6.30 p.m.

CONGREGATIONAL CHURCH.—Preaching at 11 o'c'ock by Mr. Benner. Sabbath School at 12 No evening service.

Deseret News
July 2, 1879

An affray took place at Juab, (the new terminus) last Saturday, in which Canfield Young, of Mona, assaulted J. Whitbeck Jr., calling him abusive names and drawing a butcher knife upon him. The bystanders interfered or in all probability blood would have been shed The affair grew out of a trial, by jury, of Young's son, on which occasion Whitbeck was the foreman, and the verdict rendered, guilty. Young was arrested, and is to be examined at Nephi.

A few days ago while Mr. P. Thygessen, of Levan, was riding out, the hind seat of the wagon got loose and was thrown out on the road, carrying its occupants, Miss Caroline, his daughter, and two other young ladies, with it. The first-named had her collar bone broken, the others were uninjured.

Deseret News
July 9, 1879

DIED.

At Nephi, June 29, 1879, of diphtheria. JOHN HENRY, son of Edward and Martha Jones, aged 5 years and 2 months.

Salt Lake Herald
July 11, 1879

Burglary at Nephi.

On Wednesday night, a burglary was perpetrated at Nephi, the house of Mr. John Hawkins being entered and robbed of a watch and several pieces of jewelry, and boxes and trunks turned topsy-turvy, and the young fellow who was suspected was arrested last evening, after arriving here, and lodged in the city prison, until "proof positive" is brought against him. His name is given as John Lillard, from Chicago, and he has a record. On the trip up, in his interviews with members of the fire brigade, fellow-passengers and gents who were instructed to "spot him," it is alleged that he gave himself so completely away that he was held until evidence can be accumulated to convict him, which appears certain.

Deseret News
July 16, 1879

The Nephi Burglary.—The examination of J. W. Lillard, arrested on suspicion of having robbed the house of John Hawkins, at Nephi, on Wednesday night, is going on in the Police Court this afternoon. It appears that while the members of the household were away enjoying the Firemen's display on that night, some man entered the house and stole some broaches, a pair of earrings and several other articles of value, and was seen escaping from the window by a lady of the family who returned unexpectedly. Her description of the burglar led to the suspicion of Lillard, and he was closely watched until the train started for home. He tried to jump the train at Sandy, but was prevented by Messrs. W. J. Hooper and R. C. Frye, (the latter a nightwatchman) who had charge of the excursion. His manner was so uneasy and suspicious, that with the sanction of the entire company, the gentlemen above named arrested him on arriving in this County and handed him over to the police. Two watches were found on his person, but none of the property Mr. Hawkins had lost. More will be known to-morrow.

Salt Lake Herald
July 20, 1879

Serious Accident.

By private telegram we learn that on Friday, Joseph Darton, son of James B. Darton, met with a sad accident, the cars on the Utah Southern, at Nephi, having run over his arm, which will necessitate amputation. This accident will be regretted by many, as he was a useful member of the brass and string bands of that place, and bid fair to be as proficient as he was a natural musician.

Deseret News
July 23, 1879

Accidents.—On Thursday even-
a Miss Wandell, of Nephi, while
sitting in a chair, tipped over backwards, her head striking a flatiron,
and receiving a severe wound about
two inches above the right ear.

On the day previous to this accident, M. A. Holley, of Richfield,
Sevier County, while tussling with
a companion, fell and broke the
small bone of his right leg. Dr.
Crockwell attended both these
cases, and the patients are doing
very well.

Salt Lake Herald
August 2, 1879

A Rare Bird.

Some weeks ago John W. Lillard
was arrested and fined for larceny in
this city, and is now working out
that fine. He went south on the last
firemen's excursion, and while there
a robbery was committed at Nephi.
On the return trip the impression
that he was the culprit became very
manifest among the party, so much
so that Lillard must have perceived
it. It now transpires that he was
guilty of breaking into the house in
Nephi. The articles stolen were found
along the Utah Southern track,
where he must have dropped them,
and a razor which he had sold to Mr.
Sam Rogers, his keeper, was yesterday identified as the property of Mr.
J. S. Hawkins, at whose house the
robbery was committed. Lillard was
taken before Judge Pyper yesterday,
and waiving an examination, was
bound over in $1,000 to await the
action of the next grand jury.

Deseret News
August 6, 1879

NEPHI.

We had a very pleasant time yesterday in celebrating the 24th. An
assembly of our citizens, a procession of the various quorums, societies and schools meeting in the
Tabernacle. The choir sang "Lo
the Gentile chain is broken;" Father C. H. Bryan, chaplain of the
day, offered prayer; our brass band
played in their usual good style,
and Elder M. McCune, the orator
of the day, delivered an interesting
oration; the Sabbath school choir
sang "White Lilies;" an address
from Elder George Kendall was followed by a pleasing song by Sister
E. Grace, then Patriarch J. G. Bigler delivered an address, and the
band again made lively music; Bro.
C. Morris sang "Slavery's Day;"
President Teasdale and Elders D.
Cazier and K. H. Brown delivered
short addresses; a song "There's a
rainbow in the clouds," was sung
very sweetly by Sister Grace. A
vote of thanks to the committee—
Bros. K. H. Brown, T. Crawley, B.
Richas, L. A. Bailey, Silas and
Samuel Jackson. After singing,
the assembly was dismissed by the
chaplain.

In the afternoon to the Sabbath
school scholars afforded amusement
and pleasant associations at J. S.
Hawkins' Bowery, which he kindly placed at the service of the committee.

In the evening the grown folks
had a pleasant gathering in the Social and Union Halls, and enjoyed
themselves in the dance. We had
a quiet, pleasant day.

L. A. B.

JUAB.

Juab City, August 11, 1879.

Editors Herald:

The little railroad city of Juab is at present in a flourishing condition. The company has brought water to the town in pipes, from a spring about a mile and a half from the station. The business men here are in the best of spirits, and if business continues there will be no room for them to complain. Prominent among the business men and firms are Warnock & Co., dealers in wagons, carriages, reapers, mowers and hay rakes, also forwarding and commission merchants; the Utah Forwarding Company also does a good business in wagons, plows, grain, etc; Fred. G. Willis is the leading merchant and popular agent of the stage company, and is happy since he was elected justice of the peace. E. Stoddart is the proprietor of the Railroad Hotel, where travelers will find the best meals in town. J. M. Joel-son is a dealer in general merchandise; the branch store of the Levan Coop is doing a pretty good business. Elmer Taylor is running a butcher shop, and Charles L. Olson is running a lunch house. W. P. Read is making the harness and saddles, W. C. Whitbeck is building a large frame house where he will furnish the poor weary pilgrims with pretty good hash. W. M. Pepper is doing a very good business, shoeing horses and mules. Ade Chalmers keeps a wholesale and retail liquor store. A large substantial freight house is here and so is Mr. John Bueb, who, with the rest of the boys in the freight house, is always ready to receive and ship freight.

The Railroad Company is now building a large engine house, which, when completed will loom up in the distance and greatly improve the appearance of Juab. The railroad extension is now about thirty miles from here, and in a few months will be booming into Frisco. TICKUP.

DIED.

At Nephi, August 2nd, 1879, TIMOTHY SABEN HOYT, son of James and Bula Hoyt.

Born March 4th, 1818, at Boonville, Oneida County, New York. Joined the Church in 1839; emigrated with his father to Illinois; was on a preaching mission to the Eastern States when Joseph the Prophet was martyred; enlisted in the Mormon Battalion, and suffered the privations of the march to California; arrived in Salt Lake City in 1848, and soon afterwards married Elizabeth L. Sperry; moved to Nephi in the spring of 1853; in the spring of 1857 was ordained a president of the 49th Quorum of Seventies; in the year 1866 was ordained a High Priest and set apart as High Councilor in that Stake of Zion, which position he held faithfully until his demise. Was down to St. George Temple last spring, and performed a good work for his dead.

On Sunday, the 3rd August, he was conveyed from his residence to the tabernacle by the members of the High Council, and Battalion boys as pall bearers. After singing, etc., many of his old friends spoke of his past life in a very praiseworthy manner; a great many followed him to his last resting place. He leaves a wife, two sons and four daughters to mourn the absence of a kind husband and an indulgent father. L. A. B.

"Enquirer" Items.—Riley Stewart, a crazy man at Diamond, Tintic District, has been on the rampage lately, having obtained a knife and axe and threatened to depopulate the whole district. He attacked a young man named Starr, with the knife and several others with the axe. He has been secured and sent to Nephi to the care of the sheriff.

A 14 year old thief has appeared at Juab. A few days ago he went up to two men camped a little way from the station, and seeing that one of them was sleeping in an alcoholic stupor, devised a plan to rob him. He told the sober man that a friend wanted to see him at a certain saloon, and while he was absent robbed the inebriated man of $15 and decamped. He was caught, however, and is now in durance at the Juab county jail.

Augustus Royer, the alleged child poisoner of Payson, was brought to Provo Monday and placed in jail. When brought before a justice he waived an examination. He seems to feel deeply the loss of his child and strenuously protests his innocence. He said the druggist did not give him a direct answer when he asked how much morphine was a dose. The druggist, however, declares he told Boyer that the ten cents' worth he bought would kill four men.

Kicked.—By letter from Nephi we learn that Father Wm. Goble, of that place, was recently kicked so severely as to badly break and crush the upper bone of his right arm. The blow rendered him insensible for a few minutes, but on recovering he walked two miles, from his field to the house, where Dr. Crockwell attended him, setting the bone, and making him otherwise comfortable. Our correspondent doesn't state from what kind of animal the kick was received, but in the absence of better information, we will say it was a mule.

From the same correspondent we learn that on the 5th instant, Mr. Stephen Ostler, son of Mr. John Ostler, of Nephi, was badly hurt; while riding, his horse fell with him, breaking his left arm just above the wrist. Dr. Crockwell also attended upon this gentleman, who is doing well.

A correspondent at Nephi informs us that on the morning of the 24th inst., Mr. William Osborn, of Gooseberry Valley, while oiling a threshing machine, had his left arm accidentally drawn into the cogs, to the centre of the muscle of the forearm. Part of his forefinger was crushed and all of his thumb, and his arm terribly lacerated. Dr. Crockwell amputated the fractured portion of the finger and thumb, and removed some of the ragged flesh of the forearm. The patient was doing well at Nephi, under Dr. Crockwell's care. As the patient would necessarily be thrown out of employment for some time, and has a family to support, his friends generously came to his assistance with a purse of $125; the owner of the threshing machine giving 20 bushels of wheat, and others similar amounts.

ELDER GEORGE Q. CANNON presented the following names of missionaries. Those who have already gone to Europe and the United States are indicated by *.

GREAT BRITAIN.

*Chas. R. Savage, Salt Lake City
*George M. Ottinger, "
Wallace Willey, Bountiful
Thomas Duce, Hyde Park
Hyrum Evans, Salt Lake City
Enoch Lewis, Bountiful
*Thomas Davis, Wales, Sanpete
James Birmingham, Bountiful

Robert F. Gould, Washington
Joseph C. Bentley, St. George
Samuel L. Adams "
Zera P. Terry, Hebron
Abraham H. Cannon, Farmers' Wd.
Howard Coray, Mona
William Coray, "

UNITED STATES.

*Solomon Clinton Stevens, Ogden
*Wm. W. Fife, Ogden
*George H. Carver, Plain City
*Hyrum Belnap, Hooper
*Henry Bartholomew, Slaterville
*Noah L. Shirtliff, Harrisville
*Teancum W. Heward, Draper
*Gordon S. Bills, South Jordan
*Samuel Butterfield, Fort Herriman
*Francis McDonald, Big Cottonwood
*Levi P. Helm, Mill Creek
*Moroni Pickett, Tooele
*James H. Moyle, Salt Lake City
*John Wm. Gibson, North Ogden
*David H. Peery, Ogden
*Newell W. Taylor, Harrisville
*Squire Gaeen Crowley, Lynn
Richard Hill, Ogden
*George H. Butler, Marriottsville
Lorenzo Hunsaker, Honeyville
*Benjamin Harker, Taylorsville
Franklin Spencer, Richfield
John R. Murdock, Beaver
Richard A. Ballantyne, Ogden
John H. Williams, Coalville

Crandel Dunn, Beaver Dam
Aaron Thatcher, Logan
Israel D. Olphin, Pangwitch
George Nebeker, Salt Lake City
Gronway Parry. "
John Ellison, Kaysville
John C. Witbeck, Levan

SCANDINAVIA.

*Niels B. Adler, Spring City
*Niels Thompson, Ephraim
*Mons Nielsen, Ephraim
*Christian Jensen, Moroni
*Christian Olsen, Fairview
*Niels C. Larsen, Manti
*Errick O. Byland, Santaquin
*Lawrence C. Mariger, Kanab
*Carl John Oberg, Provo
*Christian L. Hansen, Gunnison
*C. Anthon Christensen, Fountain Green
*Ludwig Suhrke, Soda Springs
O. N. Stohl, Brigham City
Jacob Hansen, Bear River City
Harmon F. F. Thorup, City, First Ward
John T. Thorup, City, First Ward
Peter Nielsen, Washington
Peter Nielsen, Smithfield
Fred Lundberg, Logan
Hans Funk, Lewiston
Israel Sorensen, Mendon
Anton L. Skankie, Logan
Peter A. Nielsen, Draper

Deseret News
October 22, 1879

Accidents.—On the 15th inst., Mr. V. L. Thomas, one of the proprietors of a saw mill in Salt Creek Cañon, Juab County, while cleaning away some sawdust, accidentally slipped in such a manner that his hand came in contact with the swiftly revolving saw. His fingers were badly cut and serious consequences were feared, but later accounts say he is doing very well.

On the 16th inst., Wm. Read, of Nephi, was undoing the windlass of an ox-shoeing rack when the iron handle slipped from his hand, striking him on the forehead over the left eye, and cutting a gash to the bone nearly three inches long. The blow knocked him down, and in falling, he struck a rock, cutting another deep gash on the left eyebrow.

A son of Reuben J. Downs injured his leg some time ago while playing at school. On the 16th the wounded member was discovered to be ailing from an abscess between the bones, extending from the knee to the ankle. An incision 10 inches long was made, from which a large amount of offensive matter came forth, and at last accounts the sufferer was improving, with every prospect of a speedy recovery.

In all the foregoing cases, Dr. J. M. Crockwell, lately of this city, rendered the medical aid necessary for the comfort of the patients.

Deseret News
October 29, 1879

A Bovine Treasure. — Brother Jacob Bigler, of Nephi, has a cow of the half breed Devon stock that is a small fortune in herself. As a sample of what she can produce, we give the following: One evening last week Sister Bigler set away the milk from this cow and let it stand thirty-six hours. She then skimmed it, taking the whole coating of cream in her hand at once and without its breaking, deposited it in the scales. It weighed just sixteen ounces. She then put it into a pan, took a spoon and stirred it three minutes and it became butter, so nice and hard it was with difficulty she could stir in the salt. The butter was then put into the same scales and weighed exactly thirteen ounces; the buttermilk exactly three ounces. We are also told that the milk from the same cow, mixed with that of ordinary cows, when setting away, not only increases its richness, but causes the cream of the latter to rise much quicker than usual.

At Nephi, October 16th, 1879, AMANDA MORGAN (Miller).
Deceased was born August 10th, 1795, at Bolton, Essex County, Vermont. Married to Josiah Miller in 1815, and embraced the gospel in the town of Holland in 1834; traveled in the Kirtland camp; came to Winter Quarters in 1846; emigrated with the first company to this country; moved to Nephi in 1850, and was one of the first settlers here. She was the mother of eight children. She leaves a son and two daughters, 56 grandchildren, 48 great grandchildren.

The funeral services took place at the residence of her son-in-law, Bishop C. Sperry, on Saturday, October 18th. After singing and prayer, etc., many of her old friends spoke of her faithfulness and long standing in the church. She has gone to meet with her husband and Joseph and Hyrum and Brigham, and those she loved. A good many followed her to her last resting place.—COM.

Salt Lake Herald
November 25, 1879

More Railroad.

It is stated that an English company, represented by Mr. Bamberger, has invested sufficient money to build a narrow-gauge railroad from Nephi to the coal beds in Wales, Sanpete County, but when the company will get returns the most intelligent Nephite is unable to predict. Messrs. Grover & Tulley have a contract for grading six miles of the road, and the rails are expected in February.

Deseret News
November 26, 1879

At Mona, Juab County, Utah, November 9th, 1879, of Diphtheria, ELIZABETH R. daughter of the late James Berry and his wife Mary Yates, formerly of the Upholland Branch of the Liverpool Conference, aged 8 years and 10 days.

Also at the same place, November 14th, 1879, of diphtheria, WILLIAM, son of the above parents, aged 7 years, 7 months and 25 days.

Mill. Star, please copy.

At Mona, Juab County, Utah, November 17th, 1879, of membraneous croup, JOHN T., son of John and Elizabeth Partington, formerly of the St. Helens Branch of the Liverpool Conference, aged 7 years, 2 months and 15 days.

Mill. Star, please copy.

Deseret News
December 10, 1879

Highway Robbery.—A few days ago a young man named George Howard, a resident of Nephi, while returning from Piocbe, was stopped a few miles south of Deseret Springs, near Ben Tasker's ranch, by two armed and masked men, who demanded his money. He gave up $24 in money and a silver watch, but afterwards begged that he might have his watch back again, as it was a family relic or something of that kind. The highway robbers manifested, under the circumstances, a remarkable degree of generosity, for they returned the watch but preferred retaining the money. On the following morning Howard went to see Ben Tasker, and laid before that worthy the facts in the matter, at the same time requesting him to investigate the affair. Ben was very indignant about the robbery and assured Howard that he would look into the matter and let him know the result in due time. If Howard waits long enough he may learn all about it in "due time," but somebody must look after Ben in the meantime.—*Enquirer.*

NEPHI, Juab County, U.T.,
January 1st, 1880.

Editors Deseret News:

Your welcome paper comes regularly to hand, and we enjoy reading what is done in other towns. I suppose it will not be uninteresting to know how we have spent our holidays here.

On Christmas Eve we had a very enjoyable dance in the Social Hall. On Christmas day we had a grand gathering at the Sabbath School. Our Nephi brass band, with their genial leader Captain John S. Hawkins, who are ever on hand to make our holidays a success, favored us with their excellent music. We had short addresses from our County Superintendent Elder G. Teasdale and Supt. W. H. Warner and his assistants Elders A. Orme and Langley A. Bailey, Counselor Joel Grover, Elder George Kendall, Sisters Amelia Goldsbrough and Hannah Grover. Bro. S. Shaw sang a comic song. Brothers Jno. S. Hawkins, Henry McCune and Joseph Darton played solos on the clarionet and cornet, and the Sabbath School choir and children sang their sweetest pieces. Presents of candy and nuts were passed around, and I can assure you we had a most enjoyable time.

In the afternoon the juveniles "tripped it" on the "light fantastic toe," and the "big boys" and girls did likewise in the evening.

On New Year's eve our Nephi Amateur Dramatic Company furnished us with a drama entitled "Wenlock of Wenlock" and a laughable farce "That Blessed Baby," which were very creditably rendered. Messrs. C. Haynes, F. Teasdel, R. C. Blackett, F. F. Hudson, I. Gadd, J. Black, F. W. Chappell and T. Parkes; Misses E. A. Udall, U. A. Knowles, C. Webb and Mrs. C. Haynes, playing the characters. On New Year's Day there was a matinee for the children, and a crowded house on New Year's night. This was gotten up for the purpose of defraying an indebtedness on the vestry. The company worked very hard, and we cannot say too much in their praise.

On New Year's morning we held our fast meeting, the meeting was crowded, and we enjoyed one of the finest fellowship meetings it has been my privilege to attend.

We are enjoying real old fashion Christmas weather, plenty of the "beautiful," good for sleighing, and a pleasant prospect for plenty of water, *for* which we are very thankful.

Wishing you a "Happy New Year," with peace and prosperity,
Your friend,
NEBO.

Deseret News
February 4, 1880

Juab County Y. M. M. I. A.

NEPHI, Juab Co., Utah,
Jan. 20th, 1880.

Editors Deseret News:

On the 18th inst., in the Nephi Tabernacle, at 7 o'clock p. m., the Young Men's Mutual Improvement Association of the Juab County Stake of Zion met, President Thos. Crawley presiding.

After singing and prayer, the reports of the different branches were then read by Thomas H. G. Parkes, secretary pro tem., which show that this Association is prospering, that their meetings are well attended, and appropriate subjects are duly given out to lecture and debate upon, many of which are handled with zeal and ability; that their meetings *are becoming* more and more interesting, and the young people are gradually losing all diffidence about expressing their ideas, and lecturing or debating upon subjects assigned to them; that this Association has been a great benefit to those who have attended its meetings.

Members, E. Shepard, of Mona, James Jenkins, of Nephi, and Wm. Tunbridge, of Levan, addressed the meeting, making remarks appropriate to the occasion, and expressing themselves well pleased with the congenial and energetic spirit of their co-laborers.

At the solicitation of President Crawley, Elder K. H. Brown addressed the young people, giving them good instruction and encouraging them to go on in their good work.

Meeting was then adjourned. Benediction by J. G. Bigler.

Yours respectfully,

A NEPHITE.

Deseret News
February 18, 1880

In Nephi, January 31st, 1880, of croup, WILLIAM R., son of David and Elizabeth Udall; aged 5 years lacking 12 days.

Deseret News
February 25, 1880

NOTARIES PUBLIC.

Juab County. — Wm. R. May, Nephi; Jas. M. Wayne, Diamond; John Pyper, Nephi; Patrick Cusick, Eureka; C. H. Blanchard, Jr., Silver City.

MARRIED.

In this city, on the 14th inst., Mr. ROBERT A. PYPER, son of Bishop A. C. Pyper, of this City, and Miss CORDELIA WEBB, daughter of Mr. David Webb, of Nephi.

Deseret News
March 10, 1880

DIED.

At Levan, Juab, Co., U. T. Feb. 16th 1880, of lung fever, after suffering from the measles, SARAH ELIZABETH, daughter of Andrew and Elizabeth Hendricksen, aged 10 years 1 month and 12 days.

Deseret News
March 24, 1880

DIED

At St. George, March 2nd, 1880, ALBERT G. FELLOWS.

Deceased was born September 5th, 1799, in Luzern County, Pennsylvania; was baptized into the Church of Jesus Christ of Latter-day Saints at Brownstown, Michigan, in February, 1839; was ordained a High Priest in Nauvoo, January, 1846; gathered to Utah with the Saints in Bishop Edward Hunter's company; has been during his long association with the Church an unpretentious but an earnest Saint of God. He came to St. George from his home in Nephi in October last, to attend to ordinance work in St. George Temple for his dead kindred and friends. He has entered into his rest in full faith and sure hope of a glorious resurrection.—COM.

Deseret News
April 8, 1880

DIED.

At Nephi, April 21st, 1880, of whooping cough and measles LEO LEROY, son o, Henry and Ellen Goldsbrough, born May 16th 1880.

First District Juries.—Following is the list of grand jurors for the First Judicial District empanelled in Ogden, yesterday.

1. Loren Roundy, Springville
2. John Rockhill, Spanish Fork
3. M. Tanner, Provo
4. C. H. Davis, "
5. Shaderack Empy, Springville
6. E. Healey, Alpine
7. John E. Hills, Provo
8. James Armistead, America. Fork.
9. H. M. Alexander, Provo
10. James Preston, Springville
11. George White, "
12. George T. Pay, Provo
13. Edwin Healy, Nephi
14. Hosea Sterritt, Pleasant Grove
15. Wm. Carten, Springville

DIED.

At Nephi, Juab County. May 2nd, 1880, of inflammation of the brain, BENJAMIN BAMFORD, son of Benjamin and Mary Jane Riches. Born January 31st, 1856.

CENSUS ENUMERATORS.

JUAB COUNTY.

First District— A. S. Kendal. Mono precinct.

Second District—J. F. Hartley. Nephi precinct.

Third District— A. S. Kendall. Levan precinct.

Fourth District—Patrick Cusick. Tintic precinct.

Respect for Dead.—Our correspondent "Nephite," writes from Nephi, Juab County, under date of the 20th inst., giving a description of ceremonies over the grave of Bro. Benjamin B. Riches, whose death was noticed in this paper a short time ago. Deceased was a workman on the Utah Southern Extension, and his fellow laborers, as soon as the were apprised of his death, which was an unexpected blow to them, appointed a committee, con- of Messrs. David Latimer, James Duncan, John H. Brough, William C. Wheeler and Levi Hunt to draft sentiments of respect and condolence, and wait upon the bereaved family and obtain permission to manifest their love and esteem for the departed by placing a marble tombstone on his grave. The father was much moved at the kindness evinced by the deputation and their friends, and freely gave his consent. Accordingly, on the 18th inst., the stone was put in its place with appropriate ceremonies. It is a well executed piece of work from the establishment of Morris & Evans, of this city, and bears upon it an inscription and some verses. A large number of the citizens of Nephi attended the ceremonies, and during the placing of the stone the Nephi Brass Band, under Captain Hawkins, played appropriate music. Remarks were made by Elders L. A. Bailey and David Latimer, and by the father of the deceased, who thanked the assembly for the respect shown to the memory of his son.

Deseret News
June 2, 1880

Report Confirmed.—Last evening we published the announcement that a man named Amos Chase was reported drowned in the Sevier River, several miles from Juab station, on the U. S. R. R. Mr. L. A. Bailey, of Nephi, writes that Mr. John D. Chase, of that place, father of Amos, received a telegram from Juab on Wednesday evening, informing him that his son had been drowned and the body not recovered. The father and relatives immediately started for the scene of the fatality, 21 miles from Nephi. Amos Chase owned a ranch on the Sevier, seven miles from Juab station, and was engaged in building a dam in the river to take out water. The deceased leaves a wife and six children.

Salt Lake Herald
June 6, 1880

The Sanpete Valley Railroad.

Work on the Sanpete Valley narrow-gauge railroad is progressing with great rapidity. All of 400 persons are working on it, with probably 175 teams. Contracts for the entire grading of the road have been let, and the contractors are now at work. Contracts for ties have also been let, amounting in all to 80,000. The road will run a distance of thirty miles, from Wales to Nephi, and it is expected the grading will be completed by July 4th. An effort is now being made to have the road running within three months, in which event it will commence the hauling of coke and coal from the coal beds at Wales. Messrs. T. Marshall, S. Bamberger and M. T. Burgess constitute the local board of directors.

LIST OF AGENTS.

The following gentlemen are authorized to canvass for the SALT LAKE DAILY, SEMI-WEEKLY and WEEKLY HERALD; also to receive payment and receipt for the same:

M. Muir....Bountiful, Woods Cross and Centreville
H. A. Lewis...Georgetown, Bear Lake Co.
W. A. Stewart,..Inverury, Sevier County
John Hortin,.....Rockport and Wanship
Wm. Hulme,.....Bloomington, Do.
H. Tuft,.........Monroe, Sevier County
Thos. Wallace.....Ogden and Weber Co
L. T. Shepherd,.........Bear Lake County
A. W. Babbitt.............Spring Lake and Santaquin
O. F. Lyons,.............Summit County
E. Henriod ....American Fork
A. Leslie................Fountain Green
B. W. Driggs, Jr. ....Pleasant Grove
E. S. Cowdell ....Beaver County
W. O. Creer.............Spanish Fork
W. L. Watkins,............Brigham City
D. G. Brian,.............Piute County
Thomas Crawley,............Juab County
J. S. Moffat ....Meadowville
Walter Walker,........ ..Farmington
Jos. T. Ellis...............Spring City

John Shields,............Tooele City
John Batty,............Toquerville
J. R. Clark,............Grantsville
Wm. Mendenhall............Springville
J. E. Johnson,............Silver Reef
John Pymm,............St. George
H. McMullin,............Heber City
R. W. Hayborne............Cedar City
J. F. Walters............Mill Creek
S. Williams............Ephraim
F. H. Wright,............Coalville
H. P. Miller,............Richfield
S. Francis ....Morgan
John Swain,............Fayette
Edw. Reid,............Payson
T. Greener,............Kanosh
Wm. Probert, Sen............Holden
Charles C. Shaw............Hyrum
John S. Black............Deseret
Wm. Probert,............Scipio
Charles Foote,............Nephi
John W. Shepherd............Levan
William Burbeck,............Provo
George Scott............Manti
John Woodhouse,............Lehi

Deseret News
July 7, 1880

Kicked and Killed.—A special to the NEWS, from Nephi, states that this morning a son of Benjamin Midgley, of that place, was kicked to death by a horse. He was leading the animal to water, when it became frightened and ran away. The boy got entangled in the rope and was dragged quite a distance and so badly bruised and mangled that he expired in about 45 minutes. The scalp was stripped from the skull. The lad was about 11 years of age.

Deseret News
July 14, 1880

At Nephi, Juab County, the day was ushered in by an artillery salute. The Stars and Stripes were unfurled, and Captain Hawkins' band played inspiriting airs. At 10 a.m. meeting convened in the Tabernacle, when the reading of the Declaration, songs, music by the band, recitations, readings, instrumental solos and duets, reading of a poem composed by Enoch Bowls, orations, etc., occupied the time till noon. In the afternoon the young folks had a dance, and in the evening the adult portion of the community gave one also. A genuine good time was experienced, for a well written description of which our correspondent "Nebo" is entitled to our thanks.

Deseret News
July 21, 1880

DIED.

At Nephi, July 7th, 1880, SUSANNAH HARRIS, wife of John Harris, and daughter of Geo. and Hannah Jackson.

Deceased was born at Berlymore, Derbyshire, England, July 22d, 1837.

Salt Lake Herald
August 5, 1880

Harness Makers.

Two GOOD Harness Makers wanted. Those who have worked in Utah preferred. Apply immediately to Grover, McCune & Read, Nephi, Utah.   au3

Deseret News
August 11, 1880

DIED.

At Levan, Juab County, August 2, 1880, of inflammation of the bowels, while his mother was on a visit, ANDREW ADOLPHEN, son of Wm. L. and Ann E. Draper, aged three months and 29 days.

He was taken to his parents' home at Freedom, Sanpete County, for burial.

Deseret News
August 25, 1880

DIED.

At Levan, Juab County, August 10, 1880, after a severe illness of 14 weeks, from dropsy and other ailments, WILLIAM H. TUNBRIDGE, son of Wm and Abce O. Tunbridge, aged 7 years, 11 months and 10 days.

He was followed to the grave by numerous friends and laid away in peace to await the morning of the resurrection. He was a loving child, and a member of the primary association. —Com.

Deseret News
September 15, 1880

Another Marriage.—We extend our congratulations to Mr. Joseph F. Hartley and his happy bride, nee Miss Leonora A. Pitchforth, both of Nephi, Juab County, who were united in the sacred bonds of wedlock, yesterday, at the Endowment House, by Counselor D. H. Wells. Mrs. Hartley is the young lady we mentioned several weeks ago as owning a printing press of her own and doing the job work for Nephi and vicinity. She is a worthy young woman and has a worthy husband. May they be happy.

Salt Lake Herald
September 16, 1880

The Shooting Accident.

On Wednesday morning we published that Mr. C. S. Burton had been accidentally shot at Moroni, Sanpete County. The party who left this city by special on Tuesday evening, arrived at Moroni at 3.45, and found Mr. Burton in an easy condition and not in danger. On Wednesday he was taken to Nephi and from there brought to this city on the regular passenger, arriving at 6.30 last evening. It appears that Mr. W. H. Rowe and Mr. Burton were shooting at a target with a small 22 calibre rifle. A clerk in one of the stores came to shoot with them, and was handed the rifle. It was discovered that the rifle had no cartridge in it and Mr. Rowe took it back to load it. Meantime Mr. Burton stood off about some sixty feet, with his side towards the parties. When the gun was loaded Mr. Rowe handed it back, and the clerk was just in the act of taking it, when it went off and Mr. Burton dropped to the ground. Whether the clerk pulled the trigger or not is unknown. They ran to Mr. Burton and picked him up, when he walked alone to the house. The little ball entered the fleshy part of the neck where it lodged. It was not known how serious the wound might be so a doctor was telegraphed for. The ball is still in Mr. Burton's neck, it being deemed inadvisable to take it out at present, but the wound is not considered in anywise dangerous, and should nothing untoward occur, it is expected he will be out in about a week.

Deseret News
September 22, 1880

POPULATION OF TOWNS IN UTAH.

THE Supervisor of Census for Utah, Secretary Thomas, kindly furnishes the following list of Utah towns and their population. The statement is incomplete, several towns and cities being omitted in consequence of the returns from those places being now in Washington. We give the imperfect list, however, as it contains information that will be useful to many:

Town	Population	Town	Population
American Fork,	1,300	Meadowville,	75
Brigham City,	1,880	Midway,	285
Bingham,	1,025	Nephi,	1,700
Beaver,	1,450	Ogden,	6,000
Coalville,	910	Orderville,	510
Corinne,	280	Provo,	3,440
Escalante,	350	Pleasant Grove,	1,780
Ephraim,	1,700	Paragoonah,	260
Fairview,	815	Parowan,	970
Fillmore,	975	Payson,	1,780
Goshen,	395	Randolph,	300
Grantsville,	1,000	Salt Lake,	20,900
Gunnison,	550	Spring City,	1,000
Garden City,	125	Silver Reef,	1,050
Glendale,	175	Stockton,	250
Heber,	1,290	Springville,	2,315
Kanosh,	300	Spanish Fork,	2,300
Kanab,	300	Santaquin,	680
Lehi,	1,400	St. George,	1,830
Levan,	395	Tooele,	920
Manti,	1,760	Toquerville,	385
Morgan,	450	Willard City,	400
Mona,	400	Wallsburgh,	200
Mount Pleasant,	2,000		

Salt Lake News
December 5, 1880

PERSONAL.

Hon. John Sharp started from New York, homeward, on Friday night.

Mr. E. H. Williams, the enterprising merchant of Nephi, is in the city on business.

District Attorney VanZile left for Beaver on Saturday morning. He goes to attend the opening of the Second District Court, on Monday, under Judge Emerson.

Salt Lake Herald
December 18, 1880

DIED.

OSTLER.—At Nephi, Dec. 12, 1880, of nervous debility, after acute suffering for several weeks, Emily, wife of William G. Ostler, daughter of Jeffrey and Mary Perkins, born March 19, 1849, at Irchester, Northamptonshire, England.

Deceased leaves two sons and two daughters. She was born in the Church She lived and died a faithful Saint.

Millenial Star, please copy.

Deseret News
December 29, 1880

NEPHI, Juab Co.,
Dec. 14, 1880.

Editor Deseret News:

A number of the citizens of this town had the pleasure of attending a very pleasant party last evening at the home of the late Timothy Hoyt, Esq. It was a wedding party gotten up for a very auspicious occasion—a dual wedding. The grooms were John Henry Love, the son of our much respected townsman, Andrew Love, and Henry Dewit Goldsbrough the son of the well known Henry Goldsbrough, of the Nephi House, etc. The fair brides were the Misses Sarah Hoyt and Elizabeth Elmer, whose parents were early settlers in this county. The supper was excellent, the guests enjoyed themselves exceedingly. It was one of those pleasant gatherings of families and friends long to be remembered. Many handsome presents were presented to the young couples with many earnest wishes for their future peace and happiness in the "battle of life."

They were married last Thursday at Salt Lake City, returning last evening. President Geo. Teasdale and Bishop C. Sperry were among the guests. NEBO.

Deseret News
January 5, 1881

DIED.

At Nephi, Juab County, December 23, 1880, SUSAN, daughter of John and Susannah Harris. Born June 13, 1880.

At Nephi, Juab County, December 22d, 1880, of old age, JAMES ROLLIN, born in Vermont, June 30th, 1788, baptized into the Church of Jesus Christ of Latter-day Saints, 1839.

Salt Lake Herald
February 6, 1881

Nephi Notes.

NEPHI, February 4th, 1881.

Editors Herald:

It is very wet and disagreeable in our small town. Rain has been tumbling for thirteen hours, and is still falling.

The firm of Crockwell & Son has changed hands, and the business is now run by G. W. Crockwell.

Goldsbrough's stage failed to connect with the train on the 3d and 4th, being several hours behind.

We enjoy very good health.

Professor Hamill is busy here.

J. W,

Deseret News
February 23, 1881

Heavy Bereavement. — In our death column will be found notices of the demise of four children of Brother James Harvey Mangum, of Nephi, Juab County. One from lung complaint, the others from diphthertic croup. Two of the deaths are of recent occurence, and have happened while the father is away from home, working on the Denver and Rio Grande Railroad. The mother is Amy Lorette Bigler Mangum, daughter of Patriarch Jacob Bigler, at whose residence the funerals of the last two decedents took place. President Teasdale, Counselor K. H. Brown and other local authorities of Juab attended the funerals, and much sympathy is expressed by all for the deeply bereaved household. We add our sincere condolence. The sad news was transmitted by Bro. L. A. Bailey.

Deseret News
March 2, 1881

JUAB STAKE CONFERENCE.

The Quarterly Conference of the Juab County Stake of Zion was held in the Nephi Tabernacle, Saturday and Sunday, January 22d and 23d, 1881.

Present on the stand at 10 a. m., 22d inst., K. H. Brown, of the Presidency of the Stake; J. G. Bigler, Sen., Patriarch; George Kendall, Wm. H. Warner, Daniel Cazier, Abraham Orme, John D. Chase members of the High Council; the Bishops of the several wards and their counselors, and other members of the priesthood.

The Bishops gave in their reports on Saturday morning. Reports that the people are feeling and doing well, attending to their meetings, and paying their tithing and Temple donations fully as well, and generally better than they have hitherto

to done. The remainder of [the]
morning's meeting was taken up [by]
some of our home brethren w[ho]
spoke to the point and in an enco[ur]
aging manner.

Apostles F. M. Lyman and J[ohn]
Henry Smith, of Salt Lake City, a[nd]
Elder David John, of Provo, arr[iv]
ed on the 11.40 a. m. train, and we[re]
with us during the remainder of t[he]
Conference.

At 2 o'clock p. m. Apostle Jo[hn]
Henry Smith presented the gene[ral]
authorities of the Church, who we[re]
sustained unanimously by the [as]
sembly as presented and sustain[ed]
at the last General Conference [at]
Salt Lake City, after which t[he]
clerk presented the authorities of t[he]
Stake, who were by the Conferen[ce]
unanimously sustained as follows:

The Presidency of the Stak[e]
George Teasdale, President; J[o]
Grover, First Counselor; K. [F.]
Brown, Second Counselor.

Patriarch—Jacob G. Bigler.

Members of the High Counci[l]
George Kendall, Wm. H. Warn[er]
Samuel Cazier, David Cazier, J[o]
Vickers, Thomas Ord, Abraham Orm[e]
Charles H. Bryan, John Keith[?]
John D. Chase, Elmer Taylor, M[a]
thew McCune.

Of the High Priests Quorum—A[n]
drew Love, President; J. T. Bel[s]
ton, sen., First Counselor; T.
Schroder, Second Counselor.

First Ward—John Andrews, Bi[sh]
op; Edwin Harley, First Counsel[or]
Wm. Knight, Second Counselor.

Second Ward—Charles Spen[cer]
Bishop; Samuel Ringrose, Fir[st]
Counselor; L. A. Bailey, Seco[nd]
Counselor.

Levan—Niels Aagard, Bish[op]
Eli Curtis, First Counselor; E[li?]
Peterson, Second Counselor.

Mona—John M. Haws, Bish[op]
Wm Newton, First Counselor; Ge[o]
W. McConkie, Second Counselor.

Elders' Quorum—Silas L. Jacks[on]
President; Chas. House, First Cou[n]
selor; Enoch Bowles, Second Cou[n]
selor.

Bishop's Agent—George Teasda[le]
Stake Superintendency of Sabba[th]
Schools—George Teasdale, Presiden[t]
Matthew McCune, First Counselo[r]
Samuel Jackson, Second Counse[lor]

A motion was also put and unan[i]
mous vote given to sustain the Sa[b]
bath schools, day schools, Relief S[o]
cieties, the Young Men's and Youn[g]
Ladies' Mutual Improvement Ass[o]
ciations, the choirs and brass band[s]
and that we sustain each other [in]
all good works.

From Brothers Lyman, Smit[h]
and Johns we had splendidly inte[r]
esting and instructive discourse[s]
full of love and kindness, filling o[ur]
hearts with joy and a determinatio[n]
to live better lives in the future th[an]
we have in the past. Such men ca[n]
not come too often nor stay too lon[g]

Yours respectfully,
WM. A. C. BRYAN, Clerk.

Nephi, Juab Co., U. T.,
January 7th, 1881.

Territorial Enquirer
May 11, 1881

Nephi Jottings.

Editor Enquirer:

A few words about Nephi.

Our farmers generally agree that the
crops have never looked more promising
for a bountiful harvest than they do at
present, not only in fields but in gardens
and orchards. We have two powerful an-
tagonists to fear, viz: the grasshopper and
the frost.

If we can be spared their deadly bite,
we shall, no doubt, have a good harvest.

Nearly all our boys have returned from
the Denver and Rio Grande R. R. and
very nearly broke. They have experienced hard times, small salaries and high
prices for goods. Another company leaves
this morning for Hams Fork on R. R.
building.

The Invincible Phil (adelphia) Margetts
has been here with his talented troupe.
On the evenings of the 6th and 7th inst.,
they gave good performances to two full
houses, that is, jammed the first night and
crowded the second.

This company cannot be too highly
praised, considering the artistic and masterly manner in which they present their
performances, for it denotes good taste,
careful training and study.

One actually forgets that he is merely
looking upon a stage and watching a play,
so faithfully and truly are the emotions
and passions of human nature represented.
The audiences were highly pleased.

We could have given Phil. another good
house or two, but not his previous en-
gagements South, prevented him. The
Nephi orchestra, under the direction of G.
Henriod, was in attendance, and much
credit is due to them for their delightful
music.

CAMERA.

Nephi, May 9, 1881.

Second Company of the Season.

List of passengers who sailed from Liverpool per S. S. Wyoming, Saturday, May 21st, 1881:

Juab.

Joseph, Elizabeth, Samuel and John T. Gerrard.

Nephi.

David Storrar.

Nephi Notes.

It is a problem that the good folks of Nephi are unable to solve: why the Sanpete railroad is not ere this completed and running. The grading is nearly all finished, the iron has been on the ground for months past, two locomotives were to have been there three months ago, when, it was said, they were on the road somewhere between here and the East. A little more energy, or money, is evidently needed to complete this narrow-gauge road.

It is sanguinely expected by some citizens that the Juab station will be discontinued ere long and Nephi be made a home station for passenger trains on the Utah Southern, now that the consolidation of the three roads has been accomplished and when the expected, new time table shall be put into effect. It is certain that Nephi, by reason of its central position and importance as a junction for travel and traffic with Sanpete, Tintic and the South, has advantages over mostly all other southern towns, and consequently offers superior inducements to the railroad companies.

The Nephi Co-op. is to have a change of superintendent, Mr. Chas Foote having resolved to resign and enter the field of enterprise, either at Nephi or elsewhere, on his own account. Who his successor will be is not yet known, but the election will be held at the next Directors' meeting.

Hyde & Whitmore are live and prosperous men. They are doing a big business, are courteous and accommodating and, consequently, capture a large proportion of the mercantile trade of Nephi and the adjacent settlements.

Ed. H. Williams has a steady going trade and understands how to retain it. He has his friends, and "their name is legion."

The affable and facetious Hawkins, who has for several years conducted a quiet and respectable business as a liquor dealer, intends soon to retire, and leave the field to others. His son, Harry, runs a good restaurant, an occupation he thoroughly understands.

Wilcock's and Goldsbrough's hotels are doing only a fair business at present, travel having seriously fallen off since the advent of the railroad at Nephi.

Goldsbrough has recently renewed his contract for another year, to carry the Sanpete and Sevier mails. In the stage business Henry has no peer in Southern Utah.

Chas. Andrews is still the agent for H. B. Clawson, of Salt Lake, and will pay as much as anybody for wool, hides, furs and skins. His place is in the rear of the Co-op.

Judge Grover, who with A. W. McCune and W. P. Read, has large contracts for building portions of the D. & R. G. railroad in Colorado, is at home again.

G. W. Crockwell, assignee for Crockwell & Son, purposes selling by auction on July 15th all the remaining stock, fixtures and furniture of the firm.

John C. Ostler is doing a heavy trade as successor to W. P. Read, in the saddle and harness business. It is here the teamster and railroad outfitter will find "square dealing," low prices, first class work, promptness and dispatch.

Our blithesome young friend, W. A. C. Bryan, was made trebly blithesome a week ago to-day by the advent of a new comer to the domestic circle—a juvenile manipulator of electricity of the masculine persuasion. The gratified mamma smiles to see William, senior's, parental glee.

A two-year old son of Mr. Cyrus Mangum, of Nephi, was drowned in the creek running near the parents' residence on Thursday last. The little fellow had crawled on to a slab that crossed the creek, fell into the water, and was swept down to the dam with such force as to break his neck. The child was dead when taken out.

Nephi Notes.

The prospects for fruit and crops in and about Nephi have not been so good for years.

In the western part of the valley, the grasshoppers are very numerous, but for some strange and fortunate reason, they seem to do but very little damage.

All the bridges up the canyon for the narrow guage road going to Wales, are about finished, and the grade is ready for the rails.

H. Goldsbrough has again secured the contract for the mail between Nephi and Richfield.

The Nephi brass band recently underwent a reorganization, and the membership was increased to twenty-eight, with J. S. Hawkins, captain; and Gustave Henroid, leader.

On Thursday — the 23d — the ladies of the Relief Society held a grand picnic festival and gave a ball in the evening.

Last Wednesday morning Mr. John Sharp, jr., and Dr. H. J. Richards arrived by the train and took the Goldsbrough stage to Sanpete. They are on a pleasure out.

DIED.

At Ephraim, June 21, 1881, CHRISTINE CHRISTIANSEN McCARTY, born in Nephi Sept. 11, 1858, only daughter of Christian Christiansen and Hedevig.

She left a husband and three beautiful children; two boys and a girl.

Our Mona Letter,--A Terrible Thunderstorm and Other Items less Terrible.

Editor Enquirer:

A very remarkable circumstance occurred in this vicinity on the 3d inst. A heavy thunderstorm was raging and about 3 o'clock p. m., the railroad hands miraculously escaped with their lives. At the time stated a flash of lightning was seen and simultaneously with the thunder following, the four men were prostrated to the ground. The shock was terrible to think of and is almost indescribable, but it came with a force like the shot of a gun, and it was several seconds before the men recovered (one of them did not recover consciousness for nearly an hour) and on taking observations found a telegraph pole a few yards away shattered to pieces, the insulators being broken and poles shattered and scattered over a radius of two miles north of them. One of the men actually states (and his word is reliable) that he could sense the taste of gun powder in his mouth for twenty four hours after. There were also a number of posts in town badly shattered by lightning but no lives were lost.

We do not celebrate the glorious Fourth on account of the attempted assassination of President Garfield.

There were a concert and exhibition on the evening of the 2d under the auspices of the Y. L. association which reflected credit on all concerned therein.

The grasshoppers have been very selfish here this season, having consumed nearly all our crops.

Mostly all the men of this place are working on the D. & R. G. railroad, in search of more visible means of support for themselves and families.

We are improving admirably under the wise leadership of Bishop John M. Haws.

M. U. Sic.

Mona, July 4, 1881.

Salt Lake Herald
July 10, 1881

LIST OF PASSENGERS

sailing from Liverpool, per steamship *Wyoming*, Saturday, June 25th,
1881. ... SCOTCH AND WELSH.

Nephi.

Ane M. S. Jensen; Gertrude Sun-
derguard Jensen; Ane K., Anders,
Peter, Johan and Severin Sunder-
guard; Antoine M. Christensen;
Lars Larsen; P. Thomas; Anthon-
ette, Ane, Martine; Ane Marie and
Jens Alma Jensen; Mette K. Peter-
sen; Kirstin M. Larsen; Maren, An-
drew, Trine, Annie and Martinus
Nielsen; Dortine M. Jacobsen;
Johanne E. Christensen; Caroline
and Krutine Petersen; Petrea M.,
Ingvald P. Sewerine and Peter P.
Jensen; Anders M., Ane Marie,
Christine P. Martin; O. Jensena
Birgitte; Anders O. Kirsten; Niels
P., Anders, Ane M. and Thomas
Andersen; Jens C., Ane C., Mette
M., Marie, Johanne K., Annie and
Hans Carl Hansen; Christian Sevew
Poulson; Jens Laursen; Kristine
Andersen; Niels, Berthe T., Soren,
Dortha and Marie Mikkelsen; Nico-
lene Jensen; Stine Madsen; Chris-
tian and Ane K. Christensen;
Magdamas Rasmussen; Niels and
Ane Johanne Madsen; J. B. Y. and
Johanne Nielsen; Rasmus, Maren,
Christoffer W. and Carl C. Rasmus-
sen; Rasmus P. and Oline M.
Laursen; Lars, Nicoline, Carl and
Caroline Andersen; Anthon Soren-
sen; Herman H. Andersen; Maren
Rasmussen; Jens and Peter Peter-
sen; Neils and Laust Mikkelren;
David Madsen; Mette M. Madsen;
Jens S, Wilhelmine S, Frantz P, O.
J, Kirstine S and Christian Smith
Petersen; Jorgine S. Sorensen;
Julius P. Petersen; Emma Mad-
sen; Mads P, Clara, Hans A,
Maria S and Anne C. Nielsen; Ja-
cob, Karen, Marthen, Peter Jens,
Anders, Johanna and Oluf Jensen;
Niels, Johanne, Henrik and Anders,
P. Andersen; Johanne K Petersen;
Nicoline A. Larsen; Ane S and Carl
M. Hansen; Hans, Maren K. and
Clara Andersen; Hans C. Klansen,
Lars A. Anders S. and Carl E. Gau-
fin; Emma C. Hupnore; Adolf F,
Britha D and Johan A. Wisterman;
Caroline, Albert and Axel Nord-
quist; Anders Larsen, Anders E,
Anna C, Maria C and Erikka C.
Walnider; Lavina Magensen; Jo-

han Wengren; Wilhelm Frear; Cor
gren Freder; Johan P. Herman;
Kenthi, Bergtha, Elna and Johanna
Nielsen; Martinens Larsen; Ane
M. Andersen; Marilsen Nielsen.

Deseret News
July 13, 1881

CAZIER'S CAMP,
Ham's Fork,
June 22nd, 1881.

Editor Deseret News:

We have been on this river somewhere near five weeks, and during
that time we have had considerable
sickness. Men who have had a
great deal of experience, say it is
mountain fever, there has been several cases of it in our camp, and
Samuel Cazier, of Nephi, has had a
severe attack of the disease,

JUAB CONFERENCE.

The Primaries held their Conference on Friday morning, July 15th, 1881. The Tabernacle had been thoroughly renovated and was as clean as a new pin. There was a good attendance.

Reports from Sisters Hannah Grover, S. A. Andrews and Armelia C. Bigler, of the various primaries, were very interesting.

A number of the little folks sang and recited very well.

Encouraging remarks were made by Sisters Nuttall, Goldsbrough, Pitchforth and A. L. Bigler.

President Teasdale blessed the children and all who had the care of them.

Bishop John Andrews dismissed.

In the afternoon the Relief Societies held their Quarterly Conference. Reports very satisfactory, a lively interest being taken by our good sisters to fulfill the responsibilities imposed upon them. Excellent singing and short lively discourses rendered the meeting very profitable.

In the evening, the usual quarterly Priesthood meeting convened and had a very profitable time.

On Saturday morning, at 10 a.m., the Conference opened with the usual devotional exercises.

The Bishops reported the condition of their Wards. Statistical and financial reports were read, all satisfactory.

In the afternoon Presidents Geo. Q. Cannon and Wilford Woodruff were present, also Presidents Geo. Teasdale an K. H. Brown, of the Stake, Patriarch J. G. Bigler, Sr., and others.

Presidents Cannon and Woodruff occupied the afternoon, enjoying much freedom and speaking with great power.

The choir, under the able management of Professor Darton, favored us with some very delightful singing.

In the evening the Y. M. and L. M. I. Societies held their conference, Superintendent Thomas Crawley presiding. After the usual exercises Supt. Crawley reported for the Stake.

Sister Hannah reported the Young Ladies' Association.

Reports statistical and financial were read.

Sister Georgie Parks read the "Young Ladies' Journal" in a very artistic manner, demonstrating the steady improvement in this praiseworthy association.

Presidents Woodruff and Cannon gave some most excellent instructions and encouragement to these societies. It was indeed a very agreeable time.

On Sunday morning at 10 a. m. the Sabbath schools held their quarterly conference. A crowded meeting of happy, joyful children and their teachers. President C. Petersen, of the Sanpete Stake, with Elder Lunt, of Ephraim, and George Bean, of Richfield, were present on the stand.

After the usual singing by the Sunday School Choir and prayer, there were reports given of the various Sabbath Schools, and most excellent instructions on the necessity of purity of life, chastity and virtue were given by Presidents Woodruff and Cannon. Between the reports and instructions the Nephi brass band, under the able leadership of Captain John S. Hawkins, and the Sabbath School choir under Brother Charles Morris, charmed us with their delightful playing and singing.

In the afternoon Stake Conference continued. Devotional exercises. Music by the band. Sacrament administered. President Geo. Q. Cannon delivered a very able discourse on marriage. Sister Sarah A. Andrews and choir sang. "Who's on the Lord's side? Who?" President George Teasdale presented the authorities. Benediction by Elder Allred.

In the evening there was a crowded congregation which was addressed by Presidents George Q. Cannon and George Teasdale who referred to the spirit of improvement manifested in the Tabernacle that had been so thoroughly cleaned and which looked like snow. Complimented Messrs. Trinnaman and Jackson, of Lehi, for the good work they had performed, and the industrious sisters who had lent their valuable aid in cleaning the room and seats.

On Monday morning the congregation assembled at 10 a.m. The

time for instruction was occupied by Presidents Cannon and Woodruff in answering some interesting questions in a very able and masterly manner.

We had a glorious conference; it seemed as if the Lord poured out His blessings upon us as an acknowledgment of our exertions and labors to have a good, sweet, clean building to meet in to worship the Lord our God. WM. A. C. BRYAN,
Clerk, per T. C.

Deseret News
September 14, 1881

DIED.

At Nephi, Sept. 3rd, 1881, NANCY WILSON HARTLEY, born Feb 12th, 1838, at Barknowleswick, Yorkshire, England; emigrated May 23rd, 1863.

She died firm in the faith, and was a true Latter-day Saint.

Ogden Herald
September 20, 1881

Departure of Missionaries.

Elders James Jenkins, Samuel Jackson, and Charles Andrews, all of Nephi, Juab County, proceeded east on this morning's train. They are Church Missionaries destined for the Southern States mission. Their present objective point is Nashville, Tenn., where they will probably meet President John Morgan, and, by him, be assigned to their several fields of labor.

The same train took Elders P. F. Goss, of Salt Lake City, and Jacob Walser, of Payson, who are destined for the Swiss and German Mission. They expect to sail from New York for Liverpool on Tuesday, on the *Arizona*.

Salt Lake Herald
September 22, 1881

LIST OF PASSENGERS

Sailing from Liverpool, per S. S *Wyoming*, Saturday. September 3d, 1881.

Nephi.

Kirstine and Anna Anderson; Niels, Christine, Niels P. N. and Christine M. Steffensen; Jens Peter and Anders P. Petersen; Petrine M. Jensen; Birgitte, Jorgeg, Line C., Maren S., Peter Chr. and Nephi Nielsen; Martin C. Christensen; Kirsten M., Soren S. and Cicilie Nielsen; Else C. Petersen; Hogan P. Sjostedt; Christine W. H. Andersen; Niels Julius Rasmussen; Niels Petersen, and Marie P. Motter; Dorthea K. Madsen; Andreas M. and Stephen M. Petersen; Ane Christian Madsen; Ane Chr. Christensen; Jensine P. Frandsen; Anders P. Jensen; Anne Magdalene Petersen; Hans P., Hansine, Christoffer M. and Helene Andersen; Soren M. Johansen; Niels M., Mette K., Sophie L., Nicoline M. and Mads Michaelsen; Anne and August N. Larson; Albert and Christine Johannessen; Louise Caroline Carlson.

Ogden Herald
October 12, 1881

Hurt His Hand.

Last Monday forenoon, an orphan boy, Thos. Kay, from Mona, 90 miles south of Salt Lake City, who was working for Mr. S. P. Ewing, eight miles southwest of Soda Springs, on the Oregon Short Line grading, was shooting ducks with an old double-barreled shot-gun, when one of the rusty barrels burst and the contents were emptied into the boy's left hand. Mr. Ewing brought the boy down, this morning, and placed him in care of Dr. A. S. Condon, who attended to the wound, after which Kay started for his southern home.

Deseret News
October 19, 1881

The Nephi Lightning Disaster.— We are under obligations to Mr. L. A Bailey for an account, by mail, of the killing, by lightning, of George J. Belliston, at Nephi, on the night of the 10th. We have already published a statement of the occurrence, received by telegraph. Our correspondent states that the unfortunate lad was, at the time he was struck, walking hand in hand with his brother. The flesh of the boy's body was partially consumed by the electric fluid. The other lad's arm was slightly burned and he was rendered insensible by the shock. Other parties in the vicinity were so severely shocked that they were also rendered temporarily insensible. George had the reputation of being a very good boy.

DIED.

At Nephi, November 1st, 1881, ELISA WIL-SON, wife of John Sidwell, born August 26, 1844, in Coldike, Scotland.

She leaves her husband and seven children to mourn her loss. She lived and died a faith-ful Latter-day Saint.

Mill. Star please copy.

THE FATAL ACCIDENT AT NEPHI.

NEPHI, October 20, 1881.

Editor Deseret News:

In the dispatch from Nephi on the 11th inst., published in the DESERET NEWS, it is stated that George James, son of *Thomas* and *Sophia* Belliston, "was killed by lightning last night about 10 o'clock."

As it might be inferred that Bro. Belliston allows his children to run loose at late hours of the night, (which I know is not the case) and that if he did not, the accident would not have happened; it is the earnest request of many friends that, in justice to Brother Belliston, the fact that the accident occurred a few minutes after 7 o'clock, be sent to the NEWS for publication.

George and his younger brother John were running hand in hand to their grandmother's, and while George was speaking, he was in-stantly killed by lightning, his clothes were nearly burnt off and his boots torn to pieces; but not a par-ticle of his flesh was consumed.

He was born on the 15th of Oct., 1870.

John was knocked against a shade tree and fell in the ditch. At the same instant he saw by the light of the flash, a door key, and afterwards told a neighbor where to find it.

Before J. Elliston, who saw the accident, could reach the spot, John had crawled out of the ditch and cried for help, exclaiming: my brother is dead! These facts show that he was not at any moment in-sensible, although he was burnt from the right hand to the armpit, thence obliquely across the body and down the left leg, and his shoe torn off. His clothes were not injured.

The lightning struck the ground about three feet from the trunk of a shade tree, making a hole nearly a foot square and three inches deep. The tree was uninjured.

J. G. B.

Correspondence.

Not Killed as Reported.

BILLING's A. & P. R. R.,
Arizona Territory, Oct. 8th, 1881.

Editor Deseret News:

You have no doubt long since seen an account of the killing of Brother Hendrickson and party by the Apache Indians, at or near Black River, A. T., about the 25th of August. It has been currently reported in this Territory and also in New Mexico, that I, with my traveling companions, viz.: Nephi Spafford of Springville, Israel Evans of Lehi, and Charles Ingram of Nephi, were killed, at or near the same place about that time. Thank kind Providence I am able and happy to state that the report is not true as to the killing of myself and party. We left Smithville, on the Gila River, August 21st, the same day that Brother Hendrickson and party left, with all calculation of traveling together for safety. We traveled down the south side of the river, 18 miles, to Camp Thomas, a U. S. Post; two or three companies of troops stationed there. I called to see the Quartermaster to get the use of his small boat to ferry our buggy, grub, blankets, etc., across the river, as it was very high. To the credit of the Quartermaster he gave me the use of his boat to cross the river, and sent a soldier to man the boat for us. We crossed that evening in good shape. Brother Hendrickson and party declined crossing in this way, choosing to keep down on the south side, some 18 or 20 miles to the old ford, thinking they could ford it, but in this they were mistaken, consequently they turned back at the ford, with the understanding that they would go to Camp Thomas and ferry at that place, and follow us on the north side. I saw nor heard anything of them till a few days ago. The sad news reached me at my old camp in the Zuni mountains, where I had left three sons and one daughter to spend the summer, while I journeyed south, that I and my company, with Bro. H's were all killed. The best information I have is that Bro Hendrickson was following close after me, and was, as near as I could learn, about 24 hours in our rear. The fight with the troops and Apaches took place just after we passed Camp Apache. There was great excitement all along our line of travel. We saw quite a number of the natives, they treated us kindly, asking who we were, where we were going, and what we wanted, &c., and we would reply "waner-amigo."

I send you this communication in order that all may know that I still live in the flesh, and my weight is 185 pounds net.

I remain your brother,

J. D. HOLLADAY.

Deseret News
November 16, 1881

The Missing Names.—When the names of the last company of emigrants that sailed from Liverpool Oct. 22d were published, we stated that a portion of the list had not reached us. It has now come to hand, and we herewith publish it that the record may be complete:

NEPHI.

Mary Wood; Jas., Mary, Elizh. and Mary Glover.

NEPHI.

Christian Hansen; Signa Hansen; Kristen Anderson.

A Veteran Gone.

The Logan *Leader* records the death of another good man, and one of the first settlers of Utah. John Anthony Woolf, Sen., of Hyde Park, Cache Co., died of pneumonia on Monday, the 7th of November, after a short illness of five days.

Deceased was born in Westchester County, State of New York, on the 31st day of July, 1805. He joined the Church of Jesus Christ of Latter-day Saints in July, 1841, and moved to Nauvoo in 1844, and was driven from there with the rest of the Saints, and spent one winter near Council Bluffs. He came to Salt Lake with the first company, in 1847; went to Iron County with the first settlers of that place; returned from there to Salt Lake and soon removed to Willow Creek in Juab Co., where he opened a farm and made a comfortable home for his family, which he enjoyed only a short time, being driven foom it by the Indians, after which they settled in Nephi, where they lived several years and then removed to Cache Co., and was among the first to settle Hyde Park. Deceased was widely known and won the love and respect of all who became acquainted with him, always being a friend to the needy, none of whom were ever known to be turned away empty handed. He was kind and forgiving almost to a fault. He was the last of three brothers, whose father was one of the Hessians pressed into the British service in the Revolutionary war. His children, grandchildren and great-grand-children number over 100, who deeply mourn his loss. He died as he had lived, firm in the faith and full belief of a glorious world hereafter.

The funeral services were held in the meeting house, which was filled to overflowing, there being few, if any persons in the settlement who were not present. Apostle Moses Thatcher and Prest. Preston delivered very impressive addresses, which were highly appreciated by the relatives of the deceased.

Recovering.—We are happy to hear that Elder Andrew Love, of Nephi, County Superintendent of District Schools for Juab, who has been suffering severely from pneumonia, is on the high road to recovery. He is seventy-three years of age.

Ogden Herald
December 1, 1881

Fatal Accident.

Yesterday the *Deseret News* received a special telegram from Silver City U. T. in relation to a fatal accident. The dispatch says:

Thos. Connell fell 130 feet in the Eureka Hill mine, this district, at 1 p.m. to-day. He was killed, the body being terribly mangled. They have sent to Nephi for the Coroner. Deceased leaves a wife and three children.

Salt Lake Herald
December 17, 1881

MARRIED.

TEASDALE—BRENETTA.—In this city, December 1₹, Francis Charles Teasdale, son of George Teasdale, and Delphia Brenetta, both of Nephi.

Deseret News
December 21, 1881

United.—In another part of the paper will be found a notice of the uniting in the bonds of matrimony, of Francis C. Teasdale and Delphia B. Hague. The bridegroom is the son of our old friend President George Teasdale. He has opened business for himself in Nephi and is pursuing a very exemplary course. The bride is the daughter of Brother John Hague, and is an intelligent and amiable young lady. The young couple have our hearty congratulations and best wishes.

Salt Lake Herald
December 25, 1881

DIED.

WINN—At Nephi, Juab County, Utah, December 18, 1881, of heart disease, Emily A. Sanders, wife of George Winn, aged 42 years, 6 months and 21 days.

Born at Woolwich, Kent, England; emigrated to Utah, 1862. She leaves her husband and five children to mourn her loss. She lived and died a true Latter-day Saint —[COM.

Mill. Star please copy.

Salt Lake Herald
January 17, 1882

DIED.

PAY.—At Nephi, January 11th, 1882, of inflammation of the lungs, Richard William, oldest son of Richard and Mary Pay, aged 21 years, 3 months and 21 days.

Deseret News
February 8, 1882

Councilor Teasdale presented a petition from Joel Grover, and 211 other taxpayers and business men of Nephi, praying for a bill for an act incorporating Nephi City, with full power of chartered cities. The bill was read and referred to the committee on municipal corporations.

JUAB STAKE CONFERENCES.

The Primary Association Conference was held in the Tabernacle, Nephi, commencing at 10 a. m., on Friday, Jan. 20, 1882.

Sister Hannah Grover, President of the Stake Primaries called the meeting to order.

After singing and prayer the minutes of last meeting were read and accepted.

A few excellent and encouraging remarks were made by Sister Hannah Grover. The various Ward associations were represented by their presidents to be in excellent condition.

Then followed recitations, dialogues and songs by the children which demonstrated the truth of the Presidents' reports.

At the close of the Conference a Primary Fair was opened at the Nephi Relief Hall. All who attended were well repa'd. It was exceedingly interesting to view the works of industry performed by little hands. Beautiful boquets of flowers in wax, wool and tarleton, chaste samples of mats, worked mottoes, knitting, fancy crochet and needle work. There was also a presentable exhibit of cookery in the shape of bread, tartlets and candy by the little girls, and some talent displayed by the little boys in drawing, painting and wood work.

2 p.m.

The Relief Societies held their fifteenth Conference, Sister Amelia Goldsbrough of the Stake organization presiding.

After the usual devotional exercises, reports were received from the various Ward associations, financial and statistical reports were read by the secretary.

After the reports several of the sisters expressed their feelings and Elders K. H. Brown and George Kendall gave some excellent instructions.

6:30 p.m.

The priesthood meeting was very well attended. The presidents of quorums reported their members. The High Council had passed a resolution approving of and adopting the action taken by the High Council, and approved by the Conference of the Salt Lake Stake of Zion with regard to to the liquor question. This met the approbation of those present, and it was resolved to adopt the same resolutions in this Stake of Zion. An excellent spirit prevailed and much good instruction was given.

Saturday, 10 a. m.

The Quarterly Conference of the Juab Stake of Zion convened. On the stand were the Presidency of the Stake, members of the High Council, Bishops and Counsellors.

After opening exercises President Teasdale expressed gratitude to our Heavenly Father for benefits received, relating his reasons for such feelings. Bishops Andrews, Sperry, Hams and Aagaard represented their wards, and spoke very encouragingly of an improvement manifested by their people and the blessings of God received, both spiritual and temporal, the past season, thus occupying the morning session.

2 p.m.

Usual opening exercises.

Elders Eric Petersen of Levan, and Prest. K. H. Brown spoke.

Clerk read the statistical report.

Presidents Grover and Teasdale addressed the congregation on intelligent obedience to correct principles, the law of tithing, recommends, magnifying the Priesthood and true integrity were the subjects treated upon, an excellent spirit prevailing.

6.30 p.m.

The Y. M and L. M.I. Associations held their Quarterly Conference.

After singing and prayer Elder Thomas Cramley, Stake superintendent make a few opening remarks.

Elders Israel Bale, Wm. Tunbridge and John Evans, also Sisters Kate Sene and Hannah Grover represented their associations in a very interesting manner.

Apostle Erastus Snow gave some valuable instructions to the young people, relating some very interesting circumstances in his own experience.

Sunday, 10 a. m.

The Sabbath school conference was held.

The brass band was in attendance and demonstrated a marked improvement in their playing.

After opening exercises the superintendents of the various Sabbath schools reported.

The choir and Primaries sang.

President A. O. Smoot, of Utah Stake, and Apostle Erastus Snow imparted to the children some valuable advice and exhortation.

2 p. m.

After devotional exercises President Teasdale presented the sacrament service, consisting of two flagons, four baskets and four cups that had been donated by the voluntary subscriptions of the people for the use of the Tabernacle.

Apostle Snow, offered the dedicatory prayer and blessed the bread. Choir sang an anthem. The congregation was addressed by Apostle Snow, who gave a masterly discourse on the eleventh chapter of Romans.

President Teasdale, presented the authorities, which were unanimously sustained.

6.30 p. m.

President A. O Smoot and Apostle Snow occupied the evening, bearing testimony to the truth of the latter-day work, and showing the bearing it should have upon our every day conduct spiritually and temparally. Encouraged the Saints to be patient and full of integrity to our Heavenly Father, His laws and the Constitution of our beloved country.

We had an excellent Conference. All seemed to enjoy the spirit that prevailed. Our choirs and band did excellent service.

THOMAS CRAWLEY,
Clerk of Conference.

THE FROZEN FEET.

A Different Version of the Affair— The Boy's Story False.

MONA, JUAB Co., Feb. 21st, '82.

Editors Herald:

Dear Sir—We have to-day read an account in your paper of the 18th inst., of one Christian Alfveson, in regard to his being mistreated and abused by Mr. Sidney Swasey, and then driven away from his home poorly clad and with but very little food. It is an entire misrepresentation in every respect. Mr. Sidney Swasey has been falsely accused, and we the undersigned, citizens of this place, make a true statement of the case. In the first place we have been told that the boy was brought to the country by one John Dorro's, who resides at Fort Ephraim, Sanpete County. From there the boy went to Castle Valley, Emery County, with his sister and brother-in-law some two years ago. He ran away from them while there and went to Mr. Charles Swasey's house, in the middle of the night. Mr. Swasey told him that he could make it his home there if he would do a few chores about the house and that he (Mr. Swasey,) would board and clothe him and send him to school, all of which he did. While the boy was with Chas Swasey he was well cared for in every respect. From Charles Swasey's the boy went to live with Sidney Swasey, who was at that time living in Castle Valley, Emery County. Shortly after that time Sidney Swasey brought the boy with his family, over to Mount Pleasant, Sanpete County. He lived with his family while there and was treated the same as one of the family. In October last Sidney Swasey moved his family to this place, Juab County, and brought the boy with them. While here the boy had very little work to do, and in fact did as near as he had a mind to.

as it was possible for anybody to do. He never herded sheep a day in Dog Valley, but simply went there once with Sidney Swasey, and stayed but two days. The boy ran away from Sidney's about the 1st of December, and stole a saddle-horse to go with. Mr. Swasey followed him and overtook him about four miles from this place, and tried to persuade him to go back home with him. He refused to do so, and said he was going to Sanpete County. Mr. Swasey took the horse away from him and put him on a wagon that was going to Sanpete. Since that time none of us have seen or heard or know anything of the boy's career, where he has been or what he has been doing. He did not leave here in January, as the paper states, but left about the first of December, when the weather was warm and pleasant, and was obliged to pass through four different towns, where he had acquaintances, to get to the place where the paper states that he was found with his feet frozen. When he left here he was well clad with plenty of warm clothing, and might have had any amount of food to take with him if he could have been persuaded to do so.

R. D. SWASEY,
JOHN A. MILLER,
FRELAM ENGLER,
FRANK R. BROOKER,
FANNY LOVEL,
SARAH Y. BUNNELS,
F. D. EVANS,
MARY ROWE,
ASA B. YORK.

I also make the following statement in regard to Christian Alvenson: He came to live with me of his own free will and choice; he was well treated and cared for in every respect, and he also left my house of his own accord and while I was away from the house. He was a boy that was very difficult to manage, and would not mind scarcely anything that he was told to do, and was continually running away from home and would be gone the whole day and often half of the night roaming around through the hills, fearless of anything or anybody. I kept the boy more out of pity for him than his usefulness.

SIDNEY SWASEY.

Salt Lake Herald
March 7, 1882

Levan Burglary.

The Levan Co-op. was robbed on the evening of the 4th inst, of $40 and a quantity of books, flannel, blankets, tobacco and other goods. The same day the robbery occurred the taking of stock had been completed, and a former clerk had turned the business over to a son of Mr. Elmer Taylor, who had been appointed to take charge. It appears the robbers had stolen an axe from another house, with which they broke open the door. With the same instrument they also broke open the small safe in which the money was kept. At last accounts no arrests had been, and no clue had been gained as to who the robbers were.

Ogden Herald
March 13, 1882

Murder at Levan.

What appears to be a cold-blooded murder was committed at Levan, a week ago. On Monday last, Charles Taylor, a nephew of Elmer Taylor, was shot in the back by Chris Tinker, of that place. Taylor died from the effects of the wound, at 11 p. m. the same day. Tinker either gave himself up or was arrested by Sheriff Cazier of Nephi. It is reported that Tinker is of disreputable character.

A. G. Sutherland, Esq., of Provo, was summoned on Friday by telegram, to act on the part of the prosecution in the examination of the case.

It seems that a few days previous to the shooting, Taylor and Tinker had got into an altercation at a party. They had met several times since and tried to settle the difficulty, but it seems could not agree. On the day of the shooting they met at Tinker's corral, when Taylor accused him of telling lies about him (Taylor). The discussion becoming warm, Tinker struck the deceased with two rocks—one on the arm and one on the head, the latter missile knocking him down. After throwing the rocks he ran into his house, when Taylor pursued, firing one shot from his revolver. On entering the house, Tinker procured a gun and discharged it at Taylor from the window, the shot taking effect in the back. Tinker's plea is self-defense.

The above is the version of the case as given to the *Territorial Enquirer* by an informant.

Salt Lake Herald
March 19, 1882

MARRIED.

HARRIS-JACKSON—On March 5, 1882 by Justice Borroman, John Harris, o Nephi City, and Harriett Jackson, of Salt Lake City.

Deseret News
March 22, 1882

DIED.

At Nephi, Juab County, Utah, MARY, wife of William Sidwell, and daughter of William and Grace Wignal.

Deceased was born at Lenwortham, Lancashire, England, died March 6th, 1882. She leaves a husband and two children to mourn her loss, and died in full faith of the Gospel Aged 35 years and 18 days.

In the 15th Ward, Salt Lake City, Feb. 6th, and buried at Mona, Juab Co., Feb. 8th, 1882, MARGARET PARTINGTON, relict of the late Thomas Partington, formerly of the St. Helens Branch of the Liverpool Conference. Born Feb. 8th, 1806.

She will be remembered by many of the Elders for her kindness in former times.—

Ogden Herald
April 10, 1882

Shooting Scrape.

The *Terr. Enquirer* is informed that a shooting affray took place at Mona, Juab County, last Monday. A young man by the name of John Young, met another man, named Dick Netherly, and without any cause or provocation, Young drew his pistol and fired at Netherly, the ball taking effect in the arm. Young escaped to the mountains. It is supposed the cause of the shooting resulted from a previous dispute. Netherly is not seriously hurt.

Deseret News
May 10, 1882

LIST OF PASSENGERS

Sailing from Liverpool, per S. S. Nevada, Wednesday, April 12th, 1882, in charge of John Donaldson

NEPHI.

Jens Christian Christiansen; Thos. Bytheway; Thomas Jones; Ada James; Sarah, George, Arthur, Heber, John and Mary Hollands.

JUAB.

Martha Febbel.

Deseret News
July 26, 1882

Correspondence.

The Old Folks of Nephi.

NEPHI, Juab Co., U. T.,
July 12, 1882.

Editor Deseret News:

Dear Sir—Please to express through your columns the thanks of the Old Folks of Nephi for the kind and generous manner in which they were cared for and entertained at the festival in Salt Lake City on that occasion; we shall ever remember the kindness and good feeling which was shown to us there. The committee have our warmest thanks for the kind attention to us all, and we shall, we hope, ever appreciate their kind services to us on that occasion.

We are yours,
EVA ———,
JOSEPH HYDE,
In behalf of the Old Folks of Nephi.

DIED

July 10th, 1882, at West Jordan, in the house of William Cooper, Sarah Jackson, aged 69 years. She was baptized in 1842, at Mattersea, Nottinghamshire, England, being the first member of the Church in that Branch. The Elders always found a good home in her house and never left it penniless, although at the sacrifice of many comforts. She traveled many miles often, in company with her husband when he was preaching the Gospel in the surrounding villages, and was a faithful and industrious wife. She was left a widow 20 years ago, and by her own labors raised her family consisting of 9 children.

Mother Jackson emigrated to Utah in 1862, and made her home in Nephi, where she was buried. She has always been an advocate of "Mormonism," and will surely receive her reward for the integrity she manifested.

She leaves 39 grand children and many friends to mourn her loss.—*Millennial Star*, please copy.

Deseret News
August 9, 1882

PIONEER DAY.

NEPHI.

After the usual salutes in the morning, hoisting of the Stars and Stripes, Captain John S. Hawkins' brass band serenaded the citizens.

At 10 a.m. the Tabernacle was filled to its utmost capacity.

The committee, Bros. Wm. H. Warner, Jos. W. Vickers and John Foot furnished a very good programme, as follows:

Music by the band; "On the mountain tops appearing," by the tabernacle choir; prayer by Patriarch Jacob G. Bigler, chaplain; a patriotic song by choir; speech, "Pioneer's Day," Hon. Geo. Teasdale; music by band; speech, Patriarch J. G. Bigler; music by band; song by Sister Elizabeth Grace; reading by Prof. F. W. Chappel; chorus by the Sabbath School choir; recitation, sister Elizabeth Schofield; cornet solo, Brother John Foot; comic song, Brother Robert Pyper; speech by Brother George Kendall; song by Sister Grace; recitation, by Georgina Parks; chorus, "Hark, the Song of Jubilee; toasts and sentiments. Congregation sang, "Praise to the Man."

Benediction, Elder John Squires.

In the afternoon, the children had a joyous time at Captain John S. Hawkins Bowery, dancing, songs, and recitations, a happy assembly. A dance for the adults in the evening finished a very agreeable day.

Salt Lake Herald
August 17, 1882

HORRIBLE ACCIDENT.

A Young Man Literally "Cut" in Two by Cars.

On Wednesday morning as the Utah Central passenger train was on its way north from Riverside to Lexington, Juab County, David Bigler, of Nephi, employed as a brakesman on the train, accidentally fell between the engine and the caboose, when eleven cars passed over his waist, literally cutting him in two. It appears that he was passing along the train in company with another brakesman, whose—though each had a lantern—was the only one that was lighted. In the darkness it is supposed the unfortunate man's foot either slipped or was misplaced which precipitated him between the cars with the result stated.

Deceased was a middle-aged man, having a wife and six children. His body was conveyed to his home in Nephi upon the train which had crushed out his life.

At the time of the accident he was a short distance in advance of his companion—James Bringhurst, and he saw Bigler's head and shoulders disappear between the cars. He immediately gave the notice, and the cars were stopped as soon as possible, but not until they had all passed over the poor man's body. When they found him he was breathing his last. The news of death was broken as gently as possible to his wife, and the railroad has taken the customary steps in the sad case.

Deseret News
August 23, 1882

DIED.

At Nephi, Juab County, July, 31st, 1882, of whooping cough and bronchitis, JENETTE, daughter of Samuel and Sarah J. Tolley, aged 22 months and 12 days.

Deseret News
August 30, 1882

Returned Missionary. — This morning we received a call from Elder Charles Andrews, of Nephi, just returned from a mission to the Southern States. He left here on the 20th of September last. He labored three months in East Tennessee, a new field. In consequence of being inhospitably received, the school houses being closed against him and his companion, only six meetings were held and no opening made. In company with Elder Joseph Ford he next labored five months in Wilson and Coffee counties where they baptized six new members.

Elder Andrews next labored in Alabama in company with Elder Samuel Jackson. There they were attacked by a mob who pelted them with stones, so they retired from that field and returned to Wilson County, Tennessee, where Brother Andrews remained until released, on account of failing health. Two more were there added to the Church by baptism.

OBSEQUIES OF D. G. BIGLER.

NEPHI, Juab Co.,
Aug. 16th, 1882.

Editor Deseret News:

The funeral obsequies of Brother David George Bigler, who lost his life whilst in the discharge of his duties, on the U. C. R. R., reported in the DESERET NEWS of the 16th inst., took place here to-day.

The ceremonies were under the direction of President George Teasdale and Elder James Latimer, who represented the railroad authorities. The body was taken from the residence of his father, the Hon. Jacob G. Bigler, to the Nephi Tabernacle. The pall bearers were, Sisson A. Chase, James Bringhurst, Robert Simpson, John Russel, Wilford and John Henry Wilson, his friends and fellow-laborers on the U. C. R. R. The bereaved wife, supported by his brothers Abner and Mark Bigler, family, relatives and friends following. The Tabernacle was soon filled with a sympathizing multitude, whose presence demonstrated the affection in which he was held and the respect for our aged Patriarch whose first-born had been so suddenly taken from this sphere of action.

The stand was occupied by the leading authorities of the Stake, supported on the right and left by the railroad officials and his fellow-laborers on the line. The body was placed on a rest draped in white and black.

The tabernacle choir sang, "O, Lord, Responsive to thy call."

Prayer was offered by Elder Thos. Crawley, the Stake superintendent of the Y. M. M. I. Associations.

Choir sang, "O, God, our Help in Ages Past."

President Teasdel made the opening remarks, followed by the following brethren: A. W. Caine, James Lattimer, Robert Simpson, Sisson A. Chase, John Russell, Wilford Wilson, John Kinder, John H. Wilson, Bishop Charles Sperry, George Kendall and Apostle Erastus Snow, who bore testimony to his native worth as a citizen, companion, officer, husband and father, and offered consolatory remarks. A letter of condolence, from Supt. John Sharp, was read.

The choir sang:

Nearer my God to Thee.

Apostle Erastus Snow pronounced the benediction, and the vast congregation took a farewell glance at the familiar face that they had been acquainted with ever since Nephi has been a settlement.

A large procession of fifty-five vehicles followed the body to its resting place.

David George Bigler was born on the 8th of February, 1846, at Nauvoo, Illinois. He came with his father to the mountains in the year 1852, and in the fall moved to this place, which was then first being settled, and he has grown up

with us, through all the difficulties experienced in new settlements, always being a "minute man" in all cases of danger, and as constable or deputy sheriff, cool, brave and manly in his bearing, always willing to assist, he has made hosts of friends who propose to aid in taking care of his invalid wife and five small children. This untimely end seemed to shock the whole community.

Yours truly,
REPORTER.

Salt Lake Herald
September 10, 1882

Mrs. Sarah Johnson Dead.

MONA, Sept. 8th, 1882.

At 8 a. m. Mrs. Sarah Johnson passed away after a lingering illness. Her disease was hastened by injuries received through a fall from a carriage during the Old Folks' excursion to Salt Lake City. She was a great sufferer but died firm in the faith, after thirty-seven years of faithfulness in the church of

Jesus Christ of Latter-day Saints. She was 74 years of age and leaves a large family of children and grandchildren to mourn her loss. She was loved by all, and none could censure. The body was accompanied to Salt Lake by Pres. Geo. Teasdale, Bishop J. M. Haws, and several of her children. It was her request to be taken to Salt Lake and laid beside her husband.

J. Z.

Deseret News
September 13, 1882

Deputy Registrars.—The following deputy registrars have been appointed in the counties named:

JUAB COUNTY.

Nephi Precinct—Alma Hague.
Levan Precinct—H. F. McCune.
Tintic Precinct—C. H. Blanchard, Jr.
Mona Precinct—T. W. Chappell.

Deseret News
September 27, 1882

LIST OF PASSENGERS
Sailing from Liverpool, per S. S. Wyoming, Saturday, September 2nd, 1882, in charge of of William Cooper.

NEPHI.

Ola Gouthe; Anne and Johanne Larsen; Hans P. Johanns N., Maren K., Juliane F., Karen M., Hans H. and Rebecke E. Hansen; Maria Sophie Fredriksen; Anna C. Andersen; Jens Fredriksen; Martine K. Jensen; Karen and Anne Rasmussen; Mads Knudsen; Maria C. Christensen; Marten C., Else M., Jensine and Niels C. Neilsen; Elisa S. and Soren N. Thyring; Anna M. Poulsen; Johan P. Petersen; Jens C. Larsine M. and Susanna Christensen; Ole C. and Soren M. Sorensen; Soren P. and Ingeborg K. Svensen; Christen Valdemar Svensen; Lars C. Larsen; Karen Olsen; Marinus Jensen; Anders C. Anderson; Sophia Augusta Harder.

JUAB.

Karen P. Madsen; Sorine Caroline Gregersen; Carl and Charlotta Anderson.

Ogden Herald
October 2, 1882

Fire at Nephi.

On Thursday morning, about 4 o'clock, the Presbyterian church at Nephi was discovered to be on fire.

A lady named Warwood first observed it, being awakened by hearing the glass falling from the windows. She gave the alarm, a crowd soon gathered and the flames were extinguished. Some carpenters had been at work and left the floor covered with shavings. The origin of the fire is unknown. The loss is about $150. The building is insured for $2,000.—*Deseret News.*

Ogden Herald
October 16, 1882

List of the Presiding Judges in the Precincts.

·The following additional appointments of judges of election have been made by the Utah Commission:

JUAB COUNTY.

Nephi—Charles M. Fraser.
Levan—A. L. Jackman.
Tintic—Sanford Johnson.
Mono—E. W. Williams.

Salt Lake Herald
November 7, 1882

LIST OF PASSENGERS.

Sailing from Liverpool per S. S. Abyssinia, on Saturday, Oct. 22nd, 1882.

JUAB.

Peter Crosbie, James H, Emma and Willie Ludweeks.

NEPHI.

Anders C. Anderson; Johanne Eskilsen; Susanna Olson; Jobanna M., Loren P. T., and Jens C.M. Christensen; Nils Anderson.

JUAB.

Axel, Maren C. and Nilsine M. Henriksen; Johan B. Jensen; Inger, Ane and Maria Emilia Christensen; Christen M. Andersen; Larsine Simonsen; Harriet and Eliza Anderson; Christine Maria, Hansine M. Christin A. and Marthea Henrika Hansen.

Deseret News
November 8, 1882

What was done at Mona.—James Gledhill, Jr., speaks thus of the Mona ratification of Tuesday.

Ratification meeting held here to-day, by the People's Party, stirring speeches were made by Delegates from Nephi, Hon's Wm. May, and John Chase. There was singing by the Choir, under the supervision of Jas. Gledhill. "Hold the Fort," and "Strike, Strike for Victory." Speeches were also made by John M. Haws, Geo. W. McOnkie, throwing hot shot into the "Liberal" ranks. There was a unanimous expression for the candidacy of John T. Caine. The Nephi brass band led by John Foote, was on hand, and supplied inspiring music.

DIED.

GOLDSBOROUGH.—At Nephi, Juab County, U.T., October 27th, 1882, in childbed, Ellen Jackson Goldsborough, daughter of Thomas and Joice Jackson. She was born in Kent, England, August 23rd, 1840; emigrated to Utah, crossing the plains in the hand-cart company in the year 1857; married in the year 1858; is the mother of ten children—three daughters and two sons survive her. As a wife, mother, confidential friend, she was beloved by all who knew her. Her demise is not only a loss to her family, but to the community, who will miss her faithful labors in the Relief and Primary Societies.—[Com. *Mill. Star*, please copy.

Deseret News
November 22, 1882

ELECTION RETURNS.

The following are the returns of the election of November 7th, as received by the Canvassing Board. The returns of a few precincts that appeared in the NEWS are not in this list, while several in the outlying districts have not been received at all by any parties, so far as we are aware:

Precinct.	Caine.	Van Zile.

JUAB COUNTY.		
Nephi	893	8
Pintle	2	60
Levan	84	5
Mona	54	—
Total	533	73

Deseret News
November 29, 1882

MONA, JUAB COUNTY, U. T.,
October 13th, 1882.

Editor Deseret News:

We had a two days' meeting held here Saturday and Sunday, October 11th and 12th insts. President Teasdale, Counselor Brown, George Kendall, John Kinkey, Jacob Biglar, Jr., attended, the latter three being members of the High Council, Besides these Brothers Bailey, John Ostler, Chas. Andrews, Jos. Vicars, from Nephi were present, besides the Ward Authorities.

The people rejoiced exceedingly to have spiritual food given to them in such abundance. It was a time to be long remembered by the Saints in Mona, the people of this portion of the Lord's Vineyard always rejoice to receive what the Lord has to say to His Saints. The short time

that our beloved President has been with us in this Stake of Zion; he has been the instrument in the hands of God in bringing about much righteousness, and we say may the blessings of heaven attend his labors in the future as they have in the past, may the Lord grant unto us a man to fill the office of President of this Stake of Zion, that will build upon the foundation that President Teasdale has laid, and carry on the work of the Lord victoriously. I will say, before concluding, that a portion of the people are more energetic than they have been in the past. The instructions that were given during the two days' meeting will not be soon forgotten by the wise.   G. W. M.

GOLDSBROUGH—At Nephi, Juab County, November 14, 1882, Harold Jackson, son of Henry and Ellen Goldsbrough Born Oct. 27, 1882. His mother died at his birth.

Ogden Herald
December 5, 1882

Mr. John Ostler, of Nephi, was in Ogden, to-day. He came up as far as this city with his son Charles, one of the missionaries spoken of elsewhere. Mr. Ostler spent the day with his brother Oliver in this place.

Salt Lake Herald
December 29, 1882

DIED.

HAWKINS —At Nephi, Juab County, December 22, 1882, of old age, Ann Hawkins, wife of John S. Hawkins, and daughter of James and Ann Hibbard.

She was born in London, England, June 10th, 1804; embraced the Gospel in 1851, emigrated to New York in 1854, moved to St. Louis, and arrived in Salt Lake City in the fall of 1856, and moved to Nephi in 1858, where she resided ever since. She lived the principles of the gospel; performed works like unto Sarah of old, and died in full faith and fellowship in hope of the reward promised to those who obey the Gospel of our Lord and Saviour Jesus Christ.— COM.

Deseret News
January 3, 1883

DIED

HAWKINS—At Nephi, Juab County, Dec. 22nd, 1882, of old age, Ann Hawkins, wife of John S. Hawkins, and daughter of James and Ann Hibbard.

She was born in London, Eng'and, June 10, 1804. Embraced the gospel in the spring of 1851. Emigrated to New York in 1854, from whence she went to St. Louis, arriving in Salt Lake City in the fall of 1856, and moved to Nephi in 1858, where she resided ever since. She lived the principles she professed, performing the works like unto Sarah of old, and died in full faith and fellowship with the Saints, in hope of the reward promised to those who obey the gospel of our Lord and Savior Jesus Christ—COM.

PRACTICAL RELIGION.

A NEW WAY TO MAGNIFY THE OF-FICE OF A DEACON.

SALT LAKE CITY,
January 29, 1883.

Editor Deseret News:

I consider the following worthy of a place in the NEWS:

While we were holding a Conference of the Juab Stake, at Nephi, on Saturday, the meeting house could not hold more than half of the people who desired to assemble. A quorum of Deacons gave up their seats to other persons, and to amuse themselves they obtained some axes, surrounded President George Teasdale's woodpile of several cords, cut it all up into stove wood, and piled it up nicely in his woodshed. They then went and served half a dozen widows in the town the same way, and also performed the same ceremony for one of the deacons, who had met with an injury so that he could not cut his own wood. They continued this work through the day for those who were needy. When Brother Teasdale returned home he did not discover that hoodlums had carried off his gates, but, to his astonishment, he found all his wood pile missing, and on looking around to see if he could find enough left to make a fire of, to his surprise he found it all nicely piled up in his woodshed. I consider this a good example for other deacons to follow, for if they would go and do likewise, many deserving and needy persons might be benefited. The following are the names of the Deacons who officiated in their office as above related.

Alfred Miller, Heber Fowkes, Saml. Gadd, Oliver Wilson, Daniel Tranter, Robert Turner, Edwin Udall, John Watwood, William Gadd, John Chase, James Chase, David McCune, Langley Bailey, Thomas Bailey, John Coleman, Peter Sorensen, Owen Cazier, John Wilson, Solomon Chase, William Littley, Frank Paxton.

Yours respectfully,
W. WOODRUFF.

JUAB STAKE CONFERENCE.

On Friday evening at 7 o'clock, a priesthood meeting was held in the Tabernacle at Nephi. Present: Of the First Presidency, John Taylor and Joseph F. Smith; of the Apostles, Wilford Woodruff and George Teasdale; visitors, Elders George Reynolds, Wm. Paxman and George F. Gibbs; the Presidency of the Stake and all the leading authorities. The hall was filled with the local Priesthood.

After the opening exercises the Presidents of the various quorums represented their quorums in a satisfactory manner.

President Teasdale thanked the Priesthood for the manner they had sustained him as President of the Stake, and bore testimony of their advancement and faithful labors.

President Joseph F. Smith gave an excellent discourse upon the duties of the Priesthood, and the glory and exaltation resulting from the magnifying of their various responsibilities and callings.

President W. Woodruff gave a very interesting account of his early labors as a Priest, his experience in magnifying the Aaronic Priesthood and the power of God demonstrated in his early labors.

President Taylor concluded by expressing his pleasure at meeting so many of the Priesthood, and briefly alluded to the change about to be made in the Presidency of the Stake, etc.

———

Saturday, 10 a.m.

The Tabernacle was full.

The Nephi Brass Band was out, and a most lively interest was manifested by the people.

The morning was occupied by the Bishops representing their several wards.

President Taylor on hearing of the burning of the Mona Ward meeting-house, introduced the following resolution, which was carried unanimously:

Resolved, That we assist in rebuilding that meeting-house. The following amounts being appropriated:

By the Trustee-in-Trust, - $400.
" Nephi Wards, - 200.
" Mona " - 200.
" Levan " - 100.

President Teasdale spoke upon the pleasant and profitable experience he had enjoyed during his Presidency of the Stake, and referred to the works of the people, demonstrating their steady progress.

President Taylor expressed pleasure at the reports, and gave a most excellent, fatherly discourse, filling the hearts of the Saints with joy.

———

2 p.m.

The afternoon was occupied by Presidents Woodruff and Taylor.

The statistical report was read.

———

Sunday, 2 p.m.

After the usual exercises, the General Church Authorities were presented, and then the Stake Authorities, as follows:

William Paxman, President of Stake; Joel Grover and Chas. Sperry, Counselors.

Andrew Love, President of the High Priests; Jas. T. Belliston and Thos. G. Schrouder, Counselors.

Members of the High Council—Geo. Kendall, K. H. Brown, Saml. Cazier, David Cazier, John Vickers, Thos. Ord, Abraham Orme, Chas. H. Bryan, John D. Chase, John Kinkle, Matthew McCune, Jacob G. Bigler, Jr.

Patriarchs—Jacob G. Bigler, Sr., Knud H. Brown and John Andrews.

Presidents of Seventies—Benjamin Riches, John Adams and Thos. Wright, Sr.

Presidents of Elders Quorum—Silas L. Jackson, Chas. House and Enoch Bowles.

President of Priests' Quorum—Bishop David Udall.

Nephi, First Ward—Wm. H. Warner, Bishop; Edwin Harley and Thos. Crawley, Counselors.

Nephi, Second Ward—David Udall, Bishop; Langley Allgood Bailey and Thomas Bowles, Counselors.

Mona Ward—John M. Haws, Bishop; Geo. W. McConkie and Wm. Kay, Counselors.

Levan Ward—Niels Aagaard, Bishop; Eli Curtis and Eric Petersen, Counselors.

Bishop's agent, Wm. Paxman, who was also sustained as Stake Superintendent of Sabbath Schools.

President Taylor, Apostle Teasdale, Presidents Joseph F. Smith and Wilford Woodruff occupied the rest of the afternoon and evening.

The Tabernacle was crowded to excess, and the universal verdict is that it was the best conference ever

held in Nephi and much good is expected to result therefrom.

On Saturday evening the Y. M. and Y. L. M. I. Associations held a conjoint conference; reports very favorable. Instructions were given by Presidents W. Woodruff and Jos. F. Smith.

On Sunday morning the Sabbath School Conference was held; over 600 scholars were present besides teachers and visitors. Reports from the various superintendents were given, very suitable instructions from Presidents Taylor, W. Woodruff, Jos. F. Smith and Geo. Reynolds; a time long to be remembered.

THOS. CRAWLEY, Clerk.

Deseret News
March 28, 1883

DIED.

JAQUES—At Nephi, March 10, 1883, Sarah
Jaques. Born Oct. 6th, 1815, at Foles Hill
Warwickshire, England.
She joined the Church in 1850; emigrated to
Utah in 1862 with three daughters and one
son. She lived and died a faithful Saint.—COM.

Deseret News
April 11, 1883

DIED.

MILLER—In Nephi, Juab County, March
26th, 1883, of a paralytic stroke, Mary Hannah Miller.
Deceased was born April 14th, 1834, in St.
Peter's Parish, Derby, Derbyshire, England.

She was married to Thomas Parkes in the
year 1850. Her husband died, leaving her
with two sons and four daughters; one
daughter died in England, one son on the
plains. Emigrated to Salt Lake City in 1868;
was married to brother Thomas Miller April
16th, 1865; moved to Nephi in 1866; had three
children by Thomas Miller. She was baptized
into the Church of Jesus Christ of Latter-
day Saints December 13th, 1848. She was
respected by all who knew her. She died as
she had lived, a true wife, a good mother and
a faithful Latter-day Saint.—[COM.

Salt Lake Herald
June 3, 1883

DEPUTY REGISTRARS.

JUAB COUNTY.
F. W. Chappell, Mona precinct.
Alma Hague, Nephi precinct.
H. F. McClune. Levan precinct.
C. H. Blanchard. jr., Tintic pre-
cinct.

Deseret News
June 6, 1883

LIST OF PASSENGERS,

Sailing per S. S. Nevada, May
16th, 1883

Nephi.

Axel Bellander; Frederikke Frederick and Christian Larson; Georgun Peterson; Anne Christine Hansen; and Kann Johanne Tonne

Juab.

Wm. Field.

Deseret News
June 20, 1883

DIED

GOLDSBROUGH.— In Nephi, Juab County, June 11th, 1883 Amelia H. Goldsbrough, wife of Brother Henry Goldsbrough. Deceased was born December 7th, 1814, at Little Common, Yorkshire, England. Was baptised by Samuel Wood, Oct. 29th, 1847.

Emigrated with her husband in 1851 to Salt Lake City. Came to Nephi in 1864. Was called and set apart by Bishop C. H. Bryan to preside over the Nephi Relief Society, June 23d, 1868, which position she filled with honor and satisfaction until February 18th, 1878, when she was chosen and set apart by President Teasdale to preside over the Juab Stake Relief Societies—Nephi, Mona and Levan. Ever faithful to her duties, she won the love and affection of the officers and members over whom she presided.

The remains were followed from her residence to the meeting House by her family and relatives, her Counselors and Secretary, the Board and Teachers of the Nephi Society, the President of Mona Society, and officers of the Levan Society; also a number of members of the Nephi.

President Paxman, Patriarch J. G. Bigler, C. H. Bryan, G. Kendall and C. Sperry made very appropriate remarks, aided by the Spirit of God, comforting the bereaved that were present, and a fervent prayer by Brother Joel Grover to God our heavenly Father for His blessings to rest upon the bereaved family, and upon her husband now on a mission to England.

The Nephi Brass Band were in attendance, and her remains were conveyed to the cemetery, followed by her family and many friends.

Salt Lake Herald
June 24, 1883

The Nephi Suicide.

NEPHI CITY, June 23, 1883.

Editors Herald:

On last Thursday evening, 21st instant, Alexander Gardner was found dead in bed at his house in the city, having previously locked his doors. He was last seen between 7 and 8 o'clock a.m. that day, and to all appearances seemed to be in no worse condition of mind and body than had been usual for him of late. His health had been poor for some time and no doubt had much to do with the manner of his sudden death, as the following will explain: G. H.

TERRITORY OF UTAH,)
NEPHI PRECINCT, JUAB Co. {

An inquisition holden at Nephi City, in Nephi Precinct, Juab County, on the 21st day of June, A. D. 1883, before William Sperry, coroner of said county, upon the body of Alexander Gardner, there lying dead, by the jurors upon their oaths, do say that he came to his death by strychnine administered by his own hands, and in a fit of temporary insanity.

In testimony whereof the said jurors have hereunto set their hands, the day and year aforesaid.

CHARLES FOOTE,
CHARLES ANDREWS,
GUSTAVE HENRIOD,
Jurors.

Attest my hand this 21st day of June, A. D. 1883,

WILLIAM SPERRY,
Coroner of Juab County.

LIST OF PASSENGERS

Sailing from Liverpool per S. S. "Nevada," July 20th, 1883, in charge of Hans O. Magleby.

Nephi.

Oloff and Karin Person; Anders C Dahlrod; Gjetnia M, Anna M, and Josephine Petersen; Dorthea Albrechtsen; Anna Maria Olson; Jens Jorgen; Hanna Marie and Serine Cathrine Sorensen; Anders, Elvira, and Anders Oscar Fredricksen; Karn J, Petrea, Anna, Serena M, and Ole West Sorensen; Mariane Sorensen; Maren Sophie Fredriksen; Christine J Rasmussen; Christine Hansen; Maren Larsen; Anne Kerstine; Wina and Axel Petersen; Cathrine Olson; Elna Olson; Ola, Carl W, John, and Mary Person; Anne Person; Ole Rasmussen; L Peter and Elof Nilson; Bashan Hansen; Mikkel and Cawhuo Anderson; Jorgen, Johanne M, Cecilia M, George A, and Christine F Petersen; Hansine Knudsen; Johaune M Sorensen; Anders, Kjerstine, and Niel P Petersen; Rasmus and Sline Rasmusson; Mads Nielsen; Genge W Fredriksen; Fredrika, Petrea, Sophia, and Christian Andersen; Anne C Sorensen; Anne, Maria K, and Melvine E Petersen; Christen S Christensen; Christian N and Nicoline C Nielson; Sven Sorensen; Christian M, Waldemar, and Mariana Svensen; Mariana Larsen; Eline M and Johanne M Christensen; Mariana K and Sina Johanna Jensen; Christian Joseph Nielson; Lars and Ch. Andersen; Rasmussen Carl Christien.

Juab.

Hans S and Anna Johanna Petersen; Johanna M Hansen; Olive M Olson; Karen Petersen; Lovise M Petersen, Rudolf Petersen; Niels, Larsine, and Albertine A Lauritzen; Peter Christensen; Sino M K Nielsen; Peter, Fredrick and Amaine M Mikklesen; Christian, Anne Christine, Nicoline, and Anders Mannus Hansen; Alvine Christinsen; Christine Larsen; Alvine, Victoria, and Emilie V Sorensen; Marie Christiansen; Alfred Jensen; Anna Christine and child; Trine, Niels, and Christian Jensen; Nils, Mano, Sophie, and Auna K M Andersen; Hulda L Sander; Sophus B Goldsmith; Hugo E D Peterson; Maline S Ring; Hans C Nielsen; Magnus C Nielson; Anna M Thompson; Anders P Andersen; Gertrude M Heyldahl; Johannes Christensen; Carolina K Nielson; Johanna and Maria Mork, Christian Joseph Nielson, Petrus and Anton Christensen, Ramele Nillsen; Karen Gregorsen, Peter Christian Rasmusen.

Juab.

Inger and Jens Nielsen.

Nephi.

Annie Holmes.

Died Away from Home.—A little over five weeks ago Brother David V. Bennett, of Mona, Juab County, brought his invalid wife, Mrs. Amanda A. Bennett, up to the city in the hope that her health would be benefitted by the change, she being affected with consumption. The lady gradually sank, however, and expired at the house of Brother Thomas Mitchell, of the 3rd Ward, this morning. The funeral will be conducted at the 9th Ward school house at 10 o'clock to-morrow. Deceased was a native of Sweden, having been from near Stockholm. She had been a member of the Church since 1873, and was a faithful and consistent Latter-day Saint.

Deseret News
September 5, 1883

Back From Wisconsin. — This morning Elder Andrew Hendrickson, of Levan, Juab Co., arrived from Wisconsin, where he had been laboring as a missionary since last May. In consequence of being severely afflicted with acute rheumatism he was released to return home. He is still suffering from that complaint. He baptized three persons into the church and found a number of others who were greatly interested in the Gospel message. While his health was good he enjoyed his labors, and regrets much his inability to continue them longer.

Deseret News
September 19, 1883

LIST OF PASSENGERS,

SAILING FROM LIVERPOOL PER S. S.
"NEVADA" WEDNESDAY
AUG. 29. 1883.

LIST OF SCANDINAVIAN EMIGRANTS.

Juab.

Jacob Nicklas Gustafson; Christian and Heovig Larson; Kristine Nicoline Nielson; Gregers n Soren.

Sorensen; Hannah Sorensen; Peter Anna, Perine and Ottohio Andersen; Soren A. T. and Carl Magnus Sorensen; Christian T. Johnson, Mari Anne, Rasmus, Leverin Magnus and Anna Hansen Jacobsen; Maria Knudsen; Els Johanne Knudsen; Kjers in, Marmus, Anton Martinus, Johan Ludvig and Martin Christian Frandsen; Else Brigette, Niels, Bodil Maria, Else Margrete

Nephi.

Christin Peter, Anne Christine, Liron Christian, Else Christian Harald, Waldemar and Hannah

and Wilhelm Sorensen; Martin, Martine, Axel, Anne Caroline and Martin Peters n; Anne Katrine and Niels Larsen; Mette Kerstine and Laura Onire Mortensen; Peterson Thorvald; Niels Holm; Bahlke Christian F., Thomas C. Bartelsen, Anne K. Jensen; Anders Anderson; Aspas and Carl A. Peterson; Mads C. Petersen.

Deseret News
September 26, 1883

Deseret News
September 26, 1883

FROM THURSDAY'S DAILY, SEPT. 20.

He Caught Them.—John Rowley, of Nephi, informs us that he had at last caught the boys who injured his concrete piping by stopping up the mouth. They begged so hard to be let off, however, that he concluded to let past offences go on their agreeing to behave better in future. Should a similar occurrence take place again, however, he asserts his purpose of prosecuting without fail. He gives us the names of the offenders.

Ladies' Work.—Sisters E. B. Wells and H. M. Whitney, returned this morning from Nephi, where they had been attending the Relief Conference of Juab Stake.

On Saturday the Relief Society held their Conference, at which time a re-organization of the officers of that Society took place, rendered necessary by the demise of Sister Amelia Goldsbrough, the late President. The following officers were nominated by President William Paxman, and sustained by the unanimous vote of the conference. President, Mrs. Mary Pitchforth; First Counselor, Mrs. Amy L. Bigler; Second Counselor Mrs. Necolena Brown; Secretary, Mrs. Mary Hoyt; Treasurer, Mrs. Thirza Maria Vickers. Mrs. Mary Pitch-

forth having presided over the Relief Society of Nephi for several years, a reorganization of the Ward was also effected by President Paxman and his assistants in the Priesthood. Mrs. Maranda Bryan, President; Mrs. E. R. Udall, First Counselor; Mrs. Ann Midgely, Second Counselor; Mrs. M. E. Teasdale, Secretary; Mrs. Hannah Grover, Assistant Secretary; Mrs. C. Evans, Treasurer; Mrs. Julia Bryan, Assistant Treasurer.

The meetings were very interesting—Sunday morning, Primary Conference, in the afternoon Y. L. M. I. A., and in the evening, the joint meeting of Y. L. and Y. M. I. Associations. The meeting-house was filled mostly with young men and women.

MILLER.—At Nephi, September 15th, 1883, of gastric ulcer, Thomas Miller; born Sept. 17th, 1829, at West Nantmeal, Chester County, Pennsylvania; joined the Church of Jesus Christ of Latter-day Saints in 1856; emigrated to Utah in 1861. He lived a true Saint, a good husband and father and an agreeable neighbor.—[Com.

Salt Lake Herald
November 6, 1883

Painful Accidents.

We glean the following particulars from the Provo Enquirer:

On Tuesday last, George Bagley, son of Mr. William Bagley, of Charleston, met with quite a painful accident. He was engaged in blasting some rock with giant powder, and while making a charge, the powder accidentally exploded, burning his face terribly, and almost destroying one eye. He was brought to Provo and is now under Dr. Hannberg's treatment.

Yesterday, Bishop John M. Hays, of Mona, brought his son to Provo and is receiving skillful treatment from Dr. Hannberg. The youth had been running a molasses mill, and accidentally got his left hand caught in the machinery, by which the member was badly lacerated. Though his hand will be stiff and incapable of doing him much service in the future, it will fortunately be spared amputation.

MISSIONARIES FROM THE SOUTH.

RETURN OF ELDERS JOHN MORGAN, CHARLES F. MARTINEAU, JAS. JENKINS AND SAMUEL JACKSON.

Yesterday morning's train over the D. & R. G. Railway, brought to Salt Lake City the above named Elders from the Southern States; President Morgan, accompanied by his wife, returning from a flying visit to the region in which he has labored so long and successfully, and the other brethren having filled up terms of various length in endeavoring to promote the interests of the Lord's work in that land. Elder Morgan we have not yet had the pleasure of meeting. The other brethren called in yesterday and to-day.

Elder Martineau, whose home is in Logan, left here on the 11th of April, 1882, and proceeded to Middle Tennessee, where he labored the whole time with the exception of two months spent in the Western part of the State. In the latter region, he and his companion Elder were threatened by a mob, who assembled with hickories to whip them if they did not leave the neighborhood. Deeming it wisdom to go, the brethren left accordingly. He baptized and assisted to administer that ordinance during his ministry to 18 persons.

Elder Jenkins left Nephi, his home, on the 17th of September, 1881, and labored altogether in South Carolina, in Burke County principally, though he also preached in McDowellCounty, and after the 20th of last March, being appointed to preside over the Conference, moved about generally. He was well treated as a rule, by the people at large, and though often threatened, especially in a place in Burke County, (from which Elders W. H. Clayton, Richard A. Robinson and Joseph Belknap were expelled some time ago,) he afterwards preached there and was not molested. He officiated in thirteen baptisms and assisted in performing a number of others. He met many kind-hearted people, not of his faith, who were willing to share every comfort with him.

Elder Jackson, who also resides in Nephi, left home on the same date as Brother Jenkins, and on arriving at his destination was assigned to labor in Alabama. He was with Elder B. L. Bowen for the first eight months, in Cullman and Morgan Counties, and afterwards traveled with Elder Charles Andrews. They were mobbed in Cullman County, having rocks thrown at them, and being threatened with death, an account of which was published in this paper at the time. Elder Jackson then went to Tennessee, where he and Elder Joseph J. Adams opened up a new field in Jackson and Putnam Counties. From the 20th of last March, he had charge of the East Tennessee Conference, until he was released to come home. He baptized in all 13 souls, and assisted other brethren to perform that ceremony in numbers of other cases. As a general thing he was treated very kindly, and he, as well as the rest, places high value on his missionary experience.

Twenty-two immigrants from Elder Martineau's district, accompanied the brethren from the Southern States. A portion of them went to the San Luis Valley, Colorado, others came to Utah, and one family was destined for Franklin, in Idaho.

Mona Mentions.—Ex-Bishop Edward Thay, of Mona, Juab County, was the recipient of a pleasant surprise party on December 1st, his 54th birthday anniversary.

The people have been blessed with abundant crops and at present enjoy general good health.

The new meeting-house is up to the square, and has been standing quite a while for want of lumber. This having lately arrived, work will be pushed ahead. The building will be a great public benefit, as the people have had no place to meet in since last January.

AT REST. — Thomas Sorrensen, of Nephi, Juab county, whose death notice appears elsewhere, was a faithful Saint, a loving husband and a kind father. He joined the Church in Denmark, his native country, from which land he also emigrated at his own expense over fifty poor Saints, at a cost of $5,000. He did not suffer pain previous to his death, and only a few hours before walked from one room to another. He called his children to him and blessed them as his voice grew weaker, and finally fell peacefully asleep, in the 44th year of his age.

SORRENSON.—At Nephi, Juab Co., Utah, Dec. 30th, 1883, of consumption, Thomas Sorrenson; aged 43 years and 17 days. Deceased was born Dec. 16th, 1840, at Franberg, Denmark. He leaves a wife, two sons and four daughters. He joined the Church in 1875, and emigrated in 1879.
Scandinavian Papers please copy.

NEPHI.

A City that Has the Educational Fever.

The County Showing—Its Future Prospects.

Nephi is the capital of Juab county, and one of the thriftiest and most enterprising places in the Territory. For a number of years she has made application for a city charter, and the Legislature has given it the privilege, but Governor Murray in his inscrutable wisdom, and knowing a great deal more about the needs of the people than they knew themselves, has seen fit to veto enactments looking to the incorporation of Nephi as a city. It is a consolation to know that in a community where the people are so given to extravagance as they are in Utah generally and in Nephi in particular, that his high-mucky-muckiness, without a dollar's interest in the place, should put a stop to their wild career and forbid such an unnecessary expenditure of the people's money and stop them in their mad rush and thirst for a municipality. His course was the more to be commended for the reason that express provision had been made that all officers elected should serve for two years without any remuneration whatever. But his excellency is a great man, and a colossal civilizer, and he knows how it is himself.

Notwithstanding this heartrending rebuff the Nephites are pushing ahead, and in more respects than one are to be commended. The strides made in the last year in the interest of education are remarkable and greatly to be admired. The election of the present school trustees was beyond all question a very judicious move, and was in all probability a premeditated and deliberate choice, for the cooperation of prominent citizens and the people generally has been so pronounced that the labors of the trustees are a source of pleasure, rather than a task of as disagreeable a nature as can well be imposed on a willing citizen, as is too generally the case.

Nephi is divided into five school districts, with a school in each. The County court house—or the building formerly used for that purpose, including the lot, was sold for school purposes by the county recently, and is now used as a school. It is by long odds the most eligible place in the city, and has been fitted up at a cost of over $1,100. The interior has been cleaned, painted and finished, and made both comfortable and attractive; while new seats and desks, of the latest and most improved pattern, have taken the place of the old and delapidated ones. Two schools are held in this build ing, one up and the other down stairs. The former is presided over by F. W. Chappell, County Superintendent, and the latter by Miss Schofield, a graduate of the University of Deseret, and naturally an admirer of Dr. Park. In these two departments there is an attendance of close on 150 pupils. The establishment of this school was the beginning of a graded system in Juab county, and the result has been all that could have been looked for. The other schools are located in different parts of the city and it is a lamentable fact—and a rare one—that the accommodations are unequal to the number of applicants. It is said 100 more s u-dents would attend if accommodations could be found for them. This is not due to a lack of interest, but to a sudden awakening of interest, which has been so rapid that facilities could not be had to keep up with the remarkable growth of the demand. The people have paid their school tax willingly. and in the spring further building will be prosecuted with a view to giving adequate facilities for existing and increased requirements.

The Probate Court appropriated $250 out of the money to be paid by the trustees for the building purchased by the county, provided it will be used in planting trees and beautifying the grounds.

Let any place in Utah show a better disposition.

Juab County is one of the poorest counties in population in the Terri-tory, one of the wealthiest in minerals, and has a financial record that can be eclipsed by none. Nephi, the county seat, has a population of about 2,000, or nearly one-third of the whole county. By judicious management, by the probity and good sense of its county officials, it has not only been liberal and just in its expenditures, all the while looking to the best interests of the people of the county, but it has managed to keep its paper, or scrip, as near par all the time as it could be. The people of that county look forward to a bright future, and that with confidence. The county has limitless mineral resourc-s varied in their nature, the land is of the best farming kind, and the developments of the near future may place the county as one of the richest and most cer tain agricultural sections in the west. We hope so; the people there have sense enough to appreciate such a condition and they will never lack the enterprise and breadth of soul to seize the opportunity.

R. W. S.

Nephi, January 23, 1884.

Artesian Well Company. — We learn from Apostle George Teasdale that the good people of Nephi have organized "The Nephi Artesian Well Company," and have just received from the Peirce Well Excavation Company, a 600-foot artesian well drilling rig. It arrived last week and the officers of the company, with their superintendent, immediately set it up and commenced working to give it a trial and get acquainted with its powers of labor.

It was their first trial, yet in one hour they drilled ten feet, which, considering they were all inexperienced hands, certainly speaks well for their future labors. It is an excellent machine and they are all sanguine that a corresponding result will follow their efforts.

The company have secured the agency for the Territory of the Pierce Well Excavator Company, for their excellent machinery, and they hope in the near future to have to record the success of their work in Juab County, or wherever their labors may be needed.

The officers of the company are: President, Wm. Paxman; Directors, Charles Sperry and David Broadhead; Treasurer, Langley A Bailey; Secretary, Alma Hague. John Kinkie is the superintendent.

Resolutions of Respect, etc.—A committee of the Y. M. M. I. A., of Nephi, Juab County, composed of the following; Israel Bale, Silas L. Jackson and Richard T. Schroder, have drafted resolutions of respect and grateful recognition of the services of W. S. Connell, James Paxman and Isaac Gadd, in aid of the above named association. The young men last named, it seems, are about to leave home on missions.

DEATHS.

TRANTER.—At Nephi, April 6th, 1884, Thomas Tranter, aged 67 years and 4 months.

He was born at Codsall, Staffordshire, England; baptized into the Church October 23rd, 1849, by Elder E. Timmins, of Spanish Fork. He leaves a wife and 4 daughters and 2 sons. He died in full faith of the Gospel,—Com.

Deseret News
May 14, 1884

The Sanpete Valley Washout.—
The floods in Nephi Cañon are still
raging and the washout on the Sanpete Valley Railroad is not yet repaired. Superintendent Bamberger, with
a force of men, is actively at work on
the damaged track, and the bridge,
which was wholly or partly swept away,
is being replaced. The Utah Central
Company will send a spile-driver out
on the morning freight train, for use
at the point indicated.

Deseret News
July 2, 1884

LIST OF PASSENGERS

*Sailing from Liverpool per S. S.
Arizona, June 14th, 1884.*

SCANDINAVIANS.

Nephi.

Lars P., Bertha K., Anthon, Nielson
and Anders C. Andersen; Ingri, Chris-
tine, Niels, Maria A. and Soren H.
Larsen; Niels Peter, Else Maria,
Anton A., Anne K. Nielsmine,
Old Peter and Marius Nielsen;
Christed K. Mine N. Maria P. and
Jemine Bush; Niels P. Mars K. Mar-
tinus L. and Anne K. Peterson; Sine
Maria, Henny F. F. Kera E. J. Carl W.
and Davins E. Schultz; Peter C. Peter-
sen; John Hyrum Jacobson; Ole Jen-
sen; Jens Peter Frandsen, Lars E.
Jensen; Carl J. Andersen; Karen M.
Jensen; Mine S. Jorgensen; Anne
Nielsen; Valdemar M. Mortensen;
Nans C. Mare, Anne K.M. and Hans A.
J. Rasmussen; Lars Jorgensen; Chris-
tine Svendsen, Svend J. M. Jorgensen;
Anders Miekelsen; Mariane N. Peter-
sen; Gotfred Lorentzen; Anders Aug.

Johansen; Seline Olsen; Margrete
Teadore, and Margrethe Larsen;
Martha A. Hildus O. Orson M. Johan
A. Hjalmas A. Jenny A Jensen; Olava,
Maria, Olga, Parley, Hjalma and Karla
Hassel; Caren, Olaf E. and Emil J. Ol-
sen; Mine, Maria, Hortha and Olga
Nielsen; Broghamine Hansen; Chris-
tian, Andrea M. Laura and Danfred
Larsen; Wilhelm Ditmar; Jens, Maria,
Dorthe and Dagmar Larsen; Ane M.
Andersen.

Juab.

Jens C. Abelone; Lauritz T., Anthon
C., Marimus and Christen Christensen;
Erick N., Line M., Mette M. and Erick
Busk Christen Nielsen; Anne S., Jens
C. and Vilhelm C. Jensen; Klava Jacob-
sen; Otte, Martha, Dagmar, Einar and
Thyra Sorensen; Jensine Juhl, Ida C.,
Clausen Christen and Karen Nielsen;
Axel Nielson; Jens C. and Frederikke
Larsen.

Nephi.

Lauretz Petersen.

ITEMS FROM NEPHI.

NEPHI, JUAB CO., U. T.
June 19th, 1884.

Editor Deseret News:

On Saturday and Sunday last, the conference of the Relief Societies of this Stake, the Primaries and the Y. L. M. I. A. were held. They were well attended and the reports very satisfactory. The young ladies read a most excellent paper. "The Young Ladies Journal" showing a very marked improvement. On Saturday a very interesting dedication took place. Our good sisters with the assistance of their liberal brethren, had built a two room house for the needy on a lot where they already had a building which they bought with the lot some time ago. Apostle George Teasdale offered the dedicatory prayer. President W. Paxman and others expressed their satisfaction at this, another movement of the faith, unity and good works of the people of Nephi encouraging them to continue in the landable work of kindly taking care of the aged and needy. To visit the widow and fatherless in their affliction and keep themselves pure and unspotted from the world. It was indeed a very interesting occasion.

On Wednesday evening, our respected Patriarch, Jacob G. Bigler, gave a wedding supper in commemoration of the fortieth anniversary of his wedding day to Sister Amy Lorette Bigler. They were married in Nauvoo on the 18th day of June, 1844, a short time previous to the martyrdom of the Prophet Joseph Smith and his brother Hyrum. They have had quite an experience since that time, but their faithfulness has brought the recompense of reward. Speeches, songs and recitations with expressions of gratitude to our heavenly Father for the restoration of the gospel and our redemption from priestcraft, ignorance and death was the order of the evening. It was a very pleasant evening, one never to be forgotten. May our Patriarch live to celebrate his fiftieth wedding anniversary.

Health of the people good. They are putting a gallery in the meeting-house, which we hope to be able to use at our next Conference. Improvement, unity and good feeling amongst the Saints is the order of the day.

NEBO.

Deseret News
September 24, 1884

LIST OF PASSENGERS

Sailing from Liverpool per S. S. Wyoming, Aug. 30, 1884, Elder Benjamin Bennett in charge.

SCANDINAVIAN.

Nephi.

Maria Sorensen; Arild C. Nielsen; Inger, Peter S. and Lows W. Larsen; Johannes and Hansine C. Hansen; Johanne, Petrea K., Wilhelmina and Else M. Petersen; Jensine, Niels K., and Jens P. Petersen; Eline Hendriksen; Karen M. Svendson; Sine Sorensen; Albertine M. Christensen; Nickoline and Peter C. Andersen; Anthon Nielsen; Andreas Svendsen; Else M., Martine M. and Wilhelmine Hansen; Benedicta Hansen; Kirsten and Dora Johansen; Peter, Ane K., Nielsine Caroline, Anina and Josephine Andersen; Maria Christensen; Niel P. Sorensen; Peter and Hannah Lindberg; Christine Svensen; Ellen K. and Christine Andersen; Stine E. Carlsen; Inga Avensen; Margrethe Bjork; Maren Andersen.

Juab.

Namy Sadusannah Larsen; Ane J. and Peter Nielsen; Axel F. Nielsen.

Nephi.

L. I. Bonnekson; Mads Sorensen; Peter Frederiksen.

Salt Lake Herald
September 30, 1884

NECK BROKEN.

A Young Man, of Mona, Suddenly Killed.

We learn from Mr. William Yates, at whose house the young man, John Green, was stopping in this city, before the operation performed by Dr. Benedict, that while taking the body from the car last Saturday evening, a messenger arrived in hot haste, on horseback, and sent a thrill of horror through the sorrow-stricken company, by announcing to Mr. Newton, superintendent of the Co-op. store, that his son, William, had had his neck broken in the canyon. On learning the particulars, it was found that Wm. Newton and another boy, by the name of John W. King, had gone after a load of wood. While working, the horses of both boys got loose and started down the canyon, but were subsequently captured. Young King went on down, riding one animal and driving the other, of his. After proceeding some distance he missed young Newton. Tying his team, he returned up the road and found his companion lying in the wagon track, breathing his last. The supposition is that in going up part of the way which was very steep he had reached over to hit the animal to increase his speed, when the horse kicked him on the left side of the neck and jaw; but whether the kick or fall broke the unfortunate young man's neck was not determined. From all we can learn, the deceased was a promising, moral young man, and his untimely death has cast a gloom over the community in which he was best known.

Deseret News
October 15, 1884

Names of missionaries who have been called since the April Conference, 1884, and now in their fields of labor, and whose names are now submitted:

HINDOOSTAN.

William Willes, 20 Ward.
Milson R. Pratt, 16th Ward.
Henry F. McCune, Nephi.
George Booth, Calcutta.

GREAT BRITAIN.

George Osmond, Bloomington.
Peter Winward Payson.
Thos. Butterfield, Herriman.
Joseph H. S. Bodell, Herriman.
Jesse B. Martin, Jr., Scipio.
Willmer D. Thompson, Scipio.
William Horsley, Brigham.
George Gidney, Brigham.
George H. Fowers, Hooper.
L. L. Hatch, Franklin.
John Rowley, Nephi.
William Rex, Randolph.
Thomas Slight, Paris.
Robert W. Sloan, 18th Ward.

SWISS AND GERMAN MISSION.

Gustave Henroid, Nephi.
Godfrey G. Fuhriman, Providence.
Conrad Faterlouse, Paris.
Joon Kunz, Jr., Bern.
David Kunz, Bern.
Arnold Henry Schulthess, 1st Ward.

UNITED STATES.

John D. Chase, Nephi.
Joseph Shipley, American Fork.

SCANDINAVIA.
Jeppa Jeppsen, Brigham.

Niels Hansen, Manti.
Rasmus Borgquist, 10th Ward.
S. A. Wannberg, 20th Ward.
Christian Nielsen Lundsteen, Levan.
Matts S. Mattson, St. Charles.
Thomas C. Petersen, Ovid.
Niels C. Christensen, Levan.
Christian Christiansen, Levan.
Thomas R. Schroder, Nephi.
Mads Peter Madsen, Ephraim.
Andrew C. Anderson, Redmund.
Christian Anderson, Ogden.
Nephi Anderson, Petersen.
Johan Peter Mortensen, 8th Ward.
August K. Anderson, Grantsville.
Chas. J. Stromberg, Grantsville.
Peter M. Anderson, Grantsville.
John Alfred Eliason, Grantsville.
Anders Gustaf Sandberg, Grantsville.
Erasmus P. Marquerdson, Elsinore.
N. P. Peterson, Pleasant Grove.
Carl G. Anderson, 19th Ward.
John J. Johnsen, Logan.
Andras Olsen, Gunnison.
Lars Foolson, Smithfield.
Peter W. Peterson, Smithfield.

Salt Lake Herald
December 11, 1884

Mr. ALLISON, of Mona, is up purchasing goods for their thriving town.

Deseret News
December 17, 1884

DEATHS.

HOYT—In Nephi, Juab county, Nov. 25th, 1884, Elizabeth Lamont Sperry Hoyt; was born Oct. 2, 1816 in Henrietta, Monroe county, New York; emigrated with her parents from Illinois in the fall of 1847; was baptized into the church in the spring of 1848; married the late Timothy S. Hoyt, April 15, 1849; resided with her husband in Mill Creek, Salt Lake County till the spring of 1853, when they moved to Nephi; was the mother of six children, two sons and four daughters; six grandchildren and two great-grandchildren. He died a faithful Latter-day Saint.—COM.

Deseret News
December 31, 1884

DEATHS.

JORGENSEN.—At Levan, Juab County, December 17th, 1884, nine days after giving birth to a boy, Ovenia Andrea Jorgensen, wife of H. C. L. Jorgensen.

Deceased was born March 15th, 1851, in Randers, Denmark; received the Gospel in 1870; emigrated to Utah in 1873, and married the the same year; was the mother of seven children, all of whom with her husband are left to mourn the departure of a faithful Saint and a dearly beloved wife and mother, loved and respected by all who knew her.

Bikuben and *Scandinavian Star*, please copy.

JACKSON—At Nephi, Juab County, Utah, December 5, 1884, Thomas Jackson; aged 82 years, 4 months and 28 days.

Deceased was born in Chelsfield, Kent, England; emigrated to this country in 1866. He died in full faith of the Gospel. He leaves a wife, one son and two daughters to mourn his departure.

Millennial Star, please copy.

Salt Lake Herald
January 9, 1885

NEPHI POINTS.

EDWARD BOOTH, of this place has had the misfortune to lose a son. The child was 5 years of age and died this, 7th, inst., of croup.

H. GOLDSBROUGH, the accommodating proprietor of the Nephi House, is yet at his place of business, where he is prepared to convey travelers by team to all points of interest in southern Utah. His accommodations for travelers are ample and his teams excellent.

PRESIDENT PAXMAN, the superintendent of the Nephi Co-op., appears to be an enterprising business man. He has just completed a very neat and attractive building for the Tithing office, which is an ornament to the town.

THE THRIFTY firm of Hyde & Whitmore occupy a very large and well stocked store of general merchandise. Their place is well patronized.

The Home Dramatic Company have been giving some very fine entertainments to crowded houses during the holidays. Amusements now appear to be taking a rest for a season. B. R. S.

Nephi City, Juab County, Utah,
January 7th, 1885.

Salt Lake Herald
January 15, 1885

NEPHI NOTES.

KIRKHAM'S PANORAMA exhibited here last night; but owing to the long run of entertainments here during the recent holidays, the attendance was not so large as it would otherwise have been.

THE YOUNG people of the town have lately given some very fine entertainments for the benefit of the Sunday school. They were well patronized and gave general satisfaction.

THE OLD pioneer harness shop of Nephi, under its proprietor, J. C. Ostler, has lately established a branch house at Gunnison. Both houses are doing a fair business and carry a complete stock of harness and saddlery. They also deal largely in sportsmen's outfits and are an enterprising business firm.

THE YOUNG men have started a crusade against the rabbits. They went forth this morning well armed with all the shot guns of the town, leaving the place to be defended by the less harmless members of the community. Judging from the wagons they took to cart the dead bunnies home, and the determined look on their faces, we may expect to hear some wonderful tales of slaughter. S.

Nephi, January 13th, 1885.

Another Veteran Gone.—We learn from L. A. Bailey of the death of Father Charles H. Bryan, who died at his residence at Nephi yesterday morning, at 6 o'clock. He was an old and respected member of the community.

A Returned Missionary.—We had a call this morning from Elder Charles P. Ostler, of Nephi, who returned to our city last evening from a mission to the Southern States, upon which he started on the 5th of December, 1882. He labored while absent in North Carolina and Virginia, first in company with Elder John H. Barlow and subsequently at various times with Elders James Jenkins, Amos Cook, John E. Rouesche, B. F. McKinney, John S. Willie, Charles Noakes, Joseph Belknap and E. G. Farmer. He met with considerable opposition, and upon one occasion was pursued by a armed mob with guns, but escaped without injury. He also found many kind friends in the South, both inside and outside the Church, had some success in his labors and on the whole enjoyed his mission very much, and appreciates his experience while abroad. He had some difficulty in getting home, owing to funds sent from here to pay his fare having failed to reach him. He was one month on the way, being delayed at several points, but returns in excellent health and spirits.

A CAREER OF USEFULNESS.

INTERESTING BIOGRAPHICAL SKETCH
OF THE LIFE OF THE LATE
W. H. BRYAN.

NEPHI, Utah, Jan. 16, 1885.

Brother Charles Hinkle, son of John and Elizabeth Hinkle Bryan, was born at Bryan Farm, Floyd's Fork, Ky., Dec. 14th, 1807; died at his residence in Nephi, Juab County, Utah Territory, January 14th, 1885, aged 77 years and 1 month.

He was baptized by Andrew Love and confirmed by President Brigham Young a member of the Church of Jesus Christ of Latter-day Saints at Mosquito Creek, Iowa, on the 14th day of July, 1846.

WHAT LED TO HIS CONVERSION.

In the summer of 1833 he was out hunting in the woods of Little Okaw, Moultrie County, Illinois, and while in the pursuit of game was attracted by the sound of a loud voice speaking in emphatic tones, and being curious to know the cause, leaned his gun against a tree and noiselessly approached the speaker. When he drew near enough for observation he found that the speaker was a man poorly clad, being barefooted, and standing upon a log preaching to a small company of people encamped at that spot. He sat down upon a fallen tree, and unobserved listened to the speaker, who was teaching his companions in the duties of their several callings, and though the first principles of the Gospel were not mentioned by the speaker, Brother Bryan there and then became convinced that the little company of travelers were the true followers of the Lord Jesus Christ and that the speaker was uttering inspired words. He learned that the travelers were a company of Latter-day Saints, and though he did not join the Church immediately, from that time he advocated and sustained the principles of "Mormonism" and for that cause was driven from his possessions at Little Okaw, Moultrie County, Ill., with the Latter-day Saints in the early spring of 1846, when he started west, reaching Highland Grove, Iowa, in July of the same year.

The mob drove from that place Andrew Love and family, Wm. Cazier and Family and George Best and family, "Mormons," and Brother Bryan and family who had not then joined the Church.

The mob offered to give Brother Bryan further time to make preparations for moving, saying they had nothing against him except that he would harbor the "Mormons," but he refused the proposal and moved at once with the company.

He built a house and remained at Highland Grove until the 19th day of May, 1848, when he started west,

REACHING SALT LAKE VALLEY

on the 22d day of September of the same year, where he took up a city lot and farm and remained until the 22d day of October, 1851, when he moved to Nephi, Juab Co., Utah, reaching that place on the first of November.

In November, 1852, he was ordained a High Priest by Bishop Jacob G. Bigler, Sen., and chosen and set apart to act as his First Counselor, in which position he acted until June, 1861, when he was ordained and set apart by Bishop Edward Hunter to act as Bishop of Juab County, and he acted in that capacity until October 25th, 1869, when he went on a mission to the western and middle States, returning from his mission on the 10th day of March, 1870. He took a prominent part in the

INDIAN WAR

of 1853, and was one of the committee appointed and who acted in the location and building of the Fort Wall around the town of Nephi, the dimensions of the wall being 105 rods square, 6 feet thick at the bottom, and two feet at the top, and 12 feet high, having gates on the north and south sides.

He held a commission from Governor Brigham Young, appointing him to the office of "Surgeon's mate of the Battalion of Infantry of Juab Military District," with the rank of Second Lieutenant of Juab Military District of the Nauvoo Legion, and of the Militia of Utah Territory, to take rank from the 21st day of January, 1854.

June 1st, 1877, he was ordained and set apart by President Brigham Young to the office of a member of the High Council of the Juab Stake of Zion, which office he held until his death. He took a leading part in the building of the Nephi meeting-house, and Social Hall, and in the locating of the townsites and fields of Juab County; also in the establishment of co-operative institutions, and he presided over the Nephi Co-operative Mercantile and Manufacturing and the Nephi Mill and Manufacturing Companies for sevral years.

He organized the Nephi Relief Society, June 23d, 1868.

He held the office of a Selectman in Juab County Court from 1854 to 1861.

He entertained President Brigham Young with many of his company on nearly every occasion of his passing through Nephi, and kept an open free house to the traveling public for many years.

He acted as physician and surgeon free of charge on every occasion to any and all who called upon him in that capacity—Mormon, Jew, Gentile or aborigine, numbering thousands of cases from the time of his arrival until his late sickness, and there is scarcely a home in Nephi that does not remember him in kindness and gratitude for his many benevolent acts.

His death came like sleep to an infant, passing away quietly and resignedly, feeling that his earthly work was complete and that God would receive him into His kingdom.

His funeral rites were held at the Nephi Meeting House, commencing at 11 o'clock a. m., Jan. 16th, 1885, Apostle Teasdale conducting the services. In his remarks he dwelt principally upon the benefit of a well spent life, drawing the sympathy of the Saints in such a manner as to cause each to comprehend the grand reward of faithful works in the Kingdom of God. Presidents Paxman, Grover, Sperry and Elder Love, Bishop Udall and Patriarch J. G. Bigler also spoke, each bearing upon the subject advanced by Brother Teasdale, and giving testimony of the faithfulness and usefulness of the deceased.

He leaves two wives, two sons and several grandchildren to mourn his loss.　GEORGE TEASDALE.

Deseret News
February 18, 1885

DEATHS.

BALE—At Nephi, Juab County, Utah, February 5th, 1885, Thomas Bale; born at Lenton Docks, Nottinghamshire, England, January 20, 1809; embraced the gospel at Coalville, Leicestershire, July 1844; emigrated to Nephi, Utah, September 1869, where he remained till death, continuing faithful and true to the gospel.

Mill. Star please copy.

Salt Lake Democrat
March 10, 1885

Hon. JOEL GROVER, of Nephi, left for a visit to his old home at Pottsville, Pa., this morning.

Deseret News
March 25, 1885

DEATHS

PLATT.—At Mona, Juab County, Utah, March 16th, 1885, of brain fever, after an illness of four days, James Platt, aged 70 years and 9 months.

Deceased emigrated from the St. Helens Branch of the Liverpool Conference, in the year 1862.

Salt Lake Herald
April 4, 1885

THE LEVAN ROBBERY.

The Two Men Supposed to be Guilty Still at Large.

Further particulars have reached us of the recent burglary at Levan. Very strong suspicion points towards two young men named Martin and Fred Moss, brothers, as being the guilty parties, and warrants are out for their arrest. Soon after the burglary occurred they were missing from Levan. It subsequently transpired that they had taken a trip, per team, to Sevier County. They managed to get up a row in Salina, and assaulted several of the inhabitants. It becoming too warm for them in that town, they borrowed two saddle horses, without asking the owners' consent, and made for the mountains between there and Juab County. The horses giving out, were turned loose and the riders footed it to the hills, where it is supposed the plunderers are hidden. They have several times been seen in the mountains near Juab, but have so far eluded capture.

Martin Moss is of slim build, has light hair, bright eyes and a medium fair complexion. Fred Moss is heavy and stout and the possessor of rather a bad looking countenance. Ages 20 to 24 years.

The money stolen from Levan amounted to nearly $200, consisting of gold, paper currency and silver. A reward of one half that amount will be paid for recovery of the treasure and capture of the thieves.

Utah papers please copy.

Salt Lake Herald
April 14, 1885

COUNTY REGISTRARS.

List of the New Officers Appointed by the Commissioners.

Juab County—Edward Booth, Nephi.

Deseret News
April 29, 1885

The Levan Robbers.—Last evening

Sheriff Cazier, of Nephi, returned from Iowa, bringing with him Fred and Martin Moss, charged with having committed a burglary in Levan, and this morning they were taken before Commissioner McKay, and pleaded not guilty. Bail was placed at $300 each, in default of which the accused will repose in the penitentiary. The further examination of the case will be continued on Saturday.

CORRESPONDENCE.

ON THE WAY TO SAN JUAN.

NEPHI, Juab County,
April 6th, 1885.

Editor Deseret News:

Saturday the 28th ult. we left your fine city and drove eight miles to

BIG COTTONWOOD,

where we were entertained in a right royal manner by Sister Harriet Brinton, widow of the late David Brinton, and her sons, until Monday morning. Doctor Seymour B. Young and wife, Elder John A. Groesbeck and wife and Sister Elizabeth Nebeker joined us on Saturday evening and remained with us until Sunday evening. We spent a very enjoyable time together. I met quite a few old friends here whom I had not met for thirty-five years. I lived here in 1849.

On Monday, the 30th ult., we bade farewell to our friends on the Cottonwood and journeyed to Lehi, Utah County. We passed through a continuous chain of settlements, beautiful orchards, well tilled fields and fine, cosy farm houses. The lucern was always in sight, and to it, in a great measure, I attribute the thriving condition of most of our settlements on the line of travel we are pursuing. Farms on the Little Cottonwood that a few years ago would not produce enough to justify cultivation are now yielding good paying crops.

I find the settlements crowded up to their utmost capacity, land and water all appropriated, and our young people as they marry off have no place to settle near home; hence I would say, not exactly as Horace Greely, "Young man,

MARRY AND GO SOUTH

into San Juan County, Utah." I am going there and like company. I don't want to go even to heaven alone. I would not have you infer by this that San Juan is heaven, or even a paradise at present, but we propose to make it such in time, as the Saints have made their pleasant homes in these sterile valleys, by persistent and unremitting toil. And now the devil covets the results of our labors, or rather his pious emissaries of the clerical persuasion, and government carpet baggers, do and they think it awful that we don't quietly move out and give them possession; but then I do not feel to complain because of their treatment towards us, for it is doing us, as a people, great good. I perceive, as I travel among and mingle with the people that there is a better feeling prevailing among the Saints than I have witnessed for years past—more determined feeling to maintain their faith in God and in his work as now being established through the labors of his holy Priesthood even unto death. And thus will the Lord turn the efforts and labors of the devil and his aids for the advancement of His cause and the establishment of His kingdom upon the earth, and no power of the devil or man can prevent it.

Now, Mr. Editor, I do not wish our friends, the clergy, or our Federal officials any harm, for about forty years ago I was in the same school of sectarian folly, without hope or any definite idea of God; but having found the truth, I can afford to be generous.

The City or County of Salt Lake, should fix up some of the

BRIDGES CROSSING THE CANALS

in the southern part of the county, below Sandy and north of the Point of Mountain; they need side rails, and one which spans a deep gulley might be widened about two inches, as it is only about eight feet in width, barely wide enough for a sober United States Marshal to drive safely over, and I should dislike very much if any of those gentlemen should come to grief through any neglect of our City or County officials.

There is also a very bad piece of road south from the point of the mountain, and north of Lehi, deep narrow gullies washed out through the melting of snow, I judge, from the near foothills; there is a mile or two of this kind of road, where every few rods you have to throw on the brake and come to a dead halt, or run the risk of breaking an axle-tree or jerking your false teeth out. Either case would be a sad affair to a poor pilgrim bound for a country where such things could not well be replaced.

On the evening of the 30th we arrived at Lehi, which is a pretty little city, well governed and quite prosperous, but like most of our towns, overpopulated, for the resources of the people are about exhausted, unless they go into manufacturing.

On Tuesday, the 31st, we passed on south through American Fork and Battle Creek, and over the great Provo Bench to the

RENOWNED CITY OF PROVO,

with its great woolen mill, grist mills, banks, fine stores filled with merchandise from every land, and drug stores with drugs from every land—enough, if carefully used, to kill all the Saints in the land and a few of the U. S. marshals. Here I enjoyed the hospitality of my old and dear friend, President A. O. Smoot. Judge Dusenberry also showed me through the magnificent edifice built for the accommodation of the unfortunate of our race—the lunatics. Here, it seems to me, that everything that can in any way contribute to the pleasure, happiness, comfort and convenience of its inmates has been carefully studied and provided for. The Judge informed me that the entire cost

up to date had only reached $80,000. I certainly feel that the money has been

WISELY EXPENDED,

and the tax-payers have need to be proud of the result. The committee, too, who have had this subject in hand deserve great credit for the praiseworthy manner in which they have discharged their trusts. If the institution had about 40 acres more land to add to its grounds it would be a great blessing.

I also called upon Professor Maeser, at the B. Y. Academy, who very kindly showed me through all the departments of learning over which he is presiding, with which I was highly gratified.

The good people of this Stake have almost completed a most magnificent building for a

STAKE TABERNACLE,

which, when completed, will be one of the finest places of worship in the Territory. Utah County is a rich district, and signs of wealth and prosperity are displayed on every hand. Continuing my journey to the beautiful city of Springville, I again halted. For location I know of none that I consider superior to Springville, except Salt Lake. Here we were entertained in a sumptuous manner by my sister-in-law, Ann Bringhurst, widow of the late Bishop Wm. Bringhurst. In the evening the brass band came around and gave us a sweet serenade.

On the 1st of April we pursued our journey to Spanish Fork. Here we were entertained by my brother-in-law, Carl Morgenson and wife. This town has also grown to be a fine place, filled with enterprising citizens.

The following day we continued on to Santaquin, passing through Pond Town and Payson, and put up at Widow Holladay's, widow of the late David Holladay, Bishop of Santaquin. Here I met with some old friends whom I had not seen for 34 years, and spent the afternoon and evening with Brothers John M. Holladay and Henry G. Boyle, like old soldiers fighting our battles over again. Brother Boyle while preaching to save others nearly all his days, has not been able to save himself temporally. He is in a crippled condition, having lost the use entirely of one hand, and has a large family and little or no income. He has spent his best days in preaching the Gospel and gathering the people to this land, and deserves to be better situated.

The prospects for fruit and crops generally are exceedingly good through all our settlements, and the present fine rains are making the farmers to rejoice.

On Saturday, the 4th, we left Santaquin and proceeded to Nephi, 13 miles, passing through Mona, a nice little village, where everything seemed neat and orderly. At this place I overtook my teams, and found them nicely provided for. I was entertained by Brother Henry Goldsbrough, in old-fashioned "Mormon" style, and spent the evening in a most pleasant manner. Brother Goldsbrough, being an old timer, had many fine bits of experience to relate, almost equal to Brother Woodruff's "Chapter of Accidents."

While in Nephi I attended the

SABBATH SCHOOL

in a very nice, comodious hall, where the Ward meetings are held. I was much pleased with the good order and large attendance. There were over 500 pupils enrolled, besides a large primary school in the vestry. I noticed many of the pupils were middle aged men—men of experience. I was told by the Superintendent, Brother W. H. Warner, that they were mostly Seventies. I noticed those having charge of the Sacrament, when they blessed the bread knelt dnown, and as soon as the bread was blessed, without arising, the water was blessed also. This, I think, is to save time, as the Priests who serve the water can follow up those serving the bread, and the exercises of the school soon be allowed to proceed.

I also attended the Ward meeting. I was called upon to address the Saints by Prest. Chas. Sperry. I saw some old familiar faces, among others that of Brother John Borrowman, a member of the famous Mormon battalion, whom I had not seen since the spring of 1849.

NEPHI

is a very enterprising town, filled with a go-ahead sort of people, judging from their works, and if they had a nice stream of the fine water from Ogden Valley flowing through their town I think it would be a very desirable place to live in. There is but one well here, which, I am informed, is some 200 feet deep, and supplies but poor water; hence the people are dependent upon the water from the creek for domestic use, which at this time, I think, would be good for making adobes, as it would require but very little mud to make it the required consistency.

About 6 o'clock p. m. Brothers Harmon, Bellnap, Wardsworth and Messervy, from Hooper, and Adam Russell from Riverdale, overtook me, all well. They had remained one day at Santaquin in consequence of horses having got poisoned on some hay obtained at Payson. They will proceed by way of Sanpete, and join me at Salina.

From your traveling friend and brother,   F. A. HAMMOND.

Salt Lake Herald
May 20, 1885

DIED.

ADAMS.—At St. George, Utah, on May 9th, 1885, Emma J. Adams, aged 54 years.

Emma Jackson Adams was born in Milnthorpe, England, December 9th, 1830, and was baptized a member of the Church of Jesus Christ of Latter-day Saints at Kendal, England, in the fall of 1851. She married Elder Samuel L. Adams, at Liverpool, England, February 6th, 1852, and sailed a few days after for Zion, arriving in Salt Lake City with her husband, in Elder A. O. Smoot's company, September 3, 1852. She resided in Nephi, Juab County, from 1854 till 1864. In the latter year her husband being called upon to go to St. George, Washington County, she removed with him to that place in the winter of that year. With the exception of intervals, amounting in all to about three years, she has continued to reside in St. George until her death, which occurred on May 9th, 1885. She leaves her husband, four children, sixteen grandchildren and a very large circle of friends to mourn her loss. She was an affectionate wife, a tender mother and a consistent member of the church with which she had united herself. She has been a confirmed invalid for ten years past, and during that time has suffered intense physical pain yet she was patient, cheerful and considerate in all her sufferings. She passed away peacefully, and died in the hope of a glorious resurrection. We feel that she is "not lost, but gone before." A large concourse of her brethren and sisters, her old friends and acquaintances paid their last tribute of affection at her funeral services, which were held in St. George on the afternoon of May 10th, 1885.—COM.

Salt Lake Herald
June 12, 1885

Boards of Equalization.

The county clerk of Juab County, Mr. W. A. C. Bryan, announces in THE HERALD that the board of equalization for Juab County will sit in Nephi on July 6th, when all complaints as to over (or under) assessments may be made. Clerks of other counties should forward their notices to the daily or semi-weekly HERALD—whichever circulates most largely in their neighborhoods—in order that the people may be apprised when and where complaints may be made.

Salt Lake Herald
July 4, 1885

THE COMING ELECTION.

The Judges Appointed by the Utah Commission.

List of the names of Judges of election appointed by the Utah Commission to serve at the ensuing election to be held in the Territory of Utah, August 3d, 1885:

JUAB COUNTY.

John H. McChrystal, John H. Saville, James L. Yates, Eureka.

Ephraim Ellertson, Elias W. Williams, Mormon Ellertson, Mona.

George Lar-en, William Brown, J. W. Shepherd, Levan.

Charles Foote, Edwin Boothe, F. W. Chpapell, Nephi.

J. E. Clinton, W. P. Read, James E. Taylor, Juab.

Salt Lake Herald
August 21, 1885

MR. GOLDSBOROUGH, of Nephi, met with quite a serious accident in Beaver a few days ago. Through some cause he fell backwards into a cellar, alighting on his head and shoulders. At last accounts his injuries were considered critical.

Deseret News
September 16, 1885

DEATHS.

RANDERSON—At Nephi, Sep. 1, 1885, Samuel Randerson; born in Rocklington, Yorkshire, Eng., Aug. 24, 1829, emigrated from Hull to Utah in the year 1881.

Deseret News
October 14, 1885

DEATHS.

FAULKNER—At Central, Arizona, October 1, 1885, after a protracted illness, of malarial fever, Rebecca, wife of Wm. Faulkner, late of Nephi, Utah, who removed with his family to Arizona last fall. Sister Faulkner embraced the Gospel in early youth, emigrated to Utah from Hertfordshire, England, in the year 1868, led a consistent, exemplary life, and was beloved by all who knew her. Her age was 39 years and 15 days.

Deseret News
November 4, 1885

A Double Wedding.—A couple of marriages occurred at the Logan Temple, on Wednesday last, Oct. 28, 1885, two of the parties to which were Ortherus and Clomenia (Phelps) Pratt, son and daughter of the late Apostle Orson Pratt, and Juliette (Phelps) Pratt, the bride of the former being Miss Emma Louise Taysum, daughter of Andrew J. and Mary Ann (Mears) Taysum, of the 20th Ward of this city, at whose residence a reception was held last evening, 30th inst., in honor of the young bride and groom. The bridegroom of Miss Clomenia Pratt is Brother Wm. Bailey, of Nephi, the son of Langley Allgood and Sarah (Andrews) Bailey, also of Nephi.

A reception in honor of both these couples will be held this evening (31st inst.) at the residence of Mrs. Juliette Pratt Crabb, 17th Ward, this city, where it is expected that a large assembly of the relatives and friends of the contracting parties will enjoy the proceedings of the occasion, as was the case at last evening's reception.

Brother William Bailey expects to start for his home at Nephi next Monday morning, to which place his new bride will accompany him, and where the prospects are favorable for another reception.

Brother and Sister Ortherus Pratt will start next Tuesday morning for Scipio, Millard County, at which place the groom will resume his duties at the store.

We wish these fortunate couples all the felicity they desire in their new estate.

Ogden Herald
November 9, 1885

LIST OF PASSENGERS

Sailing from Liverpool per S. S. Nevada, October 24th, 1885, in charge of A. H. Lund.

Nephi:

Alice A. Tomlinson; Ann, Louisa, Emma, Jane, Elizabeth, Henry and Arthur H. Burton; Wm. Baines.

Juab.

Micael, Ursula M. Henrietta K. Kaunna, Thogra, Hans R. Hansen; Amanda and Alexander Nielsen; Johanno M. Jensen; Peter Rasmussen.

Hjalmar Eriksen; Mikkel Petersen; Karen M., Karen H., Marinus M., Petra Petersen Kong; Niels Beck; J. C. N., Pauline M., Anne E. and J. C. N. Clansen; Johanne Clanson; Olga, Thora, Nielsen, Hans Johansen; Hugo Jacobsen; L. P., Birthe M., Dorthea. Martin and Emily Jacobsen; Frederik and Johanne Olsen; Sorn O. Sorensen; Jensine M., Jens J., Andreas M., Christine M, Frederik and Thomas Jensen; J. O. Jensen; Christen and Martha Johansen, Thor Thoresen, Joseph Andersen; C. Sunderup.

Deseret News
November 25, 1885

Commissioned.—On Saturday the Governor issued commissions to the following officers:

James Jensen, constable, Mona precinct, Juab County.

H. W. Hartley, justice of the peace; Charles Mangelson, constable, Levan precinct, Juab County.

Salt Lake Herald
December 23, 1885

NOTES FROM NEPHI.

THIS PLACE has outgrown its village suit and can now with propriety don the garb of a full fledged city, and it would not require any great expansion of one's imagination to rank it as the commercial centre of Southern Utah, as car after car is daily being loaded with grain brought to this point from Sanpete, and surrounding counties, to be shipped north, east and west; the result is that the city is at present in a much healthier condition—financially—than for several years back, and merchants are correspondingly jubilant.

THE TAYLOR & SCOTT Sea of Ice Company closed their engagement here last night to a jammed house, repeating their success of the previous night, on which occasion people were turned away by scores, as the house was by far too small to accommodate those who wished to witness the performance. The play, company and scenery combined, make the strongest attraction ever presented in Southern Utah; and the public show their appreciation of its merrits by turning out in force and crowding the houses upon each presentation, and the company leave each town under a promise to repeat it upon their return. They also present the Life of an Actress as a companion piece, and have scored a success in that as well as the Sea of Ice.

To ALL appearances the Sanpete Valley Railroad is upon the eve of a genuine boom, for the the people of this section of the country are just awaking to the fact that a railroad is a public convenience as well as a benefit.

THE WEATHER here is beautiful over head but muddy under foot.

TRIX.

NEPHI, December 20, 1885.

Salt Lake Herald
December 29, 1885

Kendall-Parkes,

On Christmas afternoon the elegant parlors of Wm. A. C. Bryan, Esq., at Nephi, were filled by a host of relatives and friends, who assembled to witness the marriage of Mr. A. S. Kendall, of Salt Lake, to Miss Georgia A. Parkes, of Nephi, the lovely and talented sister of Mrs. W. A. C. Bryan. The bride is a lady well-known and esteemed for her many fine qualities of heart and mind. The bridegroom is widely known here for his good nature and social qualities, having been principal of the Eleventh District School for a number of years. The ceremony was performed by Hon. Joel Grover, and when concluded, the guests adjourned to the dining-room, where the tables were loaded with all the delicacies of the season. We wish the newly-married couple an ocean of joy and happiness.

Salt Lake Herald
January 12, 1886

A FATAL AFFRAY AT NEPHI.

H. H. Pearson Kills Forrest Green ---The Effect of Drink.

The following particulars of a fatal shooting affray have reached us: "Forrest Green and H. H. Pearson had been drinking and were in a yard east of Abe Chalmer's saloon, when Pearson drew a pistol, and placing the muzzle against Green's face said, 'I will shoot you!' Green answered, 'Shoot me, if you want to!' at which Pearson reiterated his former threat, and, stepping back about four or five feet from Green, took deliberate aim and fired. Green fell upon his face, exclaiming. "You have killed me!" Pearson then turned his weapon upon a man who was standing near, and commanding him to turn Green over and see where the bullet had hit him. The person addressed turned Green over and told Pearson he was shot in the breast near the heart. Pearson mounted his horse, which was standing near, and 10's away, flourishing his pistol. He was, however, immediately followed by the sheriff and posse, arrested and lodged in jail. An inquest was held and a verdict rendered in accordance with the above facts."

Pearson was to have had an examination yesterday.

Deseret News
February 3, 1886

Run Over.—Yesterday Mr. F. Soreusen, roadmaster of the Sanpete Valley Railway, while going up Salt Creek Cañon, hitched his hand car behind the train. When he went to uncouple his car he fell forward on the track and was run over by the trolley, receiving severe injuries. He was taken to his home in Nephi, where medical assistance was rendered.

LEES.—In the 19th Ward of this city, Jan. 28, 1886. Father John Lees, who was born at Hurst-brooks, Lancashire, England, Feb. 25, 1800; was baptized into the Church at Ashton-under-Line, June 10th, 1848, by Elder John Albiston; emigrated to Utah in the fall of 1853, and settled in the 19th Ward, which has been his home ever since, except during the time of the general removal southward, at the time of the approach of Johnson's army to Utah, when he located at Nephi for a few months. He has held the office of Elder and High Priest, which he faithfully filled. He has reared a very large family to maturity, most of whom have been of substantial aid in settling and developing the resources of our Territory. His immediate family numbers upwards of 65 souls, most of whom are inhabitants of Utah. He has never wavered in the testimony he was always borne to the truth of the everlasting Gospel.

Salt Lake Democrat
February 4, 1886

Sanpete Valley Railw'y

—:0:—

Trains leave daily as follows:

Leave Moroni.....................9.00 a.m.
Arrive at Nephi..................11.00 a.m.

Leave Nephi......................1.00 p.m.
Arrive at Moroni.................3.00 p.m.

Stages connect at Moroni for all parts of San Pete and Sevier.

Private teams and spring wagons can be ordered by telephone at Nephi, to be ready on arrival of trains at Moroni. Price, $4 per day, driver paying all his own expenses.

S. BAMBERGER, Manager.

LEGISLATIVE PROCEEDINGS.

The Council.

FEBRUARY 3.—Mr. Hammond, from the Committee on Judiciary, reported a substitute bill for H. F. 26, relating to estates of decedents.

Mr. Barton, from the Committee on Municipal Corporations and Towns, reported back C. F. 24, incorporating Nephi, with three amendments, and C. F. 14, apportioning legislative representation, with six amendments.

A message was read from the House giving notice of the adoption of the report of the Board of Directors of the Insane Asylum. Also, of the passage of C. F. 18, prescribing the punishment for a misdemeanor. Referred to Committee on Engrossment.

INTRODUCTION OF BILLS.

By Mr. Francis—C. F. 30, amending Section 817, Chapter 7, Laws of 1884, regarding civil suits. Committee on Judiciary.

C. F. 24, incorporating Nephi City, was read the first and second times, the amendments reported by the Committee adopted and the bill ordered printed.

Salt Lake Herald
February 4, 1886

MR. BARTON, from the committee on municipal corporations and towns, reported back C. F. No. 24, incorporating Nephi City, Juab County, with three amendments, and recommended the adoption of the amendments. Report of committee adopted.

The amendments recommended by the committee on municipal corporations and towns, C. F. 24, incorporating Nephi City, were adopted, the bill was read the second time by its title, placed on file for third reading, and ordered printed.

Salt Lake Democrat
February 5, 1886

THIRD READING OF BILLS.

C. F. No. 24, incorporating Nephi City in Juab county. On motion of Mr. Sharp the bill was recommitted to the Committee on Municipal Corporations and Towns.

Salt Lake Herald
February 5, 1886

· ELECTRICITY IS LIFE.

H. E. GROW, ELECTROPATHIST,

No. 112 W. SOUTH TEMPLE STREET, Opposite Valley House, Salt Lake City Next to J. C. Sandberg's.

The following testimonial shows that Dr. H. E. Grow is doing exactly what he professes to do, to help all parties suffering with chronic rheumatism, sciatica, neuralgia, nervous diseases, coughs, colds, chills, fever, etc., and in many cases will effect a permanent cure. We refer you to the following persons, who, having received treatment from him, and cheerfully give their testimonials to its efficacy:

Hon. John T. Caine and wife, Apostle John H. Smith, Mrs. Rachel Grant, James Townsend, Esq., Bishop Jas. Watson, W. C. Morris, artist, Mr. and Mrs. Nephi W. Clayton, Hon. Judge F. R. Clayton, Beaver City, R. H. Ford, Esq., Mrs. Virtue Clift, Henry Grow, architect, Mrs. Nettie James Spencer, Mr. and Mrs. John Pickett, Mr. and Mrs. M. H. McAllister, John C. Sandberg. Esq., Paul Cardon. Esq., Logan, James Needham, Esq. Mrs. L. Pierce Mrs. A. Farr and Mrs. Minnie Madsen.

SALT LAKE CITY, November 28, 1885.
Mr. H. E. Grow:

Dear Sir. — Having suffered from deafness for over thirty years and been under your treatment for one month, I gladly make it known that I have been greatly improved—yes, so much that I can now hear the whistle from the engine at the depot two miles away, and recommend your treatment to all who are afflicted as I was; being one of four brothers, who are all deaf, as is also my father.

ROBERT ROCKET.
Twenty-first Ward.

Salt Lake Herald
February 7, 1866

UTAH TERRITORY.

Official Directory, comprising the names of the Federal and Territorial Officers, and the Officials of Salt Lake County and Salt Lake City:

Federal.

Governor—Eli H. Murray, of Kentucky.

Secretary—Arthur L. Thomas, of Pennsylvania.

Chief Justice—Charles S. Zane, of Illinois.

Associate Justice—Jacob S. Boreman, of Missouri.

Associate Justice — Orlando W. Powers, of Michigan.

Marshal—E. A. Ireland, of Utah.

Register—H. McMaster, of New York.

Receiver—Hugh C. Wallace, of Missouri.

Surveyor-General—F. Salomon, of Missouri.

Deputy Collector—O. J. Hollister, of Indiana.

Commissioners Under the Edmunds Anti-Polygamy Act:

Alexander Ramsey, of Minnesota, President.

A. B. Carleton, of Indiana.

G. L. Godfrey, of Iowa.

A. S. Paddock, of Nebraska.

J. R. Pettigrew, of Arkansas.

Territorial.

Delegate to Congress—John T. Caine, Salt Lake.

Superintendent of District Schools—L. John Nuttall, Salt Lake.

Auditor—Nephi W. Clayton, Salt Lake.

Recorder of Marks and Brands—Nephi W. Clayton, Salt Lake.

Sealer of Weights and Measures—Joseph A. Peck, Salt Lake.

Treasurer—James Jack, Salt Lake.

Librarian—Nephi W. Clayton, Salt Lake.

Salt Lake County.

Judge of Probate—Elias. A. Smith.

Clerk of County Court—John C. Cutler.

Selectman—Ezekiel Holman.

Selectman—Jesse W. Fox, Jr.

Selectman—Frank Armstrong.

Assessor—W. S. Burton.

Collector—N. V. Jones.

Recorder—George M. Cannon.

Treasurer—M. E. Cummings.

Sheriff—John A. Groesbeck.

Prosecuting Attorney—Isaac M. Waddell.

Coroner—George J. Taylor.

Surveyor—J. D. H. McAllister.

Superintendant District Schools—Wm. M. Stewart.

Salt Lake City.

Mayor—James Sharp.

Alderman First Ward—Adam Spiers.

Alderman Second Ward—Isaac M. Waddell.

Alderman Third Ward—Joseph H. Dean.

Alderman Fourth Ward—Robert Patrick.

Alderman Fifth Ward—George D. Pyper.

Councilors—George Stringfellow, O. H. Pettit, Thomas G. Webber, John Clark, A. W. Davis. Joseph A. Jennings, A. N. McFarlane, Heber J. Grant, Junius F. Wells,

Recorder and Auditor—Heber M. Wells.

Treasurer—O. F. Whitney.

Assessor and Collector—M. W. Taylor.

Marshal—William G. Phillips.

Attorney—F. S. Richards.

Deseret News
February 20, 1886

THE LEGISLATURE.

C. F. No. 24, amending the charter of Nephi City in Juab County, was read the second time by its title, placed on file for third reading and ordered printed.

Salt Lake Herald
February 13, 1886

PERSONALS.

CHARLES ANDREWS, the Nephi hide and wool dealer, is in the city.

Salt Lake Herald
February 21, 1886

PERSONAL.

WM. EIMBECK, of the United States Coast Survey, goes east to-morrow.

TOM DOBSON leaves to-day on a brief visit to Call's Fort. His brother will act in his stead during his absence.

WM. BURTON, of Sells, Burton & Co., leaves to-morrow for a short trip east.

WM. FULLER and E. J. Swaner purpose starting to-morrow (Monday) for a trip to Eureka, Tintic, Nephi and the intervening settlements, on business bent.

Salt Lake Herald
February 24, 1886

The committee on municipal corporations and towns reported back C. F. 24, the Nephi City charter, with a substitute, and recommended the adoption of the substitute. Adopted and ordered printed.

ors. Committee on elections.

Substitute for C. F. No. 24, incorporating Nephi City, in Juab county, passed its third reading.

After numerous amendments the bill passed.

A message from the House was read

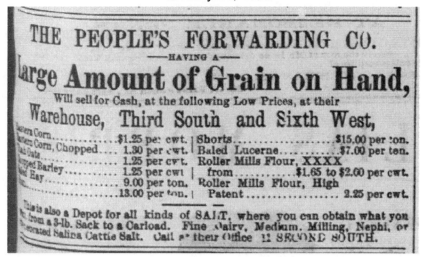

THE PEOPLE'S FORWARDING CO.

—— HAVING A ——

large Amount of Grain on Hand,

Will sell for Cash, at the following Low Prices, at their

Warehouse, Third South and Sixth West,

Eastern Corn	$1.25 per cwt.	Shorts	$15.00 per ton.
Corn, Chopped	1.30 per cwt.	Baled Lucerne	$7.00 per ton.
Oats	1.25 per cwt.	Roller Mills Flour, XXXX	
Chopped Barley	1.25 per cwt	from	$1.65 to $2.00 per cwt.
Hay	9.00 per ton.	Roller Mills Flour, High	
	13.00 per ton.	Patent	2.25 per cwt.

This is also a Depot for all kinds of SALT, where you can obtain what you want from a 3-lb. Sack to a Carload. Fine Dairy, Medium, Milling, Nephi, or Evaporated Salina Cattle Salt. Call at their Office 12 SECOND SOUTH.

James Dunn returned from the capital yesterday. He has made arrangements for the erection of a wool warehouse at Nephi, which he will open on April 1st.

Hon. N. C. Larsen went by the D. & R.

ing expenses already.

Councilor Joel Grover, of Nephi, said he was in a former session of the Legislature, some eight or ten years ago, when the Government did precisely the same thing. He could not see the consistency in the Legislature making appropriations to pay a debt which the Territory and its representatives had no voice in creating. In his opinion the amount of debt which was standing on the books at Washington against Utah had grown from such needless expenses as the Utah Commission, and he thought there was no justice in holding the legislators responsible for it.

the News bill for printing same, $602.50.

After a long list of items were added by the Council, the bill was passed, with the understanding that other items could be added, two of which were passed at once, one for $750, for Nephi City to pay them for money expended on the Salt Creek road, and the other for $1,000 to Davis county to fix the road through Devil's Gate.

Salt Lake Herald

March 9, 1886

Mr. HAMMOND reported C. F. 24, incorporating Nephi City as correctly enrolled, signed and forwarded to the Governor.

Salt Lake Herald

March 13, 1886

24—The Nephi charter; still in the Governor's hands.

Salt Lake Herald

March 14, 1886

THE LADIES' APPEAL.

The Memorial to Be Forwarded to Congress.

A VERY STRONG DOCUMENT.

A Powerful Plea for Justice, and a Recital of the Wrongs Endured in Utah.

The committee of ladies appointed at the mass meeting held in the Salt Lake Theatre one week ago to memorialize Congress, calling attention to the injuries and wrongs inflicted upon the people of Utah, have presented the following, which will be properly engrossed and forwarded to headquarters:

To the Honorable President, and the Senate and House of Representatives of the United States in Congress Assembled:

GENTLEMEN—We, your memorialists, respectfully represent that at a mass meeting of the women of Utah, held in the Theatre, Salt Lake City, March 6, 1886, attended by over two thousand ladies, representing the wives, mothers, sisters and daughters of the whole Territory, the following resolutions were unanimously adopted:

PREAMBLE AND RESOLUTIONS OF THE WOMEN OF UTAH IN MASS MEETING ASSEMBLED:

Whereas, The rights and liberties of women are placed in jeopardy by the present cruel and inhuman proceedings in the Utah courts, and in the contemplated measure in Congress to deprive the women voters in Utah of the elective franchise; and,

Whereas, Womanhood is outraged by the compulsion used in the courts of Utah to force mothers on pain of imprisonment to disclose their personal condition and that of their friends in relation to anticipated maternity, and to give information as to the fathers of their children; and,

Whereas, These violations of decency have now reached the length of compelling legal wives to testify against their husbands without their consent, in violation both of written statutes and the provisions of the common law, therefore, be it

Resolved, By the women of Utah in mass meeting assembled, that the suffrage, originally conferred upon us as a political privilege, has become a vested right by possession and usage for fifteen years, and that we protest against being deprived of that right without process of law, and for no other reason than that we do not vote to suit our political opponents.

Resolved, That we emphatically deny the charge that we vote otherwise than according to our own free choice, and point to the fact that the ballot is absolutely secret in Utah as proof that we are protected in voting for whom and what we choose with perfect liberty.

Resolved, That as no wife of a polygamist, legal or plural, is permitted to vote under the laws of the United States to deprive non-polygamous women of the suffrage is high-handed oppression for which no valid excuse can be offered.

Resolved, That the questions concerning their personal condition, the relationship they bear to men marked down as victims to special law, and the paternity of their born and unborn children, which have been put to women before grand juries and in open courts in Utah, are an insult to pure womanhood, an outrage upon the sensitive feelings of our sex and a disgrace to officers and judges who have propounded and enforced them.

Resolved, That we honor those noble women who, standing upon their rights and refusing to reply to improper and insulting questions such as no true man nor any court with any regard for propriety would compel them to answer, have gone to prison and suffered punishment without crime, rather than betray the most sacred confidence and yield to the brutal mandates of a little brief authority.

Resolved, That the action of the District Attorney and the Chief Justice of Utah in compelling a lawful wife to testify for the prosecution in a criminal case involving the liberty of her husband and in face of her own earnest protest, is a violation of laws which those officials have sworn to uphold, is contrary to precedent and usage for many centuries, and is an invasion of family rights and of that union between husband and wife which both law and religion have held sacred from time immemorial.

Resolved, That we express our profound appreciation of the moral courage exhibited by Senators Call, Morgan, Teller, Brown and others, and also by Mrs. Belva H. Lockwood, who, in the face of almost overwhelming prejudice, have defended the constitutional rights of the people of Utah.

Resolved, That we extend our heartfelt thanks to the ladies of the Woman Suffrage Association assembled in Boston, and unite in praying that God may speed the day when both men and women shall shake from their shoulders the yoke of tyranny.

Resolved, That we call upon the wives and mothers of the United States to come to our help in resisting these encroachments upon our liberties and these outrages upon our peaceful homes and family relations, and that a committee be appointed at this meeting to memorialize the President and Congress of the United States in relation to our wrongs, and to take all necessary measures to present our views and feelings to the country.

The following ladies were selected as a committee to draft and present a memorial to the President and Congress: Mrs. S. M. Kimball, Mrs. E. S. Taylor, Dr. R. B. Pratt, Mrs. M. I. Horne, Salt Lake City; Mrs. Mary John, Provo; Mrs. Mary Pitchforth, Nephi; Mrs. H. C. Brown, Ogden; Miss Ida I. Cook, Logan; Miss Ida Coombs, Payson.

In pursuance of this appointment we present the following in behalf of the women of Utah:

On the 22nd of March, 1882, an act of Congress was passed which is now commonly known as the Edmunds law. It was generally understood to have been framed for the purpose of settling what is called the Utah question, by condoning plural marriages up to that date and preventing their occurrence in the future, and also to protect the home, maintain the integrity of the family and shield innocent women and children from the troubles that might arise from its enforcement. But instead of being administered and executed in this spirit, it has been made the means of inflicting upon the women of Utah immeasureable sorrow and unprecedented indignities, of disrupting families, of destroying homes, and of outraging the tenderest and finest feelings of human nature.

The law has been so construed by the courts as to bring its penalties to bear upon the innocent. Men who had honestly arranged with their families so as to keep within the limits of the law, have been punished with the greatest possible severity, and their wives and children have been forced before courts and grand juries, and compelled to disclose the most secret and private relations which in all civilized countries are held sacred to the parties. The meaning of the law has been changed so many times that no one can say definitely what is its signification. Those who have lived by the law, as interpreted in one case, find, as soon as they are entrapped, that a new rendering is constructed to make it applicable to their own. Under the latest ruling, a man who has contracted plural marriages, no matter at how remote a date, must not only repudiate his families and cease all connection with them, but if he is known to associate with them in the most distant manner, support them and show any regard whatever for their welfare, the offense of unlawful cohabitation is considered to have been fully established, and he is liable to exorbitant fines and imprisonment for an indefinite period, one district judge holding that a separate indictment may be found for each day of such association and recognition. In the case of Solomon Edwards, recently accused of this offense, it was proven by the evidence for the prosecution, that the defendant had lived with one wife only since the passage of the Edmunds Act, but after having separated from his former plural wife, he called with his legal wife at the former's residence to obtain a child, an agreement having been made that each party should have one of the two children, and the court ruled that this was unlawful cohabitation in the meaning of the law, and defendant was convicted.

In the case of Lorenzo Snow, now on appeal to the Supreme Court of the United States, the evidence for the prosecution showed that the defendant had lived with only one wife since the passage of the Edmunds law, that he had not even visited other portions of his family except to call for a few moments to speak to one of his sons, but because he supported his wives and children and did not utterly and entirely cast them off, under instructions of Judge Orlando W. Powers, he was convicted three times for the alleged offense and sentenced in each case to the full penalties of the law, aggregating $900 fine besides costs, and eighteen months' imprisonment, the Judge stating in his instructions to the jury: "It is not necessary that the evidence should show that the defendant and these women, or either of them, occupied the same bed, slept in the same room or *dwelt under the same roof*." "The offense of cohabitation is complete, when a man, to all outward appearances is living *or associating* with two or more women as his wives." Thus women who are dependent upon the men whom they regard as their husbands, with whom they have lived, as they have regarded it, in honorable wedlock, must not only be separated from their society and protection, but must be treated as outcasts and be driven forth with their children to shame and distress, for the bare "association" of friendship is counted a crime and punished with all the severity inflicted upon those who have not in any way severed their plural family relations.

In order to fasten the semblance of guilt upon men accused of this offense, women are arrested and forcibly taken before sixteen men and plied with questions that no decent woman can hear without a blush. Little children are examined upon the secret relations of their parents, and wives in regard to their own condition and the doings of their husbands. If they decline to answer they are imprisoned in the penitentiary as though they were criminals. A few instances we will cite for your consideration:

In the Third District Court Nov. 14, 1882, Annie Gallifant, having been asked by the Grand Jury a number of questions which she declined to answer, one of them being as to the name of the man to whom she was married, she was brought into court, and still declining, was sent to the penitentiary where, although daily expecting to become a mother, she was kept till the

Grand Jury was discharged. On the trial of John Connelly. She was again brought into court and asked: "When did you first cohabit with your husband?"

"How long after you commenced cohabiting with your husband was it that your child was born?"

Miss B. Harris was sentenced to fine and imprisonment in the Second District Court at Beaver, by Judge Twiss, because she declined to answer whether she was a married woman, and if so, who was her husband. She was taken to the penitentiary, a building used for the confinement of criminals of the most hideous types, with her babe in her arms, and leaving one behind with her mother. When asked the questions mentioned, by the grand jury, she answered, "Gentlemen, you have no legal right to ask this question, and I decline to answer it."

The question was an insult and a vile insinuation of departed virtue; and yet were she a public prostitute, no such question would ever be asked. She was fined $25 and imprisoned three and a half months, when she was released by Judge Twiss. She is a lady with strength of character, who was defending a principle; her right as a witness was as sacred as any right recognized in courts. She was a martyr to personal right, and in defense of a vital principle of freedom. The question was not directed to her knowledge of any crime, but to her social relation to another, she not being charged with any crime.

On May 22, 1884, in the same court, Nellie White for refusing to answer personal questions in regard to her relations with Jared Roundy, was sent to the penitentiary, under the same roof with murderers, burglars and other convicts, and confined there until July 7th, the Grand Jury being kept over and not discharged for the purpose of protracting her imprisonment until the beginning of a new term.

In the court of U. S. Commissioner McKay, June 20, 1885, Elizabeth Ann Starkey was brought in as a witness against Charles S. White. On refusing to answer the question, "Have you ever in this county, within the last two years, occupied the same bed with defendant," she was sentenced to one day's imprisonment and a fine of $50, and placed in the custody of the U. S. Marshal until payment.

On June 22d, she again declined to answer, and was fined $100 and committed until payment.

On June 24 h she refused to answer similar personal questions to the grand jury, and was committed to the penitentiary until August 21st, but was again imprisoned and kept till October 6th. While in prison she was approached and grossly insulted by an employe of the Marshal's.

On the 15th of September, 1885, Eliza Shafer was sent to the Penitentiary for refusing to answer the question "Have you, within three years last past lived and cohabited with J. W. Snell as his wife?" The Court ordered her imprisonment until the question was answered.

On February 15th, 1886, Mrs. Martha J. Cannon was brought into the Third District Court, and the Grand Jury complained that she would not answer certain questions, among them the following: "Are you not now a pregnant woman?" "Are you not now with child by your husband, George Q. Cannon?" On still declining to answer, the Court adjudged her guilty of contempt, and pending sentence she was placed under bonds of $2,500, which were subsequently raised to $5,000.

On March 2d, 1886, Miss Huldah Winters was arrested by Deputy Marshal Vandercook at her home in Pleasant Grove, forty miles distant, no charge being preferred against her, but it was suspected that she was a plural wife of George Q. Cannon. She was brought to Salt Lake City and conducted to the Court House, where she was required to furnish bonds for $5,000 for her appearance from time to time as she might be wanted.

Under the suspicion that any woman or young lady is some man's plural wife she is liable at any time to be arrested, not merely subpoenaed, but taken by force by deputy marshals and brought before a grand jury and examined and brow-beaten and insulted by the Prosecuting Attorney or his minions. But this is not all. In defiance of law and the usages of courts for ages, the legal wife is now compelled to submit to the same indignities.

On Feb. 20, 1886 in the Third District Court in the second trial of Isaac Langton upon whom the prosecution had failed to fasten the slightest evidence of guilt, Prosecuting Attorney Dickson exclaimed: "If the Court will allow me I would like to call Mrs. Langton" (defendant's legal wife.) After a strong protest from the attor-

neys for the defendant, the Court permitted the outrage and against her and her husband's consent, she was compelled to testify for the prosecution; the evidence however completely exonerating the husband, who was discharged.

But this has now been set up as a precedent, and within the past few days a legal wife has been taken before the Grand Jury, as many have been before, who refused to give evidence, but this time was compelled to answer the questions propounded by the public prosecutor against the lawful husband.

We also direct your attention to the outrages perpetrated by rough and brutal deputy marshals, who watch around our dooryards, peer into our bedroom windows, ply little children with questions about their parents, and when hunting their human prey, burst into people's domiciles and terrorize the innocent.

On Jan. 11, 1886, early in the morning, five deputy marshals appeared at the residence of Wm. Grant, American Fork, forced the front door open, and while the inmates were still in bed, made their way up stairs to their sleeping apartments. There they were met by one of the daughters of Wm. Grant, who was aroused at the intrusion, and despite her protestations, without giving time for the object of their search to get up and dress himself, made their way into his bedroom, finding him still in bed and his wife *en dishabille* in the act of dressing herself.

Early on the morning of Jan. 13, 1886, a company of deputies invaded the peaceful village of West Jordan, and under pretense of searching for polygamists, committed a number of depredations. Among other acts of violence they intruded into the house of F. A. Cooper, arrested him and subpoenaed his legal wife as a witness against him. This so shocked her that a premature birth occurred next day, and her system was so deranged by the disturbance that in a few days she was in her grave.

Feb. 23, 1886, at about 11 o'clock at night two deputy marshals visited the house of Solomon Edwards, about seven miles from Eagle Rock, Idaho, and arrested Mrs Edwards, his legal wife, after she had retired to bed, and required her to accompany them immediately to Eagle Rock. Knowing something of the character of some something of the character of one of the deputies, from his having visited the house before, when he indulged in a great deal of drinking, profanity and abuse, she feared to accompany them without some protection, and requested a neighbor to go along on horseback while she rode in the buggy with the two deputies. On the way the buggy broke down and she with an infant in her arms, was compelled to walk the rest of the distance—between two and three miles.

They could have no reason for subpœnaing her in the night, and compelling her to accompany them at such an untimely hour except a fiendish malice and a determination to heap all the indignities possible upon her because she was a "Mormon" woman, for she never attempted to evade the serving of the warrant, and was perfectly willing to report herself at Eagle Rock the next day. She was taken to Salt Lake City to testify against her husband.

On Feb. 23, 1886, Deputy Marshal Gleason went to Greenville, near Beaver, Utah. The story of their conduct is thus related by the ladies who were the subjects of their violence:

MRS. EASTON'S STATEMENT.

About 7 a. m. deputies came to our house and demanded admittance. I asked them to wait until we got dressed, and we would let them in. DeputyGleason said he would not wait, and raised the window and got partly through by the time we opened the door, when he drew himself back and came in through the door. He then went into the bed-room; one of the young ladies had got under the bed, from which Gleason pulled the bedding, and ordered the young lady to come out. This she did, and ran into the other room, where she was met by Thompson. I asked Gleason why he pulled the bedding from the bed, and he answered, "By G—d, I found Watson in the same kind of a place." He then said he thought Easton was concealed in a small compass, and that he expected to find him in a similar place, and was going to get him before he left.

MISS MORRIS' STATEMENT.

Deputy Gleason came to my bed and pulled the clothing off me, asking if there was any one in bed with me. He then went to the fire-place and pulled a sack of straw from there and looked up the chimney. One of them next pulled up a piece of carpet, when Gleason asked Thompson if he thought there was any one under there. Thompson said "No," and Gleason exclaimed, "G—— d—— it, we will look any way!" They also looked in cupboards, boxes, trunks, etc., and a small tea chest, but threw nothing out.

WILLIAM THOMAS' STATEMENT.

The deputies called at our place about daybreak, and came to my window and rapped. I asked who was there, but received no answer. They then tried to raise the window, when I called again, and they said they were officers. I asked them to wait until I was dressed, but they said no, or they would break in the door. I told them they had better let that out, and they went around to mother's door, which was opened, and father was summoned. The deputies next went to the bed of Mrs. Elliotts and subpœnaed her. Gleason said, with a frightful oath, that he knew there was another woman in the house, and searched in boxes, trunks, etc.

These are a few instances of the course pursued towards defenseless women, who are not even charged with any offense against the law. We solemnly protest against these desecrations of our homes and invasions of our rights. We are contented with our lot when left unmolested, and would enjoy the peace of quiet homes, the society of our husbands and children, and the blessings that only belong to God-fearing families trained to habits of thrift, temperance, self-restraint and mutual help, if it were not for these outrages which are committed in the name of law, under the false pretense of protecting home and preserving the family.

We learn that measures are in contemplation before your honorable bodies to still further harass and distress us. We protest against the movement to deprive us of the elective franchise, which we have exercised for over fifteen years. What have we done that we should thus be treated as felons? Our only crime is that we have not voted as our persecutors dictate. We sustain our friends, not our enemies, at the polls. We declare that in Utah the ballot is free. It is entirely secret. No one can know how we vote unless we choose to reveal it. We are not compelled by any men, or society, or influence to vote contrary to our own free convictions. No woman living with a bigamist, polygamist, or person cohabiting with more than one woman, can now vote at any election in Utah. Why deprive those against whom nothing can be charged, even by implication, of a sacred right which has become their property?

We ask for justice. We appeal to you not to tighten the bonds which are now so tense that we can scarcely endure them. We ask that the laws may be fairly and impartially executed. We see good and noble men dragged to jail to linger among felons, while debauched and polluted men, some of them Federal officers who have been detected in the vilest kind of depravity, protected by the same court and officers that turn all their energies and engines of power towards the ruin of our homes and the destruction of our dearest associations. We see pure women forced to disclose their conjugal relations or go to prison, while the wretched creatures who pander to men's basest passions are left free to ply their horrible trade, and may vote at the polls while legal wives of men with plural families are disenfranchised. We see the law made specially against our people, so shamefully administered that every new case brings a new construction of its meaning, and no home is safe from instant intrusion by ruffians in the name of the law. And now we are threatened with entire deprivation of every right and privilege of citizenship, to gratify a prejudice that is fed on ignorance and vitalized by bigotry.

We respectfully ask for a full investigation of Utah affairs. For many years our husbands, brothers and sons have appealed for this in vain. We have been condemned, almost unheard. Everything reported to our detriment is received; our cries to be heard have been rejected. We plead for suspension of all measures calculated to deprive us of our political rights and privileges, and to harass, annoy and bring our people into bondage and distress, until a commission duly and specially authorized to make full inquiry into the affairs of this Territory, have investigated and reported, And while the blessing of Him who will one day deal out even-handed justice to all, shall rest upon your Honorable Bodies, your memorialists, as in duty bound, will ever pray, etc.

Mrs. SARAH M. KIMBALL,
Mrs. M. ISABELLA HORNE,
Mrs. ELMINA S. TAYLOR,
Dr. ROMANIA B. PRATT,
Mrs. H. C. BROWN,
Mrs. MARY PITCHFORTH,
Miss IDA I. COOK,
Mrs. IDA COOMBS,
Mrs. MARY JOHN,
Committee.

Salt Lake Herald
March 17, 1886

TRAVELERS' GUIDE.

When to Start and Time of Arrival.

UTAH CENTRAL RAILWAY.

Southward.	Stations	Northward.
Lv.... 6 30 p m	....Ogden.	Arr,... 9 15 a m
Lv.... 6 48 p m	..Summ t.	Lv .... 8 58 a m
Lv.... 7 06 p m	..Kaysville.	Lv.... 8 41 a m
Lv.... 7 18 p m	.Farm ngton.	Lv.... 8 30 a m
Lv.... 7 33 p m	Wood's Cross	Lv .... 8 16 a m
Arr.. 7 50 p m	{ Salt Lake }	Lv .... 8 00 a m
Lv.... 7 20 a m		Arr.... 6 40 p m
Lv.... 7 40 a m	..Francklyn	Lv.... 6 20 p m
Lv.... 7 47 a m	Lovendahl's	Lv.... 6 13 p m
Lv.... 7 58 a m	...Sandy ...	Lv.... 6 02 p m
Lv.... 8 09 a m	..Draper..	Lv.... 5 51 p m
Lv.... 8 40 a m	.Lehi Junct..	Lv.... 5 20 p m
Lv.... 8 55 a m	.Am Fork.	Lv.... 5 05 p m
Arr.. 9 35 a m	{ ..Provo.. }	Lv.... 4 25 p m
Lv ... 9 50 a m		Arr... 4 10 p m
Lv....10 18 a m	Spanish Fork	Lv.... 3 42 p m
Lv....10 54 a m	..Santaquin	Lv.... 3 06 p m
Lv....11 45 a m	...Nephi...	Lv.... 2 15 p m
Arr...12 20 p m	{ ..Juab .. }	Lv.... 1 40 p m
Lv.... 1 00 p m		Arr... 1 00 p m
Lv.... 2 50 p m	Lemington.	Lv....11 10 a m
Lv.... 4 25 p m	...Deseret..	Lv.... 9 35 a m
Lv.... 7 20 p m	..Black Rock.	Lv.... 6 50 a m
Lv.... 8 30 p m	...Milford...	Lv.... 5 30 a m
Arr...10 15 p m	...Frisco...	Lv.... 4 00 a m

SANPETE VALLEY RAILWAY.

Southward.	Stations.	Northward.
Lv ... 11 45 a m	...Nephi	Arr...10 40 a m
Lv.... 1 00 p m	Fountain Gn	Lv.... 9 40 a m
Lv.... 1 55 p m	..Moroni...	Lv.... 8 40 a m
Arr... 2 10 p m	.. Chester...	Lv.... 8 25 a m

Deseret News
March 31, 1886

Rates from all stations on the Utah Central to Provo and Salt Lake, good going, from April 1st to 6th inclusive. Tickets good for return to and including April 10th:

FROM	To Provo and Return.	To Salt Lake and Return.
Frisco............	$10 50	$12 75
Milford	9 50	11 75
Deseret...........	5 85	8 10
Lemmington.....	4 40	6 65
Juab.............	3 10	5 35
Nephi............	2 85	4 60
Moun.............	1 90	4 15
Santaquin........	1 25	3 50
Payson...........	1 00	3 25
Benjamin.........	80	3 05
Spanish Fork.....	60	2 85
Springville.......	30	2 55
Provo............	......	2 30
Pleasant Grove...	50	1 85
American Fork...	65	1 65
Lehi	80	1 50
Draper...........	1 45	85
Sandy............	1 75	65
Lovendahl's......	1 80	50
Francklyn........	1 90	35
Salt Lake	2 30	......
Wood's Cross	2 75	......
Centreville.......	3 00	......
Farmington	3 15	......
Kaysville........	3 35	......
Kay's Creek......	3 50	......
Hooperville	3 90	......
Ogden............	4 30	......

Return tickets will not be sold from stations north to Salt Lake, but lay-over will be allowed at Salt Lake on tickets purchased to Provo.

A NEW COMPANY.

Influential Members to be Added to the Co-op. Furniture Company.

The Co-operative Furniture Company, who have heretofore been doing business at the corner of West Temple and South Temple, the principal members of which are Messrs. Williams, Neve and Schoenfeldt, will be incorporated sometime during the present month. The capital stock will be placed at $50,000 and the new company will include such well-known names as S. R. Marks, W. N. Williams, S. P. Neve, F. Schoenfeld, O. H. Petit, H. J. Grant, A. H. Cannon, John Henry Smith and F. M. Lyman of this city, also Thomas R. Cutler and John Beck of Lehi, W. C. Rydalch of Grantsville, Mark Jeffs of Heber City, John Jones of Spanish Fork, Lyman G. Wood of Springville. It is also contemplated to start a branch house at Nephi, and probably in other parts of the Territory.

This change is necessitated, we are informed, by the constantly growing business of the house, and the additional prestige and capital thus gained will add materially to the fame already enjoyed by it.

QUARTERLY MEETING

Of the Utah Cattle and Horse Grower's Association Last Evening.

The quarterly meeting of the Utah Cattle and Horse Grower's Association was held at the office of William Jennings last evening. F. H. Meyers presided, and O. A. Hardy, the Secretary, kept the minutes. There were present, besides John Q. Leavitt, Isaac Jennings and William McIntyre, of Salt Lake City, Samuel McIntyre, of Tintic, George C. Whitmore, Alma Hague, John Hague and James Mynders of Nephi. Minutes of the last meeting were read and approved. It was ordered that the Secretary be authorized to procure 250 copies of the stock law framed by the last Legislature from THE TRIBUNE Publishing Company, for circulation among the members and Utah cattle men.

The Secretary read a communication from the National Cattle and Horse Grower's Association, presenting a bill of $7.50 for the dues of 1885, and a special assessment of $10 additional. It was ordered that the bill be paid, and a resolution was passed withdrawing from the National Association. A motion was then made that the Utah Association should join the International Range Association, headquarters at Denver. This was discussed at length, and finally postponed until the next meeting. Mr. Meyers favored the idea of joining the Range Association because it enabled them to secure government assistance for the quarantining of foreign cattle, and the killing of diseased stock, and would assist in the passage of a bill permitting the lease of public lands to stock raisers. Charles Felt, Frederick K. Snively, H. Henroyd, Wm. Mallory and Perry Potter of Ibapah, Henry Chipman of American Fork, and Thomas Fleming of Diamond City were admitted to membership in the association which has now forty-three members. An assessment of one cent per head was ordered to secure funds to carry out the purposes of the Association. The next meeting of the Association will be held at Nephi.

Salt Lake Herald
April 6, 1886

Geo. Wexx, of Nephi, was in the city on Monday.

Deseret News
April 7, 1886

A New Incorporation.—The last but by no means the least important of the projects lately started for establishing incorporated companies for carrying on business of various kinds is that in connection with the Co-operative Furniture Company, whose place of business is on the corner of South and West Temple Street, immediately west of the Assembly Hall. The company, of whom Messrs. Marks, Williams, Neve and Schoenfeld have been the principal members, have built up a very good business, both in the line of manufacturing and importing furniture, and now find the increasing demands of their trade require additional capital and extension of facilities, to secure which and add to the prestige and influence which the firm already enjoys, it has been decided to increase the number of their stockholders and incorporate with a capital stock of $50,000. The new organization will be effected some time during the month of April or not later than the 1st of May, and will include as stockholders: S. R. Marks, W. N. Williams, S. P. Neve, F. Schoenfeld, O. H. Pettit, H. J. Grant, A. H. Cannon, John Henry Smith and F. M. Lyman of this city, also Thomas R. Cutler and John Beck of Lehi, W. C. Rydalch of Grantsville, Mark Jeffs of Heber City, John Jones of Spanish Fork, Lyman G. Woods of Springville, and a number of other substantial business men, including several country dealers in furniture.

A branch house of the company is also about to be established at Nephi, and others probably will be erected in other parts of the Territory.

It affords us pleasure, as it must do all who are interested in the prosperity of the Territory and its inhabitants, to learn of such worthy men as compose this company uniting their interests and establishing various branches of business upon a permanent and substantial basis and to know that they are succeeding in that which they undertake.

PRESBYTERIAN PERFIDY.

The Presbyterian preachers and teachers of Utah have been holding a sort of convocation at Nephi. The following ministers were present:

F. L. Arnold, Evanston, Wyoming; J. F. Flero, Evanston, Wyoming; H. A. Newell, Salt Lake City; F. M. Blohm, Salt Lake City; S. L. Gillespie, Box Elder; Josiah McClain, Ogden; R. G. McNiece, Salt Lake City; Peter Van Houten, Salt Lake City; J. A. L. Smith, Payson; David Houe, Payson; A. B. Cort, St. George; G. W. Martin, Mantl; T. F. Day, American Fork; E. N. Murphy, Mt. Pleasant; S. J. Neilson, Mt. Pleasant; E. W. Greene, Richfield; Philip Bouback, Hyrum; H. D. Stoops, Parowan.

The following teachers were in attendance:

Miss M. Beekman, Mt. Pleasant; Miss M. S. Byers, Box Elder; Miss K. J. Bingham; Salt Lake City; Miss E. S. Dickey, Salt Lake City; Mrs. M. M. Green, Gunnison; Miss L. H. Hindman, Spring City; Miss M. E. Knox, Fillmore; Miss E. M. Knox, Fillmore; Miss L. L. Lockwood, Nephi; Miss K. McPheeters, Nephi; Prof. J. F. Millspaugh, Salt Lake City; Miss L. P. Moore, Salt Lake City; Miss L. G. Morton, Parowan; Miss M. H. McCullough, Payson; Miss J. A. Olmstead, Richfield; Miss M. Evans, Scipio.

Besides these there were present:

W. E. Renshaw and E. M. Knox from the Presbytery of Wood River; Judge Osborn; Mrs. H. A. Newell and Miss Annie McDowel of Salt Lake City; Mrs. J. A. L. Smith of Payson; Mrs. L. A. Lockwood of Nephi.

Little interest attaches to their proceedings except the construction of the following resolutions which, after a full discussion of their contents, were unanimously adopted:

"In regard to the statement recently telegraphed over the country from Washington that no further Congressional legislation is needed for Utah, because of the work which the churches and schools are accomplishing, it is recommended

First—That this statement be declared unwarranted by the facts and calculated to do great mischief.

Second—That while the Christian churches and schools are doing a most salutary work, which is increasing in power every year, there is still great need of radical legislation by Congress.

Third—That if our Government had done its duty as faithfully as the great Christian denominations have done theirs, Utah would have been Americanized years ago, as is shown by the fact that since the Government has begun to assert its authority, by putting the transgressors of its laws in any community in the penitentiary, the freedom of the people to attend the churches and schools has been greatly augmented."

These enunciations are much gentler in tone than many that have emanated from a similar source. And considering that such reckless and unscrupulous defamers as McNiece and Gillespie participated in the proceedings, they are rather remarkable for their mildness. With the wilful and barefaced falsehoods of each of those hypocrites, who are a disgrace to the name of Christian and a burlesque on the title of minister, the Utah public are pretty well familiar. They have both appeared in print as the concoctors of "infamous libels against the 'Mormons,'" and have struggled, in vain, to appear to the country as martyrs to the cause of Presbyterianism. Their attempts to show that they had been persecuted were proven to be absolute lies without the shadow of excuse, and their shameful mendacity will stand against them on earth and in heaven, in time and in eternity.

But beneath the quietness of the language of the resolutions there lurk both the falsehood and the vindictiveness which are the chief characteristics of the snappy Salt Lake declaimer and the flabby exhorter from Box Elder. At the close of the Resolutions is an untruth that implies more than it speaks. The impression conveyed and intended is that the people here have been prevented in times past from attending Presbyterian meetings. That the freedom which is admitted to exist at present has been denied in times past. And that the liberty enjoyed is in consequence of the imprisonment of a few Latter-day Saints, for practicing a principle of their religion. The inference is that if more "Mormons" are put into the penitentiary the Presbyterians will be able to flourish with greater freedom. Therefore the aid of Government is requested that force may accomplish what Presbyterian persuasion and Presbyterian doctrine have failed to effect. That is after the straight McNiece style and method.

The falsehood implied in the Resolution is patent to every resident of this Territory. But it is not intended for home use. It is manufactured for exportation. It is for manipulation at a distance. It will help fill up the Utah Presbyterian money-bags—the grand desideratum of all these libels upon the "Mormon" community. There is no more liberty to attend sectarian churches and chapels to-day than there was before the passage of the Edmunds law. The Latter-day Saints are advised now, as much as then, not to send their children to schools taught by their enemies, not to entrust the care of the little ones to those whose main object is, to turn them from the faith of their fathers. The wisdom of this advice must be clear to every thinking mind. The folly of rejecting it is apparent to all who are possessed of common sense. Advice has been the only influence used in that direction. And no man or woman has been coerced in relation to this matter. Those who insinuate to the contrary, either by preaching or resolution, know that they are guilty of gross falsehood.

And what a confession of abject impotence is conveyed in the plea that the influence of Presbyterianism is so small that it cannot hope to prevail without the employment of force? What a weak and watery religion that must be, which cannot make headway in a free land without the government puts its opponents into prison! Meeting-houses and schools built for them by others' money poured out like water in their aid, with scarcely anything to do but draw their hireling's wages, these sleek and snuffling men of gab, unable to convert because they cannot convince the "Mormons," try to goad the Government into measures for their destruction.

We can understand why the political adventurers who want to control the Territory are anxious for "radical legislation," for that means the disfranchisement of the "Mormon" majority for the benefit of the anti-"Mormon" minority. But on what Christian principle can professed disciples of Jesus strive to accomplish the same end, and that too under the plea of a palpable lie? They see men who would be an honor to any community thrust into jail because they will not promise to renounce what they know to be right; virtuous wives dragged from their homes and forced in violation of law and religion to give testimony against their husbands; children compelled to answer prurient questions in relation to the bedroom privacy of their parents;

homes disrupted, families scattered, hearths made desolate. All this they endorse, and ruthlessly cry for more radical measures. It is not enough for their pious purpose that people who do not agree with their views are thus hunted and despoiled, but in their religious wrath they demand further oppression and more extreme legislation.

And what is the reason for this holy outcry? Why, these "Mormons" will not yield to the principles of Presbyterian doctrine. "Mormonism" cannot be controverted by scripture nor by argument, and the only way to accomplish our Presbyterian purpose is to put their leaders in prison, break up their homes, confiscate their Church property, and disfranchise every man and woman who is a member of the Church that we cannot put down by ordinary measures. Our reasonings fail, our renderings and wrestlings of holy writ, our nasal-twanged prayers and our sanctified demeanor count for nothing with these obstinate believers in old-fashioned Bible Christianity, and therefore the Government must step in to our aid with pains and penalties and the most "radical legislation."

Oh! ye plotting and mendacious priests who preach for hire and teach for money; who distort the truth, who wrest the scriptures, who plot against the innocent, who join with the political shark, the carping infidel, the

sneaking place-hunter, the roystering ruffian, the conspirator, the spotter and the spy; who formulate falsehoods that ye may gather in dollars, and foster prejudices that ye may get gain; how shall ye appear in the great day of judgment and of justice? Who shall hide you from the gaze of the Eternal and cover you from the scorn of the just? When you reap your full reward, what can save you from the doom of the liar and the hypocrite—the deep damnation of the lowest hell?

Utah Journal
April 14, 1886

TIMELY TOPICS.

Proceedings of the Courts Severely Criticised.

EDITOR JOURNAL:—As the times are full of events especially interesting and significant to Latter-day Saints, and expressions from the people being always in order, allow me to say a few words through the columns of your worthy paper. You know we have often heard talk of "one man power," "church and state in Utah," etc. Of the former I have never seen it exhibited only in the Chief Executive and other Federal appointees, who frequently wield it against the voice and interests of an entire Territory. Of the latter, it is only manifest in Utah when a conclave of religious pro-

fessors assemble like that recently convened in Nephi, calling for anti-Mormon legislation to suppress that which those pious (?) ones are totally unable to overthrow from either a Biblical, scientific, social, or any other respectable platform. Is it not cowardly for an individual to call for the hands of those he despises to be secured and made helpless, while he gives them a lashing? It certainly is, and yet this is the position taken by Sectarians in Utah. They asserted that since our brethren had been incarcerated in prison "the freedom of the people to attend the churches and schools has been greatly augmented." Being a young man born in Utah, I have only lived here twenty-seven years and several months, but during that short period no one, either parents nor church authorities, has ever laid a straw in my way of attending churches of any denomination, and the more I have listened to the preaching of these learned (?) religionists, the more I appreciate the plain, Biblical teachings of "Mormon Elders," who neither preach for money nor divine for hire, but, being freely given, freely impart, speaking as men having authority, and not as the Methodist, Presbyterian, etc.

As for the schools, how many Sectarian children attend the Mormon schools in this Territory? It is the right of parents to educate their children where they think proper, and our Sectarian friends should recognize this fact.

Another exhibition of the church attempting to rule the state occurred in the winter of '81 and '82, when a great religious furore was raised throughout the Union by the churches calling Congress to pass inimical laws relating to "an establishment of religion and prohibiting the free exercise thereof." Congress yielded, violated the sacred oath of office to support the Constitution, laid its freedom at the feet of religious hypocrisy and as the fruits of this "unlawful cohabitation" of church and state, brought forth the Edmunds law. To those who are thoughtful, intelligent, and truthful, the evidence is abundant to prove that plural marriage is with us "an establishment of religion," and embraced by Latter-day Saints in sincerity, knowing full well that the animosity of the world will be waged against them. The Utah Commissioners in one of their reports to the general government reported that polygamy was as much a part of their religion as baptism, remission of sins, etc. Then in the passage of the Edmunds act and the decision of the U. S. Supreme Court thereon it appears evident that the three departments of the general government are involved in violating their solemn oath of office as provided in Art. 2, Sec. 1, Par. 9 of the Constitution, and also the 1st amendment to the same, providing that

"Congress shall make no law respecting an establishment of religion, or prohibiting the free exercise thereof." But the law extends farther upon the forbidden domain of Constitutional rights, reaching backward, and deprives citizens of the right of franchise who entered into plural marriage before there was any law against it, thus becoming ex post facto, and in depriving citizens of this franchise it is done by the administration of a test oath, and not according to due process of law, thus transgressing Art. 1, Sec. 3, Par. 3 of the fundamental law, viz: "No bill of attainder, or ex-post facto law shall be passed. If the franchise becomes the property of the citizen by possession, then he cannot be justly deprived of it, except as provided for in Art. 5 of the amendments to the Constitution, that is, "Without due process of law." Now the law is passed. In the natural course of events it is to be enforced, and were this done impartially, in a manner becoming the dignity of a great nation, it would not be quite so galling. It is natural for people, who look upon their nation as the best of human governments, designed as an asylum for the oppressed of every land and clime, to expect that its representatives in every department, at home or abroad, shall be men of honor, virtue and truth, who would not stoop to anything mean in their official acts, but hold themselves above prejudice and selfish motives. We also look to the officials of government to mete out the law as it reads especially when there is nothing doubtful in the wording thereof. One might suppose who reads the Edmunds act, that it was designed to prohibit and punish immorality, regardless of who the offenders were. But it has been announced by the Prosecuting Attorney in open court, and voiced by the Judge that the law was not intended to strike at sexual sins, but to reach this "peculiar system of marriage." If this assertion be true, then the law is incorrectly worded and does not mean all that it says, and the assertion of Federal officials in Utah, do not cast a very exalted reflection upon congress. If the statement is not correct, then the general government is slow to vindicate her honor, or willing that her citizens should be oppressed, corrupt and dishonorable men. Let the President of the United States verify his promise to see the law impartially administered, and there would shortly be more anti-Mormons and fewer Latter-day Saints in the penitentiary for "unlawful cohabitation." There would be fewer of the latter class unwilling to come into court and stand trial, but who can honestly blame men for evading such tyranny? In the process of the Judiciary, officers of the court are sent out to arrest men, and in doing so frequently visit the peaceable homes of citizens in the quiet of night or before the dawn of the morning, and in the absence of male members will insult helpless women and children, and conduct themselves in a manner becoming only to thieves, burglars and vagabonds, etc, and sometimes without proper warrants, and thereby disregard and violate Art. 4 of the amendments which says the right of the people to be secure in their persons, houses, papers, and effects, against unreasonable searches and seizures shall not be violated; and no warrant shall be issued but upon probable cause, supported by oath or affirmation, and particularly describing the places to be searched, and the persons or things to be seized. "Let officers observe this rule, instead of transgressing it, and all good people will respect them more. Then comes the empaneling of the Jury, by which to secure justice, our forefathers provided in Art. 6 amendments to Constitution. "In all criminal prosecutions the accused shall enjoy the right to a speedy and public trial by an impartial Jury" and further Art. 6 of the Constitution and paragraph 3 says that "no religious test shall ever be required as a qualification to any office or public trust under the United States." The proceeding of Federal courts in Utah will not stand this constitutional test. Men of a certain class are denied an impartial Jury of their peers because by the open venire process, parties are secured for Jurors who are the avowed enemies of the accused, and who we have good reasons to believe are guilty of "unlawful cohabitation" in its grossest form. The religious test is applied so that if a man is a member of the same church with defendant, he is excluded though he promise to convict, if the evidence warrant it, as did Mr. Shields who was excluded in the case of the U. S. vs. A. M. Cannon. Neither is the Grand Jury exempt from this dark aged inquisition, and what justice can the accused anticipate in this condition of affairs? The 8th Article of the amendments to the Constitution also provides that, "Excessive bail shall not be required, nor excessive fines imposed, nor cruel and unusual punishments inflicted." A glance at the history of proceedings in the courts, will show that excessive bail is required. Frequently witnesses are placed under bonds in excess of the full fine imposed upon the defendant should he be convicted. In the case of Prest. Geo. Q. Cannon, had he been tried and convicted on the three indictments, the fine would have aggregated but $900 and costs of prosecution. This is enough, and more than justice would demand, but in the bonds required of him this sum was multiplied by fifty. What more is needed to prove that the accused was not wanted for "unlawful cohabitation" but because he is prominent in the Church of Jesus Christ of Latter-day Saints? And if more proof is needed, we have it in the threats of crusaders, who declared their determination to deprive him of his liberty, and thus aim a blow at the church and people of whom he is a prominent, most honorable, and respected member, with a character above reproach. Unworthy would be the people of the association of righteous men, who would not gladly furnish the amount demanded, rather than see the accused made the object of bitter persecution, when it can be honorably avoided. Reading a little more of court doings, not satisfied with conviction the court urges a promise of the defendant, whether or not he will obey the law in the future as interpreted by the courts. By what authority and under what law is such a promise demanded? On condition of a promise in the affirmative, the defendant's sentence is either lightened or suspended, while the man who has too much regard for his honor, and the Constitution of our country to make such a promise, gets the full penalty of the law even if he had attempted in the past to conform to the law as the law reads, and as honest men understand it. But two men are alike guilty according to the verdict. Why then should partiality be shown? Are they on trial for what they may or may not do in the future, rather than for what they have been charged with doing in the past? But how can a man promise to abide the law as interpreted by the courts, when the interpretation is given to fit the case and conflicts with itself from time to time. This is apparent from rulings given in the cases of the United States, vis: Rudger Clawson, A. M. Cannon, A. M. Musser, Lorenzo Snow and others, making the law very broad when a Mormon is on trial, but very narrow for an anti-Mormon seducer and the like. But suppose it is just to base the leniency of the court upon such a promise, what assurance has the court or any one else that the promise will be kept? The defendant once made a covenant with God of a most solemn character, that he would be true to God, his wives and children; and if a man will break so solemn a promise, he might possibly violate the promise made to the court, and his apparent integrity to the unjust demands of the court, would only be in profession. If I honor the Constitution of my country how can I thoroughly honor and respect that law, and the modus operandi of enforcing it, that tears away from that Constitution which is the basis of our civil government, many of the most vital safeguards of human liberty? Who are the friends of human freedom? Can it be those who will twist the law in every conceivable shape to convict men for marrying women and protecting female virtue, while the same officials will refuse to prosecute the libertine who revels in lust, despoiling virtue and opposing the peace and good order of society? I think not; and we have a right to speak and write freely; to protest against such villainy, and appeal to the nation to treat us fairly, asking no favors. Nothing but our rights. If they refuse, as in the past, we leave our cause in the hands of God, feeling rather to suffer wrong than to do wrong, and the day is not far distant when they who have misapplied the law and overstepped the bounds of their authority and hated us without a cause, will be either had in derision by the inhabitants of this land, or their names will be lost in oblivion. Patrick Henry said in his immortal speech in favor of the Declaration of Independence: "As God lives, my friends, I believe that to be his voice. Yes, were my soul trembling on the wing of eternity; were this hand freezing in death; were my voice choking with the last struggle, I would still, with the last wave of the hand, with the last gasp of that voice, implore you to remember the truth: God has given America to be free."

M. F. COWLEY.

Salt Lake Herald
April 21, 1886

TIMOTHY B. FOOT, an old resident of Nephi, and veteran of the war of 1812, died at that place on Sunday, ot old age. He was the first settler in Juab County, and the original founder of Nephi City.

Deseret News
April 28, 1886

A Veteran Gone. — Timothy B. Foot, a notable character of Nephi, Juab County, one of the veterans of the war of 1812, who has long been a Government pensioner, died at his home in that place on Sunday evening last, at 8:30, of old age. He joined the Church in a very early day, and shared in the persecutions endured by the Saints in Missouri. He used to like to dwell upon his loyalty to the Prophet Joseph Smith, and often recounted his experience in connection with the siege of Far West, when he ventured into the camp of the mob-militia to learn the fate of Joseph and Hyrum Smith and the other prisoners betrayed into their hands through the treachery of Colonel Hinkle and was used pretty roughly as a result, being hustled along between two horsemen, who held him by the collar while they rode at a full gallop.

He was the first settler of Juab County and the original founder of the City of Nephi, in which for many years he was one of the leading spirits, taking a prominent part in all public work. For some years past he has been in his dotage and hardly responsible for what he said or did. He was a remarkably healthy man, scarcely ever having any sickness in his life, and was quite active until a few months ago when he lost his sight, since which time he has not been able to get about much.

Salt Lake Herald
May 15, 1886

DEATH OF JOEL GROVER.

The shock caused by the sudden and unexpected death of Hon. Joel Grover, at his home in Nephi on Thursday night, will not be confined to the locality of his late residence, but will extend throughout the Territory. He was widely known and as widely admired and respected for his nobleness of character, his business and social integrity, his devotion to principle, and his keen sense of right and justice. His death will be most keenly felt in Juab County, where he has long been a central figure; but many industrial enterprises in this city and elsewhere in Utah will miss him. When such a man dies the sorrow and mourning are not confined to the relatives, friends and immediate acquaintances of the deceased, but extend throughout the community.

Our correspondent at Nephi states that the funeral will be held at Nephi on Sunday, and that a special car will be run to convey parties from this city who desire to attend. Many will undoubtedly take advantage of this opportunity to pay the last respects to one who was so much respected in life.

Deseret News
May 19, 1886

MARRIAGES.

BOSH-LUNDBLAD—At Levan, May 10th, Mr. H. C. Bosh and Miss Florentine Lundblad.

ELDER J. W. PAXMAN

of Nephi, left this city for Great Britain April 15th, 1884, and on reaching England was appointed to labor in the London Conference. He remained there, his field being the Sussex, North London and Lambeth Branches, up to the time of his release, with the exception of about six weeks spent at various times in visiting relatives. He was quite successful in his labors, finding in the midst of the prevalent indifference and opposition to "Mormonism" many persons willing to listen to his testimony and quite a few willing to embrace the Gospel as presented to them by him. He had the pleasure of baptizing 33 persons. Two of these were his relatives, and one of them accompanied him home.

He was very kindly treated generally, especially by his relatives, many of whom live in the vicinity of London and are quite wealthy. Though the latter were pleased to have him visit them, however, with very few exceptions they wanted to hear nothing whatever about his religion, being too worldly-minded or bigoted to even investigate it. Brother Paxman performed a faithful mission, gained a valuable experience while abroad, and returns feeling thankful alike for having gone and for being once more in his mountain home.

ELDER T. R. SCHRODER,

also of Nephi, was perhaps the youngest of the returning Elders. He was only nineteen years of age when he started upon his mission in the autumn of 1884. Though born of Scandinavian parents, he had but a very limited knowledge of their native language, so that he was placed at a slight disadvantage on his arrival in Denmark. However, he was soon able to speak in public, and labored with great satisfaction in the Aasbus and Aalborg Conferences until he had to leave there to avoid being banished. Under a law passed some years ago for expelling German laborers who were overrunning the country, and at the instigation of the sectarian priests of the land, quite a number of the Elders have been banished from Denmark within the past few months. In December last Elder Schroder and two others were brought before the magistrate twice and questioned as to whether they were American citizens, where they and their parents were born and reared, when they emigrated to America, where they were laboring, by whom they were sent and whether they received any pay for their services. The magistrate acknowledged that it was not right to banish such men as they were, who had committed no offense, but said the priests of the country had unitedly demanded their banishment, and he expected to have to expel them. The Elders were subsequently searched for by the officers and it being no longer safe for him to remain there and attempt to labor as a missionary, Elder Schroder was released earlier than he otherwise would have been. He received kind treatment in general during his absence, and greatly enjoyed his mission.

Deseret News
May 26, 1886

HON. JOEL GROVER.

A BRIEF SKETCH OF HIS CAREER.

By the aid of Brother W. A. C. Bryan we are enabled to give some details in relation to the late Hon. Joel Grover. He is the son of Thomas and Hannah T. Grover, was born at Farmington, Davis County, Utah, March 11th, 1849. He died of *hepatic colic* (passing of gall stones) at his residence in Nephi, Juab County Utah, at 11:55 p. m., May 13th, 1886. He was the first white male child born in Davis County. He was baptized into the Church of Jesus Christ of Latter-day Saints, when eight years of age. At the April Conference of 1867 he was called by President Heber C. Kimball to go on a mission to Europe. He started on his mission May 12th, 1867, crossing the plains most of the way by team, and arrived in Liverpool, England, July 26th. He labored faithfully in the Kent and Glasgow conferences two years, preaching the Gospel, and after having completed his mission, to the satisfaction of the

Presidency, was released on the 14th and departed from Liverpool in the steamship *Colorado*, homeward bound, July 28th, 1869, arriving at his home in Farmington, August 20th.

December 5th, 1869, he was married to Mary Asenath, daughter of Dr. Willard Richards, upon which occasion President Brigham Young predicted that Brother Grover would yet occupy prominent positions of usefulness in the Kingdom of God.

November 10th, 1871, he was ordained a High Priest and called to preside over the Juab Stake of Zion. Subsequently there being changes in the presidency, he has been First Counselor therein. He has been a leading figure in the management of all of the important matters pertaining to the welfare and prosperity of the Stake.

In 1873 he was elected a Representative to the Legislative Assembly of the Territory of Utah, and has since that time been repeatedly elected Representative and Councilor, and has been well recognized and admired as a wise and able Representative of the people. In 1875 he was elected to the office of Selectman, and in 1878 to that of Probate Judge for Juab County, and he held the latter office at the time of his demise.

He was an extensive stockholder in the Nephi Mercantile and Nephi Mill and Manufacturing Institutions, and held the offices of President and Superintendent of the store and Secretary and Superintendent of the Mill. He was prominently identified in all of the public institutions of the Stake, and was a very liberal subscriber to every legitimate enterprise and industry organized since his arrival in Nephi.

In the First National Bank of Nephi, about to be organized, he was a subscriber for a considerable amount, and at the preliminary meeting was chosen for one of its directors.

As a financier he was of the first order, and his judgment and executive ability were quick and firm. He was a close, affectionate and lasting friend, and while being a faithful Latter-day Saint and having the love and confidence of the authorities and people of the Church, he was broad, liberal and charitable, to such an extent as to gain the admiration and confidence of every class.

On the evening of the 13th inst., Brother Grover and his wife had been out riding and had only just returned home, when he was seized with a violent cramp in the stomach, it being then about 7:30 o'clock. Doctors Don and Atkin were immediately summoned, and the Elders of the Church were sent for and everything was done that could be done to counteract the disease, but nothing seemed to have any effect, and after much suffering in so short a time, he passed away at 11:55 o'clock.

The news of his death caused a most sudden shock and spread a gloom over the entire community. The town was draped in mourning and flags put at half-mast.

During his lifetime Brother Grover having expressed his desire that when he should die his remains should be taken direct from his home to the tomb, and that there should be no funeral sermon over his remains, his wish was carried out, the obsequies commencing at his late residence, and after singing by the Nephi Tabernacle Choir and prayer by Apostle H. J. Grant, the multitude assembled to attend the funeral passed through the parlor, viewed the remains, and the procession then being arranged, in order, proceeded to the cemetery. It was the largest attendance on any occasion of the kind ever known in this county. A great many friends and prominent citizens from Salt Lake, Utah and other counties were present, among them were quite a number of his co-laborers in the Legislature.

The funeral procession returned at 4 p. m. and adjourned to the Nephi Tabernacle, where the afternoon's services were devoted to remarks in relation to the deceased. The Tabernacle was draped for the occasion, and combined with the devotion expressed, presented a most solemn aspect.

The speakers were President Charles Sperry, George Kendall, Mathew McCune and Wm. A. C. Bryan, personal friends and intimate acquaintances of the deceased.

Deceased leaves a wife, five children, a mother and numerous other relations to mourn his departure. His friends and the entire community retain an affectionate remembrance of the departed, who was loved and respected by all who associated with him in life.

Juab County Judges.

The Utah Commission have appointed the following Judges of election for Juab County.

Gus Shepherd, H. W. Hartley and Geo Larson, Levan precinct.

Wm. D. Goodwin, A. Vom Baur and Harvey K. Tempkins, Eureka poll, Tintic precinct.

John W. Morehouse, Peter Sutton and James Larson, Nephi precinct.

James A. Boyack, John V. Hampton and James E. Clinton, Juab precinct.

S. P. Ewing, Elias W. Williams and William A. Starr, Mona precinct.

H. H. Sowles, P. H. Connell and Jas. Shearer, Silver City poll, Tintic precinct.

LIST OF EMIGRANTS

Passengers per S. S. Nevada, May 22, 1886.

Juab.—George, Andrew, Jane Alex, Annie Janet and Jane Easton; Jas. and Andrew Monson, Wm. Latimer; Mary Yates; Jesse and Ann Hopkinson.

Nephi.—Wm., Ann, Maria, Lydia, Wm., Henry and Emily Rowbury; Benj., Esther and Hannah Price.

FROM SATURDAY'S DAILY JULY 31.

Killed.—Yesterday, at Grantsville, James G. Burton, of Nephi, was killed by a horse. The animal was a vicious one and kicked the unfortunate man, inflicting injuries from which he died in a few minutes. No one else was present in the barn at the time of the occurrence. The wife of the unfortunate man was telegraphed to and came up to take charge of his body.

DEATHS.

JORGENSEN.—At Levan, Juab County, August 15th, 1886, of diphtheria, Hertha Wilhelmine, daughter of H. C. L. and Oline Jorgensen; aged 5 years and 4 months.

LIST OF EMIGRANTS.

Sailing per S. S. Wyoming, August 21 1886.

Nephi. —Alfred, Sarah Jane, John H. and David Haycock; Kate and Sarah Golding; Maria Shering; Annie Baker.

Nephi.—Eva Almquist; Johan H. Gustapson; H. H. F., Jens F. and Alfred Jorgensen; Jens, Kesstine and Peter Andersen; Marie, Johan, Hedvig, Thora, Peter and Ernest Nielsen, Mariane Christensen; Jens, Karen, Dorthia, Elsa, Christen, Mette and Jens Pejstrup; Johanna Nielsen; Ingrid and Maria Sandstrom, Karen Johannesen; Lette and Mine Anerson; Maria Olson; A. J. Anderson.

Juab.

Hilda Soderberg; Lorents, Carl and Hermaus Okander; A. U. Mellquist; Johanna Anderson; Soren C. Jenson.

THE WOOL GROWERS' ASSOCI-ATION.

THE CONVENTION AT NEPHI ON THE 10TH INST.

Our correspondent at Nephi, Juab county, sends the following relative to the Wool Growers' Association, under date of Saturday, September 11th:

The convention of the Wool Growers' Association of Southern Utah completed an organization last evening.

The subscribers to date represent 81,625 sheep, in value $185,000.

Officers for the Association were elected as follows:

J. H. Erekson, President.

Edwin Booth, Vice-President.

Edwin Booth, A. A. Cahoon, Thos. Wright, Jr., David Collins, T. W. Ross, L. J. Jordan, John Lowry, George C. Bean, G. W. Bean, Thos. Hunt, John H. Seeley, Directors.

J. E. Clinton, Secretary and Treasure.

E. H. Booth, Assistant Secretary.

The object of the association is for the purchase and sale of wool, hides, pelts, etc., with headquarters at Nephi, Utah. That city is chosen for headquarters on account of its central location. Owners of sheep all over the the Territory winter their flocks on the Desert, west and southwest of Nephi and as the snow melts away near spring, they gradually move east and north to their shearing grounds, many thousands being shorn near Nephi.

I am informed by the Utah Central Railway that there was shipped from Nephi, during four months of the season last past, 1,871,000 pounds of wool.

We well know that middle men have made a profit of from five to ten cents per pound this season, which means that the wool-growers who shipped from Nephi alone have given away, at the lowest estimate, $68,550.

The association is composed of solid men who have gained their flocks by persistent toil, and having already paid fortunes to middle-men, now propose to consolidate their energies and harvest their honest earnings.

It is the object of the Association to handle the business with the least possible expense, to obtain the actual value, including the profits hitherto enjoyed by middle and commission men, on all sales, and to pay to the wool growers the net profit.

It is thought that before the next season the Association will represent 200,000 sheep, and next year will handle at least 2,000,000 pounds of wool.

There is no doubt that the Association is a success, and will be of great benefit to all parties interested.

W. B

Territorial Enquirer
September 17, 1886

DIED.

On Sept. 13, 1886. At Mona, Juab county, of heart disease, Christina, wife of C. Neilsen, aged 35 years. Deceased has left a husband and nine children the smallest one a month old.

Sister Neilsen was the daughter of Hans and Berget Knudsen.

Funeral services were held at the family residence, and consoling remarks were made on the occasion by Elder H. Coray.

Deseret News
September 29, 1886

DEATHS.

SALISBURY.—At Nephi, Juab Co., Sept. 20, 1886, of fever, Inger Marie daughter of David and Ann Salisbury; born Sept. 29, 1870. She was beloved by all who knew her.—COM.

Deseret News
October 6, 1886

DEATHS.

HAWKINS—At Nephi, Juab County, Utah September 22nd, 1886, after a lingering illness, John small Hawkins, aged 64 years, born at Wormester, Wiltshire, England; baptized into the Church July 24th, 1850; emigrated to Utah in 1851; ordained a High Priest in St. Louis, in 1855.

Territorial Enquirer
October 8, 1886

Fatal Accident in Mona.

Editor Enquirer:

A fatal accident occurred here yesterday which has cast a gloom over our village, and again reminded us of the absolute uncertainty of life.

A number of boys had gone as usual to herd the cows belonging to their parents and others, and were spending the day at a spot on the creek bottom where the soil had been worn away by the water, leaving a perpendicular embankment six or seven feet high. This they had perforated with holes which they used in some of their games. At the mouth of one of these holes Hiram Owing was sitting, when suddenly, and without any immediate cause, a portion of the bank gave way, striking him on the neck and back and causing a concussion of the spine, which completely paralyzed the lower limbs. The quantity of earth that fell, was quite small, only partially covering the boy's body. He was lifted to his feet, only to find that he had lost all use of them, and was again laid down. He next asked to have his legs straightened out—they being quite stiff and straight already. He expressed himself as being in no particular pain, but felt "funny." He expired almost immediately thereafter.

This is the second terrible accident that has happened to Brother Porter Ewing's family and he absent from home; this time he was at Sanpete, but arrived late in the night. Of course the family are all but distracted over their loss. The youth was aged 14 years and 9 months and 6 days.

The funeral will take place at 2 p. m. to day.

AMITIE.

Mona, Juab Co., Oct. 4, 1886.

FIRST DISTRICT COURT.

In this court at Provo, on Monday the 18th inst., the Pearson case was resumed. Three witnesses were examined through the day.

Frederick W. Chappell was sworn; was justice of the peace at Nephi; acted as coroner at the inquest over the body of Green; saw the bullet hole in the body near the heart.

Ernest Green was sworn; was brother to the deceased; identified the body; had his clothes, memorandum and pocket books that were sent to me after the shooting; thought the defendant and the deceased were on good terms before the shooting; saw the body in the court house at Juab.

W. P. Boreman was sworn; had seen the defendant at a saloon about 4 p.m. January 10, 1886; Pearson had a knife and pistol; he said he had spared Green's life once but would not do it again; they went out of the saloon towards their horses; Pearson told Green not to advance or he would shoot him; still advancing, Green told him to shoot if he wanted to; Pearson said he would, and at the same time fired; Green fell and expired in about ten minutes.

Mr. Jas. Hartly was called and sworn; was bartender in the saloon at Juab; saw the proceedings; thought Pearson and Green had drank several times at the bar, and took some beer with them.

On Tuesday morning court resumed. Testimony was continued.

Mr. Hartly testified to the shooting; saw Pearson shoot Green; was only a few feet away; some conflict arose about paying money at the bar; part of the money went on the floor and a scuffle ensued; this was before the shooting.

Testimony of the same witness on cross-examination was being given Tuesday afternoon.

LIST OF EMIGRANTS

Sailing from Liverpool October 13th, 1886.

Nephi.—Adam and Jemima Brown; Elizabeth, Esther and Chas. Kiddle.

Nephi. — Augusta Hogberg; Agnes Soderberg; Carl and Gustaf Carlsen; Laurits C. Anderson; Carl Drejen; A. F. Christensen; A. F. Pehrson; M. A., Julia, Anna, Anders and Hanna Nauman; Hanne, Hanna and Hildo Andersen; M. A. Salmonson; Else M. Andersen; Christian Johansen.

Juab.—Pauline M. Olsen; C. A. Lundell; Sofia Mellguist; Ane Rasmussen; Christine Christensen; H. J. Lindhard; Stine and Henry Rhode; N. C. Mikkelsen; Dorothea M. Jensen; Kirstine Skjelegaard; Christen Jensen.

JUAB STAKE CONFERENCE.

The quarterly Conference of Juab Stake was held in Nephi on Saturday and Sunday last, with the exception of Sunday morning, which was occupied by the Sabbath School Conference, which was moderately well attended.

Apostle Heber J. Grant was present on Saturday afternoon and remained with us over Sunday, speaking at every meeting. His remarks were of a thorough, practical character, and were fully appreciated by the Saints.

Brother Seegmiller, of the Panguitch Stake Presidency, occupied a part of the time Sunday afternoon and evening.

The only changes made in the officers of the Stake was caused by the resignation and honorable release of John M Haws from being Bishop of Mona. John Kienke, from the High Council of this Stake, was set apart to succeed him.

THOMAS CRAWLEY,
Stake Clerk.

Pleasant Party.—A Mona correspondent informs us of a pleasant party given there on the 2d instant. It being the birthday of Bishop's Counselor Edward Kay. A number of friends congregated, and an old-fashioned, enjoyable time was had.

Deseret News
December 29, 1886

Bound Over.—We learn from the Ogden *Herald* that the man Jones, who forged a certificate on Hon. D. H. Peery in the sum of $200, and who, when the certificate was presented at Nephi, was arrested, after it was ascertained that the certificate was a forgery, has been committed in default of bail, to await the action of the grand jury. Hon. D. H. Peery has returned from Nephi, whither he went to give his testimony in the case. Jones, it appears, succeeded in raising $3.50 from one person, and $1 from another, on the spurious document. The certificate was a bungling affair, and did not even bear evidences of shrewdness on the part of the forger.

Deseret News
January 19, 1887

Information Wanted.—Brother J. Kissick, of Nephi, Juab County, Utah, requests us, through Brother William Willes, to publish the following, with a request for other papers to copy:

I have two brothers and three half-sisters in some part of the Eastern States, and I would like to know their whereabouts.

1st. I enlisted in her Majesty's 57th regiment on the 16th of December, 1840, at Belfast, and landed in the East Indies on the 2nd of July, 1841, where I remained until the 6th of April, 1853.

2nd. I was born in Lifford, County Donegal, Ireland; lived at Magherafelt, County Derry, Ireland, before I enlisted. My father's name was Joseph.

Should this meet the eye of anyone who would like to know the particulars of John Crawford, of Magherafelt, who enlisted in her Majesty's 64th regiment a short time before I did, I shall be happy to furnish any information, as I was personally acquainted with him for 14 years.

DEATHS.

BRYAN—At Nephi, Juab County, Utah, Julie F. Leroy Bryan, born Jan. 2, 1812, at Agincourt, France; she was baptized by Curtis E. Bolton, November, 1851; emigrated in 1853; married to C. H. Bryan July 23d, 1855; died December 31st, 1886.

Deseret News
February 9, 1887

OBITUARY.

BRAFFORD.—George Brafford died at Levan, of old age, January 3d, 1887, being 94 years old. He was born at Shenango, Olston County, New York; his father, George Brafford, was killed in a battle at Sackett's Harbor; his grandfather on his mother's side was aid de camp to Geo. Washington during the war; his grandmother King was cousin to Washington's wife and lived in the same house during the war; his grand-father Brafford was in the war at the same time. Father Brafford became a member of the Church of Jesus Christ of Latter-day Saints at an early day, was personally acquainted with the Prophet Joseph Smith, and passed through the mobbings and was robbed and driven at different times. When asked upon his death bed in regard to the Latter-day work, he said "I have borne my testimony thousands of times and it is my testimony now."—COM.

Deseret News
March 23, 1887

DEATHS.

KENDALL.—At Payson, Utah, March 11th, 1887, of jaundice and fever, Elizabeth Kendall, beloved wife of Joseph S. Wignal, and daughter of George and Elizabeth Kendall; born at Bridport, England, November 15th, 1849; baptized at the age of eight years, at Nephi City, Utah. She was married to Brother Wignal October 5th, 1865, had eight children and all are living. She was a good and faithful mother, and maintained her integrity as a Latter-day Saint, and was well respected.

The funeral services were held in the meeting-house on Sunday the 13th, at 2 p.m., when consoling remarks were made by Elders J. D. Irvine, D. Lamb and C. Brewerton. A procession of 35 vehicles filled with relatives and friends followed the remains to the City Cemetery—COM.

Salt Lake Herald
April 5, 1887

Death of D. M. Brown.

Mr. George Whitmore, of Nephi, who arrived in this city on Sunday evening, yesterday received a dispatch from home announcing the death of Mr. D. M. Brown. The dispatch failed to convey any intelligence as to the exact hour of his demise, but it is supposed to have occurred in the morning. Deceased was about 62 years of age, and had been a resident of Nephi for the past quarter of a century. He was extensively engaged in the cattle and sheep business, in which he had made considerable money, and is supposed to have been worth over $30,000. Eight days ago, while on his way to his ranche, his team ran away, and for twenty-four hours he was exposed to the cold and without food. He had been confined to his bed for nearly a week at the time of his demise. He had no family there, and so far as known the only living relation is a son, who now resides at Canker City, Kansas.

The death of Mr. Brown will be generally regretted by all who knew him. He was open-hearted, free and generous, and highly-esteemed by all, for his fair and honorable dealings.

Mr. Whitmore leaves for home this morning to attend the funeral.

Deseret News
May 4, 1887

THE EMIGRANTS.

THE NAMES OF THE FIRST COMPANY OF THE SEASON.

The following is a list of the emigrants sailing from Liverpool per steamship *Nevada*, April 16, en route to Utah:

For *Nephi*.—Jens, Maren, Martin, Ole and Christoffer Larsen; Kirsti Jensen; Anna M. and Ane Jorgensen; Sophie Petersen; H. J. Jorgensen; Soren P. Sorensen; Hulda E. Nielsen; A. C., Anna M. and Niels Andersen; Jens C. Silmousen.

For *Juab*.—Anna M., Augusta, Alfred Gustavsen; Emma Sanders; Pauline Madsen; N. C. and Kristie Nielsen.

For *Nephi*.—Anna Sarau Leighton.
For *Juab*.—Ellen Twins.

Deseret News
May 25, 1887

DEATHS.

WRIGHT.—At Nephi, Utah, May 9th, 1887, Tabitha Matilda Wright, wife of Thomas Wright, Jr., and daughter of David and Tabitha Norton, born Dec. 26th, 1855, at Willard, Box Elder Co., Utah, from hemorrhage. She died in full fellowship, beloved by all who knew her, leaving a husband and four children to mourn her loss.

SHAW.—At Nephi, Utah, May 13 1887, Eve, relict of James Shaw, born July 16th 1822, in Lancashire, England; embraced the Gospel and emigrated in 1848, and resided in the Fifth Ward, Salt Lake City, till the more, when she removed to Nephi where she resided until her death.—[COM.

Deseret News
June 8, 1887

THE IMMIGRANTS.

List of Passengers En Route to Utah.

☞The following is a full list of the immigrants that left Liverpool May 21st, per the *Nevada:*

FOR NEPHI.

Robert, James and John Hoggan; Elizabeth, Henry, Emma, Elizabeth, Jr., James, Mary, Ann, Louisa and Thomas Warren; Alfred, Leah, Emily and Alfred Blakeman.

Ogden Herald
June 20, 1887

A Nephi Newspaper.

The *Nephi Ensign* is the name of a weekly paper which has been added to Utah journalism. James T. Jakeman is the publisher and as its name indicates, it makes its appearance at Nephi. The number received is an interesting one and we wish the venture success.

Deseret News
June 22, 1887

The "Nephi Ensign."

This is the title of a new six-column, four-page weekly, published by J. T. Jakeman at Nephi. Its typographical appearance is somewhat superior to that of the paper issued in Manti by the same gentleman; it is well patronized in the matter of advertising, and with good management should do well. It has our best wishes for its success. Brother Jakeman's enterprise is commendable.

DEATHS.

CHRISTENSEN.—At his residence in Levan, Juab County, Utah, Niels C. Christensen. He was born in Aastrup, Aalborg County, Jytland, Denmark, February 5th 1847. He embraced the Gospel in 1861; emigrated to Utah in 1862; was ordained a Seventy January 26th, 1884, and went on a mission to his native land in the fall of the same year. On account of ill health he was honorably released in the spring following and he returned, but never recovered from his sickness. He used his means freely in assisting the poor. He leaves two wives, six children, other relatives and numerous friends to mourn his loss.

Scandinavian Star please copy.

PEXTON.—In Nephi, Juab County, Utah May 1, 1887, of heart disease, James Pexton. Deceased was born at Elliston, Yorkshire, England, March 9, 1831; embraced the Gospel February 24, 1851; emigrated to Utah in 1853. He leaves a large family to mourn his loss, and died in full fellowship.—COM.

Their Names.

Following are the names of the emigrants who left Liverpool June 4th 1887:

Nephi.—Olef E., Ida A., Olof E., Oliva, Julia C. Ohlson; A. L., Mathilda, Albertina, Carl, Johan Ramstrom; G. T., Beata Hillberg; Ida M. Andersen; Carl T. Statlund; Hulda A. Ramstrom; Augusta Hettberg; Anna L. Svederus; Alfred P. Andersen; Anna C. Magnusen; Per. A. Nordin; Erik L. Malus; Thorn, Anna C., Hulda Andersen; And. Andersen; Anna N. Pehrson, H. C., Christen Jensen; Theodor, Anna, Soren Petersr Maren Sorensen; Emma, Johansen, Niels P., Johaunes Nielsen.

Juab.—K. Peter, A. E. Funk.

Raid on Levan.

On Friday night, about midnight, two of the nocturnal prowlers, Deputies Dykes and Clawson, raided Levan, Juab County, and arrested H. A. Peterson on the charge of unlawful cohabitation. Information reaches us that his first wife and her brother are the complaining witnesses. The latter with a formidable pistol by his side guarded the prisoner on Saturday in Nephi while making the necessary arrangements for the conveyance of himself and witnesses to Spring City, Sanpete County. Brother Peterson was obliged to furnish his own conveyance. His first wife Lillie, his daughter Fredericke, and his brother-in-law, Charles P. Olsen, were subpœnaed to appear against him before Commissioner Jacob Johnson.

Deseret News
June 29, 1887

DEATHS.

GARRETT.—At Bountiful, June 10, 1887, after a lingering illness, William Garrett, born December 26, 1817, at Willenhall, Warwickshire, England; joined the Church October 28th, 1852; was ordained an Elder and subsequently a High Priest, and presided over the Coventry Branch for twelve years; migrated to Utah in 1866; resided at Bountiful for three years then removed to Nephi, Juab Co., and finally returned to Bountiful, where he remained until he died.

He was a faithful Latter-day Saint, was highly respected and besides many friends leaves a wife, nine children and forty-two grandchildren to mourn his death.—COM.

Mill. Star, please copy.

Deseret News
July 13, 1887

Death of a Young Man.

By letter from L. A. Bailey we learn of the death of George, son of President William Paxman, of Juab Stake, which occurred at Provo, July 1st. Deceased had been laboring on the Manti Temple at carpentry for two years. He was afflicted with rupture and, becoming ill, took stage for Nephi. On the way the trouble was aggravated, and he was sent to Provo to have it treated. An operation was performed for his relief but was too late, and he succumbed. He is spoken of as an excellent young man [illegible]

Ogden Herald
July 20, 1887

Lucky for the Hammer.

Nephi Ensign.

Bro. Robert Stevenson was swinging a heavy 14lb. striking hammer on Friday last when the head flew off and struck Mr. S. on the left leg just above the knee. The hammer having glanced his leg was not broken but badly bruised. He was carried home and medical aid was secured.

Juab County.

The Utah Commission has provided judges of election for Utah County:

Mona—Elias W. W. Williams, Wm. A. Starr, C. P. Ewing.

Nephi—Henry Adams, James Larsen, Peter Sutton.

Juab—Moroni Howarth, Anthone W. Brown, Orrawell W. Williams.

Levan—Geo. Larsen, P. C. Paterson, Charles I. Olson.

Silver City—H. H. Sowles, James A. Shearer, J. A. Beaman.

Diamond—P. H. Connell, W. T. Mathews, Wm. T. Dennis.

Tintic—Alfred H. Hames, James D. Yates, Wm. Hatfield.

Trunk Lost.

A correspondent writes as follows from Mt. Pleasant:

A trunk was lost belonging to Annie Person, who came in with the June company of immigrants. It was lost between Nephi and Salt Lake. Her name appears on some part of it, as given above.

Any one knowing of it will confer a favor by communicating with Peter Matson, Mt. Pleasant, Utah.

Nephi Notes.

THE GEODETIC survey on Mount Nebo has been discontinued for the season. Captain William Eimbeck and party have gone to their homes for a time.

HARVEST is keeping the majority of people very busy just now, and for that reason our streets are partially deserted. In spite of dull times, the smile of satisfaction is on everybody's face. Nephi takes lead in prosperity.

BLACKSMITHS ARE at work repairing and putting in trim threshing machines. We shall soon hear their busy hum, and although the crops are not exceedingly heavy, yet we believe many of the farmers will smile.—*Ensign*.

Ogden Herald
September 7, 1887

"Mr. J. E. Clinton, secretary and treasurer of the Wool Growers' Association, Nephi, and well known in Salt Lake, leaves for Boston, Tuesday morning, Sept. 6. He expects to be absent about four months, and will look after the interests of his association. Already over 2,000,000 pounds of wool have been shipped and over 400,000 pounds sold. The fall clip, which will reach probably 250,000 pounds is not yet in, therefore is not included in the figures given above.

"While East Mr. Clinton will also familiarize himself with buildings, machinery, prices, etc., of woolen mills, with a view to the ultimate establishment of factories at Nephi, if the undertaking appears feasible."

Deseret News
September 7, 1887

WEBB.—At Lehi, Maricopa County, Arizona, August 29, 1887, from the effects of being over-heated, Chauncy Edwin, son of Parden and Margaret Webb, born May 9th, 1874, in Moon, Juab County, Utah.

Deseret News
September 14, 1887

THE IMMIGRANTS.

Names of those in the Company Now En Route to Utah.

The following is a list of the names of the Saints who sailed for Liverpool August 27th, per steamship *Wisconsin*. They will probably reach Utah on Monday, Sept. 12th:

SCANDINAVIAN PASSENGERS.

Nephi—J. P., Raoirer and Hilda Amunds-n; Petra Andersen; Oscar Jensen; Johan Andersen; Peter and Bettie Larsen; Anders, Maria, Beda and Ester M. Andersen; Erik D. Andersen; Hedvig Almquist; Jensioe C. Jensen; Niels C., Anna M., Niels M., Hans M., Chris. P. and Helena R. Hansen; Maren Christiansen; Anna K., Maria and Christian Jensen; Niels C. Larsen; Peter H., Christiane, Maria, Lauritz, Peter and Hedvig Larsen; Ellen Pehrson; Hans Hermansen; Riza K. and Angta Sorensen; Chris. Jensen.

Juab—Wilhelmina and Agda Ochander; Chris., Maria, Ellena M., Alfred C., Eliza M., Lovase F., Wilhilmine, Cemine C. and Christiane A. Larsen; Lars P., Marin K. and Martine Jensen; Hans P., Christian, Hatra and Christian Sanders; Hans C. Nielsen; Nielsen and Marius Sorensen; Inge Sorensen; Ingeberg Christiansen.

Deseret News
September 21, 1887

Henry Forrest met with a very painful accident last Wednesday evening. He was hitching one of his horses to a buggy with the intention of taking an evening drive and happened to let the shaft touch the animal on the leg. The horse kicked striking Mr. Forrest just above the ankle of the right leg, fracturing the bones. Dr. Atkins is in attendance.—*Nephi Ensign, Sept. 9.*

UP WITH THE TIMES.

Nephi Proudly Coming to the Front.

A LIVELY, PROGRESSIVE TOWN.

A Brief Glimpse of Some of Her Industries—A Needed Move for Water.

Nephi is the liveliest town in Utah for its population. It has more money and does more business per head than any other part of the Territory. It also displays more enterprise, and that enterprise is not confined to the young, who ordinarily have to pull along the aged as a dead load. In Nephi you will find some young men dusting with their coats off and running like hares to keep up with the energy and grit of their sires. It is almost phenomenal.

In all parts of this thriving place, building is going on, new dwellings and new stores. Mr. W. P. Reid and Hon. W. A. C. Byran are now breaking ground for a structure which it is promised will be the finest and most imposing in Nephi. The lower part will be used for a retail and wholesale business, or both; the upper part as a large hall, and will supply a want long felt.

The First National Pank, which has been in operation for about a year, and over which Judge Alma Hague presides, has been of incalculable benefit in keeping money in that remarkably thriving place, and in bringing more to it.

Last week a new company was incorporated, the parties to the incorporation being Peter Greaves, Charles Andrews, Joseph Christianson, John Williams and John Yorgason. The capital stock is placed at $25,000, being equally divided between the five gentlemen named. The business of the firm will be to deal as buyers and sellers of wool, hides, pelts, grain, machinery and live stock; or they will handle goods as commission merchants. Mr. Andrews is general manager and Mr. Greaves president of the company; and as the members are all practical men and propose to give personal attention to the several branches, each attending to that in which he has the greatest knowledge, there can be no doubt of the success of the firm.

The gentlemen of this company are closely identified with the interests of Southern Utah, and to their efforts much of the prosperity in their vicinity is due. The company's headquarters are at Nephi, and that city will be benefited in consequence.

One thing Nephi lacks; that is, good drinking water. Judge Hague, Hon. W. A. C. Bryan and others are satisfied that Nephi has attained her rapid growth, unless this difficulty be removed, and as a consequence steps are being taken to supply Nephi with an excellent quality of water which can be had four miles distant from springs that are now available. It will cost about $30,000, and it is understood that the greater part of this sum has already been subscribed. A mass meeting of citizens is called for to-night, when the question of establishing a system of water works and piping good drinking water to the town will be discussed. If the citizens do not undertake the work, private capital will be put into the enterprise, and as the future growth of Nephi will depend on its water for culinary purposes, it is apparent that the private company will make a fortune out of the undertaking if the citizens neglect the opportunity afforded them. The public spirit of Nephi, however, will be equal to this emergency, and the public will control the water system, as it should.

The Nephi Co-operative Harness and Saddle Manufactory is up to the times, and its manager, Mr. W. H. Pettigrew, is pushing his trade all through the south. They mean to hold what trade they have and get a great deal more.

Quarries of excellent building rock have been discovered within two and four miles of Nephi. Both red and white sandstones are obtainable in abundance, as well as a handsome quality of marble. There is no doubt of the value of the quarries when their proximity to the town is considered.

Messrs. George Hyde and J. W. Morehouse, of Nephi, are the lucky possessors of a splendid parafine location. Specimens of the article, as reduced by a Salt Lake chemist, are as clean and pure as could be desired. In its crude state, it is exceedingly valuable for a number of purposes, and refined it is even more valuable. If a fair tariff on the railroads can be obtained, it is not unlikely that a large export trade will be opened. It will come in time.

Mr. J. C. Ostler has one of the largest establishments in Nephi, and his harness display is correspondingly attractive. Above him the Nephi *Ensign* floats and bids a welcome to money, muscle and grit.

It is claimed that Nephi ships more goods over the Utah Central than any place south of Salt Lake, if the coal trade be not counted in.

Deseret News
September 28, 1887

FROM FRIDAY'S DAILY SEPTEMBER 23.

Arrest at Nephi.

Mr. John Warwood, of Nephi, was arrested yesterday on the charge of unlawful cohabitation. He was placed under $1,000 bonds to await the action of the grand jury.

Salt Lake Herald
November 18, 1887

A NEPHI SENSATION.

Attempt to Rob the First National Bank There.

CLOSE CALL FOR THE CASHIERS.

The Two Young Would-be Robbers and Murderers Chased, Caught and Jailed.

Yesterday morning the startling announcement was made that a bold attempt had been made to rob the Nephi First National Bank, the foundation for the rumor being the following telegram, received at the Deseret National Bank, in this city:

Nephi, November 17.

L. S. Hills, Cashier, Deseret National Bank:

A bold attempt to rob the bank was made at 10 30 this morning, by two men. Two shots were fired at the cashiers. No injury was done and no money taken. The parties were captured, and are now in jail. Find Whitmore, and show him this.
ALMA HAGUE.

In the afternoon, a HERALD reporter took the south-bound train for the scene of the attempted robbery and murder, and telegraphed the subjoined account of the affair:

Nephi, Utah, November 17, 1887.—[Special to THE HERALD.]—Nephi indulged in a genuine sensation to-day. At 10.30 this morning two young fellows named Charles B. Allred and Joseph Justesen walked into the First National Bank here, and walking up to the cashier, asked Cashier Hague if he could exchange some greenbacks for gold. Both of them had their faces blacked and had hitched their horses a short distance away. Mr. Hague replied that they were a little short of greenbacks and did not care to make the exchange. Assistant Cashier Stone was also in the bank and was just in the act of walking out of the bank when Justesen covered him with a pistol and ordered him to stop. Mr. Stone stopped, and at this instant Justesen fired. Stone dropped and the bullet missed its mark, his assailant being at the time only a foot distant. Stone went on out when he was again called upon to stop and was covered by the gun. As he followed Stone out, Justesen said to Allred, "Take care of that s—— of a b——," meaning Mr. Hague. Just about the same moment, Allred snapped his pistol at Hague, but the weapon failed to respond. Mr. Hague dropped down behind the counter, and as he again raised, Allred evidently thinking he was coming up with a gun, broke and ran outside, where Justesen still had Stone covered. In their haste to get away they failed to mount their horses and sped away on foot. In a few moments nearly the entire town was astir and about fifty horsemen were in pursuit of the fugitives and for a time the excitement raged high.

Allred was captured about half a mile from the bank, where he had taken refuge in a cellar and Justesen was caught in the hills a couple of miles away. During his flight, the latter held up a farmer and compelled him to give up his horse, which he mounted, but finding the animal was not fast enough, he stopped another man and borrowed the best horse of a span he was driving and abandoned the one he had previously taken. Both were brought back and safely lodged in jail, where they will be held until 1 p.m. to-morrow, at which time they will have an examination.

It is understood that two charges will be entered against them, one of assault with intent to kill, and the other assault with intent to commit robbery.

Both the young fellows are well known here. Allred is a resident of Chester, where he was raised. Justesen's home is at Mount Pleasant. Allred at the present time is under indictment on the charge of grand larceny.

The scheme was well laid, and there is little doubt but the fellows intended to murder both the cashiers, if such an act had been necessary to accomplish their ends. They had fresh horses hitched about twelve miles out of town, which they intended to take in case they had succeeded in their game.

Public feeling ran high, and as both the gentlemen attacked stand well here, there is little doubt but that had either been killed there would have been a lynching bee. Both Allred and Justesen talked freely after being placed in jail, and did not appear to be very downcast over their failure.

It was a desperate deed, and especially so when the youth of the disciples of Jesse James is considered, Allred being about 21 and Justesen 24.

It is now said that the fellows stole the horses they rode into town on, and the horses stationed twelve miles away were their own.

Sheriff Turner is here at the request of the bank officials, and is looking into the matter.

Deseret News
December 7, 1887

DEATHS.

WILKINS.—At Nephi, of old age, November 22nd, 1887, Elizabeth Wilkins, aged 83 years, 8 months and 14 days. Deceased was born March 8th, 1804, at Coventry, Warwickshire, England; was baptized June 1st, 1851; emigrated to Utah in 1861. She lived and died a faithful Latter-day Saint. She was the mother of nine children, and leaves a large number of relatives and friends to mourn her loss.

Millennial Star, please copy.

Salt Lake Herald
December 9, 1887

Bishop Udall Arrested.

NEPHI, December 8.—[Special to THE HERALD]—Bishop David Udall was arrested on the going charge, at his residence, to-day, at noon, by United States Deputy Marshal McClellan, and taken to Provo. Hon. Alma Hague and J. A. Hyde have signed bonds for his appearance.

Salt Lake Herald
January 4, 1888

That Attempted Bank Robbery.

The two young disciples of Jesse James—Jas. Justensen and Charles Allred—whose bold but unsuccessful attempt to rob the First National Bank of Nephi, some few weeks since, and who have been confined in the Utah Penitentiary since that time, awaiting the action of the Grand Jury, were yesterday released on bail, each furnishing sureties in the sum of $13,000. Allred's father went out to the Pen later in the day, and drove the young hopefuls to this city, leaving for home in the afternoon. The old gentleman seemed much affected yesterday, but had very little to say to anyone. It is understood that Mr. Dickson has been retained in behalf of Justensen and Allred.

Deseret News
January 18, 1888

PICKUP.—At Antelope, Alturas County, Idaho, at 5:35 p. m., December 27th, 1887, Emily, beloved wife of J. E. Pickup. Deceased was born at Nephi, Juab County, Utah, April 14th, 1865. She died as she had lived, in full faith of the Gospel.—COM.

Salt Lake Herald
January 29, 1888

Names of Jurors.

The United States Marshal was yesterday commanded to summon the following gentlemen to serve as jurors of the First Judicial District for the present term:

GRAND JURORS—Charles Andrews, Nephi; James Crookstron, American Fork; John Moulton, Heber; R. A. Coates, Ogden; George Bowman, Ogden; Isaac Cummings, Heber; James Dunn, Provo; John Cownover, Springville; Joseph E. Tibbetts, Spanish Fork; E. Yount, Ogden; Barney Tibbles, Ogden; B. P. Critchlow, Ogden; Lester Taylor, Payson; George H. Trine, Ogden; B. W. Brown, Lehi; Adam Sindberg, Trenton; William Bailey, North Ogden; Henry Rawlins, Provo; Cyrus Sanford, Jr., Springville; Robert A. Hills, Provo; Joseph Smith, Huntsville; J. D. Page, Mount Pleasant; William Hall, Springville; Newell Knight, Provo; Peter Adamson, American Fork; James Wotherspoon, Ogden; Lyman Hudson, Nephi; George W. Jarques, Provo; William Wallace Boyle, Ogden; Charles W. Middleton, Ogden; Andrew Madsen, Lake View; James Barton, Manti; Lars O. Lawrence, Spanish Fork; John Greer, Provo.

Deseret News
February 15, 1888

Arrest at Nephi.

Bishop Wm. H. Warner of Nephi was arrested on the 8th inst. at his residence, by deputies McClennan and Clawson. He was taken before Commissioner John Moorehouse and gave bonds to the amount of $1,000 to appear again before the Commissioner on the 25th of this month. One of the Bishop's daughters and two sons were subpœnaed, but were not required to appear before the Commissioner.

Deseret News
March 7, 1888

Deputy Registrars.

The Utah Commission yesterday made the following appointments:

Juab County—Eureka, J. H. McChrystal; Levan, Geo. Larson; Mona, J. H. Mendenhall; Nephi, James Larson; Silver City, P. H. Connell.

Deseret News
March 14, 1888

The Third Bank Robber.

Ever since the attempted bank robbery in Nephi, the officers and other interested parties suspected that another, or others than the boys Justesen and Allred, were connected with the affair. Their suspicions led them to make plans for the detection and arrest of these parties, have recently matured and proved very effective. Everybody is now satisfied that there was only one man connected with the robbery other than Justesen and Allred—E. A. Billington, of Spring City, and he passed through Nephi yesterday in the custody of Deputy Clawson.

The two boys held out firmly for some considerable time that they were alone in the robbery, but it seems that Justesen is the best one of the lot—at least the one least accustomed to crooked ways—and he finally admitted that there was a third party, named Billington. A scheme was concocted which brought Justesen and Billington in conversation, supposedly to the latter private, which was overheard by three concealed parties. During this conversation the plan was rehearsed and Billington was heard to plead not to be given away by Justesen, and now no doubts are entertained but that he was the originator of the whole scheme and that he will suffer equally with the other two if not more. On Wednesday evening, about two hours after the conversation referred to, Billington was arrested and taken before Commissioner Johnson. He waived examination and bonds were placed at $5,000. He tried hard to raise the bonds but could not get them, so little sympathy does the man have over there. Suspicion has been resting on him ever since the robbery was attempted, from those who knew him and in fact he is a man of very poor character. Rumor has it that it is through his influence that many of the young men of Springtown and vicinity who together have gained the name of a "tough crowd" have been ruined, and the only sorrow that is felt is for the young wife he has recently married. She is an estimable young lady and now is almost distracted. Billington hails from the States.—*Nephi Ensign, March 9.*

Salt Lake Herald
March 15, 1888

NEPHI NOTES.

THE *Ensign* is now entirely in the hands of Mr. J. S. Rolls.

YESTERDAY morning Nephi was a veritable "sleeping village."

THE streets of Nephi are muddy, but not so muddy as those of our own city.

MR. SELLS is just now completing a two-story brick building for a furniture store.

THE two-story brick hotel building of C. R. Foote is rapidly nearing completion.

A PLANT for the manufacture of Plaster of Paris is being placed in the mouth of the canyon.

THE principal streets of Nephi are now lighted by ample coal-oil lamps fully equal to our gas burners.

CITIZENS of Nephi are jubilant over the prospect of a city charter, one of the first benefits of which will be the piping of water from springs in the canyon to the city.

THE new Nebo Block is the property of W. A. C. Bryan and W. P. Read, who will shortly open a general merchandise store in the lower part, the upper being kept as a dancing hall.

Deseret News
April 4, 1888

Charles Allred and Joseph Justesen pleaded guilty to the Nephi Bank assault case, and were sentenced as follows: Charles Allred five years and Justesen four years; the sentence in the larceny of wool was postponed until after the expiration of these sentences.

Southern Utonian
April 6, 1888

The town of Nephi which by the way has relegated unto itself the title of the "Little Chicago," has decided to establish a system of waterworks to supply its citizens with aqueous fluid for domestic purposes. It is proposed to pipe the water from Marsh Springs, a place some three miles distant from the town. The estimated cost is between $3000 and $4000.

DIED.

BROADBENT.—At Mona, Utah, March 25, 1888, of measels and congestion of the brain, Alice Ann beloved daughter of James T. and Sarah A. Broadbent, aged 5 years and 4 days. She was born March 21, 1883 at Santaquin, where her remains were interred Thursday March 29, 1888.—*Deseret News* please copy.

Deseret News
April 11, 1888

Free Again.

John Warwood, of Nephi, and Chas. Anderson, of Hyrum, have been released from the penitentiary, where they have served terms for unlawful cohabitation.

Salt Lake Herald
May 3, 1888

The Grand Ball at Nephi.

The ladies of Nephi are to be congratulated on the success of the grand calico leap year ball, given in Nebo Block Hall, Tuesday evening. More than a hundred couples were present, and each came there to enjoy the entertainment, and unquestionably did so. Everything passed off pleasantly, and dancing was continued well into the morning. An interesting feature was a character dance, in Highland costume, by Mrs. Abbott.

Ogden Standard
May 15, 1888

From Nephi.

Nephi Ensign.

On Monday last, May 7th, Edward Jones, of Nephi, breathed his last. He was aged 57 years on the 10th of last March, and has been a faithful member of the Church of Jesus Christ of Latter-day Saints, and an extremely hardworking man. Hard labor brought about the trouble from which he has suffered all the winter, and which caused his death. He was buried on Wednesday last, and was followed to his resting place by a large concourse of people, there being over fifty vehicles in the cortege.

Robert Wilson, the tailor, who was a hopeless victim of alcoholic stimulants, was found dead in his bed yesterday morning. He was living alone in a house on the east side of Main Street, Nephi, three blocks south of the Co-op., and had been on a "spree" for the last three or four weeks. On Wednesday his nephew, from Tintic, and a young man of Nephi, named Crawley, were sleeping in the house and were awakened several times by the old man asking for a drink. In the morning they found him dead. The coroner was notified, a jury secured, and an inquest held. The jury returned a verdict of "death by over-potations of alcohol."

Deseret News
May 16, 1888

DEATHS.

Pass.—At Nephi, May 2d, 1888, of pneumonia, Mary Ann. beloved wife of Thomas Pass; born Jan. 8th, 1812, at Stockport, Lancashire, England.

Millennial Star, please copy.

Nephi Nuggets.

THE bakery is progressing

FLOWER gardens and lawns are increasing in number.

BRICKYARDS are in full blast, running a large force of men.

FRANK SELL's immense stock of furniture is getting into ship-shape.

ANOTHER new street lamp has been erected. It is in front of Foote's hotel

SEVERAL new dwelling houses are being finished and erected in the suburbs of town.

OLD fences are being replaced by new ones that are neat and substantial, by many of the citizens.

BLACKSMITHS and carpenters are busy, and the merchants are adding continually to their already large stocks

CHARLES FOOTE is excavating preparatory to erecting a large and handsome dwelling house just north of his store.

A LARGE force of men have been employed on the Plaster of Paris works at the mouth of the canyon for some time. The works will commence in a week or two.

IT is in contemplation to change the flour mills at the mouth of the canyon into roller mills, but nothing can be done in the matter till after the meeting of the stockholders the present month, when new officers will be elected.

THE old Court House is no longer. It has been torn down and is now being cleared away. The new $10,000 Court House is to be erected in its place, and building will commence in a day or two. The contract will be awarded to some of the bidders on Monday.

THE livery stable is doing a good business and the room just west of the stable, which is a portion of the building, is being fitted up for a harness and saddle store and manufactory. The gentlemen who will compose the firm are Thomas Booth, and William Broodhead. The goods have arrived and they will commence business on Monday next. Mr. Booth enters into the business willing to learn while Mr. Broadhead is master of his trade, and success is sure to attend the boys in their enterprise.

ROCKS are being hauled for the foundation of a store to be built by E. N. Pyper, in which will be carried a stock of hardware, and in which will also be conducted a tinner's business. The building will be completed in a few weeks, when J. E. Cooper, tinner of Manti, will form with Mr. Pyper a copartnership. Mr. Cooper leaves Manti and comes to a town of enterprise, and is well known as a thorough and competent workman in his trade besides being a wide awake business man Mr. Pyper's abilities are well known and it is at once a "sore go" that this firm will corral the work and trade in tin of southern Utah.

PLANS and estimates for a $15,000 Opera House have reached town. Articles of incorporation for the organizing of a stock company to erect the building are also here and subscribers will be solicited. No doubt the building will go up this summer.—*Ensign.*

Nephi Items.

The citizens of Nephi, Juab County, are manifesting a good deal of enterprise in the way of building, and otherwise improving their town. Quite a number of new business houses have lately been built and still others are in course of erection, including a rather pretentious looking livery stable for D. B. Broadhead, a harness shop for Booth & Broadhead, a new bakery for James Woods, a furniture store for Sells & Dinwoodey and a tin shop for Pyper & Cooper. A new County Court House, about 50 x 65 in size, and two stories high, is also being erected on the corner opposite the meeting house westward, besides a number of dwelling houses. The co-op. grist mill in Nephi has not been doing a very successful business for some years past, and as a result the stock had become so depreciated that a number of citizens not previously interested in it recently bought a controlling interest at fifty per cent of its face value, and are now about to make it first-class roller mill of it.

Scarcity of money is complained of by those who are in business in Nephi, but from the metropolitan airs which the place is fast assuming one would scarcely think that such was really the case. However, it is quite possible that the late extensive improvements have been made with a view to future rather than present needs.

An effort is being made now to have the shipping business of the southeast, of which Juab has enjoyed the monopoly heretofore, transferred to Nephi, which seems a more appropriate place for it, especially as it is the junction of the Utah Central and Sanpete Valley Railway and a much more important place than Juab is ever likely to become. About the only reason which is urged why such a transfer should not be made is that the water of Nephi is not first class. There are, however, a number of large springs in what is known as Marsh Hollow, same distance up Salt Creek Cañon, which are owned by the city and yield an excellent quality of water, which it is proposed to convey to Nephi through pipes. If this were done it would make Nephi a much more desirable place of residence and doubtless enhance its business interests.

LIST OF PASSENGERS,

Sailing from Liverpool May 19th, per S. S. "Wyoming."

Nephi—James, Mary J., Thomas W. and George H. Bagnall; Catherine Cooper.

LIST OF EMIGRANTS

Leaving Copenhagen, Denmark May 24th, 1888.

The following is a list of the Scandinavian Saints who sailed from Liverpool on June 2nd, 1888:

For Nephi.

Amalia Dreier; Joh. O. Johanna, Johan F., Edith M. and Bertha S. Hellberg; Carl E. and Peter G. Bergstrom; Olof Nilsen; Erik A. Lundell; Elna Ekberg; Jens C., Christine, Oline and Henriette Olsen; Ane Nielsen; Jergen L. Anderson; Carl C. Srensen; Dorothea Johanson; Ernst Erestsen; Olof Amundsen.

For Juab.

Johan Emanuelson; Johan and Johannes Johanson; Christian F. Johanson.

Nephi Notes.

Deputies McClelland and Norrell have been making themselves conspicuous again about Nephi. They caught in their meshes Richard Jenkins and L. A. Bailey, charged with unlawful cohabitation.

L. A. Bailey's case, which was brought before Commissioner Morehouse on Wednesday, was continued until the 2d of July because of the failure of the deputies to get witnesses.

John C. Ostler met with a very severe accident last Monday evening. He was leading a horse from one portion of the field to another. The horse made a lunge forward and pulled Mr. Ostler to the ground. Just as he was falling the horse kicked, striking Mr. Ostler squarely in the face with both feet. The horse was shod, but luckily no bones were broken. Mr. Ostler's face is in a very bad condition, but he is progressing favorably.—*Nephi Ensign.*

Election Judges.

The Utah Commission have made the following additional appointments of judges of election for the places named:

JUAB COUNTY.

Eureka—H K Tompkins, J S Yates, A Von Bohe.

Juab—A W Brown, Wm May, Wm Burholt.

Levan—J M Thompson, Wm Brown, Chas J Olsen.

Mona—W A Starr, W E Mendenhall, S m Ewing.

Nephi—Robert Bagley, O R Foot, Henry Adams.

Silver City—James Shearer, H H Sowles, J F Croxall.

Deseret News
June 27, 1888

Arrested.

John C. Ostler, of Nephi, who was arrested on June 14th for unlawful cohabitation, was released on $500 bonds to appear for the preliminary examination before Commissioner Morehouse on July 2d.

Salt Lake Herald
July 1, 1888

The Provo Dramatic people — the original Home Club — have obtained the Silver King manuscript from the Home Club of this city, and are now at work upon it. W. C. A. Smoot will have the leading male role and Miss Atkins, of Nephi, will be the leading lady. Our home company has also furnished the Second Ward Club, of Ogden, with the manuscript of the Green Lanes of England.

Deseret News
July 4, 1888

Nephi Notes.

We were called upon yesterday afternoon by L. A. Bailey, Esq, of Nephi, from whom we gleaned the following facts relating to that town:

A $15,000 court house is in course of erection. John Adams & Sons are the contractors. A good district school building is also being erected.

Crops are light, hay especially so. On some of the farms near the town the grasshoppers almost entirely destroyed the grain.

Business is dull, money is scarce and a stringency prevails in business circles. The unfavorable condition of the wool market has a marked effect on business interests of Nephi.

Salt Lake Herald
July 18, 1888

PATRIARCH JOHN ANDREWS, of Nephi, was thrown from a hay rake on Monday morning and so severely injured that his recovery is despaired of.

Patriarch Andrews Dead.

NEPHI, Utah, July 17.—[Special to THE HERALD.] — Patriarch Andrews, who was, yesterday, thrown from a horserake while returning from his farm, died about 7 o'clock this evening. He has not been conscious and has struggled between life and death constantly since the accident. He was one of Nephi's oldest and most respected citizens.

Deseret News
July 25, 1888

Patriarch Andrews' Death.

The following dispatch to the News was received last evening:

NEPHI, Utah, July 17, 1888.—Patriarch John Andrews, who was yesterday thrown from a horse rake, while returning from his farm, died about 7 o'clock this morning. He has not been conscious and has struggled between life and death constantly since the accident. He was one of Nephi's oldest and most respected citizens.

Our correspondent at Nephi sends the following particulars in addition to what was published yesterday:

Yesterday, July 16, Patriarch John Andrews was driving home from his field, on a sulky rake, with his adopted six-year-old son. In passing the Utah Central depot some cars were close by the road, and the horse became a little frightened. Just at this time a San-pete Valley Railway locomotive whistled, causing the animal to be more frightened and to run with great speed over the railway track, throwing Brother Andrews off with great force, breaking his collar-bone. The teeth of the rake cut up his face fearfully. He also received some internal injuries. He was picked up unconscious and remained so up to his death. The family had no hopes of his recovery from the first.

The boy hung to the rake until the horse neared home when the rake struck against a tree and broke off both shafts. The boy was badly frightened but not hurt much.

Brother Andrews was an old resident at Nephi and is widely known throughout the Territory for his hospitality and generosity.

Ogden Standard
July 29, 1888

Arrest at Nephi.

NEPHI, Utah, July 28 —Special to the *Deseret News.*—Deputy Marshal McClellan arrested President Charles Sperry yesterday evening, on the charge of unlawful cohabitation. He and the main witness were taken before Commissioner Morehouse and released on their own recognizances, to appear before the grand jury at the September term. Three others were arrested at the same time.

Deseret News
August 8, 1888

Juab Notes.

Deputy McLellan has been quite busy in and around Nephi this week. He has made eight arrests and helped put out the fire.

John Adams yesterday gave bonds before Commissioner Morehouse to appear before the grand jury to answer to the charge of unlawful cohabitation.

At Levan, Juab County, on the evening of the Twenty-fourth, a serious accident occurred. While the fireworks were being set off one little boy, who was near, had one of his eyes burned very seriously.

Deputy McLellan arrested six members of a North Bend, Sanpete County, family, named Cox, and brought them over to Nephi on Monday. They were bound over in the sum of $300 each to await trial on a charge of horse stealing.— *Nephi Ensign.*

DEATHS.

ANDREWS.—At Nephi, on July 17th, 1888, in consequence of being thrown from a horse rake, John Andrews.

Deceased was the son of James Andrews and Ann Knight, and was born November 24th, 1817, in the parish of Bestford, in the county of Worcestershire, England, and was baptized on February 24th, 1841, at Naunton, Beacham, Worcestershire, by Elder Thomas Smith, who also confirmed him. He was first ordained to the office of Deacon, then to the office of Priest, then to the office of Elder, then to the office of Seventy, Forty-ninth Quorum, and after that to the office of High Priest, and set apart a Bishop over the First Ward of Nephi. Subsequently he was ordained to the office of Patriarch. He was a fervent worker in the Church, and a respected citizen, and lived and died a faithful saint. He leaves a wife, one son and two daughters.—[COM.

Salt Lake Herald
August 12, 1888

EMIGRATING SAINTS.

List of the Company of Scandinavian Saints.

Following is a complete list of the emigrants who left Scandinavia on July 19th, and their destinations:

For *Juab*—Anna Gustafson; Karen Carl E. Fredricksen Thomine M. and Jens P. Thomsen.

For *Nephi*—Hanna Clemenson, Anna Anderson, Elsa Pherson, Maria, Albin Belander, Kjersti, Josephina O. Berlin; Inger M. Nikolaison; John L. Christianson; N. P. Neilson; K. N. C. Jensen; Maria Jensen.

Deseret News
August 15, 188

ESTRAY NOTICE.

I HAVE IN MY POSSESSION:

One black MARE, 4 or 5 years old; spot in forehead; branded 15 on left shoulder.

One roan MARE, 7 or 8 years old; both hind feet white; branded F on left thigh.

One bay HORSE, 5 or 6 years old; branded P on right and left thigh.

One roan HORSE, 1 year old; right hind foot white; branded JT on left shoulder.

If damage and costs on said animals be not paid within fifteen days from date of this notice, they will be sold to the highest cash bidder, at Nephi estray pound, at 9 o'clock a. m., on the 23d day of August, 1888.

Dated at Nephi Precinct, Juab Co., Utah, this 8th day of August, 1888.

PETER SUTTON,
Poundkeeper of said Precinct.

Salt Lake Herald
August 19, 1888

Baseball at Nephi.

Following is the score of a game of baseball played at Nephi on the 16th instant, between a Nephi nine and a Provo nine: Provos—5 runs in nine innings; Nephis—7 runs in eight innings.

The Nephis invite every club in Southern Utah—Fairview and Mt. Pleasant barred—to come here and play. We will make everything agreeable for them, and if they beat us, will take our defeat good naturedly.

T. O.

Nephi, August 17, 1888.

Salt Lake Herald
August 21, 1888

DIED.

Scofield—At Nephi, on the 20th inst., of of premature confinement, Athalia Hyde Scofield, wife of Thomas Scofield, Nephi.

Salt Lake Herald
August 23, 1888

MRS. SCHOFIELD'S FUNERAL.

It will Take Place on Friday Afternoon.

To the Editor of THE HERALD.

The sad and untimely death of Mrs. T. J. Schofield, Jr., (nee Athalia Hyde) has caused the well springs of affectionate sympathy to flow out freely to the grief-stricken family. The occasion is one of more than ordinary sadness. Mr. Schofield some three months ago had his leg broken, and is now hobbling around on crutches. His infant child died only the morning before his wife passed away, and surely the world must look dark to him. Mrs. Schofield's parents, who live in San Juan, were telegraphed for, but it is doubtful if they will reach here in time for the funeral, which will take place on Friday, the 24th, at 2 o'clock p. m. The body has been carefully embalmed, and a vault prepared, so that the parents, should they not arrive in time, will have an opportunity to view the remains and bid a sad good-bye to their beloved daughter. The relatives and friends of Mr. and Mrs. Schofield in your city are cordially invited to attend the funeral.

J. E. Clinton.

Nephi, Utah, August 22.

NEWS NUGGETS FROM NEPHI.

Crops Light—Mineral Wax—Wool Season Over—General.

THE crops at Nephi are not good this season.

B. P. KINENKE, of Mona, was arrested this morning on the going charge.

THE wool season is practically over Over 2,000,000 pounds have been shipped

THE court house is nearly completed

CONSIDERABLE grain is now going out of Nephi.

THE funeral services of Mrs. T. J. Schofield were held at Nephi on Friday. Forty-five carriages filled with relatives and friends, followed the remains to the grave.

THE Nephi Mineral Wax Mining Company has been formed. George C. Whitmore is president, and J. R. Hickman, secretary. The capital stock is $1.100,000, divided into 220,000 shares of $5 each. The location of the works is in Emery County, Utah. The directors are J. E. Clinton, J. A. Hyde, and Alma Hague.

Out of Prison.

Today Thomas Harding, of this city, Joshua Adams, of American Fork, Jas. Latimer, of Nephi, Jas. Higginson, of Spanish Fork, L. Loveridge, of Provo, and E. E. King, of American Fork, were released from the penitentiary, where they have been serving a term for living with their wives. Some of them were kept in custody longer than necessary because of the failure of the clerk of Provo to report the payment of fines. It is said there are some still in prison simply on account of this neglect their terms having expired.

Another Arrest.

The following came this afternoon in the form of a dispatch to the News, dated Nephi, Utah, Aug. 25:

Bishop John Kienke, of Mona, was arrested last evening at his residence in Nephi, on the charge of unlawful cohabitation.

Names of the Immigrants.

List of passengers sailing from Liverpool, Sept. 15, 1888, per S. S. Wisconsin, Wm. G. Phillips, President of company.

For Nephi—Rebecca, James, Elizabeth and Thomas Thomas; Elizabeth Yoxall; Fanny Bailey.

Deseret News
October 17, 1888

DEATHS.

MILLER.—In the Twentieth Ward, this city, at 11:30 p. m., October 10th, 1888, of the results of an operation for the removal of an ovarian tumor, Ellen, wife of John Miller, of Nephi.

Deceased was born in Lancashire, England, June 12th, 1823, and hence was aged 65 years.

Deseret News
October 31, 1888

DEATHS.

TINGEY.—At Nephi, Juab County, Utah, Oct. 24, 1888, of scarlet fever, Ray Stafford, son of Charles S. and Sarah L. Tingey, aged 3 years and 1 months.

Deseret News
November 7, 1888

THE IMMIGRANTS.

Names of the Saints who are En Route to Utah.

List of the Saints sailing from Liverpool October 20th, per steamship Wisconsin, John Quigley President of company:

For Nephi.—Alfred, Sarah, Ethel and Chas. Stanbridge.

SCANDINAVIAN.

For Nephi.—Gustaf, Josephina, Emma and James Alinqvist; Ivar Walbou.

Deseret News
November 14, 1888

DEATHS.

WRIGHT. At Nephi, Nov. 3, 1888, after an illness of seven weeks from typhoid fever, John S., son of Thomas and Sarah Wright. Deceased was aged 34 years, and leaves a wife, two children, father and mother, three brothers and two sisters. He bore an excellent character and was loved and respected by all who knew him. He had been called to go on a mission to the southern states, and was expecting to go.—[Com.

Arrests Made.

Friday morning Deputy McLellan arrested E. T. Harper, of Payson, on the charge of unlawful cohabitation. Brother Harper has but recently returned from a mission to the Southern States. He waived examination and was bound over to await the action of the grand jury.

On Wednesday Deputy McLellan arrested Thomas Richard Jackson in Nephi on a charge of unlawful cohabitation, and took him before Commissioner Moorehouse of that place. Jackson asked for his discharge on the ground that he had not been living with his first wife. This admission brought Deputy McLellan to his feet, who asked the court to dismiss the charge of unlawful cohabitation, and hold him on a charge of adultery. The Commissioner concluded, however, to bind him over on the unlawful cohabitation charge in $1500 bonds. The second wife was held in $300 bonds.

Deputy McLellan arrested George Ostler in Nephi on Monday on a charge of polygamy. He was taken before Commissioner Moorehouse and bound over to appear in this city next February. It will be remembered that Ostler was discharged a few months ago on a similar charge, as the alleged plural wife could not be found. Recently, however, Deputy Franks arrested the plural wife in Salt Lake City, and she freely admitted having married Ostler on Oct. 9, 1888. Some six months ago, however, she married a soldier named Bartolio. She was held in $250 bonds to appear against Mr. Ostler.—*Provo Enquirer.*

NEPHI MARKET.

Nephi City, December 8, 1888.

	Buying.		Selling.
Wheat ⅌ bushel.....	80@	85	85
Oats ⅌ cwt.........	1	00	1 25
Barley ⅌ cwt........		90	90
Hay (loose) ⅌ ton..	9	00	
Lucern (loose) ⅌ ton	7	00	
Wool ⅌ lb.........	12@	16	
Hides 1st class ⅌ lb		8	
Hides 2d class ⅌ lb.		5	
Hides 3d class ⅌ lb		3	
Deerskins ⅌ lb.....	12@	25	
Beef ⅌ lb..........	4½@	5	9
Mutton ⅌ lb........		5½	10
Pork ⅌ lb..........		7½	10@ 15

Salt Lake Herald
December 15, 1888

IN LOVE, BUT HER HEAD LEVEL.

It is a matter of considerable astonishment among persons who are inclined to be careful, that others should be so loose in their way of doing things. A letter of utmost importance, placed carelessly in the pocket, may sometimes find its way into the hands of persons whom it was never intended to reach. In proof of this the following. On account of the prominence of the parties names are, for the present, suppressed:

NEPHI, December 3, 1888.

Dear —— The ring was received by this morning's mail. I am sorry you did not send along some acid by which I could have tested it, as I observe from the box in which it was enclosed that it was not purchased at the store of E. J. Swaner & Co.—whose reputation for good goods and fair treatment of their customers has reached further south than Nephi, and is among the bits of social gossip daily retailed in Goshen. The chances are that, had you made the purchase at SWANER's you would have saved enough to buy a washboard and perhaps a wringer. But this is your first offense, and I'll forgive you, for I know it will be your last.

Ever your own,

†   M—— M——.

Deseret News
December 26, 1888

JAMES LITTLEY HURT.

He Falls With a Load of Ties, and Has a Leg Broken.

James Littley, of the Sixth Ward of this city, met with a serious accident, a short distance above the end of the Salt Lake & Eastern Railway, in Parley's Cañon, yesterday. He was engaged by the railway company in hauling ties from the terminus to where they were needed on the grade. The ties being peeled and wet were quite slippery. Mr. Littley was sitting on the load, and as the front wheels of the wagon went into a small ditch across the road, the ties commenced to slip. Before he could free himself the unfortunate man fell with the load. He was thrown in front of the wheels, one of which passed over his left leg. He was in a cramped position, and the result was that the limb was broken just below the thigh. It was turned so badly that a piece of the broken bone protruded through the skin. His team did not run away, but continued up the cañon until a man stopped them. Mr. Littley called for help,

and his cries were heard by Mr. David Ostler, who was at the carpenter's camp, a short distance below where the accident occurred. He went to where the unfortunate youth was lying, and with others conveyed him to where the construction train was standing. He was immediately brought by rail to the Salt Lake & Fort Douglas depot in this city, and then removed to his brother-in-law's, Mr. John Watson's. Dr. H. J. Richards attended him, and set the broken limb, which he hopes to save, though it will be

several months, with the best fortune, before the young man can get around again. Today he was removed to the hospital, his condition requiring the attention that can only be given there. His father lives in Nephi, Juab County, his mother being dead.

DEATHS

RICHES.—At Nephi, j i .... from the
effects of injur... rec.......... the mount- ... to Riches A.
tains, getting fir.... d. ... Ap.. Eng'and.
  Deceased was bor...la No......... widow... a...
Nov. 5, 1826, and was senior p..............
7.st Quorum of seventi.... at the ....
his death. He leaves a wi... rec ...
two daughters —COM.

Millennial Star please copy.

THE CITY OF NEPHI.

The Wisdom of Her People Evinced on Monday.

SHE WILL NOW BOOM AHEAD.

The Officers Elected Receive a Hand some Majority Over the Non-Incorporation Votes.

Owing to the many previous attempts and failures to obtain a city government for Nephi, interest in the election which took place Monday ran high.

Several weeks ago the following ticket was nominated: For Mayor—Hon. Alma Hague, Councilmen—James H. Mynders, Joseph A. Hyde, Charles Andrews, A delbert Cazier, Peter Sutton, E R. Booth, James Jenkins, Jr. Recorder—J. R. Hickman. Treasurer—E Harley. Assessor and Collector—W. A. C. Bryan. City Marshal—W. P. R ad. Justices of the Peace—James B. Black, and William Stout. The opposers were numerous at first but the question of securing waterworks to furnish pure water for culinary purposes under a city government, being well ventilated, squelched them, and every evidence seemed to favor the election of the straight ticket. Many of the voters were surprised Monday morning to find another ticket in the field with the names of Herbert Burton and James R McPherson, as Councilmen, substituted for Adelbert Cazier and Charles Andrews, for the purpose of giving better representation, as the former two live in extreme north and south of town respectively. Straightway Mr. Andrews had some stickers printed, and prevailed upon many voters to use them. The new ticket and the stickers were used almost exclusively, making the chances run close between Booth and Andrews, resulting in favor of Booth. Although interest was deep the day passed off quietly. Only 212 votes were polled; 37 against incorporation, and 174 for incorporation. The new ticket was elected. One envelope was found by the judges to contain two tickets, one for and the other against incorporation, and this was thrown out.

The Nephi Brass Band, under the leadership of Charles H. Sperry, serenaded the town, and did a great deal towards waking up the sluggards. Saloons were closed. Peace and good will prevailed.

THE NEW OFFICIALS.

Below are the officers elected, and the votes received by each:

Mayor—Alma Hague, 172.

Councilmen—Joseph Alonso Hyde, 172; James Jenkins. Jr , 171; Edwin R. Booth, 110; Herbert Burton, 139; Jas. H. Mynd rs, 172; James R. McPherson, 145; Peter Sutton 172.

City Marshal—Walter P. Read. 182.

Assessor and Collector—William A. C Bryan. 168

City Recorder—John R. Hickman, 172

Treasurer—Edwin Harley. 173.

Justices of the Peace — James R. Black, 172; William Stout. 158.

Deseret Weekly
March 2, 1889

F. A. Petersen, of Levan, Juab County, was released from the penitentiary Jan. 25. He has served an eighteen months' term on a conviction of adultery. This was a case where a charge of unlawful cohabitation was construed into adultery, as it was for living with his plural wife that he was prosecuted.

Salt Lake Herald
March 15, 1889

People vs. E. A. Billington is the sensation of the day in court. J. L. Rawlins was associated with the counsel for the prosecution, Dickson and Powers defending. The testimony given so far is to the effect that the defendant was the instigator of the attempt of two years ago to rob the Nephi First National Bank. According to the testimony of Justeson who is down from the penitentiary as a witness, Billington was to act as a co-worker at home, he and Allred doing the work.

Deseret Weekly
March 30, 1889

Richard Jenkins, of Nephi, Juab County, was released from the Penitentiary March 28, having undergone a sentence of four months for unlawful cohabitation. A fine of $50 and costs was also imposed, for the non-payment of which he served an additional month.

Salt Lake Herald
April 10, 1889

Mr. H. Burton, for some time superintendent of the Co-op. at Nephi, has severed his connection with that institution. He will go into business for himself in connection with Mr. Pettigrew, also of Nephi. The gentlemen expect to open out in a couple of months, and are building a store, which they will occupy.

NEPHI CITY WILL CELEBRATE.

The Centennial Anniversary of the Inauguration of the Father of Our Country.

In response to a call made by the mayor and several of our prominent citizens, a mass meeting was held in the Nephi tabernacle for the purpose of nominating a committee of arrangements for the coming centennial celebration. Mr. F. W. Chappell was appointed chairman of the meeting, and James W. Paxman secretary. The following gentlemen were nominated as a committee: Rev. W. N. P. Dailey, of the Presbyterian mission; Hon. Alma Hague, F. W. Chappell, H. F. McCune, Henry Adams, Charles Sperry and James W. Paxman. Mr. Dailey the next day, declined to serve, and the committee appointed Mr. Charles Sperry as chairman. A programme is being arranged, and the prospects are that the citizens of Nephi will celebrate right royally.

Prospects for a dry season are imminent. The streams are small and very little snow in the mountains. Grasshoppers are plentiful.

Dr. M. McCune, one of our old-timers, is in a very critical state of health. Hopes are strong for his recovery.

Mr. Charles Abbott one of the lucky ones in THE HERALD drawing, is jubilant over his splendid set of furniture, and says THE HERALD is all right.

The gypsum works of Nephi have been leased to an eastern firm.

Judge Charles Foote has completed a beautiful brick residence.

Wool is coming in fast and the wool merchants are kept busy.

The Nephi philosopher, D. Cazier, has commenced well-boring with steam power, and says he will strike water or bust. Success to the first Dave.

Where, oh where is our telephone line?

JUAB.

NEPHI,

Woman Suffrage in Nephi.

NEPHI, Utah, May 11.—[Special to THE HERALD.]—The ladies of Nephi met in the tabernacle at 2 p.m. for the purpose of organizing a Woman Suffrage association. The meeting was called to order by Mrs. Mary Pitchforth. Mrs. Pitchforth was nominated chairman of the meeting and Mrs. M. E. Teasdale secretary. Singing by the choir; prayer by Mrs. S. A. Andrews. The secretary then read the call. The following officers were elected: President, Miss L. A. Schofield; first vice-president, Mrs. E. B. Bryan; second vice-president, Mrs. M. E. Neff; third vice-president, Mrs. M. A. Cazier; secretary, Miss Lou Udall; corresponding secretary Mrs. Annie Atkin; treasurer, Mrs. L. A. Hartley; executive board, chairman, Mrs. M. A. Grover; Mrs. M. E. Whitmore, Mrs. Mary Wright, Miss Emma Adams, Mrs. Ella Jones, Mrs. S. E. Abbott, and Mrs. Julia Paxman, members of the board.

The constitution was then read and adopted. Speeches were then made on woman suffrage by the following named ladies and gentlemen: Miss L. A. Schofield, Mrs. M. Pitchforth, Mr. F. W. Chappell, Mr. W. H. Jones, Mr. J. W. Paxman and Mr. Charles Sperry. The Payson brass band rendered sweet music at intervals. The meeting adjourned until the 31st of May. The meeting was well attended by the ladies of Nephi, and a very pleasant and profitable time was spent.

NEPHI NEWS.

Nephi presented quite a holiday appearance this morning. Hundreds of children dressed in their best were on the street in front of the tabernacle at 10 o'clock. Wagons loaded with people from the neighboring towns came rolling in all morning. The stars and stripes floated on the breeze, and music, enchanting the ear, foretold that the good people of Nephi were about to participate in something extraordinarily grand; and so it proved, for at 11 o'clock the Sanpete railway train arrived with two passengers whom the people of Juab county revere—Presidents Wilford Woodruff and George Q. Cannon. The Sunday-school and primary children formed on each side of the sidewalk as far as the tabernacle, and the illustrious visitors walked up the long aisle of beautiful children, accompanied by Presidents Sperry and Paxman, bishops and other leading men of Nephi, with the band at the head, passing under an arch with the inscription, "With Joy We Greet Our Leaders," to the tabernacle, which we found entirely too small to accommodate the vast number of people who had assembled for the purpose of seeing and hearing the men they had not seen nor heard for years. Meeting opened and Presidents Cannon and Woodruff occupied the time in good teaching.

. . . . . up the children of . . . . .
Elder H. G. Parkes, of Nephi, Juab County, returned on May 10 from a mission to the Northern States. He left Utah on May 2nd, 1887, and first went to Pittsburg, where he remained for about a month. He was next assigned to the State of Ohio, and labored chiefly in Hamilton, Brown and Clinton counties. There he continued for some fifteen months, having as his co-workers Elders David McMullin, Edwin Bodily and J. A. West. This being almost a new field (not having been visited by missionaries for nearly forty-five years), the work was attended in the outset with some little difficulty. For the first eight months of their sojourn in Ohio the Elders did not make many friends, but as they became better known they were hospitably treated by the people. There was not, however, much spirit of inquiry manifested. The "White Caps" are in strong force in the localities named—notably in Brown County. Elder Parkes was on several occasions threatened with personal violence, but the threats were never carried into execution.

The opinion of Elder Parkes is that in the future the mission in those parts will be attended with greater success than has been the case thus far, as the people are seemingly becoming more anxious to investigate the Gospel. After leaving Ohio he proceeded to Wetzel County, West Va., and there was well treated by the residents, who were found most ready to receive the instructions imparted to them. Elder Parkes went to the Pennsylvania Conference, on the 13th and 14th of April, and was then released. He informs us that he baptized thirteen persons during his absence. He has greatly enjoyed his mission, and is now in first-rate health and spirits.

NEWS FROM NEPHI.

War of Extermination Against the Grasshoppers.

IMPROVEMENTS AND PROGRESS.

A Mine on Mount Nebo—The Gypsum Industry —The Festive Drummer—Margetts and His Troupe.

NEPHI, May 31, 1889.—[Special Correspondence of THE HERALD.]—Decoration day, yesterday, was very quietly observed as a holiday here, no business being done by the mercantile houses, banks or professional men.

The curse of the country, the grasshoppers, are giving the farmers a great deal of trouble and worriment, and the war of extermination now in progress is being waged fiercely and steadily. Children, for the most part, are enlisted in the pest-killing crusade, and the satisfactory results of their work are manifest in the decrease in the number of the 'hoppers. The army of children and adults engaged in the warfare so effectually do their duty that in about two hours, day before yesterday, seven bushels of grasshoppers were piled up ready for the crematory. It is believed that in consequence of the present war of extermination, a good percentage of the crops will be saved.

The staid conduct of Nephites generally, has had the effect of giving to their city

A TRULY METROPOLITAN ASPECT,

on a small scale, of course. The buildings recently erected are all of the substantial order, imposing and agreeable to the view. The court house is notably a handsome structure. The store of Read & Bryan, the Co-op., the Cyrus Foote hotel, the residences of Charles Foote, Sandroen Lunt, James Miner, William Gaze, and others, are evidences of good taste and an abiding faith in the future of "Little Chicago." Herbert Burton is erecting a nice little brick building on the main street.

Ed Williams, the pioneer merchant of this place, has moved from the principal thoroughfare to a snug little place half a block west of Read & Bryan's.

John Hague, one of the live men of Nephi, although somewhat crippled by rheumatism, is still a rustler, and is a moving spirit in improvements and undertakings for the good of the community. Among the many of the enterprises he is identified with, is the extensive plaster of paris mine in Salt Creek cañon. This manufactory is an increasing one, both in the employment of men and the output of its product, and will shortly be recognized as one of Utah's leading industries. Already shipments are being made all over the country, and the calculation is to so order the work at the deposit that a car load a day will be sent over the Utah Central. Plasterers who have used the plaster in different cities attest its superiority over the imported article, and Mr. Hague says that it can be furnished cheaper than the eastern. Mr. Hague is also interested in a galena-yielding

MINE ON MOUNT NEBO,

about four miles from the railroad, and if the 700-pound specimen I saw in his front garden this morning is a specimen, the hole in the ground referred to will furnish him and co-partners wealth galore. While the percentage of silver is small, the richness in lead evens it up sufficiently to make it a paying ore, so close to the railroad. It is understood that some Salt Lake capitalists will pay the find a visit with a view to an early and extensive development of the property.

The presence of members of the drummer corps is very noticeable in this and other cities, and all seem to do well.

THE OPERA HOUSE,

or theatre here, last night was packed with an appreciative audience, who attested their satisfaction with "Joshua Whitcomb," by Phil Margetts and his clever company, by continued and vociferous applause. At the conclusion of the performance, a request was made for a repetition of the drama, and an announcement given that the company would repeat it on their return from Manti, next week.

Here, as at Payson, the streets are lighted at night by kerosene lamps, on respectable-looking posts. The ones at the former city, nine in number—seven belonging to the city and two private property—are manipulated by F. H. Wilson, chairman of the committee on streets, and justice of the peace. They are self extinguishers, and so regulated by a slide, that they will burn four hours at a time and then wink out.

WATER IS SOMEWHAT SCARCE

here just now, and irrigating is punctually and sharply looked after by all interested. Every drop of the aqueous fluid is placed where it will do the most good.

Joseph Darton, a leading musician of Nephi, is suffering from a curious freak of nature, as a following from an attack of erysipelas he had a short time ago. His left leg, from the knee down is swollen to double its natural size and the flesh is as solid as India rubber, almost. It has been designated "elephant leg." Mr. Darton has the sympathy of all who know him.

In traveling through the country, I have noticed the absence of THE HERALD on the trains and have asked myself and others, "How is this?" but have not yet received any satisfactory reply.

Shale is being plentifully used here on the sidewalks, and where it has been down a year or so is compact and firm as rock.

To-day, I have just learned, the gypsum works start up in full blast, with new, improved machinery, by means of which the plaster of paris is bolted and refined as it never was before, and rendered A No. 1.

Success to "The Giant of the Rockies." More anon.   FLEWELLYN.

Salt Lake Herald
June 29, 1889

A Nephi Savings Bank.

The mania for savings banks is spreading. Impelled by the example of the Deseret National and the Provo bank, the First National of Nephi has decided on organizing a savings bank. The incorporation was made on the 26th, with a capital of $50,000, 25 per cent. of which has been paid up. The officers are the same as those of the First National of Nephi, George C. Whitmore, president, and Alma Hague cashier. The directors are the same, with the addition of J. E. Forshee and James M. Peterson. Following are the incorporators:

	SHARES
George C. Whitmore, Nephi, Utah	50
James E. Clinton, Nephi, Utah	50
W. I. Brown, Nephi, Utah	48
Alma Hague, Nephi, Utah	30
Mary A. Grover, Nephi, Utah	20
Tacy W. Grace, Nephi, Utah	10
Willitta Gaye, Nephi, Utah	10
Edwin R. Booth, Nephi, Utah	20
J. A. Hyde, Nephi, Utah	10
Charles H. Grace, Nephi, Utah	5
Charles S. Tingey, Nephi, Utah	5
James W. Paxman, Nephi, Utah	5
David O. Miner, Nephi, Utah	5
William O. Key, Nephi, Utah	5
Charles L. Hyde, Nephi, Utah	5
Gustave G. Henroid, Nephi, Utah	3
John R. Hickman, Nephi, Utah	2
Andreas Jensen, Nephi, Utah	2
Langley A. Bailey, Nephi, Utah	2
M. Don, Nephi, Utah	2
Henry McCune, Nephi, Utah	2
Adelbert Cazier, Nephi, Utah	1
George Q. Cannon, Salt Lake City, Utah	10
Lewis S. Hills, Salt Lake City, Utah	10
Frank W. Jennings, Salt Lake City, Utah	10
William Probert, Provo, Utah	10
William H. King, Provo, Utah	10
John B. Milner, Provo, Utah	10
J. H. Erickson, Mt. Pleasant, Utah	35
A. A. Cahoon, Mt. Pleasant, Utah	5
J. E. Forshee, Grass Valley, Utah	50
James M. Peterson, Richfield, Utah	40
Jacob Johnson, Spring City, Utah	5
John Lowery, Spring City, Utah	3
N. P. Rasmussen, Levan, Utah	5
G. W. Nixon, Cedar Springs, Utah	15

THE CONTEST OVER.

The Twelfth District Sends Thomas Adams and the Tenth Sends W. A. C. Bryan.

The councilors to the next legislature have all been chosen by the People's conventions, and the full ticket appears at the head of THE HERALD's columns this morning.

The following dispatch was received from Nephi last evening, and is self-explanatory:

NEPHI, July 11.—[Special to THE HERALD.]—The Tenth Council convention convened at Nephi July 10. Following are the names of the delegates: Juab county—Alma Hague, Adelbert Cazier, N. P. Rasmussen, C. E. Neilson and C. A. Tingey. Millard county—Alma Greenwood, Joshua Greenwood, James A. Melville, Thomas Memmett and L. R. Cropper. Sanpete county—John Carter, Andrew Madsen, L. Larsen, J. E. Allred, Peter Sundwall, Peter Graves, Jr., J. C. Peterson, M. Fox, A. L. Jensen and Lars Neilsen.

On motion of Mr. Hogue, Mr. John Carter, of Mt. Pleasant, was elected chairman, and Mr. C. S. Tingey secretary. After the organization was made permanent and a committee on credentials appointed, the convention adjourned for one hour. Pursuant to adjournment, the convention convened, and the report of the committee on credentials reported the names of the individuals entitled to seats in the convention.

Hon Jas. A. Melville moved that it be the sense of the convention that the councilman to be nominated be a resident of Juab county.

The matter was elaborately discussed, and the motion being put, a tie was the result of the voting. The convention remained in dead lock on the question and adjourned until 4:30 p. m. The convention was again called to order by the chairman.

Mr. J. Greenwood moved that the motion be rescinded. Carried. The nominees were then named and balloting commenced and continued from time to time during the two days, including a night session, until 3 p.m. to-day, when W. A. C. Bryan was nominated.

CRUSHED TO DEATH.

Stephen Stephenson Gets Under the Wheels of a Locomotive.

Deseret News.

A lamentable accident occurred on the Utah Central and Milford early this morning, resulting in the death of a young man named Stephen Stephenson. The first announcement of the sad affair in this city was the following telegram, received by Hon. John Sharp:

"MILFORD, Utah, July 13, 1889.—Steve Stephenson, one of the train hands south of Juab, was killed this morning. He was riding on the back of the tender after putting the freight on a switch, and must have been crossing the drawhead when he fell off the tender, and part of the engine passed over his body. One leg was cut off, his bowels cut open and several bad cuts made about his head. He died instantly. His parents and family live at Levan "

An inquest was held at Milford, the result being announced in the following dispatch:

"The coroner's verdict is that Stephenson came to his death by falling from the tender of an engine, the same passing over him while in the performance of his duty, and that no blame can be attached to anyone."

The Utah Central sent a special down with a coffin, and the body will be taken to Levan for interment.

NEPHI NOTES.

"Water!" is the cry of thirsty Juab. Nothing is more refreshing, after a dusty and wearisome ride through Juab, than to emerge into the green pastures, fields and orchards of Utah County. Juab County has perhaps a greater area of arid desert land — irreclaimable for want of water — than almost any other county of Utah. The only inhabitable valley is the Great Uah Vant, extending north and south across the eastern part of the county and thence appropriating the Sevier. A vast stretch of desert covers the western nine-tenths of Juab and the greater part of the two adjacent counties, and is useful only as a great winter pasture for flocks and herds. Here, when the winter snows furnish water for its only organic life, sheep men find sustenance for thousands of flocks from all parts of the Territory.

The crops of Nephi have been threatened incessantly by the grasshopper and the drought. The people have exhibited much enterprise and perseverance in fighting the one enemy, but the other is invisible only in its effects. The schools have been known to join wholesale in the fight against the grasshoppe which, being of the native species, is not migratory, and to be got rid of must be exterminated. As it is the people of Nephi anticipate scarce half crops.

Fancy spreads wide her magical pinions and future prospects loom up buoyant with hope regarding the prospective visit in August of the Senate water commission. Already do we see with the eye of imagination countless silvery lakes pent up, at the nation's expense, in our mountain fastnesses ready to assuage the thirst of barren plains below. I see these plains becoming populous and thrifty of wealth and civilization; but oh! beware then of the danger impending in these reservoirs, over the settlements so cosily skirting the Wasatch's fastnesses. Our civil engineers must needs remember the

Nephi City, lately assuming incorporation habiliments, is without dispute the greatest wool market of Utah. The Wool Growers' Association has its headquarters here, and many another nabob association swells the annual shipment of wool to Boston, Philadelphia and other eastern marts, what with loads and loads of wool continually thronging the street and several cars of wool being shipped. Daily the "Little Chicago" resembles an enterprising Gulf port engaged in the cotton industry.

Speaking of heat, the mercury of the thermometer hereabouts, for several days past, has been seen to play and hang affectionately upon the neck of 100 deg. F.

cruel fate of Johnstown and build reservoirs with due regard to fitful and unseasonable storms.

The white cliffs to the east of Nephi, shimmering in the heat of an almost tropical sun are anything but grateful to the eye, but nevertheless that white gypsum earth will yet prove a valuable and inexhaustable source of wealth to Nephi. The gypsum works are again running full blast, turning out an excellent quality of plaster of paris. The process and principle of the operation is this: Gypsum is composed of calcium, and hydrogen and oxygen in the proportion to form water. The rock being crushed and ground fine as flour is then heated to drive off the water elements. The product is then ready for use, and to be utilized needs only the water of its original hard condition restored, when it sets as plaster of paris.

The Nephi roller flouring mills are making an excellent quality of flour. They will shortly utilize Salt Creek's water power to aid and economize the steam power heretofore used.

Nephi has no street cars, electric lights, and such fashionable metropolitan paraphernalia, but it now boasts of telephone connection with Provo, Salt Lake and Ogden. Merchants now do much of their business through the "hello!"

It may be hard to catch a weasel asleep, or for that matter the "Liberal" party. Last year in Nephi, while the People's Party were napping, the "Liberals" put in their trustee. Last Monday night found the citizens more wide awake to their educational interests. The main hall of Nephi's elegant court house was crowded. After the report of the trustees for the last year was received, nominations were in order for a new trustee. The liberals advanced for the position Mr. C. S. Tingey who, though of the People's Party, seemed to satisfy at once the "Liberal" and the dissatisfied factions. The People's Party nominated the outgoing trustee, Jas. W. Paxman, and Thos. Crawley. Mr. Crawley withdrawing from the field, Mr. Paxman, the regular nominee of the People's party, was elected by a vote of 16 over that of the Liberal candidate.

The educational conditions of Nephi, as shown by the trustee's report of Monday night, were never in a better condition. A system of gradation of schools has been rigidly enforced under the principalship of Mr. Wm. H. Jones. This with the establishment of an academic department, ably conducted, has given general satisfaction, and awakened a rousing interest in educational matters. A new brick schoolhouse of ample proportions and elegant architecture, and costing some $4,000, has been erected in the northern part of the district.

The Central School building should be overhauled and refurnished with necessary school apparatus and teaching appliances. A set of encyclopædias for reference should constitute the foundation of every school district's library.

It was a wrong report lately published in some of the Salt Lake papers that the grand celebration in Nephi of Independence Day was a "Liberal" affair. There was but one "Liberal" on the committee; while of the local talent figuring on the programme there were none of that faction. Of course in the procession all the enterprising firms were represented—and gorgeously too. But without the People's Party participating in that day' events the occasion would have wanted sadly in its proprieties, patriotism and genuine success.

An incident occurred in Nephi in the grand procession on Independence Day, which would better have not been witnessed. With a bottle in each hand and a half dozen empty bottles sticking out of his several pockets, a man was seen staggering along behind the whisky float which graced (?) the procession.

Tuesday night a grand ball was given in the Court House by a coterie of our political aspirants, with a view doubtless to develop fraternal and uniform relations between representative delegates of Millard, Juab and Sanpete. Today the convention was held but at 2:30 p. m., after much wrangling and wire-pulling, the choice for candidate had not been determined. Mr. Whittemore, banker and merchant, was the nominee (defeated) of those "Liberally" inclined.

Mr. Wm. A. C. Bryan has a majority of the votes of the Millard and the Juab delegates; but the Sanpeters have a choice of their own in the person of Mr. A. Lund. The last named gentleman, in his character and parts, is admirably possessed of legislative qualities. Mr. Bryan has been to the Legislature before and has proven himself a capable and conscientious worker.

"Little Chicago," peers eagerly forward, anticipating in the near future to become something other, in the commercial world, than a mere nomenclature on paper. Her citizens are concerned materially in the proposed enterprise to extend the Utah Central to the Pacific, and with scarce less eagerness are they watching for the Sanpete Valley Railway Co. to thread Manti and other more southern cities of Utah on the line of its contemplated projection into Arizona. Nephi will then become a southern "hub," lacking, perhaps, only the noisy self-praise of our northern junction City—a neighbor of Salt Lake.

The city fathers of Nephi have been considering for some time the advisability of supplying the town with canyon spring water, to be conducted in pipes some ten miles—to the tune of $30,000. This water, for culinary purposes, is now brought in portable tanks and retailed at a few cents per gallon. This is made necessary from the fact that Salt Creek, the stream on which Nephi is built, is signific-

antly named, being strongly impregnated with salt.

The street lamps of Nephi are striking reminders of the allegory of the five foolish virgins. They are indeed more ornamental in the daylight than useful in the night. The moonlight at present helps out wonderfully; but of a night a short time ago one might with perfect sobriety run against a street lamp or have to strike a match to apprehend its identity.

In a town newly organized there is much to do by way of converting the chaotic into organized conventional forms. And to straighten the street surfaces and improve the sidewalks of Nephi will be an expensive, but one of the first achievements of the solons.

The suggestion in the Fourth Council District convention is a good one, that in each school district and precinct People's political clubs

be formed aiming at improvement in the knowledge of civil government. The want of a knowledge of parliamentary law was painfully evident at the school meeting of Monday night at Nephi. Everybody seemed to have something to say and much of it was said in such a pandemonium as cannonading and grape shot may occasion in other circumstances. One gentleman facetiously recommended that certain of the citizens join the Woman's Suffrage club and study parliamentary decorum and law.

There is plenty of clay in Juab County to make the Salt Lake canals impervious to water, and enough gypsum to have settled at once the Salt Lake sewerage question.   JAY.

NEPHI, July 10, 1889.

Salt Lake Herald
July 26, 1889

THE TWENTY-FOURTH.

Pioneer Day in Nephi and in Warship.

The inhabitants of Little Chicago were aroused this morning from their slumbers by a salute of forty-two guns. At sunrise the stars and stripes were unfurled to the breeze from several conspicuous places and Darton's cornet band serenaded the citizens. At 10 a.m. the people assembled in the Tabernacle (which was most artistically decorated for the occasion) and a very entertaining programme was rendered.

Orator of the day, D. Cazier, delivered a very able discourse on "Church History," referring to the persecutions and driving of the saints out of the United States, and their journeying to the Rocky Mountains, etc., etc. T. H. G. Parkes also delivered an elegant address on the same subject. In the afternoon the little gem of Utah had a most enjoyable time dancing in Hoyt's grove, and in the evening the older folks had a good time in the court house. Peace and good will seemed to pervade the breasts of all.   PIONEER.

NEPHI, July 24, 1889.

Deseret Weekly
August 17, 1889

The result of Monday's election battle in Juab County gives the county to the Independent-Liberal party. Their victory comes from the complete amalgamation of these two parties against the People's. The successful candidates are: Geo. Whitmore (Nephi) and Delos Lombard (Tintic) for Selectmen, and Chas. S. Tingey (Nephi) for Superintendent of Schools of the county. The defeated People's candidates are: Chas. Andrews and C. E. Neilson named for selectmen, and F. W. Chappell for county superintendent of district schools. The People elected their candidates for the Legislature, and also their precinct officers everywhere except in Tintic, the stronghold of the "Liberals."

Seventy-two suffragists of Nephi were absent from Monday's election. They could have turned the tide in favor of the People.

Monday's suffrage contest gave to Nephi a wide-awake, exhilarated character. Everybody seemed intensely interested in the election, and all the registered voters not out of town, save five, appeared at the polls. The total number of votes polled was: In Nephi 293, of which 67 were "Liberals" and Independents; in the entire county, People's 354, "Liberals" (with their Independent allies) 388.

Salt Lake Herald
August 17, 1889

Another Account.

NEPHI, Aug. 16.—[Special to THE HERALD.]—Nephi has just passed through one of the hardest storms experienced in its history. After a very hot day to-day, a strong wind set in and blew for about twenty minutes, at the end of which time a rain and thunderstorm came up. Some of the thunderbolts were so severe that they shook several buildings and one struck the roof of Read & Bryan's store at the northeast corner, setting the woodwork on fire. The electricity followed the iron roof to the southwestern corner, and from there down the telegraph wire clear to the telegraph instruments, almost completely ruining them and setting many papers on fire. It also went down into the cellar, igniting some wooden boxes, but the goods were removed before any great damage was done. The storm was traveling in a southeasterly direction; in its course, it struck one William E. Henroid, a young man of eighteen years of age, who now lies insensible from the effect. A few moments later another bolt struck the residence of George Atkin, Jr., shattering the roof completely. No further damage was done other than that Mrs. Atkin, who was in an upper room, was badly frightened and is now quite ill in consequence.

Salt Lake Herald
August 27, 1889

DIED.

COOPER—In Nephi, Friday, August 23, 1889, Mrs. Isabella L. Cooper. Born September 9, 1830, in Meerut, India.

Ogden Standard
August 31, 1889

The Emigrants

List of the emigrants who sailed from Copenhagen and Christiania, Aug. 8th and 9th 1889.

Nephi.—Peter Johanna, Alvin, Exel, Elin and Emil Anderson; Marie Johansen; Andrear, Elsie, Niels L., Marie Maren, Andrea Kristine and James Christensen; Ane Kristine Berg; Christine Lareen; Josephine, Vigo and Anders Bolander; Ane Larsen.

Juab —Thora Jorgensen; Maren Christensen; Jens Jensen; Marie Larsen; Josefine Thonesen; Thomine Bolander; Johanne K , Johannes K., Johannes T , Caroline, Josefine and Marie Johansen; Jacobine Ibsen.

Salt Lake Herald
September 12, 1889

MARRIED.

ROLLO-FENN—September 11, in Provo, at the residence of the bride's parents, Mr. John Rollo, of Nephi, to Miss Jennie Fenn, Judge William Brown officiating.

The wedding took place at 3 o'clock yesterday afternoon, in the presence of a host of the happy couple's friends. The presents were elegant and numerous. The bride is one of Provo's pretty and popular belles, while the groom was a gay young bachelor and editor of the Nephi *Ensign*. Mr. and Mrs. Rollo will take up their residence in the "Little Chicago," beginning life with the best wishes of the people of both Provo and Nephi. A reception will be tendered Mr. and Mrs. Rollo by their friends this evening, on their arrival at their new home.

Deseret Weekly
September 28, 1889

NEWS FROM NEPHI.

Two flourishing banks are now representing Nephi in the financial world.

The three district schools of Nephi have, together, an attendance of 160 pupils.

An assay, made the other day, of a metallic "find" in the mountains eastward, runs—silver, 6.5; gold, a trace.

Good drinking water piped from the mountains will add a specially inviting feature to Nephi's material conditions.

Willie Bryan, aged 12, a bright little son of Hon. W. A. C. Bryan, died today of diphtheria after a week's illness. The bereaved family have the sympathy of the entire community.

The autumn days have come, when sombre hues and hollow winds and rustling leaves seem to favor those who are peculiarly inclined to indulge in gentle, dreamy melancholy.

city for $10,000, to add to this sum probably $1,500 or $2,000 of the city's revenue, and to complete as much of the work this season as the latter sum will permit.

A party from Nephi, interested in the limestone deposits four miles to the west of here, made a trip thither last week. They report that the deepest explorations in the marble deposits have, as yet, discovered only broken, and consequently valueless, marble. As, however, the mineral is said to be of very fine grain, of snowy whiteness and chemical purity, if, at greater depths, massive, unbroken stone be found, the deposit will prove of inestimable value because of the scarcity in the United States of statuary marble.

The public are notified of the dissolution of the Ensign Publishing Company. Mr. J. S. Rollo, the former editor, now assumes entire ownership of the paper and announces that it "will undergo no change either in policy, principle, style or tone."

The subject of matrimony is at present claiming special attention in this borough. Last week two couples were united in hymenial bonds; today Mr. J. S. Rollo, of the *Ensign*, and Miss Jennie Fenn, of Provo, were made happy by the silken knot; while cards are out announcing the wedding, Sept. 18, of Mr. J. S. Ostler and Miss Louie Udall, both of this city.

A proposition offered by the City Council to establish a system of waterworks to convey to Nephi City the water of Marsh Springs, about four miles up Salt Creek Canyon, has been accepted by the city. It is proposed to bond the

Last Wednesday evening a ball was held in the Court House, the proceeds to be given to immigrate from the East Indies one Captain John H. Cooper, whose little children, by the recent death, in Nephi, of their mother and grandmother, are left orphans. Everything connected with the ordinary expenses of a ball was, in this instance, given gratis; and the youth of Nephi are deserving of commendation for their liberal patronage of the charitable scheme. Many gave donations who did not attend the party; and, in all, over a hundred dollars will be realized.

Salt Lake Herald
October 20, 1889

NEPHI NUGGETS.

President Charles Sperry met with a very painful accident two days ago, by being thrown from a horse. His collar-bone was broken and he was severely bruised in other parts of the body, but he is progressing favorably under the treatment of Dr. Don.

The citizens of Nephi are anxiously looking forward to the completion of the water works, which are retarded in their progress by the non-arrival of the piping.

Sheep herds are on the move for the winter ranges, and as their pathway lies down Salt creek cañon, our water is something that we cannot recommend.

Mrs. Isabel Ord Pitchforth, daughter of Thomas Ord, and wife of H. H. Pitchforth, died this morning of typhold.

Bishop Harrison Sperry, of Salt Lake city, is paying his many friends a visit.

R. G. Lambert, of the *Deseret News*, is in town.

The Wool Growers' association of southern Utah has shipped this season 1,500,000 pounds of wool and three car loads of hides and pelts, the latter to local tanneries. Andrews & Co. have shipped 1,250,000 pounds of wool and five car loads of hides and pelts, and have sold five carloads of wagons this season.

Our potato crop is almost a total failure, and the tubers are in great demand.

We are sadly in need of a first-class hotel, and there is a right smart chance for some enterprising boniface.

Nephi city bonds amounting to $12,000 were sold on the 10th inst. to James H. Bacon, president of the Bank of Salt Lake.

Our quarterly conference convenes Sunday and Monday, 20 and 21.

JUAB.

NEPHI, Oct. 19, 1889.

Salt Lake Herald
December 2, 1889

COLONIZATION.

NEPHI, October 28, 1889.

O. W. Powers, Esq.,

DEAR SIR:—The bearer of this wants to vote, look after a job for him.

JOHN WITBECK.

TONY, Levan, Juab co., Utah.

Deseret Evening News
December 19, 1889

Nephi Notes.

From a gentleman just in from Nephi we learn that the crops in that section were very short. There was very little fruit, very few potatoes, and not half enough wheat for home consumption.

There have been storms in the mountains and much snow has fallen, which gives the farmers good prospects for next spring.

Owing to its having been a bad season many of the young men of the town have been compelled to seek employment elsewhere. A number have gone to Pioche, others to Tintic, and some to this city to get work.

What is called Marsh Spring has been piped into Nephi, and conveyed in pipes through most of the principal streets, which is a great improvement to the town.

About four miles west of Nephi is a red oche (paint) mine, which is being developed and promises to be very rich. The capacity of the gypsum works at Nephi is to be increased until ten cars per day can be shipped.

A BIG INSTITUTION.

A Nephi Company which Will Turn Out a Car of Plaster Per Hour.

A rapidly growing institution of Nephi, concerning which Salt Lakers have hitherto known but little, is the Nephi Plaster and Manufacturing company, which has been incorporated, with the following board of directors:

John Hague, President, Nephi.

John McCraken, Vice-President, Portland, Oregon.

J. A. Hyde, Secretary and Treasurer, Nephi.

Alma Hague, Nephi.

George C. Whitmore, Nephi.

F. W. Fowler, Superintendent.

The gypsum mines which this company operates are located about a mile east of Nephi, and were discovered by John Hague over twenty years ago. He was aware that the time would arrive when the value of the mines would be recognized, and for two decades he kept his eye on the property, waiting for that time to come. Last March Mr. Fowler, the present superintendent and an expert on gypsum, was notified of the existence of these mines by J. S. Tebbets, of the Union Pacific.

Mr. Fowler is a member of the firm of Fowler Brothers, Blue Rapids, Kansas, who are extensive plaster manufacturers, and at Mr. Tebbets' suggestion, he went to Nephi to look at the property. He was at once struck with the excellent quality of the gypsum and concluded arrangements by which he became interested in the company; and the corporation was made with the above named board of directors.

At present the company is shipping two carloads a day from Nephi and in the spring they expect to be able to turn out one car per hour, having contracted for machinery and a new plant at a cost of $25,000 which Mr. Fowler thinks will enable them to make this achievement without difficulty.

In an interview with a HERALD reporter recently, Mr. Fowler stated that he was well acquainted with the quality of the gypsum mines in Kansas, New York and Nova Scotia, but none of these mines could equal in quality the gypsum in Utah. The mine here is practically inexhaustible, consisting of a mountain 4,000 feet high and producing a plaster which, according to Mr. Fowler, is the best on earth. They now work sixty men and supply the whole of the west with plaster, fifteen carloads having been sent to Salt Lake alone.

The Union Pacific railroad has lent a friendly hand to the operations of the company; and by giving a good freight rate an immense trade in the northwest has been opened up. With John McCraken, of Portland, Oregon, and the Tacoma Trading company, of Tacoma, Washington, as general northwestern agents, the future of the Nephi Plaster and Manufacturing company will be an immense one; and the company promises to be one of the great factors in the prosperity of the "little Chicago."

BUILDINGS OF 1889—THE DYER BLOCK, COMMERCIAL STREET.

Salt Lake Herald
December 29, 1889

NEPHI PROGRESSING.

Her System of Waterworks is Rapidly Assuming Shape.

Although little has been said lately about the labors of our energetic city council, they have been working assiduously one night each week regularly. Waterworks and railroad matters have occupied a great deal of their time. We understand they have an ordinance drawn out and adopted concerning the granting of right of way and other details pertaining to the U. N. & C. railway.

The waterworks question has been solved for some time and much work has been expended in putting the plan into operation with success. Supervisor Sutton has at last got a stream of pure water conducted into Nephi from Marsh springs, and the council have applications for the putting of it into private houses by the score. Regulations will have to be made and ordinances formed to put them into effect.

A stroll over the system yesterday amply repaid our reporter for his trouble. The water is brought from the spring to the mouth of the cañon in a four-inch pipe and from there down along side of the railroad in an eight-inch pipe to Evans' corner, four blocks east of Main street. At this point six-inch cross mains are laid four blocks south, one west and again one south, also one block north from Evans' corner, west a block, thence north to the big hollow. It will be brought at once down Railroad street and Mill street in four-inch pipes to Main street, when other cross mains will be laid, the necessary public hydrants placed in and the job will be completed, of course there will be a vast amount of private work done in putting in the service pipes.

At Evans' corner is a spill pouring forth a large stream of water with terrific force as it flows sparkling through the trough and goes from there rippling to the ditch its ever happy murmur seems to speak in plain words, Nephi's redemption is here. It is a sight to make the heart of every Nephite glad and proud to see a large stream of pure, sparkling water running in our ditches. When the houses are supplied with water, which will be soon, then we will see Nephi's boom awaken, real estate begin to change hands more rapidly, the town grow and everybody happy. Our city council are to be congratulated on their success.—*Ensign.*

Made in the USA
Middletown, DE
09 May 2017